INTERPRETATIVE REPORTING

INTERPRETATIVE REPORTING

EIGHTH EDITION

CURTIS D. MACDOUGALL, Ph.D., Litt.D.

Professor Emeritus of Journalism,
Northwestern University

MACMILLAN PUBLISHING CO., INC.
NEW YORK
COLLIER MACMILLAN PUBLISHERS
LONDON

Printed in the United States of America.

Macmillan Publishing Co., Inc.
866 Third Avenue, New York, New York 10022

Collier Macmillan Canada, Inc.

Library of Congress Cataloging in Publication Data

MacDougall, Curtis Daniel (date)
Interpretative reporting.

Includes index.
1. Reporters and reporting. I. Title.
PN4781.M153 1982 070.4′3 80-28615
ISBN 0-02-373120-6

Printing: 1 2 3 4 5 6 7 8 Year: 2 3 4 5 6 7 8 9

PREFACE

This is the Golden Anniversary edition of a book that has topped the best-seller list in its field for a half century. The first edition, published March 22, 1932, was called *Reporting for Beginners*. When, in 1938, the second edition was renamed *Interpretative Reporting,* copyright rules made it necessary to start counting again. Thus, although called the eighth, this is really the ninth edition.

Study of the changes that have occurred from edition to edition—1932 to 1938 to 1948 to 1957 to 1963 to 1968 to 1972 to 1977 to 1982—would have value for a researcher concerned with developments in newspaper reporting and in education for journalism and, of course, in me.

At the first convention that I attended of the American Association of Teachers of Journalism and the American Association of Schools and Departments of Journalism (long since superseded by the Association for Education in Journalism), Dec. 29–31, 1930, in Boston, Ralph Casey of the University of Minnesota spoke on "The Present Status of Journalistic Literature." He advised journalism teachers to rely more on periodical material and independent investigations than on textbooks. He quoted another professor to the effect that, because of the low quality of textbook material available, book publishers should be urged to submit manuscripts to a committee of representative teachers "to see whether there is any demand for the book in question and whether it is any credit to the present standards of teaching."

I shared the low opinion Casey and his unnamed colleague expressed regarding the dozen or so reporting texts in print at the time. I had tried most of them in my classes at Lehigh University and was confused by the differences between them. Journalism as an academic discipline was still in its experimental infancy, or at best its adolescence. Curricula were mostly offered within departments of English. In 1930 there were only 21 members of the American Association of Schools and Departments of Journalism and 35 other professional curricula not eligible for membership in the AASDJ. During the school year 1928–29, nationwide there were 3,051 journalism students being taught by approximately 500 teachers, not more than 100 of whom belonged to the American Association of Teachers of Journalism. Today the American Association of Teachers has 1,800 members, there are 80 accredited schools, and during the 1979–80 academic year, 71,594 students majoring in journalism in 188 schools that cooperated in a poll. In addition there are thousands of others in unaccredited and/or noncooperative schools and still more thousands who take journalism courses without becoming journalism majors. Approximately one-third of the nation's 1,200 community colleges offer one or more courses in journalism.

Reporting is the backbone course of any journalism curriculum. The early texts reflected the lack of any generally accepted idea as to how the subject should be taught. The books, and probably also the courses, cited the qualifications needed for success as a newsgatherer and discussed ethical problems and the history and social importance of journalism. These aspects now are generally considered in other courses but they do not provide the answer to a beginner's quest for specific instruction in how to do a good job. The books lacked definite instructions, the nitty-gritty of reporting, the nuts and bolts of news writing.

My first attempt to provide what I thought the existent books lacked was a 140-page manual for the staff of *Brown and White,* the semiweekly undergraduate newspaper at Lehigh University. President Charles E. Richards told me when I took over that the paper was ''worse than a seventh-grade high school paper.'' Less than a decade later it was called ''the prize winningest daily of all time'' by *The Epsilog.* Many other eastern colleges emulated the Lehigh system of a curriculum of courses for students participating in extracurricular journalism.

The approach that proved successful in college journalism and which I expanded in *Reporting for Beginners* was what I envisioned during a year in the Chicago bureau of the United Press when I assisted Prof. Harry F. Harrington in an evening class in reporting on the Chicago campus of the Medill School of Journalism of which he was the first director. A large proportion of the class exercises included in the *Teacher's Manual,* which was a bonus for teachers who adopted *Reporting for Beginners* and the first edition of *Interpretative Reporting,* were ones that Harrington and I worked out for that adult education class.

So, *Reporting for Beginners* was an expansion of the Medill School's approach to the teaching of reporting. Almost immediately Dr. Frank Luther Mott, then journalism dean at the University of Iowa, included it in his list of ''Fifty Books on American Journalism'' with the annotation: ''probably the fullest manual for the reporter.'' Inasmuch as the Pulitzer Prize-winning Mott was regarded then, as he still is, as the most outstanding scholar journalism education has produced, his endorsement of the work of a previously unknown author was important.

Within a few years competing books were imitating my approach. Most of them never had a second printing. In my opinion *Interpretative Reporting* has survived because it has persisted in stressing the fundamentals. Although I have taken cognizance of new theories and practices, both in professional newsgathering and in the teaching of it, the book has always been a ''how to do it'' manual for journalistic fact-finders. Laudably most journalism students want to become star reporters, specialists, experts, columnists, editorial writers or editors. My old-fashioned idea is that the best approach is mastery of the basic principles of reporting and writing, step by step, and that attempts to shortcut the learning experience are unwise.

The broadening of my own perspective regarding the function of the journalist is indicated by the change of attitude in *Interpretative Reporting* as contrasted with that of *Reporting for Beginners.* When I wrote the first book I drew on seven years of reporting experience on the Fond du Lac (Wis.) *Commonwealth,* a daily, and the Two Rivers (Wis.) *Chronicle,* a weekly, and a year in the Chicago bureau of the United Press where I was an awe-stricken cub from beginning to end. In those days Fond du Lac and Chicago were 1,500 rather than merely 150 miles apart. The big city provided a romantic escape if things became too rough at home. I was starry-eyed, largely because the former Chicago *Tribune* reporter who taught the first journalism course I ever took at Ripon College related anecdotes of the exciting life of a reporter during the *Front Page,* Al Capone, and William Hale Thompson days in the Loop. Even though I observed considerable bootlegging and racketeering in City Hall, as well as other parts of the city, I retained my belief that journalism was a romantic experience.

The Rover Boys, Horatio Alger attitude was expressed in the first few paragraphs of *Reporting for Beginners* as follows:

> The newspaper reporter who elbows his way through the crowd at the scene of an accident or fire, flashing his police card and gaining access to important personages, is an object of awe. Whereas the average citizen is acquainted with his barber, his doctor, his lawyer and his minister by name (some of them even by their first names), the writers for his favorite newspaper generally remain unknown. At best they are only by-lines. The reader seldom recognizes a writer on a streetcar or in society; he almost never knows one well enough to invite him to his home.
>
> It is this aura of mystery surrounding the relatively anonymous profession of journalism that is responsible, in large part at least, for the rapidly increasing number of young men and women who believe that they want to be newspaper reporters, or as they put it, journalists—a term that includes "column" conducting, theatrical reviewing, editorial writing, feature and magazine writing and authorship in general.
>
> Journalism means mystery. Mystery means romance, and romance attracts youth. What to do with the hundreds of young people who are being graduated each spring from schools and departments of journalism is becoming a problem. Threats of long hours, few vacations, considerable drudgery and low wages seem to be of no avail. Neither are these youngsters frightened by knowledge of the opprobrium with which a rather large portion of the populace regards newspaper workers.

By contrast the Preface to *Interpretative Reporting* in 1938 read as follows:

> *Interpretative Reporting* grew out of an attempt to revise the author's *Reporting for Beginners* (Macmillan, 1932). The general outline and about 25 per cent of the contents of the earlier volume have been retained, but both its scope and size have been increased.
>
> The principal difference between *Reporting for Beginners* and *Interpretative Reporting* is one of point of view towards the task newsgatherers of the immediate future will be asked to perform. A clue as to the writer's present attitude is in the present volume's title; it is his belief that changing social conditions, of which students of the principal media of public opinion have become increasingly aware during the past six years, are causing newsgathering and disseminating agencies to change their methods of reporting and interpreting the news. The trend is unmis-

takably in the direction of combining the functions of interpreter with that of reporter, after about a half-century during which journalistic ethics called for a strict differentiation between narrator and commentator.

What caused the disilllusionment or awakening was my year on the St. Louis *Star-Times* and three years as editor of the Evanston *Daily News-Index,* the details of which are given in my *Spilling the Beans.*

I didn't invent interpretative reporting and I called the book "interpretative" instead of "interpretive" because that was the preference of all the standard dictionaries. It still is but some either don't know or ignore it and the publicity value of satisfying their curiosity has been considerable. I certainly helped popularize interpretative reporting even though I didn't invent it. When the book appeared many reviewers spent more time discussing the title than they did the contents. The highlights of objectivity vs. interpretative debate are related in Chapter 1.

Throughout the book's lifetime journalistic fads have come and gone. In the '40s publishers went overboard for Rudolf Flesch and readability testing. They spent millions in the futile effort to discover the proper word and sentence lengths to increase circulation. Finally, rebelling writers convinced them of the impossibility of writing by formula. However, for several editions of this book I had to devote considerable space to the phenomenon, as some journalism teachers were taken in also. A few post-mortem remarks on readability tests and on semantics, another onetime fad, appear in Chapter 8.

More recently it has been *New Journalism,* a term used to include a great many supposedly innovative techniques about which a quantity of articles have been written. The sixth edition of this book appeared two years earlier than was originally planned to take cognizance of the situation. Today it is recognized that the term *New Journalism* grew out of the practice of some magazine writers and novelists to use the literary devices of the fiction writer to retell factual journalistic accounts. Thus, Truman Capote's *In Cold Blood* and Gerold Frank's *The Boston Strangler* read like novels but are only recapitulations of facts familiar to any careful newspaper reader. Some critics pointed out that John Bartlow Martin did it better a generation ago in *Why Did They Kill?* an account of multiple murders in southern Michigan. All these authors and others, of course, did additional research, as would any reporter assigned to do a weekend roundup.

There is nothing new about writers drawing on newspaper stories for plot material. Many a great novel has been a thinly disguised account of real people and real events, and some libel suits have resulted as a consequence. See Chapter 3 for more details.

So, even though not new, the term *New Journalism* meant a system of fact-gathering and a style of writing suitable for certain magazines and novels but hardly applicable to everyday newspaper reporting. Furthermore, Tom Wolfe, Jimmy Breslin, Gay Talese and the other modern self-styled new journalists had plenty of counterparts in the past among newspaper feature and special writers and columnists. Youngsters impressed by their writings will be dumfounded if they dig into the files and read many masterly descriptive and detailed accounts—eyewitness and imaginative both—by past masters such as Meyer Levin, Meyer Berger, James O'Donnell Bennett, Bob Casey, Ben Hecht, Howard Vincent O'Brien, Irvin S. Cobb, Heywood Broun, Simeon Strunsky and scores and scores of others. They practiced New Journalism a generation or more before the name was invented and mostly they did it better.

A feature of early editions of this book was facsimiles of the front pages of the same day's edition of ten metropolitan newspapers from coast to coast. They illustrated wide differences in editorial judgment, mostly because of a greater emphasis on local news. Today the products have become so standardized that if the flags were concealed it would be difficult or impossible to tell whether the paper came from Miami or Minneapolis.

World government still is only a dream of the future, but the consciousness of increasing interdependence grows steadily as transportation and communications facilities improve and energy and environmental problems are recognized as worldwide in scope. The journalistic media have tried to keep up with the changing world. A generation ago there were few specialists except in the sports department. Today, from sheer necessity in an over-populated, polluted and hazardous nuclear world, the opposite is true. The elevation of school of journalism graduates into executive positions has helped accelerate the improvement of the product.

A concomitant of the increased attention paid national and international news today has been a corresponding downplaying of local news not only on the front page but throughout the entire paper. It has been increasingly difficult from edition to edition to find outstanding examples of local coverage of speeches, meetings, court trials, obituaries and other types of local occurrences once given prominent attention. On the other hand, there has been a proliferation of syndicated columns and features pertaining to social, economic and political problems of universal interest or concern: gardening, child care, fashions, housing, health, travel and family life.

As a consequence of the broadened scope of editorial interest, there has been a great trend toward departmentalization. No generally accepted formula has as yet been developed. The Minneapolis *Tribune,* for instance, has sections on Family Living, Entertainment/Arts, Travel/Adventure, Home/Gardens and Marketplace. The Saginaw (MI) *News* has replaced the traditional Women's page, which in turn had succeeded the Society page, with a Living section: "with more modern-day social concerns of both women and men. Every Wednesday the stress is on food; every Thursday it's consumerism; on Friday it's local things to do; on Saturday it's on parenting; Sunday contains the major shot of weddings and engagements. Fashion gets in every other week. The other days are a variety of everything under the sun," according to George E. Arwady, editor.

As the schools of journalism have developed, their curricula have been expanded to include separate courses to acquaint students with the nature of the business, the history of journalism, newspaper law, newsroom problems and policies and the social role of the media. Hence, portions of the earlier editions of this book that dealt with such topics have been eliminated or reduced in emphasis.

Interpretative Reporting is intended for beginning reporters and is not a complete course in journalism. Ideally it could be the basic text for two or three semesters and thereafter serve as a reference work. Legal and ethical matters are considered as they affect the reporter. Similarly the technological changes that have occurred, fast making the typewriter as obsolete as the horse and buggy, are evaluated according to the extent they change news gathering procedures. Old-timers generally view the innovations with alarm but learn to adjust. Young staff members catch on easily and soon everyone gets used to having clean newsroom floors rather than overflowing wastebaskets. Editors continue to think up assignments and reporters continue to cover them.

Features of earlier editions that have been eliminated include pictures of newspaper buildings with unusual architectural features, snapshots of various departments of a newspaper, including the mechanical department, along with lengthy descriptions of all departments, illustrations of reporters' copy with headlines written by copy readers, copy reading symbols, proofreading symbols, a bibliography of journalism books, chapter footnotes, vignettes or skits to brighten every chapter and an author's style book.

The major problem in revising a book is deciding what to eliminate to make room for new material so as not to increase the size of the volume. Dated examples naming former presidents or mentioning streetcars and the like obviously must be replaced, but I have learned that teachers who have used the book for a long time do not like wholesale changes. They become fond of certain examples that they have learned to use effectively in the classroom. My rule is: don't replace unless there's something better. In early editions there were examples of foreign correspondence and national news. In recent editions there have been only examples with immediate educational value for the cub reporter. They illustrate assignments he might expect to receive comparatively early in his career or to which he might aspire before long. I wish there were room for many more examples, but teachers and students can find good ones in the daily press.

In addition to explaining past journalistic practices, the early editions of this book included accounts of quite a few historical events, as the London naval disarmament conference, the New York Easter parade, the Marian Parker kidnaping, the execution of Ruth Snyder and Judd Gray, the Republican national convention of 1928, the overthrow by veterans of a corrupt Tennessee political machine, the William Heirens murder case, recollections of Hermann Goering by Ferdinand Kuh and many more. There were accounts of interviews with Marilyn Monroe, Robert Maynard Hutchins, Joseph R. McCarthy, Vyacheslav Molotov, James A. Farley, Irvin S. Cobb, Ann Todd, Katharine Hepburn, Cloris Leachman, Dorothy Lamour and others. And the obituaries of William Howard Taft, Sidney Hillman, Will Rogers, H. L. Mencken, Sam

Rayburn, A. A. Milne, Vince Lombardi, David Belasco, W. C. Fields, John D. Rockefeller, Harry Byrd, Connie Mack, Jack Benny and others.

Pressure is increasing on the schools from kindergarten through graduate school to "return to the basics." This is one book that never has abandoned the basics. It shall continue to adhere to that policy.

For additional practice on the basics or fundamentals, *Workbook for Interpretative Reporting, 8/e,* has been prepared by Daniel E. Thornburgh and J. David Reed, Eastern Illinois University.

Curtis D. MacDougall

ACKNOWLEDGMENTS

Since 1932 I have made 249 expressions of gratitude for help in keeping this book up to date. Many of the contributions of years ago still enrich this edition. It would be impossible to list all of those who have permitted me to use material or who have given me advice and/or assistance in obtaining information or examples to illustrate the text. Therefore, I must restrict myself to mention of only those who made specific contributions to this Golden Anniversary edition.

For permissions to use material I am grateful to the following:

Scripps-Howard Newspapers for use of the list of red flag words from Scripps-Howard's *Synopsis of the Law of Libel and the Right of Privacy* whose author was Bruce Sanford, through David Stolberg, assistant general editorial manager.

The National Technical Information Service for reprints of parts of *High Energy Physics, The Ultimate Destruction of Matter and Energy,* available from the service, 5285 Post Royal Road, Springfield, Va., 22161, through Frances F. Roberts, product specialist.

The *IRE Journal* through John Ullmann, editor, and to Patrick Riordan for the Miami *Herald* for reproduction of Riordan's article, ''Getting the Background Fast,'' in the May–June, 1979, issue.

Clark Mollenhoff, Washington and Lee University professor of journalism, for ''Rules for Dealing with Confidential Sources.''

Several persons provided lengthy comments on the coverage of special areas or specific news events, as noted in the text. They were as follows:

Jerry Ackerman, environmental/energy editor, Boston *Globe*.

Dennis A Britton, national editor, Los Angeles *Times*.

Casey Bukro, environment editor, Chicago *Tribune*.

William Jones, managing editor, Chicago *Tribune*.

Dale A Davenport, city editor, Harrisburg (Pa.) *Evening News*.

Charles-Gene McDaniel, Roosevelt University professor of journalism, formerly Associated Press science writer.

Charles Roberts, director of information, National Wildlife Federation.

William M. L. Briggs, meteorologist for the National Weather Service in Chicago where Raymond Waldman is meteorologist in charge, updated weather terms for years updated by J. R. Fulks, formerly with the service.

As he has for several editions, William Wylie, Pittsburgh *Press* business editor, helped update the chapter on business. John F. Lawrence, assistant managing editor, Los Angeles *Times,* also made helpful suggestions.

Prof. Don Ranly of the School of Journalism of the University of Missouri and the Rev. George R. Plagenz, Cleveland *Press* religion editor, did the same for the chapter on religion. Dr. Scott Cutlip, University of Georgia dean of journalism, criticized the section on public relations.

Among those who watched for outstanding examples of journalism in their regions were Jack Botts, University of Nebraska professor of journalism; Leon Baden, copydesk editor, Harrisburg (Pa.) *Evening News;* Edward Peeks, business/labor editor, Charleston (W. Va.) *Gazette;* Dr. Daniel Thornburgh, head of journalism studies at Eastern Illinois University; Dr. Dozier Cade, formerly journalism director at the University of Tennessee.

Others who contributed information, advice or materials included these:

Arwady, George E., editor, Saginaw *News*.

Batts, J. Partick, director of information, American Farm Bureau Federation.

Bednarek, David, education reporter, Milwaukee *Journal*.

Black, Creed, editor and publisher, Lexington (Ky.) *Herald-Leader*.

Block, Mervin, Columbia Broadcasting System, New York.

Blodgett, Cameron H., executive secretary, Minnesota News Council.

Bray, Howard, director, Fund for Investigative Reporting.

Brownlee, Lester, manager, WSSD, Chicago.

Carty, James, professor of journalism, Bethany (W. Va.) College.

Case, Leland D., Tucson, formerly editor, *The Rotarian* and *Together*.

Cento, W. F., managing editor, St. Paul *Dispatch*.

Cottrell, Bonnie, Chicago public school teacher.

Davis, Beverly, chief, Community Advocacy Unit, Governor's Action Center, Harrisburg, Pa.

Davis, Frank, director publicity and information, Pennsylvania Human Relations Commission.

Dougherty, W. B., executive secretary-treasurer, Community College Journalism Association.

Eisen, David J., director of research and information, The Newspaper Guild.

Finnegan, John R., executive editor, St. Paul *Dispatch* and *Pioneer Press*.

Flanery, James, metropolitan editor, Omaha *World-Herald*.

Gantner, Dr. George E., secretary-treasurer, National Association of Medical Examiners.

Gerard, Betty, administrative assistant, National Farmers Union.

Graham, Patrick, assistant metropolitan editor, Milwaukee *Journal*.

Greiff, Frances and George, associate professor of journalism, Georgia State University.

Haiman, Robert J., executive editor, St. Petersburg *Times*.

Hallstrom, William, Miami *News*.

Holst, Annette, United Press International, New York City.

Isaacs, Norman, chairman, National News Council.

Jensen, Dr. Carl, director, Project Censored, Sonoma State University.

Kunerth, William, professor of journalism, Iowa State University.

Lohmann, Lawrence, labor reporter, Milwaukee *Journal*.
MacDougall, A. Kent, staff writer, Los Angeles *Times*.
MacDougall, Gordon P., Washington, D.C. lawyer.
MacDougall, Priscilla Ruth, attorney, Wisconsin Educational Association Council.
Macklin, Robert A., general manager, International Circulation Managers Association.
McCormally, John, formerly editor, Burlington (Iowa) *Hawkeye*.
Merida, Kevin, city zone reporter, Milwaukee *Journal*.
McWhinnie, Charles, Action Time, Chicago *Sun-Times*.
Nofziger, Fred O., leisure editor, Toledo *Blade*.
Pearson, Margaret M.E., director of information, American Farm Bureau Association.
Perry, John L., formerly managing editor, Anderson (S.C.) *Independent*.
Reilly, Joseph, metropolitan editor, Chicago *Sun-Times*.
Renner, George A., editor and director, Religious News Service.
Ryan, Daniel M., editor, Kalamazoo (Mich.) *Gazette*.
Stark, Julia M., program director, National Conference of Christians and Jews.
Trost, Robert, editor, Grand Rapids (Mich.) *Press*.
Van Cranebrock, Allen, senior financial correspondent, Midwest bureau, Reuters, Ltd.
Wertheimer, Dr. Jerrold, professor of journalism, San Francisco State University.
Wagner, Bill, director of communications, National Farmers Organization.
Warner, Hartland W., Fraser Associates, sponsors of Action Line Reporters Association.
Wilson, Quentin, executive secretary, Association for Education in Journalism.
Witwer, Stanford, B., formerly columnist, St. Petersburg *Times*.
Zimmerman, Alice, public information secretary, American Nuclear Society.

Credit also is due Carol Olson, who typed the manuscript after deciphering my scrawls, and to my wife, Genevieve Rockwood MacDougall, for preparing and xeroxing copy.

CONTENTS

PART ONE

NEWS REPORTING

Journalism presents a continuous, never-ending moving picture of the world and its occurrences, of mankind and its conduct, depicting comedy, tragedy, vice, virtue, heroism, devotion, enterprise, discovery, calamity, beneficence, sorrow and joy—human life in all its kaleidoscopic and inexplicable changes. And accompanying all this editorial comment upon the news, interpreting the meaning of events, associating views with information, opinion with facts, and thereby aiding the reader to a better understanding and to an opinion of his own which becomes an element in the creation of public opinion, that "sovereign mistress of effects," which rules the modern world. Such is journalism, a profession that exists upon the events of the day, that mirrors all life and presents it to the view of every individual, thereby bringing all mankind to a closer unity and a clearer conception of its kinship. —CASPER S. YOST, editor, St. Louis *Globe-Democrat*

A newspaper should seek what is original, distinctive, dramatic, romantic, thrilling, unique, curious, quaint, humorous, odd, apt to be talked about, without shocking good taste or lowering the general good tone and above all without impairing the confidence of the people in the truth of the stories or the character of the paper for reliability and scrupulous cleanness.

—JOSEPH PULITZER, New York *World*

WHOSE FIRST AMENDMENT?

Whose First? It belongs to every man, woman and child.

Whose right to use it? It is the right of every man, woman and child.

Whose responsibility to protect it? It is the responsibility of every man, woman and child.

The First Amendment protects freedoms, separately defined, yet indivisible. We share these rights:

- To believe.
- To speak.
- To publish.
- To support or criticize our government.

These rights belong to the people and never are to be denied nor controlled by the government.

We share, as citizens, a responsibility to understand that the First Amendment protects, with equal force, the ideas we despise as well as those we cherish. Government infringement on any one of these fundamental rights threatens them all.

Whose First? One infringement will raise another question: Who's next?

As Irving Brant, the distinguished constitutional authority and journalist, thoughtfully pointed out in his history, "The Bill of Rights," James Madison and his colleagues "knew what they were doing. . . . English history had demonstrated to them that without complete religious liberty, without freedom of conscience and separation of church and state, there could be no freedom of speech, or of the press, or the right of assembly. Both English and American experience had taught them that without all these freedoms there could be no free government. And they had learned that even in a country where the people are sovereign, no words of lesser force than 'shall not'—enforceable in independent courts of law—could restrain the servants of the people from acting as if they were the masters."

We owe ourselves and those who follow an obligation to recapture the concern and spirit which Madison referred to as the "Great Freedoms."

If freedom is a growing thing, it can mean no less today and tomorrow than it meant to those who wrote the First Amendment.

The First Amendment distinguishes us from all other societies. And it works. Every time the First Amendment works, it makes us stronger.

The preceding was passed as a resolution by the delegates to the First Amendment Congress in Williamsburg, Va., in March, 1980.

1
THE MODERN NEWSGATHERER

When the first edition of this book appeared in 1932 there were still old-timers who wrote their news stories in longhand. Although linotypes were used for body type, in most newspaper plants headlines were set by hand. Press association copy was received by Morse telegraph and news pictures came by mail. Schools of journalism required courses in typing.

TECHNOLOGICAL CHANGES

Most technological changes in newspaper production have not affected directly reporters and writers and it has not been difficult to adjust to them.

The same is true today as the technological revolution has reached the city room. Reporters no longer type their stories and yell "boy" to transmit copy to the city editor. Instead, they compose on a keyboard which resembles that of a typewriter and they observe their stories on the screen of a video display terminal (VDT) also known as CRTs (cathode-ray tubes). Sentences can be rewritten, paragraphs moved around and spelling mistakes corrected using pushbuttons. A pushbutton also causes a story to be stored in a computer memory bank from which a copy editor can retrieve it.

Another method of getting stories into cold type is to use copy produced on an IBM Selectric typewriter for a scanner or OCR (optical character reader), which transfers the contents of the typewritten sheet or its equivalent onto computer tape that is fed into a phototypesetter.

Because of the newness of those electronic systems there inevitably will be refinements and developments. Manufacturers and their clients already are asking "what next?" Through a new subsidiary, Viewdata Corporation of America, the Knight-Ridder Newspapers have begun to test consumer interest in an electronic home information system called Viewstrom. The plan involves 150–200 Miami families using television sets adapted for use as video display terminals that allow access to news, weather and sports information. The British Post Office also is testing a similar system.

Fantastic predictions also are being made regarding facsimile, ultrafax, communication satellites, computers that can translate languages, read handwriting or typewriting and change spoken words into written words on perforated tape. Future reporters of the news may dictate their stories into microphone-like gadgets for transmission to "voice setting" machines, which in turn will correct the words into "type" ready for the page form. Other machines may "think" their words and transfer them to their assigned space in newspaper pages, together with pictures and headlines, electronically and photographically. The words may go into international newspapers, facsimiles produced in the homes of readers automatically translated into languages indigenous to the various countries in which they are circulated.

In an excellent article on the electronic revolution in the newsroom in the July–August 1979 *Columbia Journalism Review,* Dominique Wolton wrote that "the new technology necessarily makes the intellectual creative process more abstract, involving an essentially visual rather than a material or tactile relationship to writing, which now occurs within the fixed space of the display screen. Who can deny that here we have the seeds of a change in the journalist's relation to his work?"

To date, however, the reaction of most journalists has been one of relief. Old-timers have been surprised and relieved to discover that adjustment is easy, only a few days being required to master the machine. More important, no matter what Jules Verne or Buck Rogers types of invention can be put into operation, the news will have to be gathered by human beings. And the most important machine will continue to be the human reporter whose training cannot be neglected while he becomes enamored with the mechanical possibilities of tomorrow. This is true no matter what the method of distribution: slave runners, town criers, newsletters, carrier pigeons, telegraphs, telephones, printing presses, motion pictures, radio, television or thought waves; nor will it matter whether reporters use pencil or pen, typewriter or some electronic machinery.

According to the National Institute for Occupational Safety and Health, video display terminals do not emit radiation levels that present a hazard to employees. Both the Institute and The Newspaper Guild recommend safeguards to prevent eye strain and body tension, by means of shields, lighting, rest periods and other measures.

THE NEWSPAPER AS A BUSINESS

Of necessity a newspaper is a business enterprise that must be economically profitable to survive. It is a peculiar business enterprise because its social service is considered so important that it is protected by the First Amendment to the Constitution.

Freedom of the press pertains to gathering and printing the news only, however, and not to the commercial aspects of publishing. Like all other businesses, news media must obey laws pertaining to child labor, wages and hours, anti-trust, taxation and so forth.

As commercial enterprises, newspapers have been affected by the same economic trends that are present in all other phases of the economy. Most importantly that means mergers, consolidations and purchases to eliminate small independent businesses. Despite anti-trust laws there are huge monopolies, financial conglomerates and international multinationals whose holdings are widely diversified. Newspapers, magazines and other journalistic enterprises are bought and sold as are businesses dealing in food, clothing, machinery or anything else.

In 1910, when the population of the United States was approximately 92 million, there were 2,202 daily newspapers. Today there are 1,756 daily newspapers to serve a population of 220 million. Whereas in grandfather's day virtually every city of 15,000 or over had rival newspapers and the largest cities—New York, Chicago and others—had from five to ten papers each, today only a few of the largest cities have second newspapers and most of those are under the same ownership.

In 1890 there were 1,348 urban places in which 1,610 dailies were published. Today there are 7,062 urban places but 1,759 dailies represent 1,551 cities. There also are 696 Sunday papers, mostly with the same ownership as dailies, with 54 million circulation. About 1,100 of the 1,756 dailies or 63 per cent, are owned by 167 corporations, which are absorbing independent papers at the rate of 50 to 60 annually. The Gannett-Speidel chain owns 82 daily newspapers, 19 weeklies, one radio station and one television station. Knight-Ridder owns 33 dailies, 12 weeklies, four radio and TV stations. Harte-Hanks has 26 dailies, 61 weeklies, four TV stations and ten radio stations. Thomson has 65 dailies and seven weeklies in this country and about as many more journalistic properties in Canada and Great Britain. Newhouse and Freedom Newspapers each own 29 dailies.

These figures change constantly as new properties are bought and sold, as are oil companies, insurance companies, banks and other commercial enterprises. In 1977 Australian Rupert Murdoch paid a reputed $32.5 million for the New York *Post* with a circulation of nearly 400,000 daily. Three years earlier he paid $17.3 million for the San Antonio *Express* and *News* each with about 80,000 daily and, combined, about twice that Sundays.

In 1930 chains controlled only 43 per cent of the circulation and in 1960 only 46 per cent. Of the 1,500 cities with only newspapers today, 97.5 per cent have no local competition. In 1920 there were 700 American cities with competing newspapers. Today there are 40.

There is, however, competition for advertising and news from independently owned radio and television stations and from a growing number of community, suburban and special interest periodicals. There are about 8,500 weeklies with a total circulation of about 43 million and about 13,500 other nondailies, mostly community gossip sheets or throwaway shopping newspapers, which are becoming more editorial in content.

The existence of these nondailies means more job opportunities for beginners. Many of them are gadflies, often embarrassing the larger dailies by scooping them on important stories, mostly exposés. During the '50s there were a number of iconoclastic publications, first called underground and later alternative newspapers, which appealed to youthful activists.

THE NATURE OF NEWSPAPER WORK

Any experience, from the high school or college campus newspaper to the most standardized of the metropolitan dailies, is valuable. Monetary reward is seldom the prime motivation of a would-be newspaper reporter, although, as will be related in Chapter 4, the starvation wages and long working hours of yesteryear are no more.

Understandably applicants ask themselves:

1. How do I know I would like it?
2. How do I know I am qualified?
3. How should I prepare myself?
4. Can I preserve my integrity?

Old-time movies notwithstanding, newspaper reporters do not often emulate detectives in exposing murderers, kidnapers and subversives, nor do they shout "stop the presses" and compose headlines over the telephone after profanely "telling off" unreasonable superiors. Rather, they put in a regular full day's work in and out of remarkably quiet and orderly newsrooms, where they remove their hats.

In large cities, some reporters spend their entire working days in the pressrooms at police headquarters, city hall, the county buildings, the federal building and other places where it is certain important news will originate or be reported. They telephone their information to rewrite persons in note form or they dictate it, composing as they go along. Many now send copy via facsimile machines from pressrooms in outlying offices to the city room. On smaller newspapers, beat reporters visit their news sources once or twice daily, returning to their offices to compose their own accounts. They also may double as general assignment reporters, covering news that occurs at places other than the familiar spots. In all instances they are under the careful direction and scrutiny of the city editor, who in turn is responsible to the managing editor, who has general charge of the entire news-editorial operation.

To satisfy the cosmopolitan interests of their readers, newspapers are becoming increasingly departmentalized. The geographical beats are giving way to interest or subject beats. How departmentalized a newspaper operation is and how split up the managerial and operational functions are depend upon its size. Someone is in charge of handling news that reaches the office via the teletypesetters or leased wires of the press associations (Associated Press and United Press International), so there may be a telegraph or wire desk or, on larger papers, a foreign news department with a cable desk as a part of it. Some large newspapers also have a central copy desk where most stories from whatever source are checked for style, accuracy, etc., and given headlines. Makeup (deciding where stories and other, mostly illustrative, materials are to appear) may be handled by a separate makeup editor, by a news editor or by someone else performing multiple duties.

Most newspapers, large and small, have had autonomous sports departments for decades. Society pages that enjoyed equal longevity, however, have virtually disappeared in recent years. For a time they were replaced by women's pages. Today there is considerable experimentation to determine both the format and contents of a substitute department. The staff of the Anderson (S.C.) *Independent* sampled that paper's readership and, according to John L. Perry, managing editor, learned that prominent among the concerns of the residents of the area were roads, safety, women, youth, ethnic groups, inflation, entertainment, politics, sexuality, environment, public spending, drainage, education, growth, transportation, religion, personalities, law enforcement, criminal justice, civil justice, arts, health, work force, business, nuclear power, consumers, energy.

Few if any papers can afford the luxury of a specialist for every one of these interests. The trend, however, is unmistakably in that direction. Already the need is recognized for specialists on energy, environment, education, religion, civil liberties, health, housing and planning and some other fields. Beat reporters covering any of these cannot remain stationed in a single pressroom. There are a large number of offices, public and private, that the reporter must visit or maintain contact with by telephone. Service clubs, church groups, women's organizations, labor unions and other groups have become actively interested in many fields related to social welfare. The reporter must be familiar with the magazines, books, reports and other material related to a specialized field.

A warning to such colleagues is sounded as follows by Casey Bukro, Chicago *Tribune* environment reporter:

> Specialists must avoid falling into a trap, in which they begin to view themselves as "experts" and begin writing stories that have little meaning to the average reader. Specialists do this by writing over their readers' heads, giving little explanation, or by writing about rarefied issues of little consequence other than to show that the writer knows something nobody else knows. A specialist should not be an elitist. He should be an interpreter, an explainer.

Although the reporter may be haunted constantly by deadlines (the last minutes at which copy can be submitted to make editions), there is generally less monotony and consequently danger of "getting into a rut" in newspaper work than there is in almost anything else one could do today. This is the age of the Organization Man in which white-collar as well as blue-collar workers increasingly are becoming comparatively smaller and smaller cogs in huge industrial machines whose total operations (or even purposes) it is difficult for them to understand. Many recent authors have deplored the extent to which the contemporary economy puts a premium on conformity, stifles imagination and originality, causes boredom and, consequently, destroys initiative and even self-respect. They see youthful unrest, on and off college campuses, as due in considerable part to these factors.

There is, of course, considerable similarity in the news from the same source day after day. Nevertheless, no two stories ever are exactly alike. The principals at least are different and so are their reactions to whatever befalls them: arrest, accident, honor, etc. And, even though the swashbuckling days of Richard Harding Davis are long since past, there is still a thrill, or at least a satisfied feeling, with every assignment successfully concluded. There is a greater pride of workmanship and sense of accomplishment than is possible for workers in most industries and offices in the late twentieth century. Even though low on the press's totem pole, the cub reporter carries more prestige with the public than do apprentices in most other fields. At the scene of a fire or riot s/he flashes his/her press pass and is allowed to cross police lines. On the routine beat s/he is courted by those who want to get something in or to keep something out of the paper. From the very start of a journalistic career, by the very nature of the work, a reporter, "is somebody," and this fact cannot help but be gratifying to the human ego.

Reporting is not a dream world or fool's paradise. The reporter actually is a responsible person. Several others will have a part in determining how news appears in the paper. Nevertheless, the reporter has "first crack" at it, exercising original judgment to determine whether and/or how something is to be reported. The reporter, in other words, is the backbone of the newsgathering and disseminating operation. Truly, every reporter is also an editor and, conversely, the best editors continue throughout their future careers to maintain the attitudes of reporters.

The occupational disease that newspapermen and/or women must guard against is cynicism. Whereas skepticism is a journalistic asset, a hard-boiled or flippant attitude toward the so-called realities of life can lead not only to a flagrant disregard of the public interest but also to personal deterioration. Many of the public figures with whom s/he comes into diurnal contact, the reporter knows, do not deserve public adulation but are, to use the vernacular, stuffed shirts or phonies. Disillusionment comes also with discovery that the "rules of the game"—as the game actually is "played" in politics, business and many other aspects of life—are often crass, mercenary and hypocritical. Overcoming gullibility and learning the "facts of life" can be valuable, provided they lead to intelligent sophistication.

The reporter who has a professional attitude will be happier and more effective. Professionalism can be present or absent among carpenters, hotel clerks, nurses, doctors, lawyers, taxi drivers, newspapermen, and anybody or everybody else. As for journalism, there is no field that offers greater opportunities for the development of a professional point of view, idealism, public service and the like. It is the place for the starry-eyed youngster who wants to help "save the world." There is no better way for one who wants to help make democracy work more effectively to devote his talents.

Perhaps the most important advantage of newspaper reporting is that one is paid while learning. On every new assignment one gets valuable experience for any future occupational venture.

REPORTORIAL QUALIFICATIONS

Personality Traits

Successful journalists are not born; they are made. Most of the personality traits usually listed as valuable for the journalist are ones that would be equally essential for success in most other professional fields: intelligence, friendliness, reliability, imagination, ingenuity, nerve, speed, accuracy, courage, endurance, ability to organize one's activities, perseverance, mental alertness, honesty, punctuality, cheerfulness, the power of observation, shrewdness, enterprise, optimism, humor, adaptability, initiative and the like.

Altogether too many college freshmen think training for journalism consists primarily in learning how to write. They are mostly students who did well in high school English and were inspired with literary ambitions by teachers who were surprised and grateful to find fewer than the average number of grammatical errors in their themes. Unfortunately, there is no such thing as "just writing," in journalism or any other field. William Shakespeare is immortal not because of vocabulary or style but because of greatness of thought. He had an incomparable knowledge of history, psychology, geography, philosophy, and many other fields. He and other masters of past centuries are read today because they had something extraordinarily worthwhile to say.

Because great ideas rather than beautiful words and phrases make for superior writing, everything that a journalism student studies is of potential value. The subject matter of journalism includes all that is taught in courses in political science, history, economics, sociology, chemistry, physics and other subjects too numerous to mention. The student who recognizes this fact as a freshman has a big advantage. By the time s/he takes his/her first journalism course in the sophomore, junior or senior year, s/he will have more than the average liberal arts student's superficial interest in and knowledge of the contents of innumerable textbooks. The reporter's head and files should be full of information on which to rely when wandering on or off campus in search of news. Journalism courses should make textbook knowledge come to life. This background should enable the reporter to understand and interpret the contemporary scene. Through experience in hiring both liberal arts and journalism school graduates, editors have learned that a so-called broad background of general courses is not in itself adequate preparation for newspaper reporting. Since, however, the journalist deals mostly with news related to the subject matter of courses in the different social sciences, the student who has little or no interest in political science, economics and sociology should take stock to determine whether s/he really is wise to aspire to a career in journalism.

The young person who should be encouraged to go into journalism, therefore, is the one who wants very badly to spend an adulthood saying or writing worthwhile things about contemporary problems. His/her chances of success may be judged by the extent to which at an early age s/he becomes interested in the world of affairs. There is no sense aspiring to a newspaper career unless one finds newspaper reading pleasurable as a youth. The more cosmopolitan one's interests, the better.

Among the courses that relate to the kind of news the future journalist will cover are ones in criminology, urban sociology, labor problems, public finance, taxation, political parties, population problems, state and local government and others in the fields of sociology, political science and economics. Taking them is the comparatively easy way to learn what any successful journalist must know; the hard way is on the job. A student supposedly goes to college to get a head start.

Attempts to prepare a profile of the average reporter considering such factors as age, ethnic background, family background, politics, education, religion and so forth are of doubtful value. The average of 2, 3, 4, 9, and 10 is 6 but there is no such unit among the numbers listed. In other words, the composite personality may have no counterpart in actuality. Experienced journalism teachers know it is futile to judge the competence of a student reporter by personality traits. It just isn't so that to be a successful newsgatherer one must be an extrovert or a compensated introvert.

If there is any clue to be discovered in childhood by which to estimate journalistic capacity, it probably would be the extent to which the boy or girl demonstrates curiosity and skepticism. A newsgatherer's stock in trade is the ability to keep on asking questions until s/he has exhausted all angles of an assignment. The youngster who wears out his/her parents by inquisitivenesses may be worth encouraging as a potential journalistic great.

Nose for News

Usually listed first among the special qualifications that a newsgatherer needs is a nose for news, which means the ability to recognize the news possibilities of an item of information and involves

1. The ability to recognize that the information can be made of interest to readers.
2. The ability to recognize clues that may be very casual but may lead to the discovery of important news.

3. The ability to recognize the relative importance of a number of facts concerning the same general subject.
4. The ability to recognize the possibility of other news related to the particular information at hand.

The following anecdote, possibly apocryphal, is told of Deems Taylor when he first became music critic for the New York *Times*. He is said to have arrived at the premiere of an opera only to learn that the prima donna had taken poison in her hotel room and the program had been canceled. Taylor, it is hard to believe in view of the eminence he later attained, went home and to bed. He was awakened in the middle of the night by an outraged editor who told him every other paper in town had the suicide story on Page One. Taylor murmured, "Well, there was no opera performance to write about, so what else could I do but go home?"

Another, possibly fictitious, reporter was assigned to cover a speech that an important man was to deliver. He was instructed to follow the speech with the advanced copy in his hands to see if the speaker deviated at all from the manuscript. The speech, in the meantime, had been written up and its publication awaited only the actual delivery. The reporter strolled back to his editor's presence and reported that the speaker had cast aside his prepared manuscript and had talked extemporaneously. He said that it had been impossible to follow the speaker by means of the copy which he had. The reporter, however, had failed to take a single note on the speaker's impromptu remarks.

Common sense is indispensable for the reporter. In these days of public relations counsel and press releases, news sources often are difficult to see. The reporter must ask question after question to draw out whoever s/he does get to interview to learn about less obvious but important phases of the subject at hand. S/he must, in other words, be inquisitive, perceptive and healthfully skeptical.

The reporter with a cultivated nose for news realizes that, although the same elements may be present in similar stories, they invariably are there in different proportions as to importance. For instance, in an automobile accident story the reporter always must find out the names of all persons concerned, the extent of the injuries, details of the collision, etc. In Story A, however, the name of a person injured may be most important. In Story B the most important element may be the name of a prominent person who escaped injury. No two accidents ever result from exactly the same cause. In one case it may be a defective brake; in another a drunken driver; and in a third, a billboard obstructing the view. Often the cause of an accident is very unusual as when a bee makes a driver lose control of his machine.

In the same accident story there may be other important features that the reporter could not know without considerable questioning of the persons concerned. Perhaps the same two persons had been in accidents together before. Perhaps one of them recently left a hospital where he was recuperating from a previous accident. Perhaps one of them was on the way to an important engagement, a sickbed or the scene of another accident.

The possibilities of a feature in a simple accident story have by no means been exhausted. Enough has been said, however, to indicate that to report a story in depth a reporter must be constantly on his toes. The newsgatherer has to think and think and think, and s/he has to ask and ask and ask. Good reporting consists in gettintg all the pertinent facts and then some more. Otherwise the story will not be complete and may be misleading because some of the important elements are left out. The reporter who learns to do a thorough job of delving into all the potential angles of a simple straight news story is obtaining valuable training for interpretative reporting.

Smelling a rat is also an attribute of the straight news reporter and, especially, the interpretative reporter. For example, a reporter learned that a certain congressman was going to deliver a public address. He was sharp enough to inquire whether this meant that an important hearing over which the representative was to preside had been called off or postponed. Another reporter, unable to buy a certain game at several stores, investigated and learned that there was a new recreational fad in existence. Still another, noting that average school attendance in the elementary grades had gone up, investigated and came up with an article on the successful use of cold shots and other sickness preventatives.

This "smelling a rat" attitude should be the most valuable attribute of any kind of researcher, journalistic or academic. The truth-seeking reporter explores every possible avenue for information, operating with no predetermined ends to seek, no hypothesis to prove—just the truth to be determined. The manner in which information is transmitted is an important subject for scholarly research, and it is staggering to conjecture what changes the development of electronics may bring. Nevertheless, the first essential step will always be the same: to seek and to obtain the facts. They cannot be transmitted until they have been gathered, and that task will continue to be performed by human beings, not by robots.

WHAT IS NEWS?

Scholarly attempts to define news, for which the reporter is supposed to have a nose, correctly emphasize the fact that it is the account of an event not the event itself. At any given moment billions of simultaneous events occur throughout the world. Someone is born, dies, gives a speech, attends a meeting, takes a trip, commits a crime and so on ad infinitum. All of these occurrences are potentially news. They do not become so until some purveyor of news gives an account of them. The news, in other words, is the account of the event, not something intrinsic in the event itself.

Professional newsgatherers judge the potential interest and/or importance of an event before deciding whether to render an account of it, thus making it news. These newsgatherers are humans, not deities. They possess no absolutistic yardstick by which to judge what to report and what to ignore. There is nothing that cannot be made interesting in the skillful telling; and only a supernatural power could say what is important.

Understanding of the nature of news is not improved by adding such words as "timely," "concise," "accurate" or the like to definitions, as all such adjectives require explanations which differ with the editors or the circumstances. Nothing is news until it is reported, no matter when it occurred. After an important person dies hitherto unknown facts about him or her become known as in the iconoclastic anecdotes about J. Edgar Hoover, Douglas MacArthur and others. Sometimes the events occurred many years earlier, as the revelation that William O. Douglas wrote to Harry S Truman offering his support in 1948 or that Dwight Eisenhower secretly taped conversations in the Oval Office that included a criticism of Richard Nixon for attacking the foreign policy of the Democrats.

The nature of news is not changed by analysis of its effect on those who learn of it, regardless of whether the response is immediate or delayed. Valuable as the study of such factors as audience reaction may be for total understanding of social behavior, the first-rate newsgatherer acting as such persists in his search for truth. He does not ask himself what the potential use or effect of his information will be or how many "gatekeepers" will handle it; rather, his sole duty is to concentrate on discovering the truth. Annually there are numerous polls to determine public opinion regarding the year's biggest news stories. Since 1977 also Sonoma State University at Rohnert, Calif., has asked a panel of distinguished journalists, authors and scholars to cite the year's "best censored stories." The results substantiate the viewpoint that there is no simplistic definition of news.

The top stories for 1980, according to votes of the two press association editors follow:

	Associated Press	*United Press International*
1.	The election which put Ronald Reagan in the White House and gave Republicans control of the Senate for the first time in almost two decades.	Iranian hostages, including the aborted American rescue attempt.
2.	Iranian hostage crisis.	Ronald Reagan's election.
3.	The U.S. economy.	Inflation and the economy.
4.	Soviet intervention in Afghanistan.	Mount St. Helens erupts.
5.	Mount St. Helens erupts.	Iran-Iraq war.
6.	Events in Poland. The strikes. The growth of an independent union movement and the threat of Soviet intervention.	More than 100,000 Cubans flee to the United States.
7.	The murder of former Beatle John Lennon.	U.S., other nations boycott Moscow Olympics over Soviet occupation of Afghanistan.

	Associated Press	United Press International
8.	Earthquake in southern Italy which killed thousands.	Polish workers' strike.
9.	War between Iran and Iraq.	Abscam, Brilab undercover operations lead to political corruption charges.
10.	The boatlift from Cuba and the influx of thousands of Cuban and Haitian refugees and the fire that killed 84 persons at the MGM Grand Hotel in Las Vegas.	U.S. racial unrest. UPI also listed the Italian earthquake and John Lennon's murder, explaining that the two events occurred after the ballots were distributed in late November.

By contrast the Sonoma Project judges listed the ten best censored stories of the year as follows:

1. Distorted News About El Salvador. Said Prof. Carl Jensen, the project's director: "Like the Tonkin Gulf media event in 1964, this is a prime example of how the mass media . . . generated public support for a misguided U.S. foreign policy that threatened to embroil America in another Vietnam war."
2. The National Security Agency is Spying on You, by recording "telephone calls, wireless and cable messages . . . in violation of the Bill of Rights."
3. Continuing Censorship of the Nuclear Issue, the "no one died at Three Mile Island" propaganda being used to conceal the fact that nuclear war is history's greatest health hazard."
4. The Benedectin Cover-up, the drug prescribed for pregnant women, manufactured by the same company that produced thalidomide. The Food and Drug Administration is charged with covering up evidence of unfavorable reports of the drug's side effects.
5. Something is Rotten in the Global Supermarket. The transition from self-sufficient economics to food-dependent economics leaves millions of landless Third World peasants facing starvation and malnutrition.
6. The Circle of Poison with Banned Pesticides. Pesticides, banned in the U.S., are exported abroad, endangering American workers at home, Third World workers in the fields and Americans who eat the food that is returned here.
7. Space Wars: Killer Satellites and Laser Weapons. The U.S. and U.S.S.R. are developing weapons which may result in a nuclear space war.
8. Tobacco Companies Censor the Truth About Cigarettes, using advertising revenue to discourage magazines from publishing stories of the hazards of cigarette smoking.

9. Oil Companies' Monopoly of the Sun. Multinational oil companies, aerospace firms, utilities and others are buying into the solar industry, the objective appearing to be to squeeze out small competitors and control development of that alternative energy source that threatens massive investments in fossil fuels and nuclear power.
10. Toxic Waste: Poisoned Water, Poisoned Land. The Environment Protection Agency does not effectively monitor some 78 billion pounds of poisoned chemicals dumped into 51,000 sites where they enter the underground water supply.

The panelist jurors who named the top ten censored stories were: Dr. Donna Allen, editor and publisher, *Media Report to Women;* Ben. H. Bagdikian, journalist, author and professor, Graduate School of Journalism, University of California, Berkeley; Hodding Carter, journalist and former Department of State press secretary; Prof. Noam Chomsky, Massachusetts Institute of Technology; Robert Cirino, author and teacher; Ann Crittenden, economics writer, New York *Times;* David Cohen, issues politician and author; Joel Dreyfuss, executive editor, *Black Enterprise Magazine;* Nicholas Johnson, chairman, National Citizens Communications Lobby; Mary McGrory, Washington *Star* columnist; Jack Nelson, professor of social science education, Rutgers University and Sheila Rabb Weidenfeld, writer and TV host, producer and moderator.

Bagdikian is alarmed because of the shift in emphasis from quantity to quality circulation. To obtain mass circulation a century ago William Randolph Hearst, Joseph Pulitzer and others championed the cause of the underdog and crusaded for reforms in the economic system. Today, Bagdikian quotes the Detroit *News* editor as saying, "We are aiming our product at the people who make more than $18,000 a year and who are in the 28–40 group." Otis Chandler, proprietor of the Los Angeles *Times,* has said: "We cut out unprofitable circulation and we arbitrarily cut back some of our low-income circulation. The economics of American newspaper publishing is based upon . . . advertising, not circulation."

As a result of the policy to appeal to the affluent suburbs, Bagdikian notes, the New York *Daily News* goes into only 38 per cent of New York homes, the New York *Post* into 15 per cent and the New York *Times* into 12 per cent. By contrast in Illinois the paper in Freeport gets into 99 per cent of its home-city households; the one in Mattoon into 95 per cent; in Bloomington 88 per cent and Pontiac 97 per cent.

THE INTERPRETATIVE VIEWPOINT

To climb the ladder of success the journalist of the future is going to have to be more than a thoroughly trained journeyman. S/he must be capable of more than routine coverage and able to interpret as well as report what is going on.

To interpret the news it is necessary to understand it, and understanding means more than just the ability to define the jargon used by persons in different walks of life. It involves recognizing the particular event as one of a series with both a cause and an effect. The historians of the future, with their perspective, may be better able to depict the trends and currents of the present, but if the gatherer of information is well informed, through reading of history, the study of economics, sociology, political science and other academic subjects, and is acquainted with the attempts of other observers to interpret the modern scene in books and magazine articles, s/he will at least be aware of the fact that an item of news is not an isolated incident but one inevitably linked to a chain of important events.

The first important impetus to interpretative handling of the news was provided by World War I. When it broke out most Americans were surprised—dumfounded in fact—and utterly unable to explain its causes. In his doctoral dissertation at the University of Wisconsin in the mid-'30s, the late Maynard Brown suggested the extent to which the newsgathering agencies were responsible for this phenomenon. Brown wrote in part

> Where the Associated Press failed most was in preventing its reporters from sending background and informative articles based on politics and trends. It smugly adopted the attitude of permitting correspondents to report only what had definitely transpired. It wanted no interpretation of events but the mere factual reporting of the obvious. Some of its correspondents were trained in foreign affairs, but too few were able to interpret or discern significant events and tendencies.

Not only the Associated Press but other press associations and newspapers as well learned a great lesson from the experience of being totally unprepared either to understand the final steps that plunged the world into war or adequately to report the war once it started. During the '20s and '30s they peopled the capitals and other important news centers of the world with trained experts qualified not only to report but also to explain and interpret factual occurrences. Among the best of these journalistic scholars were Walter Duranty, John Gunther, Vincent Sheean, Edgar Ansel Mowrer, Edgar Snow, Quentin Reynolds, William Shirer and W. M. Fodor. In newspaper stories, magazine articles, authoritative books and radio commentaries, they and others did such a thoroughly competent job that, by contrast with 1914, for years before World War II began in 1939, an overwhelming majority of Americans expected it or at least knew it was possible if not probable.

Reader demand for more than mere drab objective reporting of domestic news grew tremendously after the stock-market crash of 1929 and during the depression years of the '30s and the period of New Deal experimentation which brought with it nationwide awareness of the increased importance in the life of every citizen of the federal government. Readership of the recently created weekly news magazines, *Time, Newsweek* and others, skyrocketed; so did the circulation of *Reader's Digest* and a multitude of other monthly digest magazines. So did the number and readership of how-to-do-it and other easily read books, allegedly compendious accounts of how to understand what was happening in a variety of fields of human interest and activity. So also did newsletters for general and specialized audiences.

Slow to modify their basic news formula, newspapers nevertheless expanded their contents to include signed columns by political analysts, most of which were syndicated at reasonable cost so as to be available for moderate- and small-sized newspapers. In the mid-'30s newspapers also experimented with weekly news reviews, some of which (notably that of the New York *Times*) have survived. They also tried out various forms of daily reviews, expanded Sunday magazine or feature sections and increased the number of supplemental articles to provide historical, geographical, biographical and other background information to help make current news more understandable and meaningful. A whole new vocabulary developed to categorize these writings. Instead of lumping them all under the general heading of "think pieces" as in the past, newsmen talked of sidebars, explainers, situationers, wrap-ups, button-ups, blockbusters and other types of explanatory, enterprise, offbeat, background, subsurface, creative, speculative or interpretative reporting and writing.

Today, the debate is virtually over, with only a few still arguing against the necessity for interpretative reporting. This means that to become more than a humdrum journeyman the future reporter must prepare himself to help meet the increasing need and demand for "subsurface" or "depth" reporting, to "take the reader behind the scenes of the day's action," "relate the news to the reader's own framework and experience," "make sense out of the facts," "put factual news in perspective," "put meaning into the news," "point up the significance of current events," and so on, to use the expressions of various authorities.

Foremost defender of interpretative reporting against its critics has been Lester Markel, longtime associate editor of the New York *Times,* who wrote

> Those who object to interpretation say that a story should be confined to the "facts." I ask, "What facts?" And I discover that there is in reality no such thing as an "objective" article in the sense these objectors use it—or in any sense, for that matter.
>
> Take the most "objective" of reporters. He collects fifty facts; out of these fifty he selects twelve which he considers important enough to include in his piece, leaving out thirty-eight. This is the first exercise of judgment.
>
> Then the reporter decides which of these twelve facts shall constitute the lead of the story. The particular fact he chooses gets the emphasis—which is important because often the reader does not go beyond the first paragraph. This is the second exercise of judgment.
>
> Then the editor reads the so-called objective story and makes a decision as to whether it is to be played on page 1 or on page 29. If it is played on page 1 it may have considerable impact on opinion. If it is put on page 29 it has no such emphasis. The most important editorial decision on any paper, I believe, is what goes on page 1. This is the third exercise of judgment.
>
> In brief, this "objective" news is, in its exponents' own terms, very unobjective

and the kind of judgment required for interpretation is no different from the kind of judgment involved in the selection of the facts for a so-called factual story and in the display of that story.

In other words, just as the Constitution is said to mean what the Supreme Court says it means, so is news what newspapers and other media of communication decide it is to be.

HOW TO PREPARE

Informational Background

The rule to follow in preparing for a career in journalism is this: learn as much about as many things as possible and stay intellectually alert. The ignorant reporter is at a tremendous disadvantage. S/he annoys news sources, doesn't obtain all of the essential facts, and may make gross errors of fact as well as emphasis.

To cover intelligently a police station, criminal court, city hall, county, state or federal office, or political headquarters, one must understand the setups of government, the nature and functions of various offices. The reporter must be able to read and quickly digest the contents of legal documents. S/he must know the meanings of such terms as *corpus delicti, habeas corpus, injunction* and *certiorari*. A reporter cannot say *divorce* when *separate maintenance* is meant, or *parole* when it should be *probation*. The reporter must be able to read a bank balance sheet, know when a financial market is bullish and when bearish and what it means to *sell short, hedge* and *stockpile*. S/he must understand what it means to *refinance a bond issue* or *liquidate the assets of a corporation*. Craft unions must not be confused with industrial unions.

It is impossible for an interpretative reporter to write that the last obstacle to beginning a slum-clearance program has been removed unless s/he knows the procedure by which such projects are developed. One can't explain the status of a pending city ordinance without understanding what the rules provide for future consideration of it. It is impossible to interview a prosecuting attorney regarding a possible course of action in a particular case unless one knows what the alternatives are.

Although most editorial offices today are equipped with good libraries, or morgues as they often still are called, the reporter has to know which reference books and clipping files to consult to obtain historical and other explanatory information to "round out" a story. As the reporter gathers experience s/he becomes a veritable storehouse of knowledge. Aware of the nature of different organizations, public and private, the trained newsgatherer knows which ones to consult on which occasion and what each group's slant or interest is likely to be.

Without background knowledge in a field a reporter cannot fill out an account by declaring that the home run was the longest ever hit in the park;

that this was the first time a certain ward gave a voting majority to the candidates of a particular party; that a fatal accident occurred at an intersection where the city council once refused to permit the erection of stop signs; that what seems to be a new proposal for civic reform really was resurrected from a decade-old report by an elder statesman.

At a recent Associated Press Managing Editors meeting, Robert Paine of the Memphis *Commercial Appeal* cited the following story:

> Grand Junction, Tenn., Feb. 19.—(AP)—A smooth-working hound flushed seven bevies of quail in a three-hour trial yesterday for the top performance of the national championship.

Commented Paine:

> I imagine that every bird-dog owner in the country shuddered in horror at the word HOUND. That would be about the same as saying a cow won the Kentucky derby. There are strictly different kinds of dogs and bird-dog fanciers have a habit of shooting from the hip when one of their dogs is called a hound.
>
> Secondly, the word FLUSH is the exact opposite of the word that should have been used. That would be about like saying Babe Ruth won the game by striking out. Flush means to frighten the birds into flying away. The correct word is point.

It was not too many years ago that a journalistic ignoramous asked the Nobel prize-winning physicist Dr. Robert Millikan what cosmic rays were "good for." Those were the days when science was treated more or less as a joke in editorial offices and reporters assigned to science news stories were capable of little more than asking when the scholars expected to fly to Mars, find the missing link or take the smell out of the onion. No wonder that many scientists still are reluctant to talk to reporters.

The interpretative reporter reads the fine print of a news story in order to answer the reader's query, "What does it mean?" To keep a particular news event "in focus," the interpretative reporter shows its comparative importance. Darrell Huff began his *How to Lie with Statistics,* a book every journalist of whatever kind would find valuable reading, with a warning that widespread reporting of a particular type of news, such as crime, easily can create a distorted impression as regards a social situation.

Mere figures showing total numbers of different types of crime committed in two or more areas only suggest the real story. Explanations of why styles in lawbreaking differ in different places at the same time, and at the same place at different times, are to be found in such variable factors as size and complexion of population, police policies and activities and many others.

To present anywhere near a true picture of the housing situation in any community, a reporter must consider the age of the community and of the dwelling units; the adequacy of zoning and building codes and their enforcement; the influx of newcomers and the effect, including that caused by prejudice against certain types of persons because of race, national origin, religion or other reasons; the extent of overpopulation; transportation and parking facilities; educational, cultural and recreational advantages; the income and cost of living indices; nearby urban and suburban growth and similar factors. With such data the reporter can provide readers with an understanding of the situation and enable them properly to evaluate proposals for change.

Mere announcement that consumer credit outstanding at any given time is such-and-such means little or nothing unless the reader knows how the figures given compare with similar ones for comparable periods in other months or years. Tables, graphs and charts help show trends; the news magazine *U.S. News & World Report* makes very effective use of them. For a broader picture of the state of the economy as a whole, more than comparative figures in any one economic category is necessary. In addition to installment buying, price indices, extent and kind (savings or checking) of bank deposits and withdrawals, a breakdown of the types of depositors (by size of deposits), purchase and cancellation of government securities (with comparable breakdown) bank loans, mortgages, new businesses, business failures, growth of chains and monopolies and other similar factors must be considered.

Often the motives of persons in the news must be known to make their actions understandable. The more a spectator knows about the strategy involved in an athletic contest, for instance, the more enjoyment s/he derives from it and the better able s/he is to second-guess the manager or be a Monday morning quarterback. If, on the other hand, the spectator knows little or nothing about such strategy, s/he won't understand why a weak hitter was given an intentional base on balls in order to pitch to a weaker one, possibly one batting from the same side as that from which the pitcher throws and supposedly more likely to hit into a double play. Or s/he will not understand why a quarterback called for a play that could not help but lose ground on the third down in order to put the ball in better position to try for a field goal on fourth down.

Just as sports writers explain the strategy of coaches, managers and contestants, so could reporters dealing with political affairs explain that precinct captains who rival the positions of ward committeemen often are made candidates for judgeships in order to remove them from active politics. The interpretative reporter knows that cornerstone layings, dedications of buildings, openings of parks and other public facilities and similar acts are timed so as to have the maximum beneficial effect for the officeholders in charge. After s/he has been around long enough, the interpretative reporter knows the tricks of the trade and can at least suggest probable causes for the behavior of many newsworthy persons. Failure to do so means that readers are in the position of just not knowing what's going on.

To write with the perspective of the cultural anthropologist or historian of a century means to be aware of schools of thought, climates of opinion and social, economic and political trends. A journalistic scholar should know when the views of an educator are consistent with those of an outstanding scholar or organization or with what has been attempted elsewhere. The education reporter should know what *progressive* versus *traditional* in pedagogical methods means. To cover social welfare s/he should know the difference between the missionary (settlement house or boys club) and the self-help (area or community project) approaches.

There is a correlation between the extent of a feeling of insecurity and attacks upon civil liberties. Quite naturally the curves fluctuate with periods of war and depression, although it always is dangerous to draw historical parallels without thorough consideration of all possible factors.

Of this the studious interpretative reporter is certain: nothing just happens. A wave of intolerance has a cause. So has a revival movement, excessive hero worship, a bullish stock market, an increase in superstition, or any fad, fashion, craze or mass movement. Sometimes what seem to be isolated phenomena in several different fields really stem from the same causal roots. At any rate, there is always an explanation for how we got that way. For instance, when violence erupts and persists simultaneously in many parts of the world, it is shortsighted to treat a local incident as an isolated phenomenon.

Academic Preparation

Although there probably always will be exceptions, present trends indicate that future journalists will be college trained. Such, in fact, is already the case on most metropolitan newspapers and, except for old-timers, most of the degree holders went to schools of journalism. The proportion of those with master's and other higher degrees also is increasing.

Modern journalism schools are not trade schools. From two-thirds to four-fifths of a student's classwork is taken in the liberal arts or other divisions. Anything and everything that a future journalist studies has potential future value and it is frustrating not to be able to take the entire curriculum in the humanities and the natural and physical sciences. Those who are ambitious to specialize ultimately in particular fields should do so, but the majority should strive for a thorough and well-rounded background in the social sciences: political science, sociology and economics in particular. The student should try to get in courses in public finance, criminology and labor problems among others. History courses provide perspective and psychology enables one to come closer to understanding both individual and crowd behavior. The reporter should have some idea about what public opinion is that journalists are supposed to influence.

In advanced journalism courses the student should expect to be taught how to utilize the background and theoretical knowledge acquired all over the rest of the campus in reporting and interpreting the contemporary scene. On assignments, the student observes theory becoming action, and by taking some philosophy s/he will be better able to comprehend and evaluate the immediate incident in terms of the general and eternal.

A strict journalism instructor, simulating the exactness of a hard-boiled city editor, can teach sound methods of research. The journalistic fact-finder does not begin with a hypothesis for which factual proof is sought. Rather, the journalist is an open-minded seeker after truth who explores every possible avenue of investigation; and only after exhausting every chance to obtain additional information does s/he attempt to draw conclusions regarding the accumulated data. This objective approach to knowledge is much sounder than that practiced by many researchers in other academic fields. In the process, the student-reporter becomes familiar with the nature of reference or source material; s/he may learn how to read and understand a county board's budget or the complicated declaration filed to begin a civil law action.

Since World War II, a number of social scientists have become interested in quantitative analysis of various aspects of social behavior and in communication theory. They use the tools of the statistician and the language of the sociologist to examine the effects of various ways to influence human thought and behavior. Many of their findings are of value to the propagandist, advertiser, public relations counsel and others who have ideas or products to sell. Knowledge of what they are up to is important for the true journalist who is a protector of their potential victims. The journalist, however, should be wary of academic fads and should examine the so-called behavioral sciences and communications theory courses to determine whether they have relevance to anything journalistic and whether the teachers of them have any practical knowledge of the profession of newsgathering. *Social Science As Sorcery* by Stanislav Andreski (St. Martin's Press, 1972) is an edifying critique by a Reading University scholar.

Prospective employers usually want to see samples of an applicant's published work. The student who has any thought of becoming a journalist should start accumulating clippings as early as possible. Certainly there should be stories written for high school and college papers. Otherwise the hiring editor will want to know why the would-be professional cub didn't have enough interest to take advantage of whatever opportunities alma mater provides.

Occupational Aids

Until recently, few reporters felt the need of shorthand since the task of translating notes, of which there was temptation to take too many, slowed rather than hastened the process of reporting and writing. Today, however, when it often is necessary to interview news sources in the company of other reporters or to attend news conferences at which only a few get to ask questions, a verbatim record of what happened often is valuable. Testimony in court or at committee hearings also can best be taken down in shorthand; thus more and more newsgatherers who specialize in this kind of work are learning it.

Those who have not done so usually develop their own system of short longhand, and may know some of the commercialized systems, which are based primarily upon abbreviations for common syllables and combinations of letters. The reporter who develops his/her own system uses abbreviations for frequently used words and phrases. For instance, "2" is used for "to," "too" and "two," and "c" for "see," "u" for "you," "r" for "are." The reporter can use simplified spelling in note taking if not in actual copy and can make use of such common abbreviations as "rr" for "railroad" and "inc" for "incomplete.'' S/he may even use foreign words that are shorter than English, as the French *selon* instead of *according to*. Instead of ''capital punishment'' s/he may jot down ''cp'' and instead of ''labor union'' may write ''lu.'' Still used by some old-timers is the Phillips Telegraphic Code patented in the late 19th century by an Associated Press official. Typical code abbreviations are xgr for ''legislature,'' bd for ''board,'' sap for ''soon as possible,'' xn for ''constitution,'' and itxd for ''intoxicated.'' There are several similar systems all using abbreviations, including Zinman Rapid Writing and Streamline.

Tape recorders today are in widespread use by magazine and free-lance writers and by newspaper reporters gathering material for feature or other articles for which the deadline is not immediate. Under all conditions the recorder is valuable at news conferences and public functions and even during some interviews as a means of protecting both interviewer and interviewee as to the accuracy of subsequent quotation. There is the danger, however, that such interviews can become too formal and stilted and that the presence of the electronic device cause the interviewee to become overly cautious in his/her remarks. The same is true if motion pictures or television recordings are made. In such case, of course, the reporter does not have to know how to operate the gadgets. On some small- and medium-sized papers, however, s/he may be expected, on occasion at least, to be able to use a camera when a staff photographer is unable to accompany him/her on assignment. Labor union contracts may forbid doing so in other places. In any case, it is unlikely that the reporter will have to know more than how to take the pictures; the development and printing will be the task of others.

The greatest drawback to using the tape recorder is the time necessary to replay and make notes of the points of use in the story at hand. Obviously, it must be necessary to take even more time for such translation as that consumed by the interview itself. Therefore, the tape recorder is of limited value to the daily newspaper reporter with immediate deadlines to make. It is of great value to a feature writer for newspaper or magazine.

If you ran for president of the Be Good and Behave society you couldn't get your face into the newspaper, unless you paid advertising rates. But if you get drunk and shoot a few dozen people, the newspapers will bid against one another for the only photo of your mug in your home.

—Bridger (Mont.) *News*

Anything really new attracts attention and is news. Hence, Amos Cummings' maxim, "If a dog bites a man, that's not news. But if a man bites a dog, that is news."

If you read, "Girl Discouraged, kills herself with gas," you pass on—so many girls kill themselves with gas.

But when Miss Mary Caprea, poor thing, buys ten dresses and ten hats and fails in the movies and kills herself, you read all of it. For Miss Caprea took the ten hats and dresses out of her trunk. Then she ran a pipe from the gas stove into the trunk, got into the trunk, pulled down the lid and died, crouching. Newspapers will have diagrams of that suicide, but if it happened ten times, they'd hardly notice it. That's why the ancient philosophical egotist jumped into the mouth of Vesuvius. And that's why, as Cibber remarked two hundred years ago:

> *The aspiring youth that fired the Ephesian dome*
> *Outlives in fame the pious fool that raised it.*

—ARTHUR BRISBANE

If I were to make a plea to the colleges and universities on behalf of the press, it would be to prepare a few all-around men and women who should be competent to perform a planetary service, not only geographically but intelligently, to be in this democratic age what Democritus was in his day to his little world. Such men as one whom I knew who was prepared when the tomb of Tut-Ankh-Amen was opened to enter intelligently with the archaeologist; who when Einstein propounded his theory had some notion of what he was talking about; whom I found one day trying to find geometrically the area of a triangle in the terms of its sides; who in the midst of the last campaign wrote a two-column editorial on the new planet, and yet who could tell you the baseball champions for the last ten years, or the presidential returns for the last century.

—DR. JOHN H. FINLEY, associate editor, New York *Times*

2

GETTING IT RIGHT

Sometimes a reporter is present at a news event as a meeting, speech, court hearing or athletic contest. More often, however, the newsgatherer must rely on secondhand information obtained by interviewing eyewitnesses, authorities and others, or from press releases, reports and documents. Even when the reporter is at the scene, facts and details must be checked with police, firefighters, convention chairpersons and the like.

Usually these sources are approachable and cooperative. As much cannot always be said of others from whom the reporter seeks supplementary background information, comments, explanations or predictions of the consequences of an event. Maybe the news source doesn't want to become involved in some matter, for fear of being summoned to court as a witness or of arousing the displeasure of public officials, gangsters and others. Possibly a person whose opinion is solicited does not want to reveal ignorance or to risk betraying a business or other secret. The reasons why a news source slams the door or telephone or clams up may be many and diverse, but the obligation of the reporter is the same, to learn any facts that it is in the public interest to make known.

INTERVIEWING

Reliability of Witnesses

Even when news sources are cooperative the shrewd reporter should seek corroboration of whatever he is told. Editors often hold stories until at least two witnesses or authorities have verified their contents.

Beginning with Hugo Munsterberg's *On the Witness Stand* almost a century ago, there have been many scholarly investigations of the reliability of human testimony. A recent excellent article on the subject was "Eyewitness Testimony" by Robert Buckhaout in the December 1974 *Scientific American*. The author concludes, "Human perception is sloppy and uneven," and "the ideal observer does not exist, nor does the ideal physical environment to make testimony trustworthy."

It is human to distort an impression to conform to one's preconceived notions, prejudices and experiences. No instant recall is possible as it is when televising sports events. The closest approximation is the classroom exercise of staging a dramatic event and then asking students to prepare memoranda on what they observed. The differences in the reports are fantastic and constitute a strong warning to the journalistic truth-seeker.

Journalists are also suggestible human beings likely to be influenced by the prestige of informants. Their visual impressions are often distorted because of their preconceptions. An outstanding example occurred when Dr. Otto John fled from West to East Germany. According to the Associated Press,

> He spoke nervously at first. Then he got over his first mild stage fright and was completely at ease. Pink-cheeked, he was the picture of German health. His low modulated voice was pleasing to hear, regardless of how one would react to the sentiments involved. He made many wisecracks that brought laughter, wisecracks appreciated only in his native German tongue which lost much of their salt in translation. Not all of the laughs came from the Communist press either.

What the United Press reporter saw was as follows:

> His press conference statement today was recited grimly and hurriedly, much in the manner of confessions made by the victims of numerous Red Purge trials.
>
> He gave the tell-tale evidence of Communist brainwashing tactics; he was wooden-faced and nervous at the conference. He never smiled, although some of his comments brought laughter from newsmen.

An International News Service writer in Washington, using material purported to be supplied by Allied counterintelligence sources, wrote

> These sources are convinced that, through use of a highly developed combination of hypnosis and hypodermic needles, Dr. John became a virtual "zombie" without a will of his own, capable of acting and speaking only at the dictates of his Communist masters.

Over the National Broadcasting Company airways, Robert McCormick commented as follows:

> John handled himself with self-confidence and assurance. He definitely showed no signs of being drugged, beaten or tortured and, in fact, seemed quite happy. If anything, he looked more content than he looked in Bonn.

It is impossible to argue with the importance of attempting to describe Dr. John's attitude after his sensational act. No deadpan recording of whatever words he spoke would have sufficed to give readers a hint of the motive for his act. Equally obvious is the fact that at least one (which?) of those who attended the press conference was a thoroughly incompetent reporter. The example does not disprove the value or necessity of interpretative reporting. Rather, it provides argument for the fact that journalists, whether they report and write objectively or interpretatively, must be highly ethical.

There have been some outstanding examples of reportorial error. One occurred when Roy Howard of the United Press reported that an armistice to end World War I had been signed Nov. 7, 1918. The False Armistice was celebrated world-wide four days before the real signing Nov. 11. In 1961 reporters waited at the airport in Ndola, North Rhodesia, for arrival of the plane on which Dag Hammarskjöld was a passenger. A plane landed and from a distance a man resembling the United Nations secretary general was seen to alight. Reporters signaled his arrival to the whole world. Actually the plane carrying Hammarskjöld had crashed ten miles north of Ndola killing all aboard.

Getting the Interview

When seeking additional facts about a fast-breaking overt incident, a reporter does not have time to write or telephone for an appointment. A great deal of such interviewing is by telephone. For best results the reporter should be straightforward, identifying her/himself by name and newspaper. Pretending to be a police official or coroner's deputy is self-defeating, because the untruth is bound to be discovered, at least when the paper appears. Since the first 30 seconds of a telephone interview may be the most important, come to the point at once, at least to make clear the nature of the information that is being sought. When seeking opinions as well as fact, avoid a negative approach as "You wouldn't want to say something on this matter, would you?" Rather say, "We want your opinion."

If someone has recommended that the reporter contact the interviewee that fact usually can be stated unless the tipster requested that s/he remain anonymous and the reporter gave his/her word. Unless it seems necessary to gain the confidence of the interviewee, it usually is better to postpone mention of other mutual acquaintances as one never can be certain what the relationship between the interviewee and the third party is.

In all situations, whether face-to-face or by telephone, the interviewer must be flexible. Ordinarily it is better to postpone asking potentially embarrassing or irritating questions until after a friendly relationship has been established. However, when using the telephone, if the reporter fears the interviewee will hang up, it may be expedient to reveal whatever the reporter already possesses with a request that the interviewee comment upon it.

When the time factor is not urgent, appointments can be made by mail or telephone. Some important people surround themselves with secretaries, public relations counsel, bodyguards and others to protect their privacy, which they often believe all journalists want to destroy. In such cases the reporter is lucky if s/he has influential friends to put in a good word. It is important to make friends with people on the way up as well as those who are already in influential positions. One makes contacts of value in the future, no one can predict when. Friendly secretaries can be of great assistance.

Reportorial perseverance is usually rewarded. If a man deliberately evades the press by refusing to answer the telephone or by hiding in an office or at home, he plays a losing game. If he is a person whose information or opinion the newspaper has a right to request, his refusal to grant an interview does not make him appear in a very favorable light to readers. The reporter must be careful in stating that a man has disappeared to avoid being interviewed or facing charges but it can be said that a person could not be reached. In fact, such a statement should be included to let readers know that the effort was made. If a person grants an interview but still refuses to talk, his silence may be even more important news than any statement would have been. Once the reporter has questioned a person and has received a noncommittal answer or no answer at all, he can say that Mr. So-and-So refused to make any comment. Then readers can draw their own conclusions as to why Mr. So-and-So would not talk.

> Mayor Alvin R. Potter had nothing to say today regarding the accusation that city employees, including himself, obtain free gasoline from the city yards.
>
> The charge was made yesterday by Ald. Leonard Ball, chairman of the streets committee. The chief executive's only reply to inquiring reporters was: "I have no statement to make at this time."

Sometimes the reporter may be able to convince a subject that it is better to make some statement. If a person knows that the paper will run a story of his refusal to comment, s/he may be frightened into speaking against a previous resolution not to do so.

In his *Inside Story* (Doubleday, 1974), Brit Hume, then assistant to Jack Anderson, says it is a "common technique" to persuade a person that you have been told a truly lurid story to inspire him to reveal the truth. Hume often was sly in identifying himself with the syndicate that distributed the Anderson column rather than with his employer. And he recommends the two-questioner technique popular with police whereby one interrogator assumes a belligerent attitude while the other seems protective. The Washington *Post* reporters Carl Bernstein and Bob Woodward, Pultizer prize winners for the Watergate scandal exposé, reveal in their book *All the President's Men* (Simon and Schuster, 1974) that they inspired confidence when Bob said he was a registered Republican and Carl expressed a sincere antipathy for both parties. When an interviewer asked who gave the reporters his name, they could explain the necessity of protecting their sources, thus inspiring confidence from a jittery interviewee. They often called at interviewees' homes unannounced and always created the impression of seeking the truth regarding partial information they possessed. The confessions of these and several other top flight reporters inspired a great deal of soul searching throughout the entire journalistic world. The ethical beginner who is studying this textbook should become acquainted with the memoirs of many contemporary reporters.

The veteran foreign correspondent, Georgie Ann Geyer, who has interviewed the heads of most of the world's governments, relates how when foreign correspondents were not allowed to enter Cambodia, she obtained a tourist visa. That, she says, was the only time in 20 years that she misrepresented herself. On another occasion, however, she got herself invited to a dinner as a state guest rather than as a journalist.

The Reluctant Interviewee

Once the reporter has an audience his/her first task is to win the confidence of the interviewee. It is impossible to lay down rules for all occasions. Sometimes it is possible to break the ice by irrelevant conversation, perhaps inspired by a painting or other object in the room or by a comment on some hobby of the interviewee's. But unless the reporter is sincerely interested and, above all, well-informed, the effort may repulse the interviewee as being contrived.

The reporter's best bet to impress the interviewee is by making clear what s/he is after and that s/he has prepared for the occasion by learning about he interviewee and the subject of the interview. The reporter must make it clear that s/he does not know all the facts; otherwise s/he would not be there and should not be afraid to seem to be asking stupid questions.

Beginners and even some experienced reporters often yield to the temptation to argue with interviewees. If one hopes to convert the interviewee this is usually a futile effort, and one runs the risk of antagonizing the person from whom information is sought. It is possible, without being belligerent, to ask potentially embarrassing questions by requesting comments on statements or situations about which others have ideas different from those of the interviewee. Interviewers should have specific questions in mind but must be flexible enough to follow any leads to other points arising from the interviewee's responses.

If a person evades questions or changes the subject and talks about extraneous matters, the reporter must be tactful about any interruption. The source should not, however, be permitted to escape responding to the purpose of the interview. The reporter should not give up but should come back to vital unanswered questions. Continued dodging of them usually convinces the interviewer that s/he is on the right track in the quest for knowledge. The clever reporter does not terminate an interview until s/he has asked all the questions s/he had in mind and has obtained some response from the subject.

Sometimes a lucky guess disarms a reluctant interviewee as when the reporter asks whether a certain meeting is in the offing and the news source is startled into believing the reporter has more information than the interviewee had assumed to be the case.

When the interviewee is cautious or antagonistic it usually is best to take as few notes as possible. In fact, it might be disastrous to take a single note. If the reporter can get his/her subject to forget that s/he is speaking for publication, s/he will obtain much more than if the person is constantly reminded that the interviewee is taking down verbatim what s/he is being told.

Sometimes the interviewee requests that the reporter take verbatim notes. Or the reporter at the end of an interview may remark, "By the way, would you mind spelling that name for me?" Or s/he may ask for exact figures, addresses, etc., which the interviewee will be glad to have correct. The reporter must be careful in asking for such information, however, so as not to suggest to the interviewee that s/he had better start designating which remarks were for publication and which not.

The reporter must train his/her memory to recall, an hour or so afterward, all the important remarks of the interviewee. S/he should make immediate mental note of any startling statement which s/he will want to use verbatim, and should keep turning it over in his/her mind during the rest of the interview.

S/he should seize the first opportunity after leaving the scene of the interview to write down such a statement and to make any other necessary notes. If the reporter has an hour or so before s/he must write his/her story, s/he will be surprised to find that, bit by bit, virtually the entire interview will come back to him/her.

In writing an opinion interview, it often is wise, for the sake of authority, to mention that the statements were made during an interview. If so, "Mr. White stated in an interview today" is better than "Mr. White told a News reporter today." The newspaper should not boast of an exclusive interview unless it has shown ingenuity in outwitting opponents.

Off the Record

A reporter must always be reluctant to allow the interviewee to go off the record. It usually is understood that the newsgatherer expects to use whatever information s/he obtains. It can happen that, in the course of an interview, a principal says, "I'll answer that but only off the record." The reporter must make a fast decision whether to proceed on such terms. If the answer probably can be obtained from other sources, the reporter may consent but it is wise to advise the interviewee that the attempt will be made to get the desired information from others. What the reporter never should permit is for an interviewee to make statements and later designate that they were off the record. If other sources for the information do not exist, the reporter would be killing his/her own story by promising not to use it.

Reporters sometimes leave news conferences when the interviewee goes off the record, fairly certain that some colleague will fill them in later. Once the reporter agrees to accept something off the record, that promise must be kept. To do otherwise is to risk ostracism by one's fellows as well as to lose the trust of the news source. The most outstanding case of a reporter who violated a secrecy promise occurred at the end of World War II when Edward Kennedy, an Associated Press correspondent, disregarded Gen. Dwight D. Eisenhower's request on behalf of the White House that news of the German surrender be postponed until it could be announced simultaneously in London and Moscow. Kennedy's act, which put a strain on American-Russian relations, was roundly condemned by other journalists. The Associated Press publicly apologized.

The Typology of Interviewing

Interviews can be classified in several different ways, the shortest and most inclusive being fact, opinion and personality.

When he was editor of the Wichita *Beacon,* John Colburn prepared the following typology of questions useful in interviewing.

Type	*Purpose*	*Examples*
A. Factual	1. To get information 2. To open discussion	1. All the "W" questions: what, where, why, when, who and how?
B. Explanatory	1. To get reasons 2. To broaden discussion 3. To develop additional information	1. "In what way would this solve the problem?" 2. "What other aspects of this should be considered?" 3. "Just how would this be done?"
C. Justifying	1. To challenge old ideas 2. To develop new ideas 3. To get reasoning	1. "Why do you think so?" 2. "How do you know?" 3. "What evidence do you have?"
D. Leading	1. To introduce a new idea 2. To advance a suggestion of others 3. To crystalize thoughts of a person into reasonable information	1. "Should you consider this—as a possible solution?" 2. "Would this—be an alternative?"

Type	Purpose	Examples
E. Hypothetical	1. To develop new ideas 2. To suggest another, possibly unpopular opinion 3. To change the course of the discussion	1. "Suppose you did it this way . . . What would happen?" 2. "Another city does this . . . Is this feasible here?"
F. Alternative	1. To make decisions between alternatives	1. "Which of these solutions is best, A or B?"
G. Coordinating	1. To develop concensus	1. "Is this the next step?" 2. "Is there general agreement then on this plan among Board members?"

Friendships on Beats

Because nobody is as grammatically correct while speaking as while writing, it is common practice to fix up unprepared oral statements of persons in the news so as not to embarrass them or create a wrong impression. The sense of any quotation must, of course, be retained. On occasion, it may not be in the public interest to protect a source. If, for instance, despite overwhelming evidence to the contrary, a public official declares that he knows nothing of a scandalous situation with which he should be familiar, it is not unfair to quote him verbatim. When such necessity arises, the best reporter who has daily contact with the news source would be pleased to have a special or general assignment reporter sent over to handle that particular story. Often the beat reporter finds it wise to warn someone with whom s/he has made friendly contact that an unfavorable story is going to appear. In other words, a reporter cannot be effective if s/he makes enemies of those on whom s/he must depend for information. How to maintain personal relationships of friendship and at the same time fulfill one's newsgathering obligations is one of the most vexatious problems with which the best reporter has to contend. As one of them put it,

> A newspaper reporter, especially if he is assigned to a particular beat, enters into a very personal relationship with his news sources after a while.
>
> It can't be avoided, for these are the people you are talking with every day. In contrast, the public for which a reporter is writing, and to which he is responsible, is always a very impersonal and nebulous thing. There is a constant danger of giving the human being the benefit of the doubt at the expense of some quite abstract body of readers. For example, the superintendent of schools gets himself into a bad situation. Knowing him, you understand that he had the best motives in

the world, but simply made a mistake of judgment. You know he recognizes it is your duty to advise the public of his action. Or, a situation I actually ran into: a cop had been suspended for striking a prisoner. I found out about it. The cop was a guy I had talked with every day for nearly a year. He'd told me all about himself, his family and his ambitions. The suspension had been ordered promptly and there was no doubt that he was being properly punished for his action. I wondered at the time what possible good it would do the public to know of the suspension. Who was the public, anyway? Of course, I wrote the story and spent much time trying to explain to the cop and to his superior why it was necessary that the public be advised. But the point is that the reporter is called upon often to make that kind of decision, and unless he is very careful, he will unconsciously find himself giving in to the very human appeal of his news sources. I think I've found this the toughest temptation to guard against in the business.

One of the greatest pitfalls the cub reporter must avoid is naïveté. No matter how pleasing the personality of the interviewee, or how logical whatever s/he has to say, the reporter must realize that it is necessary to check, corroborate, diligently seek the other side and in general not be gullible. With complete sincerity a news source usually presents a one-sided version of whatever is at issue. A callow reporter may be tremendously impressed with the account of how a business, governmental unit or social agency operates if s/he relies entirely on what an interested party tells him/her. Omissions, misplaced emphases and distortions may become apparent only by interviewing other persons known to be critical. Otherwise the reporter may become only a messenger boy or girl for press releases or one-sided "good" news. Probing, both by intensive interviewing of original news sources and of others, will not always end in complete reversal of original impressions, but it is a necessary precaution against error through excessive exuberance.

Publicity Seekers

By no means are all persons reticent about granting interviews. The person who attempts to cajole or bulldoze reporters or to hand out statements promoting himself or a cause is ubiquitous. The reporter must be constantly on guard to spot the phony.

Entertainers and authors advertising their books are eager to be interviewed, especially on television. They have secretaries or press agents who may have typewritten or mimeographed answers to stock questions. The enterprising reporter, of course, wants much more. If the primary purpose of the interview is to obtain information or opinion on some public matter, the reporter may encounter the unhappily growing tendency on the part of celebrities to expect monetary reward. Magazines, radio and television offer huge sums for memoirs, life stories and personality sketches or profiles. Those who have such to sell are reluctant to give them away free to newspaper reporters.

When a public official or other prominent person returns from abroad, especially if s/he has been on a public mission or involved in a newsworthy experience, s/he hardly can avoid granting some kind of interview to the press.

It is obtaining an exclusive audience with the celebrity that challenges the reporter's ingenuity. Sometimes a letter of introduction from some other prominent person helps. Accosting an interviewee in a hotel lobby generally achieves little more than laconic replies to quick questions—at best an appointment for a future time.

A musician, scientist, writer, politician or any other person who has become prominent despises the reporter who betrays ignorance of his/her activities and reputation. Anyone with a speciality, furthermore, is bored to have to talk to another who is utterly uninformed concerning his/her field of interest. There are numerous biographical reference books which the reporter can consult to learn something about a person's life and achievements. The newspaper's reference department, probably computerized or about to be, should be able to supply information as to what the interviewee actually has done.

The importance of being prepared was impressed upon an Atlanta reporter who asked Vivien Leigh what part she played in the motion picture version of *Gone With the Wind* when the actress attended the premiere of the reissue of the 1939 Academy Award winner. Miss Leigh simply informed the reporter that she did not care to be interviewed by such an ignorant person.

Not only national celebrities but also local persons who have won honors, taken new positions of importance, or been in the news prominently are the frequent subjects of reportorial inquiry. Reporters follow candidates for public office around during a day of campaigning to make a full report on their activities. Articles written after interviews with newly appointed school superintendents, bank presidents, chairmen of civic organizations and the like may resemble the profiles (combined biography, character sketch and description) originally made popular by *The New Yorker*. The object is to give readers the "feel" of the person, not just statistical facts regarding him/her and his/her activities.

When a person is being written up primarily because of his/her information or opinions regarding a matter, personality traits and description should be kept to a minimum or ignored. If a man shouts, bangs on the table, hesitates before giving an answer or in some other way behaves so that proper understanding of his comments requires mention of such circumstances, they may be included. Unless such is the case, references to "the balding professor" or "the slight soft-spoken man" may be inconsistent and out of place.

By Mary Powers

Read the newspaper aloud while holding an infant. Use complete sentences when talking to a baby. And talk to the baby while driving, shopping or cooking.

Simple steps, but ones teacher Nancy Peterson said parents can take to protect their children from joining the estimated 23 million American adults who cannot read.

"Parents get very excited when their children start school. All of a sudden they begin trying to teach them to read, or learn their ABCs, or start subscribing to educational magazines. They don't realize how much time they've already wasted," explained Peterson, a VanHorne Elementary School teacher.

She also coordinates the Tucson Area Reading Council's Bathe Your Baby In Reading Program.

Parents should concentrate on preparing their child to learn, not on teaching them to read, she stressed. They should also concentrate on making the process fun, she added.

The task begins at birth. Peterson contacts mothers while they're still in the obstetrics ward. . . . [Tucson *Arizona Daily Star*]

Entirely the opposite is true when the object is to make readers thoroughly acquainted with the subject of the interview as a person. In such cases, the subject's opinions are secondary and are used to help build a total word picture. How a person appears, talks and behaves during the interview may be pertinent, especially if the reporter elects to write in the first person.

By George Esper

Rogers, Ark. (AP)—He dances the disco and partakes in transcendental meditation. At age 75.

Casual dress has replaced the dark blue suit, vest with gold chain and high collar with pin that were his trademark.

He has become a health food enthusiast.

He has taken a new wife, 40 years his junior, and moved from New York to the idyllic manmade lakes of northern Arkansas.

Life has taken some curious turns for Dr. Benjamin Spock, the grand adviser to mothers whose "Baby and Child Care" book has sold more than 28 million copies and has been translated into more than 30 languages since it was first published in 1946.

Ten years ago this month, he was convicted in Boston of conspiracy to aid, abet and counsel young men to avoid the draft for the Vietnam War. He was sentenced to two years in prison, but the conviction was overturned by a higher court.

Looking back now, he says he has no regrets except that it took so long to stop the war. . . .

These rules are applicable to all kinds of subjects including the off-the-beaten-path characters who may be the subjects of feature articles: retiring lifeguards, octogenarians, persons with unusual hobbies or reminiscences and the like. Pictures supplement and confirm written accounts in such cases, not the other way around.

High school reporters may be excused for referring to notes while asking questions. The professional, however, memorizes questions. These should be related to the interviewee's field of interest and yet should not be too elementary or questions that it is reasonable to suppose the person has been asked time and time again. The reporter should try to find some new angle of approach, some fresh subject upon which the person interviewed will be able to speak. S/he should not try to cover his/her subject's entire field of interest. To do so would mean failure to cover any aspect with any degree of thoroughness. The best stories following interviews with celebrities are on specific points about which the interviewer has questioned his subject thoroughly.

News Conferences

Persons who know that they are to be interviewed by the press often arrange for formal interviews at which representatives of all the newspapers and perhaps electronic and other media in the community are present. From the standpoint of the reporter, such an interview is undesirable because none of the information is exclusive.

An advantage of the formal interview, however, lies in the fact that there are several minds thinking up questions to ask. Frequently the person to be interviewed announces in advance that these questions must be prepared in writing and submitted some time before the hour of the interview. This procedure permits the reporter to know exactly what the subject matter of the interview is to be, but it also allows the interviewee to prepare guarded answers to questions that, if presented spontaneously, might bring forth answers more to the reporter's liking.

If the news conference is televised, as are many of those in the White House, it may take days or weeks to verify or supplement misstatements or incomplete remarks that have already been heard by large audiences. In non-broadcast interviews presidents and other prominent persons may designate what of their remarks are to be (1) on the record and usable as coming from the source; (2) background information usable but not to be attributed to the source; (3) off-the-record, for the reporter's information only, not to be used without further permission.

Even when interviewing someone in the company of other reporters, in closed conference, it is possible to obtain material on which to write a different story from those which the others will write. The keenest listener and the sharpest wit present writes the best story. Comparison of several write-ups based on a joint interview often discloses several different methods of handling the subject. One reporter plays up one statement and another reporter picks an entirely different one for the feature. Still a third writer concentrates on the personality of the interviewee rather than upon his/her remarks.

Denials

Sometimes a person quoted in an interview as having made a certain statement issues a denial. He may even aver that he never saw the reporter who wrote the story. This happens when a reporter plays up some extemporaneous remark of an interviewee's that the person would not have made in a formal interview.

A denial of the facts of an interview, of course, can be avoided by presenting the copy of the write-up to the subject, but few newspapers favor such a practice. To do so means that the interviewee will delete everything the least bit unfavorable. It also means delay which a newspaper may not be able to afford, and a surrender of the newspaper's privilege to gather its information and write its stories as it sees fit.

If the reporter is not guilty of misquotation s/he may refuse to correct or retract, and if the newspaper supports its reporter, defy the interviewee who has denied making a statement. In another story the reporter may reaffirm that the original report was accurate. Then the public can choose whom to believe. Reporters frequently do not use remarks that they suspect the interviewee would deny. If the reporter wishes to make sure that the interview will not be denied, he/she can phone or call upon the interviewee again to obtain verification of whatever s/he wishes to write. When the reporter does so, or even when obtaining his/her original interview, s/he may take a third person along as a witness to the interview. This, however, seldom is feasible, as the presence of a third person may prevent informality.

A tape recording is the best defense that any interviewer can have of his/her accuracy. Most of the problems considered so far in this chapter would be reduced or eliminated if it were possible to use electronic recording devices on all occasions. That is, of course, impossible. Unless there is surreptitious use of the devices, which would raise legal as well as moral questions, most interviewing for spot news stories will continue to be of the old-fashioned pencil and notebook kind. At present effective use of tape recorders must be limited to feature interviews with the time element not so pressing as daily press deadlines. Some people, especially those not used to being interviewed, are self-conscious when a tape recorder is used. Often their discomfort disappears. It should be the reporter's goal to put them at ease.

There is no succinct set of simple rules for a beginning interviewer to master. It is impossible to advise a cub always to do this, generally avoid doing that, etc. No two situations are the same, but it is essential that the reporter (1) know about the interviewee, (2) know the subject matter and (3) be sharp, which means flexible, perceptive, penetrating and possessed of common sense and, in the public interest, a strong ethical sense.

ACCURACY

It isn't so that most people don't believe what they read in newspapers. The truth comes closer to Will Rogers' claim that all he knew was what he read in the dailies. Today, if the polls are trustworthy, a majority think news received by radio or television is more reliable than news found in newspapers, despite the fact that the same press associations serve all media.

Public Attitudes

There has been considerable research to determine news story accuracy, usually by questioning persons involved in the news or in positions to recognize errors in the reporting. The first study, conducted in 1936 by Prof. Mitchell Charnley of the University of Minnesota, revealed that of 591 straight news stories in three Minneapolis dailies only 319, or 54 per cent, contained no errors of any kind. In 1965 Charles Brown found a 59.5 per cent accuracy score for 143 stories in 42 small weeklies. In 1966 Fred C. Berry Jr. reported

270 stories in two metropolitan and one suburban dailies were 47.3 per cent accurate and in 1967–68 Prof. William B. Blankenburg of the University of Wisconsin got a 40.1 per cent accuracy score for 332 stories in one suburban and one rural daily. A summary of these and other studies appeared in an article by Blankenburg, "News Accuracy: Some Findings on the Meaning of Error," in the *Journal of Communication* for December 1970. A more detailed review of more than 40 years of research was prepared by Prof. Michael Singletary of Shippensburg State College for the American Newspaper Publishers Association, which published it Jan. 25, 1980, as its Research Center Report No. 25.

Whereas there seems no doubt that most people mistrust newspapers, little research has been attempted to determine the reasons for that distrust. At an Investigative Reporters and Editors convention, Clark Mollenhoff, veteran Washington correspondent and Washington and Lee University journalism professor, said, "Three-fourths of those interviewed about an issue are wrong and yet traditional journalists accept their consensus." In other words, people who cooperate with pollsters may not know what they're talking about. Nearly everyone at times has questioned the news judgment of an editor. Historically the bearer of bad tidings has been scapegoated. A reader may carry a lifetime grudge against journalism because of an error in fact or judgment concerning an event of which the reader had firsthand knowledge.

A study of Ottawa newspapers showed society stories are 90 per cent accurate and sports stories 77 per cent accurate. According to researchers Gary C. Lawrence and David L. Grey, two major causes of subjective error are (1) reporters' insufficient background information and (2) news desk and editing practices and policies. These results may be explained by the facts that most society news is written from press releases and sports writers were experts long before their counterparts were considered necessary in other fields. Other studies have shown that information obtained face-to-face is more accurate than any received by telephone. News based on press releases is considered more accurate than news obtained otherwise, the judges, of course, being the parties who prepared the press releases, not exactly disinterested parties. One can be similarly skeptical about the judgments of personal friends who give news to reporters. For example, *pr reporter,* a newsletter, reported that 75.5 per cent of public relations practitioners, mostly former newspaper reporters, said newspapers tend to be accurate in matters related to their business.

Avoiding Error

The newspaper has no reason for not being 100 per cent accurate in by far the majority of the stories it publishes. Thus, one of the first lessons the beginning reporter must learn is how to avoid making mistakes. There are some newsrooms even in large cities where a certain amount of carelessness is condoned, but not many. A standard of accuracy way beyond anything to which the recent college graduate has been accustomed in his English composition classes is maintained by a large majority of those newspapers worthy of being called first-rate. Lucky is the cub who starts his/her reporting career under an editor who "raises the roof" whenever he detects a misspelled word or incorrect middle initial in a piece of copy.

The reporter who has had time to prepare for an interview by acquiring knowledge of the background of the subject matter and of the interviewee is less likely to accept misinformation than one who must handle the assignment without the opportunity to prepare.

Fairness and caution both require that, when two persons interviewed differ greatly as to what is the truth, the statements of both be included in the news story. To achieve this objective, newspapers go to extremes of which the general public hardly dreams. The sentence saying that Mr. Smith could not be reached for a statement may have been added to a story after hours of futile effort to attain either accuracy or fairness or both.

Newsgatherers increasingly are up against what has been called handoutitis, which means the refusal of many news sources to provide any more information than is contained in carefully prepared publicity releases. Between the reporter and a principal in the news is the public relations or public affairs counsel, as publicity persons and press agents like to call themselves today. On the whole, these intermediaries perform a useful function, as no newspaper could possibly employ a staff large enough to cover all a community's activities. They also can be helpful to the reporter who wants additional information not included in a press release or who is seeking an original story. It must not be lost sight of, however, that public relations or public affairs persons are employed to advance the best interests of their employers, which means that often ways to circumvent them must be sought. The reporter who is content with what is included in a mimeographed press release may become little more than a messenger boy or girl.

The veteran investigative reporter I. F. Stone warns that any newsgatherer concerned with governmental sources should assume that every officeholder is a liar and that it is the journalist's duty to discover the truth of what is being covered up.

Within our generation, presidents, vice presidents and other high-up national leaders have appeared on television to lie publicly. In September 1971 New York Gov. Nelson Rockefeller deliberately lied to the press about the Attica prison riot. He and other state officials said prisoners were responsible for the deaths of 29 prisoners and 10 guards who were held as hostages. The coroner's report proved that all bullets came from the guns of state troopers, and a Special Commission called the assault "the bloodiest attack by Americans on Americans" since the original massacre of Indians at Wounded Knee, S.D. The reporters covering the riot were held at bay and had to rely on official bulletins which they had no way of verifying.

Shortly before the disaster at the Three Mile Island nuclear plant near Harrisburg, Pa., in April 1979, the York (Pa.) *Record* ran a series of articles warning that there were inadequate safety devices at the plant. Walter Greitz, president of Metropolitan Edison Company, which ran the plant, lambasted the *Record's* series as tantamount to crying fire in a crowded theater. Two days later he confessed, "We should have listened."

James Panyard, veteran Philadelphia *Bulletin* investigative reporter, said, "We've been given complete misinformation and conflicting statements from the Nuclear Regulatory Commission here and the NRC in Washington, the governor's office and the utility." He said that authorities who condescended to meet the press seemed to talk a foreign language. If a reporter asked a straight question about how much radiation was escaping the answer would be mumbo jumbo about millirens, mansens, rods and picocuries. One needed a nuclear physics degree to come up with the proper follow-up question.

In the February 1980 *Quill* Steve Weinberg told how his students in the Washington, D.C. program of the University of Missouri School of Journalism obtained authentic information. It was the way that Izzy Stone popularized. Because of poor hearing, Stone skipped news conferences and consulted records. For years he scooped all of his competitors with better ears. In emulation of Stone the Missouri students visited the Bureau of Radiological Health at the Federal Food and Drug Administration to learn the results of tests. From public documents at the Nuclear Regulatory Commission they learned how many times a particular plant had been shut down and for what reasons. Other important information was available at the Security and Exchange Commission, Federal Trade Commission and Federal Communications Commission.

What is important is to know what information is to be found at what place. The Investigative Reporters and Editors, organized in 1974 with a membership now numbered in the thousands, is building a resource center on the campus of the University of Missouri at Columbia, Mo. It services members who want to know where to go to find material on the topic and makes available the results of similar projects conducted by other papers. Journalism students may become associate members. The address is 220 Walter Williams Hall, University of Missouri, Columbia, Mo. 65211. Phone: 314–882–0042. IRE has an annual convention and regional workshops. Its *Journal* is a 12-page monthly.

Verification

Verifying a story means more than checking the statements of different news sources against each other. It also means making use of the standard books of reference to check spellings, addresses, middle initials and many similar details. In many newsrooms, reporters are required to write "All names verified" on their copy, and woe be it to them if such is not true. In many police and court stories more than the newspaper's reputation for accuracy may be at stake; innocence or carelessness is no defense against libel.

The newspaper takes a chance whenever it prints an unverified story. Mere rumor it generally can detect, but when a story contains something that seems improbable it is safer to miss an edition than use the story before checking. Often persons in public life say things to reporters that they later regret. It may seem to laymen that the newspaper should quote them regarding what they have let slip and then stand by its guns and insist upon its own accuracy. It is the same laymen, however, who with few exceptions believe an important personage's denial even though it be a gross lie. For this reason many an editor has held up a story until she/he has had a chance to check on even a reliable reporter's work.

Telephone books, city directories, clippings in the newspaper's library and books of reference are available to the newspaper reporter for a purpose—so that they will be used. In interviews, it is possible to repeat information to be sure it has been heard correctly. Over the telephone, difficult words can be spelled in code: A as in Adam, B as in Boston, etc. A humorous incident once occurred on the Dayton *Journal-Herald* that emphasizes the need for great care in taking news by telephone. A reporter, doing a late phone check of police/fire, wrote a story that 2,003 pigs had been killed in a barn fire. A check by a skeptical desk man revealed that the accurate casualty list was two sows and three pigs. How the error occurred as the result of a telephone interview can easily be imagined.

If the reporter has profited by his high school and college education, he should avoid many errors that the uneducated might commit, such as giving a ship's speed as "knots per hour," the office as chief justice of the Supreme Court instead of chief justice of the United States, the Court of St. James instead of the Court of St. James's, Noble instead of Nobel prizes, half-mast instead of half-staff, John Hopkins University instead of Johns Hopkins University, and many other "teasers," mastery of which is a journalistic prerequisite.

IRE leaders stress the importance of asking the same questions of different persons, being careful not to change the wording as from "Do you think the mayor should?" to "Do you think the mayor could?" Often it is best to ask the interviewee's own views if he is knowledgeable.

Qualification

When certain about the main facts of a story but doubtful about others, a way to make the earliest edition before complete verification is possible is to qualify what is written, as

> A man believed to be Hillyer Swanson, 30, of Salt Lake City, was found by police today wandering in Forest Park, apparently an amnesia victim. Partial identification was made by means of a billfold and checkbook found in his possession.

> Fire thought to have resulted from faulty electric wiring in the coal cellar caused approximately $500 damage early today to the dwelling at 1514 Murphy Place occupied by Mr. and Mrs. O. B. Ryan and their three small children.

Stories such as the following inspire confidence in readers that newspapers attempt to give the truth as far as possible.

Mayor Ezra Hawkins today intimated that he will not be a candidate for reelection, but Corporation Counsel Fred Bacon, who managed the mayor's last campaign, declared that "when the time comes the proper announcement will be made" and that "friends of His Honor will be pleased by the announcement."

Even without editorial comment it is possible to cast doubt on a statement by someone in the news. For example, a Chicago firefighter was dismissed because he did not reside within the city limits. He insisted that whereas he often stayed with relatives in a suburb, he had a city address, which he gave. The *Sun-Times* interjected:

However, utility records show that service to the second floor apartment had been cut off since October according to Personnel Director Charles Pounian.

It is when the reporter guesses or takes a chance that error is most likely to occur. Careless habits not only are bad practice from the newspaper's selfish standpoint, but reprehensible ethically as well. The speed with which newspapers are produced and the other obstacles to accuracy in reporting make a minimum number of errors seem almost inevitable. If the newspaper is generous in publishing corrections of the most serious errors and if it gives evidence of striving to attain the ideal of absolute accuracy, the supercilious reader should not be "off" a newspaper for life because on one occasion it made a mistake in the middle initial of a great-aunt's brother-in-law.

Systematic Checking

The practice is growing among newspapers of soliciting the comments of readers in much the same way that scientific researchers do. Increasingly, also readers are urged to take the initiative in pointing out errors and many newspapers have institutionalized their handling. In addition to "The Public View," a letters-to-the-editor column, the St. Petersburg *Times* has "Hotlines," to handle criticisms of the paper's policies and performance. In 1979 the paper received 9,681 letters and 2,784 calls from readers. Reader comments called in on a recording machine totaled 1,383 and there were about 2,500 who participated in coupon polls.

The practice also is growing of soliciting comments through questionnaires. Among the earliest attempts was that of the Minneapolis *Star and Tribune* whose Bureau of Accuracy and Fair Play was founded in 1948 "to deal courteously with any person who feels that he or she has not been justly treated in any news story or business dealing involving the newspapers." Since the news and editorial staffs of the papers were separated, the *Tribune* retained the bureau and the *Star* established a similar *Reader's Referee*. Every day stories are selected at random, clipped and mailed to persons mentioned in them with a request that the recipients answer the following questions: (1) are names correctly spelled? (2) are ages, addresses, titles or other identification correct? (3) is the report accurate and unbiased? (4) are all essential facts given? and (5) is the headline clear? About two-thirds of the 36 forms sent out are returned each week.

Every week the nearby St. Paul *Dispatch* and *Pioneer Press* select about 15 articles in which inaccuracies or unfairness might be likely to occur, such as any meeting report in which two sides are presented, articles on controversial topics, reports of public hearings, trials or court rulings, labor disputes and spot news stories written under pressure of deadlines. The paper gets about a 50 per cent return on the approximately 700 clippings annually. An analysis of one year's 331 replies showed

- 93 per cent of the headlines involved were thought to have been accurate and fair. There were 23 complaints about headlines.
- 95 per cent found names, addresses and titles correct. There were 17 complaints about mistakes.
- 93 per cent found articles to be complete. There were 23 contentions that pertinent material was omitted.
- 98 per cent found quotes to be accurate. There were eight claims of misquotation.
- 88 per cent found facts to be correct. There were 41 claims that material was incorrect.

Since 1971 the Twin Cities newspapers have been under constant surveillance of the Minnesota Press Council which, in 1980, changed its name to Minnesota News Council to reflect the fact that broadcast stations also fall within its purview. The professional journalists and general public are represented equally on the council of 24. In a typical year the council received 65 grievances alleging inaccurate, unfair or biased news coverage; 17 alleging unethical conduct involving such matters as conflict of interest or invasion of privacy; 15 alleging unfair denial of access to letters columns or political advertising space; and three involving matters that do not fall within the council's purview such as truthfulness in commercial advertising and management disputes.

Similar local councils exist in several other places. All are in their experimental infancy and there has not yet been any "big issue" or "test case" to determine their value. The same is true of the National News Council, founded in 1973 by the Twentieth Century Fund to investigate complaints against the major television and radio networks, major wire services and a few prestigious newspapers. Of 4,290 complaints received during its first five and a half years, 223 were considered at 33 meetings with 45 being found warranted. There also is AIM, which means Accuracy in Media. It is a strongly conservative critic of press performance. It writes letters and inserts advertisements to correct errors in interpretation and editorial opinion. It watches Jack Anderson carefully and goes after radio and television commentators, contending that the networks never criticize each other.

In 1967 the Louisville *Courier-Journal* borrowed a Swedish idea dating from 1916; namely, the ombudsman whose role is to be as critical of the newspaper as it is of most everyone else. The idea has spread to about 20 other papers. Many who have held the positions have had great difficulty because of the conflict of interest involved in trying to serve both the paper's management and the reading public.

The opinions and complaints of readers are solicited by an increasing number of papers, the ombudsman being one way. The New Brunswick (N.J.) *Home News* and Annapolis (Md.) *Evening Capital* were among the first to run display ads with such headlines as "We Want to Be Fair," soliciting reader response.

Dick Cunningham, with the title of reader's representative, runs a column, "If You Ran the Tribune" in the Minneapolis *Tribune*. Here are a few typical leads:

> If Colin Meline of Plymouth ran the Tribune, he would not have described the people who sent American clergymen to Teheran for Easter as "a . . . group sympathetic to Khomeini."
>
> Meline protested to the Tribune after the "sympathetic" description appeared in a story last Sunday. Friday, as a result of Meline's protest, the Associated Press was deciding whether to change its description of the sponsoring group for future stories.
>
> If Tom Trites and a group of his friends at the University of Minnesota ran the Tribune, they would have rewritten the headline and the first couple of sentences of a story Thursday about money in the Minneapolis election campaign.
>
> The head said, "IR, unions big spenders in city races."
>
> The story said, "Public-employee organizations in Minneapolis and the Independent-Republican Party have become the dominant financial forces in the 1979 city election, campaign reports show.
>
> "Local branches of the IR Party and seven unions or associations representing virtually every municipal employee have contributed far more than they ever have and have overshadowed the campaign efforts of other special-interest organizations."
>
> If that's true, Trites said, how come the ward-by-ward expenditures in the same story show that DFL candidates spent $71,106 compared with only $51,740 for IR and Independent candidates combined?

Another successful consumer service is the Action Line, often a court of final appeal for help in getting responses from public agencies or business enterprises. About 500 frustrated subscribers ask the Chicago *Sun-Times* Action Time editors for help every week. It is possible to publish only 30 to 40 of the letters, but all requests are acknowledged, building good will for the paper. Under the sponsorship of the Corning Glass Works, in 1978 the Action Line Reporters Association was founded to facilitate the exchange of ideas between about 400 charter members. Increasingly the columns contain more news and information as well as consumer advice. The amount of investigative research steadily increases.

Total Effect

An account can be devoid of errors in facts, spellings and the like and still be inaccurate if the impression it gives as a whole is wrong. This can happen when pertinent facts are omitted, when motivations are disregarded, when cause and effect relationships are not made clear and in many other, similar ways.

Thorough reporting is the best protection against unintentional distortion. For example, a story telling of an arrest for reckless driving could be error free, but would it be accurate unless it were explained that the apparently careless motorist was trying to get to his injured child's side? Without the part after the "but" the following lead would have given an erroneous impression. The reporter obviously asked, "Why?"

> Chicago—The number of persons drawing unemployment compensation declined by 5,154 during the second week of this month, but indications are that more than 3,000 of them were off the rolls because their eligibility expired.
>
> [Peoria *Transcript*]

Chester Goolrick warned against incomplete reporting in an amusing article, "The Dropped Shoe Syndrome," in the July 1979 *Rural Living*. He cited a newspaper account of the ransacking of a house during which just almost everything was taken. It was reported that the burglar ate an entire pie which the man of the house had kept in his desk drawer. Goolrick conjectured that Sherlock Holmes would consider the pie the most important clue, the mystery being why it had been kept in a desk drawer, inciting the reader to wonder what kind of pie it was, whether Mr. Smith, if that was his name, was a pie addict, did he take one with him to the movies that night and many similar questions. Not too serious but a good story surely could have been made better.

The "Other Side"

Deadpan reporting of the contents of a report, speech or the like, even when the source is reputable, may be misleading in that it does not give readers the "whole" or "essential" truth. When the news source is irresponsible, grave disservice may be done the reading public. It certainly is newsworthy when someone important in public life attacks another person. Such news often cannot be ignored. It can, however, be put in better perspective if there is simultaneous opportunity for reply by the otherwise injured party. Readers want to know how those most affected by any news event react to it. Unless their curiosity is satisfied, the account is incomplete.

"Real objectivity" was attained by an interpretative reporter for the Memphis *Press-Scimitar*, who merely filled in background and, without drawing conclusions, gave readers additional information by which to judge a current news story. The incident occurred during the campaign of B. Carroll Reece, Republican candidate for United States senator from Tennessee.

In a Memphis speech, Reece lambasted the "motley crowd" of Democrats in charge of the federal government for speaking "with such a variety of accents, all of them un-American, that they sound like the tongues of Babel." Continued Reece:

> These mixed tongues are chanting many themes that are utterly offensive to our American instincts. None is more offensive than their chant that "States' Rights might give way to human rights." Under this sweetsounding slogan is a snake in the grass as vicious as any reptile we have ever encountered. Herein lie the efforts of men who are either recent immigrants to our shore or whose ideas of government are immigrant to our shore—to move in on our system of States' Rights for the kill. . . . We of the South shall throw the pretty phrases back in their teeth. We say to them that the South has always preserved human rights. . . .

Straight-faced reporting of this speech would have appeared under some such headlines as, "ALIENS CONTROL U.S. GOVERNMENT, WARNS REECE." However, the Memphis reporter included in his interpretative article the fact that in an earlier speech in Buffalo (N.Y.) Reece said,

> This element (the Southern Democrats) which of course stemmed from the slave-holding oligarchy which once plunged this nation into a bloody war to preserve the institution of slavery, is the group which still maintains itself in power in a large section of this country by the practice of outrageous racial discrimination, preventing millions of American citizens from exercising the right to vote. It is the element of the party which inaugurated Jim Crow laws; the element which had pushed discrimination into the North. . . .

The interpretative article was headed, "REECE VERSUS REECE."

Many American editors came to wish they had accorded the late Sen. Joseph McCarthy of Wisconsin similar treatment instead of printing every unsubstantiated charge of communism he brought against governmental employees and others.

ATTRIBUTION

A newspaper's reputation for credibility is the best guarantee a reader has of the reliability of the news. Nevertheless, the most authoritative publications are the most careful to attribute every important fact to some source. "Who said this?" a hard boiled city editor may bawl to a cub reporter. "Why, Mr. Smith, whose name is in the lead as having given the speech," is no defense but merely provocation for a further remark such as, "You don't say he said this unquoted part down in the fifth paragraph. I know he made the statement in the lead, but the rest of your story reads like an editorial."

Direct Quotation

To avoid such reprimands, the smart reporter "documents" his/her stories. How to attain accuracy and authority in different types of news stories will be considered more fully in the chapters devoted to them in Part Three. Including authority in the lead adds emphasis, satisfies the reader's curiosity and partially protects the newspaper against criticism.

> Promotion of W. C. Fairchild, 2308 S. 10th street, lieutenant of the Superior Railroad police in the Milltown division, to captain of police of the Logan division, was announced today by Ronal Weber, superintendent of the Milltown division.

When the news consists in the fact that an announcement or statement has been made, especially if it is one which has been expected for some time, authority should be given the greatest emphasis possible by beginning the lead with it, as

> Mayor Herbert G. Van Duesen announced today charges of irregularities in the collection of business licenses made by the Chamber of Commerce will be referred to the Board of Aldermen Friday evening.

When someone in public life makes an attack on another, the lead should begin with that person's name, as

> State Sen. Rollin A. Bishop today called Gov. Joseph B. Dilling a "crackpot" and described his plan to consolidate seven state departments as "the wild idea of a neophyte in public life."

This type of lead is much better than the following:

> Gov. Joseph B. Dilling is a "crackpot" and his plan to consolidate seven state departments is "the wild idea of a neophyte in public life," State Sen. Rollin A. Bishop said today.

It is the fact that Senator Bishop attacked the governor that is news; what he said is opinion unless he was much more definite than either lead would indicate. If he did make specific charges, then what has been said regarding efforts to obtain "the other side" applies.

In stories growing out of public reports, statements or announcements, mention of the authority may be delayed until the second paragraph but seldom should be any later than that.

> Milltown users of natural gas pay a higher rate than consumers in any other American city of comparable size, but local rates for electricity are among the lowest in the United States.
>
> These facts were revealed by a Federal Power commission report released today. . . .

Care, however, must be exercised to avoid a "tag line" type of lead that, standing alone, is misleading, as

> Rep. Y. S. Owen could defeat Mayor L. L. Wood.
> That is the opinion of Judge K. K. Wendell who spoke at noon today.

Caution must be exercised so as not to declare as certain something that still is a matter of debate or further official action. For instance, a reporter erred when he wrote

> Baxterville will have a new 20-story office building by next spring.
> Plans for it will be presented tonight to the City Planning commission.

In this instance the Planning commission disapproved the project, which the reporter might have anticipated if he had interviewed more than its enthusiastic proponents. The hoary adage which applies is never to count your chickens before they hatch.

The extent to which a careful newspaper goes to give adequate authority throughout a controversial story is indicated in the following example:

> All ships of the North German Lloyd and Hamburg-American lines may be placed on the strike list of the International Longshoremen's association along with the Cunard White Star and Furness-Withy lines, *it was announced today* by Joseph P. Ryan, president of the longshoremen, when he learned a North German liner was scheduled to arrive at Montreal today.
>
> If the ship is unloaded at Montreal by members of a union not affiliated with the I.L.A., *Mr. Ryan said,* his union will strike all German ships on the Atlantic coast from Portland to Newport News.
>
> Although peace efforts continued in a three-way conference among I.L.A. officers, steamship officials, and representatives of the Montreal independent unions, plans were made for a protracted fight if necessary, *Mr. Ryan said.*
>
> Threats of delay failed to halt the sailing of the Furness-Withy liner, Queen of Bermuda, which left her pier at 55th street and the North river promptly at 3 P.M. without tugs. The ship left behind more than a hundred tons of freight, but officers arranged to have crew members carry aboard the baggage of passengers.
>
> The presence of 700 travelers in Bermuda awaiting return to New York caused the company officials to proceed without waiting for freight. Before the Queen of Bermuda sailed *Mr. Ryan declared* that if crew members carried aboard the baggage "they can continue doing it from now on." *He also said* that if tugs were used it would be "a long time" before the tugs would again take any ships out of New York. Two tugs were ready, but were not required because of the favorable tide.
>
> A peace conference between Mr. Ryan and his associates and officers of the National Independent Longshoremen's Union apparently made some headway. *Mr. Ryan said* that he "told them what terms they (the Canadians) could have."
>
> There are 700 passengers awaiting return from Bermuda, *it was said.*
>
> *The steamship officials* regard the trouble as largely out of their jurisdiction because it revolves about an inter-union dispute. *They expressed* the hope that a

quick adjustment could be made, and offered to sit in at the union meetings as "observers."

That efforts of the C.I.O. to organize waterfront workers is behind the I.L.A. move to assert its claims was indicated by *Mr. Ryan in a statement* protesting against C.I.O. inroads. [New York *World-Telegram*]

Indirect Reference

Even the parts of the example just given that are not attached definitely to an authority imply that they were verified by a careful reporter. Note in paragraph 4, for instance, that the writer knew of "threats to delay" and that "officers arranged" to meet the situation. Possibly this paragraph and the first sentence of paragraph 5 were guesswork, but the careful inclusion of both cause and effect regarding each incident, plus the adequate authority given in other parts of the story, gives the reader confidence in the correctness of the story as a whole.

No reporter should write a story supplied by an anonymous source, which means that practical jokers and persons with grievances who telephone and write to newspapers in the hope of giving news without disclosing their identity seldom are successful. When taking, over the telephone, information about which any question may arise, the reporter should obtain the informant's number, hang up and call him back. This practice often will expose impersonators, provided the reporter also checks the telephone numbers in the directory. Sometimes, at the request of high public officials, newspapers thinly veil sources of information by referring to "sources close to," "a source known to be reliable," "an official spokesman," "a high official" and the like.

It is irritating to any reputable reporter to have to write this way, and protests against the refusals of public officials to permit their names to be used as authorities are frequent. Such vagueness weakens the confidence of readers in any newspaper that practices it on its own volition.

Sen. Joseph R. McCarthy once gave reporters a statement regarding monitored telephone calls, but insisted that it be used as emanating from "a person who declined to let his name be used publicly." Commented Russell Wiggins, Washington *Post* managing editor, "The press associations and the publishing newspapers allowed him to put out a transcript under conditions that it originated from an unprejudiced source." To this, Claude Ramsey of the Asheville *Citizen & Times* added: "Senatorial immunity is bad enough without being compounded with senatorial anonymity."

High government officials, including the president, may designate into which of four classes what they say at a press conference falls: (1) quotable directly, (2) quotable as from a reliable source, (3) not quotable but valuable as background information or (4) completely off the record. Reporters begrudgingly acquiesce unless they defiantly boycott the session and then try to learn what happened secondhand from someone who did attend. Such an informant might be another journalist. Most leaks of all kinds, however, originate with disgruntled or public-spirited underlings.

John D. May in *Columbia Journalism Quarterly* for September–October 1978, calls it "Goosing the Public" to write "Vyacheslav Kuzrin, believed to be the KGB officer, etc.," or Bishop Abel Muzorewa, "believed to have the largest following . . ." or "decisions on money . . . are expected to dominate the 1978 General Assembly." He deplores what he calls "a standardized way of treating events, in which journalists allude, often in the guise of doing 'straight' reportage, to what is believed, estimated, expected, perceived by, well—by nobody in particular, by everybody, by unidentified and yet implicitly credible witnesses, by ghosts."

When Unnecessary

In the average run of police, legislative and many other types of news it is possible to omit specific mention of the source of information. In such stories it is presumed that a reliable authority was interviewed, and the newspaper's general reputation for accuracy is the reader's safeguard, as in the following examples:

> The Keeler polygraph gave the lie today to Henry (Hank) Munson's denial that he shot and killed his nephew, Arnold Munson, Sunday in the rooming house at 717 Victoria place where they both live.

> The 95 boys and girls who came to Milltown to participate in the state spelling bee finals Friday will attend a banquet at 6:15 p.m. today at the Hotel Bedford.

One way excessive attribution can be avoided is by being careful not to cite authority for old, especially widely known, facts. You wouldn't, for instance, write: "The capital of Wyoming is Cheyenne, according to Senator Blimp." Neither, unless there was uncertainty regarding it, would you give authority when mentioning the capital of Tibet, Afghanistan or any other place. Such facts, though probably unfamiliar to most people, are easily obtained from standard reference books.

To cite authority for old facts can be misleading. It is likely to create the impression that the information is new. For example,

> To be eligible for low-cost public housing a person must not earn more than $5,000 annually, Theodore McCoughna, economist for the Public Housing administration, said today.

The statement would be bad if the $5,000 ceiling had been in effect for some time. It would be worse if "revealed," "announced," "admitted," or some similar verb had been used. When a statement of fact is inserted in a story as part of the background to enable readers properly to evaluate some item of news, it should not be attributed to any authority unless, in the newsman's judgment, it might not be accepted as true otherwise. Then dictionaries, encyclopedias, public laws and other authoritative reference works can be mentioned. Never use such vague expressions as "statistics prove" or "authorities agree."

A lead that must be handled with caution is the "opinion here today" type. Seldom is such a lead based on an exhaustive survey of the "trend of public sentiment." The danger, from the standpoint of ethics, is the creation of what social psychologists call the "illusion of universality." It may be a gross exaggeration to write that "the entire city today mourned the death of Mayor Bull," or that "the world of music lovers was turned topsy-turvy," or that "business leaders today feared. . . ."

In sports stories, which are written with a recognized good nature and prejudice for the home club, such leads may be condoned, but when used in political writing they generally are misleading. If it actually can be established that a majority of public officials or of any other group believe a certain way, there should be some indication not too long delayed that the news writer knows what he/she's talking about.

Accuracy is the most elementary thing in journalism, and yet it is never completely mastered. Its lessons may be learned by heart one day, only to be imperfectly remembered the next. No journalist regards inaccuracy, either inadvertent or deliberate, as a good thing, but nevertheless many journalists condone it as a necessary evil in the attainment of speed and the maximum of news interest, trusting in a higher general average of authenticity to maintain confidence in the paper within the margin of safety.

—L. N. FLINT in *Conscience of the Newspaper*

Without accuracy you cannot have fair play. Inaccuracy is today the greatest peril that the newspapers have to overcome. It results continually in injury to innocent persons. It causes the public at large to lose confidence in newspapers in general and the offending newspapers in particular, to question the sincerity of their professions and to distrust their motives. The reader who loses faith in the news columns will not be impressed with what he finds on the editorial page. A newspaper's real influence must be measured by the number of readers who believe in it.

—ISAAC F. WHITE, formerly director, New York *World's* bureau of accuracy and fair play

Ballade of the City Room

BY EMERSON ROBINSON

"Write me a song of the City Room,"
The editor croaked one day,
"Write of the birds who fuss and fume
And wail at the sheet's decay;
Write, but make sure that your roundelay
Will fit to a one-line head—
Damn all the news, and be sure to say,
'The paper has gone to bed.' "

"Write of the smokes that we all consume,
The nerves that we have to fray;
Write of the rewrites we have to groom
And the files where they rot away;
Write of reporters that come to stay
A year, but that leave, instead,
Owing us all—and be sure to say,
'The paper has gone to bed.' "

"Write of that pall of impending doom—
The deadline that turns us grey
Write of ye editor's constant gloom
At copy-boys who delay;
Write of the cuts that they don't display,
And linotype slugs of lead
That pi themselves—and be sure to say,
'The paper has gone to bed.' "

L'Envoi
The Reporter's Reply:

"Editor, spare me a while, I pray,
The troubles that heap your head;
Give me my leave to be off—you say,
'The paper has gone to bed.' "

The major interview is a carefully constructed transmitting device, a medium, a mirror. It is a mirror held up to remarkable personality. It is a mirror in which newspaper or other readers see the spiritual, moral, and logical features of an outstanding statesman, admiral, general, orator, poet, novelist, playwright, artist, scholar, philosopher, critic, physician, surgeon, business man, journalist.

—EDWARD PRICE BELL, Chicago *Daily News*

3

THE REPORTER AND THE LAW

THE FIRST AMENDMENT

The press in America "is operating in an environment of public opinion that is increasingly indifferent—and to some extent hostile—to the cause of a free press in America," George Gallup, Jr. told a First Amendment Congress in Philadelphia sponsored by the Society of Professional Journalists, Sigma Delta Chi. The eminent pollster elaborated:

> In fact, the survey shows Americans leaning heavily, 2 to 1, to the view that present curbs on the press are 'not strict enough' rather than 'too strict.' Tougher restrictions are favored by those who feel that newspapers sometimes publish information that is not in the best interests of the nation and should be kept confidential, distort and exaggerate the news in the interest of making headlines and selling newspapers, and rush to print without first making sure all facts are correct.

When it is realized that the first freedom that goes whenever a dictatorship of any kind assumes power is freedom of the press, it is alarming that three Americans in every four drew a blank when asked if they know what the First Amendment to the U.S. Constitution is or what it deals with.

"Perhaps more alarming," Gallup reported, "six in ten among persons with a college background indicate lack of awareness . . . Six in ten teenagers are unable to name the document that guarantees the right of a free press."

The situation is serious because of the reliance the Founding Fathers placed in a free press to help create an informed public capable of making the American experiment in democratic self-government possible. The first amendmant was not a guarantee that every journalistic attempt would be praiseworthy. Quite the contrary, the authors of the Bill of Rights (the first ten amendments to the Constitution), weighed the consequences of allowing some form of government censorship other than libel laws, and decided the risk was worth taking. A free press was, and has continued to be for more than two centuries, the most important cornerstone of American democracy.

The Right to Report

Freedom of the press thus is a means to an end, not an end in itself. It is the right of the people to know, not the special privilege of those who own the media to profit therefrom. During the current debate concerning the precarious status of press freedom, some legal and other scholars have contended that freedom of the press protects only the right to publish and not the right to obtain news. The response of the neo-Jeffersonians is that if the desideratum is an informed public, their attitude is self-defeating. As James Russell Wiggins, a former president of the American Society of Newspaper Editors, sees it,

> How futile it would have been to give constitutional and legal protection to circulation of the facts while denying the right to gather the facts. Information is the raw material of opinion. . . .
>
> A people who mean to enjoy the benefits of a free press must have a government that protects
>
> 1. The right to get information.
> 2. The right to print without public restraint.
> 3. The right to print without threat of sanguinary reprisal for mistaken publication.
> 4. The right of access to the means of publication.
> 5. The right to distribute.

Problems of Access

Unless forewarned, one of the first big surprises that the young reporter may experience is the discovery that s/he can invoke the freedom of the press clause in the Constitution from morn to night and still be denied access to some documents that his/her naïveté might lead him/her to believe are public records open to all. Should s/he be able to break down certain barriers s/he still might run the risk of being cited for contempt of court or sued for libel were s/he to use information thereby obtained.

It is regrettable that there is no place to which the reporter, or the editor either, can be directed for a clearcut statement of what his/her rights and privileges are in particular instances. Not only are the laws of different states different, but also the same law is likely to have been interpreted differently by two or more courts of law in what would seem to be cases involving identical issues. As regards a number of important legal problems involving newspapers, there is little or no law, either statute or common. For this, newspapers themselves are partly if not largely to blame because they prefer to settle law suits out of court.

The principle generally observed, regardless of the clarity of state or municipal law, is that the public—which includes the press—has the right to inspect public documents except when the public interest would be harmed thereby. The frequent clashes between newspapers and public officials result from differences of opinion as to what constitutes a public record and what constitutes public interest. Some states have been careful to define public documents; others haven't. In either case, and regardless of the fact that there have been few tests in court, newspapers do not expect to be allowed to cover grand jury proceedings, executive sessions of lawmaking bodies, or to be shown records of unresolved cases in the police detective bureau, the report of an autopsy before it is presented to a coroner's jury, the report of an examiner to either a fire marshal or public banking official or a number of other similar documents. Pleading public interest, the county clerk who refuses to disclose the names of applicants for marriage licenses, so as to protect them from commercial salesmen, probably is on sound legal ground.

The cub reporter should learn what both the law and general practice are in the community and what the paper policy is as to defiance or circumvention of public officials seeking to conceal news. Some editors encourage reporters to search for leaks whereby grand jury and executive session news may be obtained and they have defied judges' orders with resultant citations for contempt. Many years ago, the United Press forced the United States Senate to modify its rule regarding secret sessions after Paul Mallon obtained a secret roll call on the confirmation of a presidential nominee for a cabinet position. Despite resolutions to the contrary, however, congressional committees still hold closed sessions when legislation is being drafted.

Over half of the states have passed open record and open meeting laws, many of them based on Sigma Delta Chi's model laws. Nevertheless, reporters continue to be frustrated by the evasive practices of some governmental bodies, such as city councils and school boards, which go into executive session and hold informal meetings in private places. Often important matters are decided at such clandestine rendezvous so that what transpires in public legally is merely a confirmation and leaves the newsgatherer ignorant of the factors which went into the decision making.

Only one state, Tennessee, obeys all 11 criteria for an ideal open, or sunshine, law according to a study conducted for the Freedom of Information Foundation of the University of Missouri by Dr. John B. Adams of the University of North Carolina. The criteria are (1) a statement of public policy in support of openness, (2) an open legislature, (3) open legislative committees, (4) open meetings of state agencies or bodies (5) open meetings of agencies and bodies of political subdivisions of the state, (6) open county boards, (7) open city councils, (8) no closed executive sessions, (9) legal recourse to halt secrecy, (10) actions taken in meeting which violate the law are null and void and (11) penalties for violation of the law.

The United States Supreme Court has upheld the right to publish names of rape victims that are included in official documents. In the case at issue the victim was murdered. The court also ruled that the press had no right to general access to lists of welfare recipients. The United States Bureau of Prisons was upheld when it forbade prison inmates to hold press interviews.

Most serious has been a steady increase in judicial orders forbidding reporters to attend court proceedings. In July 1976 the United States Supreme Court declared unconstitutional a Nebraska judge's gag order restricting press coverage of a mass murder case. Three years later, however, in *Gannett v. DePasquale,* the Burger court, 5 to 4, in effect reversed itself. Specifically the court upheld the closing of a pretrial hearing to the press. The language of Justice Stewart's majority opinion, however, was so broad that 45 attempts were made in all parts of the country to close entire trials. Of these requests 32 succeeded, and there were about 200 other attempts, about half of them successful, to exclude press and public from preliminary hearings. And then, July 2, 1980, exactly a year after the Gannett decision, the Supreme Court, 7 to 1, declared that criminal trials under most circumstances must be public. The case involved a Virginia murder trial from which Richmond reporters were excluded. The decision left undecided the right to cover pre-trial hearings.

Until the Richmond decision many, perhaps most, reporters were supplied with written statements, of which the one provided United Press International correspondents was typical. It read as follows:

> I am a reporter for United Press International and have been advised by our legal counsel that the U.S. Supreme Court's decision in Gannett Co. v. DePasquale requires, among other things, a hearing before a courtroom can be closed to the press and public. Accordingly, I respectfully request such a hearing and an early opportunity for our legal counsel to be present to make the appropriate arguments to you since I am in no position to do so myself. For the record, I must object to any attempt to close these proceedings and I request that this card be made a part of the record. Thank you.
> Name ______________________ Date ____________

As the press learned quickly, the decision in the Richmond newspapers case did not invalidate the earlier one regarding preliminary hearings at which a sizable majority of cases are settled. Judges in different parts of the country continued to bar reporters from pre-trial negotiations. An exception was a New York Supreme Court judge who ordered a town justice to provide the Troy *Times-Record* with the record of a preliminary hearing from which it had been barred.

INVASION OF PRIVACY

In 1890 two young lawyers, Samuel Warren and future Supreme Court Justice Louis Brandeis, wrote an article for the *Harvard Law Review* in which they attempted to establish a common-law right to privacy—the right to be left alone. They deplored the yellow journalism of their times and argued that persons should have legal recourse if they were victims of gossip from journalistic overstepping of the "obvious bounds of propriety and decency" and pandering to "idle or prurient curiosity."

Although most states have laws allegedly to protect against invasions of privacy, the concept is virtually impossible to define in any but subjective terms and is hence susceptible to various judicial interpretations.

Despite the lack of specificity in privacy laws it generally is accepted that anyone who courts public attention, such as a politician or entertainer, sacrifices much or most of his/her privacy. How much it is legitimate to publicize of a celebrity's private life as distinguished from his/her professional life has been tested in many courts with no consistent results and is mostly a matter of journalistic ethics.

Some people lose their privacy temporarily through no fault of their own if they witness an accident or crime or other newsworthy event. It is not surprising in these computerized days, with everyone being the subject of many dossiers, that the press should be the object of complaint and legal action when someone feels there has been an invasion of privacy through unjustified disclosure of facts of his/her private life, by physical intrusion or trespass in the course of newsgathering, by infringement of one's right to advertise his/her own talent or by being placed in a false light.

Judicial Differences

Oliver Sipple, an ex-marine, is one who believes his privacy was invaded when accounts of his having probably saved the life of President Gerald Ford also revealed that he was gay, which his family learned for the first time from press accounts. A San Francisco judge, however, dismissed his suit against area reporters.

After two *Life* reporters posed as patients and used a secret wire recorder to obtain evidence of medical quackery for public health authorities, A. A. Doetemann sued. The United States Court of Appeals upheld a jury's verdict of $1,000 rendered in his favor for injury to his "feelings and peace of mind." In similar cases the courts have excluded evidence obtained by wiretapping but there is no uniformity in the laws of the various states. The same is true of recording telephone conversations. In some states both parties must be aware of the recording.

Hugo Zacchini won a 5 to 4 opinion from the U.S. Supreme Court that the First Amendment did not protect a television station from liability for having broadcast his act as a human canonball. James J. Hill, however, lost his suit against Joseph Hayes, author of a novel, *The Desperate Hours,* which was made into a play and was publicized by *Life.* The plot was built upon the experience of the Hill family which was held captive for 19 hours by three escaped convicts. Although the novelist added fictitious details to embarrass the Hills, the court ruled there had been no actual *malice,* which it defined as knowledge that statements are false or made in reckless disregard of the truth.

Many papers suppress the news of innocent relatives of persons unfavorably in the news, innocent victims of rape and juvenile first offenders, even though the U.S. Supreme Court had declared unconstitutional a West Virginia law requiring such suppression.

Editors deplore, as do all others, insensitivity and stupidity by newsgatherers. An example cited to show lack of common sense by television reporters was the question "How did you feel?" asked of a father who had just seen a jet plane with his daughter aboard break into flames and crash.

Passage of the Family Education Rights and Privacy Act in 1974 known as the Buckley amendment for its sponsor, Sen. James Buckley, Con., N.Y., gives parents the right to inspect, challenge and protest records of their children and denies federal funds to any school that releases such records to others without written parental permission. It was not long before some literal-minded school authorities were refusing to allow news photographers to take pictures of graduates or reporters to report on any student activities. The law was passed shortly after the United States Supreme Court ruled that no child can be suspended from public school without notice of charges.

The court struck down Florida's "right to reply" law which compelled newspapers to print responses from persons attacked in their columns. It also ruled that Georgia's law forbidding publication of the identity of rape victims was not applicable after the information became part of a public record. In the case at issue the woman had been murdered. The court made further litigation inevitable when it confined its ruling to "the narrower interface between press and privacy" rather than "the broader question whether truthful publication may ever be subjected to civil or criminal liability."

A feature story about the family of a man killed when a bridge collapsed contained "calculated falsehoods" and portrayed the family "in a false light through knowing or reckless untruths," according to the highest court in upholding an Ohio jury verdict of $60,000 against the Cleveland *Plain Dealer.* Mrs. Margaret Mae Cantrell testified that the story created the false impression that the reporter had interviewed her whereas he spoke only to the children in their mother's absence.

A Florida Appeals Court said the privacy of a patient who tried to escape from a drug rehabilitation center was not invaded by a newspaper's use of her name. The Iowa Supreme Court decided against a woman who objected to her name being used in a Des Moines *Register* story that mentioned her compulsory sterilization in a story critical of a county health home. And Michael Virgil, a champion body surfer, lost his suit against *Sports Illustrated* because it publicized some of his eccentricities as a youth. The United States Court of Appeals declared that as long as a truthful description about a person in the news is "newsworthy" a newspaper cannot be held liable for printing it. The United States Supreme Court has yet to rule in any case raising this issue.

Complete details of these and all other cases related to press matters appear in *The News Media and the Law,* the bimonthly publication of the Reporters Committee for Freedom of the Press, 1125 15th St. N.W., Room 403, Washington, D.C. 20005.

The New Journalism

In the early '70s Tom Wolfe and several other magazine writers and novelists gave the name New Journalism to their use of the literary devices of the fiction writer to retell news stories. Thus Truman Capote's *In Cold Blood* and Gerold Frank's *The Boston Strangler* read like novels but were only recapitulations of facts familiar to newspaper readers for a couple of years. Most of the writings of the new journalists appeared in magazines such as *Esquire*.

The style was neither new nor journalism, but no one was sued for invasion of privacy or libel until a California psychologist successfully sued Gwen Davis Mitchell and her publisher because she modeled a character in *Touching* after him. Doubleday thereafter tried to recover $138,000 damages from Mitchell.

Regarding the U.S. Supreme Court's refusal to review the Mitchell case, Townsend Hoopes, president of the Association of American Publishers, said: "I think it's one of the most destructive and wrongheaded decisions that any court has made in the area of First Amendment rights."

If such suits become popular a freedom that writers have enjoyed for centuries will be in jeopardy. Cervantes, Proust, Ernest Hemingway, Somerset Maugham and other literary greats have been guilty. Robert Penn Warren's *All the King's Men* was a fairly accurate biography of Huey Long. Theodore Dreiser's *An American Tragedy* was a by-product of his reportorial coverage of a murder trial; he changed the name of the murderer from Chester Gillette to Clyde Griffiths and similarly camouflaged others. Orson Welles "did" William Randolph Hearst in *Citizen Kane*. The testimony in *Inherit the Wind* is verbatim from the Scopes trial where the rival attorneys were William Jennings Bryan and Clarence Darrow, not Matthew Harrison Brady and Henry Drummond as in the play. The Barrymores are believed to have considered legal action as a result of the thinly disguised portrayal of them in Ellis Roble's play, *The Royal Family*. Alexander Woollcott softened the blow that *The Man Who Came to Dinner* would have been by joining a cast and playing himself.

New Journalism lost much of its allure after Redpants, a Detroit prostitute whose "true story" Gail Sheeby told in the July, 1971 *New York* magazine, was exposed as a composite character. The same was true of several other magazine articles whose new journalistic authors defended by saying they correctly described newsworthy conditions. Attributing several experiences or statements to one instead of several persons merely strengthened without distorting the facts.

In April, 1981, for the first time in history, a Pulitzer prize was refused because a feature story's facts were fabricated. The New Journalism was blamed by some. Others, however, found the Washington *Post* more blameworthy for not verifying Janet Cooke's background and facts and for not insisting she tell editors the identity of her sources.

LIBEL

Many, perhaps most, privacy suits also charge libel but they are only a small proportion of the total number of libel actions. There is no aspect of newspaper law about which reporters must be more knowledgeable, and that means keeping up with United States Supreme Court decisions.

Public Figures

The first of a succession of such decisions that have kept publishers and libel lawyers wondering "what next?" was *New York Times v. Sullivan* in 1964. The case began when L. B. Sullivan, Alabama commissioner of public affairs, sued the paper because of an advertisement soliciting support for Dr. Martin Luther King's Southern Christian Leadership Council. It was captioned "Heed Their Rising Voices" and charged that a reign of terror against Negro students existed in Alabama. Sullivan won in lower courts but in 1964 the United States Supreme Court declared that a public official may not receive damages for defamatory statements relating to his official conduct unless he proves that the statements were made with "actual malice" with knowledge that they were false or in "reckless disregard" of truth or falsity.

Five years later the court extended the "public official" rule to include "public figure." The case was *Curtis Publishing Co. v. Butts* as the result of an article charging that Wally Butts, University of Georgia football coach, had conspired to throw a game to the University of Alabama. Butts won because the court considered the magazine failed to investigate adequately after Butts had told the *Saturday Evening Post* writer the charge was untrue.

In 1971 the court came close to making state libel laws obsolete when it extended the "actual malice" rule to cover a private individual projected into the news limelight. The case was *Rosenbloom v. Metromedia*. George Rosenbloom, a nudist magazine distributor in the Philadelphia area, sued radio station WIP after he was acquitted of criminal obscenity charges. The station had branded him "smut distributor," "a girlie book publisher" and similar unflattering things. Rosenbloom lost his libel action. As a result, the law of libel seemed to be dead and many newspapers canceled their libel insurance.

And then came *Gertz v. Robert Welch, Inc.*, publisher of the John Birch Society magazine, *American Opinion*. In 1974 Elmer Gertz, a Chicago lawyer, successfully sued the magazine for falsely accusing him of having framed a policeman who was convicted of murdering a 19-year-old boy. The judge, however, set aside the $50,000 judgment on grounds that the publisher had not shown reckless disregard for the truth. The United States Supreme Court decided that Gertz was not a public figure and so needed only to prove that the publisher acted negligently. Abandoned was the principle that a private citizen speaking on public issues had to prove actual malice and so, as journalistic publications now declared, there were "new ground rules for the old ball game." A retrial of the case in April, 1981 resulted in a jury award to Gertz of $400,000.

Since then there have been other landmark cases. In *Time v. Firestone* in 1976 the court ruled that May Alice Firestone, a prominent Palm Beach society woman, was not a public figure except in her home area. The woman had sued because the magazine reported that her husband divorced her for adultery. Actually the decree, which followed a nasty trial, mentioned other grounds; adultery was omitted so that under Florida law she could receive alimony. The case commanded nationwide attention partly because of her news conferences.

June 26, 1979, the Supreme Court handed down two significant opinions. In one it declared that members of Congress can be sued for statements made in press releases, newsletters and television interviews. At issue was a suit by Dr. Ronald Hutchinson, director of research for a Michigan mental hospital to whom Senator William Proxmire (Dem., Wis.) awarded a Golden Fleece award adversely critical of the $500,000 Dr. Hutchinson received for research of the behavior of monkeys such as clenching of jaws when they were exposed to various "aggravating stressful stimuli." The court remanded the case for trial after declaring the grant did not obtain sufficient public attention and comment to make the doctor a public figure.

The same day the court ruled that Ilya Wolston was not a public figure despite his conviction for criminal contempt when he failed to appear before a grand jury investigating Soviet espionage. That was in 1958. In 1974 *Reader's Digest* published a book incorrectly naming Wolston as having been indicted for espionage. The court found no evidence of malice inasmuch as the book reference was based on the FBI report.

In a footnote to the *Hutchinson v. Proxmire* decision the court questioned the routine awarding of summary judgments in public figure libel cases, declaring "the proof of actual malice calls a defendant's state of mind into question . . . and does not readily lend itself to summary disposition."

By far the most significant decision was in *Herbert v. Lando,* intended to make it possible to obtain just such proof. Former Lt. Col. Anthony Herbert demanded that Barry Lando and Mike Wallace of CBS's "Sixty Minutes" be compelled to answer questions during pretrial discovery proceedings about their thoughts, conversations and conclusions while preparing their program questioning Herbert's accusation that the Army had covered up reports of civilian killings in Vietnam. Only by such questioning would it be possible to prove actual malice in public figure cases.

In January, 1981 the court let stand an appellate court ruling that consultants hired by the government are not public officials or public figures. The case concerned the accounts in the London (Va.) *Times-Mirror* of the hiring of the Iroquois Research Institute by the Fairfax County Water Authority. Specifically the institute objected to the paper's report that an archeologist was critical of its work.

A few weeks later the court let stand an order that Jan Schaffer, a Philadelphia *Inquirer* reporter, spend six months in prison for contempt of court after she refused to reveal the source of information concerning the Abscam undercover operation.

What Is Libel?

According to the *American and English Encyclopedia of Law*

> A libel is a malicious defamation expressed either by writing or printing or by signs, pictures, effigies or the like; tending to blacken the memory of one who is dead, or to impeach the honesty, integrity, virtue or reputation, or to publish the natural or alleged defects of one who is alive and thereby expose him to public hatred, contempt, ridicule or obloquy; or to cause him to be shunned or avoided, or to injure him in his office, business or occupation.

It will be seen from this definition that cartoons, photographs and other illustrations are included.

Before the advent of broadcasting, libel was considered more serious than slander because a written statement appearing in a publication with a wide circulation had greater possibilities of injury. Today radio and television reach millions and the same judicial interpretations apply to electronic journalism. This does not mean that courts will be consistent. In fact just the opposite often is the case from state to state and even within the same jurisdictions. Ordinarily, however, it is considered defamatory to

1. Charge that a person has committed or has attempted to commit a crime, or that he has been arrested for the commission of a crime, has been indicted for a crime, has confessed to committing a crime or has served a penitentiary sentence.
2. Impute that a person has committed an infamous offense, even though the words do not designate the particular offense.
3. Tend to diminish the respectability of a person and to expose him to disgrace and obloquy, even though they do not impute commission of a crime.
4. Tend to disgrace, degrade or injure the character of a person, or to bring him into contempt, hatred or ridicule.
5. Tend to reduce the character or reputation of a person in the estimation of his friends or acquaintances or the public from a higher to a lower grade, or tend to deprive him of the favor and esteem of his friends or acquaintances or the public.
6. Impute that one has a perverted sense of moral virtue, duty or obligation, or that he has been guilty of immoral conduct or has committed immoral acts.
7. Impute commission of fraud, breach of trust, want of chastity,

drunkenness, gambling, cheating at play, violation of duties imposed by domestic relations, swindling, etc.

8. Impute weakness of understanding or insanity.
9. Impute a loathsome pestilential disease, as leprosy, plague or venereal disorders.
10. Tend to expose a person in his office, trade, profession, business or means of getting a livelihood to the hazards of losing his office, or charge him with fraud, indirect dealings or incapacity and thereby tend to injure him in his trade, business or profession.

A libel may be committed by mere insinuation. It is necessary only that the insinuation contain the elements of libel and that the readers of the paper understand it in its derogatory sense.

Likewise, allegory and irony may be libelous, as imputing to a person the qualities of a "frozen snake in the fable" or heading an article in regard to a lawyer's sharp practices "An Honest Lawyer."

The following list of "Red Flag Words" is taken from the Scripps-Howard *Synopsis of the Law of Libel and the Right to Privacy* by Bruce W. Sanford. They are words that may lead to libel suits if not handled carefully in news stories.

Adulteration of products
adultery
altered records
ambulance chaser
atheist
attempted suicide

bad moral character
bankrupt
bigamist
blackguard
blacklisted
blackmail
blockhead
booze-hound
bribery
brothel
buys votes

cheats
collusion
communist (or red)
confidence man
correspondent
corruption
coward
crook

deadbeat
deadhead
defaulter
disorderly house
divorced
double-crosser
drug addict
drunkard

ex-convict

false weights used
fascist
fawning sycophant
fool
fraud

gambling house
gangster
gouged money
grafter
groveling office seeker

humbug
hypocrite

illegitimate
illicit relations

incompetent
infidelity
informer
intemperate
intimate
intolerance

Jekyll-Hyde personality

kept women
Ku Klux Klan

liar

mental disease
moral delinquency

Nazi

paramour
peeping Tom
perjurer
plagiarist
price cutter
profiteering
pockets public funds

rascal
rogue

scandalmonger
scoundrel
seducer
sharp dealing
short in accounts
shyster
skunk
slacker
smooth and tricky
sneak
sold his influence
sold out to a rival
spy
stool pigeon
stuffed the ballot box
suicide
swindle
unethical
unmarried mother
unprofessional
unsound mind
unworthy of credit
vice den
villain

Damages

Damages resulting from libel suits may be of three kinds: (1) general, (2) special and (3) punitive or exemplary.

General damages are awarded in cases of proof of libel when injury is recognized as the natural consequence of such publication. There must, however, be proof of actual injury to reputation.

A plaintiff may receive special damages when s/he can prove particular loss. When special damages are asked, proof of specific injury must be established by the plaintiff. Special damages may, however, be awarded in addition to general damages.

Punitive damages are inflicted as punishment for malice on the part of the offending publication. Proof of malice must be established by the plaintiff. Punitive damages may be awarded upon proof of gross negligence or if a newspaper reiterates its libelous statement after being warned that it is untrue.

Defenses

There are five possible defenses against libel:

1. Truth. In civil actions the truth of a publication is a complete defense, even though natural inferences of a defamatory character might be drawn which would be untrue. If malicious intent can be proved, however, truth may not be a defense. In criminal prosecutions, unless the publication was made for the public benefit or with good motives and for justifiable ends, truth is not a defense. The law in this respect differs in different states.

A publication must not only know the truth of what it has printed, but it must be able to submit legal proof. It is not a defense to claim that the libelous matter was printed upon the authority of another person. For example, publication of libelous statements made in a public address is not privileged, and the injured party can sue both the individual making the statement and all publications which reported it.

2. Privilege. Publication of the contents or of extracts of public records and documents for justifiable purposes and without malice, even though they contain libelous matter, is privileged by law. Publication of the contents of complaints or petitions before a public hearing has been held on them is not privileged; neither is publication of the proceedings of a private hearing, the contents of a warrant before it is served, confessions to police, news of arrests unless by warrant and many other exceptions.

3. Fair comment. Authors, playwrights, actors, officeholders and other public characters who invite the attention of the public to their work are liable to fair comment and criticism. This privilege, however, extends only to an individual's work and not to his private life, and there must be no malice.

In the case of officeholders, comment or criticism must be confined to official acts or actual qualifications, and there must be an honest purpose to enlighten the community upon the matter under discussion.

The language of such criticism cannot be so severe as to imply malice, and the statement or comment must, in fact, be comment and not an allegation of fact. It, furthermore, must be on a matter of public interest, such as comment on public affairs, the church, the administration of justice, pictures, moving pictures, architecture, public institutions of all kinds, other publications and the like.

4. Absence of malice. As indicated, malice is an important element of all libel actions. It must be proved, as the previous discussion indicated, in cases involving public officials and public figures. Its presence in those or any other kinds of cases leads to larger damages than its absence. Malice is either *in fact,* which means that it springs from ill will, intent, hatred and so on, or *in law,* which is disregard for the rights of the person without legal justification.

Sylvan Meyer, eminent Southern editor, has written,

> More than error is required to commit libel. Libel suits grow out of the atmosphere of a story or a campaign, out of the running relationship between the newspaper and the supposed victim of the libel. And, according to several astute editors, the gee whiz, slam bang stories usually aren't the ones that generate fear of libel, but the innocent-appearing, potentially treacherous minor yarns from police courts and traffic cases, from routine meetings and from business reports.

Absence of intent to libel is no defense, but proof of unintentional libel helps to mitigate damages. In proving absence of malice the defendant in a libel suit may show

a. That the general conduct of the plaintiff gave the defendant "probable cause" for believing the charges to be true.
b. That rumors to the same effect as the libelous publication had long been prevalent and generally believed in the community and never contradicted by the accused or his friends.
c. That the libelous article was copied from another newspaper and believed to be true.
d. That the complainant's general character is bad.
e. That the publication was made in heat and passion, provoked by the acts of the plaintiff.

f. That the charge published had been made orally in the presence of the plaintiff before publication, and he had not denied it.
g. That the publication was made of a political antagonist in the heat of a political campaign.
h. That as soon as the defendant discovered that he was in error he published a retraction, correction or apology.
i. That the defamatory publication had reference not to the plaintiff, but to another person of a similar name, concerning whom the charges were true, and that readers understood this other person to be meant.

5. *Retraction.* Often a newspaper can avoid a suit by prompt publication of a retraction. If a suit does result, such retraction serves to mitigate damages, especially if it is given a position in the paper equally prominent to that given the previously published libelous statement. A few states have passed laws making complete retraction and apology a complete defense in libel cases.

CONFIDENTIALITY

Journalistic defendants in libel actions are handicapped by the growing inclination of judges to grant plaintiff requests that they be compelled to reveal the source of their information and often to turn over all notes and other material used in the writing of their accounts. A New Hampshire judge ruled that if a newspaper refuses to disclose the source of an article, the court can presume there was no source.

Similar requests are made by attorneys engaged in almost any kind of newsworthy litigation. The Reporters Committee for Freedom of the Press reports that from 1960 to 1968 about a dozen subpoenas were served on news organizations. In the next two years the number jumped to about 150. From 1970 to 1976 about 500 subpoenas were served on reporters. After that the committee stopped counting because subpoenas were being issued all over the country and it was impossible to keep track of them. It estimates there are at least 150 new cases annually. Often lawyers use the tactic to delay a trial or to save themselves the trouble and expense of investigation.

Even when the information has not been obtained in confidence most newspapers refuse to comply with court orders. Hundreds have gone to jail and been fined as a consequence.

What inspired lawyers and judges to crack down on the press was a Supreme Court 5 to 4 decision upholding the conviction of Earl Caldwell, a west coast New York *Times* reporter, for contempt of a grand jury to which he refused to reveal the identity of sources from whom he obtained information concerning the Black Panthers.

Also upheld by the court was the contempt conviction of Paul M. Branzburg, who refused to tell a grand jury whom he saw converting marijuana into hashish as he reported for the Louisville *Courier-Journal*. The court also upheld the conviction of Paul Pappas, reporter-photographer for The New Bedford (Mass.) WTEV-TV station, who attended a Black Panthers meeting in anticipation of a police raid that did not occur.

Since then the most newsworthy cases in this category include the following:

Bill Farr, Los Angeles *Herald-Examiner* (now Los Angeles *Times*) reporter, who was in and out of jail a half dozen times for a total imprisonment of 46 days because he refused to identify a defense lawyer who told him that Charles Manson's family planned murders in addition to those of actress Sharton Tate and others. The story appeared in 1970. In 1979 the Court of Appeals ruled that further incarceration would be punitive inasmuch as the maximum punitive sentence was only five days in jail and a $5000 fine. A $24 million libel suit against Farr also was dismissed.

Farr was jailed despite a strong California shield law, which in 1980 was made a part of the state constitution as the result of a referendum. Such laws have been adopted by more than half of the states presumably to protect journalists from being compelled to reveal confidential sources. It is the same kind of protection that is provided priests, lawyers and doctors. Supporters contend that without such laws not more but fewer crimes would go undetected because tipsters would cease to confide in reporters. Until recently many newspersons opposed such laws in the belief that the First Amendment provided adequate protection and that if lawmaking bodies started legislating about journalistic procedures the results might be oppressive laws.

The managing editor, ombudsman and two reporters for the Fresno *Bee* spent 15 days in jail for refusing to reveal how they learned the nature of grand jury testimony concerning graft in granting city contracts for garbage collection. Upon releasing them the judge said, "I am persuaded that the newsman's ethic is a moral principle."

Even stronger than the California law ignored in the Farr and Fresno cases is that of New Jersey. Nevertheless, Peter Bridge spent 21 days in jail for refusing to answer some questions in a grand jury's probe of housing conditions in Newark about which Bridge had written in the Newark *Evening News*.

Another New Jersey case that attracted widespread attention was the jailing for 45 days in mid-1978 of Myron Farber, New York *Times* reporter, because he refused to reveal who caused him to write a series of articles calling for a reinvestigation of five deaths ten years earlier in a hospital. Attorneys defending Dr. Mario Jascalevich on murder charges demanded to see all of the reporter's notes in the case. The *Times* backed its reporter and paid a total of $285,000 in contempt fines. Even without Farber's notes, the doctor was acquitted.

One case that had a comparatively happy ending was that of Daniel Schorr, noted Columbia Broadcasting System reporter, who defied the Ethics Committee of the House of Representatives that wanted to know where he obtained a copy of the report of the House Select Committee on Intelligence (the Pike report), which contains information adversely critical of the Central Intelligence Agency. CBS and the New York *Times* already had used most of the pertinent parts of the report before the House as a whole voted to keep it confidential. Then Schorr gave his copy, one of 17 outstanding, to *The Village Voice,* which gave it copious coverage. The CBS management paid Schorr's legal fees but suspended him for the duration of his case. The rest of the journalistic fraternity was almost unanimously supportive of Schorr, and after spending $150,000 to try to locate the leak, the Ethics Committee was happy to drop the matter in September 1976. Schorr then resigned from CBS whose management had been sharply divided as regards his behavior, probably indicating the effect government pressure has had since 1972 when Frank Stanton, president, narrowly escaped a contempt citation by the House of Representatives, which wanted to see all of the film taken but not used in the documentary, *The Selling of the Pentagon.*

Believers in the First Amendment have additional reasons for worry, including the ruling of the U.S. Court of Appeals in Washington in August 1978 that journalists do not need to be warned that their long-distance telephone records are being subpoenaed in criminal investigations. Especially alarming was the Supreme Court's 5 to 3 decision June 1, 1978, in *Zurcher v. Stanford Daily,* in which it held that Palo Alto police acted constitutionally in 1971 when they raided and ransacked the office of the Stanford University student newspaper allegedly in search of photographs of demonstrations by which they hoped to identify participants. No member of the paper's staff was suspected of any wrongdoing. The police found nothing of any value to them.

Noteworthy raids in the wake of the Stanford case decision occurred when the Minneapolis Vice Squad raided the offices of a tabloid, the *Metropolitan Forum* and police did the same at the Flint, Mich., *Lafeer County Press,* and KBCI-TV of Boise, Idaho.

As a result of tremendous pressure from journalistic organizations, Congress acted and on Oct. 10, 1980 President Carter signed a bill, the Privacy Protection Act, which ended the practice in federal courts. President Carter declared that the Supreme Court decision in the Stanford case had had "a chilling effect" on the ability of reporters to develop sources and pursue stories. "This bill requires federal, state and local authorities either to request voluntary compliance or to use subpoenas—with advance notice and the opportunity for a court hearing—instead of search warrants when they seek reporters' material as evidence," the president explained. He urged the states to enact similar legislation, as Washington already had done.

Editor & Publisher began its March 10, 1979, editorial, "Surveillance of the Press," as follows:

> Don't make any important phone calls from your office or your home. Use public telephones. Someone may want AT&T to tell them who you called.
>
> Don't say anything important to anyone on the telephone from your office or your home. Someone may want to know what you said as well as who you called. A wiretap is possible.
>
> Don't keep any records in your house or your office about who told you when, where and what. They can search your office and, if they can do that, they can search your home.

Don't keep any records. Period. Destroy them. Don't let anyone tell you anything in confidence. You have no right to keep a secret.

This is the impact of recent Supreme Court decisions. It amounts to a potential of total surveillance of the press upon demand.

Clark R. Mollenhoff, Pulitzer prize-winning Washington correspondent for the Des Moines *Register* and *Tribune,* now also a professor of journalism at Washington and Lee University, has prepared the following "Rules for Thoughtful Dealing with Confidential Sources":

1. Know the law applicable to dealing with confidential sources in your jurisdiction. Know the limitations of that law. Do not be misled by your own notion of what the law should be. The law as it is now, and as it has been, does not provide an absolute right for reporters to keep their sources confidential. Read the applicable state and federal statutes and read the opinions of the United States Supreme Court.

2. Know the views of prosecutors and judges in your jurisdiction as well as the views of your own editors and publishers. The law permits considerable discretion for prosecutors and judges in the search for evidence. It is expensive to fight for a principle, and you would be well advised to have an informed judgment as to how far your editors and publishers will go with you even if there is a shield law that seems to afford some limited protection.

3. Try to limit your area of vulnerability in the discussions with your confidential source. In most instances the source is interested in protection only for a certain amount of time, or until after certain events take place. Do not be too quick to offer or give blanket assurances of confidentiality that could put you in jail. It is a serious business and you should give great consideration to the value of the information and to the possible consequences.

4. Do not con your source by giving the false impression that a shield law protects your confidential relationship or that the United States Constitution gives you a firm right to keep your sources confidential. The Court has stated that newsmen do not have an absolute right to refuse to disclose information to a grand jury. The Sixth Amendment rights of a defendant to subpoena all witnesses who may be favorable to him represents such a serious limitation that Myron Farber and the prestigious and wealthy New York *Times* could not overcome it.

5. If you take information in confidence keep the source totally confidential. Use that source properly as leads to public records, documents and other witnesses who may be used in support of the story. Do not mention in the story that you have a confidential source for that is waving a red flag in the face of defense attorneys, law enforcement officials, the courts and others. You are not being true to your confidential source if you risk disclosure by mentioning the undisclosed source in your story, and particularly if you mention a source and give any leads as to the position of the source in any specific agency. In the rare case in which it is believed necessary to indicate a confidential source in the story, make sure there is a specific agreement with the source as to how he (or she) will be identified in the story.

6. Do not keep notes that might identify the confidential source. In any highly sensitive situation the original notes should be destroyed after the reporter has transcribed them into "random notes" that might be produced without identifying

or pointing to the confidential informant. To destroy these notes after a subpoena is issued would risk a contempt of court charge.

7. If litigation is initiated to force you to disclose your source with threats of jail and fines, you should seek permission from your source to be relieved of the obligation of confidentiality unless it is obvious why the disclosure would seriously endanger his life, health, ability to earn a living or his family life.

8. Unless you are relieved of the responsibility of the confidential relationship you should be prepared to serve a substantial jail term, to pay a fine, and to pay legal fees. Your publisher can pay your fine and your legal fees to uphold your pledge to confidentiality, but he cannot serve your jail term for you.

9. Do not sign a contract to write a book that is related in any manner to your confidential source, until all litigation is concluded. Even if you are pure of heart in your motivation, the existence of any money contract provides defense lawyers, the court, prosecutors, and any other critics with an argument that you have a financial stake in the outcome of the litigation. It can leave the impression that you are remaining silent for a price rather than a principle.

Investigative reporting is a precarious profession, and no one with any real understanding of the business would tell you it is an easy and comfortable way to make a living. Confidential sources are important to investigative reporting, and it is vital that reporters and editors give those sources a real protection by using them properly and by avoiding any actions that may risk identification of the source even within the confines of the newsroom. Most often it is a trust the source has in an individual reporter, editor, or news organization. That personal trust is not influenced so much by the opinions of the courts or the ulterior motivations that various prosecutors and defense lawyers may have as it is by the faith in the specific news reporter, and his track record for decency and common sense.

Reports of newsmen dealing in a dishonest manner with their sources are as destructive of the confidence of sources in reporters as are the questionable tactics of any defense lawyer or prosecutor or the arbitrary overreaching of any wrong-headed or dishonest judge.

There are many situations in which confidential sources are invaluable in getting the full story, but it is a disservice to the cause to wrongly argue that Watergate (or any other big story) would have remained buried if it had not been for some "deep throat" source. Make sure that you understand the detailed development of any story situation before using it as an argument on the vital role of confidential sources. If there are good cases in your own experience, they are much better than repetition of a fallacious argument built upon a widely circulated myth.

GOVERNMENT SECRECY

The ghastly extent to which the American people were uninformed and misinformed about many matters, especially the conduct of foreign affairs, was revealed during the congressional hearings into the Watergate scandals and by subsequent exposés of the censorship and propaganda activities of earlier administrations. Revelations of infringements of the Bill of Rights by the CIA, FBI, IRS, military branches and other agencies were shocking. Some charged the press with overplaying the news but most came to realize that American democracy was saved by the so-called Fourth Estate which accelerated its activities when the three official branches floundered.

Systematic post-World War II infringement of the people's right to know began Sept. 24, 1951, when President Harry S Truman ordered all federal departments and agencies to classify and withhold news as the State and Defense departments already were doing, the categories being "classified," "top secret," "secret," "confidential" and "restricted." Under pressure from all of the journalistic organizations, President Eisenhower eliminated the "restricted" category, which proved meaningless as "classified" became the catchall.

With the support of the ANPA, ASNE, SDX and other journalistic groups, a House committee chaired by Rep. John Moss of California embarrassed a number of bureaucrats who tried to justify their censorship actions, using a 1789 "housekeeping" statute intended to help George Washington get his administration started. Congress passed an amendment to the 1789 law to state it "does not authorize withholding information from the public or limiting the availability of records to the public." Joy died when President Eisenhower, on signing the bill, declared it did not "alter the existing power of the head of an executive agency to keep appropriate information or papers confidential in the public interest."

In 1966 President Lyndon B. Johnson used virtually the same language when he signed the Freedom of Information act which established the right of the public, including the press, to inspect the *Federal Register* descriptions of the operations of federal agencies, their rules and records. Several kinds of information, mostly allegedly related to national security or privacy, were excepted and the measure was of little help to journalists. Whereas private law firms and businesses utilized the law 640 times, the press used it only 90 times. In 1975 passage of 17 amendments over President Ford's veto supposedly simplified and accelerated use of the privilege. However, bureaucratic stalling and exorbitant service charges still were obstacles.

A sizable library exists of books by frustrated journalistic scholars who tried to "set the record straight" as regards such events as the U-2 incident, the Bay of Pigs, the Cuban missiles crisis, the invasion of the Dominican Republic, the Vietnam War, America's attitude during the Indo-Pakistani War, the role of the CIA in insurrections, including assassinations in several countries such as the Congo, Guatemala, Iran, Indonesia and Chile. Fresh facts regarding these and other incidents are still emerging, in congressional investigations, from confessions of repentant principals, and, not the least, from journalistic activity. In the meantime the American public has had to wait to know the truth about important historical events.

Whereas there have been several attempts by states to impose prior restraint or to suppress periodicals (the Minnesota gag law of 1925 and the Louisiana advertising 1934 tax were the most notorious), since colonial days the federal government had made no such attempts. Then in July 1971 the United States Supreme Court ruled, 6 to 3, that the New York *Times* and Washington

Post could publish articles based on the so-called Pentagon Papers, documents detailing much of the behind-the-scenes diplomacy which led to American military involvement in Southeast Asia. The papers were leaked to the press by a former Rand Corporation researcher, Dr. Daniel Ellsberg, whose trial for conspiracy and other offenses ended with the revelation of the attempted burglary of his psychiatrist's office by members of the White House Plumbers group which also burglarized the National Democratic headquarters in the Watergate. Some of the Plumbers' leaders had been prominent in the fiasco of the Bay of Pigs invasion of Cuba a few years earlier.

In permitting publication of the Pentagon Papers the Supreme Court did not invalidate the classification system, which remains intact. Perhaps 20,000,000 documents remain inaccessible because of the actions of about 30,000 federal governmental bureaucrats with censorship powers.

A second case on which practicing newspapermen split was the injunction issued by U.S. District Judge Robert W. Warren in Milwaukee against publication of a magazine article by free-lance writer Howard Morland on "The H-Bomb Secret; How We Got It. Why We're Telling It" scheduled for publication in the May 1979 issue of *The Progressive*. Morland revealed that he had obtained all of his information from government publications, which fact American Civil Liberties Union investigations confirmed. The contention of most atomic scientists that there is no secret was substantiated in September when *The Press Connection,* a Madison daily operated by former strikers against the *Capital-Times,* ran a letter from a 32-year-old computer programmer, Charles Hansen, who used unclassified information to describe the bomb. After several other papers published the Hansen letter, the government dropped its suit and the original Morland article appeared in the November 1979 *Progressive*.

If passed by Congress, what its opponents call Nixon's Revenge would make impossible other disclosures similar to those of the Pentagon Papers and *Progressive* article and disclosures that have resulted in many Pulitzer prizes: Jack Anderson for exposing official duplicity during the Pakistani-Indian war; Seymour Hersh for exposing the My-lai massacres; Robert Woodward and Carl Bernstein for their relentless revelations concerning the Nixon inner circle following the Watergate burglary.

The bill was drafted by John Mitchell when attorney general to revise the federal criminal code. Journalistic and civil liberties groups successfully lobbied to defeat it in its first version, S 1, in 1976. Reintroduced as S 1437, it expired in committee in 1978. The 1980 version, S 1722, sponsored by Senators Edward Kennedy and Strom Thurmond, would forbid any federal employee, present or former, from leaking any restricted information and investigative reporters who used it would be subject to two years' imprisonment and fines up to $250,000.

Reporters could be accused of "hindering law enforcement" if they refused to identify sources; or for "defrauding the government" if they disclosed government information secretly leaked to them and the reporters used the information to expose corruption or to influence government policies. The penalty: up to five years, $250,000 fine.

Public servants, active or retired, who provided the information would be subject to the same penalties.

According to Jack Anderson in *Confessions of a Muckraker:* "Any government agency in which men connive to court the favor or dodge the obloquy of politicians is bound to be a spawning ground for one of the most valuable species in American life—the informer. The informer is our principal protection against the design of public wrongdoers who have built massive walls to hide their activities."

S 1722 also would allow preventive detention; make it illegal to demonstrate to influence a judicial proceeding; to improperly criticize a witness before a government hearing; put many union strike activities under the heading of extortion or blackmail; turn emphasis in sentencing toward prison and away from better alternatives and severely restrict availability of bail; lay foundation for a national police force; undo decades of work safeguarding when and how wiretaps can be used.

S 1722 died when the 96th Congress adjourned in December, 1980.

COPYRIGHT

Facts (news) cannot be copyrighted. The actual wording of an account of those facts, however, can be. A Conference of Press Experts called by the League of Nations in 1927 at Geneva stated the principle as follows:

> The Conference of Press Experts lays down a fundamental principle that the publication of a piece of news is legitimate, subject to the condition that the news in question has reached the person who publishes it by regular and unobjectionable means, and not by an act of unfair competition. No one may acquire the right of suppressing news of public interest.
>
> The Conference affirms the principle that newspapers, news agencies, and other news organizations are entitled after publication as well as before publication to the reward of their labor, enterprise and financial expenditure upon the production of news reports, but holds that this principle shall not be so interpreted as to result in the creation or the encouragement of any monopoly in news.

Although facts cannot be copyrighted, newspapers can seek redress for pirating of news as a violation of fair business practices. In the case of *Associated Press* v. *International News Service,* the United States Supreme Court declared Dec. 23, 1918:

> Except for matters improperly disclosed, or published in breach of trust or confidence, or in violation of law, none of which is involved in this branch of the case, the news of current events may be regarded as common property. . . . Regarding the news, therefore . . . it must be regarded as quasi-property, irrespective of the rights of either as against the public.

A newspaper that wishes to rewrite or quote a copyrighted article appearing in another publication either buys the copyright privilege or requests permission to quote. In either case, credit must be given to the publication that originally printed the material. If the copyright privilege is purchased, this credit line appears at the top of the article, as

> **By Larry Green and Rob Warden**
> © 1975, CHICAGO DAILY NEWS
>
> A Chicago undercover policeman operated as a double agent, spying on antiwar groups and at the same time selling those groups information on police intelligence operations, a Daily News investigation has found.

Otherwise, if permission to quote is given, the newspaper that copyrighted the article is given credit in the story itself. Unless permission is received, the paper using material in this manner is in danger of being sued for violation of copyright laws.

> Regina, Saskatchewan (UPI)—A Canadian man and woman ate the flesh of her father in order to survive after their small plane crashed in a remote area of Idaho May 5 a newspaper reported Friday.
>
> A copyrighted story in the Regina Leader-Post quoted Brent Dyer, 25, as saying he and 18-year-old Donna Johnson, his sister-in-law, suffered from hunger for days before deciding to eat parts of the body of Donald Johnson, 50, who died 30 hours after the crash.
>
> Detroit, Aug. 3.—(AP)—The Detroit *Times,* in a copyright story, said today that a Wyandotte, Mich., grandmother has identified "Little Miss 1565," hitherto unidentified victim of a Hartford, Conn., circus fire, as her granddaughter. . . .

Magazine articles and books usually are copyrighted but a newspaper seldom cares to quote enough of such material to run the risk of violating copyright privileges. Often a magazine article or book contains an important fact that a newspaper wants to quote. Credit always is given to the original publication, as

> How lobbyists for the National Federation of Soothsayers defeated a bill which would have licensed their activities is told in the May issue of Revelation, the organization's official publication.

In September 1976 more than two decades of lobbying by the Authors League of America resulted in congressional revision of the 1909 copyright law. Instead of 28 years plus renewal for another 28 years, the new law provides that a copyright shall last for the duration of the author's life plus 50 years. The new law restricts teachers in their use of photocopies of articles and book extracts. The practice is allowed for face-to-face classroom teaching but wholesale reproduction for an entire school system requires royalties to authors.

The press benefits from the law because failure to register and pay a fee does not forfeit copyright protection, which begins at the moment of completion. It is permissible to carry a notice of copyright on a newspaper's masthead without registering the copyright. Registration is desirable, however, in case of any litigation.

A newspaper certainly is connected with the public interest as much as the street car, the telephone, or the gas plant and all the other municipal utilities. An editor is really a trustee entitled to his profits if they are clean and decent to the fullest extent that he may make them, but not entitled to make his profits at the community's loss. Unless he can give the public some valuable thing—information, guidance, or entertainment—he has no right to his profits. A newspaper is certainly a public utility.

—WILLIAM ALLEN WHITE, editor, Emporia *Gazette*

Journalism is the professional name of the newspaper business. It was used decades ago before the giant metropolitan daily came into its own; before the newspaper required colossal capital, stupendous labor and trained brains for production; before it was purified by commercialism; before it appealed to the masses instead of the classes; before it became an enormous, self-supporting, ultramodern business, powerfully influential in its community, uncontrolled but controlling, the maker of money and morals, merchants and men.

—HUGH A. O'DONNELL, business manager, Philadelphia *Press*

4

REPORTORIAL ETHICS

When a presidential candidate came to town, a reporter for Paper A wrote: "Despite the rain a wildly enthusiastic crowd of thousands gave him a warm welcome at the airport." His rival on Paper B saw it this way: "Although the rain had stopped before his plane landed, only 5,000 persons—most of them loud teenagers—were present when he arrived."

Both accounts were accurate but obviously biased, one pro and the other con. To get by their copy desks their slanted accounts must have been consistent with their managements' prejudices.

BIAS, CONSCIOUS AND UNCONSCIOUS

These prejudices, on the part of either publisher or reporter, may be unconscious. To the extent that they are conscious convictions both may try not to allow them to distort or suppress the truth. A reporter's academic training should have made him/her aware of the importance of stereotypes, taboos, superstitions and other factors influencing attitudes and opinions. The journalism student is encouraged to be as open-minded and objective as it is humanly possible to be and to be aware of any emotional obstacles to be overcome in seeking so-called truth and to understand the behavior of others who may go through life unaware of their inhibitions.

Overwhelmingly newspaper ownership is conservative. A large majority of newspapers always endorse the most conservative presidential candidate. Moreover, with few exceptions the press has opposed measures generally considered liberal. The majority of newspapers fought Woodrow Wilson's New Freedom, which meant the income tax, woman suffrage, federal reserve bank, child labor laws and similar measures. The press joined the economic royalists in despising Franklin D. Roosevelt and the New Deal. It disliked Harry Truman's Fair Deal, John F. Kennedy's New Frontier and Lyndon Johnson's Great Society. Likewise, ever since the press helped drum up support for the Spanish-American war, the majority of the papers have been chauvinistic, uncritically supporting America's foreign policy. Only voluntary censorship was needed to obtain their cooperation during World Wars I and II and in support of aggressive actions in Korea and Vietnam. The press has been hawkish in support of increases in military expenditures despite their inflationary effect. Only a handful of papers vigorously opposed Sen. Joseph McCarthy, the House Committee on Un-American Activities, witch hunters and red baiters.

It has not been difficult to recruit personnel, at all levels, whose outlook coincides with that of management. Professional journalists become more liberal as the result of their firsthand observations covering assignments. It is possible to maintain one's integrity even on a paper whose policies are personally repugnant. The time to say "no" when asked to do something contrary to one's principles is on the first occasion. If anyone shows a willingness to do dirty work s/he will get the assignments. This strong warning should not be interpreted as meaning that such disagreeable experiences occur frequently. In fact, they occur infrequently enough to be newsworthy, as when a Texas editor was fired because he ran a comparative shoppers' list and when two Michigan editors were replaced because they refused to publish what they considered to be unfair criticisms of the president distributed by the chain's headquarters. On the other hand, it was news world-wide when a foreign correspondent resigned from the *Daily Worker* because it refused to publish "straightforward accounts of what I had written" about the Hungarian revolution and when another correspondent resigned from the London *Express* because of its attacks on John Strachey, British secretary of state for war.

CONFLICT OF INTEREST

There is no unanimity among journalists as to how much they, from the owner to the cub, should participate in community affairs. In the interest of objective reporting, Len Kholos, managing editor of the Erie *Daily Times,* generally says "no" except for some good causes that are mostly noncontroversial.

"We are the world's critics," Kholos told a gathering of Pennsylvania editors, "and it's almost impossible to criticize your own act. I'm not talking about correcting errors under your standing head that says 'We goofed!' I'm talking about personal criticism of your performance as a public official. If you were a school director would your newspaper compare you to the proverbial unfit dog catcher? . . ." Kholos said he includes all public service where "significant community-wide controversy is likely, where one-sided reporting can affect lives and fortunes; where the newsman's fortunes can be improved by what he does or does not report and how he writes it. Behind the scene string-pullers are just as guilty of conflict of interest as the elected officials out front."

On the other hand, Robert E. Lind, managing editor of the Connellsville (Ohio) *Daily Courier,* said, "We encourage our people to be involved in community activities. We pay their dues, their meals and any other expenses." Lind, however, has three rules; no partisan politics; no one-to-one solicitation of funds for charitable activities; no publicity chairpersonship of any group.

When a reporter for the Hackensack (N.J.) *Record* made a routine examination of campaign donation funds he discovered that William Dean Singleton, publisher of the Paterson (N.J.) *News,* had given $1,000 to the election campaign of that city's Mayor Lawrence "Pat" Kramer. He had done so through the Westfield (Mass.) *Evening News,* which he also owned. Singleton explained that he made the contribution as an individual, not as a newspaper publisher. Malcolm "Mac" Borg, publisher of the Hackensack paper, replied, "You cannot separate the individual from the publisher." Singleton said his paper covered the campaign fairly; the paper endorsed Kramer, who won handily. Then he recalled that both the executive editor and Trenton correspondent of the *Record* had at different times taken leaves of absence to act as the governor's press agent. Borg also serves on the board of the Bergen Pines County Hospital, some units of which lost their accreditation. Singleton asked what went through the mind of the *Record* reporter who covered the story.

Although some newspaper managements permit or even encourage employees to join organizations and accept positions on the boards of philanthropic institutions, most frown on staff persons being candidates for public office. When Julianne Agnew filed papers to run for the Duluth (Minn.) City Council, she was promptly discharged as Living editor of the Duluth *Herald* and *News-Tribune* by managing editor Robert. A. Knaus, who said her decision "placed her in a position of conflict of interest with her responsibilities to these newspapers." Subsequently a county grand jury indicted Knaus and other members of the paper's management for violating the state's fair campaign practices law. The case eventually reached the Minnesota Supreme court, which dismissed the charges.

In nearby Minneapolis, John Cowles Jr., owner of the Minneapolis *Star* and *Tribune,* became chairman of the Greater Minneapolis Chamber of Commerce Stadium Task Force, and gave $4.9 million of the company's money to the campaign to construct a domed stadium in midtown Minneapolis on land owned by the newspaper. The following paid advertisement signed by 49 *Tribune* newsroom staffers appeared in the *Tribune:*

> As journalists, our responsibility is to be dispassionate and fair in covering public issues. Our role is to report, not to participate in these issues. Because we work

for the Minneapolis Tribune, we recognize some people may question our fidelity to that principle when John Cowles Jr., chairman of the board of the Star & Tribune Co., is a leading advocate in the debate over whether and where the sports stadium should be built. We bought this advertisement to assure our readers that our professional principles have not been undermined by Cowles' involvement in the stadium issue. We neither advocate nor oppose building a stadium, domed or un-domed, at any location. Furthermore, neither Cowles nor any other company executive has tried to influence the Tribune's coverage of this issue. But to prevent even an appearance of such a conflict of interest, we believe management should avoid a leadership role in sensitive political and economic issues.

Unusual as the incident was, it was not the first time working journalists resorted to advertising to promulgate viewpoints at variance with those of management. The New York *Daily News* twice refused to accept advertisements signed by staff members. The first, signed by 58 employees of the paper, opposed the American incursion into Cambodia and the killing of Kent State University demonstrators by state troopers. The second, with 150 signers, called on President Nixon "to live up to his preelection promise of peace in Southeast Asia." Both ads were accepted by the New York *Times*.

In 1971 after the Chicago *Daily News* endorsed Richard J. Daley for reelection as Chicago's mayor, 88 staff members bought a half-page advertisement to oppose the endorsement. Then 61 staffers of the Chicago *Sun-Times* did likewise.

The paper's liberal attitude, by comparison with that of the New York *Daily News,* recalled the Republican candidacy for vice president of Frank Knox, when he owned the Chicago *Daily News*. The paper's editorial page columnist, Howard Vincent O'Brien, wrote several uncensored columns opposing the Landon-Knox ticket, even declaring he didn't think his boss would be good in the job.

After the officers of the Newspaper Guild endorsed Sen. George McGovern for president in 1972, the Washington *Post* ran a full-page advertisement signed and paid for by nearly 300 Washington Guild members declaring the Guild had no business interjecting its members into a partisan political role. "We in the news business have an obligation to inform the public," the ad read, "The fulfillment of this obligation depends on maintaining credibility with the public."

ACTIVISM AND ADVOCACY

Many publishers became alarmed with publication of a 16-page report, *Activism and Advocacy,* prepared for the Associated Press Managing Editors by Malcolm F. Mallette of the American Press Institute. It defined activism and advocacy as a philosophy but unfortunately included no examples of news writing that had been affected by it. Nor did it mention any newspaper or newspaperman converted to it. Nevertheless, the report viewed with strong alarm what Paul A. Poorman, then of the Detroit *News,* said is "an articulate trend," what Ed Heins of the Des Moines *Register* and *Tribune* believed is "becoming a strong tendency," what Joseph W. Shoquist of the Milwaukee *Journal* thought is a "fairly strong trend" and what Robert H. Hollingsworth of the Dallas *Times-Herald* "did not like" but which he felt "is growing and growing rapidly."

This book's author wrote to all of the contributors to the APME symposium and to authors of all the most important magazine articles. Typical responses included: "I do have a problem finding examples," "Are they real? I hear too much evidence to think otherwise" and "It is highly subjective. I cannot document this statement." Not one of the alleged authorities sent an example or even named a newspaper or newspaperman as the cause of his rage.

Maybe this is the kind of writing that was feared:

> Mayor Byrne on Wednesday nominated an attorney and family friend with no training in urban planning to become chairman of the Chicago Plan Commission, the panel that oversees most major developments in the city.

That lead was published in the Chicago *Tribune;* its author was one of the paper's veteran reporters. It is the kind of interpretative reporting, 100 per cent factual, that has been commonplace in most newspapers for decades.

An example of what those who believe in the existence of New Journalism and/or the recency of activism and advocacy in newspapering would find in the files of yesteryear is this story from the St. Louis *Post-Dispatch* for July 21, 1925, under the by-line of Paul Y. Anderson:

> A memorable scene was enacted yesterday afternoon beneath the great maples that canopy the yard of the Rhea County Courthouse. On a platform where was convened the trial of John T. Scopes, Clarence Darrow placed William Jennings Bryan on the witness stand, and what followed was an event in the intellectual history of the world. It was magnificent and tragic, stirring and pathetic, and above all it was pervaded by the atmosphere of grandeur which befitted the death grapple between two great ideas.
>
> Two old men, one eloquent, magnetic and passionate, the other cold, impassive and philosophical, met as the champions of these ideas and as remorselessly as the jaws of a rock crusher under the crumbling mass of limestone, one of these old men caught and ground the other between his massive erudition and his ruthless logic. Let there be no doubt about that. Bryan was broken, if ever a man was broken. Darrow never spared him. It was masterly, but it was pitiful.
>
> It was profoundly moving. To see this wonderful man, for after all, he was wonderful, this man whose silver voice and majestic mien had stirred millions, to see him humbled and humiliated before the vast crowd which had come to adore him was sheer tragedy, nothing less.

What some publishers fear is not any revolt against traditional techniques of news reporting and writing that would upset the validity of any of the contents of this book. Rather, what disturbs the journalistic administrative status quo is a developing demand on the part of rank-and-file editorial workers that they be given at least a consultative share in policy-making. As such, the reporters' revolt is definitely "in tune with the times," and cannot be evaluated or completely understood without relating it to world-wide demands by many minority groups, that the Establishment relent and allow minority opinion to be heard.

Impetus to development of militancy among journalists was provided by the attitude of some newspaper managements at the time of the Democratic National Convention in Chicago in August 1968. Conservatively estimated, 100 reporters and photographers were victims of physical violence during what the report *Rights in Conflict,* submitted by Daniel Walker to the National Commission on the Causes and Prevention of Violence, called a "police riot." Belief that their superiors had failed to support them led to the organization by Chicago reporters of the Association for Working Press and the publication of a monthly, *Chicago Journalism Review,* which performed a watchdog function and presented continuous critical analysis of the performance of the journalistic media in Chicago until its demise in late 1975. The former editor now edits a section on The Media in *Chicago Lawyer,* published monthly by the liberal Chicago Council of Lawyers. The *St. Louis Journalism Review* and *Feedback,* concerned with northern California journalistic activities, survive. *Columbia Journalism Review,* which predates all the others, always has been a heavily subsidized nationally oriented magazine.

REPORTER POWER

Primary concern of journalists, as of all workers, is higher wages and better working conditions. Before the Newspaper Guild was organized in December, 1933, the average weekly wage for newspaper reporters was $29.47 and working weeks of six days, 70 hours or more were not uncommon. In 1980 the average top minimum weekly wage for the 33,500 Guild members in more than 80 locals in more than 100 cities was about $375; the five-day working week was 40 hours with equal time off or time and a half pay for overtime. Starting minimum weekly salaries for reporters and photographers ranged from $135 to $528.67.

The model Guild contract also calls for severance pay of two or more weeks' salary for each year of employment; no discharges because of automation; orderly grievance machinery; paid holidays (as many as 18); planned retirement with almost all members covered by pensions; acceleration of the hiring of minority groups and similar benefits.

Integrity

In addition, the model Guild contract includes an integrity clause as follows:

> EMPLOYEE INTEGRITY: Employees shall be protected by contract against use of their by-lines or credit lines over their protest. Employees shall also be

protected by contract against having to perform under protest any practice compromising their integrity. Substantive changes in material shall be brought to the employee's attention before publication. Provision shall be made that no employee shall be required to write, process or prepare anything for publication in such a way as to distort any facts or to create an impression that the employee knows to be false. Provision shall be made that if a question arises as to the accuracy of printed material, no correction or retraction of that material shall be printed without prior consultation with the employee concerned. Any employee whose work or person is mentioned in a letter to the editor shall be informed of such letter immediately and shall have the right to respond to such letter simultaneously and adequately on the page on which it is published. Provision shall be made that no employee shall be required to use his or her position as an employee for any purpose other than in carrying out his or her work for the employer.

The Guild demands elimination of secret surveillances of employees as well as the use of electronic supervisors, tape recordings, telephone monitoring systems and similar procedures and devices. It seeks management's support of anyone who "refuses to give up custody or disclose any knowledge, information, notes, records, documents, files, photographs or tapes or the source thereof, that relate to news, commentary, advertising or the establishment and maintenance of his or her sources, etc."

Employee Voice

Citing *Le Monde* of Paris and some other European publications, the Guild seeks regular, generally monthly discussions between representatives of management and the reportorial staff, also possibly delegate attendance at regular editorial board and similar high-level meetings.

Since 1972 there has been a labor-management committee at the Minneapolis *Star*. It grew out of informal discussions the previous year when Guild and management agreed on two appointments to assist city editorships. Management retains authority for all appointments but the labor group has an "advise and consent" relationship. Later, when a permanent committee came into operation, the publisher agreed with the labor group in selecting an editor-in-chief.

Among matters that have been on the agenda of the joint committee have been policy on confidentiality of sources, how additional news space might be used, writing seminars, seminars on law and newspaper reporting, newsprint, staff size, orientation program for new staff members, free-lance policy, office redesign, criteria for selection of editor, parking, minority hiring program, production campaign and by-line policy.

When the Burlington (Iowa) *Hawk Eye* needed a managing editor, the publisher, John McCormally, invited all members of the news-editorial department and the heads of other departments to veto his first or second appointee if they wished to do so. As a result, the new man, an outsider who subjected himself to thorough interviewing by all, received unanimous approval.

The *News Policy Manual* of the Lexington (Ky.) *Leader* stipulates: "During the first week of every month a news policy committee made up of the editor, the managing editor, the city editor and two reporters or copy editors, will meet to consider suggested changes and additions."

One of the strongest deterrents to injustices is the adverse publicity that often results. That was the case when Jude Dippold was fired by the Greensburg (Pa.) *Tribune-Review* for remarking, "one down and one to go" after Spiro Agnew resigned as vice president. The publisher, Richard Mellon Scaife, had contributed $1 million to the Nixon campaign. Twelve other reporters resigned in protest.

Because she refused to shake hands with a congressional candidate, Karen Kelly was fired by the Oak Park *Pioneer Press*. Her reason was Edward Hanrahan's role, when Cook County state's attorney, in the police raid that resulted in the murders of Black Panther leaders Fred Hampton and Mark Clark. Even Hanrahan objected to the firing.

On the other hand, there was little adverse criticism when the Chicago *Tribune* fired a columnist for plagiarizing the work of another author.

SPECIAL INTERESTS

Policy decisions are made by management, with or without consultation with labor groups or any others, and are communicated to the rank and file. Nevertheless, it is to everyone's advantage for reporters to know the reasons as well as the decisions themselves. That means, among other things, understanding the special interests that seek favorable treatments by the press.

Public Relations

Many persons who quit newspapers or other journalistic media go into public relations work. Often this is because of the lure of a fatter paycheck, in which case the more basic reportorial experience the better. Others have been cynical failures in their attempt to find adequate means of self-expression where they were. They become jaded and bored, weary of being "a daily historian" and believe public relations provides a greater variety of experiences. Still others seek opportunities to promote causes in which they believe.

Their most recent attempt to improve their public image is to call themselves directors or vice presidents in charge of public affairs. Over half of the nation's largest corporations now use the terms "public affairs" or "corporate relations" instead of "public relations." The trend is also for governmental agencies at all levels to do the same.

To Edward L. Bernays, who coined the term "public relations" in 1919, the phenomenon is partly the result of "the operatives in the White House who called themselves public relations experts and who were not." Bernays is dubious about the value of name change, saying that "a group of high-binders" could commit some "kind of professional mayhem" and then "another name would have to be sought." As he has since 1923 in *Crystallizing Public Opin-*

ion, the first book ever written on the subject, Bernays advocates state licensing of public relations counsel to safeguard the public from quacks.

Adverse Criticism

Until recently, practicing journalists were almost unanimous in condemning public relations persons as brazen if not unscrupulous space-grabbers and fakers. Today, this harsh judgment has been considerably modified, partly because of the impossibility of covering the wide range of potential news without assistance, and partly because of the considerable elevation of standards within the public relations field. Once they were mostly press agents, whose forte was the manufacturing of stunts, and, more recently, they were mere publicity men whose success was determined largely by the amount of space their clients got in the legitimate news columns of the media. Now the best of them are skillful participants in top-level policy making who have the total image of their clients in mind. Instead of courting publicity they may, in fact, advise against seeking any journalistic mention. They concern themselves with internal problems of personnel and morale, advertising, product, salesmanship and total behavior. In their exalted positions they may be considered by some to be even more dangerous as hidden persuaders, pressure boys, masters of the invisible sell, space-grabbers, ballyhoo boys, hucksters or malicious engineers of public consent, to use some of the titles by which they are known to their detractors.

A great danger is the extent to which public relations people erect a barrier between the reporter and original news sources. If all news is obtained through carefully prepared news releases, the reporter becomes little more than a glorified messenger. Good newspapers and magazines consist of more than such handouts with proper headlines and picture captions added by the editors. No matter how cooperative and sensible, the public relations counsel never can lose sight of the fact that the primary obligation is to his/her employer. The reporter, on the other hand, is a public servant in a democracy. There are bound to be at least occasional clashes of interest. News releases today are usually well written and reliable but often there are omissions and obscurities that can be corrected only by personal contact between newsgatherer and news source.

Large news conferences, especially with the president and other prominent public figures, can be extremely frustrating because no reporter present has the opportunity to probe deeply into any matter. Too often a reporter is limited to a single question so that as many as possible can have a turn. Planted questions are asked by friendly reporters who have been advised by press agents. It's impossible under such circumstances to be thorough in one's fact finding. Even if better conditions prevail, a public relations counsel may hover over the shoulder of the interviewee to advise, augment and correct his statements. Reporters often are infuriated and feel that their dignity has been injured. Serving one's editor and the public is extremely difficult under such circumstances.

If the interview is broadcast live, the nonelectronic media newsgatherers may be at great disadvantage to follow up misconceptions that already have become familiar to millions of watchers. It is possible for public figures to misuse television to the detriment of all. The task of the print media to correct errors and to supplement incomplete details is becoming tremendous.

In Defense

In their own defense, the estimated 80,000 persons who perform public relations functions contend that their activities are of great social benefit. They take credit for having converted business and industry completely away from the public-be-damned attitude and say that they have humanized business, helped give it good manners and, most important, a conscience; and that they have taught it that he profits most who serves best. They define public relations or its synonym as simply doing the right thing and letting people know about it, applying the Golden Rule in everyday activities while not letting one's light shine unnoticed under a basket. To them, sound public relations means the daily application of common sense, common courtesy and common decency in accordance with a continuous program of enlightened self-interest through good works that not only earn one a good reputation but also cause him to deserve it as a good neighbor. There is a growing sense of professionalism among corporate public relations counsel and increasingly they are seeing the wisdom of training and preparing chief executives to face the media. Several major agencies run sensitivity courses for corporate executives on dealing with the media.

In further defense of public relations as it relates to news media, it is indisputable that almost every legitimate news item that appears in public print has publicity value for someone. Even unfavorable mention or scandal doesn't seem to be fatal to national heroes, especially in the entertainment world. Readers' memories are short and inaccurate and when they go to the polls the familiar name has advantage, no matter how unsavory the situation in connection with which it was publicized. Organized baseball and other professional sports are commercial enterprises that have thrived on free publicity, through good-sized sports sections, for generations. The same is true of the theater, book publishing, concert stage and other artistic enterprises, which are not entirely philanthropies.

Since John D. Rockefeller II hired Ivy Lee early in the century, the policy of the public relations profession has been increasingly toward more cooperation with the newsgathering media rather than agencies to suppress unfavorable news or retard newsgatherers in their efforts to obtain it. Public relations departments of railroads, airlines and industries today are a great asset to reporters at times of fires, accidents and other disasters, whereas a generation ago exactly the opposite was the case.

The news or publicity or information division of a public relations department provides a quantity of legitimate news handouts, full texts of speeches by important people, notices of meetings and conventions, plans for changes in policies and operations of both private and public institutions, and other services that no newspaper or magazine could afford to obtain by means of its own paid employees. To some extent, the media are today at the mercy of the public relations people to keep them informed of what is going on in large segments of society.

Freebies and Payola

Reporters covering large meetings, conventions, athletic contests and similar events expect that there will be press rooms and tables with desks, telephones, refreshments and other necessities. Newspapers differ as to how much, in addition to the mere necessities, their employees should be permitted to accept. Some even refuse passes to games or plays and pay for the books they review.

Some journalistic organizations, notably the National Conference of Editorial Writers, refuse convention gifts supplied by business establishments or even host newspapers. Such gifts at commercial affairs become less elaborate as the number of reporters in attendance increases. For example, the National Football League rewarded sports writers covering the first Super Bowl game in 1967 with sunshine baskets of cheese, fruit and a couple of bottles of scotch and bourbon. A handsome gift (once a tweed travel bag) was given out with credentials to about 200 reporters. By contrast the 2,000 who attended the game today received an inexpensive vinyl briefcase with a note pad and a commemorative coat patch.

Because it is important to make contacts with newsworthy people, the reporter finds it impossible to boycott all cocktail parties and receptions at which there often are elaborate refreshments. Reporters are guided by office rules as to what, if any, gifts they can accept at Christmas or any other time. Sometimes it is stipulated that a newsroom employee must return any gift that costs more than a certain amount, possibly the price of a fifth of whisky. Sports writers today mostly have their expenses paid by their offices rather than by the management of the teams they accompany on trips. Usually, however, they are allowed to accept season passes just as music and drama critics go free to entertainments and book editors do not have to pay for books they review.

When the Strand book store in New York wrote a letter of solicitation to a book editor whose managing editor was president of the Associated Press Managing Editors, an investigation was undertaken to reveal that for years book review editors in many parts of the country were making thousands of dollars annually by selling unreviewed books to the used book company. Most newspapers consider the books the property of the paper, not the reviewer. To avoid the gigantic payola some donate the books to libraries or charitable institutions. According to the used book stores, some of these institutions then offer them for sale.

There have been a few cases of financial writers who used their inside knowledge of the market for personal profit. The Securities and Exchange Commission has taken action against writers who purchased stock just prior to boosting it in their columns, after which they sold at considerable profit. The practice is growing for newspapers to require financial writers to reveal their holdings, to their editors at least. The St. Petersburg *Times* issued regulations that state: "It is a violation of company rules for any staff member to make or hold any investment which in any way might pose a conflict of interest." Richard J. Haiman, managing editor, explained: "In practice it means that no staff member holds any stock in any local companies or in any national companies about which a St. Petersburg *Times* reporter ever would have occasion to write."

Payola has been called bribery, but a consensus of editorial writers who contributed to a *Masthead* symposium was that highly trained journalists have the moral stamina to maintain objectivity despite the hospitality and any feeling of social indebtedness it creates.

The importance of journalists seeing something of the world cannot be denied. Only a few of the larger papers can adhere consistently to a pay-as-you-go policy. So they allow their staff people to accept invitations from foreign governments to visit other nations, usually in parties with representatives of other papers, and they are represented on junkets paid for by their own government to inspect military establishments or to visit battlefields. They take inspection cruises and go on inaugural flights as the guests of private aviation companies.

Contests

A more subtle way of influencing news judgment is the awards that are given in recognition of stellar performance in a particular field. The decision in such a case as to what constitutes good journalism is that of the donor of the prize. Some newspapers are eager to wallpaper their offices with plaques and certificates, and some keep a careful tab on announcements of such honors in the offing. *Editor & Publisher* issues an annual *Directory of Journalism Awards*. In 1980 it listed 330 competitions, most of them annual contests. Too much ambition may develop into exaggerated emphasis on news of a certain character rather than unprejudiced evaluations of the happenings of the day. In other words, conscious efforts to please the donors of prizes can badly warp good editorial performance. The commendations that accompany the certificates or plaques or medals in addition to money prizes, are flattering to recipients and creators of good will for the donors.

"I think we can say that the business journalism awards and fellowships are paying off," according to Vernon R. Alden of the Foreign Business Council reviewing the latest prestigious Gerald Loeb awards called "the Pulitzer prizes of financial journalism."

DECEPTIONS

In Front Page days it was common practice for reporters to pretend to be policemen, deputy coroners or some other public officials. To avoid deliberate misrepresentation without identifying themselves they might begin a telephone conversation with a news source by saying, "I'm calling from police headquarters." Or they might ask, "Has the sheriff arrived yet? If not would you tell me . . ."

Concealed Identities

Even today reporters occasionally crash gates merely by not identifying themselves and acting as though they were within their rights. Mark Butler of the Suburban and Wayne (Pa.) *Times* attended a Kennedy family wedding reception after chauffeuring a part of the bridal party in a car rented from a garage for which he occasionally moonlighted as an extra driver. A Detroit *News* Washington correspondent witnessed the signing of an Israeli-Egyptian peace treaty in the White House by taking the bus seat intended for a congressman who, he knew, would be absent. No special credentials had been issued and police were too busy to check attendance carefully.

Inasmuch as both of these incidents were successful evasions of security measures they led to official condemnations of reporters, the police and the Secret Service. In another case a $1 million suit for invasion of privacy was brought against a radio reporter who eavesdropped on a Panax corporation stockholders' meeting as well as a closed directors' meeting. He did it by putting on overalls and checking wall sockets with an electric circuit tester.

Gene Patterson, editor of the St. Petersburg *Times,* has said: "All of us engage in plainclothes reporting. Our restaurant reviewer doesn't wear a press card on her lobster bib; she takes pains, in fact, not to be recognized in the joints she's casing for our readers' guidance. Neither does our consumer reporter reveal her noncustomer status when she sets out to nail a bait-and-switch advertiser. She's not even above driving a rigged car into a series of garages in order to report the wildly varying cost and effectiveness of auto repairs."

Stunts

Nevertheless, Patterson has soured on such stunts as planting a masquerading reporter on a nursing home's payroll to do an inside job on the nature of the care provided patients. Most newspapers, however, do believe that the best, often the only, way to investigate a situation is from the inside. Edgar May of the Buffalo *Evening News* won a Pulitzer prize for his series of articles after working for three months as a caseworker for the Erie County Department of Social Welfare. Ted Smart of the Chicago *Daily News* won several citations for his exposé of conditions in the Chicago Bridewell, to which he got himself committed as a common drunk. Several official investigations resulted after Edward Williams, Milwaukee *Journal* reporter, spent ten days in the House of Correction posing as a vagrant. By becoming an applicant himself, Sam Washington of the Chicago *Sun-Times* exposed an examiner who was soliciting bribes from students taking a General Educational Development Test.

When William Jones, Chicago *Tribune* reporter, since then promoted to editor, heard unconfirmed reports alleging that Chicago police were bribed to steer hospital call cases to private ambulance companies, he thought it worthwhile following up. So he trained as a first-aid man and got a job as an ambulance driver. The results: a six-part exposé of official collusion; a grand jury that handed up 16 indictments; and a Pulitzer prize for special local reporting for Jones.

Other reporters have obtained employment as guards or attendants in prisons, mental hospitals and other public institutions. The existence of illegal gambling has been exposed by investigative reporters who were supplied with money and told to find bookmakers with whom to place bets. Because of the growing complaint by teachers that students are unruly, reporters with the proper credentials have obtained teaching positions or have acted as substitutes in the classroom to observe firsthand.

The opportunities for such "undercover" journalism are boundless. Usually, some properly qualified official, as a judge or social worker, is "in" on the stunt, often to legalize it and, in any case, to soften adverse criticisms of entrapment or other unethical conduct. Certainly the responsibility is great not to yield to the temptation to merely "make a case" in the interest of a sensational story. It is easy to find that for which one earnestly is looking. The reporter and newspaper are vulnerable unless the highest principles of ethical journalism are observed. Impersonation is not illegal except of police and public officials.

The investigative stunt that perhaps caused the most debate in journalistic circles was that of the Chicago *Sun-Times,* which purchased a tavern that was then operated by reporters with cameramen taking surreptitious pictures of attempts by city inspectors and others to solicit bribes or payoffs. The revelations shook the city that was supposed to work and was considered a cinch for a Pulitzer prize. Although it won eight state and national contests sponsored by organizations including the Associated Press, United Press International and the Society of Professional Journalists, Sigma Delta Chi, the public service committee judging the Pulitzer prizes decided the *Sun-Times'* enterprise involved entrapment, so the prize went to the Philadelphia *Inquirer* for exposing systematic police violence.

Impersonations

When the roles are reversed, journalists usually protest impersonations of reporters by policemen. The Welch (W. Va.) *Daily News,* however, hired an undercover policeman to pose as a reporter to gather evidence of the illicit drug traffic. After several journalistic organizations were critical of the imposture, the paper's publisher, Rollo Taylor, wrote to the Charleston (W. Va.) *Mail:*

> For over 100 years newspaper reporters have posed as ditch diggers, diplomats, welders, Indians, Jews, blacks, truck drivers, and criminals to obtain stories.
>
> Such a pose is a deception—a lie—but I don't recall that anybody was ever offended by that, nor do I recall that any newspaper ever lost its credibility by it.
>
> It now seems to offend some newspaper people that a policeman posing as a

reporter is all wrong despite the fact that a reporter is applauded for posing as a policeman.

Much more serious were the revelations by two special congressional committees, one in the Senate with Frank Church of Idaho as chairman, the other in the House with Rep. Otto Pike of New York as chairman. Both reports revealed that almost since its origin shortly after World War II, the Central Intelligence Agency had employed journalists abroad as covert agents or informers. At the time of the reports, 1976, it was estimated that approximately 50 foreign correspondents for American newspapers and news services, freelancers and stringers were in CIA's employ. They helped plant stories in publications all over the world, falsified accounts and supplied the CIA with information that didn't get into any news dispatches.

The disclosures of the Church and Pike committees and revelations contained in several books by former CIA agents resulted in new CIA guidelines containing the following: "Effective immediately the CIA will not enter into any paid or contractual relationship with any full-time or part-time news correspondent accredited by any U.S. news service, newspaper, periodical, radio or television network or station."

The order was almost universally applauded by journalists. However, when Congress began considering new legislation governing clandestine CIA and FBI activities in 1980, there were few provisions to prevent a recurrence of the old practices.

CODES OF ETHICS

"In nearly 40 years of newspapering I have never witnessed so massive a tendency toward wholesale scapegoating," wrote Sydney Justin Harris in his syndicated column. As illustrations of what he meant, among others, he cited the following:

> If a politician says what he later regrets and sees it in print, he has been "misquoted."
>
> If a movie star makes a fool of himself in a barroom, a bath house or a brothel and gets on a police blotter, its publication is the fault of a "sensational" press.
>
> If a foreign government is knocking off its dissidents and insensately violating human rights and such activities are broadcast in this country, the media are "exaggerating and inflaming" the situation.
>
> If a mass murderer and arsonist is photographed being taken into custody, the press is conspiring to deny him a "fair trial."

"Even Hitler didn't blame the Jews or Stalin the kulaks for as many crimes, sins and defects as nearly all elements in our society are now laying on the media," Harris lamented.

Verification of Harris' statement is found in the quantity of bills to limit journalistic performance in one way or another that are being introduced in state legislatures and Congress. They call for licensing, compulsory retractions, refusal of access to public records and judicial proceedings, boards to investigate and order corrective actions and more of the same.

Professional public opinion polls show an increasing number of persons favoring strict control of the media. Gallup told the First Amendment Congress in Philadelphia that 75 per cent of Americans do not know what the First Amendment is or the issues with which it deals. "The key finding," Gallup reported, "seems to be that the press in America is operating in an environment of public opinion that is increasingly indifferent and, in some respects, hostile."

This situation is one of the facts of life that the young journalist must be aware of. To combat the bad public image that newsgatherers have to the detriment of the credibility of the media, almost every journalistic organization has prepared a code of ethics for the guidance of reporters on how to be on their good behavior. The National Labor Relations Board has ruled that the management of the Madison (Wis.) *Capital-Times* can unilaterally issue a code of ethics but it cannot establish penalties without negotiating with the Guild. The paper's managing editor had declared in a speech to the New Jersey Press Association, "Can a reporter who dates news sources be objective? We can't prevent such associations but in order to protect as much as possible the newspaper's objectivity we must know about them." This inspired many reporters to prepare memoranda telling of their social engagements, including menus, size of bills and conversations. Some who received tips or ideas for news stories requested overtime pay.

The Society of Professional Journalists, Sigma Delta Chi, has the largest membership of any journalistic organization. Its code, revised in 1973, follows:

> The Society of Professional Journalists, Sigma Delta Chi, believes the duty of journalists is to serve the truth.
>
> We believe the agencies of mass communication are carriers of public discussion and information, acting on their Constitutional mandate and freedom to learn and report the facts.
>
> We believe in public enlightenment as the forerunner of justice, and in our Constitutional role to seek the truth as part of the public's right to know the truth.
>
> We believe those responsibilities carry obligations that require journalists to perform with intelligence, objectivity, accuracy, and fairness.
>
> To these ends, we declare acceptance of the standards of practice here set forth:
>
> RESPONSIBILITY
>
> The public's right to know of events of public importance and interest is the overriding mission of the mass media. The purpose of distributing news and enlightened opinion is to serve the general welfare. Journalists who use their professional status as representatives of the public for selfish or other unworthy motives violate a high trust.
>
> FREEDOM OF THE PRESS
>
> Freedom of the press is to be guarded as an inalienable right of people in a free society. It carries with it the freedom and the responsibility to discuss, question,

and challenge actions and utterances of our government and of our public and private institutions. Journalists uphold the right to speak unpopular opinions and the privilege to agree with the majority.

ETHICS

Journalists must be free of obligation to any interest other than the public's right to know the truth.

1. Gifts, favors, free travel, special treatment or privileges can compromise the integrity of journalists and their employers. Nothing of value should be accepted.

2. Secondary employment, political involvement, holding public office, and service in community organizations should be avoided if it compromises the integrity of journalists and their employers. Journalists and their employers should conduct their personal lives in a manner which protects them from conflict of interest, real or apparent. Their responsibilities to the public are paramount. That is the nature of their profession.

3. So-called news communications from private sources should not be published or broadcast without substantiation of their claims to news value.

4. Journalists will seek news that serves the public interest, despite the obstacles. They will make constant efforts to assure that the public's business is conducted in public and that public records are open to public inspection.

5. Journalists acknowledge the newsman's ethic of protecting confidential sources of information.

ACCURACY AND OBJECTIVITY

Good faith with the public is the foundation of all worthy journalism.

1. Truth is our ultimate goal.

2. Objectivity in reporting the news is another goal, which serves as the mark of an experienced professional. It is a standard of performance toward which we strive. We honor those who achieve it.

3. There is no excuse for inaccuracies or lack of thoroughness.

4. Newspaper headlines should be fully warranted by the contents of the articles they accompany. Photographs and telecasts should give an accurate picture of an event and not highlight a minor incident out of context.

5. Sound practice makes clear distinction between news reports and expressions of opinion. News reports should be free of opinion or bias and represent all sides of an issue.

6. Partisanship in editorial comment which knowingly departs from the truth violates the spirit of American journalism.

7. Journalists recognize their responsibility for offering informed analysis, comment, and editorial opinion on public events and issues. They accept the obligation to present such material by individuals whose competence, experience, and judgment qualify them for it.

8. Special articles or presentations devoted to advocacy or the writer's own conclusions and interpretations should be labeled as such.

FAIR PLAY

Journalists at all times will show respect for the dignity, privacy, rights, and well-being of people encountered in the course of gathering and presenting the news.

1. The news media should not communicate unofficial charges affecting reputation or moral character without giving the accused a chance to reply.

2. The news media must guard against invading a person's right of privacy.

3. The media should not pander to morbid curiosity about details of vice and crime.

4. It is the duty of news media to make prompt and complete correction of their errors.

5. Journalists should be accountable to the public for their reports and the public should be encouraged to voice its grievances against the media. Open dialogue with our readers, viewers, and listeners should be fostered.

PLEDGE

Journalists should actively censure and try to prevent violations of these standards, and they should encourage their observance by all newspeople. Adherence to this code of ethics is intended to preserve the bond of mutual trust and respect between American journalists and the American people.

The press is a gigantic force that, to a higher degree, governs the world, its opinions and its activities. To be a servant of this great force is a privilege which we are happy to possess. The press shall work for the uplifting and the enlightening of humanity. But with the greatness of the task follows the greatness of the responsibility. A splendid opportunity to serve our fellow-men is given us; it is our duty to serve them well. Because we love our work and venerate it we must see if anything is wrong, and ask how to improve upon it. We cannot, in a short while, change the conditions of the press, the system, the capitalistic power, the dependence upon the advertisers, the taste of the public. But what we can do is to strengthen the claims to our own respect for the truth.

—LUDVIG SAXE, editor, *Verdens Gang*, Oslo, Norway.

My own newspaper experience is that the average item is more carefully written to conserve truth than is the average business letter, lawyer's brief, historical work or sermon. The explanation is that the good news writer on the good newspaper acts on impulse without respect to objectivity other than the spread of information; he is free of interested motives.

—MARLEN PEW, editor, *Editor & Publisher*

Journalism should be put on a professional basis by the practicing newspaper men themselves. Any law or state board for the regulation of journalism suggests too strongly the stigma of politics and a jeopardy of the freedom of the press. Journalists should be just as vigilant as lawyers and physicians to segregate the shysters and the quacks. Neither law nor medicine was on a firm professional basis until each had its literature and its recognized schools. Journalism has been slower than law and medicine in providing education for its aspirants. But today journalism has both a literature and its own schools. It remains but to attain that professional standing which so long it has claimed, but without a valid foundation.

—JOHN E. DREWRY, University of Georgia

PART TWO

NEWS WRITING

A high standard of style is repeatedly found in the great newspapers; it is one of the qualities that make them great. —ERNEST BERNBAUM, professor of English.

"ONLY A NEWSPAPER GUY"

I see a man strut through a jam in the hall,
Take a seat 'mid the speakers and chat with them all.
"Is this Reagan?" I ask, "that the crowd he defies?"
"No," says someone, "He's one of the newspaper guys."

I see a man pushing his way through the lines
Of cops where a fire brightly glimmers and shines.
"Chief Collins?" I ask, but a fireman replies,
"Oh, no, why that's one of those newspaper guys."

I see a man start on the trail of a crook,
And he scorns all assistance, but brings him to book.
"Mr. Webster?" I inquire. Someone scornfully cries:
"Webster? Naw, he's just one of them newspaper guys."

I see a man walk through the door of a show
Where great crowds are blocked by the signs S. R. O.
"Is that Olivier himself that no ticket he buys?"
"Well, hardly. He's one of those newspaper guys."

I see a man knock on a president's door.
And the sign, NO ADMITTANCE, completely ignore.
"Is this Rockefeller that privacy's rights he denies?"
"Rockefeller? Shucks! It's just one of those newspaper guys."

And some day I'll walk by the great streets of gold
And see a man enter, unquestioned and bold.
"A saint?" I'll inquire, and old Peter'll reply:
"Well, I should say not. He's a newspaper guy."

Adapted from an original by Ted Robinson, Cleveland Plain Dealer

5 ORGANIZING THE FACTS

Even before the task of gathering the facts concerning a particular news event has been completed, the reporter starts thinking of how to organize them into a news story. The more experienced the newsgatherer, the more automatic or unconscious this habit becomes. As new information is obtained, earlier ideas regarding the theme or central idea coming out of the assignment may be modified.

CONTEMPORARY TRENDS

Since World War II there have been numerous studies of the traditional methods of organizing a news story. Professional journalistic organizations have devoted considerable attention to ways of making news stories more readable. In part, they were motivated by the success of news magazines in presenting the news in brighter and livelier fashion. Also, and perhaps more important, radio and television newscasters have demonstrated how the gist of a story can be presented in fewer words than are contained in the usual newspaper lead paragraph.

The press associations and some large newspapers employed experts in readability to analyze their practices. A few journalistic higher-ups became so enthusiastic over some readability formulas that they blamed widespread reader ignorance and indifference upon traditional styles of journalistic composition. Some others thought the answer was to be found in greater understanding by journalists of the philosophical and statistical aspects of the communication process. More recently critics within the newsroom have joined some laymen in insisting that the press must assume greater leadership in investigating and crusading in the public interest.

Because the five *w*'s have been taught to journalistic novitiates for several generations, they often seem to be trite and academic. Nevertheless, no matter what writing or speaking style is used, and regardless of whether the contents are objectively descriptive or subjectively analytical, the reader or listener's curiosity has to be satisfied as regards the *who, what, when, where* and *why*, as well as the *how* of a newsworthy occurrence. What has happened, largely as a result of the blandishments of the readability conscious and statistically conscious communications researchers and the socially conscious rank-and-file, is a considerable loosening of the rigid rules regarding the structure of a news story. Whereas a generation ago it was virtually mandatory that as many as possible of the five *w*'s and *h* be mentioned in the first paragraph of a news story, today considerably greater freedom is permitted in presenting them. Now that radio and television have taken the edge off the spot news, stories important enough to have been broadcast may be written with some disregard of the old principles. Nevertheless, though delayed, the five *w*'s must be included somewhere in the full account.

THE INVERTED PYRAMID FORM

Furthermore, since by far most of the stories a newspaper prints every day have not been broadcast by radio or television, the great majority, perhaps 90 per cent, of news stories still are written in accordance with the traditional rule that the first part—whether it be a conventionally written single paragraph or a half-dozen or more one-sentence paragraphs—contain a succinct resume of the story as a whole. The beginner ambitious to achieve stylistic originality does well to master the rules first in order to break them intelligently later.

The striking difference between traditional news writing in the United States and other forms of written composition, such as the essay, poetry, drama, novel and short story, continues to be this: whereas the authors of these other forms of composition usually begin with minor or incidental details and work to a climax near or at the end of their compositions, the news writer reverses this plan of organization. That is, the climax or end of the story comes first. Given a schedule of facts to arrange in the form of a newspaper article, the writer selects the most important fact or climax of the story and puts it at the beginning. The second most important fact comes second, the third most important fact third and so on.

The traditional form of news writing is called the *inverted pyramid form*.

It is said to have originated in Civil War days when correspondents used the telegraph for the first time. From fear that their accounts would not be transmitted all at one time, the war correspondents crowded as much information as possible into their first paragraphs.

Throughout the decades since that time, press associations, which transmit stories by telegraph, have perfected the system. Before the teletypesetter was introduced about mid-century, few leading stories ever were transmitted in one piece. Instead, a few paragraphs of several important stories were sent first and then the later paragraphs. Throughout a day's sending, there were numerous new or substitute first paragraphs (leads), inserts and additions.

Locally written news followed the press association pattern. The inverted pyramid form of organization was defended in several different ways:

1. *To facilitate reading.* The reading matter of the average newspaper, if printed in book form, would fill a large volume. The American newspaper reader hasn't time to read that much daily. Neither is anyone interested in all the articles appearing in any newspaper. If the climax of every story is at the beginning, the reader can learn the gist of the news quickly and, if interested, can continue to the details. No one should have to read any article to its conclusion to learn what it is about.
2. *To satisfy curiosity.* This is the natural way of telling an important item of news. If someone drowns while swimming, the average person would not begin telling of the incident by narrating the dead person's preparations for a visit to the beach with a group of friends. Rather, the important fact would be first—John was drowned while swimming. The supplementary details of how, when and where it happened would follow.
3. *To facilitate makeup.* In rectifying a page, the makeup editor often finds it necessary to cut the length of some articles. If the least important details are at the end of a story, this can be done without harming the story. The makeup editor should feel free to cut ordinary articles without consulting other editors.
4. *To facilitate headline writing.* The headline consists of the key words or their synonyms necessary to give an idea of what a story contains. If the story is well written, the headline writer should not have to look beyond the first paragraph or two to find these words.

A few years ago the Writing committee of the Associated Press Managing Editors cited the story in the right-hand column below as one of the best examples of news writing of the year. It was written in the traditional inverted pyramid style. In the left-hand column below, the same facts, using the identical phraseology as much as possible, are rearranged in chronological order.

Chronological Style

About 1 A.M. today, Mrs. Harry Rosenberg was awakened by the sound of a car

Newspaper Style

Judith Ann Roberts, blue-eyed, 7-year-old daughter of a Baltimore attorney and

Chronological Style

roaring out of the driveway of her home. She rushed to the living room where she discovered that her granddaughter, Judith Ann Roberts, 7, no longer was sleeping on the studio couch and that the front door was standing open.

Mrs. Rosenberg called her daughter, Mrs. Shirley Roberts, wife of a Baltimore attorney and labor leader, who was visiting her parents. Mrs. Roberts, the missing child's mother, notified police of her daughter's kidnapping at 1:10 A.M.

Police said the kidnaper sneaked into the home of the grandparents, stole the keys to the Rosenberg's car from the grandfather's trousers pocket and took the child away.

Four hours and ten minutes after they were called, police found the Rosenberg car abandoned in the strip of sandy land between Bayshore drive and the shore of Biscayne Bay. Its wheels were mired in the sand and the tire marks showed the driver tried frantically to get it out.

Judith Ann's nude and brutally battered body was found a block from the car in a clump of bushes off fashionable Bayshore drive. It was caked with blood and dirt, indicating she put up a brave fight for her life. The blue-eyed child had been raped and beaten on the head with a heavy instrument and a piece of gauze was knotted about her throat. Her flimsy seersucker nightgown, white with red polka dots, lay eight feet from her body.

Newspaper Style

labor leader, was kidnapped from the home of her grandparents here today, raped and beaten to death.

Police found the child's nude and brutally battered body in a clump of bushes off fashionable Bayshore drive five hours after her mother, Mrs. Shirley Roberts, reported her missing.

She had been beaten on the head with a heavy instrument and a piece of gauze was knotted about her throat. Her flimsy seersucker nightgown, white with red polka dots, lay eight feet from the body.

Judith Ann's little body was caked with blood and dirt, indicating she put up a brave fight for her life.

Police said the killer sneaked into the home of the grandparents, Mr. and Mrs. Harry Rosenberg, about 1 A.M., stole the keys to Rosenberg's car from his trousers pocket and took the child from the studio couch in the living room where she was sleeping.

Mrs. Rosenberg was awakened by the sound of the car roaring out of the driveway. She found the child missing and the front door standing open.

Police were called at 1:10 A.M. Four hours and ten minutes later, they found the Rosenberg car abandoned in the strip of sandy land between Bayshore drive and the shore of Biscayne Bay. Its wheels were mired in the sand and the tire marks showed the driver tried frantically to get it out.

Judith's body was found a block from the car.

"Note, please," the APME Writing committee asked, "the many fine points . . . 'the seersucker nightgown, white and red polka dots, lay eight feet from the body.'

"How many little nightgowns like that are all over this land? And *eight feet* . . . no guess-work there; the reporter was seeing it for you. Too, the killer sneaked in about 1 A.M. and 'police were called at 1:10 A.M.' The car was found *four hours and ten minutes later* . . . not simply later in the day."

Although few would argue with an unnamed telegraph editor with more than forty years' experience, whom the committee quoted as saying, "That Miami story is one of the finest writing jobs I've ever seen," the points cited by the committee indicate that the story's strength derived primarily from the fact that an extraordinary job of reporting, involving keen observation, had preceded its composition. In other words, *the most important step in communication is obtaining something worthwhile to communicate.* Stated still another way, the basis of all good journalism is thorough reporting. Shorter words, sentences and paragraphs, desirable as they may be for clarity, cannot add important details to a journalistic account. *There is no substitute for good reporting no matter what writing style is used.* It is the message and not the medium that counts, and journalists should not be misled by crackpot theories to the contrary.

THE LEAD

The Miami story was written in traditional inverted pyramid style. That is, the first paragraph contained the gist or skeleton outline of the entire story in a minimum of words. Subsequent paragraphs elaborated upon various aspects of the lead, making them more definite; or they supplied additional details in the order of their importance as the reporter judged them.

Since, for more than a half-century, this has been the orthodox form of news writing, the *lead* of a straight news story came to be defined as the first paragraph which contained all of the elements (five *w*'s and *h*) necessary for the complete telling of the essential facts.

This practice often led to long and crowded first paragraphs. The lead of the Miami story, for instance, might have read something like this:

> The nude and brutally beaten body of Judith Ann Roberts, blue-eyed, 7-year-old daughter of a Baltimore attorney and labor leader, was found by police in a clump of bushes off fashionable Bayshore drive here at 1 A.M. today after she had been kidnapped from the home of her grandparents, Mr. and Mrs. Harry Rosenberg, and raped.

In the effort to avoid such cumbersome lead paragraphs, and to increase readability, some newspapers have gone to the opposite extreme of invoking the "one-fact sentence" rule, which would lead to something like the following:

> A 7-year-old girl has been kidnapped, raped and beaten to death.
>
> She was blue-eyed Judith Ann Roberts of Baltimore. Her father is a lawyer and labor leader.
>
> Police found the child's body in a clump of bushes off fashionable Bayshore drive.
>
> The body was nude and brutally battered.
>
> The child's mother, Mrs. Shirley Roberts, reported her daughter missing at 1:10 A.M.
>
> That was four hours and ten minutes before the body was found by police.

It is difficult to determine exactly how many of the one- or two-sentence paragraphs of a story written in this manner constitute the lead, or first unit of the story. Every sentence relates to some word or fact in a preceding sentence, and it takes a half-dozen or more of them to present all of the information which one would have been crowded into half the space or less. This form of writing says less in more words but is scored as more readable. The original version of the Miami story was a compromise between the new and old extremes.

Since the inverted pyramid form still is adhered to, even in the staccato type of paragraphing illustrated above, in that facts are arranged in the order of their supposed importance, the traditional definition of a news story lead holds: the first unit of the story which performs the function of telling the entire story in epitomized form.

A good lead, no matter how much it is strung out, answers all the questions that a reader wants answered when hearing of a particular incident. These include the cause and result (the *how* or *why* and the *what*), the *who* and often the *where* and the *when*. These elements are called the *5 w's* and the *h*. Not all of them must be present in every lead, but no important one should be omitted. The lead also plays up the feature of the story if there is one, is attractive and induces the reader to continue with the rest of the story, It, of course, observes the canons of good writing. A good lead suggests or gives the authority on which the news is printed and indentifies the persons mentioned in the story (or the story itself) by relating them (or it) to previous or current news.

The Miami story fulfilled these requirements in this way:

Who—Judith Ann Roberts.
What—Killed.
When—July 7; time of day (1 A.M.) given later.
Where—Miami, Fla.
How—Kidnapped, raped and beaten to death.
Authority—Police and relatives obvious sources of information.
Identification—Seven-year-old daughter of a Baltimore lawyer and labor leader.
Feature—Kidnapped from home of grandparents.

THE BODY

In view of the tendency to reduce the first sentence of a news story to the fewest possible words, the function of the sentences and paragraphs that immediately follow is clearly to restate the facts of the first sentence so as to make them more definite. Loosening of the rule that the first paragraph contain all of the five *w*'s and the *h* means that succeeding paragraphs often must supply some additional pertinent facts crowded out of the lead in the interest of brevity.

It doesn't make any difference what academic labels are placed on units of a news story, and it is difficult or impossible to chart news stories so that units do not overlap. If you wish, you can consider the extreme attempt at epitomized writing ("A 7-year-old girl has been kidnapped, raped and beaten to death") as the lead and call all the rest of the story by its traditional name, *body*. Or you can insist that the lead proper include as many sentences as are necessary to make the basic elements (five *w*'s and *h*) definite.

In either case, there often remain a number of additional paragraphs which can be labeled either "body" or "second part of body." If new details are added in the same sentences or paragraphs in which there is further amplification of the lead, telling exactly where the last unit of the story begins isn't easy.

Unity

A method of obtaining rhetorical unity as one short paragraph follows another is by use of *linkage* words. Note in the following example how their skillful use creates a flow and, at the same time, enables the writer to introduce new facts. This story could be cut at the end of almost any paragraph and there still would be a rhetorically complete account.

By Associated Press

Mighty rivers on a late winter rampage surged through south central sections of Alabama, Georgia and Mississippi Wednesday, leaving wide trails of muddy ruin amounting to millions.

Except around Jackson, Miss., the highest levels of the flooding rivers were spread largely across rural areas as they continued toward their common draining point, the Gulf of Mexico.

However, more flood menace lies ahead for downstate residents, and even in ravaged mid-state sections where the worst is over, it will be days before the rampant rivers fall within their banks.

ALABAMA AT CREST

At Selma in central Alabama, *for example,* the Alabama River reached its crest of 58.3 feet Tuesday night, but the muddy waters are not expected to creep back to the 45-foot flood level until March 9.

In hard-hit Selma and Montgomery and Demopolis, Ala., *as well as* Jackson, Miss., and West Point and Columbus, Ga., thousands in evacuation centers looked to more days of waiting for water to seep out of their homes.

To relieve the tension of Montgomery refugees, many facing their fifth night in shelters, the Red Cross put on recreation programs.

Damage to Alabama's public facilities *has already topped* $10 million in preliminary estimates. That includes only roads and bridges and county and municipal places—not homes, businesses, farmland and livestock.

CATTLE DROWNED

In central Alabama's Montgomery and Elmore Counties alone, a livestock broker estimates that about 2,500 head of cattle worth $500,000 have drowned *during the current flood.*

As the swollen Pearl River swirled around the Jackson, Miss., area Tuesday night and Wednesday, cutting a three-mile swath in some places, about 850 residents left their low-lying homes and most flocked to refuge centers.

[Tampa *Tribune*]

Other useful linkage words or phrases include the following: in the meantime, before, after, earlier, later, sooner, previously, furthermore, also, therefore, because, moreover, nevertheless, however, but, by contrast, inconsistently, here, there, above, below.

Block Paragraphing

In longer stories, regardless of whether the lead was one or several paragraphs long, paragraphs are so written as to include a single subtopic each.

This type of paragraphing differs from the type that English composition students are taught is best. Because newspaper paragraphs of necessity (appearance) must be short, they do not follow the orthodox rule of rhetoric that every paragraph should include a complete thought or topic sentence. Rather, in newspaper paragraphing the idea-unit is broken up into subtopics. In other words, news writers paragraph their paragraphs.

This type of *block paragraphing* is distinctly advantageous for news writing. It permits the insertion or deletion of paragraphs without disarranging a story. Frequently it is necessary, in the light of new information, to recast certain paragraphs, to add additional paragraphs and to remove others. For example, note in the following story how additional information might be added without serious trouble. The paragraphs in italics quite conceivably could have been added after the story was written. Furthermore, several of them could have been inserted at other places in the story. Quite a few of the paragraphs, italicized or not, could be shifted around without destroying the effectiveness of the story. Often, different inserts are written by different reporters.

Flights were back on schedule Monday at Kent County International Airport after being disrupted this weekend with fog canceling most flights.

Air traffic during the busy holiday season came to a near standstill Saturday and Sunday because of dense clouds of fog which kept most planes grounded and prevented flights from arriving from other cities.

Passengers coming here from Chicago were being ferried in on buses, while those trying to leave Kent County either had to wait and hope for the fog to clear or take a bus to Detroit in hopes of catching a flight there.

The airport terminal was cluttered with luggage and impatient passengers most of the weekend.

"Fog closed it down yesterday from the early morning to about two in the afternoon. It was closed back down again at night," said an airport spokesman. "It was basically the same thing Saturday. Nobody could get in."

Flights were back to normal by 7:30 a.m. Monday. Some passengers were able to catch flights out of Kent County, while others were bused to Detroit for flights there.

"Everything got so far behind this weekend that they (airlines) decided not to

divert planes here to take out the passengers," said a spokeswoman from Republic Airlines. "Those that could not be accommodated on a flight from here are going to Detroit.

"It's better this way than to try and play catch up."

Travelers faced the possibility of a foggy Christmas in wide sections of the country with poor visibility contributing to traffic accidents that pushed the death toll toward the 300 mark in the third day of the long holiday weekend.

[Grand Rapids (Mich.) *Press*]

Chronological

A widely used method of organizing the material after the lead is chronological, at least for a number of paragraphs, after which new facts can be added in block paragraph style. This type of organization is effective in stories in which action is described, as in the following example:

A gunman yesterday robbed the Eastwood Federal Savings and Loan association of about $7,000 while scores of noonday shoppers walked past the building at 118 S. Jeffrey street.

The bandit walked in at 12:45 P.M., normally the busiest time of day, and found the office empty of customers. A teller, Miss Virginia Kole, one of four employees present, asked the man if she could help him.

"Yeah. There's a lot you can do to help me," the man answered as he leaped up on the 4-foot high counter and pulled out an old rusty revolver.

"Get back, get back," he ordered from his perch. "I'm not fooling. I'll shoot the lady first. Don't step on the alarm."

Joseph Dierks, vice-president, said he was sitting in the back of the office and did not move, waiting to see what the man would do next.

The bandit jumped down on the floor behind the counter and ordered the four to a rest room in the rear. The other two workers were Howard K. Jacobs, secretary-treasurer of the association, and Robertson Evans, a teller.

As the holdup man was directing the group to the rear room, a customer came in. He was Walter Mather, 2130 W. Otis avenue, who also was ordered to the back room.

The robber closed the door on the five and went back to the front of the office where he rifled three cash drawers and the open safe.

When Mr. Evans heard the front door close, he hurried from the back room and ran to the front door hoping to see which way the bandit fled. The man apparently became quickly lost in the crowd and Mr. Evans could not see him.

Mr. Dierks said an early count indicated the stolen money totaled $6,829.15, but he thought the final tally would be higher, perhaps as much as $8,500.

The vice-president considered the holdup man an extremely lucky amateur. He pointed out that an experienced robber probably would have looked over the office several days in advance and would have realized that the association usually was busiest between 12:15 and 1:15 P.M. when many customers come in on their lunch hours.

Mr. Dierks said the gunman was probably a very athletic person, judging from the way he hopped about the office. He appeared to be in his early twenties, about 5 feet 6 inches tall, and weighed about 140 pounds. He wore a blue cap, green shirt, and khaki trousers.

What must be avoided is making the lead sentence merely a "peg line." For example, "Alderman John F. Gates today called Mayor Henry R. Penrose a liar" is superior to "An alderman today called the mayor a liar." It is inferior to "Alderman John R. Gates today charged that Mayor Henry R. Penrose lied when he said he never owned any west-side real estate." If by some grotesque error the former lead sentence were to appear alone, there would be considerable embarrassment if not worse. There is, in other words, a limit beyond which it is unwise to be brief. Too often brevity necessitates being vague or indefinite, which requires more rather than less effort on the part of the reader who seeks the facts of a news story.

VARIATIONS

Increasingly, in stories in which the human interest is paramount, the rule that it should be possible to cut final paragraphs without ruining the news interest is violated. There are some stories that must be read in their entirety.

Sequence

In a story written in sequence style all facts are arranged in strictly chronological order. The climax or satisfaction of the reader's curiosity is postponed until the end. Thus a sequence story cannot be edited from the bottom up as could the chronological story which has a news lead.

> Three-year-old Byron Halpert, being an inquisitive little fellow, opened a second-story window Tuesday a few minutes after his mother had left to take her daughter to school.
>
> Byron leaned out to see what he could see. But he leaned so far that he lost his balance, fell through the opening and wound up hanging from the window sill by his finger tips, 20 feet above a concrete walk.
>
> Just then a police car came by. Officer William Watson, sizing up the situation, ran to the spot below the window just as little Byron let go. The boy landed squarely in the policeman's arms, unhurt but tearfully scared.

Cumulative Interest

The lead of this type of story contains some sort of news peg. In addition to emphasizing the tone or situation of the story as it progresses, this kind of story incites reader interest, which cumulates as each succeeding sequence and paragraph makes for greater definiteness.

> Long Beach, Calif. (AP)—The young woman said a friend had given a bottle to her with instructions to throw it at anyone who tried to mug her.
>
> Police officials said Miss Jackie Lynn Samay, 22 years old, had telephoned to ask them what to do with the bottle in her refrigerator, "a pint of nitroglycerine."
>
> Bomb-squad officers rushed to her residence, ordered a four-block downtown

area evacuated, packed the bottle in ice from a nearby liquor store and had Army experts transport it carefully in a thick metal box to nearby Fort MacArthur. Traffic was cleared from all streets along the route.

The next day the Army reported the liquid was glue. [New York *Times*]

Suspended Interest

A suspended interest story is one in which the writer "strings along" the reader to the very end before giving him the news peg on which the item is based. Such stories resemble magazine short stories in that they must be read in their entirety. Frequently, the climax may be a surprise; in any case, it satisfies the reader's interest which has been suspended because of the indefiniteness of early details.

An ice-cream cone failed to have a cooling effect Saturday night on Patrolman Harry O'Brien.

O'Brien, assigned to the burglary detail, was parking his car on Auburn street near Wilson avenue, when a man approached the car, mumbling incoherently.

"What did you say?" O'Brien asked.

Without another word, the man suddenly jammed an ice-cream cone into the policeman's face.

O'Brien alighted, drew his gun, seized the man and was told, "You'll have to fight to take me in."

With that, the prisoner slugged O'Brien in the mouth with his fist, O'Brien countered with an uppercut which knocked the man flat.

At the Kenton Avenue Station the arrested man identified himself as Willis C. Solano of 1768 W. Tree street and said he thought policemen were "too hot" and he wanted to "cool one off."

Delayed News Peg

Since most readers of sports pages are fans who already know how their favorite teams or players fared, sports writing has undergone a great change. Today the fan who didn't attend the game or watch it on television has to hunt for the score in the fourth or fifth paragraph. Then he may or may not return to read the description or evaluative or philosophical earlier paragraphs. Here are a couple of typical examples of this type of story or organization, both from the Chicago *Sun-Times*.

By Bob Pille

Ann Arbor, Mich.—Being very mindful of tradition and honoring the 100th anniversary of local collegiate football, the folks at Michigan should have been wary of omens Saturday.

It was equally tradition-encrusted Notre Dame against the Wolverines in the nation's biggest game of this early season with 105,111 in the house on one of those sunny autumn afternoons invented for football and most of the country watching on television—when the cameras were working, that is.

So they had to know that the Irish came in with a two-game winning streak at

Michigan—from victories in 1909 and 1943—and that Dan Devine, the Notre Dame coach, had been the last from outside the Big Ten to beat the Wolverines here. Devine, in his Missouri days, did it to Bo Schembechler's first team in 1969 just as he had to Bump Elliott's first Michigan team in 1959.

And the Irish and Devine did it again 12–10 in a moderate upset in a strange sort of game dominated by defenses and field goal kickers. . . .

By Taylor Bell

All Scott Parzych could remember was that he was the goat last year and Lockport's 6–7 All-Stater wasn't about to let it happen again. In the end, however, he could only watch as Jim Stack lofted a 20-foot shot with one second to play.

"In last year's game," recalled Parzych, "there was one second left and Kevin Boyle took a rebound away from me and he beat us. The ball rolled off my fingertips and he got it. I felt terrible. And tonight, when that shot went off, my heart was 'way down here in my stomach."

But Stack's shot rimmed out, and Lockport, which trailed by five points with four minutes left, rallied to pull out a 42–41 victory over St. Laurence Wednesday night in a showdown between the state's two ranking Class AA powers in the sectional tournament at Downers Grove North. . . .

Direct Address

Beginning reporters are admonished to keep out of their own stories, only an occasional reference to the fact that a reporter asked a certain question or made an unsuccessful effort to obtain an important fact being permitted. Use of either the first or second person is discouraged. Columnists, special writers who sign their articles, and writers of feature stories are exempt from this rule when effectiveness cannot be obtained otherwise. The following are examples to show how the first or second person occasionally may be used in an ordinary news or news feature story such as a beginning reporter might write.

> Kids, when Ma and Pa take a look at your report card then start the sermon about how smart they were in high school, do you see red? Do you want to chew nails?
>
> Relax, kids, you've got a friend.
>
> He is Dr. F. H. Finch of the University of Illinois, and he takes your side today in a monograph of the American Psychological Association.

> If you haven't heard of it, and wouldn't believe it if you had, it probably will be on display today at the National Inventors' Congress in the Hotel LaSalle.
>
> Window glass that can't be seen through, lamps that give invisible light and solid water pipes that have no hollow space for the water—those are some of the things you may expect to find.

THE REPORTER'S NOTES

Prerequisite to a well-organized news story is a careful rearrangement of the reporter's notes. For the experienced reporter, the task of dictating a story over the telephone to a rewrite person from a handful of notes scribbled on copy paper while standing in a stuffy booth is an everyday matter. The reporter who uses an electric typewriter in an electronically equipped newsroom does not jerk "false start" leads from his mill to help litter the newsroom floor with crumpled copy paper. It is to the writer's interest to make as few false starts as possible, thus avoiding the push-buttoning involved in making corrections. While learning, the cub reporter profits by an outline of the facts s/he has gathered. The reporter has, first of all, to pick the feature to go into the lead; next, to be certain essential questions are answered and there is sufficient identification and authority; then, to decide which phases of the lead need amplification in the first part of the body of the story and how it is to be provided and, finally, to arrange the other facts which should be included.

Seldom, if ever, does the reporter jot down facts in the order in which they should be used. As the reporter learns more and more about the incident one or more lead possibilities are seen. There are few if any reporters, regardless of experience, who fail to profit by a study of all notes taken and an outlining of them, if only in the head, before beginning to write or dictate. The young reporter frequently finds it profitable to number the facts included in his or her notes in the order of importance.

The necessity for rearranging and discarding notes can be seen by imagining how the reporter who covered the Judith Ann Roberts case gathered the facts. If he were stationed at police headquarters, the first information obtained was: Mrs. Shirley Roberts called to report that her child had been kidnapped from the home of her parents whose address was given. Either then or when policemen, accompanied by reporters, arrived at the residence, the mother gave a complete description of the child's appearance and habits. She and her parents told how the child's disappearance was discovered and the condition of the room, including the empty couch and open door. Mr. or Mrs. Rosenberg provided a description of their automobile: its make, model, color, license number, mileage and distinguishing features.

In the search for clues, police and reporters asked the three adults and other residents about the visit of the mother and child to Miami. They wanted to know how the family and child spent the preceding day, especially what they did during the evening. They asked about Mr. Roberts and whether either he or any of the others had any enemies who might wish them ill. They wanted to know whom Judith had met, talked with, played with, where she had gone and so on.

Before the body was found, reporters made notes on the activities of the police: how many and who were assigned to the search, where they went and whom they questioned, what alarms were sent out, what clues, if any, they considered important and the like. They inquired carefully into how discovery of the body was made—whether as part of a careful plan of investigation or by accident.

Bear in mind that the example given was written for a press association, which means it was intended for publication in cities other than Miami. In that city the story received much longer treatment with many additional details of interest to local readers.

To summarize: The first step in good news writing is good reporting. No story writes itself. The factual material must be gathered first. The person who doesn't know how to observe and gather facts never will be able to write a good news account.

DEVELOPING AN IDEA

Charles-Gene McDaniel was a prize winning science writer in the Chicago bureau of the Associated Press when his editor suggested that he write an article on baldness. "If I could have worked on it steadily I could have done it in three days," says McDaniel, who, after a quarter century of professional journalism on the York *Gazette and Daily* and the AP, now is a professor of journalism at Roosevelt University. Able to work on it only off and on while handling other assignments, McDaniel wrote the following story three years later and then waited six months before it was distributed by the AP to receive wide usage nationwide.

By C. G. McDaniel
ASSOCIATED PRESS WRITER

"The only thing that will stop falling hair is the floor."

So advises John T. Capps III, who is bald and proud of it. If you're bald or getting there, just relax and enjoy it.

"Bald is beautiful," Capps proclaims, along with about 5,500 members of Bald Headed Men of America, which includes three women and many foreign members. They range in age from 11 to 95.

And medical authorities agree. So far anyway, it is not possible to do anything to stop hair from falling out. Once it has, the baldies have the option of buying something to cover it up or—in some cases—having a hair transplant.

Otherwise, the nostrums advertised in magazines and newspapers as baldness cures do not serve any purpose other than to enrich the seller, they say.

Capps, 38, of Dunn, N.C., founded Bald Headed Men of America in 1973. Why? "I felt like bald headed men needed a little moral support," he says.

"If you don't have it, flaunt it," is one of the organization's mottoes.

"One thing about baldness is it's neat," says Capps, who apparently has the agreement of some well known public figures, such as actors Yul Brynner of "The King and I" and Telly Savalas of television's "Kojak" fame.

The list also includes singer-composer Isaac Hayes, comedian Don Rickles and football players Y. A. Tittle, formerly of the New York Giants, and Otis Sistrunk of the Oakland Raiders.

Members of Capps' organization include former President Gerald Ford, Sen. Henry Jackson, D-Wash., and sportscaster Joe Garagiola.

They're in the tradition of Julius Caesar, Socrates and Shakespeare, among other great onionheads of history.

And it's getting to be chic among some high-fashion men to have a chrome dome to go with their disco duds.

Capps said in a telephone interview that for years Madison Avenue advertisers have projected an image of how they wanted people to look and people have followed their line.

But, "skin is in," says Capps, a marketing specialist, political campaign advertiser and publisher of "The Donkey Tale Newsletter."

He comforts those who lament their plate pates with, "The Lord is just, the Lord is fair. He gave some brains and others hair."

Capps' automobile license in North Carolina is BALD 1 and the address of his organization is P.O. Box BALD.

While Capps and his fellow club members are not ashamed of their eggheads, and in fact enjoy them, it would seem that millions of others have a problem coping with their depleted pelts.

The Department of Commerce reports that $48 million worth of "hair goods" were imported in 1976. And that was before markup—which may run as high as 400 percent. An additional $3 million worth—wholesale—is being produced annually in the United States.

The yellow pages of telephone directories have pages of advertisements aimed largely at men promoting hair transplants, hairpieces, fusion, weaving and other hair replacement techniques which remain mysterious in the context of the claims.

Cranium rugs, made from natural or synthetic hair, may cost from $15 to several hundred dollars, and that's just for starters. Then there's the upkeep and the need to replace them about every three years.

Millions of dollars more are spent on hair transplants and for dubious baldness remedies, such as special light treatments and salves.

Dr. Edward Krull, chairman of the dermatology department at Henry Ford Hospital in Detroit, says of the charlatanism, "Wherever we have problems that don't have solutions, there are always going to be people moving into that area."

There is no practical way, say he and other medical authorities, to grow new hair in bald spots other than hair transplants. Once it is gone, it is gone.

Dermatologists generally agree that the major causes of baldness are age, heredity and hormones.

Hair is dead tissue, Krull points out, and there is nothing that can be put on the scalp to make it grow once it has stopped. Routine dandruff won't cause the hair to fall out, Krull says, advising that the shampoo that works best and costs the least is the one to use to take care of dandruff.

But for many people, hair transplants are available. This procedure, which should always be done by a qualified physician, involves transplanting plugs of hair from the back of the neck to bald parts of the scalp.

Care must be exercised so that the hair is transplanted so that it will grow in the proper direction and will look natural once it has grown out in a few months.

An estimated one million persons have undergone this procedure, which is usually done in a doctor's office under local anesthetic.

The cost varies from about $5 to $35 a plug and 100 to 500 plugs may be required, depending upon the degree of baldness.

Another type of hair replacement has proved to be not only unsuccessful but to result in serious complications and permanent scarring. This is the implantation of synthetic fibers in the scalp.

A recent study published in the Journal of the American Medical Association reported that in 20 patients seen at one clinic in Cleveland, nearly all of the implanted fibers had fallen out by 10 weeks. The physicians also reported that the patients suffered from facial swelling, infection, scarring, permanent hair loss and other complications.

These implants cost $1,500 to $3,500 and, the physicians said, often were performed by technicians with physicians only briefly in attendance.

Other techniques, not without their problems, involve hair weaving, or braiding remaining hairs to keep the hairpiece from falling off, and suturing of the hairpiece.

But for those who don't want the bother or expense, Utah's bald Sen. Jake Garn offers this reassurance, "God has made very few perfect heads. The rest of them he covered with hair."

McDaniel's first step in researching the article was to consult his personal file on dermatology. He found only a few items of little help. So he phoned Frank W. Chappell Jr., science news editor for the American Medical Association. From him he received a package of material, the important items turning out to be an old clipping from *Time* magazine on John T. Capps III.

To obtain Capps' address McDaniel contacted the Chicago Public Library where a friendly helper consulted a reference book on organizations. What the reporter learned during a couple of long-distance calls is indicated in several parts of the story.

From the library reference book McDaniel also learned of the American Academy of Facial, Plastic and Reconstructive Surgery and of the American Association of Dermatology headquartered in New York. From the public relations counsel of the latter organization he learned of Dr. Edward Krull of Detroit, whose contributions to McDaniel's project are apparent in the article. The New York source also referred McDaniel to a Dr. Stough of Hot Springs, Ark., who had just returned from a conference on transplants held in Lucerne, Switzerland. What McDaniel wrote as a result of his telephone interview with that authority, however, was edited out of his story, which was reduced in size about one-third.

McDaniel learned of the Department of Commerce report from a Chicago *Sun-Times* news story. As the story indicates, he consulted the yellow pages in the telephone directory to discover that reputable surgeons do not advertise there. He considered it a safe guess that millions of dollars are spent on the items that are listed. Also he based such statements as "medical authorities agree," "dermatologists generally agree" and "an estimated one million persons have undergone" a kind of hair transplant, on the basis of his interviews with Drs. Krull and Stough and his perusal of the reports and articles obtained from Chappell. He mentioned some historical and contemporary baldies of whom he knew. It was not an assignment to cause him to lose hair himself, but it illustrates how even a simple situation feature story requires painstaking inquiries of several persons and references.

6
CHOOSING THE LEAD

A. The News Peg
B. News Values
   1. Timeliness
   2. Proximity
   3. Prominence
   4. Consequence
   5. Human Interest
C. The Five *Ws* and the *H*
   1. The Who
   2. The What
   3. The Why
   4. The Where
   5. The When
   6. The How
D. Rhetorical Devices
   1. The Summary Statement
   2. Conditional Clauses
   3. The Substantive Clause
   4. Phrases
   5. The Quotation Lead
   6. The Question Lead
   7. The Staccato Lead
   8. The Explosive Lead
   9. The Dialogue Lead
E. Purposeful Leads
   1. The Cartridge Lead
   2. The Punch Lead
   3. The Astonisher Lead
   4. The Contrast Lead
   5. The Descriptive Lead
   6. The Figurative Lead
   7. The Epigram Lead
   8. The Literary Allusion Lead
   9. The Parody Lead
F. More Than One Feature
   1. Separate Stories
   2. The Crowded Lead
   3. The "Shirttail" Method
   4. Boxes
   5. The 1–2–3–4 Lead

There is no one way to write any news story. Given the same schedule of facts, equally competent writers will compose accounts that read differently and an impartial judge might find it impossible to choose the best.

THE NEWS PEG

No matter how the lead is written that part of it that contains the kernel or more of news that is the story's excuse for being is called the *news peg*. It is a matter of editorial judgment what angle or phase of the total information available should receive emphasis. It is not enough that the first part of a story answer as many of the questions Who? What? When? Where? Why? and How? as the story demands be answered. These elements must be arranged to give proper emphasis to those most important.

The entire tone of a news story is determined by the feature that is emphasized in the lead, often in the first sentence or even the first clause or phrase of the first sentence. Giving proper emphasis to the different ingredients of a news story is a simple, standard *method of interpretation* which was practiced long before words were used to describe it. The reporter who develops facility in this regard is training himself or herself well for the future.

NEWS VALUES

Disregarding considerations of policy as a determinant of news judgment, newspapers and other media of communication, despite their differences, have similar criteria by which to determine the potential newsworthiness of the thousands or millions of occurrences from which they make their selection daily. Psychologically these criteria may be superficial or erroneous, but they have been tested by years of experience and, rightly or wrongly, are in vogue in all but a negligible number of newsrooms.

Differing in arrangement, nomenclature and emphasis, the main determinants of news values, textbook writers and editors in the main agree, are these:

1. Timeliness.
2. Proximity.
3. Prominence.
4. Consequence.
5. Human interest.

Timeliness

Familiar to every journalist of the past half century is the axiom that "nothing is so dead as yesterday's newspaper." Today, possibly, should be added "or the radio or television newscast of an hour ago." Certainly the increased speed by which news is transmitted has stimulated all who are engaged in the communications business to obtain and stress "latest developments first." The rule is always to bring a story up-to-date as much as possible before going to press or on the air and, if at all possible, to avoid using "yesterday" except in early morning reports.

This "last minute" effect often can be obtained by omitting the "when" from the lead, as in the following:

> A Circuit court judge has given the owners of a slum tenement 60 days to repair their building or face losing the property to the city.
>
> The action was taken Thursday by Judge Ernest L. Eberholtz in a case involving the five-story brick building at 2122 W. Ashberry street.

In reporting speeches, announcements and the like, this form can be used:

> Elimination of all overnight street parking is necessary to reduce Milltown's traffic accident rate in the opinion of Traffic Engineer L. Scott Updike.
>
> "Many pedestrians are being injured at night because parked cars obstruct the vision of drivers," Updike told the Milltown Executive club last night.

Proximity

Wars and revolutions, political, economic and other crises no matter where they occur have expanded the home-town newspaper reader's interests. As a consequence, within a generation the old newsroom rule "It takes a very important foreign story to crowd out a fairly important local story" no longer holds true.

Nevertheless, most events occurring within the territory of a newspaper's circulation are still of greater interest than similar events outside that area. A $50,000 fire in Keokuk will get a bigger play in a Keokuk paper than a $100,000 fire in Baton Rouge. People still want to know what is going on in their communities. As metropolitan newspapers have felt the necessity to print more national and international news, there has been an increase in the number of community and suburban papers devoted primarily to local coverage and to special pages and supplements in the big city press.

Not only do people like to read of happenings in their vicinity of which they have no previous knowledge, but also, perhaps especially, do they look for accounts of events with which they are familiar. They like to see their own names in print and to read what the paper has to say concerning situations about which they already know something. When a person expects that his/her name, or the name of someone whom s/he knows well, is to appear in the newspaper, s/he looks first of all for the item containing it. S/he is eager to read the newspaper's account of a meeting that s/he has attended, an accident that s/he has seen or an athletic contest at which s/he has been present. Logically, the contrary should be true: s/he should read first that which s/he already does not know. But s/he doesn't, and editors know that s/he doesn't. This being so, newspapers try to please as many readers as possible. If they feel that there is any chance of an appreciable number of readers being interested in an item, no matter how trivial it may be, they print the item, space permitting.

This statement contradicts the supercilious attitude that it is only rural folk who delight in gossip. Just the opposite is true. We do not read in a New York paper that Mary Taylor is spending the weekend with relatives in New Haven merely because not enough people are acquainted with Miss Taylor. Those who do know her are interested in the item of her visit; if the name happens to be Elizabeth Taylor there is a strong possibility that the item will be published. There is no gossip about celebrities too trivial for publication in a metropolitan newspaper. No city reader has any right to laugh at readers of country weeklies who are interested to learn that Henry Jones has painted his barn red.

Writers are enjoined to play up the local as well as the latest angles of stories. For instance,

> Robert A. Brown Post No. 89 of the American Legion will be represented at the tenth annual convention of the state American Legion Monday, Tuesday and Wednesday at Neillsville, by a delegation of approximately 50 members, including 35 members of the fife and drum corps.

This is better than

> The tenth annual convention of American Legion posts of the state will be held Monday, Tuesday and Wednesday at Neillsville. The local post. . . .

Newspapers rewrite or supplement the stories of press associations, correspondents and press releases, which carry general leads, such as the second, in order to meet the interests of local readers. They localize national stories, as illustrated by the following:

> The nationwide airline strike is having little or no effect on air mail service in Lincoln, Postmaster Kenneth Lewis said.
>
> He said that sufficient flights are available on nonstruck lines to ship air mail cargo from Lincoln.
>
> Problems, however, are occurring at the national transportation centers such as Denver, Kansas City and Omaha. National air mail deliveries are being delayed as much as 24 hours.
>
> Mail has been moving on airlines not affected by the strike and most of them have put on extra flights. But, William J. Hartigan, assistant U.S. postmaster general, reported that the emergency scheduling cannot be maintained and some of the extra flights will be canceled.
>
> Military mail for servicemen in Southeast Asia and in Europe has been proceeding on an almost normal basis because all airlines have maintained their military contracts. [Lincoln (Neb.) *Journal*]

Prominence

All men and women may be created equal, but some grow up to be more newsworthy than others. This may be because of the positions they hold, because of their entertainment value or because they have behaved so unusually in the past that they have created interest in whatever else they may do.

What is true of persons also is true of places and organizations. All other elements being equal, a newsworthy event, such as a fire or crime, is more important if it occurs in one's home town. The reader, however, does not have the same interest in all other places. Such large population centers as New York, Chicago and Los Angeles rate ahead of most small cities and towns. Among the latter, however, there are some considered more newsworthy than others, often because they have become associated with a particular kind of news. Among such places are Reno, Las Vegas, Hollywood, Tiajuana and Monte Carlo.

To the home-town editor, news of all potential subscribers is important, and he tries to use the names of as many of them as space permits. Newspapers often print long lists of delegates to conventions, guests at weddings and social events, committee memberships and so forth. Reporters are instructed to obtain as many names as possible and are cautioned to get complete names and their correct spellings. Last names seldom are enough. News media should use a person's name as its owner uses it in business and society generally. Sometimes a telephone book or city directory may give a full name whereas the person uses one or more initials or even a nickname. The only safe way is to ask the person. The reporter must never take chances with the spellings of names. Is it Kern or Curran, Smith or Smythe, Reilly or Riley, Meyers or Myers, Pew or Pugh, Cole or Kole? The rule is this: take nothing for granted, don't guess.

If a widely known person figures in a news event, that fact may become the feature of a story, as in the following:

> State Sen. Lyle G. Fitzhugh and six other persons were injured last night when a row of temporary bleacher seats collapsed during the Milltown-Rushville basketball game.

Consequence

Not only the prominence of persons, places and things mentioned in news stories originating outside the community which a newspaper serves causes them to be published in place of local news; an equal or perhaps more vital factor is the importance of the item.

To illustrate: News from Washington, D.C. is front-page copy in Chicago and San Francisco not primarily because it contains the widely known names of a senator or cabinet member, but because the issues with which those figures are connected vitally concern the best interests of readers all over the country. Every American citizen is directly affected by an important piece of legislation before Congress. National or state political news often is more important than local political news. In a nuclear age one-world-mindedness is a necessity.

Stories concerning changes in the weather or fashions, and stories of epidemics and pestilences, are important because the immediate community may be affected indirectly if not directly. A coal strike in a distant state may lead to a local shortage of fuel; a new model of automobile will be on sale locally within a short space of time; an important scientific discovery may change a reader's way of thinking on a metaphysical problem. The interest in such stories is very personal and very real.

In addition to localizing nationally important stories, newspapers emphasize the consequence of news by seeking the *tomorrow* angle on strictly local stories. This device serves to make the item seem timely and to point up significance. Emphasis is on results rather than causes, on explaining what the present continuing or probable future effect will be.

> The cost of riding city busses in Lincoln is about to increase. The Nebraska State Railway Commission reported Thursday it has approved the application of Lincoln City Lines for a 5-cent-per-fare rate hike, effective Aug. 1.

The change will boost the adult fare from 15 to 20 cents, and the fare for children under 12 from 10 to 15 cents. [Lincoln (Neb.) *Journal*]

Students in West Mason Elementary District 67 could be in their classrooms Monday morning for the first time this fall if their striking teachers approve a tentative contract agreement to end their 10-day walkout.

Human Interest

Interest in human beings as such, and in events because they concern men and women in situations that might confront anyone else, is called *human interest*.

It is human interest, interest in the lives and welfare of others and in the well-being and progress of mankind as a whole, that causes us to read, with interest and sympathy, of loss of life and property in communities far removed from our own. When an earthquake destroys homes and takes lives in southern Italy or in Japan, there is little likelihood of our being affected directly, except perhaps as we are asked to contribute to the Red Cross relief fund; but we are interested in learning of such "acts of God" because other human beings like ourselves are involved.

It is this personal appeal which editors mean when they say that an item of news has reader interest even though it may not possess any of the other elements of news value: timeliness, proximity, prominence and consequence.

Strictly speaking, all reader interest is human interest. Because readers differ in their occupational, recreational and other interests, some news that has a *personal appeal* to one reader fails to interest another. Any reader, however, no matter how cynical or self-centered, has some *sympathetic interest* in the lives and well-being of other humans. This interest includes both extremes of the pathetic and humorous in everyday life, whatever causes a reader to feel sorry for or to laugh with or at some other fellow being.

Interest in accounts of disasters involving loss of life and property is sympathetic. There may be other elements of interest in stories of fires, wrecks, accidents and other catastrophes; but when individuals are mentioned in unfortunate situations, there also is sympathetic interest. Sickness, near death, suffering of any kind, loss of wealth and the like create attitudes of sympathy in readers.

At the other extreme, ludicrous accounts of typical men and women touch a sympathetic vein also. Americans like to laugh and are amused at almost anything in any way incongruous. In most humorous stories there is someone who suffers some inconvenience, but this does not detract from the humor of the situation any more than does knowledge of possible injury to a person who has slipped on a banana peel and fallen suffice to suppress the smile which comes to one's lips.

Such incidents also involve *unusualness*. People everywhere, and perhaps Americans in particular, love thrills and anything with an "-est" to it. Unusual people, quaint and picturesque places, exciting adventures, all appeal to us.

And when we cannot meet those individuals, see those places, experience romance ourselves, we like to read of them all the more. We take vicarious pleasure from stories of adventure and romance.

Once news of new theories and discoveries in the field of science was considered unusual. In the present nuclear age the element of surprise has disappeared, but the interest in *progress* continues. Likewise, unfortunately, the element of reader interest which probably outweighs all others—that in *combat*—also continues. Critical examination of the lists of "biggest" news stories of any year indicates that there is no other single element of reader interest that is present more frequently. Americans, it must be, like a good fight and consider life as a whole to be a struggle. The element of combat is found most prominently in stories of athletic contests, crime, politics, adventure, disaster and heroism. Man against man or man against nature always draws a big crowd, which usually roots for the underdog.

If there is *suspense* in the story of combat, or any other story for that matter, the interest is heightened. Frequently, the attention of an entire nation is centered upon a single news event, as in the case of a mine disaster when rescuers work frantically to save human lives. Illness, especially of a prominent person or from an unusual cause, may be reported so as to emphasize the element of suspense. There is suspense in political campaigns, in law cases and in athletic contests.

The so-called human interest in any kind of story is enhanced if the principals include a child, an animal or a woman, preferably a good-looking young woman. Hieroglyphic warnings against the increasing immorality of youth have been discovered by excavators, proving that adolescence always has been a problem. Furthermore, since before the days of chivalry, the female sex has caused more worry than the male.

Times haven't changed much and "flaming youth" still is having its inning, with debutantes, coeds, waitresses and heiresses flaming perhaps a bit more brightly than ever before. The growth of newspapers and of newspaper photography has helped satisfy the desire for accurate information of just what our allegedly wayward sons and daughters are doing and how they look.

So-called middle age is, from the news standpoint, the drabbest of man's several stages. Precocious infancy and childhood and virile old age vie with hilarious adolescence in front-page importance: the little girl who calls on the mayor to let her doggie out of the pound, and the grandma who takes her first ride in an airplane. The thirties, forties and fifties are the trying years if one is a publicity seeker. At those ages s/he really has to do something to get by the copy desk; or else s/he must employ an adroit public relations counsel.

Interest in animals is similar to interest in children and old age. Sometimes the reader is sympathetic, as in the case of a dog who refuses to leave his master's grave; sometimes he is resentful, as when a tame animal turns on someone and hurts him.

Stories of unusual intelligence in animals always are good copy, especially if the well-being of humans thereby is fostered. Also, anecdotes of admirable qualities, as faithfulness, have an appeal. Any freak from the animal kingdom attracts attention, as Barnum knew, and there is plentiful interest remaining in the disappearing sport of hunting, especially of big game.

The beginning reporter must learn to recognize the human interest possibilities of stories and to brighten up a story by giving it the twist that turns a drab yarn into a bright one without, of course, exaggeration or distortion.

The following are sprightly leads to factual news stories made so by adroitness on the part of their authors in picking and playing up phases lending themselves to human interest treatment or emphasis:

> Toronto—(UP)—John Brock, 32, began serving a two-year penitentiary term Tuesday because he hates women.
>
> He was convicted of assault for breaking into the ladies room of a downtown tavern and mussing up a young housewife who was fixing her makeup. The housewife told police that Brock crashed in and shouted, "I hate women and you're one." [Duluth *News-Tribune*]

> Roars and snarls of protest raged around the Denver zoo Friday, but the noise was emanating from the city and county building, not City park.
>
> The hubbub concerns the plans of Mayor Nicholson's administration to sign over management of the zoo to the Denver Zoological Foundation, a group of citizens long interested in the zoo's problems who believe they can operate it better than the city. [Denver *Post*]

These examples illustrate that it is possible to adhere to the rules regarding the news story form and at the same time avoid "wooden" leads.

THE FIVE *W*'s AND THE *H*

The *who* or the *what* usually is the feature of a short one-incident (simple) news story. It often is difficult to determine which is more important, as most news concerns people and what they do. For instance, in the following short item many readers will be interested primarily in the young man mentioned as a friend or acquaintance. Others, however, will be interested chiefly because of the extent to which the local schools will be affected by the news. When the news is about a definite person the name usually comes first, as

> Peter L. Clay has resigned his position as instructor in history in the local high school to accept a teaching fellowship in history at Booster college.

The *Who*

The *who* is unmistakably the feature in the following story:

> George L. Rose has been elected ninth vice-president of the American Council of Civil Service Employees.

Often the interest in the *who* comes from the kind of person involved judged by his occupation, religion, sex, age and so on, or by the circumstances in which he figures in the particular story, or from the number of persons involved, as

> A private watchman shot a safecracker Tuesday when he and his accomplice resisted arrest.

The indefinite *who* is used increasingly as cities become larger and persons in the news are known to fewer other persons in proportion to the population as a whole.

The *What*

The *what* is more important than the *who* when the circumstance would be significant no matter who the persons involved, as

> One man was shot and another was beaten today in an outbreak of violence as strikers tried to prevent operation of the Johnson-Smith corporation.

> A youth who went beserk with a butcher knife was captured and held by police tonight as a suspect in two recent murders in Milltown.

Press associations usually write their stories in this way, as names may not mean anything outside the immediate vicinity in which the event occurred. The writer of a news story always must decide which is more important, the name or the event.

Often a *what* lead begins with the *who* as an easier rhetorical method or to emphasize authority. Note in the following example that, although the *who* comes first, the *what* is more important:

> President Joseph E. Jennings today announced that the county board is able to pay off current expenditures as they arise, despite the fact that it has retired $568,910 in outstanding debts since he assumed office three years ago.

In the following example the *what* is unmistakably predominant:

> Vandalism against cars was reported in Southside Milltown Friday.
>
> Vice squad detectives began an investigation after auto windshields and windows were reported smashed on Haberkorn road, Lakeside drive, Alcott drive and Norton road, SW.

In action stories readers usually are interested in results rather than causes, as

> Two infant brothers perished and three firemen attempting a dramatic rescue of them were injured Monday in a blaze at 3142 N. Patzin St.

The *Why*

Sometimes, however, it is the cause rather than the result that is the feature of the story, as

> Trying to pass another car while travelling at high speed brought serious injury to two men last night when their automobile overturned twice on Washington boulevard at Potter avenue.

Taxpayers want to know the reasons for the actions of public officials.

> In order to save money and to allow men to spend New Year's Day with their families, the Sanitation Department, in its early planning, has decided to cut back sharply on its force for tonight's midnight-to-8 A.M. shift, leaving only a thin force of 188 men on duty.

The *Where*

In advance stories of meetings, speeches, athletic events, etc., the *where* must be very definite. Room numbers, street addresses, etc., should be given. In local stories, it is not always necessary to mention the name of the city or a street address. The immediate community is understood, as

> Eight testing lanes on which motorists must submit their automobiles and trucks to examination for safe driving qualifications will be opened tomorrow.

The *where* may be the featurized element:

> In her 400-year-old ancestral home, the only daughter of an English general recently became the wife of a gypsy, who worked as a handyman on the estate.

In each of the following examples, the *where* definitely was the feature, although, in the second example, the *when* rhetorically came first:

> A tract of approximately 30 acres at Forest boulevard and Kerwood avenue, assessed at $90,000, has been sold by Herschel Steel, represented by the Wray-Graw Co., to John L. Finch.

> Beginning today, parking will be permitted in the Underground Lakeside Exhibition hall of Citizen's hall by patrons of events at the hall and the Civic auditorium, at a rate of 40 cents per car.

When a place is more familiar than the names of those associated with it, the following style may be used:

> The operator of a candy store at 717 S. Ninth street pleaded guilty Monday in U.S. District court of the purchase, possession, and sale of 5 ounces of heroin.
>
> He is Andrew Solberg, 41, of 141 Oak street, who was arrested by narcotics agents last month.

The *When*

About the same may be said of the *when* as of the *where*. It ordinarily is included inconspicuously in the lead, as

> Fur thieves hit two Milltown stores early Wednesday and got away with a total loot estimated at $230,000.

Frequently the *when* may be left until the second paragraph, as

> Commissioner William Wheat has appointed a seven-man hospital committee to look into the situation surrounding construction of a county-wide hospital for pay patients.
>
> The members were appointed at a Monday afternoon session with the commissioner.

Such omission of the *when* from the first paragraph is common practice with press associations, especially when preparing news of one day for use in the morning newspapers the following day.

The *when* may be a matter of "continuous action," as

> A couple of perky oldsters who defied the wilderness for ten days on a can of beans, a bit of jelly and a small packet of powdered milk are recovering from exhaustion and hunger in Milltown hospital.

The *when* may be the featured element, as

> Midnight tonight is the deadline for 1982 automobile license plates and vehicles in use after 12:01 A.M. tomorrow must carry 1983 plates, the Bureau of Motor Vehicles reminded automobile owners yesterday.

A type of *when* lead is the "duration of time" lead, as

> After deliberating five hours last night, a Superior court jury returned a verdict of guilty in the steel purchase fraud trial of four Gruner county highway employees.

A similar type of *when* lead is the "since when" lead, as

> After being gone for two weeks, Duke, a wistful looking Collie-Spitz hybrid, decided he liked his old home better and trudged 40 miles to return to the residence of his former owner, Humane Officer Thompson Meredith.

The *How*

By definition the *how* means details to explain how something occurred. Consequently, when the feature unmistakably consists in such details, care must be exercised to avoid wordiness:

Mrs. Frederick Bascom managed to drive off an Alberto Expressway ramp yesterday in Evergreen, tear a tree completely out of the ground, knock a corner off a garage two blocks away, bounce off a car and come out of the whole incident without a scratch and with only one traffic charge.

Sports stories frequently are given *how* leads:

Fritz Tech used seven pass interceptions to throttle the Ironton Academy attack and converted one of them into a a one-yard scoring plunge by Peter Baldwin for the winning touchdown Saturday in a 28–27 win over the Eagles.

RHETORICAL DEVICES

Skillful use of the ordinary rhetorical devices enables the news writer to play up a feature.

The Summary Statement

Most news leads are mere summary statements consisting of simple sentences or of compound or complex sentences with the principal clauses first. Many examples given so far in this chapter illustrate how the feature of a story can be emphasized by means of such simple straightforward writing. Observe, in addition, the following example:

A 23-year-old woman was fatally injured early Friday morning after a car in which she was riding went out of control and slammed into a mailbox and a light post. Rene Fudala of 524 E. 24th died at Milltown Hospital at 4:20 a.m.

Conditional Clauses

Often, however, it is difficult to get the feature into a main clause. This is so when the feature is present in addition to the main news idea which the writer must include in his lead. Features to be found in accompanying circumstances, conditions, coincidences in the *when* and *where* and so on often can best be played up by beginning the lead with a complex or complex-compound sentence with the conditional clause first.

In the following examples note how the conditional clause contains the feature, whereas the main idea, which is the excuse for the story, still is in the main clause.

Because Paul Gregg, 17-year-old high school boy, was caught as a stowaway and locked in the infirmary of the liner *Justice,* he started to burn the ship to seek his freedom, he admitted to steamship authorities here today.

This emphasizes the feature much more than would inversion of the clause order, as

Paul Gregg, 17-year-old high school boy, today admitted to steamship authorities here that he set fire to the liner *Justice* to obtain his freedom after being caught as a stowaway and locked in the infirmary.

The Substantive Clause

The substantive clause usually takes the form of a "that" clause which has been much overworked by news writers because it is easy to write and is consequently taboo in many offices. Occasionally the substantive is forceful, as

That the present legislative appropriation must be doubled if minimum essentials are to be provided relief clients, is the warning contained in the monthly report made today by Harold G. Todd, local relief administrator, to the State Department of Public Welfare.

Return to the pioneer days, when youths in their early teens could assemble a muzzle-loader and pick off game 50 yards away, was sought in a bill before the state legislature today.

Phrases

Infinite, participial, prepositional and gerund phrases and absolute constructions also may be used to emphasize a feature when it happens to be one of the minor *w*'s or *h*. In such constructions, the main clause contains the *who* and *what,* one of which is modified by the phrase.

Inverted sentence structure may be used to identify (tie-back) the news with previous news (see Chapter 9) and to identify persons, places and events. Use of phrases and of the absolute construction for different purposes is illustrated in the following examples:

WHEN

After a three-hour search by police and relatives, James Fillmore, 30, his wife and four children who had been missing since Saturday, were found early yesterday in a friend's home.

WHERE

Beside the Ring river, which he made famous in song and verse, the body of Feodor Vladik today was buried with only a handful of close relatives present.

WHY

Delayed somewhat by recent hurricane alerts, work to complete Harris Civil Defense Headquarters in the basement of the Carnegie Free Library was pressed anew last week.

HOW

Citing a permissive 1867 ordinance which never has been repealed, Henry Bucher today won the right to raise geese in his backyard at 10 Cherry Lane.

TIE-BACK

Disregarding three previous failures, Grace Slawson, 21-year-old grocery clerk, tomorrow will attempt to set a new record for swimming across Lake Malthusia.

Care must be taken to avoid what Roy Copperud calls "linguistic smog," illustrated by the following example by Howard C. Heyn in an article, "A Newsman's View: Writing With Precision," in the 1970 *Montana Journalism Review:*

Two firemen fought their way into the smoke-filled building where a boy was trapped on the second floor and died of asphyxiation.

To make it clear who died the phrasing had to be converted to a direct approach in this manner:

Two firemen were asphyxiated while trying to rescue a boy trapped on the second floor of the smoke-filled building.

The Quotation Lead

In reporting speeches, public statements and the like, it is almost always better to epitomize the feature in the reporter's own words rather than by means of a direct quotation.

Weak

"A sharp decrease in maternal mortality, medical progress, and greater economic prosperity have enabled welfare agencies to solve most of their problems except that of the emotionally disturbed child," Horace V. Updike, Council of Social Welfare director, said yesterday.

Strong

The emotionally disturbed child is the "No. 1 problem" facing welfare agencies today, Horace V. Updike, Council of Social Welfare director, said yesterday.

In news stories which are not accounts of speeches or documents, however, it sometimes is effective to begin with a direct quotation, as in the following examples:

"In this country, as in yours, we take a rather dim view of serious infractions of this kind," Provincial Judge P. J. Bolsby said yesterday to a 22-year-old New York City man charged with assaulting a police officer while trying to gate-crash Saturday's rock festival at the Canadian National Exhibition.

[Toronto *Globe-Mail*]

"Don't be an old grouch on the road!"

This advice for those who wish to stay alive although they drive in Labor Day weekend traffic comes from Francis Carroway, 18, judged Milltown's best teenage driver.

The following was the lead to a story judged best by 37 journalism professors and 32 city editors to whom nine writeups of an interview with an Ohio State University campus editor were submitted:

> "To get ahead in journalism, you have to do a little more than people expect of you."
>
> This is the advice Lantern Spring Quarter editor-in-chief Ron Shafer gave freshmen journalism students today.
>
> "You may not think that anybody notices that extra work, but they do," Shafer continued.

The partial or broken quote often can be used to add authenticity without making the lead unwieldy, as

> The city manager of Cresswood refused today to "commit myself" on revoking the liquor license of a saloon raided five times by sheriff's police in a year.

The Question Lead

Ordinarily the reporter should answer, not ask, questions in his news stories. To do otherwise merely delays telling the news, as in the case of a lead beginning. "What causes delinquency?" followed by a summary of a new idea advanced by some authority. It would be much better to start: "Failure of teenagers to obtain jobs causes them to become delinquent in the opinion of . . ."

When the story concerns a problem of public interest or a matter likely to provoke debate among readers, however, it may be possible to obtain interest by means of a question lead, as

> Baltimore, Aug. 7 (AP)—Could one man in one night at one bar on The Block, Baltimore's strip-tease row, run up a bill of $1,900? Or $1,349.50? Or $1,722.11 at three clubs?
>
> The Baltimore Liquor Board investigating complaints from credit card holders about the bills they found on their vouchers, had its doubts. . . .

> **By Norman Mlachak**
> LABOR WRITER
>
> Can a labor union shut down an industrial plant even though the union isn't the officially elected bargaining agent for the workers?
>
> Teamsters Local 507 is proving that it can.
>
> It struck the American Screw Products Co. in Bedford Heights five weeks ago today.
>
> Is it legal? . . .
>
> [Cleveland *Press*]

The Staccato Lead

When the time element—either fast action or the intervals separating a series of related events—is to be emphasized, the staccato lead occasionally suffices. It consists in a series of phrases, punctuated either by periods or dashes and usually is a form of descriptive lead. The style suggests the tone of the story, its feeling.

By Timothy McNulty
CHICAGO TRIBUNE PRESS SERVICE

Ft. Worth—An oil multimillionaire . . . his beautiful but straying wife . . . her murdered lover . . . a lawyer named "Racehorse" . . . the oilman's faithful mistress . . . the mysterious "man in black" in the woman's wig . . . a young girl killed . . . a murder-for-hire revenge plot secretly videotaped . . . the "carnival" trial . . . a secluded and bloodstained mansion . . .

It all may sound like dust-jacket blurbs from a racy new novel, but these are the elements of the strange double case against T. Cullen Davis, which is still unfolding on a backdrop of Texas wealth and society.

Almost thirty years ago—back in 1953—in a different era, in a different life, after 40 years of happiness in her simple home, the light went out for Mrs. Hattie Downs, of Gregoryville and she became blind—stone blind.

Years passed—thirty of them—long and torturous—and suddenly her prayers were answered, and Mrs. Hattie Downs could see.

The Explosive Lead

Similar to the staccato lead but consisting of grammatically complete sentences, the explosive lead is especially useful for feature articles. It can, however, be used for straight news stories as well.

A fellowship wooded retreat, freeing the human mind, communal living, Renaissance songs, sensitivity training—they're all there in the next six weeks of the Near North Unitarian Universalist Fellowship. [Chicago *Daily News*]

Cloudy, lazy afternoon on Thanksgiving Day, no school, nothing to do.

On the North Side, two boys jump on the back of a bus to hitch a ride. One of the trolleys snaps and hits one of the lads on the head and he dies of a fractured skull.

On the South Side, four boys are playing cards in an apartment. One of them is horsing around with a gun he bought on the street earlier in the week. The gun goes off and a 16-year-old youth dies. . . .

The Dialogue Lead

It is difficult, if not impossible, to begin a serious news story of an important event with dialogue. Minor court stories, with strong human interest, and occasionally stories of a more significant nature, however, can be handled effectively by means of a dialogue lead, as

"Wouldn't it be terrible," asked Hazel Muller, 22, of 1864 E. Payne avenue, "if I got locked in that record vault and couldn't get out?"

"Ho, ho," replied Thomas Keyes, production manager of the Majestic Foundry company at 146 E. Belmont avenue, where Miss Muller is a secretary, "It couldn't happen."

But it DID happen Tuesday and it WAS terrible.

Here's a play-by-play account. . . .

PURPOSEFUL LEADS

The Cartridge Lead

When war is declared or ends, when a president or some other widely known figure dies and on similarly important occasions, it is customary to tell the gist of the news in the fewest possible words, as

> Galvania has declared war on Powry.
> Mayor Charles A. Brinshaw is dead.
> The Maroons are conference champions.

Stories written entirely in such staccato fashion have a breathtaking quality. Consequently, the style should not be used too extensively but reserved for occasions of particular importance.

The Punch Lead

What has traditionally been called a *punch lead* performs a function similar to that of the cartridge lead, but it is not so short, abrupt or definite. Since World War II, it has grown in popularity and on some newspapers is used for almost any kind of story, not just stories of presumed extra newsworthiness. It has been called the "blind" lead because of its emphasis on situations rather than specific persons and details. It is a form of writing easily open to misuse (1) in stories whose importance is thereby exaggerated and (2) by being excessively indefinite or "empty." An example of the latter is "Politics has a different look in Congress today," a sentence which tells exactly nothing. Paragraphs two and three of a well-written story with a punch lead should supply definite details:

> A policeman has been suspended on charges that he deserted his school-crossing post.
>
> Placed on indefinite suspension by Police Chief Patrick C. O'Brien Tuesday was Albert Murchison, 27, of 885 W. Strong avenue, attached to the Vickers station, 1412 E. Vickers avenue.
>
> Lieut. Ira Walters of the Vickers district said a routine check at noon Monday disclosed that Murchison was absent from his post at Bristol and Sacramento roads.

The Astonisher Lead

Beginning writers are discouraged in the use of superlatives and expressions of opinion. When deserved, however, superlatives should be used, as

> For the first time since the December 1974 fire, Gillespie now has a complete home decorating shoppe, which offers a custom-made drapery service.
>
> [Gillespie (Ill.) *Area News*]

The Contrast Lead

Sometimes the feature of a news story consists in the contrast between the immediate and a former situation or between the event at hand and another of which, for any of a number of reasons, it is a reminder. Note that the news peg is retained in the following lead, though not so definitely, the emphasis being upon the unusual situation:

> Behind the same walnut desk which he used to dust 25 years ago as an office boy, Virgil F. Stimson yesterday received congratulations upon becoming president of Andalia Trucking company.

The Descriptive Lead

The feature or key to the spirit of a story may be in its setting, in the physical appearance of some person or object involved or in an unusual phase of the action with which it deals. In such cases, a graphic or descriptive lead may be the most effective to give the tone or feeling necessary to proper understanding and appreciation. Before he can describe, the reporter must know how to observe; the best descriptive leads are written by eyewitnesses. To be avoided are superfluous and inapplicable adjectives, extraneous matter serving no purpose except, perhaps, to prove the writer's possession of an extensive vocabulary of trite and hackneyed expressions—clichés. The following leads to important stories avoid these hazards:

> With lists in their hands, shopping bags on their arms and fire in their eyes, hundreds of thousands of Christmas shoppers are swarming through the glittering stores as if the recession, unemployment, fear of the streets and the vogue to denigrate middle-class values all belonged to the Ghosts of Christmas Past.

> For more than a minute today the sun hung over central Minnesota like a twinkling, slate-blue Christmas ornament as the moon moved between it and the earth. In the awesome half-light that covered the area, hundreds of scientists and thousands of other persons had a perfect view of the total solar eclipse.
>
> [New York *Times*]

The Figurative Lead

Triteness must be avoided in the use of metaphors, similes and other figures of speech, either in the lead or in any other part of a news story. Many expressions have become so common through usage that they are hardly noticed by casual readers as figurative. Among them are "ax to grind," "shoe on the wrong foot," "hitch his wagon to a star," "put all its eggs in one basket" and many more. If the writer uses such expressions naturally, without strain, possibly even without awareness that they are figurative, the result is more likely to be good than if he deliberately tries for effect:

> Knocked on the ropes by a wet and windy one-two punch, Milltown's July heat wave refused to call it quits Friday.

The following lead was a winner in a Best Lead contest at the San Angelo (Tex.) *Standard-Times*. It described a potential flood.

> Cold, dirty water lapped and licked at Pecos Tuesday evening like a patient cat toying with a cornered mouse.

The Epigram Lead

The tone or moral of a story also may be emphasized by means of an epigram lead, in the writing of which bromides and platitudes must be avoided. The epigram is a concise and pointed expression, usually witty. The epigram lead may be either a familiar saying or a moral applicable to the story at hand, as

> Silence can be golden in more ways than one, Shortstop Tommy Jacobs of the Maroons has discovered.
>
> After striking out three times against Bristol Aug. 12, Jacobs complained to his manager, Bucky Johnson, that he had been the victim of several debatable strike decisions.
>
> "The trouble with you," said Johnson, "is that you spend so much time turning around to squawk that you're not ready to hit the ball. Just for the fun of it, forget to turn around and look at the umpire for any reason and concentrate on hitting the ball."
>
> Tommy followed the advice and compiled the following record . . . .

The Literary Allusion Lead

The writer with a normal background of knowledge in literature or history will have frequent chances to use it to advantage. Care must be taken to limit references to fictional or historical characters and to literary passages familiar to the average reader. The following examples illustrate how it is possible effectively to make use of one's general knowledge to improve his writing:

By Ralph Blumenthal

A desire named streetcars is growing—a desire for the return of one of America's oldest forms of urban public transportation. [New York *Times*]

By Mary Jane Gustafson

Brooklyn Center's winter skating program has grown like Topsy!

From seven warming houses in 1970, the program included 16 warming houses this winter plus additional hockey rinks at seven of the parks or 23 skating rinks to maintain. [North Hennepin (Minn.) *Post*]

The Parody Lead

Popular song hits, bons mots by famous persons, titles of best-selling books or of motion pictures or new-coined phrases or expressions of any sort may be used while still fresh, usually in parodied form, to brighten an occasional news story lead. Well-established expressions may be used similarly. The following leads avoid the ever-lurking danger of triteness in such writing:

Sheridan, Wyo., Jan. 29.—Maybe it's a case of absence of water makes the heart grow fonder, but citizens of this northern Wyoming city have risen nobly to the call to help the flood-stricken dwellers along the Ohio River Valley.

Actor Charles Keller says you can't take it with you because the government takes it first.

The 77-year-old stage-and-screen star Tuesday urged outright repeal of the federal income tax, which he called an "economic cancer."

MORE THAN ONE FEATURE

So far, only stories containing simple features relatively easy to pick even though related to important events have been considered. Not infrequently, an item of news presents so many angles that the rhetorical devices described in this chapter are inadequate. There are several ways out of this difficulty.

Separate Stories

The easiest way is to write more than one story. When there are sidelights or interviews of opinion or features connected with a news event, the assignment usually is split between two or more reporters. Some repetition usually occurs but is not discouraged; in fact, in some cases it is encouraged, and a paper may run several stories of the same event written by different reporters.

The Crowded Lead

When the various elements of interest are of nearly equal value, a number of facts may be crowded into a single lead, as

By Diane Amann

Stagnant air, overcrowded halls, inadequate toilet facilities, and jacked-up food prices at the International Amphitheatre, 43d and Halsted streets, infuriated many people taking their nursing board examinations there Tuesday and Wednesday.

[Chicago *Daily Tribune*]

Standing committees were appointed, the street-lighting contract was continued for one year and a proposed new ordinance regulating business licenses was referred to the Finance committee last night at the weekly meeting of the Board of Aldermen.

Succeeding paragraphs naturally would take up each item mentioned in the lead, providing full details.

The "Shirttail" Method

To avoid crowded and vague leads, one item deemed the most important can be played up. Paragraphs containing mention of other items then can be introduced by such expressions as "In other actions the City Council . . ." or "In a similar accident . . ." and so forth.

Ald. Val G. Grauer (17th Ward) has been elected chairman of the powerful Finance committee of the Board of Aldermen.

Other standing committee chairmen, named at last night's board meeting, follow . . . .

The board also voted to continue for one year its contract with the Republic Light company for street lighting . . . .

In other actions, the board referred a proposed new ordinance regulating business licenses to the Finance committee and rejected a request by Front street property owners that all-night parking be permitted in the 400 block.

Boxes

Often, statements, tabulations, data, side features and the like can best be presented by means of a box set either ahead of the lead, within the main article or in an adjoining column. There are many other uses for the box, most of them connected with makeup. Material most frequently boxed includes the following:

1. Lists of dead and injured in accidents.
2. Telling statements from speeches, reports, testimony and so on.
3. Statistics.
4. Summaries of facts included in the story itself or in two or more related stories.
5. Brief histories of events connected with the story.
6. Local angles on press association stories.

After requiring 12 employees and six customers to lie face downward on the floor, three armed and masked bandits shortly after 8 A.M. today removed approximately $75,000 in currency from the cashiers' cages of the First National bank, 109 N. Main street, and escaped in a waiting automobile driven by a fourth man.

FOURTH IN TWO YEARS

Today's burglary of the First National bank was the fourth in two years in Milltown. Others, together with losses and outcomes, were:

March 3, 1980—First National bank, $17,451 cash, recovered upon arrest of Abe Mason, now serving a ten-year term in the state penitentiary.

Sept. 21, 1980—Milltown State bank, $41,150 cash and bonds, recovered when sheriff's posse killed John "Gunman" Hays three miles south of town the same day.

July 15, 1981—Citizen's National bank, $50,000 removed by blowing open safe at night. Still unsolved.

The men were described by Wilmer Asher, head cashier, as all apparently under 25 years of age. They wore blue overalls and caps which were drawn down just above the eyes.

The 1–2–3–4 Lead

After a short summary statement of the situation constituting the news, the different features can be emphasized by tabulation and numbering, as

The wishes of Mayor Louis T. Tupper were ignored by the new Board of Aldermen in several votes at its organizing meeting last night. Most importantly the board did the following:

1. Elected Ald. Val G. Grauer (17th ward), political rival of the mayor's, chairman of the powerful Finance committee.
2. Referred a proposed new ordinance regulating business licenses to Ald. Grauer's committee. The mayor has called the new ordinance unnecessary.
3. Continued for one year the contract with the Republic Light Company for street lighting. The mayor opposed the renewal in campaign speeches last month.
4. Rejected a property owners' petition for all-night parking in the 400 block on Front street which the mayor had approved.

The preceding lead, of course, is interpretative. It plays up the significance of the board's actions rather than merely reporting them deadpan. It does not editorialize for or against the board's insurgency, and the treatment probably could be adversely criticized only if it could be shown that every board action was taken despite rather than because of any attitude toward Mayor Tupper.

The article as written does not say the four actions indicated hostility by the board toward the mayor. Nevertheless, there is no mistaking the fact that such an impression is given. If, at a subsequent meeting, the board were to vote in favor of a number of measures sponsored by the mayor, the facts as they existed after the earlier meeting would have to be reexamined. If, however, the facts as stated in the first story are accurate, the reporter could not be accused of coloring his account. Certainly readers were given background information whereby it would be possible for them to draw conclusions, whereas a strictly factual account of the actions of the Board of Aldermen, without attempt at any perspective, might have created a wrong impression.

It cannot be pointed out too often that essential for this kind of interpretative reporting is knowledge. Without it, the newsgatherer will consider as new something that is very old and will have news sources "revealing" and "disclosing" information that is common knowledge among a wide circle of readers.

In other words, you can't play up a feature unless you have brains enough to pick it.

The persistent use of the stereotype robs much newspaper news of any news value, in the sense of being new to us. The stuff is interesting in the same way as the account of a play, a street accident, or a baseball game which we ourselves witnessed.

—SILAS BENT in *Ballyhoo*

So I have conceived that the news properly presented should be a sort of crosssection of the character of the human events, current experiences, should delineate character, quality, tendencies, and implications. In this way the reporter exercises his genius. Out of current events he does not make a drab and sordid story but rather an informing and enlightening epic. His work becomes no longer imitative but rises rather to an original art.

—CALVIN COOLIDGE

7
JOURNALISTIC STYLE

A. Conciseness
   1. Superfluous Details
   2. Superfluous Words
   3. Superfluous Phrases
   4. Superfluous Clauses
   5. Redundancies
   6. Simplicity
   7. Passive and Active Voice
   8. Proper Emphasis

B. Avoiding Banality
   1. Figures of Speech
   2. Bromides; Clichés; Platitudes
   3. Shopwork Personifications
   4. Journalese
   5. Gobbledygook
   6. Academic Obscurity

C. Readability Formulas

D. Semantics
   1. Unfamiliar Words
   2. Connotations
   3. Puffs and Boosts
   4. Evaluative Words

E. Correct Usage
   1. Grammatical Faults
   2. Parts of Speech
   3. Troublesome Words

Of eight eminent American novelists studied, "the style of four with journalistic backgrounds displayed a tendency toward the elimination of semantic noise, characterized by compressed syntax, clear and active word choice and concrete, objective detail," according to Donald A. Sears and Margaret Bourland, whose article "Journalism Makes the Style" appeared in the Autumn 1970 *Journalism Quarterly*.

The journalist-novelists and their periods of creativity were Stephen Crane (1880–1900), Theodore Dreiser (1900–1920), Ernest Hemingway (1920–1940) and John Hersey (1940–1960). The nonjournalists were Henry James (1880–1900), Edith Wharton (1900–1920), Thomas Wolfe (1920–1940) and Truman Capote (1940–1960).

Today's recognizable journalistic style evolved during the past century and is economical and suited to the needs of the medium. Its characteristics include the following:

1. Compact, usually short, sentences, every word selected and placed for maximum effect.

2. Short, terse paragraphs, each complete in itself and generally capable of being removed without destroying the sense of a story.
3. Conciseness, directness and simplicity, through elimination of superfluous words, phrases and clauses and through proper emphasis.
4. Factualness, without editorial opinion, puffs and boosts, unwise superlatives, adjectives, nouns or other dogmatic words.
5. Avoidance of "fine" writing, strong verbs and nouns being preferred to trite, hackneyed and obsolete words and expressions.
6. Observance of the rules of good grammatical and word usage.

CONCISENESS

The objective of effective journalistic writing should be to avoid cumbersomeness without becoming choppy or repetitious through the excessive use of referents.

Superfluous Details

Relaxing of the rule that all of the five *w*'s and *h* must be included in the first paragraph of a news story generally achieves the objective of uncluttering the lead.

Cluttered

Clifford Britt, 38, 1459 Grove street, and another passenger on an eastbound Mitchell boulevard street car were injured about 8 A.M. today when the car jumped the track and collided with a westbound car at Mitchell boulevard and Perkins street.

Scores of other passengers en route to work who filled both cars were heavily jostled and shaken up as the two cars came together, according to Mitchell boulevard police who also said another man was injured but disappeared from the scene of the accident.

Britt was taken to Municipal hospital with cuts and bruises on the head and hands.

Uncluttered

Two men were injured and scores shaken when two street cars collided at Mitchell boulevard and Perkins street about 8 A.M. today.

One car was going west and the other east on Mitchell boulevard.

Hitting an open electric switch, the eastbound car jumped the tracks, struck the other, and derailed it.

One of the injured men was Clifford Britt, 38, 1459 Grove street. Police said another man was injured but disappeared from the scene of the accident.

Britt received cuts and bruises on the head and hands. He was taken to Municipal hospital.

Both cars were filled with passengers en route to work. They were heavily jostled as the two cars came together.

General wordiness is "a famous barrier" to effective news writing according to Howard C. Heyn, who cites this loose sentence as an example:

> The police officer accompanied the two to Utah last week inasmuch as it was felt that the young Marvin could be of use in helping to locate or identify the killer.

Heyn suggests that the "message" of this 31-word sentence really was this:

> The policeman took them to Utah last week, hoping Marvin could locate the killer.

Superfluous Words

The articles *the, a* and *an* often can be eliminated, as

WEAK: The Booster students who heard the talk—
BETTER: Booster students who heard the—
WEAK: It is for the men who make good.
BETTER: It is for men who make good.

Erling H. Erlandson warns against excess in adherence to this rule. Otherwise the result might be "nonsensical writing," as "Cause of the dispute was the overtime clause. Union had demanded time and a half for work after 5 P.M." Says Erlandson: "Two words saved at the expense of communication."

Sentences may be shortened and made more forceful by making verbs more direct, as

WEAK: The committee arrived at a conclusion.
BETTER: The committee concluded.
WEAK: The society held a discussion on the matter.
BETTER: The society discussed the matter.
WEAK: They did away with the old building.
BETTER: They razed the old building.

In their *The Art of Editing* (Macmillan, 1972) Floyd Baskette and Jack Sissors list 48 "pet" circumlocutions that can be reduced to save 100 words:

A good part of (much)
A little less than (almost)
Accidentally stumbled (stumbled)
As a general rule (usually)
At the present time (now)
At the rear of (behind)
Bouquet of flowers (bouquet)
Basic fundamentals (fundamentals)
Commuted back and forth (commuted)
Concentrated his efforts on (concentrated on)
Continued on (continued)
Disclosed for the first time (disclosed)
Drew to a close (ended)
Due to the fact that (because)
Easter Sunday (Easter)
Entered a bid of (bid)
Estimated at about (estimated at)
Filled to capacity (filled)
Gave its approval (approved)
Grand total (total)
Hot water heater (water heater)
In the not too distant future (eventually)
In the immediate vicinity (near)
Invited guests (guests)
Jewish rabbi (rabbi)
Kept under surveillance (watched)

- Long chronic illness (chronic illness)
- Made arrangements (arranged)
- Made an arrest (arrested)
- Mental telepathy (telepathy)
- Officiated at the ceremony (officiated)
- New recruit (recruit)
- Soothing balm (balm)
- Once in a great while (rarely)
- Paid a visit (visited)
- Personal friendship (friendship)
- Present incumbent (incumbent)
- Private industry (industry)
- Promoted to the rank of (promoted to)
- Put in his appearance (appeared)
- Reached an agreement (agreed)
- Referred back (referred)
- Rough estimate (estimate)
- Strangled to death (strangled)
- Tendered his resignation (resigned)
- Voiced objections (objected)
- Went up in flames (burned)
- With the exception of (except)

It is not necessary to include the state with the names of large cities, or to mention the state with the name of a city in the same state as the place where the newspaper is published.

WEAK: He lives in Los Angeles, Calif.
BETTER: He lives in Los Angeles.

But:

VAGUE: He lives in Springfield.
CLEAR: He lives in Springfield, Mass.

Don't waste words in giving dates, as

WEAK: The Chemical society will meet on Saturday.
BETTER: The Chemical society will meet Saturday.
WEAK: The meeting will be held this coming Friday.
BETTER: The meeting will be held Friday.
WEAK: The meeting was held at 12 o'clock noon.
BETTER: The meeting was held at noon.

Sometimes a series of related facts can be presented in *series* form, in chronological order, as a word saver. Robert G. Martin cites the following example:

> He was born in Russia, reared in Austria, graduated in 1914 from the University of Vienna, and then served throughout World War I as an Austrian artillery officer on the Italian and Russian fronts.

Erlandson, on the other hand, correctly warns against misuse of this style, as "Born in Tennessee, he served on the Los Angeles Board of Education from 1935 to 1941." Wrote Erlandson: "When two unrelated facts are jammed together, it may be tight writing but it's also faulty subordination."

Superfluous Phrases

WEAK: The meeting was held for the purpose of discussing the matter.
BETTER: The meeting was held to discuss the matter.
WEAK: We met at the corner of Spring and High streets.
BETTER: We met at Spring and High streets.

What someone who makes this mistake means is "intersection," where there are four corners, not just one.

WEAK: We reached him by the use of telephone.
BETTER: We reached him by telephone.
WEAK: The color of the cart was red.
BETTER: The cart was red.
WEAK: He will be here for a period of three weeks.
BETTER: He will be here for three weeks.

Often a strong verb, adjective, adverb or possessive form can be substituted for a phrase.

WEAK: A baby with brown eyes.
BETTER: A brown-eyed baby.
WEAK: The arguments of Brown.
BETTER: Brown's arguments.
WEAK: They assembled with little commotion.
BETTER: They assembled quietly.
WEAK: The howitzer went off with a boom.
BETTER: The howitzer boomed.

Before emulating the last preceding example, the writer must be certain that he has not distorted meaning. There is great temptation to use shorter action verbs that create a feeling of excitement not justified by the facts of the story. Some newspapers have been accused of offending considerably in this respect through frequent use of such words as *hits, slaps, traps, raps, rips, flays, slays, breaks, looms, dooms, lashes, kills, fires, cracks, nabs, grabs, quizzes, grills, curbs, blocks* and *foils,* to use a list compiled by Sydney J. Harris.

Superfluous Clauses

WEAK: All citizens who are interested should come.
BETTER: All interested citizens should come.
WEAK: He will speak at the meeting which will be held Monday.
BETTER: He will speak at the meeting Monday.
WEAK: John Farrell, who is secretary of the Engineers' club, will be there.
BETTER: John Farrell, secretary of the Engineers' club, will be there.

On the other hand, clauses can be used effectively for word-preserving interpolations.

Even though he lost them both, 8–6 and 9–7, he outscored Segman in earned points, 46–43, and his passing shots, often executed while he was running full tilt, were beautiful to watch.

Redundancies

The Minnesota Newspaper Association prepared the following list of redundancies.

absolutely necessary
advance planning
ask the question
assemble together
at a later day
attached hereto
at the present time
canceled out
city of Chicago
close proximity
consensus of opinion
carbon copy
continue on
cooperate together
each and every
enclosed you will find
exactly identical
fair and just
fall down
first and foremost
friend of mine
gathered together
honest truth
important essentials
necessary requirements
open up
other alternative
patently obvious
plain and simple
postpone until later
reasonable and fair
redo again
refer back
refuse and decline
right and proper
rise up
rules and regulations
send in
small in size
still remain
temporarily suspended
totally unnecessary
true facts
various and sundry

Simplicity

Simplicity is obtained in large part by avoiding "elegant" words when simple ones would do better. Usually

about is better than *with reference to*
agreement is better than *concordance*
although is better than *despite the fact that*
before is better than *prior to*
body is better than *remains*
buried is better than *interred*
burned is better than *destroyed by fire*
city people is better than *urban people*
clear is better than *obvious*
coffin is better than *casket*
danger is better than *precariousness*
died is better than *passed away* or *succumbed*
dog is better than *canine*
farming is better than *agriculture*
fear is better than *apprehension*
fire is better than *conflagration*
forced is better than *compelled*
funeral is better than *obsequies*
horse is better than *domesticated quadruped*
if is better than *in the event of*
leg is better than *limb*
man is better than *gentleman*
marriage is better than *nuptials*
meeting is better than *rendezvous*
money is better than *lucre*
nearness is better than *contiguity*

normal is better than *traditional*
since is better than *inasmuch as*
theft is better than *larcency*
understand is better than *comprehend*
well-paying is better than *lucrative*
woman is better than *lady*

When two words are synonyms, brevity can be obtained by using the shorter, as

after for *following*
ask for *request*
buy for *purchase*
car for *automobile*
expect for *anticipate*
get for *obtain*
try for *attempt*
use for *utilize*

Passive and Active Voice

The active voice usually is more emphatic than the passive. The passive should be used, however, when warranted by the importance of the grammatical object of a sentence. In the following sentences, for example, the passive voice is preferable to the active:

Henry Binger has been appointed chairman of the County Republican campaign committee.

Earl Kromer, prominent local merchant, was killed instantly early today when a bolt of lightning struck his home, 34 E. Wilson street.

Increased rates for the Middletown municipal water works were ordered by the public service commission in an order issued Thursday.

In other cases the feature can better be played up by use of the active voice, as

WEAK: The accident was witnessed by ten boys.
BETTER: Ten boys witnessed the accident.
WEAK: The report was received by the mayor.
BETTER: The mayor received the report.
WEAK: The keynote address was delivered by Governor Furman.
BETTER: Governor Furman delivered the keynote address.

Proper Emphasis

Vagueness and indefiniteness are avoided, and clarity is obtained, by placing important ideas at the beginnings of sentences. Also by playing up the action, significance, result or feature of the paragraph or story, by avoiding vague and indefinite words and by eliminating superfluous details, words, phrases and clauses.

VAGUE: Some 50 persons were present.
BETTER: About 50 were present.

WORDY: People of Chester will be asked to contribute $4,000 to the National Red Cross campaign to relieve suffering in the drought area of the United States, according to announcements made yesterday by John Doe, local chairman.

CONCISE: Chester's quota in the National Red Cross campaign for drought relief is $4,000, John Doe, local chairman, said yesterday.

WEAK: When asked what he thought of the compromise plan of unemployment relief, Senator Sapo today said that—

DEFINITE: Senator Sapo today condemned the compromise plan for unemployment relief as demagogic, unconstitutional and inadequate.

WEAK: The purpose of the Student Council meeting at 7 p.m. Monday in Swift hall is to discuss the proposal to limit student activities.

BETTER: The Student Council will discuss limitation of student activities at 7 p.m. Monday in Swift hall.

WEAK: It was decided by the Men's club at its meeting last evening to hold a smoker next Monday evening in the club room.

BETTER: The Men's club will hold a smoker Monday evening in the club room, it was decided at last evening's meeting.

Newspaper style books and journalism texts once admonished reporters never to begin a story with an article or indefinite pronoun. Like every other rule, this one could and should be broken on occasion. Such a lead as "There will be a meeting, etc." ordinarily should be avoided. Such effective writing as the following, however, should be encouraged.

> There was to have been a birthday party Saturday in the Rose Rest Home, 625 N. Kenmore. But instead there was quiet sadness.
>
> The party was to have celebrated the 102d birthday of Miss Lillie Hayes, a resident of the home.
>
> Miss Hayes, a retired schoolteacher, died Friday after suffering a sudden stroke.

AVOIDING BANALITY

The day of the grammatical purist is gone. Contemporary authorities recognize that language makes dictionaries and not vice versa. Many words in common use today were once frowned upon as slang or vulgarisms. Every year prominent writers coin new words or resurrect archaic ones that meet with popular acceptance. The fault of young writers as regards word choice is not so much selection of what might be called undignified words but tactless use of bromides, platitudes, and clichés. What constitutes tactfulness in using slang, trite and hackneyed expressions is for the English department, not the school of journalism, to teach. Nevertheless, the journalism teacher and certainly the newspaper copyreader can spot a threadbare word or phrase used in a threadbare way.

There isn't a word listed below, as one to be used cautiously, that can't be used effectively on occasion. This is decidedly not a don't section, merely one of precaution.

Figures of Speech

The following figures of speech generally should be avoided because they are likely to be misused. They are whiskered with age and mark their innocent user as callow.

a checkered career
acid test
alike as peas in a pod
ax to grind
blessing in disguise
busy as a bee
busy as a one-armed paperhanger
clutches of the law
cool as a cucumber
departed this vale of tears
dull as dishwater
eyes bigger than his stomach
flow like water
hail of bullets
hangs in the balance
heart of the business district
honest as the day is long
in the limelight
innocent as a newborn babe
long hours of the night
loomed like sentinels
met his Waterloo
never rains but it pours
nipped in the bud
old as Methusaleh
picture of health
pillar of the church
police combing the city
pretty as a picture
rains cats and dogs
round into shape
sea of upturned faces
silver lining
since Hector was a pup
slow as molasses in January
smell a rat
sober as a judge
something the cat dragged in
spread like a house afire
stormy session
the crying need
the great beyond
the wings of disaster
threw a monkey wrench into
to swing the pendulum
watery grave
went by the boards
white as a sheet
won his spurs
worked like Trojans

Bromides; Clichés; Platitudes

Generally considered too trite or hackneyed for effective use are the following:

all-out effort
almost fatally injured
any way, shape or form
as luck would have it
augurs well
bated breath
beaming smile
better half
bids fair
bigger and better
blushing bride
bright and shiny
broad daylight
burly Negro
crisp bill
dances divinely
departed this life
doing as well as can be expected
doomed to disappointment
dull thud
each and every
easy prey
fair maidens
favor with a selection
feature
few and far between
green-eyed monster

hale and hearty
head over heels
hectic
he-man
host of friends
in the offing
internal fury
laid to rest
last but not least
last sad rites
leering ghost
light fantastic toe
loomed on the horizon
making it a whole new ball game
many and various
method in his madness
music hath charms, etc.
no uncertain terms
order out of chaos
point with pride
powder keg
present day and generation
received an ovation
red-blooded
resting comfortably
scintillating
sigh of relief
signs of the times
smashed to smithereens
sparkling eyes
take a hard look
thick and fast
threw his hat into the ring
trend of public sentiment
variety is the spice of life
view with alarm
vital stake
weather permitting
wild and woolly

Shopworn Personifications

The following mythical characters have been introduced into all kinds of writing so often that they have lost their ability to impress or amuse:

Betty Coed
Dame Fashion
Dame Rumor
Dan Cupid
Father Neptune
Father Time
G. I. Joe
Grim Reaper
Jack Frost
Joe College
John Q. Public
Jupiter Pluvius
Lady Luck
Man in the Street
Mother Earth
Mother Nature
Mr. Average Citizen
Old Sol

Journalese

Newspapers have not contributed so much as one might expect to the coinage of new words, but they have helped exhaust the effectiveness of a large number through indiscriminate repetition. Among these are the following:

blunt instrument
bolt from a clear sky
brutal crime
brutally murdered
cannon fodder
cheered to the echo
clubber
crime wave
cynosure of all eyes
death car
fatal noose
feeling ran high
focus attention
grilled by police
gruesome find
gumshoes
hot seat
infuriated mob
man hunt
moron
mystery surrounds
news leaked out
police drag nets
political pot boiling
probe
quiz
rush
sleuths
smoke-filled room
smoking revolver
solon
speculation is rife
swoop down
thug
usual reliable sources
war clouds
while thousands cheer
whirlwind tour
will be staged

Lazy journalistic habits include use of such meaningless descriptive phrases as "a policeman's policeman," "a lawyer's lawyer" and the like and overuse of the word "controversial" presumably to heighten interest in a person, event or thing.

At any time there are words and expressions that are popular and that are used by many who don't fully understand their meaning. Among recent examples are viable, bottom line, scam, top drawer, ripoff, syndrome, do your thing, macho, connection, name of the game, panic button, bite the bullet, get the show on the road, and get the act together. Some of these fortunately are classifiable as slang fads and are not easily adaptable to newspaper copy. Columnists, editorial writers and feature writers, however, should beware.

Gobbledygook

Heyn warns against "pretentious phrasing, guaranteed to scare the reader away from the story." He cites this example:

> National Association for Advancement of Colored People attorneys told the Supreme Court today that overt public resistance is insufficient cause to nullify federal court desegregation orders.

He also warns against governmentese and other gobbledygook and cites some clauses and phrases that "should have a familiar ring," as follows:

> Since over-all policy was brought into focus . . .
> . . . under mandate to achieve conformity.
> Suspension of the principle is all the more important . . .
> . . . finalize a program for federally impacted school areas.

Wallace Carroll, when editor and publisher of the Winston-Salem *Journal Sentinel,* lamented the extent to which Emerson's law has become Nosreme's law. He recalled Ralph Waldo Emerson's aphorism: "If a man can write a better book, preach a better sermon or make a better mousetrap than his neighbor, though he builds his house in the woods, the world will make a beaten path to his door."

Carroll lamented the decline in quality in many areas of life, both material and immaterial. Specifically, as regards "the realm of words and images," he commented:

> Here, too, Emerson is in full retreat. All of us know that if an obscure man can take two clear, simple words like "hot" and "cool" (words that cannot be misunderstood even by a retarded four-year-old), and if that man can so twist and mangle those words that everybody in his right mind will wonder what in the name of McLuhan he means by them—if a man can do this he will be hailed as a genius in "communications"; foundations will be richly endowed for him so that he can perpetuate his befuddlement among succeeding generations.

The McLuhan whose activities Carroll deplored was the late Prof. Marshall McLuhan who insisted "the medium is the message." In *Understanding Media* and other books, McLuhan cited the growing importance of television and other electronic media and came close to predicting the disappearance of the printed word. To Carroll and others, however, it does not necessarily follow that the contents of a message are unimportant. Rather, the essence of good journalism remains good reporting, which means having something to say—the content rather than the medium is the message. It just is not so that what you don't know won't hurt you. In a democracy widespread knowledge is essential. Carroll strongly warned against adoption of Nosreme's law, which he defined as follows:

> If a man can write muddier prose than his neighbor, if he can arrange words in ways that befuddle the brain and grate on the ear, he will never have to monkey with a better mousetrap.

Carroll described the difficulty the newsgatherer today encounters:

> Do you want to be recognized as an authority on reading in the public schools? Then you have only to write like this:
>
> "Perhaps the task of developing proper motivation is best seen, at least in a nutshell, as limiting the manipulation of extrinsic factors to that of keeping homeostatic need and exteroceptive drive low, in favor of facilitating basic information processing to maximize accurate anticipation of reality."
>
> Do you want to become a professor of the behavioral sciences in a great university? Then you simply need to express yourself in this way:
>
> "If the correlation of intrinsic competency to actual numerical representation is definitely high, then the thoroughly objective conclusion may inexpugnably be reached that the scholastic derivations and outgrowths will attain a pattern of unified superiority."
>
> Do you want to become the chief of a government bureau? Then learn to write and talk like this:
>
> "The Board's new regulatory goal is to create a supervisory environment conducive and stimulative to industry adaptation to its fundamentally altered markets. We will give you the options to restructure both sides of your statement of condition, but the decision-making and the long-range planning function is management's . . . We will look to you for input of information which we shall rely on in making our decisions."
>
> Or do you want to become an expert on business management and go around lecturing to leaders of industry? You can if you will learn to talk like this:
>
> "The focus of concentration rests upon objectives which are, in turn, centered around the knowledge and customer areas, so that a sophisticated awareness of those areas can serve as an entrepreneurial filter to screen what is relevant from what is irrelevant to future commitments."
>
> This bastardization of our mother tongue is really a disaster for all of us in the news business. The English language is our bread and butter, but when ground glass is mixed with the flour and grit with the butter, our customers are likely to lose their appetite for what we serve them.

The popularity of fuzzy writing indicates the widespread existence of fuzzy thinking by pseudo-intellectuals who, in their frustration, accept what they don't understand as probably profound and who then struggle to interpret. As a result, shallow books such as *The Greening of America* by Charles Reich and Thomas A. Harris' *I'm O.K.—You're O.K.* become best sellers. The best exposure of the superficiality of this sort of thing is *Social Sciences As Sorcery* by Stanislav Andreski (St. Martin's Press, 1972).

Academic Obscurity

Because of the growing evidence of the functional illiteracy of many high school graduates, there is an increasing demand for a return to the basics, meaning the traditional 3 r's—reading, 'riting and 'rithmetic. The behavioral scientists who have been in the majority in schools of education and teachers colleges are in retreat with their arguments that training in sensitivity, social responsibility, creativity, and the like are more important than course content. Of the professional exponents of obscurity the *Wall Street Journal* has editorialized:

> Complexity and obscurity have professional value—they are the academic equivalents of apprenticeship rules in the building trades. They exclude the outsiders, keep down the competition, preserve the image of a privileged or priestly class. The man who makes things clear is a scab. He is criticized less for his clarity than for his treachery.

In a New York *Times* column entitled "Why Profs Can't Write," Donald Holden wrote, "Book publishers know that most professors are bad writers. The professor's grammar, spelling and punctuation are usually passable but his prose is apt to be pretentious, unclear and chaotic." Holden wrote that "dissertationese is the language that professors use to disguise self-contempt with pomposity." In her *America Revisited* (Little, Brown, 1979) Pulitzer prize-winner Frances FitzGerald documents Holden's charge as regards American history books intended for high school use during the past century.

In his "Light Refractions" column in *Saturday Review,* Thomas H. Middleton frequently berates the behavioral scientists. He is especially aghast at the endorsement by the National Council of Teachers of English of the viewpoint expressed by Leonard Bloomfield: "Writing is not language but merely a way of recording language by means of visible marks." Middleton comments: "Shakespeare, Milton, Pope, Melville, Jefferson, Twain and so on and on are no longer part of the English language. The English language is now the rap session."

A good summary of the situation is *What's Happening to American English* (Scribner's, 1979) by Arn and Charlene Tibbetts. The viewpoint of the downgraders of grammar and writing is presented in Stanley Berne's *Future Language* and Arlene Zekowski's *Image Breaking Images.* The authors, professors of English at East New Mexico University, want a new grammarless language. According to Berne, "Grammar and spelling are the property of a once privileged minority class imposing its order on a willing majority anxious to rise out of its own supposed ignorance and vulgarity."

Another crusader against the belief held by many English teachers today that it is unimportant for students to learn to spell and write grammatically is Richard Mitchell, professor of English at Glassboro State College. On request anyone can receive his four-page newsletter, *The Underground Grammarian*. He also is the author of *Less Than Words Can Say* (Little, Brown, 1980). He scoffs at sociologists and educators who say "individualized learning station" when they mean "desk." It is impossible to conceive how newspapers or other periodicals could adopt the antigrammarian viewpoint or, in fact, publish anything for anyone who does. The behavioral scientists, however, have infiltrated schools of journalism where the Ph.D. communicologists, with little or no professional journalistic experience, write articles for *Journalism Quarterly,* the publication of the Association for Education in Journalism. In the October 1979 *Quill,* Creed C. Black, publisher of the Lexington (Ky.) *Leader,* wrote about *Journalism Quarterly,* "I must confess that I found little there I could understand, much less apply." He quoted the following from a *Journalism Quarterly* article:

> We hope to accomplish two aims in this paper. We intend to explore the use of collective behavior conceptualizations in the press, focusing on the New York *Times*. We intend to test the specific hypothesis that there is a direct relationship between the reported presence of a control agency at a collective behavior event and the attribution of spontaneity, out-of-the-ordinary nature, depersonalization of participants, violence, emotionality, and the use of unit terms of reference. This hypothesis (more accurately, this set of hypotheses) will be tested by using the Spearman rank-order correlation.

In the Winter 1976 issue of *Masthead,* publication of the National Conference of Editorial Writers, Jake Highton, formerly chairman of the Department of Journalism at Wayne State University, asked, "Does Anyone at *Journalism Quarterly* Speak English?" and explained his quandary by quoting from a dozen scholarly articles in the magazine, a typical excerpt being the following:

> Overall differentiation among the six-party performance groups by the seven factors was significant (Wilks-Lamba = 0.857) five roots extracted 100 per cent of the variance, but only the first root was significant (Chi square = 35.7p < .001.)

Highton despaired and returned to professional newspaper work. So did another experienced reporter when he attended an Association for Education in Journalism convention and received the abstract of a paper, "Subject Abilities to the Metric MDS; Effects of Varying the Criterion Plan." The abstract began:

> This study addresses the problem of selecting a criterion pair to present to subjects in a metric MDS task and, more importantly, the subject's ability to reliably use that standard to describe or characterize their conceptions of a given set of

elements. It was hypothesized that: (1) The structure produced by a criterion pair involving the extremes from the concept domain will be statistically identical to the structure produced by providing the same scale base with no concept anchors; (2) As the distance between the criterion pair is increased the resulting judgments of distances among concepts will increase but the pattern of interrelationships will remain the same; (3) A criterion pair that is closer together in the space will produce a larger structure than using the extreme pair, yet the concept interrelationships will remain the same.

READABILITY FORMULAS

Shortly after World War II the two major press associations and several magazines and newspapers experimented with readability formulas that stressed brevity—shorter words, shorter sentences, and shorter paragraphs—in the belief that thereby the average American, who had only a ninth-grade education, would find the result easier to read and comprehend.

The formulas grew out of studies of several researchers, most important of whom were Rudolf Flesch of New York University and Robert Gunning, director of Readable News Reports of Columbus, Ohio. Following the recommendations of the former, the Associated Press reduced its average lead sentence length from 27 to 23 words and its average word sentence length from 1.74 to 1.55 syllables. Upon the advice of the latter, the United Press simplified its writing style so as to be suitable for readers with 11.7 years of education, whereas formerly it presumably was writing for those who had gone to school 16.7 years.

Flesch's formula allegedly estimated "reading ease" and "human interest." The former was measured by the average length of words and sentences—the shorter, the easier to read, 1.5 syllables and an average sentence length of 19 words being considered best for newspapers. Human interest was measured by the percentage of "personal words" and "personal sentences." Flesch said 6 per cent of the former and 12 per cent of the latter made for good newspaper reading.

Gunning considered three factors: (1) sentence pattern, difficulty beginning when the average number of words per sentence exceeded twenty; (2) Fog Index, a measure of complex or abstract words as "rendezvous" for "meeting," "undoubtedly" for "no doubt," etc.; (3) human interest—the frequent use of names of people, referents to those names and other human interest words.

As an APME Readability committee once reported: "The virtue of the Flesch experiment is that it *has* made writers think more of their writing."

The same, of course, could be said of the Gunning and several other formulas.

Brevity does not necessarily equate with clarity. A short word can be as vague as a long one, and a short sentence can be a misleading as a book. Unless the syllable-length criterion advanced by Flesch, such words as *beauti-*

ful, patriotism, vacation, prearrange, improbable, candlestick, bracelet, watermelon and other familiar ones would be considered difficult whereas use of *ohm, joule, watt, erg, baize, arn, tweak, volt* and *tort* would contribute to a high readability score.

Different from either the Flesch or Gunning system, in that it takes account of the reader's probable familiarity with words, is the system devised by Prof. Edgar Dale and Mrs. Jeanne S. Chall of the Bureau of Education Research of Ohio State University. The Dale-Chall system takes into account average sentence length but also uses a list of 3,000 words familiar to fourth-graders.

Dr. Dale discounts the value of counting affixes, suffixes and prefixes, as advocated by Flesch, by declaring that no two skilled judges ever get the same count. He also rejects Flesch's personal referent principle and is fond of citing a quotation from Koffka's *Principles of Gestalt Psychology* which contains personal pronouns equal to 5.8 per cent as follows:

> In the first case, real moving objects present in the field, the shift of the retinal pattern leads to behavioral motion of objects, whether I fixate a nonmoving object or follow a moving one with my regard; in the second case, when my eyes roam stationary objects, such a shift will not have this result. . . .

That would be considered very readable by both the Flesch and Gunning systems.

Proper names, other critics of these formulas have pointed out, do not necessarily lead to greater understanding unless the reader knows the persons mentioned and understands the references to them. "He was as mad as Hamlet," for instance, is about as readable as you can get; but, if the reader never has heard of Hamlet, its meaning is lost on him.

In recent years there have been several studies which show that 21 million Americans, perhaps as many as 57 million, over the age of 16 are functionally illiterate. In addition there are about 1 million who cannot read or write at all. According to the United States Office of Education, 20 per cent of adult Americans have trouble coping with necessary skills as shopping or getting a driver's license. In addition 19.7 per cent of Americans over 16 "function only with difficulty" and another 33.9 per cent are "functional but not proficient."

SEMANTICS

Despite its length, the following sentence probably would be considered readable by the readability experts:

> Many boys and girls are working at too young an age, for too long hours, too late at night, in dangerous and other undesirable conditions.

A general semanticist, however, would be quick to point out that no matter how clear the sentence may be, the information it conveys is vague and biased. How many is "many"? When you say "boys and girls" do you mean little children, such as used to work in sweatshops, or do you mean teenagers? What determines when one is too young to deliver newspapers, set pins in a bowling alley, run errands for a grocer, sew buttons or work on a lathe? How long is "too long" and how late is "too late"? What is a "dangerous" condition? Especially, what are "other undesirable" conditions?

No experienced newsgatherer would fail to ask these questions if such a statement were made during the course of an interview. Often, however, such "glittering generalities," as the Institute for Propaganda Analysis (1937–1942) would have called them, appear in publicity releases and in public addresses, especially by politicians. They need amplification to convey important meaning to others, and it will be a happy day when editors toss them into the wastebasket unless it is possible to obtain such amplification.

On assignment, the interpretative reporter must be sharp enough to ask the proper questions to clarify vague statements and define "virtue" or "smear" words. Often, if not always, this requires more than the usual amount of knowledge on the reporter's part regarding the field of interest. In other words, the more one knows about a subject, the better able s/he is to interview someone regarding it. All the readability formulas and other aids to good writing cannot substitute for thorough fact-gathering.

"Pin the man down" should be the newsgatherer's first rule. If his/her subject talks about "progress," the reporter should ask him what he means by the term and for the facts and figures that justify its use. If the person being interviewed mentions "special circumstances," s/he should be asked what s/he means by "circumstances" and what makes them "special" and to give specific examples of what s/he's talking about.

Unfamiliar Words

If the words an interviewee uses are specific but nevertheless unfamiliar, the reporter should overcome any sheepishness and ask for a little elementary shop talk from his subject. Otherwise, s/he might neglect to inquire deeply enough into the potential facts of the story at hand. Lacking such an opportunity for "depth" reporting, the reporter should consult dictionaries, encyclopedias and other reference works to fill the gaps in his own knowledge.

If a reporter has to ask or look up the meaning of an expression, s/he can be fairly certain that a goodly number of his/her readers will need explanation of it. Perhaps s/he can even avoid use of the unfamiliar word in his/her story. S/he can, for instance, say, "Union A is attempting to persuade members of Union B to change their membership from B to A." Then s/he can explain, "This is called 'raiding' in labor circles." Or, if s/he uses "raiding" in his/her principal statement, s/he can define it, perhaps in an italicized parenthetical insert.

"Jurisdictional strike," "mass picketing" and "secondary boycott" are among the other terms in a story of a labor dispute which may need explanation. In weather stories, it probably is wise to make clear the difference between hurricanes, tornadoes, cyclones and just plain gales or wind storms. Few readers probably remember what a nautical knot is or a French kilometer or an English mile. With the world becoming more complex daily and the areas of specialization growing, the need for such explanatory journalism is increasing. Thorough reporting is the best safeguard against the misuse of words.

Connotations

"The workers *won* a wage boost" has one connotation. "The workers *were given* a wage boost" has quite another. Only painstaking reporting can determine which is correct in any particular case. There can be no laziness or carelessness when the public interest is involved, as it usually is in stories pertaining to labor relations, governmental activities and the like.

Perhaps a news source condemns government "interference" when s/he really means s/he opposes government "regulation" in a particular area. Such words are loaded. Reportorial questioning should lead to specific details rather than vague charges or mere name calling. If loaded words are used from some necessity, they probably should be included in quotation marks or some explanatory matter should be added to indicate the alternative words for the same thought.

Newspapers propagandize if they use the labels of those with whom they agree editorially to describe pending legislation or situations. Examples of such editorializing would be "slave labor bill" for a measure regulating the mobility of the labor force in time of emergency, "dictator bill" for a proposal to increase the power of an executive, "goon" for labor union pickets and the like. It makes a great deal of difference whether you write

crop relief *or* farm dictatorship
foreign *or* alien
labor organizer *or* labor agitator
nonstriker *or* loyal worker
picketing *or* mass picketing
a company's earnings declined 36 per cent *or* they plunged to that extent
regulation *or* regimentation
UAW chieftain *or* UAW dictator
open shop *or* right to work
bombing *or* air support
affirmative action *or* reverse discrimination
mandatory busing *or* assignment for racial balance
right to life *or* right to choose
right to work *or* closed (or open) shop
scab *or* replacement *or* strikebreaker
liberate *or* change governments

Sydney J. Harris, whose column originates with and is syndicated by the Chicago *Sun-Times,* is a fervid semanticist. The following, entitled "More Antics with Semantics," is typical of his writings:

Why is it that Our secret agents are "patriots," while Their secret agents are nothing but "spies"?

When I have one over the limit, I become "the life of the party"; when you have one over the limit, you become a "loudmouth."

I am "strongminded," but you are "opinionated."

My candidate's plan for the future shows he has "vision," but your candidate's plan for the future makes him a "wild-eyed dreamer."

I am about the only capable and careful driver on the road; all other motorists are either "stick-in-the-muds" or "reckless maniacs."

My failure to laugh at your dirty jokes shows my "good breeding," but your failure to laugh at my dirty jokes shows "stuffiness."

* * *

The British are too "reserved," and the French are too "effusive"; the Italians are too "impulsive," and the Scandinavians are too "cold"; the Germans are too "arrogant," and the Japanese are too "diffident"—surely God must be an American.

My new two-tone car is "bright," but your new two-tone car is just "loud."

I give an inexpensive present because "it's the spirit behind it that counts," but you give an inexpensive present because you're cheap.

My son hit yours over the head with a block because he is "playful," but yours hit mine over the head because he is "vicious."

A "sound" man is a man who sounds like me.

When I spread gossip, it is always a "harmless tidbit," but when you spread gossip, it is "malicious rumor-mongering."

A "realistic" novel is a novel that agrees with the idea of reality I held before I even opened the book.

* * *

My family, which is poor, lost its tremendous fortune during the Depression; but your family, which is rich, made all its money profiteering during the War.

Why is it that "modern" is an approving adjective for plumbing, but a disapproving adjective for art?

My wife's dress is "simple," but your wife's dress is "dowdy."

Likewise, my summer wardrobe is "casual," but yours is "sloppy."

Our relatives may "get into trouble," but your relatives have illegitimate babies, go to jail and take up dope. (ours, are, of course, "unfortunate," but yours are "bad.")

Puffs and Boosts

Against one type of editorializing most newspapers are sufficiently on the alert. That is the practice of making gratuitous complimentary remarks regarding a person or event rather than stating the facts and allowing them to speak for themselves. Some such expressions, obsolete in most newsrooms, are the following:

a big success
a good time was had by all
a stellar performance
an enjoyable occasion
an impressive sight
an interesting program was offered
attractive decorations
charming hostess

- everything went along nicely
- fills a long-felt need
- happy pair
- in a very entertaining manner
- it beggars description
- it bids fair
- likable personality
- prospects are bright
- proud possessor
- replete with interest
- talented young man
- the trip was the most popular ever taken

Such expressions are taboo if for no other reason than that they have been overworked.

Evaluative Words

In quite a different category are attempts to improve the reader's understanding by the use of qualifying adjectives, other parts of speech and expressions. Even some editors who have been outspoken in adverse criticism of interpretative reporting have for years allowed and encouraged their reporters to write "One of America's *leading composers* will play his own compositions," "The two *top contenders* for the championship will meet in the first round," "An *unusual* workshop class in creative writing for talented children will be organized," "The court will hear arguments on the *complex, controversial and crucial questions*" and the like.

There is no denying that such expressions involve judgment and, to be socially responsible, the judgment must be based on adequate information. When a sports writer, for instance, writes that the outcome of a contest was "a stunning upset," s/he must know that leaders in the sports world and fans expected it to be different. No competent reporter uses superlatives without investigating to determine whether they are justified: "most devastating fire," "largest audience," "longest report," "rare appearance." Nor does s/he call every gruesome murder "the crime of the century" or assert that something is "unparalleled in human history" or "the greatest outrage ever recorded" unless s/he has done considerable scholarly research to verify his/her contentions.

Nouns

When, however, can you call a disturbance a "panic" or "riot"? When can you use such words as "catastrophe," "fiasco," "disaster," "climax," "zenith" or "debacle"? All you can say is that such terms should be used judiciously. To make common use of them would be to devitalize them. It would be like crying "wolf" when there was no wolf.

What, therefore, is judicious use? The experienced reporter who has covered many similar stories has a basis for comparison, and his/her own experience usually is better than that of most everyone else, especially ax-grinders with motives for hoping s/he uses this word instead of that. Competent reporting and integrity are more likely to give readers correct information than writing formulas and communication theories are.

Adjectives

When is a girl pretty or beautiful? Not every time she gets into a newsworthy situation certainly. Since the development of photography, reporters have become more cautious over indiscriminate use of such descriptive adjectives. Since there is no similar restraining influence in other areas the best that can be done is to advise caution in the use of such words as the following:

brave	ferocious	popular
brilliant	gigantic	remarkable
clever	happy-go-lucky	successful
cowardly	huge	tasteful
eloquent	illimitable	unpatriotic
enjoyable	impressive	valiant
exciting	nice	widely known

Verbs

Verbs must be exact. If a news source answers "yes" to a reporter's question, it is not always proper to say s/he "admitted" something. When s/he makes an announcement, s/he cannot be said to have "revealed" or "disclosed" something unless the matter previously had been kept secret intentionally. "Charge" is a strong word implying an accusation which the news source might have had no intention of making. "Claim" suggests that someone is trying to correct a wrong impression or obtain possession of something that he considers rightfully his/hers. "Probe" implies detectives of some sort are afoot.

Since very few words are exact synonyms for each other, a good dictionary or thesaurus is a better companion for the writer seeking to impart correct information than Gunning's formula to determine the Fog Index. The practice of intentionally using a strong synonym for maximum visceral effect on readers instead of the word that comes closer to stating the situation correctly cannot be condoned.

Here is a list of verbs that the reporter should be hesitant about using:

allege	laugh	sneer
beg	object	squeak
confess	plead	threaten
flee	prowl	urge
grimace	roar	whine
implore	shout	whisper
insult	sneak	yell

Adverbs

A properly placed adverb can change the entire meaning of a news story. Consider the potential power of the following:

accidentally	calmly	facetiously
angrily	carelessly	grimly
boastfully	casually	immodestly

inadvertently
intentionally
ironically
jokingly
laughingly
mockingly
seriously
stupidly
viciously

PHRASES

Evaluational phrases can "make or break" a news story and also, perhaps, some of the principals mentioned in it. Consider the potency of the following:

angry response
in an arrogant manner
in an unprecedented personal statement
in top oratorical form
pale with anger
shaking with grief
showing great dignity
under duress
with profound feeling

CORRECT USAGE

It is presumed that the student has completed a course in English grammar and composition and, therefore, that s/he knows the rudiments of good English. Although some reputable writers still split their infinitives without losing effect, few misuse "lay" and "lie," get "don't" and "doesn't" twisted, misplace "only" or use "like" when they mean "as if" or become confused over the difference between "its" and "it's." If the student of this book is deficient in his knowledge of grammar, s/he had better concentrate on it constantly. Cubs who cannot make their subjects and predicates agree and who can't spell ordinary words don't last long.

In every newspaper office some rules of grammar, word usage and punctuation are emphasized more than others. Many newspapers issue style sheets for the guidance of new staff members as to what kind of writing is preferred.

Grammatical Faults

Several years of correcting journalism students' papers have convinced the writer that the following are among the most common grammatical errors about which aspiring reporters need caution.

WRONG: Neither the mayor nor the city clerk are willing to talk.
RIGHT: Neither the mayor nor the city clerk is willing to talk.
WRONG: The Chamber of Commerce will begin their annual membership drive Monday.
RIGHT: The Chamber of Commerce will begin its annual membership drive Monday.
WRONG: Howard is not as tall as Harold.
RIGHT: Howard is not so tall as Harold.
WRONG: He gave it to John and I.
RIGHT: He gave it to John and me.
WRONG: Less than 35% of the group favor the idea.
RIGHT: Fewer than 35% of the group favor the idea.

The next two examples do not illustrate infallible rules; in some cases, the constructions listed as weak may be better:

WEAK: He has always wanted to go.
BETTER: He always has wanted to go.
WEAK: He was ordered to immediately arrest Jones.
BETTER: He was ordered to arrest Jones immediately.
WRONG: Having arrived an hour late, the audience had begun to disperse before Smith began to speak.
RIGHT: Having arrived an hour late, Smith found his audience had begun to disperse.
WRONG: After Graham and Mitchell had shaken hands he turned to greet the senator.
RIGHT: After Graham and Mitchell had shaken hands the former turned to greet the senator.
STRONGER: After Graham shook hands with Mitchell he greeted the senator.

Parts of Speech

To obtain originality of expression, writers (not all of them journalists) sometimes change the part of speech of a word. In many cases the dictionaries have caught up with popular usage. For instance, it is proper to say "chair a meeting," "jail a prisoner," "hospitalize a sick person" or "table a resolution." Even such words as "alibi," "probe," "host" and "torpedo," to whose use as verbs objection often is heard, are listed as such. President Kennedy used "finalize" as a verb and the practice of inventing verb forms of nouns is widespread; thus we say "victimize," "contact," and the like indiscriminately.

In view of the dynamic character of the language, one hesitates to become crotchety when a newspaper columnist says someone "week-ended" or "house-guested" another or that a dowager "lorgnetted" a stranger. In recent years such words as "babysit" and "moonlight" have come into common usage as verbs. Use of "-wise" as a suffix (businesswise, timewise, bookwise, saleswise) still is regarded as somewhat flippant, however expressive.

The congressional hearings of 1974 popularized many expressions and new usages that dictionaries probably will take note of. For example, "Watergate" may become a synonym for political intrigue and "stonewall it" may be defined as maintaining silence on a matter. Comedians and others are understood when they make clever use of such expressions as "at this point in time," "inoperative," "hardnose it" and "expletive deleted." An Associated Press poll revealed that 30 per cent of the papers surveyed did not censor Nixon's profane and vulgar language as revealed by the tapes. However, a year later Charles T. Alexander was fired because he permitted a four-letter word to appear in the Dayton *Journal-Herald* of which he was editor.

Usually it is left to special writers who sign their stories, sports writers and feature writers to invent unusual word usages. Authors of formal stories are more conservative and wait until the dictionaries have sanctioned an innovation before using it casually. When Webster's *Third New International Dictionary* appeared, however, it created a storm for allegedly going too far in legitimatizing new usages. Among the leading liberal authorities in this field is Rov Copperud, who conducts a column for *Editor & Publisher,* and the most recent of whose several books is *American Usage and Style* (Van Nostrand Reinhold, 1980). Another was the late Prof. Bergen Evans of Northwestern University, who coauthored *A Dictionary of Contemporary American Usage* with Cornelia Evans. Defenders of the Webster dictionary pointed out that in 1800 such words as "banjo," "hominy" and "possum" were considered too slangy for its edition that year. On the other hand, there is Edwin Newman who argues powerfully in *Strictly Speaking* (Bobbs-Merrill, 1974) and *A Civil Tongue* (Bobbs-Merrill, 1976) against too much license, especially by journalists.

Troublesome Words

No matter what the viewpoint regarding definitions, there can be no disagreement that words should be used to convey the meaning intended by their employers. Caution, therefore, is advisable in deviating from standard usages.

The following are some words and expressions that often cause difficulty:

Above. Should not be used for *over* or *more than*.

Accord. Do not use in the sense of *award*. *Give* is better.

Act. A single incident. An *action* consists of several acts.

Actual facts. All facts are actual.

Administer. Used with reference to medicine, governments or oaths. Blows are not *administered,* but *dealt*.

Adopt. Not synonymous with *decide* or *assume*.

Affect; effect. *Affect* means to have an influence on; *effect* means to cause, to produce, to result in.

Aggravate. Means to *increase;* not synonymous with *irritate*.

Aggregate. Not synonymous with *total*.

Allege. Not synonymous with *assert*. Say the *alleged* crime, but "He *said* he is innocent."

Allow; permit. The former means *not to forbid;* the latter means *to grant leave*.

Allude. Do not confuse with *refer* or *elude*.

Almost; nearly. *Almost* regards the ending of an act, *nearly* the beginning.

Alternative. Indicates a choice of two things. Incorrect to speak of *two alternatives* or *one alternative*.

Among. Use when more than two is meant; for two only, use *between*.

Annual. Don't write *first annual*. It's not annual yet.

Antecedents. Do not use in the sense of *ancestors, forefathers, history* or *origin*.

A number of. Indefinite. Specify.

Anxious. Implies worry. Not synonymous with *eager,* which implies anticipation or desire.

Anyone or *none*. Use in speaking of more than two. *Either* and *neither* are used when speaking of only two. All take singular verbs.

Appears, looks, smells, seems, etc. Take an adjective complement.

As the result of an operation. Avoid this expression. Usually incorrect and libelous.

At. Use *in* before the names of large cities: He is *in* New York, but the meeting was held *at* Greenville.

Audience. An *audience* hears, *spectators* see.

Autopsy. An *autopsy* is *performed*, not *held*.

Averse; adverse. The former is an adjective meaning *opposed to;* the latter is an adjective meaning *bad*.

Avocation. A man's pleasure, while *vocation* is his business or profession.

Awful. Means to *fill with awe;* not synonymous with *very* or *extremely*.

Balance. Not synonymous with *rest* or *remainder*.

Banquet. Only a few meals are worth the name. Use *dinner* or *supper*.

Because. Better than *due* in "They fought because of a misunderstanding."

Beside; besides. The first means *by the side of;* the second, *in addition to*.

Bloc. Don't confuse with *block*.

By. Use instead of *with* in such sentences as "The effect was gained by colored lights."

Call attention. Do not use it for *direct attention*.

Canon; cannon. The former is a *law;* the latter is a large *gun*.

Canvas; canvass. The former is a *cloth;* the latter means to *solicit*.

Capitol. The building is the *capitol;* the city is the *capital*.

Casualty. Should not be confused with *disaster, accident, mishap*.

Childish. Not synonymous with *childlike*.

Chinese. Don't use *Chinaman*.

Claim. A transitive verb. One may "claim a dog" but not that "Boston is larger than Portland."

Cold facts (*or statistics*). When is a fact hot?

Collide. To collide both objects must be in motion.

Commence. Usually *begin* or *start* is better.

Compared with. Use *compared with* in speaking of two things coming under the same classification; use *compared to* if the classes are different.

Completely destroyed. Redundant.

Comprise. Do not use for *compose*.

Confess. A man confesses a crime to the police, but he does not confess to a crime. Don't say *self-confessed*.

Conscious. Not synonymous with *aware*.

Consensus. Don't say *consensus of opinion;* simply say *consensus*.

Consequence. Sometimes misused in the sense of "importance" and "of moment," as "They are all persons of consequence" (importance); "A matter of no consequence" (moment).

Consist in. Distinguish between *consists in* and *consists of*.

Consummation. Look up in the dictionary. Do not use in reference to marriage.

Continual; continuous. That is *-al* which either is always going on or recurs at short intervals and never comes (or is regarded as never coming) to an end. That is *-ous* in which no break occurs between the beginning and the end.

Convene. Delegates, not a convention, *convene.*

Correspondent; co-respondent. The former *communicates in writing;* the latter *answers jointly* with another.

Council; counsel. The former is a *meeting for deliberation.* The latter is *advice* or *one who gives advice.*

Couple. Used only when two things are joined, not of separate things. Use *of* with it.

Crime. Do not confuse with *sin* or *vice. Crime* is a violation of the law of the state; *vice* refers to a violation of moral law; *sin* is a violation of religious law.

Cultured. Don't use for *cultivated.*

Cyclone. Distinguish from *hurricane, typhoon, tornado, gale* and *storm.*

Dangerously. Not *dangerously* but *critically* or *alarmingly ill.*

Data. Plural. *Datum* is singular.

Date from. Not *date back to.*

Depot. Don't use for *station.* A *depot* is a storehouse for freight or supplies; railway passengers arrive at a *station.*

Die of. Not *die from.*

Different from. Not *different than.*

Dimensions; proportions. The former pertains to *magnitude;* the latter to *form.*

Divide. Don't say, "The money was divided between Smith, Jones and Brown." Use *among* when more than two are concerned.

Dove. Should not be used for *dived.*

Drops dead. Falls dead is what is meant.

Drown. Don't say *was drowned* unless it was murder; just say *drowned.*

During. Do not confuse with *in. During* answers the question "How long?" *in* answers the question "When? At what time?" as "We were in Princeton *during* the winter"; "We received the letter *in* the morning."

Each other; one another. The former pertains to *two;* the latter to *three* or *more.*

Either; neither. Use when speaking of two only.

Elicit. Means to "draw out against the will."

Emigrant: Do not confuse with *immigrant.* An *emigrant* leaves, and an *immigrant* comes in.

Envelop; envelope. The former means *to surround;* the latter is a *covering* or *wrapper.*

Event. Do not confuse with *incident, affair, occurrence* or *happening.*

Experiment. Don't say *try* an experiment. Experiments are *made.*

Fail. To *fail* one must try. Usually what is meant is *did not*.

Fakir; faker. The former is an Oriental ascetic; the latter is a deceiver or cheat.

Farther. Denotes distance; *further* denotes time.

Final; finale. The former means *last;* the latter is a *concluding act* or *number*.

Fliers; flyers. The former are *aviators;* the latter are *handbills*.

Flout; flaunt. The former means *to scoff* or *mock;* the latter means *to make ostentatious display*.

Frankenstein. He was the monster's maker, not the monster itself.

From. A person dies *of,* not *from,* a disease.

Graduate, as a verb. Colleges *graduate;* students *are graduated*.

Gun. Don't confuse with *revolver* and *pistol*.

Had. Implies volition. Don't say, "Had his arm cut off."

Head up. The *up* is superfluous.

Healthy. A person is *healthy,* but climate is *healthful* and food *wholesome*.

Heart failure. Everyone dies of heart failure. There are several *heart diseases*.

Hectic. "Hectic flush" is the feverish blush of consumption. Not to be used in the sense of *excited, impassioned, intense, rapturous, uncontrolled* or *wild,* except when a jocosity is intended.

High. Distinguish from *large*.

Hoi polloi. "The many." Do not use "the" before it.

Hold. Use advisedly. The Supreme Court *holds* a law constitutional, but one *asserts* that one man is a better boxer than another.

Hung. A criminal is *hanged*. Clothes are *hung* on a line.

Inaugurate. Does not mean *begin*.

Incumbent. It is redundant to write *present incumbent*.

Indorse. Not synonymous with *approve*.

Infer; imply. The former means *to deduce;* the latter *to signify*.

Initial. A man may sign his initial, but he does not make an *initial payment*. He makes the *first payment*.

Innumerable. Not synonymous with *endless*.

Invited guests. Most guests are invited; omit the adjective.

Last. Not synonymous with *latest* or *past*.

Leave. Don't confuse with *let*.

Leaves a widow. Impossible. He leaves a *wife*.

Lectern. A reading desk; a *podium* is a small platform.

Less. Use *less* money for *fewer* coins.

Like. The slogan "Winstons taste good like a cigaret should" has helped make the use of "like" legitimate as a substitute for "as."

Literally. Often the exact opposite, *figuratively,* is meant.

Locate. A building is *located* when its site is picked; thereafter it is *situated*. A person is *found,* not located.

Majority. The lead over *all* others; a plurality is a lead over *one* other.

Marshal; Marshall. The former is a title; the latter a proper name.

Mathematics. Singular.
Media is plural; *medium* is singular.
Memorandum. Singular. *Memoranda,* plural.
Mend. You *mend* a dress but *repair* a street.
Minister. Distinguish between *minister,* a term used in Protestant churches, and *priest,* used in Catholic churches. Every *preacher* is not a *pastor;* a *pastor* has a church, a *minister* may not.
Musical; musicale. The former means *rhythmic;* the latter is a *recital* or *concert.*
Name after. The correct form is *name for.*
Near accident. There is no such thing.
Née. Give only last name, "Mrs. Helen Kuenzel, née Bauman."
Nice. Means *exact,* not *agreeable* or *pleasant.*
Notorious. Different from *famous.*
Occur. Accidents *occur* rather than *happen,* but weddings take place.
Old adages. There are no *new adages.*
Oral; verbal. The former emphasizes use of the mouth; the latter applies to either spoken or written words.
Partly completed. Has no meaning. The words are contradictory.
Past. Not synonymous with *last.*
People. Refers to population. Do not confuse with *persons.*
Per cent. Do not say "large per cent" when you mean "large proportion."
Point out. Use when something is true or clear; is not synonymous with *assert.*
Politics. Singular.
Practically. Not synonymous with *virtually.* Different from *almost.*
Principle. Always a noun. *Principal* is generally an adjective.
Prone on the back. Impossible. The word means "lying on the face." *Supine* is "lying on the back."
Provided. Not *providing* he will go.
Public. Singular.
Put in. You *occupy, devote* or *spend* time, never *put in* time.
Quite. Means *fully* or *wholly.* Do not, for example, write "He is *quite* wealthy," but "He is *rather* wealthy."
Raised. Animals are *raised;* children are *reared.*
Render. You *render* lard or a judgment, but you *sing* a song.
Rumor. It is redundant to write *unverified rumor.*
Secure. Means *to make fast.* Don't use it for *obtain, procure* or *acquire.*
Sensation; emotion. The former is *physical;* the latter is *mental.*
Ship. Cattle are *shipped* but corpses are *sent.*
Since. Not synonymous with *because.*
So. Use in a negative comparison instead of *as.*
Someone, somebody, etc. Take singular verbs.
Suicide. Do not use as a verb.
Sustain. Injuries are not *sustained* but *received.*

To the nth. An unspecified number, not necessarily infinite or large. Do not use for *to the utmost possible extent*.

Transpire. Means *to emerge from secrecy into knowledge, to become gradually known*. Not to be used in the senses of *happen, occur*, etc.; must not be followed by an infinitive.

Treble; triple. The former means *three times;* the later means *three kinds*.

True facts. Facts never are false.

Try and. Use *try to*.

Unique. Its adverbs are *absolutely, almost, in some respects, nearly, perhaps, quite, really* and *surely*. It does not admit of comparison. There are no degrees of uniqueness. It means *alone of its kind. Different* means *out of the ordinary*.

Unknown; unidentified. The former means *not recognizable by* anyone; the latter means *not yet recognized*.

Various. Not synonymous with *different*.

Vender; vendor. The former is a *seller;* the latter is a legal term.

Want; wish. The former means *need* and *desire;* the latter means only *desire*.

We. Don't use the editorial *we*. Name the paper.

Well-known. Usually *widely known* is meant.

Whether. Do not use for *if*. Don't add *or not*.

While. Means "at the same time"; not synonymous with *although*.

Widow. Never use *widow woman*.

Yacht. Do not say *private yacht*. There are no *public* ones.

A clever warning against misuse of the language was contained in the following information feature article:

By Dennis Montgomery

Centralia, Ill. (AP)—Inflation is devaluing the language as well as the dollar.

For instance, when you want to point out a ridiculously low price you might say, "It's dirt cheap." But dirt's not so cheap anymore.

Illinois highway officials building Interstate 64 say they paid 72 cents a cubic yard for dirt fill in 1972, $1.30 last year and $1.55 this month.

Chicken feed has been another synonym for cheapness, but it has doubled in price in two years. A 100-pound sack, about as much as a chicken eats in its life, now costs $9.50. That's $7 more than the purchase price of a chicken.

Then there's the American expression: "Not worth a continental."

Inflation spawned that one when the Continental Congress issued so much unsecured currency it wasn't worth the paper it was printed on. But inflation has pushed the worth of a 1776 vintage continental in good condition to $40, compared to about $15 two years ago.

The paper it's printed on? Well, the paper you have in your hand, standard grade newsprint, costs about $11 a hundredweight. Fifteen months ago it was about $8.50.

If you're angry at something you might say: "It's not worth the powder it takes to blow it up." Gunpowder prices have shot up 22 to 40 per cent, depending on grade, since last year. A pound will cost you $2.03, or 68 cents more than a year ago.

Finally, there is a phrase the colonists brought with them: "Not worth a tinker's damn." It's hard to find a tinker anymore, but there does happen to be one here in Centralia—and he gets $8 an hour.

Now, if the tinker gave you a particularly soulful curse, say a 15-second ear-bender for hitting his thumb with a hammer, it would be worth 2.5 cents.

Journalism is literature in a hurry

—MATTHEW ARNOLD

There is no reason, despite the pressures of time and space, why the journalistic writer, especially, may not turn out as fine literary work as the purely "literary" writer.

—R. R. BARLOW, professor of journalism

A good reporter sees things of interest in an event which a mediocre reporter does not see. Why? Because his mind has been so trained that, at a glance, he sees all sides of the event, around it and through it, discovers all the various facets, each one of which may reflect a ray to which the eye of one or many of the readers of his newspaper may be focussed. I have sometimes described it as unselfish thinking, in contrast with the common manner of observation, which is inspired by and largely serves self-interest, which detects chiefly that in which the observer individually is interested. The reporter sees with the eye, thinks with the mind, of his readers and discovers that in which they will be interested, and that is news. His mind must be trained to catch and react to all angles or facets. And when that eye and mind are so trained that almost automatically they search out the latent interest in men and things, curiously enough we say that man has a nose for news.

—FRED FULLER SHEDD, editor, Philadelphia *Bulletin*.

The best men in American journalism are plain, honest, wholesome, hardworking souls, fairly alive to the world's bunk, who through experience, whether directly or indirectly gained, report the progress of civilization with accuracy and feeling and in fair proportions. The best newspapers are those which are edited by such men and owned by those who operate them, free of all entangling alliances. What the future will demand of our craft we may only surmise.

—MARLEN PEW, editor, *Editor & Publisher*

PART THREE

PERSPECTIVES

The primary purpose of a daily newspaper is admittedly not the cultivation of letters but the presentation of news, but I believe that very few of us rightly estimate the educative value of the modern newspaper, and when we talk of the education of journalists we are talking of the education of perhaps the only professors under whom enormous numbers of our modern reading public study. We must not be tempted to regard our profession solely as an industry and not as an art. To write and to write well is an art. It is true that by overstressing the technical side of education you would not deprive journalism of its literary merit.

—E. F. LAWSON, editor, *Telegraph,* London, England

STAFF MEETING

By B. F. Sylvester

Mr. Edgeworth, publisher: "Well, the Meteor has done it again. What's the matter, Hoops?"

Hoops, managing editor: "I thought the Star was pretty fair today, Chief."

Mr. Edgeworth: "Why didn't we have the interview with Mr. Doddle on his trip to California?"

Hoops: "Isn't news. Millions of people have been to California."

Mr. Edgeworth: "But he said he was glad to be home, to the garden spot of the country. That's constructive."

Hoops: "Our readers would call it boloney."

Mr. Edgeworth: "I notice the Meteor is getting ahead by just such 'boloney.' Get it out of your head that we are publishing a New York city paper. We can't high-hat people like Mr. Doddle. People want the paper that prints the news about their friends."

Hoops: "If we printed all the Doddle items there wouldn't be room for Reagan. We had some big exclusive news today—"

Mr. Edgeworth: "Of course, Hoops, you're supposed to use judgment. I don't want a small town sheet. But don't let the Meteor get ahead of us."

Hoops: "The Meteor didn't have a word about the elopement of Jerry Gold and the Evergreen club dancer."

Mr. Edgeworth: "An unsavory article, Hoops. The marriage was to have been annulled. Nobody would have been the wiser and there would have been no embarrassment. I'm sure the best people don't care for such news. Sorry it was in our paper. It will give the Meteor standing. And another thing, we had very little on Kissinger."

Hoops: "We try to keep stories short, Mr. Edgeworth."

Mr. Edgeworth: "You have to use judgment, Hoops. There is a time to keep stories short and a time to give details. Well, gentlemen, that's all. Good day."

At the Meteror office:

Mr. Hawkins, publisher: "The Star has done it again. What's the matter, Watts?"

Watts, managing editor: "I thought the Meteor was pretty fair today, Chief."

Mr. Hawkins: "What about this elopement story?"

Watts: "It wasn't constructive. We'll gain in standing among the best people because we didn't use it."

Mr. Hawkins: "The best people! We want circulation. The Star could print it. That's the way the Star gets ahead. And another thing, why this tripe about Old Man Doddle?"

Watts: "He has lots of friends."

Mr. Hawkins: "He'll ask us to give him six copies of the paper and his friends will buy the Star to get the news. We've got to be more metropolitan. And will you tell me why we have to print 800 words on Kissinger?"

Watts: "The public wants details."

Mr. Hawkins: "I see the Star was able to tell it in 200. Well, gentlemen, that's all. Good day."

Editor & Publisher

8

KEEPING UP-TO-DATE

There is nothing so short as a newspaper reader's memory. No matter how carefully someone reads a news story—and most newspaper purchasers read newspaper stories hurriedly if at all—when the next day's issue appears with news of later developments about any event, the reader has forgotten many if not most details of the first account.

As with events, so also with persons in the news, no matter how prominent they may be. Results of current-events quizzes in which college students and other supposedly well-informed persons make bad boners are amusing, but instructions for such tests usually indicate that a very low score is average. Names, like faces, may be familiar, but try to identify them! It is part of the interpretative reporter's responsibility to refresh readers' memories so that the immediate news account is more meaningful.

IDENTIFICATION

The obligation of the newspaper adequately to identify persons, groups, places and events in straight news stories is recognized in any efficient newsroom. The rule is never to presume that the reader has seen yesterday's story.

It is seldom that the name of a person is mentioned in a news story without some identification. Even the occupant of the White House is given his title, and other persons mentioned frequently in the news are identified by their news past or importance. Ordinary persons may be identified in several ways. The most common methods of identification include the following:

1. Address
2. Occupation
3. Age
4. Title
5. Nicknames
6. Race, nationality
6. War record
8. News past
9. Achievement
10. Life span
11. Reputation
12. Relationship
13. Marital status
14. Description
15. Occasion

Address. "Where do you live?" is one of the first questions asked anyone from whom information is desired. A person's address in a news story locates him/her and the reader does not have to ask, "I wonder if that is the Newton Blue who lives in the next block?" Readers are interested in news pertaining to persons residing in their own or in a familiar neighborhood, even though not personally acquainted with them.

Great care must be taken to get correct addresses. Libel suits have been brought by persons with names similar to those of others mentioned in news stories. Rare cases have been reported of two persons by the same name living at the same address. It is important to ascertain whether it is "street," "avenue," "place," "boulevard," "terrace" and so on, as there may be both a Ridge avenue and a Ridge terrace. Whether it is East, North, West or South also must be mentioned.

> Peter R. Farrel, 159 E. Trembly place, was taken to Municipal hospital today after he had accidentally cut his right foot while chopping wood.

Emmett Dedmon, when executive editor of the Chicago *Sun-Times,* modified what he called "a journalistic shibboleth of long standing" with the following memorandum:

> The Sun-Times does not wish, as a matter of policy, to cause undue hardship or to invade the personal privacy of persons who are in the news through no fault of their own.
>
> While it is usually necessary to identify persons with their home address in a city as large as Chicago, The Sun-Times will refrain from doing so when good judgment would indicate such identification unnecessary or undesirable.
>
> In general the rule is: Don't use the address if it is secondary to the main point in the story, or if the address does not add to the identification of the individual.
>
> In all instances good judgment and clarity will be the criteria.
>
> Following are a few examples of situations where an address is not necessary:
>
> —John Smith is held up in his drug store. Use the address of the drug store but not his home address.
>
> —Mary Smith is posed in a weather picture.

—Richard Rowe is a witness in a crime trial. His connection with the case is sufficient identification.

—Five girls are arrested for prostitution at 1976 N. Dearborn. The Dearborn street address is sufficient.

—John Doe, a printer, found the body, called police, gave the alarm, identified the suspect etc. As long as he is identified in some way the home address is not necessary.

—A police officer captures a bandit. His station or section is sufficient identification.

These examples are not meant to be a complete list but should give enough of an idea to explain the general rule. There are of course countless other situations which will have to be evaluated as they arise.

Occupation. "What do you do?" also is high up in the list of questions asked when data are being sought about a person. The reader wonders if H. R. Snow, 1516 Chestnut street, is the carpenter by that name who worked on his/her new garage.

> Donald C. Sorenson, 51, Edwardstown, district representative for the Common Laborers Union, Monday was sentenced to a two-year jail term and fined $1,500 for income tax evasion.

The occupation of a person mentioned in the news may be the feature, as

> A butcher today used his knowledge of animal anatomy to save the life of his hunting dog, Romeo, accidentally caught in a bear trap.

Sometimes the feature is in the fact that a person in a particular position has done a certain thing, whereas the same thing done by another would not be so newsworthy.

> An assistant postmaster general charged here today that Sen. Edwin F. Dietz has been talking out of both sides of his mouth in criticizing the Post Office department.

Age. It is customary to give the age of a person who is involved in a lawsuit or who is the victim of an accident. Otherwise, unless age has importance in the story, it may be omitted. Many persons do not like to have their ages known but readers are eager to find out how old popular heroes and heroines are.

> William Murphy, 16-year-old Greenwich high school junior, today identified John Pratt, 21-year-old bootblack, as the armed bandit who robbed him of his clothing and $15 in cash Sunday night on W. Totze avenue.

Age frequently is the feature, as

> An 18-year-old girl will marry a 73-year-old man on Saturday because "our common religious beliefs are of far more importance than the disparity in our ages."

Title. When a person has a title by which s/he is known, the news writer should use it. A short title is better placed before a name; a long title should be placed after a name, as

> City Clerk George Johannsen will deliver the commencement address at 10 a.m. tomorrow at Craven Junior High School.

> James R. Wesley, commissioner of public works, will represent the city tonight at. . . .

Nicknames. Nicknames seldom are used without first names; rather, they are inserted between the first name or initials and the surname. In sports stories and in feature articles, nicknames may be used alone. Often persons prominent in the news are better known by their nicknames than by their real names, as "Ike" Eisenhower, "Bing" Crosby, "Babe" Ruth etc. When such nicknames become widely familiar, the quotation marks usually are omitted. It is a common practice with some newspapers to invent nicknames for persons mentioned in the news, frequently in crime stories. In doing so, care must be exercised so that the connotation given the nickname is not prejudicial to the proper administration of justice or otherwise socially harmful. Even so, such details are more appropriate in personality sketches than in straight news stories.

> William "Wee Willie" Swayne, pint-sized killer-bandit of the 1940s, died Wednesday evening in the Stateville prison hospital. Death was attributed to a liver infection.
>
> The baby-faced killer, who got his nickname because he was only 5 feet 3 inches tall, was serving a life sentence for the slaying in 1947 of Hilltown's police chief.

Race, nationality. Deciding when to pass copy containing "Negro," "Puerto Rican," "Polish-born," "of German descent," and similar identifications has caused many an editor many a headache. Members of racial and nationality minority groups understandably object to persistent use of such identifications in crime stories, especially in headlines: "Negro Rapist Sought," "Italian Gangster Shot." When someone is in the limelight—a politician, athlete or entertainer—fans are eager to learn every picayunish fact regarding the celebrity including ancestry; certainly no injustice is intended when such details are given. For some people, as musicians and artists, a foreign background may be considered an asset.

It is only since World War II that a majority of newspapers have capitalized *Negro*. For a period in the '60s most Negro leaders preferred to be called "colored," to emphasize the idea that differences are only skin-deep. Most recently militant Negroes have promoted the slogan "black is beautiful" to stress pride in color; they resent being called anything but black. A minority of others, however, prefer *Afro-American*.

During the past few decades there has been a great increase in the mainland population of former residents of Puerto Rico, Mexico and other Spanish-speaking areas. Although victims of economic and social discrimination, in many respects they enjoy advantages never provided earlier immigrants from Poland, Italy, Greece and other European nations. There are bilingual schools in many cities, Spanish columns in newspapers, Spanish programs on radio and television. Because of their desire to retain their identity it is not surprising that newspapers use the identifications, Hispanic, Latino, Puerto Rican and Chicano.

> Alfred M. Bowler yesterday became the first black to be elected to public office in Calhoun county since Reconstruction Days.

War record. Under pressure from veterans' organizations, most newspapers have ceased identifying veterans as such in crime stories. Often, however, veteran status is a legitimate, even necessary identification. It may, in fact, be the feature.

> Thomas Thomas, a former paratrooper, just couldn't get his training out of his head. He was sleeping in the apartment of a friend when he awoke and jumped out of a third floor window. He landed on a roof a few feet below the window sill. He was not hurt, and he explained that he had dreamed he was back in the army and had been given an order to jump.

News past. After having once appeared in the news in connection with an important event, a person continues to be potentially more newsworthy than others. Should s/he become "copy" again, his/her former exploits are a means of identification.

> Miss Jane Boynton, 22, winner of a "most beautiful baby" contest 20 years ago, today filed suit against Dr. N. O. Holten, for $15,000, charging that his plastic surgery "disfigured her for life."

> Leon L. Desmond, star witness in the Fox-Delaney murder case four years ago, today was appointed chief deputy inspector of Raymond county by Sheriff L. L. Tyler.

Achievement. The achievement of one's early life may be his/her identification in later life or after death, as

> Dr. Hal Foster, first Kansas City physician and surgeon to specialize in the treatment of eye, ear, nose and throat, died at 6 o'clock this morning at his home at the Brookside hotel, Fifty-fourth street and Brookside boulevard. He was 88 years old.

Life span. Sometimes it is pertinent to identify a person in relation to the historical events or changes that have occurred during his/her lifetime, especially as they relate to the news at hand.

Harry Thom, who joined the internal revenue staff 58 years ago, when relatively few persons paid income taxes, and stayed long enough to see virtually everyone pay, will retire Saturday.

Mrs. Eliza Addis, who was born in Philadelphia when City Council met in Independence Hall and City Hall was just a blueprint, is celebrating her 100th birthday today. [Philadelphia *Bulletin*]

Reputation. When identifying a person by means of reputation, it is necessary to be careful that the reputation is deserved. It is possible for a newspaper to make or break a person by referring to him/her constantly as the foremost authority on a certain subject, or as a mere pretender or charlatan.

James (Jimmy) Eder, reputedly the wealthiest and most successful jockey in the history of the Latin American turf, yesterday was named defendant in a suit for divorce or separate maintenance filed in Superior court by Mrs. Ruth Eder.

Relationship. A person's news importance may depend upon the prominence of a relative or friend. How much the families of persons important in public life or in the news of the day should be written up and photographed is another problem for debate by a class in newspaper ethics. Relationship may be used as identification even when the members of the family referred to are not of particular importance. Minors often are identified by parentage.

Legitimate use of relationship in identification is illustrated in the following examples:

Maj. James R. Garfield, II, training officer of the 107th Armored Cavalry Regiment, Ohio National Guard, and great-grandson of James Abram Garfield, 20th President of the United States, is taking summer training at Fort Know.
[Louisville *Courier-Journal*]

Robert Campbell MacCombie Auld, 80, a descendant of Robert Burns and an authority on the Scottish poet's life and Scottish history, died yesterday after a five weeks' illness.

A different kind of identification by relationship is illustrated by the following example:

A 30-year-old father of five was stabbed to death Saturday night in a dispute on the street near his home in the Porterfield section of Avon. The victim was identified as . . . .

Marital status. Many newspapers have accepted the feminists' viewpoint that it is unequal treatment to distinguish between single and married women without doing the same for men. The title Ms. is in widespread use, as is the practice of using only last names after a first mention in accordance with how s/he wants to be known. Alternatives would be Miss for an unmarried woman, Mrs. for one using her husband's name and Ms. for those who retain their birth names after marriage. There is some support for M. for single men and Mr. for married.

Description. Sometimes the writer brightens up an identification by a bit of personal description, without which it would often be impossible to obtain a true impression of the story's importance. In the following example, note the use of descriptive identification throughout:

> Their shoes didn't squeak. They didn't talk out of the sides of their mouths. They showed no inclination to clip anyone on the jaw.
>
> Yet the dozen plain-looking fellows who gathered at the Hotel Sherman last night were honest-to-goodness private detectives. They were holding their first postwar meeting of International Investigators, Inc.
>
> Head man is Ray Schindler, world-famed New York detective. Other members include Leonarde Keeler, inventor of the lie detector, Dr. Le Moyne Snyder of Lansing, medical-legal director of the Michigan State Police, and Clark Sellers, Los Angeles handwriting expert and document ace who worked on the Lindbergh kidnaping case.
>
> Most of the men, unlike such movie detectives as Alan Ladd, Humphrey Bogart and Dick Powell, are in the 50s and 60s and are quite calm about their work.
>
> But one, at least, was not without a kind word for their movie counterparts. Said Harry Lewis of Sioux City, Iowa: "Those boys talk pretty tough and seem to run into an awful lot of trouble. But they get their job done and that's what counts."
>
> [Chicago *Sun*]

Occasion. A person's part in a news story must be explained no matter how else he is identified.

> Prince Otto of Norway, who is on a two-month study tour of the United States, will visit Chicago Oct. 12–13.

> A mother, burned in a school bus-gasoline trailer crash which killed 31 persons Aug. 14, 1977, won a $30,000 out-of-court settlement Monday.

Picking the Identification

The proper method by which to identify a person must be decided in every case. The appropriate identification should be sought in the case of a person with a number of achievements or a considerable news past, as

> Harold Bank, president of the senior class, today announced committees for class day.
>
> Harold "Bud" Bank, football captain, will not be a candidate for the basketball team this winter.

The Associated Press Managing Editors once debated the propriety of identifying former New York Governor Thomas E. Dewey as "a two-time failure as a Republican presidential candidate" years after his candidacies and in stories that did not deal with national politics. The consensus was that in many instances recalling that part of Dewey's "news past" was poor journalism. The same arguments applied to Adlai Stevenson II.

Often the occasion calls for special identifications for prominent persons, identifications that would be inappropriate at most other times.

> Cleveland, July 25—(AP)—Federal Judge Paul Jones, once a football player himself, will hear injunction suits against Bobby Freeman and Jack Locklear, who jumped contracts with a Canadian pro team to join the Cleveland Browns. [Baltimore *Sun*]

Double Identification

Sometimes, especially in obituary stories, more than one identification may be crowded into the lead, as

> William Jay Schieffelin, retired chairman of the board of Schieffelin & Co., wholesale drug concern, and a crusader for government reform, education for Negroes and many other humanitarian causes, died Friday night at his home, 620 Park Avenue, after a long illness. He was 89 years old on April 14.
> [New York *Times*]

Synonyms

It is impossible, however, to use more than two or three identifications without making the lead awkward. One way out of this difficulty is to use the points of identification as synonyms for the person's name after the name itself has been used once. In this way, nicknames, reputation, news past, various titles and so on can be brought in and repetition of the name or of personal pronouns avoided, as

> Former Alderman Guy L. Millard today charged that the local Fair Employment Practices commission is failing to perform its functions.
>
> Chief backer of the commission when he was a member of the City Council, Millard now believes the agency's work is being sabotaged. The 78-year-old president of the Royal Dye Works said he has personally interviewed 20 local workers who had sought the commission's help in vain.

Identification as the Feature

When the achievement, reputation, occasion or news past by which a person may be identified seems more important or better known than the person's name, the identification should precede the name, as

> Murray, Ky., July 28—(AP)—The man who wrote the official history of General Dwight Eisenhower's unified European command will deliver the commencement address at Murray State college's summer exercises next Friday.
>
> He is Dr. Forrest C. Pogue, commissioned by President Eisenhower to write a history of his World War II record, "Supreme Command."

INDEFINITE "WHO"

When the *what* of the story is more important than the *who*, the identification may be featured, names being delayed until the second paragraph, as

> A 32-year-old Congregational minister has been named director of Youth Inc., a new nondenominational religious research agency.
>
> The Rev. Ernest S. Ernst, minister of the Westchester Community Church since 1973, will take over direction of the agency in January at Boone, Iowa.

DELAYED IDENTIFICATION

Similarly, overcrowding a lead already packed with important facts can be avoided by postponing identification until the second paragraph, as

> The eloquence of Reginald Burnett held a crowd of 1,200 farm delegates and their wives spellbound for an hour and 20 minutes here.
>
> The sandy-haired president of the United Plastic Workers amused and delighted his National Farmers Union audience Tuesday night with raps at big business, Wall Street and the Department of Agriculture.

WHEN UNFAIR

Experts in the field object to use of "former mental patient" even when accurate. They contend its use is as unfair as it would have been to refer to St. Paul as "a former persecutor of Christians" or to Gandhi as "a former convict" or to Thomas Jefferson as "a former slaveholder."

To be avoided is any attempt to correlate appearance with personality or character. Fads and fashions change. From the Revolutionary War to the Civil War, all American presidents (Washington through Buchanan) were clean shaven. From the Civil War to World War I every president (Lincoln through Taft with the exception of McKinley) had a beard and/or mustache. From World War I to the present all of the presidents (Wilson through Reagan) again have been clean shaven. This should be sobering evidence when it is attempted to classify hairy hippies or others. No personality traits scale, including ones based on bodily characteristics, ever has stood the test of scientific scrutiny.

Organizations

Organizations as well as persons must be identified adequately:

BY TYPE

> Directors of the Monument Builders of America, Inc., a national association of retail monument dealers, today condemned as "a national disgrace" the unkempt condition of the Statue of Liberty.

BY PURPOSE

> Milltown's Transit Authority, set up to bring order out of the city's long existent transportation muddle, has ended a year of operation with a record of substantial accomplishments although difficulties still lie ahead.

The eight-man board held its first meeting Jan. 29, 1981, in offices at 35 Elm street, beginning operations with the backing of a $200,000 fund made up of two equal contributions from the city and state, joint sponsors of the enterprise.

As a municipal authority, it has the power, fixed by state law, to acquire and operate transportation lines in and around Milltown.

BY ACHIEVEMENT

The Alameda County Fair, which has been America's "jockey incubator" since the close of World War II, has a record crop of apprentices on hand for its 12-day race meeting opening here Friday.

BY REPUTATION

The Milltown Associates, which for 23 years was the leader in promoting city beautification, will disband Jan. 1.

In stories related to important public issues—controversial matters—brief identification of an organization usually is not enough. The interpretative reporter may have to write a parenthetical paragraph, sidebar or full-length feature to provide proper understanding of what is involved. Readers cannot judge the true nature of a group by a high-sounding title. Typical situations in which full-length identification of an organization may be necessary include the following:

1. When the name resembles closely that of another group whose outlook is different. Example: the National Council of the Churches of Christ in the United States of America and the American Council of Christian Churches.
2. When a powerful group takes a stand on a public issue or a pending piece of legislation. In such cases it may be wise to point out whether the immediate action is consistent with previous activities by the same group. It may be possible to throw light on any selfish motives by revealing the business or other connections of the group's leadership or the general nature of its membership.
3. When a new group is organized, especially when its aims are expressed in semantically vague terms or it seems interested in only a single measure or matter of public interest. In such cases it may be a "front" organization for some other older interest group. Identification of the leadership may cast more light on the organization's real purposes than a quotation from its charter or constitution.
4. When an organization is involved in an act of force or violence. In such cases it may be necessary to seek reasons for the group's very existence in the social, economic or political conditions that brought it into being. Care must be taken not to place the blame for any disturbance on the victims of it rather than on its perpetrators, regardless of the prestige factor involved.

Places

Places must be identified when they are not widely known or when significant or the feature of the story, as

> Purchase of the 1600 block on Palmer road for a new junior high school was announced today by the Board of Education. Twenty-three private dwellings, almost all of them condemned by the Department of Health, now occupy the site.

A place's news past or its proximity to another place previously in the news may be the best identification; often it is the feature:

> Within a few feet of the spot where once grew the elm under which George Washington accepted command of the Continental Army, 25 Boston University students yesterday organized the Army of American Liberation. Its purpose is to "wage incessant warfare against forces which are destroying American democracy."

Places, as individuals, have reputations that may be used to identify them, as

> Sauk City, Minn., the "Gopher Prairie" of native son Sinclair Lewis' "Main Street" . . .
>
> Reno, Nev., divorce capital of the United States . . .
>
> Tarrytown, near which Rip Van Winkle allegedly took his long nap . . .

Events

Events may be identified and explained

1. By their significance (the occasion).
2. By their importance in relation to other events (comprehensive leads and stories).
3. By relating them to the "atmosphere" in the light of which they must be understood (the situation).
4. By their probable consequence (prediction).
5. By definite reference to preceding events to which they are related (tiebacks).
6. By the coincidence between them and other events.

Occasions

Circumstances of a news event—purpose, importance, significance and so forth—must be made clear, as

> The most crippling airline strike in the nation's history entered its 16th day Saturday and continued to strand travelers, disrupt tours and snag air freight service.
>
> [Lincoln (Neb.) *Journal*]

Often the feature of the story may be found in the purpose or importance of the occasion that is the subject of the story, as

> Fort Washakie, Wyo.—(UP)—An age-old tradition was broken here when an Indian woman with white blood in her veins became a "chief" of the Arapahoe tribe.

The comparison between the immediate event and preceding similar events may be pointed out, either in the lead paragraph or shortly thereafter, as

> For the first time in memory, neither political party has a contest for any office in Crow county in the April 8 primary election.

COMPREHENSIVE LEADS AND STORIES

The comprehensive lead is correlative and explanatory. Used in straight news writing, it is not opinionated, however, because it deals with the incontrovertible.

One kind of comprehensive lead attempts to interpret the immediate news in the light of previous events, as

> Six more witnesses Friday were called before the federal grand jury investigating the distribution of juke boxes in Farwell township.

> Further evidence that the voters of this city really elected a "reform" administration last month was provided by today's order by Mayor L. O. Oliver closing all amusement places in violation of municipal health ordinances.

A comprehensive lead emphasizes situations. When several stories related to the same general news event are received, they may be combined into one story and a general roundup or comprehensive lead be written. This type of lead is suitable particularly for election stories, stories of wrecks and other disasters, accidents, weather stories, etc. Facts on which a comprehensive lead and story of this sort are written usually are gathered by more than one reporter or correspondent.

Atmosphere

In these days of fast communication, new ideas, movements, slang expressions and almost anything else that comes to mind, spread rapidly.

> Evidently encouraged by the success of similar organizations in scores of other nearby cities, more than 200 owners have organized to prevent spraying of elm trees.

PREDICTIONS

The significance of an event may be explained by pointing out the probable consequences or likely "next steps."

The City Council's Big 10 crime commission starts five days of public hearings Wednesday—probably the last hearings the committee will hold.

Drastic revision of the curriculum of Serena Junior High School will result if the Board of Education approves the unanimous recommendation of its Educational Policies committee.

Among the changes which Mrs. Rose Blakely's committee says should be made are the following . . . .

THE TIE-BACK

The tie-back is the part of the lead of a story that shows the relation between the immediate news and some previous news event. In the following examples, the tie-backs are in italics:

Miss Colista Connor, 10, reputed heiress to a $500,000 fortune, *who disappeared mysteriously a week ago and returned Wednesday night to explain she was "on vacation,"* was gone again yesterday.

Five hundred and fifty-two *additional* influenza cases were quarantined in Will county today, *a slight increase over yesterday's figures,* while six deaths were recorded from flu and 14 *more* from pneumonia.

The tie-back to a previous story may be made by emphasizing coincidence. In many cases, the immediate incident may be newsworthy primarily or solely because of the coincidence, and the prior event may have received no publicity.

A second tragedy within two months today deepened the sorrow of Mrs. Mary McKinley, 26.

On June 1, her husband, Thomas, 35, a tuckpointer, was killed in a 12-foot fall. Yesterday her son, Robert, 4, was crushed to death by a truck.

Words

Parenthetical sentences or paragraphs sometimes are necessary to define or explain the context in which unusual words or expressions appear. Rep. Clarence Brown of Ohio, for instance, sent reporters to the thesaurus when he accused the president of "ingannation." At that time, the Louisville *Courier-Journal* interjected the following in a United Press account:

(The word is not in *Webster's New International Dictionary*. The United Press said it meant to confuse or bewilder, and the Associated Press reported solemnly "on consulting a thesaurus, reporters found the word ingannation listed as a synonym for deception.")

When President Truman accused a senator of raising many "Macedonian cries or yells," the Chicago Daily News used the following italized parenthetical paragraph:

(A Macedonian cry is a cry for help, so called from Acts XVI, 9, "Come over into Macedonia and help us.")

When the President told the nation that it could achieve a production goal of $500 billion a year within ten years, the same newspaper explained as follows:

(Five hundred billion dollars is half a trillion. A trillion is a 1 with 12 zeroes behind it.)

Sometimes it is a legal term that needs explaining or a diplomatic proceeding, as the following which was once used when the United Nations received a plea for the application of sanctions:

(Sanctions are positive measures that may be taken against aggressor governments under the U.N. charter, such as cutting off trade, communications, etc.)

THE FOLLOW-UP

Much of the news in any edition of a newspaper is related in some way to other news. It usually takes more than a single article to tell any story. After the first account has appeared, there usually are new developments.

Ability to sense phases of a news story which must be investigated further (followed up) is a valuable asset to a reporter or editor. Newspapers are read carefully for stories that in their original form are incomplete or should be watched for further development.

The Second-Day Story

The second-day story of any event may include (1) new information not available when the first story was written, (2) causes and motives not included in the first story, (3) more recent developments, results and consequences since the first story and (4) opinions regarding the event.

Latest developments always are emphasized in follow-up stories, and the use of a tie-back is a rigid rule. Never should the writer of a news story presume that a reader has seen the previous story or stories. Just as each installment of a serial story is prefaced by a brief summary of what has gone before, so each news story related to a single event has a short reference to previous news stories.

The tie-back usually is inserted in the lead in the form of a phrase or dependent clause, but any grammatical device may be used; sometimes the tieback is delayed until the second paragraph.

New Information

A 44-year-old Ardmore woman who was found unconscious on Coulter street near Sibley avenue, a block from her home, was in serious condition at Bryn Mawr hospital today while police searched for an unidentified man believed to have attacked her without motive. [Philadelphia *Daily News*]

CAUSE—MOTIVE

Four firemen who perished in a flaming back-draft that surged through the Backstage night club early Tuesday morning died while fighting a fire which was deliberately, criminally set.

That flat charge came yesterday from Fire Marshal Frank Kelly, chief of the San Francisco fire prevention and investigation bureau.

"The fire was not accidental," Chief Kelly declared following more than 24 hours of investigation. . . . [San Francisco *Chronicle*]

NEW DEVELOPMENT

By Frank Ryan

UNITED PRESS INTERNATIONAL

Rep. James Lewis (R-West Bend)—convicted of lying to a grand jury about a bizarre laser gun scheme—was sentenced to six months in prison Wednesday.

U.S. Judge James E. Doyle said Lewis—who also will surrender his seat in the Legislature—had to go to prison "to send the words to others" the penalty for lying under oath will be severe.

OPINION

Angry parents today charged the "L" system with neglect in the crossing death of an 8-year-old boy.

A system whereby one man controls two crossings at Flournoy and Lexington at Long endangers the lives of children in three schools, the parents declared.

Donald Kieft, 5227 Lexington, was crushed to death Monday when he attempted to cross the tracks at Flournoy on a bicycle.

The crossings are protected by gates. So many trains traveling at a high rate of speed pass the intersections in the residential district that the lone gateman keeps the gates lowered even when trains are not approaching. . . .

Metropolitan morning newspapers frequently use the follow-up technique on stories that broke for the afternoon papers the day before; afternoon papers do the same for stories the first news of which appeared in the morning papers.

Featurizing the Follow-up

An important news story breaks too fast to permit investigation of its feature possibilities. By a later edition or the next day, however, the features are developed either in a rewritten story, or in supplementary stories (sidebars). If the reporter finds himself/herself stuck with new facts, s/he may simply retell the story in feature style:

Laramie Boomerang

A freak accident was investigated early this morning when an automobile belonging to Ralph Conwell, 803 Flint, crashed into a parked pickup belonging to C. H. Melvin, 657 North Eighth, and then crashed into the front of the Melvin home.

Police said apparently the Conwells were starting on a trip and after taking the car out of his garage, Mr. Conwell got out of the car to check if the garage was locked and the lights were out inside.

The car started creeping forward headed west on Flint. Mrs. Conwell, who was in the car and had on a safety belt, attempted to halt the car by applying the foot brake and inadvertently applied pressure to the accelerator.

The car surged forward hitting the curb and climbing it at the corner of Flint and Eighth and then headed north, striking glancingly on the outside of the Melvin pickup, also headed north, which was parked next to the curb, knocking the pickup upon the curb.

The Conwell car continued and jumped the curb to the right and came to a stop after uprooting a large lilac bush and smashing into the front of the Melvin home.

The impact of the car was just beneath the window of the bedroom where Mr. and Mrs. Melvin were sleeping. Although the wall was driven in about ten inches from the impact, the window pane remained intact.

Police said there were no injuries reported to them.

Laramie Bulletin

It was 4 A.M. Tuesday.

Mr. and Mrs. Ralph Conwell were parked in front of their home ready to leave for a vacation at their ranch near Daniel, Wyo.

Conwell started the car. Mrs. Conwell was secure in a new safety belt next to the driver's seat.

Conwell remembered he left the garage door open and left the car to close it.

The car began rolling.

Mrs. Colwell struggled to get out of her "secure" position, gave up the idea and reached for the steering wheel and the brake.

She got the wheel, but hit the accelerator with her foot.

Around the corner she went, her husband running after her, the horn honking.

The car struck a parked ton truck, threw it 40 feet, jumped the curb, hit a 25-year-old lilac bush, threw it several feet, and smashed into the bedroom of Conwell's next door neighbors—Mr. and Mrs. C. H. Melvin.

Said Mrs. Conwell:

"It was the safety belt that saved me. You can never tell when an accident is going to happen."

Said Mrs. Melvin: "I thought it was a drunken driver."

Said Mr. Melvin: "My mother-in-law planted that bush here 25 years ago. I never thought it'd save our lives."

Mr. Conwell wasn't available for comment—he went back to the ranch, leaving his wife behind.

Second-Day Comment

Whenever the president delivers an important message, the Supreme Court hands down a significant decision, a new scientific discovery is announced or any one of a number of unusual events occurs, newspapers and press associations scour the country to obtain opinions from persons qualified to comment cogently. In such stories exaggeration must be avoided, as in the following piece in which generalizations were limited to the principals who are mentioned specifically.

By Brian Sullivan
AP SCIENCE WRITER

Linus Pauling's claims for Vitamin C as a powerful weapon against the common cold have resulted in a spurt of sales at many of the nation's drugstores. But in the scientific community, with a notable exception, the response has been more subdued.

At Herzog's Drugstore in Buffalo, N.Y., pharmacist Howard Carpenter said sales had at least quadrupled. He said the store has put bottles of Vitamin C into a basket adorned with Pauling's picture.

Many scientists remain generally skeptical, however. Some refused to be drawn into the matter at all, and others were cautious: A Baylor University Medical School virus-cold researcher said Pauling's ideas are based on an uncontrolled experiment.

Another warned against continued, mass dosage without investigating it first.

The exception is Dr. Albert Szent-Gyorgyi of the Marine Biological Laboratory at Falmouth, Mass., who won the 1937 Nobel Prize in medicine for isolating Vitamin C in 1928.

Localization

A news item originating in a faraway place may have a local "angle," or it may cause readers to ask, "Could it happen here?"

Local parents need have no fear that babies in local hospitals will become confused and cause another Pittman-Garner baby mix-up a generation or so hence.

So thorough is the identification system employed in this community's three hospitals that their authorities consider mix-ups like Madeline Louise Garner-Pittman's in Georgia last month an impossibility.

Although many hospitals throughout the country supplement foot and palm printing as an added precaution, adequate supervision is the only real safeguard, in the opinion of H. James Baxter, superintendent of General Hospital since 1980. . . .

Reminiscences

Similarly, readers may ask, "Has anything like that ever happened before?" Old-timers draw parallels between the present and the past and relate anecdotes brought to mind by the immediate news item.

By Zay N. Smith

If there is a hall of infamy for murderers, John Wayne Gacy, killer of 33 men and boys, has found his place: No one in U.S. history has been convicted in as many deaths.

But others have tried for the distinction—and may have killed more.

One was Herman Webster Mudgett. He came to live at 63rd and Wallace in Chicago in 1883. Police searched his three-story home 10 years later and found torture chambers, vats of acid and a pit of lime.

Mudgett would woo women, gain their property and then take them on a house tour. He confessed to the murders of 47. He was suspected in the disappearance of as many as 200—all visitors to the Chicago World's Fair of 1893.

Mudgett was known as a pleasant enough neighbor. He took 15 minutes to die on the gallows.

Johann Adolph Hoch, another Chicagoan, was less forthright. He lived as bigamist at the turn of the century. He was accused in the deaths of as many as 50 wives. He told police he had married "too many unhealthy women."

The list grows crowded after that:

- Bella Sorenson Gunness was the most efficient murderess in U.S. history. She lived on an Indiana farm in the early 1900s. She butchered hogs—and boyfriends. She would drug their coffee, bash in their heads, dissect them and bury them in the barnyard. The number came to at least 16—possibly as many as 28.
- Elmer Wayne Henley Jr. and David Brooks made money on the side by procuring boys for Dean Corll of Houston. Each of the boys was worth $200. At least 27 were molested, mutilated and murdered. Henley shot Corll dead at an acrylic-sniffing party. Henley and Brooks were convicted in the murders.
- Juan Corona was convicted in the murders of 25 migrant laborers. All were mutilated with a machete and buried in California orchards or along a riverbed. Corona's conviction was overturned because of incompetence of counsel and he awaits a new trial.
- Herbert Mullin was voted most likely to succeed by his 1965 high school class. He learned about LSD in San Francisco after that and succeeded in killing three women, four men and six boys in northern California in 1973. He said he was trying to prevent an earthquake.

Howard Unruh walked out on a Camden, N.J., street one day in 1949 and shot 13 people dead.

Charles Whitman climbed a tower at the University of Texas in 1966 and killed 16 with a high-powered rifle. That was the same year Richard Speck stabbed eight student nurses to death on Chicago's Southeast Side. Then came Charles Manson and his California murder cult. Then came "Son of Sam"—David Berkowitz—who murdered six in New York City.

And then came Gacy. [Chicago *Sun-Times*]

The Running Story

Newspapers continue to follow up stories as long as there are new angles or developments to investigate or until reader interest lags. Each succeeding story is written to bring the situation up to date.

In case of a flood, war, important court trial or political contest (to mention only a few of the possibilities), daily, almost hourly, stories are written to give the latest developments. A murder story frequently occupies the front page for weeks.

Note how the following story developed day by day, as shown by three successive leads from the Kansas City *Star:*

> About 124,000 women here today are being given the opportunity to state whether they desire to serve as jurors. The ballots should be returned to the Jackson County courthouse by June 10.

Eighty-six ballots on jury service for women had been received this afternoon at the jury commission office in the Jackson County courthouse. Twenty-nine indicated a desire to serve on juries here. Fifty-seven declined to serve.

The number of women desiring jury service was increasing this afternoon when 314 of the 1,440 ballots received by the jury commission indicated that more than one in four women responding to the poll were willing to be jurors. The remaining 1,136 do not desire to serve on Jackson County juries other than federal.

The Revived Story

Days, weeks or months later a reporter may be assigned to find out "what every happened to so-and-so" or regarding "such-and-such."

By B. J. McFarland

PORTLAND, ORE. (UPI)—

What happened to D. B. Cooper, history's first and only successful parachuting sky bandit?

Where is he and where did he stash the cash?

Three years ago on Thanksgiving Eve Cooper boarded a Northwest Orient Airlines flight in Portland for a short hop to Seattle.

The plane wasn't off the ground five minutes when it all started.

Cooper, threatening to set off an explosive, demanded and got $200,000 in $20 bills delivered, along with three parachutes, to the plane in Seattle.

After allowing the passengers to get off, he ordered the crew to fly the 727 to Reno, following a course down western Washington and Oregon before cutting across the mountains. Somewhere en route he bailed out the tail exit.

NO TRACE OF COOPER OR THE MONEY EVER WAS FOUND

It set off a chain of similar skyjackings that changed the face of air travel.

But only Cooper beat the law at taking the money and jumping. The law still is looking for him.

"The case is an active one, not only here but throughout the United States," said Julius Mattson, agent in charge of the Portland FBI office.

"We're still getting leads," he said, "but not quite as heavy as we were. The case still is in the public mind and when the public thinks of it, it also thinks of us.

"There really has been no substantive development. The work now is mostly eliminating possibilities, proving or disproving tips.

"Not one of the $20 bills has turned up."

Cooper apparently strapped the money to his body for the jump. A theory that he may have fallen into Lake Merwin east of Woodland in southwest Washington about 30 miles north of Portland could not be proved following an exhaustive search by the FBI and Army troops from Ft. Lewis, Wash. [Pittsburgh *Press*]

Some newspapers, notably the New York *Times* and the Chicago *Sun-Times,* have a weekly follow-up feature column to bring readers up to date on stories that were once in the news and have disappeared from the headlines. Typical items from one *Times*' column were the following:

PILOT ON THE SPOT

In some other circumstance, James D. Schwartz might have been complimented as a gallant warrior who refused to accept defeat. After undergoing open-heart surgery in 1975, he applied in 1977 to resume his old job. The Federal Aviation Administraton balked. Mr. Schwartz wanted to fly again as an airline captain.

The National Transportation Safety Board, noting contradictory testimony by two cardiologists, overruled the F.A.A. in October 1979.

Mr. Schwartz is flying again as a pilot in command for Frontier Airlines. He is in the final phase of checking out in a Boeing 737 twin jet, and Capt. Richard Orr, the airline's vice president of flight operations, rates his performance as "average or above average."

Commenting on the 51-year-old flier's health, Captain Orr says: "He is probably less of a risk than many other airline pilots flying, because I think the medical people know more about Captain Schwartz and his condition than they do about most other people."

VANISHING CHURCH

Harry Joe Brown Jr., the theatrical producer, bought a surplus Roman-Catholic church on Manhattan's 13th Street in 1969, intending to convert it to an Off Broadway theater. The plans went awry. The church, which had cost Mr. Brown $155,000, just stood there, empty. When he returned from a trip to Europe in 1972, the church was gone.

"I thought I was hallucinating," he said. "The church—my church—had vanished." Then he found out why: New York had torn it down as a public nuisance. Mr. Brown sued the city.

Nine days ago the verdict came down in State Supreme Court. The city must pay $280,000 in damages, with 6 percent interest for eight years. A total of $108,000 will go to the Archdiocese of New York to pay off the existing mortgage; Mr. Brown gets the rest.

The city inherits the land, valued in 1972 at $26,500. Mr. Brown abandoned it rather than pay taxes on a vacant lot for eight years.

Investigations

Often follow-up assignments are for policy purposes, but the disclosures from the resultant investigations may be definitely in the public interest. Newspapers frequently keep after someone, particularly a public official, to correct an evil brought to light by some news event.

By William Clements

Last year a team of Sun-Times reporters and photographers took an in-depth look at nearly 100 of the city's neighborhood parks.

They found the parks beaten up, abused, misused, neglected and rejected. Scores of once-proud parks and playgrounds were engulfed in litter and broken equipment, beset by rowdies, rife with graffiti and riddled with fear.

Today, over-all conditions haven't changed much.

This despite the addition of sorely needed maintenance crews and recreation workers to the hardest hit and most neglected of the parks.

Sun-Times photographers returned recently to find out what improvements the

Chicago Park District has made at several sites spotlighted in last year's series. They found that:

• The arching, once beautiful boathouse at Humboldt Park is still marred with graffiti, broken sidewalks and battered benches. The park's meandering lagoon is cluttered with cans, broken bottles and discarded fence railings. The walkway behind its famous garden is still broken and messy.

• The basin of Garfield Park's unique lily pond, once a quiet haven for West Siders seeking an interlude from some of the harsher realities of city life, remains pockmarked, crushed and unusable. The boathouse roof, an architectural treasure, is a wreck.

• Outdoor washroom facilities, such as those in Garfield and Douglas parks, remain boarded up and broken, posing major security problems for park users.

• Many benches in nearly all of the large inland parks, including Columbus, Washington, Douglas, Ogden and Garfield, are broken and unusable.

The Park District says that as the summer progresses, needed repairs will be made. The fact remains, however, that not much has changed during the past year in the 7,289-acre system which employs 4,300 and spends more than $160 million annually.

[Chicago *Sun-Times*]

The Resurrected Story

Sometimes a mystery is years in the solving, or a new fact is discovered which casts new light on some historical event or personage. In writing such a story the "tie-back" rule must be observed, although the lead seldom is adequate to supply all of the "resurrected" facts that must be told. For instance, if a criminal who has long evaded capture is arrested, the story may include a recapitulation of his crime and may even be accompanied by pictures and diagrams taken or made at the time of its commission. Later, when the person is brought to trial, the story may be repeated, and again if the criminal is put to death legally.

In every news office there are notations of stories which are said to be "hanging fire," and which may break at any time. Verdicts are withheld, a committee delays its report, there is a postponement in the filing of a suit, or an important person does not make an announcement of which he has hinted.

North Manchester, July 4.—Midnight lights burned by a Dr. Elies Ohmart prior to 1885 were explained here when Tom Richardson came across an ancient, handwritten record book in the attic of the John W. Ulrey home which he recently purchased.

The book contained notes of scientific inventions including a telephone patented by Bell in 1876, an electric arc lamp, the separation of aluminum from clay, a mechanical table of logarithms and an electric sign board.

[Fort Wayne (Ind.) *News-Sentinel*]

REWRITE

The day of the major newspaper scoop is gone. In the first place, except in a small and dwindling number of large cities, there is no competitor for the one surviving daily newspaper to scoop. Furthermore, the important day-by-day news of the world is gathered mostly by two press associations (Associated Press and United Press International) and transmitted simultaneously to all subscribers. Most important, radio and television have made it impossible for any periodical to be first with such news.

Newspapers and magazines amplify, explain and interpret the news sometimes shortly after its occurrence, but, often, weeks, months or years later when new information becomes available or the passage of time gives new perspective. Newspapers today often are competitors of magazines in the attempt to obtain first rights to the memoirs of persons able to cast new light on old events.

The Nature of Rewrite

Within newspaper offices the title rewriter now is used to designate a person who remains in the office taking news over the telephone, mostly from the paper's own reporters. There persists, however, a considerable amount of rewriting in the old sense; "borrowed," with little or no attempt to obtain additional facts, from other printed sources.

Such sources include press releases, community newspapers, trade journals, house organs, public and private reports and announcements, newsletters intended for special interest groups and out-of-town newspapers (exchanges). Some papers run a column of news briefs or oddities from the exchanges or the day's wire report. Stories in the earlier editions of one's own newspaper may be rewritten for later editions, when new facts are obtained or for reasons of space, clarity, etc.

Usually, the rewrite person attempts to compose an item that will read as though it had been written up on original information. In the attempt to play up a new fresh angle the writer must avoid killing a good lead and burying an undoubted feature. Awareness of the extent to which radio and television have taken the edge off some of the news may lead to this error unless there is conscious effort to avoid it.

Picking the Feature

The rewrite person must obey the rules of good news writing which, among other things, means that the lead of his/her story must play up the feature of the item. The difficulty is obvious when it is realized that this feature probably already was played up in the original story. The poorer the first story, the easier the task of the rewrite person who must do more than merely restate or reword the original lead.

The rewrite person, with no facts in addition to those of the original story, therefore, asks him/herself several questions, including these:

1. Did the writer play up the real feature of the story or is it buried some place in the article?
2. Is there another feature of equal or almost equal importance as the one which the writer used that might be played up?
3. Can I make my story read like a follow-up story by emphasizing the latest developments mentioned in the first story, or by suggesting the next probable consequence?
4. Can I write a comprehensive lead that will interpret this item of news in the light of other news?
5. Is there any other news today with which I can combine this story?
6. In the case of stories appearing in publications outside of the immediate community, is there a local angle that can be played up?

Buried Feature

If the writer of the original story has missed the feature, the task of the rewrite person is simple, as

Original Story

The question of submitting to the voters of Milltown at a special election Mayor A. L. Hunter's proposal to issue $400,000 worth of street improvement bonds again was the major "bone of contention" at last night's City Council meeting.

Ald. Joel Oldberg, 15th ward, presented a list of streets which he said are badly in need of repair and urged the holding of the special election. Opposing him was Ald. Arthur West, 21st ward, who said the city already has too large a bonded indebtedness.

After three hours of debate the Council voted 21 to 17 in favor of Alderman Oldberg's motion to call a special election Sept. 14.

Rewritten Story

Milltown voters will decide Sept. 14 at a special election whether the city's bonded indebtedness shall be increased $400,000 to finance Mayor A. L. Hunter's street improvement program.

Decision to submit the matter to voters was made by the City Council last night after three hours' debate. The vote was 21 to 17.

The motion was passed over the opposition of Ald. Arthur West, 21st ward, who argued that the city already is heavily indebted. Maker and chief supporter of the motion was Ald. Joel Oldberg, 15th ward, who presented a list of streets which he says need repairs.

Secondary Feature

Note in the following example how the writer found a second feature equally as important as the one played up on the original story.

Original Story

Loss of between $75,000 and $100,000 resulted from a fire which raged for three hours early today in the Central Chemical company plant at Calumet City. The

Rewritten Story

Firemen of Hammond and Calumet City braved the dangers of huge stores of highly inflammable nitric acid yesterday to battle a fire which destroyed the Central

Original Story

plant, which manufactured nitric acid, was a subsidiary of Wilson & Co., packing firm.

Spontaneous combustion is believed to have been the cause of the fire which was noticed about 2:30 A.M. by two workmen, only occupants of the building of the time. In the attempt to save acid valued at about $50,000 in storage tanks, the two men, Abel Puffer and Jared Bean, shut off safety valves to the tanks.

Exact loss cannot be determined until the tanks are opened today and tests made as to whether water reached their contents. Because nitric acid is highly inflammable, Hammond and Calumet City firemen were in constant danger as they fought the fire.

Rewritten Story

Chemical company plant at Calumet City. The loss was estimated at $75,000 to $100,000.

The plant, a subsidiary of the packing firm of Wilson & Co., is devoted entirely to the manufacture of the acid. Quantities of acid valued at $50,000 were in storage tanks.

The blaze raged for three hours. The acid tanks will be opened today to determine whether water seeped into them and spoiled the stores.

Two workmen, the only persons in the plant, shut off safety valves to the tanks when the fire began, apparently from spontaneous combustion.

FOLLOW-UP FEATURE

In rewriting the following story, the writer certainly was safe in assuming the next probable consequence. Note how this story contains a tic-back and reads as a follow-up story, although no new information is included.

Original Story

After strangling her three baby daughters with a clothesline, Mrs. Gilda Heyda last night hanged herself in her home at 423 S. Reba street.

The bodies of the three girls, Roberta, 4, Ruth, 2, and Hazel, four months, were discovered by Mrs. Sylvia Priem, mother of Mrs. Heyda, when she arrived about 8 P.M. for a visit. The children were lying on a bed with the body of their mother nearby.

The father and husband is Wilfred A. Heyda, unemployed carpenter, believed to be somewhere in the middle west on his way to Texas to seek employment.

Chief piece of evidence at the inquest which was to open this morning will be a note to her mother left by Mrs. Heyda, reading:

"It's pretty good! Wilfred has kids and can't even send them a card while on a trip."

Heyda left three weeks ago and was last heard from in Cincinnati from where he

Rewritten Story

Somewhere in the middle west today tragic news followed a father who is in pursuit of employment to support his wife and three small daughters.

The young husband and father, Wilfred Heyda, unemployed carpenter, was sought by authorities who were to inform him his wife, Mrs. Gilda Heyda, strangled their three baby girls and then committed suicide last night in their home at 423 S. Reba street.

As an inquest opened into the deaths this morning, police expressed the belief that Mrs. Heyda had become despondent from loneliness. She left a note to her mother, Mrs. Sylvia Priem, saying:

"It's pretty good! Wilfred has kids and can't even send them a card while on a trip."

The last word from the father, who left home three weeks ago, was from Cincinnati. From there he wrote he was on his way to Texas by way of Indianapolis, Springfield, Ill., Chicago, and St. Louis.

Original Story

expected to go to Indianapolis, Chicago, Springfield, Ill., and St. Louis before heading for the southwest.

Police believe Mrs. Heyda's act resulted from loneliness because of her husband's absence and failure to write more frequently.

Rewritten Story

The slain children were Roberta, 4, Ruth, 2, and Hazel, four months. Their bodies were discovered by Mrs. Priem lying on a bed when she came to visit. Nearby was the body of Mrs. Heyda who apparently had used a clothesline to strangle her daughters and then take her own life.

COMPREHENSIVE LEAD

The rewrite person's knowledge of recent news events is valuable. In the following example, the writer was able to supply additional information from memory. If time permits and the story merits the trouble, the rewrite person may consult the newspaper's library and reference department to obtain information of this kind.

Original Story

Virgil Miner, 17, son of Mr. and Mrs. Charlton Miner, 386 Coates street, last night won first place in the annual state high school extemporaneous speaking contest. Speakers from 11 other high schools competed at Beardstown Municipal auditorium.

Representing the local high school, Virgil drew "Neutrality" as his subject. All contestants were given 30 minutes in which to prepare and each spoke ten minutes. Judges were . . .

Rewritten Story

For the second time in five years, the Milltown high school entry won first honors in the annual state high school extemporaneous speaking contest when Virgil Miner last night was declared the winner at Beardstown Municipal auditorium.

Three years ago, Leland West, now a student at Booster college, won the contest which was held at Lincoln. By an odd coincidence, both boys drew the same topic, "Neutrality."

Virgil is the 17-year-old son of Mr. and Mrs. Charlton Miner, 386 Coates street, and a senior at the high school.

Rules of the contest give each entrant 30 minutes in which to prepare to give a ten minute speech. Twelve students competed last night. Judges were . . .

COMBINED STORIES

The following example shows how one rewrite person combined two items into a single story:

Original Stories

Losing control of his automobile when a butterfly flew against his face, Edgar Lewis, 33, 1301 Sherman street, crashed into a fire hydrant about 6:30 P.M. yesterday at the northwest corner of Simpson and Michigan streets. He was taken to

Combined Story

Insects were responsible for two odd automobile mishaps in Milltown early last evening.

Ants crawling on the ankles of one driver led to a smashup which sent him to Municipal hospital with two fractured

Original Stories

Municipal hospital with only minor bruises.

Sylvester Finger, 28, 1428 Grove street, is in Municipal hospital today with two fractured ribs as the result of an automobile accident about 7 P.M. yesterday. Finger's car struck a telephone pole at the southeast corner of Michigan and Central streets after he took his hands off the steering wheel to drive away ants which were crawling on his ankles.

Combined Story

ribs. In the other accident, a butterfly flew against the driver's face and caused him to lose control of his machine.

The injured man is. . . .

LOCAL ANGLE

The rewrite person who reads newspapers from other cities, official reports and documents, press agent material and the like, should look for a local angle to feature, as

Original Story

PEORIA NEWSPAPER

A state-wide membership drive of the Fraternal Order of Leopards will be planned here next Thursday at a meeting of representatives of the eight original chapters in as many cities.

Goal of the campaign will be 25 chapters and 2,000 members before July 1, according to J. S. Kienlen, Peoria, state commander, who called the meeting.

Cities to be represented at Thursday's meeting and delegates are: Wayne Lueck, Danville; R. S. Kirschten, Cairo; Lowell Watson, Freeport; S. O. McNeil, Aurora; Silas Layman, Springfield; Richard Yates, Elgin; O. L. Moss, Bloomington; and Mr. Kienlen.

Rewritten Story

FREEPORT NEWSPAPER

Lowell Watson, 34 W. Bushnell place, commander of the local chapter of the Fraternal Order of Leopards, will attend an organization meeting next Thursday at Peoria to help plan a statewide membership campaign for the order.

Representatives from all eight original Leopards chapters in the state will take part in the meeting called by J. S. Kienlen, Peoria, state commander.

Objectives of the proposed campaign are a membership of 2,000 and 25 Illinois chapters. To attend Thursday's meeting, in addition to Watson and Kienlen, are. . . .

9

GIVING IT SUBSTANCE

Experienced reporters who develop specialties often become recognized experts. They write not only authoritative newspaper articles but magazine pieces and books as well. Their vast amount of background knowledge enables them to give meaning to current happenings. More than that, they become critics in their fields and can warn and forecast and even give advice to policy leaders, including heads of state. They may have a powerful effect upon public opinion.

Later journalistic success is determined by early experience. Nobody, that is, is catapulted into a top position of prestige and influence without having served a long apprenticeship to learn correct work habits and attitudes. Local reporting provides the first and best opportunity for the development of such essential traits as thoroughness, accuracy and resourcefulness. The aspirant for future fame and fortune as an interpretative reporter and writer begins by becoming a superior gatherer of so-called straight news to be handled objectively. In addition, the future interpretative expert gets around more than his/her competitor, digging deeper for often neglected facts that provide understanding and perspective. Such a newsgatherer asks regarding every assignment:

1. What happened? That is, what *really* happened—the complete story, not just the end results of a series of incidents.
2. Why (or how) did it happen? That is, what is the explanation?
3. What does it mean? That is, how interpret it?
4. What next? In the light of today's news, what may be expected to happen tomorrow?

5. What's beneath the surface? What are the trends, ideologies, situations and so on, of which one should be aware so that an overt news incident will make sense?

COMPLETING THE ACCOUNT

Factual Background

When an event of major significance occurs, because of the mass of detailed information involved and from lack of time and space, first news stories may be in the straight news-writing tradition, leaving the interpretation for another edition or day. If, however, the reporter has an adequate knowledge and understanding of preceding events related to the one at hand, even the first story, prepared in haste, will have greater substance.

If there are both a morning and an afternoon newspaper, any news story inevitably breaks to the comparative advantage of one over the other. The publication with the earlier deadline will be able to print the story first, but the other paper should be able to prepare a more detailed account. For instance, the Peoria (Ill.) *Journal-Star,* a morning newspaper, once reported that an attempt by an alderman to have a painting contract awarded to the second-lowest bidder was defeated when the mayor cast the deciding vote. The Peoria *Transcript,* that afternoon, with more time, cast new light on the incident by revealing that the alderman and contractor were brothers-in-law, that the alderman was attending his first meeting following election and that the mayor's vote brought about a tie, not a majority.

The knowledgeable reporter will recall the history of a bill or ordinance and of previous attempts to promote similar legislation. S/he knows whether lawmakers are behaving consistently, the identity of individuals and groups in support or opposition and other facts of the same sort that enable readers to come to a better understanding of the immedate occurrence.

Eyewitness Accounts

To supplement the formal stories, it is common practice to ask victims of disasters (train wrecks, floods, fires) to relate their personal experiences. Often, such accounts are ghostwritten or are printed under the by-lines of the principals "as told to" some staff writer. Reporters themselves write eyewitness accounts of important scenes they have witnessed. Such stories are more informal than straight news accounts and usually provide graphic word pictures of what happened.

By William Michelmore

Dead workers were hanging from a safety ladder, and other workers frantically tore open their shirts in a desperate struggle to breathe and then "dropped dead like flies."

That was how rescue squads described the grisly scene Friday night after a carbon monoxide leak at the Jones & Laughlin Steel Co. plant in East Chicago, Ind.

Six employes, including three foremen, died from inhaling the gas. . . .

[Chicago *Tribune*]

Photography, including motion pictures and television, has not yet made written descriptions obsolete. Nor is it likely to do so for some time, if for no other reason than that cameramen are not always present at news events when we need to answer the question "What did it look like?" in order to present a complete account. Before a reporter can describe well, s/he must be able to observe. Careful observation means noting features that escape the untrained spectator. A bizarre vocabulary containing innumerable adjectives is not essential. The reader, in fact, will "see" best what the writer is describing if the words are familiar. Ambiguous qualitative adjectives such as "handsome" or "delicate" should be omitted, and figures of speech, historical and literary allusions and other rhetorical devices must be readily understandable.

In selecting anecdotes to relate and persons to describe, caution must be exercised so that they are either important in their own right or typical of a general situation. Otherwise a distorted impression can be created. A typical situation in which this might occur is a mine cave-in or flood or similar disaster. At the scene, probably accompanying rescue workers, the reporter is attempting to describe the reaction of victims and others so the reader can get the "feel" of the story. It must be realized that one sobbing woman does not constitute a hysterical mob. The reader must be able to depend upon the integrity of the reporter.

Sidebars

When an important news event occurs, reporters often use sidebars to round out the complete account. A sidebar deals with phases of a story as a whole which conceivably could be included in the main account but not without either lengthening it too much or sacrificing some details. When an office building in Chicago's Loop exploded, among the anecdotal sidebars were the following: (1) 105,000 square feet of new glass being rushed to city to replace show-window glass broken; (2) analysis of city ordinances covering gas leakage which allegedly caused the blast; (3) description of army of glaziers at work in area; (4) police pass system to admit workers employed in area; (5) refusal of pass to a window washer, obviously because there were no windows left to wash; (6) symposium of eyewitness accounts; (7) narrow escape of nearby elevated tower operator; (8) instructions on how to enter area; (9) Red Cross activities; (10) list of buildings whose windows were blown out.

When the news relates to a scheduled event, several reporters may be assigned to cover different angles. A woman reporter, for instance, may stay close to the wife of a visiting celebrity; at the same time, another reporter may concentrate on the crowd, noting its size and nature, ever watchful for unusual personalities and incidents. Still another may observe the behavior of the police, marshals, secret-service men and the like, or s/he may interview members of the party of either the guest or the host or both. Someone else, who might not even need to be present, can compare the occasion with similar ones in the past, here and/or elsewhere. Some of the information obtained by members of the reportorial team may be used by whoever writes the main story of the event but each probably will have enough left for a separate piece.

Team Reporting

The page 1 streamer headline of the Los Angeles *Times* was DAY OF DISASTER and the two-line head read "Quake Leaves 42 Dead, 1,000 Hurt; Periled Dam Forces 40,000 to Flee." A picture and an area map occupied about one-third of the page. There were two inside pages devoted entirely to pictures and there were enough other scattered pictures to total the equivalent of a third page. The main account began in the right-hand column on page 1 and jumped for about the equivalent of a full page on inside pages. The headlines of 26 other stories related to the disaster suggest their contents and consequently the extent of the coverage. William Thomas, since then promoted from metropolitan editor to editor, who directed the operation, says it was perhaps "the closest we have come to accomplishing" the objective of bringing "some of our interpretative and analytical techniques to the spot news story."

Virtually all of the stories were finished within six hours of the quake. The headlines: (1) 39 Still Missing in Hospital Ruins; (2) Reservoir Dwarfs Old One in Baldwin Hills [there was fear that it might give way]; (3) First a Rumble, Then Houses Catch Fire, Glass Shatters [an eyewitness impressionist account]; (4) Reagan Favors Gas Tax Rise to Repair Streets; (5) Antelope Valley Cut Off as Bridge Collapses; (6) Shock Stronger Than One That Hit Long Beach; (7) New Skyscrapers Ride It Out, Damage Slight; (8) Disaster Planning Brings Quick Aid; (9) Olive View Hospital Termed Total Loss; (10) City Schools Will Stay Closed Today; (11) Some Guard Units Activated for Duty; (12) Partial Death List Gives Scant Details; (13) Beagle Was the Alarm for Sleeper [terrified dog jumped on bed]; (14) Sea Bubbles Off Malibu Most of Day; (15) Phone, Water, Electric, Gas Services Disrupted; (16) It Was A-Test to Las Vegas; (17) Little Quake Insurance in Effect, Broker Says; (18) Quake Talks Delayed by the Quake [relates to meeting of Structural Engineering Association on subject of laws on earthquake safety]; (19) 7 Emergency Shelters Open to Quake Victims; (20) Special Loans to Be Offered; (21) Homeless Offered Vacant VA Houses; (22) Expert Tells What to Do in a Quake; (23) Care Urged in Drinking Water Use; (24) Quake Interferes with Apollo Lines [Apollo 14 was homeward bound]; (25) Eclipse Lineup Linked to Quake by Scientist; (26) Hundreds of Aftershocks.

Thomas reminisces concerning the experience,

> One editor was in charge: I, along with considerable help from two assistants. Any complex coverage has to be directed by one person or it becomes incoherent.
>
> From there, you play it by ear. You send out to cover all conceivable action,

which really is not difficult, and everything stems from this. A guy at the shattered hospital comments that it seemed a long time before help came, and that gets you to thinking about the disaster warning setup. Did it work and how well and exactly how? A report comes in that the injured are going to such a place, and as you send a team there you wonder how the evacuation process was planned and did it do the job, etc. A reporter wonders how much of the damage is covered by insurance, and you say, "That's a good idea" and you assign a man to that aspect.

As you're doing all this, you are listing your areas of coverage and deciding how to break them into dovetailing stories. Here is where our earthquake coverage differed from, say, our Watts riot coverage. The same thing was done during Watts but, instead of interpretative pieces, as we did on the riots, we assigned them for immediate publication.

Several things made this possible. First and most important is a staff who can do it. You could never do this under the old rewrite setup, where there are eight guys suitable mainly for leg work for every one who is a competent writer. We did away with the rewrite concept almost entirely some time ago, and for some years I have hired only writers. So everybody can communicate his own findings, which gives us several desirable things; greater authenticity, greater speed, better and more believable stories all around, a happier staff.

Was it organized, you asked, or random? You'd have to say it was organized in a random manner, or random in an organized manner, whichever you like best. In other words, the story was unfolding as the interpretative package was being put together so it certainly was random to that extent.

But there are certain procedures which experience dictates will bring the best results in such situations (i.e., keeping a number of the best writers in the office to handle the complex interpretative stories you know will develop, even though the temptation is to fire them out into the general area; putting the guys strongest on action reporting into those situations, the guys best on reflective stories into those, etc.). This isn't very clear, but to this extent—and to the extent that you retain a very clear idea where everybody is and what he can be expected to contribute—it is an organized procedure.

I guess you try to be organized to deal effectively with random happenings.

Another outstanding example of teamwork by the Los Angeles *Times* news staff occurred May 25, 1979, when American Airlines Flight 191 crashed shortly after take-off from Chicago's O'Hare field. Most of the 273 killed in the United States' worst commercial aviation disaster were homebound Los Angeles residents or delegates to the American Booksellers Association convention being held in L.A. Dennis A. Britton, national editor of the *Times*, tells how his staff went into action:

We first heard of the DC-10 crash from one of our Midwest Bureau correspondents who was monitoring a Bearcat Scanner in the Chicago office. He alerted us about half-an-hour before the wires carried the first bulletin. Our second correspondent was out of Chicago and unreachable. So we first sent Bob Secter of the Chicago office to the scene. We then got a Washington Bureau reporter in the air (about an hour after the crash). We talked to every section of the paper here to determine if any other reporters were in the area. We located a sports reporter covering the Angels for us and sent him to headquarters at O'Hare.

While all of this was going on we located a reporter in our lifestyle section who was a multiengine-rated pilot and got him started calling safety experts. Our Business/Financial staff had already made contact with McDonnell-Douglas.

Within two hours of the crash we dispatched a reporter from our Denver office and one from Washington to go to Oklahoma City where the FAA keeps all flight records on all planes which fly in the United States. From this we hoped to determine if the DC-10 had experienced earlier safety problems and how its safety record stacked up against other jumbo jets.

We assigned three editors—two in Los Angeles and one in Washington—to begin monitoring and handling all DC-10 stories.

We kept about five reporters full time on the crash for three days and covered the standard air disaster stories. We then, however, assembled a team of 10 reporters under an assistant national editor (James O. Bell) and set out to find everything we could about the DC-10, how it was certified and its record. We spend hundreds of dollars on computer runs at the FAA facility in Oklahoma City and at Arizona State University's crash study unit. We were forced to file Freedom of Information requests to get public information from the FAA (we *just* got our third of five batches of material March 13, 1980). Over three months we wrote more than a dozen stories. We disbanded the team as a formal entity after three months but three reporters continue to process the FOIA material. We envision more stories, some of which will detail how the manufacturer and the FAA combine sometimes to short-circuit the certification process.

I'm proud to say that we were ahead of most national publications on the DC-10 crash coverage and ahead of all on aftermath coverage.

The day following the crash the Los Angeles *Times* devoted nine columns to stories of the disaster. Coverage in the Chicago papers was, of course, even greater. The *Tribune*'s report follows.

The *Tribune* news staff bolted into action even as the black smoked billowed toward the sky.

The ensuing hours would see 41 reporters and writers, 19 photographers, and five artists, along with dozens of copy editors, graphics experts, caption writers, assignment editors, news editors and supervisors putting together the tragic story of the worst aviation disaster in American history.

The responsibility for coordinating the entire operation fell to William Jones, a former Pulitzer Prize winning reporter, city editor, and managing editor-news. Just an hour before the crash a story was written for the Saturday paper announcing his promotion to managing editor.

Jones immediately huddled with Maxwell McCrohon, newly-named editor of The Tribune, and John Wagoner, news editor, to advise them what was in the works and what to expect.

"We had a series of news conferences as our coverage developed," Jones said. "In all, it was a magnificent effort by the city desk. It was really a city desk operation."

"Damn near the whole financial and feature departments volunteered," said Bernard Judge, city editor. "If I had needed 60 people to cover the crash I had them. At least 20 reporters not from our staff, including one columnist, were standing by to help."

The final deadline for copy to the composing room for the Green Streak replate was only minutes away when the plane went down.

The replate was held up for 25 minutes while reporters in the office telephoned various sources and relayed their information to a rewrite man, who was able to make a 10-inch-long story for the day's final edition.

Then, with a 4:45 p.m. copy deadline, the rewriteman, working closely with an assistant city editor who was coordinating information from the scene, rewrote and polished his original story for the Saturday Midwest edition—first of the next day's run.

Within the next six hours the entire story was wrapped up. Tribune readers picked up their morning papers Saturday to read: Worst U.S. Crash; 272 die at O'Hare.

The main story on page one was accompanied by a picture, the entire width of the page, of the crash scene with sticks marking spots were bodies had been located. There was also a page one overview story under the headline: 'There was rain of fire falling.'

A page one box listed related stories inside:

A chaplain describing the scene as "Too hot for anything but the last rites"; a report on confusion at the plane's Los Angeles destination; a sidebar on the history of the DC-10; a list of previous air disasters; and a story on other major plane crashes in Chicago.

There was also a full page of photos including an aerial view of the crash site; a story with graphics on the DC-10's statistics and seating arrangements; a sidebar on celebrities aboard the fatal flight; a vivid description of the task of trying to match bits and pieces of flesh; a sidebar on a streetcar crash that killed 34 in Chicago on the same date 29 years earlier; more photos; and a passenger list.

The Sunday paper, which had a 9:25 a.m. Saturday copy deadline for its first edition, picked up from there, starting with a front page strip of exclusive color photos of the DC-10 going down and crashing.

Also on page one was the main story on the investigation into the cause of the crash; an airline pilot's description of the crash; a hospital interview with a man injured on the ground when the plane hit; and a box describing inside stories and where to find them.

First word of the crash reached the city desk simultaneously from police reporter Philip Wattley, who heard a fire chief calmly request crash vehicles via the emergency radio, and from photo assignment editor William Kelly, who was monitoring police and fire calls in the office.

Wattley next used a police line to contact airport security officials who confirmed, "We've got a big one down here!"

On receiving the initial call from Wattley, Associate city editor Donald Agrella and day city editor Sheila Wolfe began dispatching reporters to the scene. Agrella notified day news editor Max Saxinger of the crash, and alerted Judge.

"I figured we'd need at least 10 people on the way, not counting people to hospitals," Judge said. "You've got to move a drove of people to the scene, the morgue, the hospitals. Most of the good stories come from hospitals if there are survivors."

After determining who had already been sent out, Judge began to assign specific reporters and writers to various aspects of the story. On learning there were no survivors, reporters on the way to hospitals were diverted to the scene, the airport, and airline offices.

"Two-way radios were very helpful here," he said. "We're going to get more of them."

While reporters raced to the scene in the midst of the evening traffic rush, others in the office talked by phone to O'Hare tower, police, fire dispatchers, airline officials, and witnesses in the area.

"Agrella and I sat down and cut a schedule of the stories we expected to have for the Saturday editions," Judge said. "Wolfe was assigned to work solely with Dave Schneidman, the rewrite man doing the main story. William Sluis, assistant night city editor, was put in charge of everything else."

Working with Stephen Lough, national editor, Judge arranged to have Los Angeles correspondent Michael Coakley at the LA airport to talk with friends and relatives waiting in vain for the plane to arrive. David Young, transportation editor, who was aboard a private rail car en-route from Fremont, Neb., was rushed home with the help of rail officials.

Kelly, on the photo desk, meanwhile was sending photographers to the scene, diverting men from other assignments, and calling night workers to come in early. Assistant photo assignment editor James O'Leary kept abreast of developments by monitoring police and fire calls, and lined up a helicopter for aerial photos.

Picture editor Richard Leslie and chief photographer Anthony Berardi Jr. coordinated photo operations.

Enroute to the crash scene photographer Karen Engstrom was redirected to the American Airlines terminal to look for friends and relatives of passengers.

It was there she encountered Michael Laughlin, a free-lance photographer, who had made color shots of the ill-fated plane as it went down. Engstrom out-talked and out-bid competing news media and obtained the photos exclusively for The Tribune. She arranged to have the films processed under the watchful eyes of a Federal Bureau of Investigation agent who had taken official possession of them.

At the same time the city desk and photo desks were mobilizing into action, the graphics department began to prepare visual coverage of the disaster.

After discussions between graphics editor Howard Finberg, Gus Hartoonian, graphics art director, and Anton Majeri, his assistant, the Art Department staff was put on stand-by status.

Finberg and graphics coordinator Susan Popson worked with artists, photographers and reporters to prepare a location map; graphics of the plane; a drawing of the engine that fell off; and a sequential graphic of the aircraft's takeoff from runway to crash.

"There must have been a dozen conversations with the art directors about the shape of the graphics, who would do them, when they would be done, and who would come in the next day," Finberg said.

McCrohon, Jones, Judge, Berardi, Hartoonian, and Joseph Leonard, editor, editorial operations, worked through to 3 a.m. to assure that all Saturday stories were cleared and everything was organized for the Sunday editions. Jones came back in early Saturday to supervise the Sunday operation.

"It was a relatively uncomplicated disaster to cover," Judge said afterward. "Everyone was dead. There were no human errors involved. The engine fell off, the plane crashed, and there were no survivors."

> Reporters returning from the scene said there was no "feeling of disaster" usually encountered in such tragedies. "There was no identifiable carnage," said Judge. "No looting. Just a field of debris."

The Chicago *Sun-Times* used 28 reporters, ten photographers, two news editors, 12 copy editors, three picture editors, six graphic experts, eight free-lance reporters and two free-lance photographers. For its coverage the paper received a National Headliners Club award. Intensive daily coverage of the disaster and its aftermath continued for more than a fortnight before it began to taper off.

In similar critical situations, smaller newspapers respond in the same way as their larger contemporaries. Dale A. Davenport, city editor of the Harrisburg (Pa.) *Evening News* tells how his paper handled the radiation leakage at the nuclear plant on nearby Three Mile Island:

> I learned of an accident involving "some sort of cloud of something" from my Capitol Hill reporter, who got a telephoned tip at home about 8:50 a.m. March 28, 1979, from a colleague who said: "I'm not really interested in this, but your city desk might be since it looks like (just) a local story."
>
> I was fortunate to have three reporters on the staff who at one time or another had covered Three Mile Island nuclear doings, so I assigned one of them to check the tip. Within 10 minutes she had verified that radiation had escaped and that Civil Defense (which now calls itself Pennsylvania Emergency Management Agency) had declared an alert.
>
> I immediately assigned another two reporters to travel to Middletown, one to the TMI observation center where Metropolitan Edison Co. was keeping the press, the other to cover whatever man-in-the-street reaction he could get in Middletown. He later interviewed the mayor and filed a story for the noon edition.
>
> I sent another reporter to the western river bank town of Goldsboro across the river from TMI and he and a reporter from our York bureau covered the story from the York County angle, i.e., what officials and civilians on that side of the river were doing. I also assigned two photographers, one to TMI observation center, which is across the road from the bridge and main entrance to the plant, the other to Goldsboro.
>
> The woman who checked the tip, Mary O. Bradley, remained on telephone and, working with what notes she gathered from telephone conversations and initial Associated Press reports and a statement phoned in by a Capitol Hill reporter from the lieutenant governor, compiled a story for the first edition, with a closing time of 10:15 a.m. By 10:45 a.m., that edition was on the street.
>
> Within about 20 minutes, she had updated that story and we replaced the front page for the remainder of our 17,000 first edition run. By that time, reporters were filing their first stories from the field and another reporter in the city room, who had been assigned to assist in telephone contacts, also was contributing to the lead story.
>
> By noon, I had compiled and/or edited three sidebar stories and the lead story, which by that time carried three bylines and, in an italic notation at the end, credited three others. Various editors and suburban bureau chiefs also worked on aspects of the story.

Within minutes, by about 12:30 p.m. we filed the fourth lead. In all, 10 reporters contributed facts for it, it was written by two of them and merged electronically into one story by me.

Of course, in succeeding days, all my eight reporters, and those eight assigned to the various bureaus, covered TMI for The Evening News. For about a week, it was virtually the only local story. Decisions about what sidebars were developed were made on a spot basis and in many instances were the ideas of reporters. I turned all my routine duties over to my assistant city editor and supervised solely the TMI story.

On succeeding days, primary assignments were to the TMI observation center for press briefings and Met-Ed and the Nuclear Regulatory Commission (these later were moved to a community building in Middletown), to the state Civil Defense command post, and to the communities surrounding the plant, where human interest sidebars were always available.

Localization

The effects of some news events are felt at considerable distances. Without mention of some of the repercussions, the original story is not complete. For instance, whenever the president of the United States or some other leader of government makes an important announcement, there are reverberations on Capitol Hill, where congressional leaders abandon or alter old tactics or institute new ones. The stock market may be influenced by mere rumor. A Supreme Court decision may affect governmental practices and legal procedures in the states and cities.

In all such and similar cases, the reader wants to know, "How will this affect me?" That is the perspective from which the interpretative reporter should approach his task. In that spirit, the Evanston (Ill.) *Review* figured out the average cost for every man, woman, and child in Illinois of a newly announced federal budget. Similarly, when the United States Supreme Court upheld the blue laws of some Eastern states, the United Press International bureau in Topeka compiled a list of laws still on the books in Kansas regulating behavior on the Sabbath. The Baltimore *Sun* used a similar story to explain how a Supreme Court decision regarding motion-picture censorship would affect Baltimore and Maryland. When Sen. George McGovern revealed in March 1971 that the Vietnam War had caused 920,028 deaths, the Chicago *Daily News* figured out that "If all those killed in the Vietnam war had lived in the same U.S. city, only seven other American cities would be larger." Michigan State University Prof. James Anderson told a House Defense Appropriations subcommittee that the nation's projected $1 trillion five-year military budget would cost the average American family of four $19,400.

Many a newspaper has investigated to determine how long the local supply of coal or steel or some other commodity would last in the event a strike continued affecting the faraway source of supply. How a new federal or state law will affect the community specifically, probably always should be explained by the public-spirited local press.

By Robert M. Lewin

What will the new steel price increases do to the cost of things you buy?

The price of steel used in a 30-gallon water heater will go up 21 cents, according to the arithmetic of Armco Steel Corp., the first to follow Inland Steel Co. in increasing steel prices.

Armco's estimates also showed:

The cost of steel in a home gas furnace will go up 32 cents; 23 cents in a washing machine; 16 cents in an automatic dishwasher; 28 cents in a refrigerator; 15 cents in an automatic clothes dryer, and $3 in an automobile.

Armco contends that the increases of $2 and $3 a ton on the price of hot-rolled steel sheets and strip and cold-rolled sheets "are so modest they cannot be consequential."

The auto and appliance industries are chief users of those products. The increases are scheduled to go into effect Wednesday. . . . [Chicago *Daily News*]

There are, of course, a pro and a con regarding every public issue. The ethical newspaper considers itself a public forum for the airing of diverse opinions. The obligation, however, is not just to the person who wishes to express himself/herself, but primarily to readers so that they can be fully informed. When a new curfew law for adolescents is under consideration, for instance, the paper should seek out persons who are in positions to have intelligent opinions on the subject. This is not the inquiring-reporter technique, which often results in obtaining uninformed and unrepresentative viewpoints. Rather, it is a search for the best opinion available.

INTERPRETATIONS

It decidedly is not true that "what you don't know won't hurt you." On the contrary, in a democracy it is essential that everyone have access to as many facts as possible in order to form proper judgments and influence public affairs. For almost a century, however, there has been increasing recognition that mere reporting of objective facts is not sufficient to serve the informational needs of a self-governing people. The result: interpretative reporting.

The Interpretative Viewpoint

In gathering information about a news event, the reporter seeks answers to the *who, what, where, when, why* and *how* of whatever happened. Of these, the first four are basic to virtually any account. Offhand, it might be held that not all stories have a *why* or *how* element important enough to engage much of the newsgatherer's attention. Actually, exactly the contrary is the case. In delving into the *what* of most stories, the reporter really is asking "why?" even though the answers he receives may become part of the *what*. The beginning journalist should be aware that doing a thorough job of interviewing for what may seem to be a minor or simple story is training for more penetrating assignments in the future. The skilled reporter develops an attitude or frame of mind toward the job.

To illustrate,

> Police arrested Carter Davis, 14, son of Mr. and Mrs. George Davis, 4513 W. Coral street.

Why?

> Because he used a knife to stab his eighth-grade teacher at Tyler Junior high school, 1216 N. Marshall street. She is Mrs. Vivian Heller, 48, 5141 W. Falconer avenue.

Why did he do it?

> The assault occurred just after she had told the boy that he would fail his course in English.

But other teenagers fail in their school work without committing violence against their teachers. *Why is this boy different?* The Behavior Clinic psychiatrist is examining him now in an attempt to find out. While waiting for the report, further facts can be obtained: the circumstances and sequences of the events, the victim's condition, police activities and so forth. Questioning of school authorities reveals Carter's academic and deportment records. Classmates tell of his behavior toward and reputation with his peers, expressing either surprise or the opposite as regards the immediate situation.

Further clues as to the answer to the *why* are obtained by a visit to Carter's home and neighborhood, by talks with parents and other relatives, neighbors and friends and recreational and other workers with whom the boy has had contact.

The reporter is able to ask penetrating questions to a considerable extent because of his knowledge of modern thinking in the fields of psychology, social psychology, psychiatry and sociology. Not too many decades ago he would presume, with most everyone else, that there is a dichotomy of good boys and bad boys, determined largely by the individual's exercise of free will. A more lenient attitude would be to consider the social misfit a victim of some sort of demoniacal possession. In any case, harshness of punishment was the only known corrective. Police operated on the "catch 'em and kill 'em" philosophy and were goaded on by journalists who reflected the indignation of most of their readers whenever a particularly heinous example of misbehavior occurred.

Within a generation, the attitude of a majority of enforcement officers, judges, educators, journalists and others has changed. Today it is recognized that there is "something wrong" with a boy who commits an act like Carter's. Psychiatrists still are reluctant to discuss cases with newsgatherers until they have made their formal reports to whatever public authorities are involved. In the meantime, reporters must refrain from making medical diagnoses on the basis of their own investigations. They can, however, publicize such pertinent facts as that a misbehaving child comes from an underprivileged, broken slum home, or from a wealthy family where everything was lavished upon him except the most important ingredient of all—parental attention.

Why do some youngsters reared in the same neighborhood "go bad" whereas others do not? The answer concerns the behavior clinician who may conclude that the boy who does not act in accordance with group standards is the problem child rather than others who "go along" with the gang in committing antisocial acts. Human motivation is an extremely complex subject for scientific research, with multitudinous influences in and out of the home and other primary institutions affecting different children differently. The journalist should be warned against acceptance of "panacea" explanations such as broken homes, poverty, slum environments and especially television, comic books, the movies and so forth as providing easy answers to explain intricate situations. Especially must all journalists not panic when "law and order" advocates seek a return to the philosophers of the Middle Ages.

Even if a reasonably clear picture emerges as regards an individual case, the probing reporter can continue to ask "why?" at several different levels of inquiry. If social statistics indicate that there are correlations between various factors, as slum conditions, racial, religious or nationality backgrounds, economic status and so forth, for understanding it is necessary to ask "why?" as regards each item. What are the cause-and-effect relationships? And how explain the type of behavior that results? Why violence instead of suicide or something else? Because of the extreme frustration or sense of insecurity in the individual from whatever cause—an organic or biological reflex? Or because violence is an accepted or admired form of behavior in a group whose respect is desired? Or because there is violence in other aspects of the environment, including the international scene? These are matters that concern many different specialists in the social sciences whose erudition and research the newsgatherer cannot hope to duplicate. The reporter, however, can solicit their information, assistance and advice. Most important, the reporter can benefit more from assignments, both for immediate journalistic usage and for development of a general understanding through recognition that the isolated news event is not really isolated.

It would be impossible or at least superfluous to attempt extensive probing into the broader aspects of every incident such as the hypothetical one of Carter Davis. Space will not permit usage of exhaustive analyses of every vagrant, jack roller, tough juvenile, prostitute or others of society's "problem children." There is no beat to compare with police, however, to provide an opportunity to begin cultivation of a querying attitude toward life. When the time comes to attempt to fathom the causes of a depression, war or major issue of any kind, the experienced newsgatherer utilizes the habits of mind learned while a cub. If one doesn't take advantage of the opportunities provided early in one's career his/her grandchildren will be visiting him/her in the same pressroom where s/he started.

A typical defense of interpretative reporting by Lester Markel follows:

> Interpretation, as I see it, is the deeper sense of the news. It places a particular event in the larger flow of events. It is the color, the atmosphere, the human element that give meaning to a fact. It is, in short, setting, sequence, and, above all, significance.
>
> There is a vast difference between interpretation and opinion. And the distinction is of the utmost importance. Three elements, not two, are involved in this debate; first, news; second, interpretation; third, opinion. To take a primitive example:
>
> To say that Senator McThing is investigating the teaching of Patagonian in the schools is news.
>
> To explain why Senator McThing is carrying on this investigation is interpretation.
>
> To remark that Senator McThing should be ashamed of himself is opinion.
>
> Interpretation is an objective judgment based on background knowledge of a situation, appraisal of an event. Editorial judgment, on the other hand, is a subjective judgment; it may include an appraisal of the facts but there is an additional and distinctive element, namely, emotional impact.
>
> Opinion should be confined, almost religiously, to the editorial page; interpretation is an essential part of the news. This is vital and it cannot have too much emphasis.
>
> I see no difference between "interpretation" and "background." Of course, part of interpretation may be the setting out of some antecedent facts—and this many editors consider "background" as distinguished from "interpretation." But interpretation is much more than shirttail material; it is in addition to the presentation of the pertinent facts, present and past, an effort to assay the meaning of those facts.

Causes and Motives

In search of the news behind the news, the probing reporter keeps on asking "why?" Official proclamations and carefully prepared press releases may conceal causes and motives that preceded the spot or "end result" news of the moment. So the interpretative reporter digs beneath the surface.

Sometimes it is possible to conjecture. For instance, if a mayor and corporation counsel have disagreed frequently in public, the reasons for the latter's impending resignation would seem to be obvious. Too often, however, newspaper columnists and others, acting on rumors and tips from "persons close to" or "usually reliable sources," may be wrong. If, for instance, the mayor and corporation counsel announce after a conference that they have settled their differences and, in fact, now "see eye to eye," only a naïve journalist would accept the announcement on its face value. To obtain the "real lowdown," however, may be difficult or impossible. Perhaps the counsel threatened to make a public statement that would be embarrassing to the mayor. Perhaps he agreed to "go along" on some current matter in exchange for a promise of political support at some future date. Perhaps the mayor indicated he would withdraw some patronage from the counsel's followers. The possibilities are many and the responsible journalist must be careful not to give currency to gossip, rumor and surmise.

Once a large company with plants in several cities announced it intended to close its factory in City A and shift operations to City B. The announcement included a strong statement of regret by management, praise for City A and the like, but explained that it had become necessary to retrench, operate closer to its supply of raw materials and avoid the necessity of investing in costly new machinery. This sounded reasonable but an experienced reporter "smelled a rat" and started snooping. Before long he learned that months earlier the company had negotiated a contract with a union local in City B at a wage rate much lower than that which prevailed in City A. The City B union accepted the deal as it would mean jobs for several thousand unemployed members. Further probing revealed that this act was considered by City A unionists to be a "sellout" and was part of the campaign of a certain national labor leader to increase his strength. The City B union consisted mainly of his followers whereas those in City A belonged to a rival faction within the national organization. Facts such as these are necessary for a proper understanding of the news. The free press has been called a watchdog on government. It can perform no more worthwhile function than to scrutinize carefully everything that affects the public interest.

By John Junkerman

On the eve of his announcement of the school closing recommendations that will be acted on tonight, Superintendent Douglas Ritchie treated a group of black south Madisonians to a catered dinner at the school administration building. Before supping on prime rib, Ritchie revealed his plan to close Longfellow elementary and convert Lincoln middle into a new elementary school.

In a clear attempt to head off criticism that his plan discriminates against Madison's minority and low-income populations, Ritchie assured the southsiders that special programs and resources would be funneled into the area to compensate for the loss of the schools. Prime rib or no, the ploy did not work.

Within a week, Ritchie was informed that south Madison opposed his plan and would fight it with legal action if necessary. Since then, opposition has spread to more than 40 community organizations, the mayor's office and the city's teachers. Educators from the university, realtors, economists and accountants have warned that the plan is ill-conceived and potentially disastrous to the school district.

The breadth and unity of the opposition are probably due to two facts: first, since five schools are involved, the plan will directly affect about 10 per cent of the district's students and the indirect impact will touch one quarter of the city. Second, the closings will come before the full consequences of closing three schools last spring are known.

In the face of this opposition, the administration and its supporters on the school board have abandoned the public relations approach and assumed a bite-the-bullet determination. It was best summarized by pro-closing board member Hermine Davidson even before the public had its turn at an open hearing. "My advice to opponents," she said a month ago, "is to cut your losses and make the best of it."

[Madison (Wis.) *Press Connection*]

Significance

Referring a proposal to a committee may mean either that its enactment into law is being accelerated or that it is being killed. The perspicacious newsgatherer should know which and should so inform his/her readers. The same for all other acts of all branches of government. Readers are able to understand the significance of parliamentary and diplomatic maneuvering, but it must be pointed out to them by someone who keeps close check.

When a convicted person is sentenced to a long term of imprisonment, it is customary to point out the minimum time to be served before being eligible for release on parole. When a deadline passes for filing or withdrawing a petition, it should be pointed out what thereby becomes possible or impossible. If a diplomat attends one function and boycotts another, there may or may not be significant repercussions. In some cases, in other words, it is not difficult to explain consequences objectively. In others, a certain amount of guesswork may be necessary, in which case the rule of caution must be invoked.

By Don Warne

Maricopa County Recorder Bill Henry, who is beginning to assert himself after three months on the job, today announced plans to stage a major "post-mortem evaluation as soon after the Nov. 7 general election as possible."

The former Motorola executive and management consultant also wants to streamline the recorder's office to provide better service for the public. The office will take in about $12 million in fees this year and Henry thinks it should be modernized.

Invited to the post-election session will be leaders of the two major political parties, which Henry said will include district chairmen and other Republican and Democratic stalwarts. [Phoenix (Ariz.) *Gazette*]

Analysis

Long and/or complicated documents, including ordinances and statutes, must be analyzed so that they can be understood. This often is merely a job of tedious objective reporting to explain what now is forbidden, allowed or required and who will be affected in what way. Often the analyst will discover ramifications and repercussions that escaped even the lawmakers.

Speeches by important persons are analyzed almost immediately by journalists and later by scholars. What the speaker emphasizes, the number of times a particular matter is mentioned and omissions are noted. Qualitative judgment enters into evaluating the importance of gestures, facial expressions, tone of voice, pauses in delivery and the like and also in estimating the reaction of a visible audience. It is not difficult to note the amount and duration of applause, of course, but the intangibles are so many that great restraint is needed by the reporter. The audience, for instance, may be easily identifiable as partisan to begin with. Nevertheless, how it reacts is part of the complete coverage. Sometimes explanation is needed for proper analysis. This is often true of crime records. Changes in the frequency of certain types of offenses may be seasonal.

The population complexion of areas may change during a reporting period. Police departments have been known to alter their methods of reporting, often with the intention of making the results seem better than they should. An example would be to list automobiles as missing instead of stolen.

By Bob Kuttner
THE WASHINGTON POST

If one had to pick the political myth of the decade, the leading candidate could easily be what lay behind "the great tax revolt of 1978."

Business conservatives, muttering about government spending and ending up as the biggest beneficiaries of Proposition 13 and its clones, have managed to convince people that taxpayers were rebelling against growth in public outlays. But the real problem, it turns out, was that businesses were already getting too big a tax break, that property taxes increasingly were being shifted *away* from them and onto homeowners.

Though the idea might give a Howard Jarvis apoplexy, in reality the tax revolt of 1978 was created largely by business tax relief at the expense of homeowners.

Consider what happened in California, incubator of the revolt. Taxes on homes there increased about 110 percent between 1975 and 1978—while business assessments rose only 26 percent. By 1978, when Proposition 13 was ratified, single-family homeowners were carrying about 44 percent of California's property tax load; five years earlier they had paid only 32 percent. Small wonder that California homeowners were angry, especially since their excessive share of tax payments was contributing indirectly to a massive state budget surplus.

Why has the tax revolt been misunderstood, continuing to provide pressure for reduced government spending?

Comparisons

As with crime statistics, so with the budgets of public and private bodies, achievements of athletes, votes received by candidates and numerous other matters, the reader wants to know how the present compares with the past. Is something more or less, higher or lower, better or worse? Answers to such questions must be given with all possible influencing factors considered so as not to be deceptive. It would, for instance, be misleading to cite an expenditure as twice that for a comparable item some time in the past without taking into consideration changes in the value of the dollar, population increases, changing needs and demands and so forth.

Political party platforms can be compared with each other and with those of previous years. Faced with a vexatious local problem, public officials and newspapers may send representatives to other communities to study what steps were taken there by way of solution. Whenever a disaster of importance occurs, it is common journalistic practice to prepare sidebars, often in the form of charts or tabulations, to show how the immediate catastrophe compares in intensity with others of the past.

Old-timers are prone to draw historical parallels, to feel that some contemporary event is "just like" one they recall from years before; they feel they have "lived through this before," possibly when they observe a widespread practice that they consider undesirable, as excessive installment buying, stock market speculation, real estate booms and the like. There is no gainsaying the fact that history teaches many valuable lessons, but what may seem to be history repeating itself may not be that at all. Numerous cities previously tried and abandoned services that today are orthodox, as parking meters, traffic signals, one-way streets and off-street parking, to mention only examples in one area. Increasing populations and automobile ownership created new conditions for which new remedies no longer were premature.

Reform movements come and go in many communities. One reason for their failure to last often is the tendency of many supporters to become lackadaisical after the immediate first objective has been attained. History does prove that eternal vigilance is a prerequisite for a properly functioning democracy.

By Edward Peeks
BUSINESS/LABOR EDITOR

In the wake of Proposition 13 that slashed California property taxes, momentum is increasing in the nation for a cut in federal taxes.

But as matters now stand, West Virginians, like other taxpayers, will pay more this year in federal taxes, not less, according to the U.S. Chamber of Commerce.

"Federal taxes for the average West Virginia family are estimated to increase by $55 during 1978, increase $121 by 1979, increase $144 by 1980 and increase $392 by 1985," the chamber says. "This is the largest increase in federal taxes in West Virginia history."

Higher federal taxes appear in the offing while tax relief recedes in the fog of tax proposals before Congress, including the latest informal proposals by Howard Jarvis of Proposition 13 on his visit to Washington this week. . . .

[Charleston (W. Va.) *Gazette*]

Forecasts

Giving a news story a "tomorrow" angle often is a form of interpretation. After analysis of an action by the city council, a reporter can predict new employment, building, police activities and the like. S/he can see "trouble ahead" for certain groups as the result of a sweeping court decision and business advantages to others. A drastic price cut by one retail establishment usually results in a price war among competitors. Tightening child labor laws may have the immediate effect of throwing a certain number of minors out of work.

When it comes to predicting beyond the immediate effect, as that unemployed juveniles will become delinquent, the reporter may be merely speculating. One should draw on expert opinion and historical example and still be slow about making deductions. The death of a prominent figure may or may not clear the way toward a reconciliation between disputing factions, lead to a struggle for succession to a position of power or destroy the chances for achieving a certain goal. The expert can point out the possibilities but should not forget that some pundits have lost the confidence of their audiences by excessive smugness, which the future exposed as such.

By Bill Bank

As the nation finally slides into one of the most predicted recessions in its history, Tucsonans can gear up for more of everything this winter.

More jobs, more unemployment, more inflation, more money, more construction and more people.

How much more remains to be seen, say a host of local economists and business leaders. But there is a consensus that a recession elsewhere will be a slowdown here.

"There is no compelling evidence that Tucson and Arizona will have to parallel the national economy," observes John Buehler, head of the University of Arizona's economics department. "The evidence is that Tucson is not in a recession as of now. But on the basis (of comparison with) the 1974 recession, Tucson might lag behind a national downturn by 9 to 12 months."

Homebuilders have been predicting a downturn locally in their industry for more than a year, but it hasn't yet happened. Starts are ahead of last year, and almost all builders now agree they will equal last year's near-record pace.

[Tucson (Ariz.) *Daily Star*]

Unfortunately most people do not take seriously warnings of imminent danger unless precautionary actions are taken. After the race riots following the murder of Dr. Martin Luther King, several newspapers in cities where the disorders occurred produced clippings of articles published over a period of several years exposing conditions destined to foment trouble.

Yet many who ask, "Why didn't the papers warn us?" call the press sensational when it does expose misdeeds and conditions needing attention.

IMPRESSIONISTIC REPORTING

To Tom Wolfe, the saturation reporting in which the New Journalists engaged involved "a depth of reporting and an attention to the most minute facts and details that most newspapermen, even the most experienced, never dreamed of." Fully a generation earlier Thomas Sanction pleaded for "gestalt journalism," which he defined as "journalism which seeks the whole truth in any given field of politics, deeming the whole truth, or even the mere effort to discover it, greater and qualitatively different than piecemeal, selective reporting of the parts—gestalt journalism in this sense describes only what serious reporters have tried to do since writing began."

Sanction cited several news situations when "my on-the-scene notes contained, as a reporter's notes invariably do, more of the total mood and meaning . . . came closer to its 'gestalt' than their ultimate rewriting would ever have done."

Still earlier, Newbold Noyes Jr. advocated "impressionistic reporting" by which he meant attempts by skilled and impartial reporters to create in the reader the same feeling about an important event as the reporter had as an eyewitness of it. This, of course, was something quite different than the strictly objective reporting that had been advocated by his grandfather, Frank Noyes, one of the founders of the Associated Press.

Prof. J. K. Hvistendahl calls it "truth-as-I-see-it reporting" which he describes in this way: "It is an honest attempt on the part of the reporter to bring together all the material that he can on a subject on which he has strong feelings. The article may be onesided or it may be balanced."

It is because of the risk that personal bias will distort the reporter's effort that some editors still are cautious about granting their expert reporters too much leeway. As a result, as the late Elmer Davis put it, "Objectivity often leans over backward so far that it makes the news business merely a transmission belt for pretentious phonies."

Such, most editors agree today, happened when Sen. Joseph R. McCarthy was making headlines by unverified charges against innocent public officials and others. After he cross-examined Senator Joseph R. McCarthy during the Army-McCarthy hearings, Chief Counsel Joseph N. Welch "went outside into the hallway where he broke down and wept," the Associated Press reported. Some managing editors objected to inclusion of this fact in the AP report. Others didn't like the statements "Stevens bowed to the demands of McCarthy," and "Many spectators in the jam-packed steaming hearing room broke into loud unchecked applause after Welch denounced McCarthy." Still others thought it was bad to report during the subsequent Senate committee hearing that Sen. Francis Case slammed down a report "with a force that scattered papers." A majority of those who expressed opinions, however, favored inclusion of such details in the interest of completeness and accuracy.

In the same edition of the APME *Red Book* in which appears the report of the discussion of the service's handling of the McCarthy hearings, there is also a résumé of other parts of the Managing Editors' conference. The first few paragraphs of one section were as follows:

> Mary Margaret McBride, AP Newsfeature columnist, stole the show and the hearts of many of the editors when she matched them quip for quip in an hour of verbal sparring touched off by her contention that it is wrong to departmentalize all women's news under a "woman's page" label.
>
> This widely known writer, wearing a mink stole and a colorful orchid, beamed beneath an upswept hair-do as she prodded, argued, baited and cajoled while appearing at the two-part session on Newsfeatures, directed by Roderick J. Watts, of the Houston *Chronicle,* chairman of the News-feature committee.
>
> On one occasion, Miss McBride even shouted. And the editors loved it. Some were seen to wipe tears of laughter from their eyes as their colleagues sought to match wits with Miss McBride in an unsuccessful attempt to beat her at her own game—the art of interviewing.

This obviously violated the Associated Press' own rules for proper sentence length, but everyone who read it probably caught the spirit of the occasion.

That the account includes "value" judgments there can be no doubt. The writer thought Miss McBride "prodded, argued, baited and cajoled," for instance. Quite possibly another observer might have thought she was becoming histrionic in the attempt to conceal inadequacy in the face of a barrage of questions.

The clever writer who attempts to convey his impressions of an occasion substantiates such statements as "And the editors loved it," by reporting that "Some were seen to wipe tears of laughter from their eyes." Not always, of course, is there such tangible reportable evidence available. In such cases the reporter's experience, informational background, record of past achievement and, most of all, integrity are his weapons and his readers' protection.

Warren J. Brier gives scores of examples of good impressionistic journalism in an article, "The Lively Language of the Pros: A Glimpse at their Technique," in the 1963 *Montana Journalism Review*. Typical is the following from a UPI story about the Adolf Eichmann trial:

> Hausner, a small, hawk-faced, baldheaded man in a black legal gown, faced the defendant with both hands on his hips. An angry flush appeared on Eichmann's ashen-grey cheeks as the prosecutor pressed his attack.
>
> A nerve in Eichmann's jaw twitched and he licked his lips nervously between questions. His voice rose angrily as he answered some of the more pointed questions.

Wallace Carroll recalled a complaint the New York *Times* received after it included the following in its account of a United States Supreme Court decision: "In a passionate and despairing dissent, Justice Hugo Black rejected the majority opinion." According to a dissatisfied reader, who identified himself as a former newspaperman, "passionate" and "despairing" are "editorial words and you can't use them in a news story." According to Carroll, who was responsible, his "betters" on the *Times* commented, "We agree." Nevertheless, Carroll responded as follows:

> It is possible that this alumnus of the A.P. in Seattle has a better "feel" for the story than we had in Washington. But before I cleared the offending passage, I read Justice Black's dissent—all 18,000 words of it. And what impressed me from beginning to end was the passionate and despairing tone. And because passion and despair are seldom encountered in a judicial opinion, I thought this was news and worthy of noting in the *Times*.

In the cases cited, typical of what happens almost daily in any newsroom, the reporters were present as eyewitnesses, with no preconceived opinions, no causes to promote, intent on subduing their personal prejudices. So they acted as impartial critical experts. Admittedly there never will exist the completely emotionless reporter, editor or reader, but in the instances cited any bias was unconscious and deliberate efforts were made to avoid it. All anybody can do is his/her best to be scientifically neutral.

William Braden, an expert on the subject he had investigated exhaustively, began the first of two articles for the Chicago *Sun-Times* as follows:

Cook County Jail is not so bad as recent publicity has made it out to be.

It is much, much worse.

Even now, only a few people know how bad it really is.

It is evil. It is unjust. It is dangerous.

Those who know describe it as a cultural sink, a breeding ground for next summer's riots—and a deadly weapon aimed at the heart of the community.

After several more paragraphs of editorial conclusions, Braden began to produce his painstakingly gathered evidence:

There are two essential factors relating to the jail and its inmates.

1. The jail (as a building) was designed for the short-term incarceration of the most vicious and dangerous sort of criminals.

2. The vast majority of inmates do not fit that classification.

It is in the public interest to have scholarly minded journalists like Braden on the job, protecting the public interest by investigating such places as the jail. It would be utterly absurd to insist that a man of his caliber should not state his opinions after he has done his prowling in the public interest.

A type of impressionistic reporting more within the realm of the possible for the ordinary small city reporter is represented by the following example:

By Cal Turner

Elizabethtown—Dick Gregory is still at it. Swift, sharp and close to the bone, he cuts the U.S. into little pieces, tidies up its heart and puts it back together, and his listeners love it.

Appearing at Elizabethtown College yesterday, he held a press conference before taking the podium. In a style ranging from instant indignation to a beguiling placidity, he shot down questions from the old and weary, the young at heart and those with no cause but to sit and listen. The acid sometimes dripped.

Coming off a long fast which had as target the nation's anemic attempt to snuff out the narcotics traffic, he stroked a bearded jaw, rolled his eyes, gestured extravagantly and pictured doomsday just around the corner.

"The country is sick," he said. "Nothing will change it until its people learn how to deal with human problems on a human level. Why today, the automobile is more important than the youth."

If the tune sounded antique, the mood he wrought wore long after the conference ended. Calling himself, a "social doctor," he looks at America's ills with a venomous glee.

"I don't like to go into my predictions of the past," he said. "And I don't like to place myself as a prophet." Lacing his thin fingers together, it was here that he ripped into the CIA (Central Intelligence Agency).

"There's a good chance of this country being overthrown by the CIA within the next 18 months," he snapped, his eyes riding to the edge of their sockets. "And if they don't do it, you may see one of the damnedest blood baths the world has ever seen within the next five years."

Digging deeper, he emphasized this was possible because the American people just don't believe it can happen.

"The CIA doesn't have to answer to nobody," he said. "Not even the President. We just don't believe it can happen, yet the CIA goes all around the world, creating incidents, toppling governments. Why, they called off those trials about Vietnam (the massacres). They tap our phones. If America doesn't awaken, then you're going to see what this all will lead to.''

Just back from Tokyo, the final lap on a world trip, Gregory said he had looked long and hard at the problems of poverty on a global scale.

[Harrisburg (Pa.) *Evening News*]

Not many, if any of the so-called straight news stories about the Yuba City mass murders came so close to giving the reader the feeling of the tragedy as the following story by Douglas E. Kneeland in the June 1, 1971, New York *Times*, especially paragraphs 3, 4 and 5.

By Douglas E. Kneeland

SPECIAL TO THE NEW YORK TIMES

Marysville, Calif., May 31—Nobody much missed the faceless men who disappeared from Lower D. and nobody much mourns them now as their hacked up bodies are dug from the soft loam of peach orchards in the outskirts of Yuba City across the Feather River from here.

More than 20 of them dropped out of sight in the last two months from the four- or five-block Skid Row here that is anchored by the lower end of D. Street. Hardly anybody noticed. Perhaps because if the men existed at all in the minds of Marysville and Yuba City, they were already lost, already dead.

They were the men New Yorkers stare hard not to see on the side streets off Times Square. The men Chicagoans brush by on Division Street. The men San Franciscans avoid in the Mission district.

The weaving, tattered men with the red eyes and the stubbly beards. The ageless men, all old beyond their years. The thousands and thousands—nobody knows how many—who drift endlessly, aimlessly across the underside of America. The men who are as invisible in the small towns and cities as they are in the big ones.

Every day they turn up dead in the dank doorways of the cities, behind a shabby village saloon, beside a lonely railroad track.

It took a lot of them dead in one place to make anyone notice much at all. But 23 bodies have been dug from the orchard graves during an investigation led by Sheriff Roy D. Whiteaker, and Juan V. Corona, a 37-year-old farm labor contractor with a history of mental illness, is being held on murder charges.

Now the nation is watching and asking how so many could have been so forgotten. . . .

This is great writing, and it certainly is not in accordance with the objectivity rules of the Associated Press of bygone days. To repeat, however, it is not new. Rather, it is reminiscent of much of what came 25 to 50 years ago from the newspaper reportorial pens of such journalistic greats as Ben Hecht, Theodore Dreiser, Stephen Crane, Meyer Berger, Vincent Sheean, Ernest Hemingway, Heywood Broun and many others. Much of the complaint against the so-called new or activist or whatever-you-want-to-call-it journalism today is, as always, from those who fear exposure of the facts that the probing and sensitive newsgatherers describe.

Definitely in the old tradition was the following column by Robert T. Smith in the Minneapolis *Tribune*.

A scene at a Minneapolis Red Owl supermarket. . . .

The small slightly-built boy of about 7 was doing the shopping for his mother and little sister. The Red Owl check-out clerk said the boy doesn't have a father and his mother works.

He had put several items in his cart, but he couldn't read part of the note his mother had given him. He got to the check-out counter and there was a long line behind him.

"Could you read this for me?" he asked the young girl clerk.

There were some grumbles from those waiting behind the boy. But the clerk studied the note a minute and said the only thing the boy didn't have were three small turkey pot pies.

The boy looked a little bewildered.

"C'mon," said the clerk and she took him to the aisle and found the pies.

The lineup became more disgruntled. Some left and got into other lines. Their places were taken by other shoppers.

"Well, for heaven's sakes," said one middle-aged woman.

"You'd think we had nothing to do but stand in lines all day," said an irritated man.

An elderly woman wearing a blue stocking cap waited patiently. She had what you often see in the carts of the elderly; a half pound of hamburger, not ground beef; a small loaf of day-old bread, a small can of applesauce and a bag of the kind of coffee you grind yourself.

There were bare leather streaks on the fur collar of her coat. There was a hole in the finger of one of her mittens.

When the clerk and the auburn-haired boy returned, a thin, nervous woman in line said: "Maybe now we can get some service here." She pushed her cart up against the man in front of her.

The clerk totaled the boy's groceries and presented him with the bill. He reached into his jacket pocket and came up with nothing.

"What now?" asked a man.

The boy blushed and he searched other pockets. Others left the line. But with newcomers the line remained about the same.

From his right rear pants pocket the boy found the food stamps. He smiled and handed them to the clerk.

"I'm sorry," said the clerk, "but you're a dollar seventy-three cents short."

"This could go on forever," said the middle-aged woman. The boy blushed again and was frightened. He wouldn't look at anybody.

"That's all I've got," he said. "And my mother's not home yet from work."

A further exodus from the line. A man and woman tangled their carts as they moved to another check-out counter.

The elderly woman with the blue stocking cap left her cart and went forward to the young clerk and the boy.

"Give him his groceries and I'll take care of it," she said.

The boy smiled and in a few minutes was out of the door. At 7, you don't always remember to say thank you. Especially when you want to hurry away from something.

When it was the elderly woman's turn to check out, she also paid the $1.73 for the boy, with her food stamps.

PROVIDING PERSPECTIVE

News does not consist only in specific incidents that can be written up with clearcut inclusion of all of the five *w*'s. Ideas are news. So are ideologies, trends of thought, psychological situations and similar intangibles. It is not highbrow to believe that it would be a better world if more newspaper readers were aware of social, political, economic and other stresses and strains that often must be written about without definite news pegs. The "think piece" is a comparatively old journalistic device, but its use constantly is being broadened to include areas previously reserved for research scholars.

As Robert E. Garst, then assistant managing editor of the New York *Times,* wrote in *Nieman Reports:*

> Too much of past reporting has dealt only with the surface facts—the spot news—and too rarely has dug into reasons for them.
>
> A race riot, a prison outbreak, a bad slum condition—even a murder—has a social background, deeply rooted perhaps in the customs, traditions, and economic conditions of a region or community; but it is there and discoverable. It's the newspaper's job, it seems to me, to discover it. Only with that knowledge can a remedy be found for many of the ills that affect us.

Résumés

News weeklies, monthly digest magazines and weekly newspaper news reviews got their start during the depression years and appealed to persons in all walks of life who sought understanding in the midst of confusion. They have continued as an adjunct to quick spot-news reporting to provide recapitulations or résumés of series of fast-happening events. Few occurrences are treated as isolated happenings but as related to other events preceding and following them.

In addition to weekly news reviews, newspapers use "wrap-up" articles on running stories such as legislative assemblies, court trials, political campaigns and the like. In such stories, the expert reporter treats the events of a number of days, usually a week, as constituting material for a single story. Readers' memories are refreshed and relationships are pointed out. Often a condensed chronological recapitulation of the news is sufficient. In other cases, interpretation is added. This week, the observant reviewer may write, a certain objective came closer to realization because of this or that train of events. Defense strategy, another may explain, became clearer as cross-examination of prosecution witnesses continued in a court trial. A public official took two steps forward and one backward under observation by a knowledgeable journalist. And so on, all in the attempt to round up the events of a period into a comprehensive single story with proper perspective.

At the end of any session of the state legislature, a résumé of its activities is a journalistic must. Annual or semiannual appraisals of the handling of his official acts by a public official are in the same category. The news reviewer often takes a second look at the cumulative record about every part of which s/he has previously composed separate accounts.

Surveys

When similar news occurs in a number of places, a journalistic medium may conduct a survey to find out what the overall situation happens to be. Perhaps attempts to enact similar legislation were made in a number of states, in which case a compilation of the results is significant. Let disaster of any kind occur in one place and a follow-up survey reveals how widespread are conditions believed to have been its cause.

Newspapers have conducted surveys to determine the death rates on transcontinental highways, the outcomes of referenda on school bond issues, the use of prison labor on private projects, the attitude of condemned prisoners toward capital punishment, the extent of racial and religious discrimination in housing, schooling and job opportunities, the increase in the ownership of yachts, and on many and many other matters. Some of the material, though not quite so up-to-the-minute, might have been obtained from public and private research agencies.

In drawing conclusions from any kind of data, the press must avoid the error that professional researchers and pollsters also must avoid, that of inadequacy or lack of representativeness of the sample. It is incorrect to write, "Public opinion today here is this or that" unless one has exhaustively questioned persons in all walks of life, something it is rarely possible for a newspaperman to do. Even an impressive group of interviewees within a given area may not be typical. There is no field in which unanimity exists among experts. Quoting leaders is good journalism but minorities also should be contacted and exaggeration always avoided.

By Frank Elam

The upsurge in teachers' strikes continued last week, with some walkouts entering their third week.

Over 500,000 students have been affected by the estimated 75–85 teachers' walkouts since the new school year began. The number is roughly double the strike figure at this time last year.

Most of the strike issues have centered around wage increases, cost-of-living clauses, work loads and benefits such as medical insurance.

As the Guardian goes to press, teachers' union leaders in Bridgeport, Conn., and Dayton, Ohio, have been jailed. School teachers in Seattle, Cleveland and Fall River, Mass., are facing antistrike injunctions. And strikes continue among college professors in Chicago and Detroit. . . . [*Guardian*]

Situations and Trends

A city editor, getting the idea from an article on the subject in a national magazine, assigned a reporter to "find out how much moonlighting there is in this community." Other editors have sought the answers to such questions as "What do we do for the mentally retarded in our town?" "What about juvenile delinquency among girls?" "Are there any independent grocers left?" "What's happening to our wildlife?"

Often such assignments result in feature articles concerning little-known or off-the-beaten-path persons or groups. In other cases, there may be forthcoming broader expositions of current situations to which the journalistic limelight is applied. The net result is a better acquaintance with all aspects of the life of the community and possibly an arousal of civic interest in improvement where needed.

No reporter should start on an assignment of this sort without adequate preparation, which should include not merely examination of the publication's own clipping files but also the reading of books, magazine articles and other material to acquaint himself or herself with the aspects of the situation that s/he should bear in mind during the fact finding. When the reporter encounters someone with views contrary to those usually considered orthodox, it is best to avoid altercation. Instead, the reporter should tactfully request the news source to comment upon the views of "the other side" as generally understood.

Fortified with information from a number of other places, the perceptive reporter may conclude that under study is not just a local phenomenon but part of a widespread trend. Farmers on the fringes of suburban areas, for instance, may be keeping land out of cultivation in expectation of selling their property to urban developers. Redlining by moneylending institutions, sit-in demonstrations, sympathetic picketing, streaking by college students, fads in games, dress, music and the like may be national or international in extent. The locally written feature can stress home-town manifestations but would be inadequate if it did not mention the broader aspects.

Ora Spaid did a colossally successful job for the Louisville *Courier-Journal* when he investigated post-basketball game fights between rival gangs of high school boys. The following extracts, approximately the middle third of the first of three articles, indicate how Spaid tackled the assignment writing as the careful reporter and specialist-expert that he is, having been a social worker before he turned to journalism:

> ATHLETICS
>
> One of those not-new conditions is overemphasis of athletics.
>
> A high-school basketball game has become an orgy of emotionalism closely resembling a voodoo ritual. Big crowds pack into small gyms. Drums pound a savage throb, and pretty little girls whip up frenzied partisan spirit that doesn't let up even when play begins.
>
> Sportsmanship is usually evident—as in the exchange of "Hello" yells at the beginning. But it breaks down easily, as when a player from the other team steps to the line for a crucial free throw and the crowd jeers and shouts to distract him.

Coaches talk of the "home-court advantage"—the fact that the crowd is so partisan you can't expect a fair contest.

EMOTIONS STIRRED

Emotional pitch is built before the game in school-wide "pep assemblies," a practice that teachers consider "a necessary evil." A psychology teacher says pointedly that pep assemblies "are a real study in mass psychology sometimes."

The question is: Where does school spirit leave off and hysteria begin?

The concept of high-school sports for participation long ago lost out to the necessity of winning. Coaches build the equivalent of farm systems to produce material for winning teams. A coach becomes as much a victim of "ratings" as a television show; there's a tendency to enlarge the point spread over a defeated opponent to gain a higher rating.

Utterly lost is the grace of losing. High-school girls weep as if death had descended when their teams lose. Fathers grumble about ineffective coaches.

But gainsaying overemphasis of athletics is not enough. Why are athletics overemphasized?

It's a result, some say, of "urbanization." The exodus of people from the cities of recent decades and attendant flight to the suburbs produces a lonely-in-the-crowd society.

It also produces the big school, a factor that men like Richard Van Hoose, superintendent of Jefferson County schools, and Sam V. Noe, his counterpart in Louisville schools, hold as the root cause of many problems.

THE BIG SCHOOL

Today's suburban high school of 2,500 or more students is almost what yesterday's college was.

Let Earl Duncan, principal of the 2,600-student Waggener High School, tell of some of the problems.

"In a school of 2,600, only 12 boys can play basketball, but certainly a lot more would like to," he said. "Only five youngsters can be elected to offices in a graduating class of 350. Think how many that leaves out."

It's a case of being lost in a big school.

A bright boy in a big suburban school came home last week with failing grades. He told his mother, "I'm not good at sports; I'm not in the band; I can't get on the school paper. I've just lost all interest in school."

Most young people don't lose interest—they plunge. If they can't find something they can participate in actively, they participate vicariously. The school is something they can belong to, something to "give them identity," as the psychologists say. So they become rabid fans, fanatic followers.

MAY BOIL OVER

But nonparticipation isn't too satisfying; there's not much opportunity to blow off steam, unless in violent rooting. And it's always possible that this pent-up steam may boil over into violence, particularly if there is some way to rationalize it, like defending the school's honor or avenging a lost game.

Big schools build up tension in ways other than pep assemblies—subtler ways, often overlooked.

Principal Duncan points out that when you have only one gymnasium and it is given over to varsity teams, there is no place for other youngsters to play. To "make the best use of facilities," in gym periods or after school, the play must be scheduled and organized. Regimentation is another word for it—constant supervision, no opportunity to just horse around.

Drop in at one of these big schools at noon hour and you will see long lines of students in the cafeteria. The sheer impossibility of feeding all students at once means they eat in shifts. And mark this: lunch hour usually lasts only 20 minutes. Not only that, but by the time a student gets his food, he may have only 10 minutes to eat it. Of necessity, he must "bolt his food" or miss his next class.

DIFFERENCE IS GREAT

Compare this with the paper-sack days when pupils brought their lunches, ate leisurely and spent the rest of a long lunch hour dozing under a tree or breaking the tension of long hours at a desk in a make-up ball game.

This means that today's school children put in a 7-hour day with little let-up, seldom released from supervision. Even recess is now a matter of "supervised play," and in some schools, children are given a grade for lunchroom conduct.

Then there is homework. There always has been homework, but it seems to a lot of students that teachers are trying to close up the missile gap with Russia by the sheer bulk of homework they assign. The youngsters respond, not by learning from homework, but merely by "getting it done."

Getting it done means more hours under supervision, this time from a Mom or Dad anxious to see a good report card.

All this adds up to this: youngsters today are under greater tension than ever before but have less opportunity to dissipate it.

The foregoing was written by an expert, which many journalists become after considerable experience in covering a specialized type of news. They deserve and receive respect and their prestige is bound to grow as social scientists and others become so engrossed with their Theory and Methodology that they become unreliable witnesses to anything real. Spaid obviously wrote with a liberal slant. The liberalism of journalists is not the result, unfortunately, of what they learn in school but results from their practical experience as they come in firsthand contact with life. Members of the Establishment, including many newspaper owners and publishers, become alarmed at what they read in newspapers. But, as they are fond of telling fellow luncheon clubbers, the newspaper is merely a mirror and should not be scapegoated. The interpretative reporter today holds the mirror the highest.

Journalism is more purposeful today than ever before; it has assumed greater responsibilities than the mere recording and interpreting of news; it has acquiesced in the general feeling that it is a quasi-public utility, which makes it an easy mark for popular criticism.

—MERLE THORPE, editor, *Nation's Business*

The reader does not want to be instructed by newspapers for the first time about things of which he has had no knowledge. He wants to learn more about things which he already knows. He does not seek first knowledge, experience, or information from newspapers. He wants to have his own knowledge, experience, and information reproduced, amplified, and sublimated by them. In other words, he wants to have himself third-personified, just as people find some pleasure in looking at their own images in a mirror.

—K. SUGIMURA, editor, *Asahi Shimbun*, Tokyo, Japan

What are required above all else in newspaper making are personal characteristics or qualities on the part of newspaper men. These qualities are to a high degree a feeling of responsibility, honesty, industry, and only a fair amount of intelligence—a sort of conviction that he can serve the public, and a determination to do so.

—E. W. SCRIPPS

10
INVESTIGATIVE REPORTING

All reporting is investigative because newsgatherers seek facts. Prof. Jay Jensen of the University of Illinois says that investigative reporting is "just old fashioned traditional exposé stuff, uncovering what is being covered up, revealing what is being hidden, nailing down lies that have been told, etc." Accurate as this definition is, it does not satisfy many would-be journalists who saw the motion picture, "All the President's Men" in which Dustin Hoffman and Robert Redford played the parts of Carl Bernstein and Robert Woodward, Washington *Post* reporters who exposed many of the scandals connected with the Watergate burglary.

Robert Greene, two-time Pulitzer prize-winner for investigative work for *Newsday,* says simply that investigative reporting is "uncovering something somebody wants to keep a secret." Similarly David Anderson and Peter Benjaminson, Detroit *Free Press* investigative reporters, say in their book, *Investigative Reporting,* "Investigative reporting is simply the reporting of concealed information."

Other authorities are more expansive. The late Paul N. Williams, who won a Pulitzer prize for exposing the financial dealings of Boys Town, wrote in his posthumously published book, *Investigative Reporting and Editing,* ''Investigative reporting is an intellectual process. It is a business of gathering and sorting ideas and facts, building patterns, analyzing options and making decisions based on logic rather than emotion—including the decision to say no at any of several stages.''

At the time of his death, Williams had quit the managing editorship of the Omaha *Sunpapers* to be a journalism professor at Ohio State University. Another long-time investigative reporter now sharing his experiences with others in the classroom is Clark R. Mollenhoff, for more than a quarter-century chief of the Washington bureau of the Des Moines *Register* and *Tribune* during which time he won a Pulitzer prize. At present Mollenhoff is a professor of journalism at Washington and Lee University. He elaborates: ''Investigative reporting is a precarious profession. For the most part it is hours, days and sometimes weeks of tedious work in combing records. It is endless interviews with people who really don't want to talk, the running out of endless leads; the frustration of having most leads end as dry holes or, worse yet, with inconclusive results; and the impenetrable stonewalling of responsible officialdom.''

Despite the tedium, Mollenhoff believes, ''We are the communication line that is vital to final government accountability to the public. We should all do our utmost to make certain that the life line of democracy is not cluttered with irresponsible debris or superficial froth.''

Mollenhoff's book, *Investigative Reporting*, was published in 1980 by Macmillan.

Any newspaper with standing in its community is constantly being importuned to ''look into'' this or that, which usually means to uncover facts that it allegedly is in the public interest to be known but that someone is attempting to conceal. Annoying and time-consuming as it may become to observe the rule, it is unsafe to ignore tipsters, no matter how unreliable or crackpot they may seem to be. Maybe the policeman whose neighbor cannot understand how he is able to afford an expensive car *did* inherit a large sum of money. On the other hand, his/her affluence may be the clue to scandal involving others as well as himself/herself.

Before undertaking the ''tedious and discouraging work,'' which Brit Hume in *Inside Story* says investigative reporting is, much of the time, it is smart to evaluate the motives of the tipster. Disgruntled employees or colleagues, past or present, may be merely satisfying grudges, but they may not be. And the same goes for divorced wives or husbands. The same public records to be consulted in tracing the background of a principal in a scandal can be used to discover the motivation and perhaps the probable credibility of a news source. Certainly it is almost always unwise for a reporter to confront someone against whom a charge has been made before she has made a thorough check of all angles involved. After the records have been exhausted, the first interviewing usually should be of those on the periphery of the story. The target of any investigation ordinarily should be the very last interviewee. By that time the reporter should be thoroughly prepared and know exactly what missing links he is after.

Actually the investigative reporter is like any other kind of reporter, only more so. More inquisitive, more skeptical, more resourceful and imaginative in knowing where to look for facts, more ingenious in circumventing obstacles, more indefatigable in the pursuit of facts and able to endure drudgery and discouragement. Investigative reporters seldom play detective in the sense of shadowing persons but they do not naïvely accept explanations. Thus they are confronted with many situations that test their integrity.

CRUSADING—MUCKRAKING

Present-day investigative reporters are carrying on a journalistic tradition that did not begin with the Bernstein–Woodward sleuthing or with many other post-World War II exploits including the uncovering of facts about the My Lai massacre, which won a Pulitzer prize for Seymour Hersh, then with the Dispatch News Service, and Jack Anderson's Pulitzer prize-winning exposure of official Washington's hypocrisy during the Pakistani–Indian War.

The Era of the Muckrakers, according to the history books, was the first two decades of the century when a small coterie of magazine article writers exposed corruption in business and government.

Outstanding examples of their work were *The Shame of the Cities,* by Lincoln Steffens; *The Jungle,* a novel about Chicago's stockyards by Upton Sinclair, which led to the first pure food and drug act; Ida Tarbell's history of the Standard Oil Co. and many magazine series and books by Ray Stannard Baker, David Graham Phillips, Charles Edward Russell and others.

Although President Theodore Roosevelt considered muckraking an opprobrious term when he adapted it from John Bunyan's *Pilgrim's Progress* to apply to enterprising journalists, the first decade of the twentieth century is today regarded as a "golden period" of public service journalism. Unquestionably the achievements of the press in exposing the Watergate and related scandals and American atrocities in Vietnam will be remembered similarly. Although the so-called Pentagon Papers were not the work of investigative reporters, their editing and publishing was an historic event as for the first time in American history the federal government attempted to suppress an important news story. By successfully taking the issue to the Supreme Court the New York *Times* won a Pultizer prize.

With many other exposés to his credit, Jack Anderson ranks with Ralph Nader as the outstanding contemporary crusader. Nader won a $425,000 court judgment against General Motors, which hired private investigators to harass him after his iconoclastic *Unsafe at Any Speed* was published. Nader is the only muckraker ever to institutionalize himself. His organizations include Center for the Study of Responsive Law, Public Interest Research Group, Corporate Accountability Research Study, Public Citizen Inc. and many others.

Activist-minded reporters, young and old, favor more newspaper initiative in emulation of Anderson and Nader, the late Rachel Carson whose *Silent Spring* inspired much of the interest in threats to the environment and Vance Packard whose *Hidden Persuaders* put advertisers on guard.

Together with many books by foreign correspondents who have set the record straight concerning episodes in recent American foreign policy, these and similar crusading efforts make the present outshine the Era of the Muckrakers. As the number of papers with investigative reporters grew, in 1976 the Investigative Reporters and Editors was organized. More than 300, double the number expected, attended the first convention in Indianapolis. By 1980 the membership had reached 1,200 and a resource center, headed by John Ullmann had been established at the University of Missouri with a full-time staff large enough to publish a bimonthly *Journal,* to issue reports and to conduct workshops in all parts of the country. Impetus to the development of Investigative Reporters and Editors was the Arizona Project in which 23 members engaged in a four months' investigation of land frauds in Arizona. There Don Bolles, investigative reporter for the Phoenix *Republic,* had been murdered after he was lured to a restaurant, presumably to obtain information, and a bomb was placed in his car which blew up. Bob Greene of *Newsday* headed the project that produced a series of 23 articles that was syndicated to papers all over the country.

Support for investigative reporting also is provided by the Fund for Investigative Reporting, which makes grants to enable reporters to "probe abuses of authority or the malfunctioning of institutions and systems which harm the public." In a decade it made 450 grants totaling more than $370,000. Executive Director is Howard Bray, 1346 Connecticut Avenue, Washington, D.C. 20036.

Among the projects supported by the Fund are these:

- Reporting the My Lai massacre and the attempted cover-up. Seymour Hersh won a Pulitzer Prize for this probe.
- James Polk also received a Pulitzer for his extensive reports of illegal political campaign contributions, helping produce statutory changes.
- Edward Roeder's reporting of campaign financing abuses since those changes were enacted.
- Victor Marchetti's detailed study with John Marks of the C.I.A., "The CIA and the Cult of Intelligence," the first book the government went to court to censor before publication.
- Brit Hume's investigation of corruption in the United Mine Workers.
- A coast-to-coast probe by William Brandon of the deliberate way in which Indian tribes are defrauded and victimized.
- Rachel Scott's articles and book, "Muscle and Blood," about unnecessarily dangerous working conditions.
- An inquiry by George Crile into fraudulent tax assessments in Gary, Indiana.
- Questionable practices of the Tennessee Valley Authority uncovered by James Branscome.
- James Healion's revelations of the police entrapment of two suspects and their fatal shooting in Connecticut. The Connecticut troopers were convicted of obstruction of justice.

- An 18,000-word magazine cover article by Ronnie Dugger on government subservience to the oil lobby, costing the public several billion dollars annually.
- The first detailed analysis for a general audience of the issues surrounding cable television, Ralph Lee Smith's "The Wired Nation."
- The politics and conflicts-of-interest in New York's surrogate courts reported by Allan Wolper, honored by the American Bar Association.
- Gross neglect in protecting humans exposed to nuclear weapons tests revealed by Paul Jacobs.

What any member of the public thinks of any investigative job depends upon his/her interests and/or prejudices. Anyone who likes the journalistic enterprise will call it crusading; for anyone who dislikes it the word is muckraking.

SITUATION FEATURES

The editor who tells a reporter to "look into this" usually acts on a tip or a hunch. Often the information needed is easily obtainable and there is no hint of criminal behavior. Nevertheless, facts important for the public to know are revealed, and the opportunity to cover such assignments is excellent training for the reporter who aspires to be a high calibered investigative reporter. Under a byline the reporter, an expert as a result of thorough fact finding, expresses opinions together with reasons for them. For example:

By David Horowitz

If you order by mail and get cheated, what can you do about it? You can fight back. You can get the U.S. Postal Service and Direct Mail organizations involved, but you've got to move quickly before the con artists have a chance to scram. In the first installment of a three-part series on protecting yourself from hucksters, consumer expert David Horowitz tells how to file a mail-order-gyp complaint that can result in a hefty jail term for the rip-off artist.

Shopping by mail has ballooned into a $75-billion-a-year business and it's easy to see why. What could be more convenient than sitting in your own comfy home, thumbing through a colorful catalog, then ordering on a form that practically flings itself back in the mailbox?

But don't get too smug. Don't think you, as a consumer, are totally protected, sitting there in the security of your home. This ought to rattle your cage: Mail-order companies generated more complaints than any other type of business in 1977 and were maintaining their lead in 1978 as this was written, according to the Council of Better Business Bureaus. What's more, a survey of newspaper and television "action line" reporters by Corning Glass Works found than mail-order selling produced more gripes than any other category.

Now, I'm not putting down the entire direct-mail industry. I am only blasting the bandits and bunko artists—the kind of crooks you find in any business.

It's important to realize that direct-mail marketing exists for only one reason: to sell you something and collect your cash. If you get real value for your money, fine. But if you get cheated, here's how to avenge yourself. Better yet, here's how to avoid it in the first place. . . . [Chicago *Sun-Times*]

Pictures of border markets and boxed lists of prices of necessary grocery items on both sides of the U.S.–Mexican border accompanied a roundup article that began as follows:

By Bill Greer
ASSOCIATED PRESS

A penny-wise consumer who does his grocery shopping on both sides of the border can make substantial savings in his monthly grocery bill, according to an Associated Press check of grocery prices here and across the border.

But there are some hazards.

For example, avocados are cheaper across the border. But the seed cannot be transported into the United States.

However, once those, and similar, peculiarities are mastered, there are bargains to be had. For this comparison, the Associated Press chose a supermarket in El Paso and its counterpart, the super mercado, across the Rio Grande at Juarez. Both were in fashionable neighborhoods.

Marketing and promotional gimmicks pushing small items were used at both stores. The Mexican super mercado perhaps held a slight edge in the sales technique.

In both stores, film, candy and razor blades were displayed near the cash registers to entice last-minute purchases.

The Mexican grocers place a real temptation at the check counter—a wooden barrel filled with ice chunks and quarts of near-freezing beer.

The mercado designers had parents in mind when they planned the lilylined, tree-filled park on two sides of the building. Children play while parents spend. The only alternative to basket-riding, display-threatening children on the U.S. side is the parking lot.

Shopping center parking lots in the United States occasionally are sites of violence. Not so often at the mercado where an armed guard watches customers and cars. . . . [San Antonio *Express News*]

The author of the following piece, which could have originated either with a citizen's complaint or with observations by the paper's courthouse reporter, did not have to dig very deep for the facts.

By James Warren

Whether you've fallen into a pothole or been shot by a police officer, suing the city is a shocking odyssey. You may win—perhaps even win big—but prepare to wait as long as *four years* to get your money.

Crane operator Robert Dils waited so long for the $246,524 a judge granted him he died waiting. Now his widow has joined thousands of frustrated Chicagoans to whom the city owes $14.8 million in judgments, and who'll be lucky to collect before the *next* election for mayor.

Lawyers here call the situation a farce, and fiscal officials in other cities laugh. But the snail-like way the city pays off is no joke and leads many to try desperately to sell their judgments for cash to brokers at discounts reaching a whopping 20 per cent. . . . [Chicago *Sun-Times*]

Almost any journalist in any American city could have gotten the idea for the following story:

By Terry Atlas

After nine years in their La Grange Park home, John and Rosemary Swanson decided it was time for a larger place. They shopped around for months before settling on a house in nearby Hinsdale, one large enough to give their three daughters each a room of her own.

"It was basically a move up, the American dream," sighed Mrs. Swanson. "It's what everybody wanted to do before the crash of '79." So now the Swansons own two houses.

Practically overnight, it seems, the real estate market has collapsed. The shortage of housing has suddenly turned into glut in the Chicago area, and buyers are as rare as 10½-per-cent mortgage money. New home construction is grinding to a halt, and existing homes that would have been snatched up at the asking prices not long ago now sit for months without so much as a bid.

"The bottom has dropped out," said one real estate agent. "Nothing is selling."

It's a fact no one knows better than the Swansons, now a two-mortgage family whose old home has been on the market for more than three months while their Hinsdale house sits vacant.

The couple has tried all the usual methods to sell the house, including slashing the initial $99,900 asking price by $10,000. And, frustrated, they've even turned to the unorthodox. Taking a neighbor's advice, they buried a small statue of St. Joseph upside down in the back yard, which is supposed to bring good luck to homesellers.

St. Joseph probably is buried in more than a few back yards in the Chicago area. Anyone trying to sell his house today can use all the help he can get. . . .

[Chicago *Tribune*]

EXPOSÉS

Explaining how his paper won six consecutive Pulitzer prizes, a Philadelphia *Inquirer* investigative reporter said, "We get 95 per cent of it from public records." So, a primary requisite is to know what and where the records related to the subject matter of the assignment are and the nature of their contents.

Home Health Care

It was by looking up the law and studying health department records that the Milwaukee *Journal*'s Margo Huston turned an apparently routine assignment into a Pulitzer prize. Seeking material on "alternatives to nursing homes for the elderly," she consulted the telephone book yellow pages to obtain the names of 12 private agencies offering service in the home.

Huston was horror-stricken by the case histories she read in the welfare department books. She visited the homes of a number of the clients, which made her feel sicker. The 12 agencies admitted they were unlicensed, so the reporter consulted the state statute book in the paper's morgue. She looked under the headings "health care," "elderly," "home care," "day care" and anything else she could think of until she found a ten-year-old law that required licensing of all profit-making health care institutions.

Next Huston went to the Wisconsin Legislative Reference Library and the Administrative Code, a public record. It detailed the qualifications employees of home care agencies should have and how such institutions were to be inspected and regulated.

On a visit to the Department of Health the reporter overheard a caseworker mention the effort to test a new law by which a person could be hospitalized against his or her will. The caseworker refused to tell the patient's name so Huston went to the County Building where the corporation counsel handling the case identified the patient. A judge refused to hear the case seeking a court order, saying that otherwise civil liberties would be violated. Huston recognized the patient's name as that of an old woman whom she had visited in her squalid home. By the time she made another visit the old woman had died in a hospital where she finally went of her own volition.

As a result of the interest aroused by Huston's articles, an ombudsman program for elderly persons either in or out of nursing homes was established in connection with the Mt. Sinai Hospital Center and several private agencies improved their services. Huston received a number of calls from persons who said they had been inspired to provide better care for their parents.

Boys Town

Few if any other investigative exposés caused a greater nationwide stir than the series on the financial status of Boys Town for which the *Sunpapers* of Omaha won a Pulitzer prize for special local reporting. Founded by the Rev. Edward J. Flanagan in 1918, Boys Town, on a farm ten miles west of Omaha, was made famous by a motion picture starring Spencer Tracy and Mickey Rooney in 1938. Paul N. Williams, managing editor of the *Sunpapers,* a group of weeklies, wondered what the return was from the large-scale fund raising drives every Christmas and Easter season. Officials refused to talk, so Williams consulted the records.

Since Boys Town was incorporated as a village, it had to file condensed annual municipal budgets and brief reports of operations. Since it was a nonprofit corporation, it had to file brief reports, a list of officers, and copies of its articles of incorporation. Since Boys Town operated an educational system it had to be accredited by the state of Nebraska and the North Central Association, which requires reports of school enrollment, curricula staffing levels, and compliance with health and safety rules. So it was ascertained that Boys Town had fewer than 700 students, not the presumed 1,000 plus.

As a licensed child care operation Boys Town had to file other routine reports with the State Welfare Department. Since Boys Town owned land there had to be records of deeds and mortgages, taxes and prices. The land records indicated that, at the very least, Boys Town property in Douglas county was worth $8.4 million.

For publicity reasons, Boys Town was a U.S. post office, which meant it had to file certain minimal public reports with the postmaster general. When the local postmaster refused to talk, Williams obtained the cooperation of his congressman to learn that from 30 to 50 million letters were mailed annually from the Boys Town post office. Then Williams conferred with some private fund raisers, who declared that such sizable mailings could not be justified unless they brought in at least $10 million. The National Information Bureau, a confidential advisory service for large donors, told Williams that it was impossible for it to reply to inquiries because Boys Town provided inadequate data.

Most officials of the Child Welfare League of America and local and regional experts in child development and child delinquency told Williams that Boys Town's large single-institution approach was not best for the kind of problem children being served.

The climax of the *Sunpapers'* investigation was Form 990 filed with the Internal Revenue System under the Tax Reform Act of 1970, of which Williams had not previously known. The 94-page report showed that Boys Town's net worth was $191,401,421, increasing at the rate of about $17 million annually. Confronted with these figures, officers and members of the board of directors had no explanation. The money-raising mailings were canceled for a few years. By 1980 Boys Town's net worth was $256 million and the student body had declined to 398. Centers for the study and treatment of speech and hearing defects and for a study of youth development were established with an endowment of $30 million, and other plans to expand activities were considered.

Since the New York *Times* exposed the corrupt Tweed political ring almost a century ago, and the New York *World* did the same for the post-World War I Ku Klux Klan, to the present there have been journalistic investigations that make dramatic and exciting reading. Among the most important recently have been the Philadelphia *Inquirer's* exposure of corruption in the police department; the Miami *Herald's* Broun prize-winning "dangerous doctors" series, which exposed laxity on the part of state regulatory boards; the persistence of the small Point Reyes *Light* in telling how the Synanon Foundation operates—an account which received a Pulitzer prize; the Gannett News Service's Pulitzer prize-winning unraveling of the financial affairs of the Pauline Fathers, the Chicago *Sun-Times* exposures of improperly run abortion clinics, swindles by phony accident victims, deficient nursing homes, and crookedness by city inspectors of taverns, unethical repairmen, and many others. The paper exposed gross laxity in the Illinois Department of Law Enforcement's Bureau of Identification, which awarded firearm owners' registration cards to the deceased bandit John Dillinger as well as to the one-time Cuban revolutionary hero Che Guevara; Travis Bickle, fictitious character in the motion picture, "Taxi Driver;" Frank James, brother of Jesse James, and Peter Gusenberg, one of the mobsters killed in the Valentine Day's massacre. Authentic pictures from the paper's morgue and completely fictitious personal data were included in the applications. The bureau did reject the application of Vito Corleone, name of a character in "The Godfather," possibly because the paper used a picture of Marlon Brando, who played the part.

PUBLIC RECORDS

The importance of easily available public records to the investigative reporter was explained by Patrick Riordan of the Miami *Herald* in the May–June 1979 Issue of *IRE Journal*. With the permission of the publication and the author, the article, "Getting the Background Fast," follows:

By Patrick Riordan
MIAMI HERALD

You're methodically researching your project on the ridiculously expensive new monorail the county wants to build at the new zoo when your editor starts flailing his arms and hollering at you.

The police desk has an update on a bust at a disco last night. It turns out they found in the back room 20 kilos of cocaine, 10 bales of marijuana and 100,000 quaaludes. A Colombian citizen was among those arrested.

The cops are cooperating with the Drug Enforcement Administration, not with you. They're giving out nothing beyond the arrest sheets.

There are a hundred unanswered questions: Who owns the disco? What else does he own—land, buildings, cars, boats, airplanes? What's his economic background? Has he ever been accused of a crime? Does he use corporations to hide behind? Is there a limited partnership involved? Who are its investors? How much did they invest? Who's in business with this guy?

Public records will answer every one of those questions in a few hours.

Let's suppose the cops are really playing hard-to-get and won't even tell you the name of the owner. You can still find it.

You have the address of the disco from the arrest sheet (or the phone book.) You go to the office of the tax collector, or the office where deeds are kept on file, and ask a clerk to help you convert the street address into a legal description of the property. In an urban area that'll be a block number and one or more lot numbers in a particular subdivision.

For example, suppose the disco is located at 3000 Coral Boulevard in Miami. Either by asking a clerk or using the county real estate atlas yourself, you find that 3000 Coral Boulevard is in Miami Urban Estates subdivision, and that your particular address is Lots 5, 6 and 7 of Block 5.

With that information you can find the owner in one of two ways:

The easy way, if your county keeps abstract books, tract indexes or a property index, is to look up the book or microfilm reel for your subdivision. In that book, you flip pages or unreel film until you come to Block 5. Then go to the very last entry under Block 5 and work backward. The first entry you come to for Lots 5, 6 and 7 is the most recent. It reflects the current owner.

The other way, if you don't have abstract books for each subdivision, is to work through the tax roll. You may need to convert the legal description into a folio number, composed of the block and lot numbers, a code number for the subdivision and municipality, and other code numbers for section, range and township—terms you'll encounter more often when you're researching rural acreage.

Each piece of property in your county has a unique folio number. Once you've got someone to show you how to determine it, go to the tax roll and look it up. It shows who's paying the taxes.

USUALLY THE OWNER

About 99 percent of the time that's the owner. (In Florida and Illinois, you may have a hidden land trust with a trustee paying the taxes. Lotsa luck.)

No matter how you get the name of the apparent owner, it's a good idea to double check. Go to the office where the deeds are kept. It's the recorder's office in some states, the register of deeds, the clerk's office or the official records office in others.

Ask for the grantor-grantee index (also known as the official records index, the deed index or the index to real estate transfers.)

In our case, the current owner appears to be something called Taca Corp. To find its deed to the disco property, look up Taca Corp. in the grantee index.

There's a reference to Book 289, Page 34 in the index next to Taca Corp.

Go find Deed Book 289 on the shelf or in a microfilm drawer. Turn to page 34 and you've got the deed.

Taca Corp., it says, acquired title to the property from Rodolfo Hernandez, a name that's vaguely familiar.

The corporation owes $50,000 on the property to First Smugglers' Bank and Trust Co.

That's its first mortgage.

It also owes another $375,000 to Hernandez, payable in quarterly installments over 10 years. That's the purchase money second mortgage.

You find out how much it owes by checking in the deed book a few pages before and after the deed for a mortgage. They're usually filed with the deed, but not always. Look in the index to mortgages under Taca Corp. to be sure.

From the deed and mortgages, you now know precisely what property was bought and sold (from the legal description), who bought it and who sold it, and who's financing it.

You can also figure out how much it cost.

The amount isn't spelled out directly, but it's indicated clearly by the amount of documentary tax paid to record the deed. Sometimes called the recordation fee, this tax corresponds mathematically to the value of the transaction.

In Florida, for example, $3 worth of stamps must be attached to the deed for every $1,000 of value. On a $100,000 transaction, there would be $300 worth of stamps.

In the District of Columbia, where the tax is one percent of the value of the transaction, the amount is shown by an imprint, not actual stamps. A $100,000 transaction costs $1,000 to record.

In other jurisdictions the tax rate varies. Find out what yours is from the county office that records deeds and charges the tax, or look up your state law.

After computing the indicated value of the transaction, you note in the index to deeds (the grantor-grantee index) that Taca Corp. seems to have several other deeds on file. But before proceeding, you decide to learn a little more about Taca.

The courthouse office where occupational licenses are kept sheds little light on the subject. Taca holds the local business license in its corporate name.

You could check the utilities office to see who pays the water and electricity bills, but you decide to pass for the moment.

You call the Secretary of State's office to ask for the corporate information office. They'll give you a lot of information on the phone, and send you more by mail.

Always ask for current officers and directors, including their addresses; the corporate address (also called the registered address); the name of the registered agent; the nature of the business the corporation engages in; and whether they're up-to-date on their franchise tax.

Also ask for the date of incorporation. If you're persuasive enough, you can sometimes get someone to go find the original articles of incorporation.

From that you can get the incorporators (the people who formed the corporation), the name of the attorney who handled the paperwork, the name of the notary public who notarized the corporate charter, and sometimes a more detailed statement of the business in which the corporation engages.

In this case, one name jumps out at you: It's Rodolfo Hernandez, the guy who sold the disco to Taca.

He turns out to be the president of Taca, its registered agent and one of its incorporators three years ago when it was formed.

His lawyer, a well-known criminal defense attorney, is corporate secretary (a little out of his line.)

Before you get off the phone, you call another agency in the capital, the Uniform Commercial Code office.

That's where people file evidence of secured debts, such as car or boat loans, or business loans backed up by accounts receivable, inventory or fixtures.

Taca, it develops, owes a restaurant supply company on its kitchen and bar facilities at the disco, but that's all.

You call the nearest office of the Alcoholic Beverage Commission or the Division of Beverage, or whichever agency licenses bars in your state.

The agency will have in its files a complete list of all owners of the disco if it has a liquor license.

Since the owner is Taca, this gives you a list of stockholders. There's only one: Hernandez.

A picture is emerging.

The disco where the cops found the dope has a complicated corporate structure, but only one man behind it all. The man receives large sums in the form of mortgage payments.

It could be a clever scheme to rip off the business and go bankrupt.

Or it might be Hernandez' way of establishing a large, on-the-record taxable income for IRS' consumption, in order to conceal his real income from smuggling.

Back to the deed books.

Those other transactions involving Taca now become much more interesting than they were before. You get copies of all deeds involving the company and your paper reimburses you. (If it doesn't, deduct it on your income tax return and look for another job.)

With each deed the pattern grows stronger:

In your county alone, Taca owns 50 acres near the new free trade zone, a key parcel next to the seaport, two old downtown hotels in the path of a new convention center, three condominium apartments and the disco where the drugs were found.

You extend your research. The Uniform Commercial Code office didn't have any record of loans on cars, airplanes or boats. Maybe that's because he paid cash for his smuggling equipment.

You call the state motor vehicle records office in the capital and explain the general nature of the inquiry.

A state employee looks up Taca and Hernandez.

He owns a new Seville in his own name with no lien on it. He paid cash. And Taca owns three big, straight-body trucks and a Jeep, all free and clear.

The Department of Natural Resources (or the agency that licenses boats in your state) looks in their files for Taca and Hernandez and discovers three Donzi speedboats, each capable of outrunning anything owned by the U.S. Customs Service.

Finally, the state motor vehicle office, or the state Department of Transportation, depending on where you live, looks up Hernandez and Taca.

The corporation, it seems, owns two aircraft, a plush, radar-equipped Piper Seneca, suitable for spotting ships at sea; and a Convair 220, capable of hauling 10,000-pound payloads.

Taca begins to look like a smuggling conglomerate.

En route to the office, you check the court clerk's office. You look up Taca in the index to see if anyone ever sued it. There's only one case: a slip-and-fall on the dance floor, settled out of court.

You look up Hernandez and find a divorce file. Not much you don't already know, except in the property settlement there's a reference to Taca Investors Ltd.

You double back to the deeds office and look up Taca Investors Ltd., kicking yourself for missing it the first time.

You find three deeds and limited partnership declaration.

CANAL FOR SMUGGLERS

According to the deed the partnership owns an apartment building, rural acreage that includes a landing strip, and some oceanfront land with a canal leading to a privately maintained channel where smugglers have been arrested before.

Best of all, the declaration of partnership lists Hernandez, his lawyer and a city councilman as limited partners.

The general partner is our old friend Taca.

According to the declaration, each investor put up one-third of the investment. But only the general partner, the corporation, can be held financially accountable. And its liability is limited by the state corporation laws.

One last stop at the criminal courts building confirms what you thought you remembered: Nine years ago, Hernandez was convicted of selling 600 pounds of marijuana and a kilo of cocaine to an undercover cop.

He's got a record as a dealer, he's tied to a public official, he owns boats, planes, trucks, a landing strip and a secluded harbor, and his criminal defense attorney is his business partner.

You put it all together and call a friendly cop. You tell him what you have. He trades you a little information in return:

Hernandez is about to be arrested, along with five of his lieutenants. He asks you to hold the story out of the first edition until Hernandez is popped.

You spend the time polishing the writing.

Everything you have is tied to a public record. Everything is demonstrably true, documented and libel-proof.

This illustration is not entirely fanciful. A similar story—minus the limited partnership—was done last year by a Miami Herald reporter. It was not done on deadline, but it could have been: All the information was gathered in a single day.

Any good reporter could have done it, with a solid knowledge of public records. The problem is finding out what they are and where they are.

There are ways to learn:

- Ask questions of anybody who'll talk to you. Ask other reporters. Ask clerks in courthouses. Ask people on the phone. Find out what they have and how it can help you. And remember: Any piece of paper in the possession of any public employee is a public record unless proven otherwise in court.
- Call the IRE Resource Center at 314-882-2042.
- Get a copy of *Real Estate Law* by Robert Kratovil (Englewood Cliffs, N.J., Prentice Hall, 1974.) It's a clearly written summary of the kinds of transactions on file, what the deeds look like and why they're public.
- Get a copy of Harry J. Murphy's *Where's What* (New York: Warner Books, 1976.) It's a recently declassified CIA manual subtitled "Sources of information for federal investigators."
- Keep up with Congressional hearing records, particularly those involving agencies that touch on your area. They provide factual data submitted under oath. Their witness lists give you the names of experts on a particular agency or subject. Be sure to get any supplemental reports published after the hearings. Often they contain written responses to embarrassing questions a witness wasn't prepared to answer on the stand.
- Get to know which federal agencies are most active in your area. And get to know your local state-level officials. Sometimes, when city hall wants to cover up a report, there's another copy floating around in a state or federal agency.

If your county's CETA program is a laughing-stock and the county manager is skirting the public records law, ask for copies of all his correspondence with the Department of Labor under the federal Freedom of Information Act. If he's misspending highway funds, get information from the state. And if the city landfill is polluting the river, get the story from records of the state environmental agency.

Records are no substitute for shoe leather or sources. To make your story come alive, you ultimately have to talk to real people on the record. But knowing how to run the records comprehensively can help you ask better questions.

Useful References

The news sources, individual and records, utilized by the hero of Riordan's piece totaled 15. Every issue of *IRE Journal* contains lists of sources for a wide variety of topics. Williams devoted ten pages to enumeration of records—local, state, school, county, state and federal. Anderson and Benjaminson list 35 most important public and private records: audit and consultants' reports; birth records; business records, including dba (doing business as) reports; campaign contributions and expenditures records; charity records, including police and firemen's benefit funds, which may be thinly disguised protection rackets; chattel mortgage records, which may contain clues to how low-paid public servants make big purchases, and interest-free deposits of public funds in banks in which public officials have an interest; city directories; city license bureaus; the *Congressionial Record;* criss-cross telephone directory with listings by street addresses rather than alphabetically by names; death records; expense account vouchers; financial information from Dun & Bradstreet and similar agencies; government directories especially the *U.S. Government Manual;*. gun registrations; income-tax records; legal newspapers; legal notices; marriage records; military records; museum records of tax-free contributions; newspaper libraries; payroll records; private organization records; professional trade and business directories; religious directories; school directories; Securities and Exchange records; state regulatory records; telephone records; trade publications; vanity directories; vehicle registrations; voting records to obtain full name, address and possibly mother's maiden name; welfare records.

To which might be added voter registration records; immigration records; divorce court proceedings; probate court proceedings and wills; federal tax courts; driver's license registrations; building permits; board of equalization reports.

Securities and Exchange Commission

Even though a story may be almost entirely of local interest, it may be necessary to consult Washington sources for information. If so, the Washington Researchers, an information service which works under contract with individual clients, believes most important are Securities and Exchange Commission reports on the 12,000 publicly owned corporations—the heavyweights even though 90 per cent of all businesses are privately owned. Most important Securities and Exchange Commission form is K-10, filed annually. It describes a company's business, number of employees, gross profits, net income or loss, changes in security or indebtedness, any bankruptcy or receivership proceedings, any major disposition of assets, balance sheet and total assets. Also listed are major lawsuits affecting the interest of stockholders.

Other important SEC forms include these: 10-Q, a quarterly report, which updates 10-K and also analyzes changes in company revenues and expenses compared with previous periods; 8-K, filed whenever a publicly held company undergoes a change in control, files for bankruptcy or receivership or changes of accountants; 13-D, submitted whenever a person or business acquires more than 5 per cent of the securities of a company listed on the stock exchange or one that is worth more than $1 million and has at least 500 stockholders; 14-D1, filed whenever a company covered by 13-D receives a purchase order from another company. The offer, principals, including broker and past dealings between the two companies, are described.

By consulting Forms 13-D and 14D-L, the Des Moines *Register* was able to explain the phenomenon of an obscure scrap-metal owner whose heavy trading the paper had learned about through the SEC's *Official Summary,* a monthly publication that outlines the trading of stocks and bonds by directors, officers and heavy stockholders. On the other hand, the Gannett News Service had to ask 38 SEC employees for help before learning that the agency has little authority over religious organizations. Gannett nevertheless won a Pulitzer prize for its series on the financial dealings of the Pauline Fathers.

For information about privately owned companies it is necessary to consult state agencies, most of which have adopted the Uniform Commercial Code, which requires disclosure of corporate debts. This code makes available names and addresses of parties involved, property used as collateral and the maturity dates of debts.

Other Federal Agencies

Three of the most important of the thousands of other federal agencies are the Federal Trade Commission, the Food and Drug Administration and the Internal Revenue Service. The FTC has the broadest authority of all agencies over domestic business practices and its decisions have nationwide effects. Its responsibility is to protect the public from anti-competitive and deceptive business practices. Its trade regulation rules have the force of law. The records of its enforcement activities are kept in its Public Reference Branch. For a fee, industry indexes and reports for individual companies can be obtained from the National Technical Information Service. The Bureau of Consumer Protection issues a quarterly *BCP Matters* sheet. The Transaction Status Sheet is updated daily. The annual Corporate Pattern Report provides information on partnerships, associations and other relations between corporations. *The Quarterly Financial Report* contains aggregate statistics on the state of the economy.

The FDA collects information in seven areas: foods, cosmetics, human drugs, animal drugs and feeds, medical devices, biologies and electronic radiological products. Its Establishment Inspection Forms and Analytical Laboratory Worksheets obtain evaluations of how food-producing industries comply with the agency's "tolerable filth levels." Because the huge agency operates through 40 divisions it is a difficult journalistic assignment. Reporters often learn of important news about it from congressional hearings. Sometimes they use the Freedom of Information Act to obtain information. Jack Taylor of the *Daily Oklahoman* probably has the all-time record for using the FOIA at least 1,200 times. About 780 of the requests pertained to the My Lai massacre; Taylor obtained six boxes of records detailing the Army's day-to-day activities related to it.

Income-tax returns are confidential and it is futile for a reporter or anyone else to try to learn what they contain. Exceptions are the 990-PF and 990-AR forms, which private tax-exempt foundations must file with the IRS. It is easier to obtain access to them from the Foundation Center of the Library of Congress than from the reticent IRS. That was how the Omaha *Sunpapers* learned the financial status of Boys Town. Doug Longhini of WLS-TV also learned that funds raised to benefit widows and orphans were instead used for the Chicago Fire Department's marching band. The returns of the Richard Nixon Foundation confirmed a payment of $21,000 to Donald Nixon as a consultant on where the Nixon Library should be located.

PLAYING DETECTIVE

If for no other reason than fear of being fired or arrested, the investigative reporter does not trespass, eavesdrop, wiretap, intercept mail or perform other illegal acts. Nevertheless, some of the techniques of a professional detective may be handy.

Newsday reporters, for instance, counted the number of garbage pickups in a certain district and compared it with the number specified in a city contract. The result was the revelation that a garbage collection firm had cheated taxpayers of about $5 million.

Robert Greene of the same newspaper suggests watching for variances in zoning permits. Otherwise, he surmises, an attractive parking space for 150 cars may deteriorate into a rundown space for 40 cars.

City hall reporters know that only enough funds should be deposited in no-interest accounts. When such accounts become too large, the suspicion arises that a politician or politician's friend may benefit.

Sometimes the names on documents such as contracts or titles to property are suspiciously unfamiliar. They may be the names of relatives or associates of the real parties involved. Or they may be fictitious. Probate, divorce, bankruptcy and other court records may provide clues. Maybe the principal has used his mother's maiden name.

An *Oregon Journal* reporter decided to read the city charter and amazed himself and his readers by discovering a secret $7,000 fund for use of the city council and mayor.

Beat reporters should be on constant alert to detect situations that the public interest requires be investigated, such as contract specifications written to favor a single bidder, contracts issued without competitive bids or to high instead of low bidders. Police reporters should take note of hearings at which motions to suppress evidence are made, because the nature of the evidence may provide clues to criminal behavior, possibly involving law-enforcement officers. The reporter also should know when prisoners are mistreated. In a Massachusetts case police testified that a retarded Negro, unable to read or write, had signed a confession. Police usually consider a case closed when an arrest has been made but the reporter's interest must continue.

A link between the Hell's Angels, a motorcycle gang, and organized crime was proved by the San Jose *Mercury-News,* which checked the security for a $1 million bail bond for a gang's leader accused of bombing a drug-enforcement officer. The paper discovered that it was property owned by three Angels, who also were among the owners of a catering service most of whose competitors had been forced out of business by bombings and other acts of terrorism.

Persistence in finding a secretary who had typed a codicil a quarter century earlier prevented the breaking of a will by distant relatives. The original typist was long since dead and so was the lawyer who composed the codicil. A reporter noted that there was a slash mark between his initials and the initials of the typist. First consulted was an old city directory, which, however, had ceased publication in 1942. So the reporter began with 1930 and took down the name of every woman with the initials S.Q. Next, he took a trip to the state capital to investigate marriage records. A woman with the proper initials had married and, it seemed like a stroke of luck, the husband's name was in the current phone book. The wife confirmed the fact that her maiden name had been Sally Quinn and it seemed that the search had succeeded. Not so, as this S.Q. had been a teacher, not a secretary. The ingenious reporter considered the year 1940–41. Maybe the real S.Q. had married a serviceman, and because at the time a 72-hour wait was required in California, had gone to Las Vegas. No luck, records from 1940 to 1955, proved fruitless. Undaunted, the reporter persisted and finally found what he wanted in the record book for 1957. The groom was still listed in the telephone book. For three nights there was no response to phone calls. Finally, on the evening of the fourth day, S.Q. answered. She had just walked in from a vacation. She acknowledged being the typist and the $15 million estate was probated as the testator had desired.

Dick Krantz, the St. Louis *Globe-Democrat*'s Criminal Court reporter, was puzzled by the abbreviations on Traffic Court records: B.P. for bench probation and T.S. for traffic school. Luckily he met a Washington University student who wanted to do a paper on the court system for the American Civil Liberties Union. She spent an entire week in one of the police courts taking down the dispositions of every case that came before the judge. If the clerk would call out "$10 and cost" she wrote it down along with the defendant's name and the charge. Using her notes, it became obvious that B.P. meant that the defendant had to pay no fine. Yet contacts with many of those involved revealed that they had paid. Bail bondsmen outside the courtroom told the motorists they could pay the marshal, who would inform the judge. Others had given their tickets to friends to have them fixed. The names of some politicians appeared on some of those tickets. In all, it was estimated that there had been a $1 million-a-year racket. As a result one judge resigned; another judge was indicted, but the charges were dropped on a technicality. A bail bondsman and a marshal of the court were convicted. Another marshal was indicted but not convicted. The chief clerk resigned on the grand jury's suggestion.

Here are a few suggestions from experienced investigative reporters:

If a competitor or court official becomes curious while you are going through records, confuse him or her by turning your attention to other records in which you really have no interest.

If it is desired to check the stories of two principals against each other, solicit the aid of a colleague to make simultaneous calls to ask identical questions of the suspects.

Emulate the Michigan City, Ind., reporter who took plans and specifications for a massive sewer project to an engineer outside the county for an opinion. It saved Michigan City an estimated $1½ million. The Indiana Association of Cities and Towns also examined a proposed budget and advised that if the proposed pay raises were granted the city would be bankrupt in three years.

Practice what is being called precision journalism, which means making your own charts to indicate trends. One such examination of IRS reports showed a growing practice of auditing the returns of taxpayers in lower-income brackets much oftener than those in higher brackets.

MASQUERADING

When the Chicago *Sun-Times* failed to win a Pulitzer prize for its Mirage series, the debate intensified in journalistic circles as to how far the press should go in practicing deception. The Mirage was a tavern, which the paper bought. It was operated by two investigative reporters and a representative of the Better Government Association. Hidden photographers took pictures to provide documentary proof, and the experiment exposed the systematic corruption that plagues businesses through shakedowns and payoffs. Despite the plaudits and other prizes that the investigative reporters, Pamela Zekman and Zay N. Smith, received, the majority of the Pulitzer Prize Board considered the project unethical, possibly entrapment.

Contemporary deceptive journalistic techniques are not the crude practices of yesteryear when reporters posed as coroners and police, eavesdropped, stole pictures and manufactured information to induce news sources to talk. Modern techniques are more refined and more effective. For instance, the Minneapolis *Star* sent a 76-year-old woman whose hearing was unimpaired to a number of hearing aid shops where salesmen invariably tried to get her to make a purchase. Similar stunts are performed to catch dishonest repairmen of automobiles, television sets and other commodities. Journalistic patients have received widely different diagnoses of imaginary illnesses from a variety of doctors.

Hal Bernstein of Jack Anderson's organization worked on the Alaska pipeline to expose faulty piping. At another time he posed as a bum and worked in a migrant camp. Gordon Chaplin of the Baltimore *Sun* posed as a Philadelphia attorney interested in purchasing Spiro Agnew's house, the value of which had tripled as a result of so-called security improvements at public expense. When the vice president succeeded in killing the story it appeared in *More* and Chaplin went to work for the Washington *Post*.

A San Francisco *Examiner* reporter once enrolled in a high school class to try to discover why students are so uneducated. Several papers have exposed incompetency, laxity or bribery on the part of examiners at drivers' testing stations. They also have exposed the existence of racial discrimination in housing by sending black and white reporters, separately, to ask for referrals from real estate agents. The lead of a typical story of this kind was that of the Saginaw (Mich.) *News:*

© Copyright 1979 by The Saginaw News

The young white couple watched the real estate agent's hand stretch across the map on her neat desk, slashing a red line through Buena Vista, Bridgeport and Saginaw's East Side.

"This I am not supposed to be doing. Across the bridge, in the East Side, I would not recommend . . . I am not prejudiced, but . . . a lot of blacks are in here which automatically means the resale value is just about nil,'' said Donna Nicklyn, an associate realtor at David J. Hill Real Estate.

This scene and others like it were found by four Saginaw News reporters, divided into black and white couples, who separately visited seven area real estate firms. The couples posed as out-of-state residents wanting to buy their first home in Saginaw.

Agents at five firms pushed or steered the white couple to the city's heavily white West Side and its surrounding townships. Only at two firms did agents avoid steering.

The black couple, although more subtly guided, were frequently nudged in the direction of racially mixed Buena Vista and Bridgeport, often with little or no mention of predominantly white residential areas.

Much of the steering focused on the suburbs, rapidly growing with whites and blacks escaping city life. Almost always, whites and blacks were pushed in opposite directions.

In one instance, the black couple was discouraged from living in Saginaw Township, an area repeatedly suggested to the white couple.

In others, the white couple was quickly and bluntly told where to live, with racial considerations the major factor.

At five firms, different agents provided varying information to the couples, painting sharply different portraits of the same area.

And in almost all cases where steering was blunt, the agents voluntarily admitted they should not give suggestions based upon race. But the information was provided, unsolicited by either couple.

There is no universal answer to the question of what is ethical when gathering information without the source's knowing the reporter's identity. Many reporters have kept their jobs after walking into meetings where they didn't belong, sometimes dressed so as not to be conspicuous. Few editors object to consumer reporters patronizing restaurants and stores without introducing themselves. There are considerable differences of opinion, however, as regards almost any other kind of masquerading. A majority of editors doubtless do not condone deliberate lying on a reporter's part. Jim Polk is bothered because he once told the government of Granada that he was writing a travelogue whereas his real purpose was to expose conditions in hospitals where Americans were treated. He also got into the office of the Rev. Guy Young, successor to Jim Jones at People's Temple, by flashing an NBC identity card and responding to a secretary's query as to whether he was from the government by saying, ''I can only discuss that with Mr. Young.''

EVALUATING THE EFFORT

Investigative reporters and editors sometimes are disappointed, even disgusted, because quick reforms do not result from their efforts. They also risk cynicism when they enumerate all of the other exposés that could and should be made. Perhaps most discouraging to public-spirited journalists are the polls that reveal public distrust and dislike of them and support for repressive measures by government.

Without police or judicial powers all the journalist can do is direct attention to shortcomings. The press could not compel Boys Town to make better use of less money nor to desist in large-scale fund-raising campaigns. Nor could it stop Stefan Cardinal Wyszynski, backed by Pope John Paul II, from restoring the Rev. Michael Zembrzinski as director of the Order of St. Paul the First Hermit, commonly called the Pauline Fathers, at Doylestown, Pa., even after the Gannett News Service won a Pulitzer prize for exposing the financial mess there.

The Miami *Herald* won only a partial victory when the Florida state legislature recognized that the medical profession could not police itself and stripped the Board of Medical Examiners of its power to investigate and prosecute doctors and gave the authority to the Department of Consumer Protection and Professional Regulation. However, the medical board retained the power to decide how or whether a doctor found guilty should be punished.

There have been unfortunate examples of public employees exposed by the press as incompetent or corrupt who have been removed from one job only to be quietly hired for another with the same political sponsorship.

On the other hand, investigative reporters and editors can find satisfaction in the fact that as a result of the 125 stories that Bill Voelker wrote over a 29-month period for the New Orleans *Times-Picayune,* the state commissioner of administration in charge of computer operations was removed from his position, two computer firm officials were indicted by a federal grand jury and the FBI, SEC and IRS all investigated charges of illegal racketeering, mail and wire fraud and perjury.

Of the Pulitzer prize-winning investigation of the recruitment and killing in boot camp of a retarded Marine, Joe Murray, editor of the Lufkin (Tex.) *News* wrote, "Before it was over there would be Congressional investigations and hearings and inquiries by the president of the United States. The secretary of the Navy would get involved personally. There would be court martials and there would be trials. More importantly there would be reform. Before it was over, no less than the commandant of the Marine Corps would say that 1976 was a year of change for the U.S. Marines because of Lynn McClure. And because of that the Marine Corps was getting well. So I guess, in the best sense, that was what it was all about. Finding something that was wrong and doing something to change it."

Stories in the Sedalia, Mo., *Democrat-Capitol* were confirmed by a grand jury report that a teenaged inmate in the county jail had been "subjected to abuse, torture, assault and deviate sexual intercourse over a period of about a week." The jury, however, included a strange and sour note that the incident "had become a media event," and that the daily had acted irresponsibly.

There was a happier ending to the five months' investigation by WLS-TV, Chicago, and the Chicago Better Government Association into the death of an old woman in a Chicago area nursing home. Needed for corroboration of the rumor that Alma Weny died because there was no oxygen to save her was the nurse in attendance; she had moved to another nursing home so a BGA attorney obtained employment there. The project almost collapsed when she took pictures of patients illegally tied in wheelchairs. When someone approached her she quickly wrapped her Minox camera in a Milky Way candy wrapper and hid it behind her back. There it was seen by another person who said, "Oh I see you like Milky Ways too," so the spy-nurse, Barbara Klien, offered a real bar of which she had a supply in anticipation of just such a situation.

The project also seemed to be failing until the very last day of Klien's employment when a case similar to that which caused Alma Weny's death occurred and, almost unbelievably, the same nurse was on duty. From her Klien obtained the verification needed.

The final episode of this investigation occurred when Douglas Longhini, a WLS reporter, impersonated an investor interested in purchasing nursing homes. To the fictitious purchaser and Peter Karl, WLS investigative reporter, the management director confessed to income-tax fraud. By frequenting Skid Row the reporters also found another elderly woman who had been taken for more then $40,000.

On the first anniversary of The Mirage exposé, Pamela Zekman and Zay N. Smith, the Chicago *Sun-Times* reporters who posed as barmaid and waiter, summarized the aftermath: "more than a dozen government employees fired, Mayor orders updated safety codes, IRS probes tax fraud, state cracks down on license fraud, probers zero in on liquor and beer distributors, firemen prohibited from selling tickets on city time."

As the *Sun-Times* competitor, the Chicago *Tribune* says on its editorial page every day:

> The newspaper is an institution developed by modern civilization to present the news of the day, to foster commerce and industry, to inform and lead public opinion, and to furnish that check upon government which no constitution has ever been able to provide.

PART FOUR

GENERAL ASSIGNMENTS (which every reporter should be able to cover)

HELP WANTED

In the first edition of his *Pennsylvania Gazette,* Benjamin Franklin wrote that to be successful an editor should

> **be qualified with an extensive acquaintance with language, a great easiness and command of writing and relating things, clearly and intelligently, and in a few words, he should be able to speak of war both on land and sea, be well acquainted with geography, with the history of the time, with the several interests of princes and states, the secrets of courts and the manners and customs of all nations. Men thus accomplished are very rare in this remote part of the world.**

"Hello, is this the reporter?"
"This is one of the reporters."
"Well, I want the reporter who writes the articles for the paper."
"This is one of the reporters who writes news for the paper."
"Are you the reporter who puts in all those articles?"
"I'm one of them. What can I do for you?"
"Well, I want to put an article in the paper. Have you got your pencil ready?"
"Yes, I'm all ready."
"Well, here it is. Take it down just as I give it to you. Mrs. J. J. Whuzzis, W–H–U–Z–Z–I–S, and her charming and talented daughter, Euphrasia, will leave their palatial home, 9999 W. 38th street today, for a motor trip through the East where they will visit her aunt Lucy in the metropolis of New York City. She has a fine home there and is very rich. These two prominent Wichita ladies will return in three months to their mansion. Now read that back to me."
"I just took down notes. I didn't take it verbatim."
"I didn't want it verbatim. I wanted you to take it the way I read it. That's the way I want it in the paper."
"I'll put it in with all the facts correct."
"That ain't the idea. I want it put in the way I gave it to you, if I have to pay for it. How much will I have to pay to get it put in the way I gave it to you?"
"You'll have to talk to the advertising department about that."
"Well, I'll take it to the other paper. I never was so insulted in my life."

—*Wichita* Beacon

11

PERSONS AND PERSONALITIES

A. Gossip Is News
   1. Home Town Personals
   2. Big City Snoops
B. Family/Living
C. Personal News
   1. Weddings
      a. Picking the Feature
      b. Style
   2. Marital Status
   3. Births
D. Society News
   1. Types of Society News
   2. Elements in Society News
E. Personalities
   1. Important Position
   2. Prominent Citizen
   3. Unusual Occupation
   4. Unusual Hobby
   5. Reminiscences
   6. Visiting Celebrity
F. Consumerism

Names—people—make news and the journalistic rule, "as many names as possible in every edition" holds, in large as well as small places. Metropolitan papers are no longer able to publicize the comings and goings of most of their readers but they do their best to satisfy everyone's curiosity as regards celebrities. Gossip columns, specializing in trivia and alleged "inside dope," multiply. A generation ago Walter Winchell scandalized many with his "blessed event" and similar personal news, while Louella Parsons and Hedda Hopper possessed the ability to make or break glamorous motion-picture stars. Today *People, National Enquirer* and their competitors provide vicarious thrills for millions of frustrated hero-worshipers and are besieged by press agents seeking mention of their clients.

GOSSIP IS NEWS

Community and suburban weeklies and dailies thrive on the inability of the large metropolitan papers to provide news of the routine happenings in their circulation areas. They cover not only news of governmental bodies and public and private organizations but also personal items, which never have ceased to be the backbone of the rural weekly. Typical of the one-paragraph personals that the small city reporter may obtain just by "hanging around," by telephone conversations with friends or by opening his/her mail are the following:

> Mrs. Edwin P. Morrow of Washington, D.C., is visiting at the home of her son, Charles R. Morrow, 636 Sherman avenue. Mrs. Morrow is the widow of the late Edwin P. Morrow, former governor of Kentucky.
>
> Miss Eva Rathbone entertained her fellow members in the Puella Sunday school class of First Presbyterian church at dinner Friday night at her home, 133 N. Prairie avenue. During the evening, the girls worked on patch quilts to be distributed by the Women's Missionary society of the church.
>
> Five Milltown students at Augustana college will spend the Thanksgiving weekend with their parents here. They are. . . .

Home Town Personals

Contemporary cub reporters do not have to frequent railroad and bus stations, hotel lobbies, clubrooms, floral shops and delicatessen stores or stop acquaintances on street corners to obtain such news. Mostly it is contributed and the editor altogether too often has to tone down banality and editorializing. Wielding too heavy a pencil, however, might destroy charming originality. For example, the homely informality of the following examples makes the papers more welcome in the family circle and to former residents of the communities who subscribe to their old home-town papers by mail.

> Happy birthday to Aunt Helen Krese of Grand Rapids, Michigan, and Janice Minner.
>
> Edith Bland, Opal Becker and Martha Narup visited Helen Nord and Irene Hayn Tuesday afternoon. Sorry to report that Irene is having trouble with her leg and is on crutches.
>
> Kathy Wallendorf and Little Gus and Opal Becker visited George and Edith Bland Thursday afternoon.
>
> Happy anniversary to Mr. and Mrs. Henry Bland of Brighton.
>
> [Calhoun (Hardin, Ill.) *News*]
>
> Son Leslie shared cukes, squash and zucchini with us. Grandson Dana up on his cycle with a pretty little blonde he introduced to me. She, Mary Drews, dare say we'd be happy to welcome in the Torsey Tribe.
>
> Via the grapevine, a party has purchased 1,000 acres in New Hampton. It's to be stripped and cut up into house lots. If true, why the secrecy? Doc didn't guess there was a hunk that big to go on the block. At that rate, will Old New Hampton be a city soon? If so, who will be our first mayor?
>
> Doc at 20A blueberries for a pie, few huckleberries and chokecherries.
>
> Two big loghaulers with more logs from Sky Pond came thru our yard stripping apples from our porter, wealthy plus cider trees. These trucks bear Colebrook names.

Maurice S. biked up. An orange rig up with backhoe for ditch-digging and tipping out stones. [Plymouth (N.H.) *Record-Citizen*]

Such informality has a limit, even in the hickiest of hick towns, as illustrated by the following:

W. P. Nelson is again on the job at the bank following a seige with chicken pox. Walt had a real mixup with his "kid" disease and he says he was sure sick. Aside from being "well marked" he is okay.

The new band leader, Don Walters, put his Hubbard group through its paces last Saturday and again Tuesday and Wednesday of this week. The youngsters are all eager and ready to go to Iowa City this coming Saturday and do themselves and their community proud. Everything points to a good chance for them to come through with shining colors. The group expects to leave town about 7 o'clock in the morning so as to give the performers time to get some of the kinks from riding out of their system.

So let's cheer them on with three big rahs. All right, here we go—rah! Rah! RAH!

We extend congratulations to Mr. and Mrs. Dave Heden, who were recently united in marriage. We are not acquainted with the groom, but his bride, formerly Agnes Attleson, is well known here as this was her former home though she has been working in Chicago for several years. She has hosts of friends who wish her much joy, for she was a very nice young lady. They expect to make their home in Chicago, where the groom has employment.

On the other hand, the rural correspondent with an undeveloped nose for news may write as a brief what should have been a longer news or feature story. The properly written personal really is a news lead. As such, it is good if it fulfills the requirements of a good lead and bad if it doesn't. Note how the following barren brevities might have been made more nearly complete and interesting while still remaining brevities:

Insufficient

A. L. Scobey, 1434 Ellis street, has returned from a two-week trip to San Francisco.

Sufficient

A. L. Scobey, 1434 Ellis street, returned today from San Francisco with the prize given the delegate traveling the farthest distance to attend the annual convention of the Fraternal Order of Leopards there last week. Mr. Scobey represented the local Leopards lodge of which he is commander. The prize was a traveling bag.

Insufficient

Mr. and Mrs. Edward L. Parkhouse, 683 Pulliam avenue, entertained 16 guests Monday night at a theater party.

Sufficient

To celebrate their 25th wedding anniversary, Mr. and Mrs. Edward L. Parkhouse, 683 Pulliam avenue, entertained 16 guests Monday night at a theater party. Formerly it was believed the Parkhouses had been married only 15 years, but they chose this belated occasion to reveal that they had been secretly wed for ten years before making an announcement.

It easily can be imagined how either of these, especially the second, could have been expanded into a much longer story with considerable reader interest. Unfortunately, it is not presumptuous to imagine a beginning reporter's getting no more than the original items cited. State or county editors often despair because of the inability of rural correspondents to sense news values. Cub reporters may be able to pick important names out of hotel registers but they may miss the fact that the out-of-town visitor listed inconspicuously among those "in town for the day" is negotiating with the directors of a bank for its purchase, consulting with Chamber of Commerce officials about the establishment of a new industry or applying for a position in the local schools or for the pastorate of a local church. The fault obviously is under-reporting.

Big City Snoops

There is hardly a large city daily that does not have more than a single gossip columnist. Today the same paper may have a half dozen or more Polly Prys. One of the most popular was The Ear of the Washington *Star,* from whose contents the following extracts are typical:

TUBED UP

We all wondered what on earth happened to Barbara Howar, when she fled for the Big Apple this year. (Remember? Those ghastly gossips all nattered and nudged about how chummy she and Ham Jordan were getting. Then bingo, she was gone.) Ear's proud to announce that she's been beavering away on a pilot for public teevee up there. It's called "Watching T.V." Barb's co-toiler on it is marvellous Marvin Titman. (Marvy Marv, as we all call him, is the tube critic for clever little *Newsday.*) This all sounded *tres originale* to Ear, which is looking for a Chic New Watching Posture. But no. On the show, Barb and Marv just sit around and dish things like "Networks used sleaze to up the gross network figures. *And gross it is.*" Ear is kind of impressed, and kind of gloomy, and kind of thinking of living on the floor *anyway*.

FINEST HOUR

A Great Moment in Anglo-American Friendship, darlings: The British Embassy's freshly-knighted defense attaché, Air Marshal Sir Roy Austen-Smith, with his Lady, purred through the White House gate for the great Maggie Thatcher Dinner Monday night, superb in their glossy black Jaguar. Well, *almost* superb: A bump in the paving at the gate knocked the Jag's low-slung exhaust system off. Britain's pride jerked under the great white portico dragging pipes, grating hideously and honking deafening razberries through the smashed muffler. The Secret Service blanched. The Knight and his Lady gallantly swept out and swept in, heads high. Ashen White Housers trundled off the Machine and patched it up with chewing gum and wire. Cost of repairs on the Jag, later: $1,500. "Worth every penny. They were *just* like the Few. The Show Went On," sighed an Anglophile, eyes moist as warm ale. Ear salutes Sir Roy. He's used to it, of course.

FINEST FLOWER

Ear's glum to catch wind of the Carl Bernstein-Nora Ephron split, so soon after Nora produced wee Max, the Divine Duo's second son. Carl's *finally* fallen in true *amour* with Another, he's telling pals. He really feels *awful* about his timing. Ah yes.

FINEST FLIER

Ear hears that Clare Crawford, a hotshot *People* maggie scribe, has some charming pix of herself with Zbig Brzezinski. He's *very* tightly zipped and buttoned throughout. So, of course, is Ear.

By contrast, Irving Kupcinet's Kup's Column in the Chicago *Sun-Times* is dignified and usually newsworthy:

A Reporter's Report: As often occurs when witnesses start talking before a grand jury, the investigation veers off into other fields. That's happened in the current county grand jury hearings on alleged mob influence in the Police Department. The grand jury, as a result of the testimony of some witnesses, now is investigating last year's ChicagoFest. . . . And members of the grand jury report they're startled by people in comparatively high places in city government who are taking the Fifth. . . . The National Organization for Women, one of whose volunteers, Wanda E. Brandstetter, is being named in the probe of an alleged attempt to bribe state Rep. Nord Swanstrom to vote for ERA, soon will strike back at the legislator. NOW will reveal the political contributions Swanstrom accepted allegedly "to stop ERA." . . . The doctor-patient relationship between actress Nanette Fabray and Dr. Howard House will culminate in marriage in Los Angeles on June 8. His surgery restored her hearing.

FAMILY/LIVING

When New York newspapers near the end of the last century began printing the guest lists of parties attended by members of the so-called 400, they made journalistic history. At first this "invasion of privacy" was resented, but through "leaks" and gate-crashing the news continued to be obtained. Today the problem of most society editors is not how to get news but how to satisfy everyone wanting "nice" notices on the page. The problem is without solution and today the society page as such has disappeared in all but some very small papers. The original and enduring appeal of the page had been two-fold (1) to the vanity of those considered important enough to receive mention, (2) to the curiosity of all others regarding the glamorous way of life of their social superiors. As the scope of a paper's coverage and circulation widened, those who argued that these values are fictitious and the whole concept undemocratic have prevailed.

For several years the successor to the society page was a woman's page, which played up club news, columns and features on marriage and parenthood, possibly also cooking and household repairs. Feminists objected to this innovation, which editors also found it difficult to develop. The formula for a satisfactory substitute for the society and/or woman's page has not yet developed. Most popular of the current experiments is a family/living page or section,

Adolph Bremer, editor of the Winona (Minn.) *Daily News* describes it as follows:

> As for contents of *Family/Living,* we have retained engagements and weddings, although sharply reducing the space for them. The picture size in both instances is down and the text for the wedding is confined to a cutline. We have continued a club (mostly women's) calendar and have expanded the listings insofar as practical to eliminate an accompanying advance headlined story. We added an Arts/Platform weekly calendar, expanded artistic reviews, concentrated most club meeting reports of a routine nature to a roundup, and reduced photos of club officers, with an exception of two, to a 5-pica pic of president. We've kept the best seller list of books and added a local column, "Books and Such," which is more (or less?) than a book review column. Dear Abby and the horoscope go on. The main changes have been in getting more controversial stuff on the pages, as opposed to the puffy society stuff. This Sunday we're doing the abortion thing, a mighty hot topic here with about half of the city population Catholic. We've done quite a bit with marital and personality problems, sexual abuse, rape and the new "in" stuff that interest women (most of them anyhow) more than the spring fashions. To the outsider the Family/Living pages may not seem revolutionary, but the evolution has been drastic and it is continuing. We did experiment with local shopping comparisons (food), but we found comparative pricing full of hazards and we discontinued without advertising pressure. We do have a syndicated consumer column. Give us a bigger newshole in this area and we'd do more of a controversial nature within staff limitations, and utilize more of the good stuff from AP, NYTNS and CST. Except for Sunday we don't have the big holes to fill in this area. And frankly on Sunday we're loaded with columns although we do insist on one open or nearly open page.

A typical Family/Living page in the Winona *Daily News* contained the Dear Abby column; Jeane Dixon's horoscopes; Dr. Paul G. Donahue's health column; a local news story of a wedding; a local story announcing a meeting of the Bah'ai Campus Club; two correspondents' stories of a dance in Whitehall, Wis. and a concert in Arkansaw, Wis. and three Associated Press items: Madison, Wis. gas customers get lower rates; egg production increases in Minnesota; and a former Nicaraguan official is on trial in Managua.

PERSONAL NEWS

Though downplayed, the traditional items of society news still have a place. The Louisville *Courier-Journal* explains its policy, which is fairly typical among newspapers of its type.

> We don't like to disappoint our readers in their moments of pride and happiness. To be sure that we don't have to disappoint you when you want to publish your engagement, wedding or anniversary announcement, here is what you need to know:

ENGAGEMENTS

It can take up to two months to get your engagement announced in the newspaper. We recommend sending in announcements (with or without photographs) no later than six weeks before you want the announcement published.

Engagement announcements received less than four weeks before the wedding date will be returned to the sender unpublished.

Photographs should be wallet size or larger. A five-by-seven-inch glossy photograph will reproduce best in the newspaper. Although a color photograph may be submitted, it will not reproduce as well as a black and white. Photos will be returned, if a stamped, self-addressed envelope is enclosed.

WEDDINGS

Information about the wedding ceremony must be in our office no later than two weeks before the wedding date. The announcement is published in the first Sunday newspaper after the wedding.

Any announcements received after that deadline will be run in an abbreviated form in a later Sunday edition. Information about a wedding more than one month old will not be used.

We do not use photographs with these announcements.

ANNIVERSARIES

Accent publishes announcements of the following anniversaries: 50th, 55th, 60th, 65th and above.

If you wish to have the announcement run on a Sunday before the anniversary celebration, we must have that information in our hands at least two weeks before the celebration.

Information for anniversaries that involve no celebration or for which the celebration has already taken place will not be published if the event is more than one month old.

We do not use photographs with these announcements either.

PROCEDURE

We have simple forms for all three announcements. You can get them by writing Accent, The Courier-Journal, Louisville, Ky. 40202, or by calling 582-4667 in Louisville.

All the announcements are published as a free service of the newspaper.

Stories are written by formula:

Mr. and Mrs. Charles J. Graf of Jeffersonville, Ind., announce the engagement of their daughter, Stacie Joe Graf, and Robert M. Eyster III, Louisville, son of Mr. and Mrs. Robert M. Eyster Jr. of Salem, Ohio. Miss Graf attended Indiana University Southeast and Western Reserve . . . [Louisville *Courier-Journal*]

Linda Darnall of rural Atlanta and Martin England of Stanford were married at 7 p.m. Saturday at Armington Christian Church. A reception followed at the church.

The newlyweds will live in rural Armington.

The bride, a daughter of Mr. and Mrs. Dale Darnall of rural Atlanta, graduated from Olympia High School. She is employed by Illinois Agricultural Association.

The bridegroom is a son of James England of McLean and Mrs. Enid England of Stanford. He is also a graduate of Olympia High School and is employed by Thermo in Armington. [Bloomington (Ill.) *Pantagraph*]

Mr. and Mrs. Lawrence A. Mitchell Sr., Gallipolis, Ohio, celebrated their 50th wedding anniversary Aug. 19 in Gallipolis.

Mitchell married the former Melva Cornell Sept. 22, 1929, in Winfield, W. Va.

They are the parents of Nancy James, Norman and Donna Sanders, all of Gallipolis; Fred of Roswell, Ga., Maxine of Buffalo, W Va., Ray of Pomeroy, Ohio, and Lawrence Jr. of Milan, Mich. The couple has 15 grandchildren and one great-grandchild.

Mitchell is a farmer and is retired from Gallipolis Locks and Dam.

[Columbus (Ohio) *Dispatch*]

Formula writing is space saving and makes it easier to refuse requests that stories be written in a certain way. Many hostesses would like to have their affairs reported as the most successful of the season. The copy desk must be alert to eliminate adjectives such as "gorgeous," "radiant" and so forth to describe guests and/or decorations. Anyone who handles social items also must be wary to check news sources, since there are pranksters who think it very funny to announce the engagement, marriage, parenthood or divorce of a friend or foe.

Weddings

Backbone of the local page where news of social events is displayed is the wedding story. Some papers usually and all occasionally deviate from formula as in the following from the Freeport (Ill.) *Journal-Standard.*

Lori Ann Fluegel and Daniel Karl Hepler were united in matrimony on Nov. 17 at Trinity United Methodist Church.

Arrangements of white and lavender carnations with wheat and heather and seven-branched candelabra adorned the church as the Rev. Karl Hepler, father of the bridegroom, and the Rev. Thomas Howard officiated at the double-ring ceremony. Bill Robbins provided the piano accompaniment as Mark Anderson sang the solos.

Mr. and Mrs. Robert Fluegel, 4584 Route 20 West, are the parents of the bride. The bridegroom is the son of the Rev. and Mrs. Karl Hepler, 1133 S. Maple Ave.

The bride carried a cascade bouquet of sterling silver roses, stephanotis and Jack Frost roses accented with ivory angel lace. She wore an ivory satin crepe gown with a blouson bodice and drawstring neckline with a self-ruffled collar. A cummerbund accented the waistline. The full raglan sleeves were gathered into a button cuff. Clusters of ivory Elegance carnations and babies'-breath were worn in her hair.

Serving the bride was Carole Holey. She was attired in a satin knit gown with a fitted tucked bodice and Sweetheart neckline with long puffed sleeves. She held a nosegay of ivory Elegance carnations tipped with lavender and babies'-breath. She wore a halo of similar flowers in her hair.

Doug Weiner and Brian Olson assisted the bridegroom.

The reception was held in Fellowship Hall.

Information for such stories usually is obtained by means of blanks sent to prospective brides after the city hall reporter has reported that marriage licenses have been applied for. In most states there is a short waiting period between application and issuance of licenses. A sample wedding blank follows:

WEDDING REPORT

Full name of bride ....
Address of bride ....
Full names of bride's parents or guardians ....
Address of bride's parents ....
Full name of bridegroom ....
Address of bridegroom ....
Full names of bridegroom's parents ....
Address of bridegroom's parents ....
Date of wedding .... Time ....
Place of ceremony ....
Who will perform ceremony? ....
Will bride wear a gown or suit? .... Describe ....
....
Will she wear a veil? .... Is it an heirloom? ....
Describe the veil ....
Will she carry a prayer book? ....
Will she carry or wear flowers? .... Describe ....
....
Who will give the bride away? (name, address and relationship) ....
....
Name of maid or matron of honor and relationship ....
Describe her gown and flowers ....
Names and addresses of bridesmaids ....
....
Describe their gowns and flowers ....
Ribbon, ring or flower bearers ....
Describe their gowns and flowers ....
Name and address of best man ....
Groomsmen ....
Ushers ....
Will ceremony be formal or informal? ....
Musicians ....
Musical selections:
- Before ceremony ....
- As bridal party enters ....
- During ceremony ....
- As bridal party leaves ....

Order in which bridal party will enter ....
....

Decorations (color scheme and how carried out; significance) ....
....
Number of invitations sent out .... Probable attendance......
Will a reception follow? .... Where?............
How many will attend reception? ....
Decorations ....
Hostesses:
In parlor ....
In dining room ....
Will breakfast, luncheon or dinner be served? .... Where?......
Will couple take a trip? ...... Where?......... When?............
When and where will couple be at home? ....
Bridegroom's occupation and business address ....
Former occupation of the bride ....
Bridegroom's education and degrees ....
Bridegroom's fraternal connections ....
Bride's education and degrees ....
Bride's sorority connections ....
Bridegroom's war record: service, rank, area in which served and duration, citations, unusual experiences, etc. ....
....
Bride's war record ....
Guests from away, names, initials and addresses ....
....
Other information ....
....

Picking the Feature

Whoever writes wedding stories welcomes any possible feature with which to lead the account. Possible features to give depth to the account include

1. The romance. The manner of meeting or the length of the engagement if unusual. Sometimes childhood sweethearts are united after years of separation. Or there may be an Evangeline or Enoch Arden complication. Ordinarily, unless the bride is a widow, the fact of any previous marriage is omitted. Exceptions to this rule are persons prominent in the news, especially motion picture actors and actresses. In their cases it is common practice to write: "It is her third marriage and his fourth."

2. The place. Perhaps some relative of either party was married in the same church. Maybe an outdoor ceremony is performed on the spot where the betrothal took place. Sometimes a couple selects an unusual site for its nuptials, as an airplane or beneath the water in diving suits. Wedding ceremonies have been performed in hospitals, prisons and by long-distance telephone or radio.

3. The date or hour. It may be the anniversary of the engagement. Perhaps the bride's mother or some other relative was married on the same date. In an effort to make its wedding the first of the year or month, a couple may be married shortly after midnight.

4. Bride's costume. Often a bride wears her mother's dress or veil or some other family heirloom. There is an old superstition that a bride should always wear something old and something new, something borrowed and something blue; many modern brides adhere to this, and some article of a bride's costume may be unusual.

5. Relationship. If the scions of two old and prominent families are married, their family connections may constitute the feature. If either is descended from Revolutionary or Colonial ancestry that fact should be played up.

The feature, of course, may be found in any one of a number of other elements. Perhaps the bridegroom wears a military uniform or the bride cuts the wedding cake with her husband's sword. Maybe the minister is a relative. The attendants may be sorority sisters or representatives of some organization. Whatever it is, the society editor tries to find it and to feature it. Anything to drive off the monotony of the stereotyped wedding lead.

Style

The trite and hackneyed style of the "country" wedding story must be avoided. To this end, avoid use of such expressions as "blushing bride," "plighted their troth," "holy wedlock," "linked in matrimony." The word "nuptials" should not be overworked.

The easiest lead sentence is the straightforward: "A and B were married—." For variety, other possibilities include

—exchanged (spoke) nuptial (marriage) vows.
Miss A became the bride of B—.
Miss A was married to B—.
First church was the scene of the marriage of—.
A simple ceremony united in marriage Miss A and B—.
The marriage of A and B took place—.
—attended the nuptials of A and B.
Nuptial vows were spoken by A and B—.
The marriage of A and B was solemnized—.
Chaplain C read the service which joined A and B in marriage—.
Chaplain C officiated at—.

Some of these phrases may be appropriate in other parts of the story. When a page includes a half-dozen or more wedding stories, it is desirable to obtain variety. However worded, the lead of the wedding story should contain the feature, if there is one, the names of the principals with the bride's name ordinarily mentioned first and the time and place of the wedding. The principals usually are identified by addresses and parentage.

Writers vary the order of details in the body of the story. Most frequently, perhaps, the bride's costume is described right after the lead, and then the costumes of her attendants. The decorations or order of march, however, may come first. If there is a procession, the order in which it entered the church or home should be described.

The account of any wedding dinner or reception follows the account of the service proper. More nearly complete identification of the principals, the wedding trip and future residence and the list of guests come at the very end. Other elements which enter into the account are included in the sample wedding blank.

Marital Status

Seldom broken has been the journalistic taboo preventing mention of extramarital affairs of persons in public life. Congressmen have slept off drunks at their desks, newspaper publishers have received employees while in bed with mistresses, presidential romances are exposed posthumously in best-selling books.

It is becoming increasingly difficult for the press to shield public figures, however, as illegal behavior becomes less clandestine. Since the principals are less hypocritical and more open in their relations, it hardly makes sense for the press to protect them from public disclosure. After all, few were shocked when a leading motion picture actor at the Academy Awards gala introduced "the mother of my children," nor when a presidential candidate was reported in news pictures and stories as taking his girl friend with him on a vacation trip.

Without sensationalizing, when it is pertinent, it can and probably should be reported that what boy friend and what girl friend probably have been living together for months or years, maybe a lifetime. It is still difficult for some journalistic old-timers, no matter how many wild oats they have sowed themselves, to get used to the new frankness in reporting language and antics that not long ago would have resulted in social ostracism or worse.

Births

A real toughie is the birth notice. When a prominent woman becomes a mother the event is newsworthy. If, however, the child is born out of wedlock or from adultery, before writing the story the reporter acts wisely if he seeks advice from his superiors. Paternity suits test the mettle of journalism as well as judges, so everyone concerned usually is willing to ignore the whole business.

For the noncontroversial birth story, the reporter should obtain

1. Names and address of parents.
2. Time and place of birth.
3. Weight of the baby.
4. Sex of the baby.
5. The name, if chosen.

The mother's maiden name may be included if she has not been married more than a few years, if the couple is living in another city and her married name is unfamiliar locally or if she uses her birth name either professionally or generally. If the date of the marriage is mentioned, care must be taken to give it correctly. Libel suits have resulted from mistakes of this sort even in these liberal-minded days.

Since all parents supposedly are proud, that fact is of no news value. And it never has been proved scientifically that newly born babies bounce. A baby's rosy cheeks, lusty lungs and dimpled chin may be taken for granted. "Daughter" or "son" is better than "baby girl" or "baby boy." Do not use "cherub" or "the new arrival to bless the home" or the like.

The name of the attending physician should not be included in a birth notice, or, in fact, in any story of illness or death. This rule is broken in the case of a person of great prominence and in stories in which the physician himself or herself plays a part, as a participant in an accident, etc. Ordinarily, however, the name of the physician is left out, frequently at the request of the local medical society.

Whether the fact that "mother and baby are both doing nicely" is to be included probably is debatable. Ordinarily, however, it seems as though good health should be assumed; if either child or mother is in danger that fact may be included. Likewise, the number, names and ages of other children of the parents of a newly born baby may or may not be mentioned.

> Mr. and Mrs. Ralph Elsasser, 711 Renrose ave., became the parents of a daughter in Swedish-American hospital on Monday. Named Marie Lynette, the infant weighed 5 pounds, 5 ounces at birth. She joins a brother, Terry Lee, 12; and a sister, Vicki Lynn, 8. [Rockford *Star*]

> Mr. and Mrs. Jimmie Collins, Stonington, welcomed their first child, a son, at 4:56 (CST) o'clock Friday night in the St. Vincent Memorial Hospital. He weighed 6 pounds and 6 ounces. The mother is the former Anna Marie Jones. [Taylorville (Ill.) *Breeze-Courier*]

A frequent temptation to a beat reporter is to turn in a story telling of how some new father on his/her beat acted or announced the event to his coworkers. Such items must be adroitly handled to avoid the common fault of banality.

> It was cigars for everybody today in the office of Mitchell C. Robin, clerk of the Probate court. He explained that his wife, Mrs. Dorothy Robin, had given birth to their first child, a girl, at the Michael Reese hospital.

> Menlo Park, Calif.—(AP)—Sammy Yates showed up in the eighth grade at Central school with a cigar box.
>
> He opened it and passed out all-day suckers, explaining: "I'm a brother."

Medical treatment of sterility has resulted in a considerable increase in multiple births so that the arrival of quintuplets is no longer the story of the year. Nevertheless, they as well as quadruplets, triplets and twins still are newsworthy. Unusual weight or size, physical deformity or the cirumstances under which birth took place may elevate the event above the level of the routine birth notice, as was the case in each of the following stories:

> Wenatchee, Wash.—(UP)—Mr. and Mrs. W. E. Robinson of Entiat Valley claim to be parents of the first baby born in an auto trailer in the Pacific northwest. A daughter, Kay, was born to them in March.

> The fire department ambulance crew in charge of Lieut. Irvin Martin aided the stork early Wednesday and a baby was presented to Mrs. Callie Burns, 21, 1216 Freeman avenue. Mother and infant were then taken to the general hospital.

Some newspapers play births more prominently than others. One way is to obtain pictures of the newly born, together with short feature stories in which source of the name, brothers and sisters, date of birth or some feature angle may be emphasized. The following is a typical entry from such a column:

> Even if she is a girl, the first child of Mr. and Mrs. William Clifford Richards Jr., 1415 Ashland Avenue, was named for her father and is called Billie Mae. Her second name is the first name of her maternal grandmother. Weighing 8 pounds 14 ounces the addition who has made the Richards family a threesome, was born Dec. 2 at St. Paul hospital.

Some papers, especially in the suburbs, interview newcomers to the community to introduce them to their new neighbors. Also residents who return from trips abroad or to vacationlands anywhere make good subjects for features based on their experiences and impressions. Similarly visitors may make interesting copy.

Much of the contents of the page commonly called women's or family is syndicated and provides advice to the lovelorn; hints on how to be pregnant, give birth and rear children; advice on how to stay happily married or to live alone and like it; also, advice on how to take care of pets and stay healthy and physically attractive and fit. Experts discuss mental health, how to garden, how to cook (with plentiful recipes provided by advertisers), take care of the hair, be stylish and fashionable. Illustrations often are provided by manufacturers, along with articles which are mostly free publicity. A few lead paragraphs that appeared on a typical up-to-date woman's page follow:

> Fashion is on a big knit-kick this season, and the look comes up fresh and new and full of energy.

> Pants have come a long way from the gardening-housework-car-pool routine. Their fashion potential along with their easy-going manner has cast them in a far more important role.

> At one time if a hostess told a man "casual dress," she could generally predict what he was going to wear. But today, a man might show up in anything from velvet jeans to a suede fringed jacket.

It remains to be proved that this commercialization of the erstwhile society page is preferable and that the contents are of greater interest than the gossip that once prevailed on it. Certainly there is no way to judge which type page is more socially beneficial. One doesn't need to take college journalism courses to prepare himself or herself for this kind of writing. In fact, it would be better for his peace of mind and that of his boss if s/he didn't.

SOCIETY NEWS

Types of Society News

The typical society page or section consists mainly of the following kinds of news:

Parties: birthday, reunions, anniversary, coming-out, announcement, showers, weekend, house, theater, card and miscellaneous.
Teas, luncheons, dinners, banquets, suppers, cocktail parties and picnics.
Meetings and announcements of meetings of women's organizations, if there is no club page.
Receptions.
Dances and balls.
Benefits, bazaars and the like.
Personal items, if not used in another part of the paper.
Engagements and weddings.

As this list suggests, the society page or section is written principally for women, although men are interested in many stories of engagements, weddings, parties and personal activities. A majority of society editors are women who have social rank themselves, although many large papers have male society editors. Of whichever sex, the editor should be able to attend major social events on an equal footing with other guests, although only a few occasions require the presence of a reporter. A large majority of society page items are contributed by persons concerned or by social secretaries, either in writing or by telephone. The society editor must be ever on the alert for practical jokers sending or phoning in bogus announcements of engagements, weddings and other social events. Nothing should be used without verification. If the society editor needs pipelines, such people as chefs, florists, hairdressers and delicatessen store operators are among the best to utilize.

Elements in Society News

Most society events of any importance have elements in common which include:
Names. Host and hostess; guests of honor; members of the receiving line in order of importance; assistants to hostess in the parlor and dining room; members of committees; entertainers; musicians and their selections; prominent guests; relation of guest of honor to hostess or of assistants to either.

Decorations. Color scheme, its significance and how it was carried out; flowers, palms and ferns to make room resemble tropical garden, an outdoor scene and so on.

Refreshments. Distinguish between luncheon and tea and between supper, dinner and banquet. At receptions, always learn who poured and who served and ask if these assistants were selected for any particular reason (relatives, sorority sisters, officers of an organization).

Occasion. Is it an anniversary or an annual event? What will be done with any proceeds? Does the place have any significance?

It is difficult to achieve variety in writing similar accounts of social events. Consequently, the society editor welcomes any possible feature.

PERSONALITIES

It probably is sad but true that most people go through life without ever being considered newsworthy. At best their birth, marriage and death receive brief mention. Otherwise, unless they get into trouble, as criminal or criminal's victim, or are in an accident or innocently a part of some unusual circumstance, they are ignored by the press. If, on the other hand, they attain a position of importance whereby others are affected, they become the objects of attention.

Important Position

Newly elected or appointed public figures, executives of private businesses and others in decision-making positions are objects of interest, especially when they enter upon their new careers.

By Gary Kiefer

In their rush to serve today's job-oriented students, colleges must guard against the danger of becoming vocational schools, Ohio State University's new provost says.

W. Ann Reynolds, who took over Sept. 1 as OSU's chief academic officer, said universities are facing difficult decisions as rising costs and declining enrollments force administrators to cut back in some academic areas.

She warns that universities which make curriculum decisions solely on the basis of student interest are shirking some of the responsibility that comes with being a center for knowledge.

"There is extra pressure on us now that kids are so job-oriented," she said. The changing goals of students, she added, can be seen in their increasing interest in fields like engineering, where jobs are plentiful, and decreasing interest in liberal arts studies like languages.

"As a university, we must take a hard look at our curriculum but I think we need to protect some programs, like language studies, that are important even if they are not the most popular," she said.

Dr. Reynolds, 41, will have a lot to say about the academic decisions made at Ohio State in coming years, according to OSU President Harold Enarson, who said university officials found in her "a person of truly superior qualifications." . . . [Columbus (Ohio) *Dispatch*]

Prominent Citizen

Even holders of important positions can go unnoticed unless the paper runs a "Know Your Neighbor" series or something of the sort, short profiles to make readers better acquainted with persons who may affect their lives and well-being. Reader interest is heightened when the profile turns out to be a success story.

By George Vecsey

Nyack, N.Y.—Once he was a bellhop at Kutsher's resort hotel in the Catskills, a black basketball player from the ghetto carrying luggage. Today he is a heart surgeon, implanting pacemakers in some of the very same people he served as a bellhop.

Dr. Fletcher James Johnson Jr. could take all the credit, say "Look what I've done," and emphasize that he had to study in Italy and Switzerland to achieve his goal. But he describes the fact of a black surgeon working in a Hasidic-owned hospital as a victory for America, a proof that the system can work.

"My father is a Bible-reading man with a third-grade education who taught me that life is short—you only get one hand," he said. "I see myself accepted as a surgeon; I feel very good about this country. People can do it."

Dr. Johnson is willing to preach a little bit because he sees good things happening around him in Rockland County, a region of green hills and views of the Hudson River 20 miles north of New York City, divided among estates and old mostly gentile neighborhoods on the one hand and the Hasidic Jewish community of New Square on the other. . . [New York *Times*]

Unusual Occupation

Some people are highly visible as they earn a living—bus drivers, second-hand car salesmen, department store clerks, policemen and the like. Others, belonging to smaller segments of the labor force, are obscure and often considered mysterious or the object of awe.

By Kathy Megan

On a hillside somewhere between Clendenin and Walton, Danny Dunn leaned on his freshly sharpened shovel and sighed, "There's no consideration for a man digging a grave.

"A gravedigger's job is the loneliest in the world," he said. "You're the first to get here before a funeral and the last to leave. After everyone pulls out of here in their Cadillacs and Lincolns you've still got an hour's worth of work."

Whether in rain, snow or ice, or on New Year's, Easter or birthdays, Danny, Dally and their father Leo Dunn are on call. The Mount Tyler family has eked out a harsh but thriving livelihood in country graveyards.

Leo, 73, figures he has dug 3,000 graves since childhood. For 28 years he sold vaults, the outer case for a casket, while digging graves on the side. At the age of 62, a time when most men are considering retirement, Leo quit selling vaults for a company and established his own business. Danny and Dally had brandished shovels for their dad for most of their lives but, in the last few years, turned professional.

The family digs graves in the traditional manner, no backhoes or tractors. Using picks, shovels and muscle power, and consuming quarts of Dr. Pepper, Danny and Dally dig about 15 graves a month.

"The trouble with gravedigging is that you can't plan anything," Leo said. "When we get called, there's no deciding. We have to go."

And the places they are going, often small family cemeteries, are not easy to get to. "We could do four-wheel drive commercials that would make the ones on television look like a piece of cake," Danny said.

A graveside life does have some fringe benefits, however. Both Danny, 30, and Dally, 26, had more conventional jobs as a retail salesman and industrial worker. Danny was fired on a personnel technicality and Dally was layed off. The grave-digging business, at $125 per grave, is more reliable.

"Years ago the families would get out there and dig the graves," Danny said. "But the younger generation would rather pay to have it done than do it themselves."

All three men said they enjoy the physical labor. Dally pulls a pick back over his shoulder with the grace of a javelin thrower. Several hard smacks and he has cleared most of the soapstone from the bottom of the ditch.

"If you know where the rock seam is it's lots easier," Dally said.

The mark of a professional is the neatness of the job. Following lines mapped out with string, Dally and Danny begin at the ends of the grave and work toward the middle.

Contrary to the jokes about 6-feet under, graves are about 4-feet down. Any deeper and most vaults would be floating in water.

On the day of the funeral a large beige tent is set up, chairs are brought out for the bereaved, and fake grass is laid to cover the fresh dirt.

"Most people don't know what goes into this," Dally said. "They think, 'Well, shoot, that's just a little ol' hole . . .

"They sit there and bless everyone," Danny said. "They even 'God bless' the undertaker. Hardly ever do they bless the digger. We set up a tent to keep them out of the rain, lay down grass to keep their feet out of the mud, and dig the hole so they can have the funeral, but there's not a thought for us."

Does the thought of death ever cross their minds as they dig? "You don't think about it as a grave," Danny said. "You just think about it as a hole that needs to get the dirt back into it. You could be digging holes for the gas company.

"Except when it's kids. We buried two kids down in Kenova . . . now that was downright touching.

"Most of the time you just think about getting that dirt back into the hole so you can go home for dinner." [Charleston (W.Va.) *Gazette*]

Unusual Hobby

Not all persons utilize their spare time watching low-brow television programs or reading trashy magazines. Some make avocations out of collecting coins or antiques and everything in between. Or they create things or in some other way exhibit originality and creativity. Elderly people are especially newsworthy when they make constructive use of their spare time.

By Dave Person

Kalamazoo—The warm heart of Mrs. May Leedy has led to warm hands for dozens of youngsters at Edison School during the past four years.

Each year at Christmastime the 96-year-old boxes up the mittens she has made during a long year of knitting and sends them off to the school.

There, Principal Richard Grushon distributes a pair to each of his kindergarteners at the school's annual Christmas party.

The children always appreciate the mittens, Grushon said. Some youngsters already have lost their first pair of winter mittens by Christmas and need a new pair. Others, he said, have no mittens to begin with.

"With this sudden cold spell, they're especially appreciated," Grushon said.

For the past two months Leedy has been doing her knitting out of her room at Provincial House Nursing Home. Before that she lived at Alamo Hills Apartments.

Leedy began giving her mittens to the school four years ago when it was suggested by Helen Coover, retired director of Senior Citizens Counter Isolation.

It was a perfect match. Leedy loves knitting the mittens for the youngsters and they, in turn, show their appreciation each year in a new way. This year some of the youngsters brought her a class picture and a poinsettia.

Making the mittens is no small task. Leedy makes about 65 pairs each year. This year she's warming 63 pairs of small hands.

Last Christmas, she said, she discovered she was ahead of her usual pace. She had knitted 83 pair of mittens. Some of them went to her church bazaar.

Leedy, who frequently puts down her knitting for a game of Scrabble says she has been knitting for at least 10 years. She proves it with a 1969 issue of Guideposts, a religious magazine, which features her in one of its inspirational stories about interesting people.

Leedy proudly points out that her descendants include 63 great-grandchildren and 31 great-great-grandchildren. But most of them live in California or Arizona, where they have no use for mittens, she says with a laugh.

At Edison, teachers save their extra yarn during the year and give it to Leedy to make sure she doesn't run out, Grushon said. And she doesn't.

"She just keeps knitting away," he says in amazement.

[Grand Rapids (Mich.) *Press*]

Reminiscences

Old people often spin stories about the good old days or recall instances of historic importance, explain why they experience *déjà vu* as history seems to repeat itself. The reporter should avoid the doddering old fools who have memories only of personal experiences, mostly trivial, and seek out the wise sages whose experiences and recollections can be newsworthy.

Grand Junction—Al Look stretched his legs, leaned back in his armchair, laughed and began telling another story, this one about a "flannelmouthed, tobacco-chewing, bulldozing" defense attorney who managed to discredit all six witnesses to a murder.

Look's rapid-fire, precise accounting of the story was fast, but the easy flow of descriptive adjectives explained how the lawyer did it.

If you enjoy first-person stories about Indians, cowboys, cowtowns, cows, fish, archaeology, paleontology, film-making, advertising, journalism, comic strips, the Holy Land, Alaskan dog races, politics or the economy, listen a while.

Now 86 years old, Look has helped chronicle a good bit of western Colorado history, made some himself, and currently is working a few hours a day on his next book. He has another at the publisher's for editing, a third at the printers and already has had 14 others published. [Denver *Post*]

Visiting Celebrity

After apotheosizing entertainers, political and civic leaders, athletes and others, people want to know the extent to which the celebrities remain human beings. They ask reporters and others in a position to know, "What is he/she really like?" When a popular hero or heroine comes to town, local reporters try to find out.

By Diane Reischel

"I was never a pretty little girl. I've got the long nose, the long face."

In other words, Nancy Sparer had the aristocratic look.

It's a persona she wears with flair in her portrayal of newspaper publisher Margaret Pynchon on CBS television's "Lou Grant."

The Emmy-winning actress stopped off in Madison this weekened to visit her son David, who is in his final year of law school at the University of Wisconsin.

A graying widow on the screen, "Mrs. Pynchon" in person is softer, less forbidding, and strawberry blonde. Yet, without question, this is a woman who could keep even the most irreverent city editor in tow.

"Mrs. Pynchon is a terrific lady. I love her," said Sparer, who goes by the stage name of Nancy Marchand.

"She's obviously quite bright. She's very brave, probably pretty lonely. She has a terrific sense of humor and a tremendous sense of responsibility."

She's also had two seasons to mellow: "Some people have said to me they find she's not quite as prickly as early on in the show."

The woman behind prickly Mrs. Pynchon is an avowed easterner. She was raised in Buffalo, educated at Carnegie Tech, and unleashed on New York City in the nascent days of television.

"Television was just starting. The war had just ended. There was a lot of creativity and energy. And there was a whole new field to explore. It was a very exciting time."

In addition to television roles in "Studio One," "Playhouse 90" and "Kraft Theater," Sparer worked in radio and on stage. She spent several seasons performing Shakespeare in Stratford, Conn. In fact, that's how she met "Lou Grant" star Ed Asner, 20 years ago.

"I hadn't seen him since," said Sparer, but she understands Asner suggested her for the Mrs. Pynchon role.

In the years immediately before she took over the mythical Los Angeles Trib, Sparer played the mother in the aborted "Upstairs, Downstairs" offshoot called "Beacon Hill." She also played a wealthy relation on the soap opera "Another World."

''Then I was on a dog of a soap opera that folded pretty quickly.''

Though Sparer didn't plan to limit herself to variations on high brow themes, she says that, at least in television, ''I've gotten sort of stuck with roles like that.''

''I was trained for classical work, so I can portray somebody who has some kind of knowledge beyond the dime store and a pack of chewing gum.''

Sparer brings this knowledge to the ''Lou Grant'' set about two days a week. Each episode takes nine days to complete, says Sparer, and she commutes from New York for the days she is needed. The shooting season runs from June through February.

The show definitely revolves around Ed Asner, says Sparer. ''But he's a totally regular person. There's never any rank pulled in any way, except to help the show. He is terrific about things like that.''

Sparer believes much of the show's appeal lies in its realistic, sometimes inconclusive plots.

''A lot of these problems don't have resolutions, and they (the writers) are trying to be as honest as they can. Sometimes an investigation opens up a whole hornet's nest of other things, and the show is only an hour long.''

She feels a recent program gave a particularly sensitive exploration of prostitution. ''It showed that she could sometimes feel she was doing something worthwhile. Lots of people with office jobs never have that feeling.''

Sparer says she is pleased with an episode she just completed about conflict of interest in the newsroom. She says she is also pestering the writers to do something on the subject of newsroom automation and the labor strikes that result.

The ''Lou Grant'' cast has a strong sense of camaraderie, says Sparer, although commuting keeps her from a lot of the socializing.

''I've mostly just stayed in Los Angeles to do the job and then go home.''

Home is a sixth floor Manhattan apartment which she shares with her actor husband, Paul Sparer, and daughter, Rachel, 17. (Aside from son David, 26, the Sparers also have a daughter, Kate, 23, who is studying acting with San Francisco's American Conservatory Theater.)

''This is the last year we will have children in the house. Next year we're going to have to reevaluate what we want to do.''

On the screen, however, count on a third season of ''Lou Grant,'' and an ever-prickly Mrs. Pynchon. [Madison (Wis.) *Press Connection*]

CONSUMERISM

Although there now are about 200 full-time consumer reporters, coverage of news events that consumers need to know about to get the most for their money is grossly inadequate. For a half century Consumers Union and a few similar groups have advised small memberships regarding the comparative qualities of competing articles, but neither governmental agencies nor newspapers have been aggressive in exposing poor goods.

The modern movement, slow and halting as it still is, began with the appearance of Ralph Nader's book *Unsafe at Any Speed* in 1966. Publicity given the attempt of General Motors, through detectives, to smear Nader, aided him in originating Public Citizen and several other educational and lobbying groups.

As yet Congress and state legislatures have not strengthened the protection consumers deserve. It always has been so. The first Food and Drug Act of 1906 followed the public outcry as a result of Upton Sinclair's *The Jungle,* describing unsavory conditions in Chicago Stockyards. Two attempts to strengthen that act have succeeded only by timely revelations of threats to the public health. In 1938 the Copeland bill seemed doomed to defeat until the news story broke of the deaths of a score or more persons in Tennessee from improperly tested liquid sulfanilomide. In 1960 even a much watered-down bill that resulted from long hearings by a Senate Committee headed by Sen. Estes Kefauver was facing certain defeat as a result of millions of dollars spent in lobbying by the drug industry. Then, however, the news of the threat of the baby-deforming drug thalidomide was released with pictures of infants born without limbs. The drug industry was exposed as having opposed measures to ban the drug's use in the United States.

In the '30s Stuart Chase was the most prolific of a number of journalists and other pioneers of the organized consumer movement. Chase's books included *The Tragedy of Waste* and *Men and Machines,* which warned of industrial accidents, pollution and threats to the health of urban dwellers. Arthur Kalett and F. J. Schlink wrote *100 Million Guinea Pigs,* James Rorty wrote *Our Master's Voice,* a blast at advertising; Kenneth Crawford exposed lobbies in *The Pressure Boys,* William H. Whyte Jr. wrote *The Organization Man,* and a decade later, Hillel Black of the New York *Times,* wrote *Buy Now, Pay Later.*

All of these iconoclasts, especially Chase, were red-baited and/or otherwise vilified. And then came Vance Packard with *The Hidden Persuaders* and a half dozen other blasts at the Establishment. His books include *The Waste Makers, The Status Seekers, The Pyramid Climbers, A Nation of Strangers, The Naked City* and *The People Shapers.*

The late Sidney Margolius, probably the first and certainly the most successful journalistic expert in this field, took an optimistic view, as follows:

> Consumer journalism is a young profession, the youngest branch of journalism, but already it is making a significant contribution to stemming the many deceptions and diversions that cause the massive waste we have in society today. Without the new interest of the press and often radio and sometimes TV, we probably would not have achieved the useful advances of the past 12 years such as truth-in-lending and other credit reforms on federal and state levels; the new product safety law; advances in regulations governing auto and tire safety; some reforms in food and cosmetic packaging; unit pricing and open dating of foods; the 1962 drug amendments requiring that drugs be proven efficacious as well as safe; the exposure and increasing regulation of multiple distributor investment schemes, and many other money-wasting deceptions whether actually illegal or barely inside the law.
>
> What consumer journalism has accomplished, however, is just a beginning to what really needs to be done, including the massive task of finding ways to curb the present galloping or at least trotting inflation.

Today steps by the Federal Trade Commission and the Food and Drug Administration to warn and protect consumers get nationwide publicity and can hardly be ignored by local newspapers. It is news from coast to coast when an automobile manufacturer recalls thousands of cars for remedial work; when saccharine is or is not declared dangerous to health; toys are banned as unsafe and so are cosmetics, detergents, candy, drugs or other processed foods. There has been improvement in labeling of foods and drugs, and advertisers have been forced to desist from making false claims. The proceedings to enforce such regulations usually are time-consuming so business is not seriously inconvenienced.

Although local newspapers print press association accounts of charges and actions directed to improve or protect the public, with few exceptions, they refrain from localizing the national stories. There is not much journalistic policing of retail business establishments. Most frequent crusades are directed at bait-and-switch tactics, short-weight swindles and comparative shopper's lists that show discrepancies among stores offering identical products for sale. The victims of such investigations are not generally the town's leading advertisers.

A leading crusader for greater newspaper activity in this area is Francis Pollock, editor of the now defunct *Media & Consumers,* who advises as follows:

> As a start toward better consumer service, the travel sections might open letters-to-the-editor columns to reader give-and-take, as the New York *Times* travel section does. Other consumer features which might be added: periodic reports on the amount of lost baggage, with, of course, the airlines' names (the publicity probably would stimulate better service); features on how to get the most economical travel rates; surveys of reader experiences with travel agents, resorts, and airlines; and any other report that would help the consumer get better value for his travel dollars. . . .
>
> News organizations could, if they wanted, advise their readers on how one bank's savings plans or mortgage loans compare with those of other area banks. . . . They could, if they wanted, compare rental car rates, or, as the Minneapolis *Star* did, print comparison charts of the octane ratings and prices of gasoline.

Typical of the syndicated Consumer Reports for use by newspapers is the following from the Freeport (Ill.) *Journal-Standard:*

> Vacuum cleaners sold door-to-door tend to be more expensive than those sold in a store—a large part of that extra cost goes toward the salesperson's commission.
>
> Four brands tested recently by Consumer Reports' engineers are sold exclusively or extensively door-to-door or by appointment. The four—Electrolux, Filter Queen, Kirby and Rexair—cost two, three or even four times as much as other, comparable machines.
>
> In addition to a sales commission, the price of the most expensive tested upright—the $459 Kirby cleaner—can be driven up by exotic options including a drill chuck, a jig-saber saw and a massage cup.
>
> Electrolux salespeople stuck pretty close to vacuuming in their product demonstrations—something that the other sellers of vacuum cleaners don't always do.
>
> For example, one of the highest-priced tested vacuum cleaners—the $550 Filter Queen—has been promoted with some questionable sales pitches.

Consumer Reports' staffers visited by Filter Queen salespeople in 1976 heard vague statements about health benefits and unsubstantiated claims that the Filter Queen was used by hospitals. Filter Queen sales literature still speaks of sanitizing upholstered furniture and of helping to "fight air pollution. . . ."

There follow the lead paragraphs of four long consumer articles written by A. Kent MacDougall (Hon. Second Son) for the Los Angeles *Times*.

By A. Kent MacDougall
TIMES STAFF WRITER

In the beginning there was just Campbell's chicken rice soup.

Today, besides chicken with rice soup, Campbell Soup Co. makes chicken gumbo, chicken noodle, chicken noodle O's, curly noodle with chicken, cream of chicken, creamy chicken mushroom, chicken vegetable, chicken alphabet, chicken & stars, chicken 'n dumplings and chicken broth.

These dozen chicken soups and the 40 other varieties in Campbell's familiar line of canned condensed soup exemplify the colorful cornucopia of consumer goods that give American shoppers a range of choice unsurpassed in history.

But to competitors such as H. J. Heinz Co., which just this month settled a $105 million antitrust suit against Campbell Soup out of court, Campbell's proliferation to three lines of canned soup with a total of 80 varieties is part of a calculated strategy to hog supermarket shelf space, keep out rival brands and protect Campbell's near-monopoly in canned soup.

Whatever the merits of such charges, proliferation on the soup shelves of the nation's supermarkets is mild compared with what is going on elsewhere. Along breakfast cereal row, in the frozen foods display case, on the dog and cat food shelves, and up and down most other aisles, a fierce struggle for shelf space and market share is being waged among the two to four big manufacturers that typically dominate each category.

Rather than undercutting one another on price, the manufacturers are locked in a big-bucks battle to see which can spew out the most new products, advertise and promote them most heavily, and tie up the most shelf space.

And far from being new, most of the new brands, sizes, shapes, colors, flavors and scents being showered on the public are only minor variations on existing products, differing mainly in form, packaging and advertised image. . . .

By A. Kent MacDougall
TIMES STAFF WRITER

The folks who brought you Twinkies, Wonder Bread and other highly processed, additive-laden foods now have something for junk-food haters, too.

It's called Fresh & Natural bread, and ITT Continental Baking Co. has just brought it out in whole wheat and white. Neither variety contains preservatives, but the white bread has been artificially enriched with vitamins and minerals to replace the natural ones that were removed during extensive refining.

If Fresh & Natural does not fit everyone's idea of natural, neither will many of the "natural," "all-natural" and "100% natural" breads, cereals, ice creams, snacks, soft drinks and other foods and beverages on supermarket shelves nowadays.

Among these are "natural" cheeses that are artificially colored and preserved, a "100% natural" cereal that is more than 20% sugar, a "100% natural" grape drink that has less grape juice than sweeteners, and frozen foods, yogurt and fruit juices that boldly proclaim they are "naturally flavored," although their ingredient labels show that they contain artificial flavoring.

Such dubious claims are possible because there is no generally accepted definition of a natural food or beverage. The Food and Drug Administration, which regulates food labeling, pretty much allows manufacturers to define the word for themselves. . . .

By A. Kent MacDougall
TIMES STAFF WRITER

Snack time on United Airlines' flights used to mean a sandwich, beverage and peanuts. No more. Six months ago United eliminated the peanuts, thereby saving $800,000 a year. "And that's not peanuts," a United official says.

A number of airlines are saving millions by packing more passengers into the coach sections of their planes. United has reduced seat width by 1.3 inches in many planes, added one seat per row in jumbo jets and reduced the distance between rows by two inches in many smaller jets. These changes began months before the recent round of fare discounts and, unlike those discounts, have not been promoted.

In putting a slight squeeze on their customers, the airlines are only doing what more and more companies in many industries are doing—reducing the quantity and even the quality of goods and services in order to cut costs, boost profits and keep prices in line.

Known variously as "downsizing," packing to price and the shrinking candy bar syndrome, size reductions have a common result: the consumer gets less for his money. The hidden inflation that this constitutes doesn't show up in the government's consumer price index, but it nonetheless affects a growing list of consumer goods and services.

Automobiles are shrinking at the same time that their prices are rising. Houses are built less sturdily and of lower-grade materials. Whisky has been watered. Warranties on cars, tires and television sets cover less than they used to. Wine comes in smaller bottles, newspapers in smaller formats. Paper towels and toilet tissues contain fewer sheets per roll. And a quarter dropped in a jukebox brings forth a single song or two, compared with three songs several years ago and six generations ago. . . .

By A. Kent MacDougall
TIMES STAFF WRITER

Americans have taken in stride the nondairy creamer, the reconstituted potato chip, "bacon" made from soybeans and other synthetic foods. So why not the ersatz chocolate bar?

Stung by sharply rising prices for cocoa beans, from which real chocolate is made, manufacturers of chocolate candy, ice cream, beverages, cake mixes and other foods are turning increasingly to substitute ingredients—some natural, most synthetic, all cheaper.

Although less discriminating chocolate lovers don't seem to be noticing the substitutions, manufacturers are proceeding cautiously lest connoisseurs of fine chocolate lose confidence in brands now known for quality.

Hershey Foods Corp. has no present plans to use substitutes in its famous milk chocolate candy bar. But it has been marketing an imitation chocolate chip for baking cookies for nearly three years. And it hopes a substitute for cocoa butter that Procter & Gamble Co. has just developed will be good enough for use in many Hershey products.

The nation's largest candy maker, Mars, Inc., which coats its Snickers, 3 Musketeers, Milky Way and other bars with real chocolate, has just introduced its first candy bar with an imitation "chocolaty" coating.

Manufacturers stand to gain a great deal by using substitutes for the increasingly costly ingredients in real chocolate. Americans spent more than $3 billion on chocolate candy last year and billions more on chocolate-flavored milk, ice cream, cookies and other foods. Yet sales of chocolate candy are down this year because of consumer resistance to the higher prices necessitated by increased ingredient costs. Profits also are down—by more than $10 million at Hershey alone.

To make matters worse, chocolate manufacturers find themselves forced to defend products they consider nutritious against charges that they contribute to tooth decay, obesity and sugar addiction. The federal government is threatening to ban the sale of chocolate candy and other sugared snacks in school lunch rooms. And it is considering restrictions on television commercials that allegedly "mouthwash" impressionable children into becoming junk food junkies.

I have been a reporter and have now become a philosopher. When I was a reporter I made mistakes and preferred my friends to my enemies; now as a philosopher I make even worse mistakes, and am frequently guilty even of preferring myself to my friends. The situation is horrible indeed. But I must say that I never blamed it on the newspaper—either the one for which I reported or the one in which I am now allowed to philosophize.

—JAMES WEBER LINN, Chicago *Daily Times*

12

MEETINGS, CONVENTIONS, SPEECHES

The French writer Alexis de Tocqueville, perhaps the all-time most perceptive foreign observer of American life, was amazed by the avidity with which we Americans form and belong to organizations. Almost a century and a half later we are, more than ever, a nation of joiners. Even small-town dwellers do not have to go far to find a group with similar interests, be they professional, artistic, recreational or whatever. It is impossible for any newspaper to give adequate coverage to any sizable proportion of the total number of groups seeking publicity. Those considered the most newsworthy are of the following types:

1. Those that take an active part in local, state or national political, legal or governmental affairs, as the League of Women Voters, Chamber of Commerce, Daughters of the American Revolution, American Legion.
2. Those that are interested in controversial issues or engaged in extraordinary tactics, as Common Cause, Right to Life, National Abortion Rights Action League, American Civil Liberties Union, National Organization of Women and others.
3. Those that have programs including widely known speakers, musicians, artists and so forth.
4. Those with large, nationwide memberships that hold elaborate conven-

tions annually. Of this type are most fraternal lodges, routine news of which may be ignored but whose yearly meetings are first-rate shows.

In small city dailies and community and suburban newspapers, almost any organization is newsworthy. The initiative may be left to the group to send in its notices voluntarily or the publication may follow a sounder policy of attempting to have complete coverage, especially of such organizations as the PTA, church groups, Boy Scouts, Girl Scouts, YMCA, YWCA and so forth.

MEETINGS

The Preliminary Story

Every meeting is held for a purpose and this purpose should be the feature of the preliminary or advanced notice. From the secretary or some other officer of the group which is to meet, the reporter should learn the nature of important business to be discussed, of committees which will report, speakers, entertainment and so on.

Note how the second of the following leads emphasizes purpose:

WEAK: The Cosmos club will hold a meeting at 7:30 o'clock Thursday evening in Swift hall for the purpose of discussing the question of whether or not undergraduate students should own automobiles.

BETTER: Undergraduate ownership of automobiles will be discussed by the Cosmos club at its meeting at 7:30 Thursday evening in Swift hall.

Other vague beginnings to avoid include

There will be a meeting—
The purpose of the meeting—
At 7:30 o'clock—
The first meeting of the year—

The reporter should ask if the meeting is regular or special, business or social. S/he should inquire if a dinner or refreshments will precede or follow, whether any entertainment—dramatic, musical or otherwise—is planned. The main attraction of the meeting may be some special program. A meeting to elect or install officers, initiate candidates, hear a particular committee report or a speaker or to celebrate an anniversary has an obvious feature from the news standpoint.

The reporter must be sure to obtain the following data:

1. The organization. Its exact name, and the name and number of the post or chapter. "Local Odd Fellows" is not enough; instead, write "Keystone Lodge No. 14, IOOF" That is the usual form: name of the local chapter first, then the number and finally the name or usual abbreviation of the national organization.

2. Time and place. In the preliminary story this information must be definite and accurate. A meeting scheduled for 8 o'clock should not be mentioned in the news story as to begin at 8:30. ''Friday evening'' is not enough; the exact hour should be given. Both the building and room should be given in stating the place.

3. The program. If there is a program of entertainment, the reporter should obtain it in detail. S/he must get names of musicians and their selections, names of casts and dramatic coaches, decorations, orchestras, committees in charge. Only the highlights of a program need be mentioned, and in order of importance, rather than in the order included in the program.

Note how purpose is emphasized in the following examples:

> The American Legion Auxiliary's 5th District will meet at 8 P.M. Saturday in the Community club rooms, 1600 South Grand avenue, to hear annual reports by district chairmen and to elect delegates to the state and national conventions. Mrs. Martha Watkins, district director, will preside.

> An informational meeting has been scheduled for next Monday to explain two proposed additions to the Waterloo health care scene: A group home project for the developmentally disabled, and a sophisticated piece of diagnostic equipment for a hospital.
>
> The meeting, to be conducted by the Iowa Health Systems Agency Inc., is a preliminary step in formulating a recommendation on the projects for use by the state health department.
>
> The state must certify a need for both projects and also must approve them before the facilities involved can receive reimbursements for procedures under Medicaid, Medicare and other programs.
>
> The group homes are planned by Exceptional Persons Inc., which intends to build three of them at an estimated cost of $658,000.
>
> Each of the group homes will have 12 beds. Two of the homes will be for moderately retarded adults and the third for severely physically handicapped and retarded persons.
>
> The group homes are to be financed with industrial development revenue bonds issued by the Black Hawk County Board of Supervisors.
>
> Also on the agenda at the meeting will be a new ''nuclear imaging system'' for Allen Memorial Hospital.
>
> The machine, which will cost an estimated $135,000, will replace what has become an antiquated system of patient scanning and diagnosis.
>
> The equipment will be purchased by the hospital with cash on hand, according to its application to the state.
>
> The informational meeting will be at 7 p.m. in the Hurwich Room of the Waterloo Recreation and Arts Center, 225 Cedar St. [Waterloo (Iowa) *Courier*]

Sometimes the preliminary notice may be the excuse for a historical sketch of the organization, as

> Having enjoyed a vigorous life for 80 years, the United Charities is pausing next week to give itself a birthday party. With a program as impressive as the

occasion demands, the celebration will take place at the Palmer House the afternoon of the 16th.

Dr. Vance L. Howland is coming out from Escot to make the principal address of the party, and a pageant and tea will supplement the speeches.

As president of the group, Allan Fort will be chief host. Mrs. Stephen Lorch heads the committee in charge of the event, and is drafting a corps of her young friends who will act as ushers and hostesses in costumes their mothers used to wear as members of the organization.

Since 1902 when 23 Milltown business men founded the organization, it has been run largely by the same families. Victor G. Stoneking, Ernest I. Silsbee, James R. Leary, Austin H. DeZutter and Milo Morgan were some of the founders who named themselves the Milltown Relief and Aid society and obtained a state charter still in use.

They confronted the first big test of their efficiency in 1910 when Mayor William R. Trumbull turned over to them the job of looking after the thousands of Milltownians whose homes were destroyed in the April floods. Until then their chief means of relief had been money, but that spring, with O. A. Thayer as chairman of their shelter committee, they bought timber to build 9,000 homes, one of which still stands on the near southeast side.

Charles W. Riegel, the father of Mrs. Lee Diamond, was president of the society that year and wrote letters of thanks to people in the Hebrides, in Japan and Ecuador, and in more familiar places, for their contributions to Milltown's rebuilding fund.

It was Mr. Thayer's task to distribute building materials, food and clothes that came in from all parts of the country, and files in the present S. Savoy avenue headquarters still contain requests made to the shelter committee.

The Follow-up

In the follow-up or story after the meeting has been held, the outcome, or result, should be featured, and the writer should look to the future. For instance, avoid.

Keystone Lodge No. 14, IOOF, last evening voted to build a new million dollar lodge hall.

Rather, emphasize the future, as

Keystone Lodge No. 14, IOOF, will build a million dollar lodge hall, it was decided at last evening's meeting.

Or, better still:

A new lodge hall to cost one million dollars will be erected by Keystone Lodge No. 14, IOOF, as the result of last evening's meeting.

Other beginnings to avoid include

The Cosmos club met last evening—
At a meeting of—

There was a meeting—
The purpose of the meeting was—
One of the most interesting—
The outcome of the meeting—

The reporter should learn the disposition of every item of business. Some matters will be laid on the table or referred to committees. Others will be defeated outright. Some business, of course, will be concluded. If the meeting or business is important, the writer should include in the story not only the result of balloting, but also the arguments presented by both supporters and opponents of every measure, both those that passed and those that were defeated.

The account of a meeting that has been held never should read as the secretary's minutes. The items of business are mentioned in the order of their importance rather than chronologically as considered at the meeting. So that s/he can interpret them correctly, the reporter must obtain the exact wordings of resolutions and also the memberships of committees. It is not necessary to mention the presiding officer unless someone other than the president or usual chairman was in charge.

In the follow-up story, the time and place need not be stated so definitely. "Last evening" is sufficient, as the exact moment at which the chairman sounded his gravel is immaterial. The name of the building in which the meeting was held is enough, especially if the organization has a regular meeting place. If the time of the next meeting is not fixed by custom it should be mentioned.

Names of everyone who took part in the program should be obtained if a complete account is desired. If a ladies' auxiliary serves a meal or refreshments, the names of the women who helped should be mentioned.

Note in the following example how the writer caught the spirit or importance of the occasion, which he interpreted interestingly:

> The so-called conservative element in the labor union movement was successful in the annual election held Wednesday night by the Milwaukee Federated Trades' council.
>
> Herman Seide was reelected secretary by a vote of 458 to 169 over Al Benson, former sheriff and now organizer for the United Textile Workers of America.
>
> Anton Sterner, nominated to oppose J. F. Friedrick for the post of general organizer, withdrew. Friedrick was reelected by 624 votes.
>
> For secretary-treasurer, Emil Brodde was reelected with 458 to 164 for Severino Pollo. Frank Wietzke, sergeant-at-arms for more than 40 years, was reelected without opposition.
>
> In the contest between conservative and liberal slates for the nine places on the executive board, the same division was apparent. Those elected and their votes are. . . .
>
> [Milwaukee *Journal*]

Style

Expressions such as "Members are urged to attend," and "The public is cordially invited" should be avoided. If the purpose of the meeting is stated correctly, the former expression is superfluous. The latter expression is poor because of the "cordially." If an invitation is not cordial, it should not be extended.

Other expressions to avoid include

—was the most important happening.
—was the main business transacted.
—was the topic of discussion.
—featured the meeting.
—was the principal transaction.

Audiences

Sometimes, as at a public meeting, the size and behavior of the audience are an essential part of the story.

By Ralph Gifford

More than 100 Northwest Siders who gathered at the Edgebrook Fieldhouse Friday night heard assurances from two aldermen that the city has agreed to postpone the closing of the building until April 1, and that by then a way will be found to maintain its unique status as a community center. . . .

[Chicago *Northwest Side Press*]

By Dean Mayer

Relatively few industry officials turned out Thursday for a session designed to tell them about a program requiring some plants to treat their toxic and hazardous wastes before they enter the public sewer system.

The Green Bay Metropolitan Sewerage District invited representatives from 166 area industries to a session at the Brown County Library. Not all 166 firms are likely to be affected by the pretreatment program—certain definitions remain to be set—but the MSD wanted to cover all bases.

Only about 45 industry officials showed up, with some firms represented by more than one person.

"Frankly, I was surprised," said MSD Plant Manager Thomas Cooper of the attendance. "I'm afraid we just don't have the industries' attention yet."

[Green Bay (Wis.) *Press-Gazette*]

By Nan Robertson

"How long does this jealousy period last?" said a plaintive woman's voice from the audience the other night. "Forever!" cried an answering chorus. And then everybody laughed—the kind of laughter that meant everybody understood.

The scene was a packed, emotion-charged room at the Barbizon Hotel for Women, where women outnumbered men about three to one and virtually everybody was a stepparent or about to become one.

The audience had come to hear "Making It as a Stepparent: An Open Forum" sponsored by Doubleday, the book publishing concern. A psychologist, a registered nurse, and two authors who had written new books on being a stepparent, one a novel based on personal experience, were the panelists. Three of the four were stepparents. . . . [New York *Times*]

The following story, which appeared in the Charleston (W. Va.) *Gazette,* is the type that every journalist sometimes in his career yearns to write.

By Chris Knap

Dale Dunbar stood shivering on the banks of Witcher Creek, looking back at the converted garage that houses VFW Post 5269.

To his left stood an honor guard of flag bearers and uniformed veterans, holding M1 rifles at their side. To his right stood the rotund and jolly members of the VFW auxiliary, crisp in their bright blue hats and uniforms.

They formed a V in front of the ramshackle building. V for Victory. V for VFW. V for Vander Clute—the national commander-in-chief of the VFW, already almost two hours late for his appearance at the post's annual membership roundup.

The cold was too much. The veterans and their ladies went back into the canteen for another round of holiday cheer. Dunbar, the canteen manager, followed after them, muttering to himself.

Inside the canteen, the veterans fell into their usual groups. Several uniformed World War II veterans were standing in one corner, drinking heavily and not really talking about anything in particular.

The vets in business suits leaned against the pool table. One smoked a big cigar. Dunbar answered the phone. "For your information," he announced, "the commander has just reached St. Albans."

The crowd groaned. One of the business-suited vets walked over to the jukebox and punched the buttons to hear "Good Girls Don't."

Finally, as dusk began to fall, Howard Vander Clute and his entourage of state and national VFW officials arrived. The old vets formed their V once more and gave a three-round salute to their leader.

Dunbar escorted him into the canteen.

Vander Clute begged the post's pardon for his late arrival. He blamed the delay on the attention given him by "the radio and TV press."

The commander launched into a defense of the VFW's children's home in Michigan, now under investigation by the FBI. He said the operation of the home will not be affected. The post members listened politely.

On the Iranian situation, Vander Clute said he felt it inappropriate for "a national organization with 2½ million members to be critical of our president."

But the commander said the United States' present position "came as a direct result of the bankrupt policy of appeasement fostered by the Carter administration."

Vander Clute called for a ban on demonstrations by non-citizen groups. . . .

Afterward, an inebriated veteran rose and asked the commander a question about something that appeared in the VFW magazine. He had to rephrase it twice before anyone understood it.

Dale Dunbar sighed as Vander Clute rose to mingle with the crowd. "I hate these formal affairs," he said.

As might be expected, the article did not please the veterans. So, two days later, under the headline, ''VFW Story Angers Veterans, Wives,'' the *Gazette* ran the following:

> A group of veterans and their wives have angrily protested a story printed in the Sunday Gazette-Mail. They say the story made them look like a ''bunch of drunks.''
>
> Calvin Hughes, post-surgeon of VFW Post 5269 in Witcher Creek, said the story about the group's annual membership drive was a ''slur against all veterans.''
>
> ''And it was very rude,'' added Mrs. Nancy Nichols, junior vice president of the Women's Auxiliary of the post.
>
> The story which ran under the headline ''Glassy-Eyed Veterans Greet VFW Chief—2 Hours Late,'' and referred to members of the post as rotund, jolly and heavy-drinking, was a discredit to all veterans, members of the post said. Veterans also said that their post office, described in the story as ''ramshackle'' is newly remodeled and valued at $53,000.
>
> That is not to say that some individuals at the affair didn't fit that description, several veterans said.''But the majority of our members were not glassy-eyed,'' fumed Mrs. Nichols, who also noted that her own tall, slim frame was far from rotund.
>
> Mrs. Nichols and Hughes, along with Charles Shumaker, a veteran of World War II and the Korean War, and his wife, Delphia Shumaker, president of the Women's Auxiliary, were quick to point out the good deeds of their organization.
>
> The group sponsors annual holiday parties for children, sends children to camp, donates medicine, books, magazines and other goods to elderly veterans and patients at the Veterans Hospital in Beckley and runs a number of programs for elementary school children on such topics as drug abuse, bicycle safety and America's heritage. Each year the post honors the mothers of veterans who were killed in service.
>
> ''And that's just a small sampling of what we do,'' said Mrs. Nichols. ''It would take an entire newspaper to print it all.
>
> ''We want people to see that we are a respectable and dignified group,'' she continued. ''We are just average people trying to do a job.''

CONVENTIONS

Some organizations, such as the American Legion, National Association for the Advancement of Colored People and Americans for Democratic Action, are influential in state and national affairs. Consequently, when one of these organizations meets, what it does is of general interest. Such conventions frequently pass resolutions concerning vital political and business situations and recommend passage of certain laws by state legislatures and Congress. They even send lobbyists to state capitals and to Washington.

Conventions of other organizations that ordinarily are nonpolitical may be of widespread interest because of their large membership. Fraternal orders such as the Masons, Elks and Moose have chapters in all parts of the country, and their conventions attract thousands of delegates from all states. Church groups, businessmen's organizations, scientific and educational bodies consider matters of general interest. Frequently the first announcement of a new scientific discovery or theory is made in a paper presented at a convention of some scientific group.

Aside from the general interest that an important convention creates, there also is local interest, provided the locality is to be represented by delegates. If any local person is an officer or has a part in the program, the local interest is heightened. Many fraternal organizations hold drill team, band, fife and drum corps and other contests at conventions, and the local chapter may compete.

The Preliminary Notice

The first story of a convention usually appears a week or two before the opening session. Almost every important organization has a secretary or publicity person who prepares notices for the press. The advanced notice emphasizes the business of the convention and the important speeches or papers to be given or read. Sometimes the nature of a report which a special committee will make is disclosed in advance.

Note in the following examples of leads of preliminary notices of conventions that the writers emphasize the most important plans from the standpoint of general interest:

> College training for women interested in the field of commerce and business administration will be studied and discussed at the 10th annual convention of Gamma Theta Phi, national professional sorority of commerce and business administration, tomorrow through Sunday in the Windmere hotel.

> The National Federation of Women's Republican Clubs will make congressional campaign issues the principal theme of the organization's third biennial convention in Philadelphia Sept. 26 and 27. Mrs. W. Glen Davis of Akron, president, will direct the sessions at the Bellevue-Stratford hotel. Several hundred delegates from 42 states and the District of Columbia are expected.

In addition to the general story of a convention, or even instead of it, a local newspaper may print a story playing up the "local" angle—the part that local delegates will play, as

> With the hope and expectation of bringing next year's state convention to Milltown, 58 members of Keystone Lodge No. 14, I.O.O.F., accompanied by wives and families, are in Petersburgh today.
>
> Occasion is the 27th annual convention of the state I.O.O.F. in which several members of the local lodge will play prominent parts.

The First-Day Story

The story that appears just before the convention begins may emphasize the purpose and main business of the meeting, or it may play up the arrival of delegates; the probable attendance and the first day's program. Often a meeting of the officers or executive committee precedes the convention proper.

Some matter related exclusively to the internal organization of the group may be of sufficient general interest to be the feature, as when a rule changing the requirements for membership, or merger with another organization, is to be debated. Frequently an internal political fight is anticipated in the election of officers or selection of the next convention city.

> The leaders of the nation's banking fraternity, 8,500 strong, are arriving for the four-day annual American Bankers Association convention.
>
> The meeting, largest since the 1920s, will focus on the perplexing problem of the banker's role in curbing, while not blighting, the boom.
>
> The program at the Conrad Hilton hotel will also include speeches on the farm price problem and the task of building the free world's strength through NATO and the nation's strength through a strong free enterprise economy.
>
> In addition, a wide range of subjects, some of interest chiefly to bankers, others with a general scope, will be discussed.
>
> While thousands of bankers and their wives flock to a private showing of the General Motors Corp. Powerama Sunday, other bankers on 22 special committees—such as those on credit policy and federal legislation—will buckle down to work.
>
> But the committee which may prove to be the most controversial does not meet until Monday. That is the 50-member nominating committee, representing each state.
>
> There's no doubt, short of catastrophe, who the next president will be. He's the vice-president, Fred F. Florence, president, Republic National Bank of Dallas. He'll take over automatically from Homer J. Livingston, president, the First National Bank of Chicago.
>
> The rub will come when a successor vice-president to Florence is named.
>
> Observers think that for the first time in a generation there may be an open fight for control of the ABA, with the issue being state versus national banks.
>
> The "state's righters" argue that they haven't had a president for the last seven years. Because they can't name one directly this year, their strategy is to name the vice-president who will move up to the presidency. [Chicago *Sun-Times*]

A newspaper printed in the city entertaining a convention joins with the rest of the community in welcoming delegates. Reporters are assigned to gather side features and anecdotes unrelated to the serious business of the convention. Statistics may be included of the oldest delegate, the delegate who has come the longest distance, the delegate who has attended the most conventions, the delegate who flew to the convention by private airplane or arrived in some other unusual manner, the tallest delegate, the shortest and so forth.

The newspaper may take advantage of the opportunity to obtain feature interviews with important or picturesque delegates and speakers. At a gathering of editors of college newspapers, a reporter obtained numerous interviews regarding narcotics on campuses, a subject entirely different from the business of the convention.

The following is a well-written first-day convention story, which "catches" the spirit of the occasion:

Cleveland, July 13—(AP)—The Shrine brought its big show to town today and made Cleveland an oriental oasis of parades, concerts, ceremonies and funmaking.

Delegates were arriving by the thousands, by special trains, by automobile by plane and by boat, and tomorrow between 60,000 and 100,000 nobles are expected here for the 57th annual convention of the Ancient and Arabic Order of the Nobles of the Mystic Shrine of North America.

Today was listed on the program as all-Ohio day, with 750 members of the six Ohio temples initiated into the order, but the arrival of delegations from all parts of the country came in for equal attention.

One thousand members of Medinah temple of Chicago, the largest in the order, arrived in spectacular fashion, on the Lake Steamer Seeandbee. The Chicagoans, bedecked in red, green and yellow uniforms and bright red fezzes, paraded from the dock behind Al Koran patrol of Cleveland, and tied up downtown traffic for a half hour.

Medinah sent a brass band, an oriental band, 500 uniformed men, and a headquarters company from its 23,000 members. This year a Chicago man, Thomas J. Houston, is to be elected imperial potentate and the windy city is a contender for next year's convention.

Lulu temple of Philadelphia sent the next largest delegation—900—and presented a quarter-mile long march of sound and color. Moolah temple, St. Louis, with 500 nobles, arrived on the Steamer Eastern States, while Iram temple of Wilkes-Barre, Pa., also came by boat, via Buffalo.

Abu Bekr, Sioux City, attracted attention with its white Arabian mounted patrol of 30 pure white horses. Syria temple, Pittsburgh, was represented by 700 nobles campaigning for the election of J. Milton Ryall for outer guard.

Band concerts, a lake cruise to Put-in Bay, patrol drills and the annual meetings of the recorders and the royal order of jesters, composed of men high in shrinedom, completed the day's program. Tonight was given over to a Mardi Gras and carnival, with Lakeside avenue roped off for the merrymakers.

San Francisco was unexpectedly put forward as a candidate for the next convention of the Shrine of North America. Pacific coast delegates got behind the move at a breakfast given by Leo Youngsworth, Los Angeles, past potentate of Islam temple. Previously Chicago had been the only city mentioned for next year's gathering.

Fourteen nobles of Hella temple, Dallas, came by airplane. Another long distance air delegate was Gerald Biles, postmaster of the Canal Zone, who flew from Panama to Cleveland.

Lou B. Windsor of Grand Rapids, Mich. is the oldest member of the imperial council present and is attending his 44th annual convention. He was imperial potentate in 1920. Another veteran in attendance is John A. Morrison of Kismet temple, Brooklyn, N.Y., known as the "grand old man of New York Masonry," who says he has attended every convention since "way back when."

Robert B. Kennan of Carnegie, Pa., the tallest delegate attending the Shrine convention, was listed by police today as the first "convention casualty."

Kennan, seven feet tall, was cut on the neck when a bottle of stench fluid was tossed in the lobby of the Hotel Winton. More than 100 persons were routed by the incident, which police blamed on hotel labor troubles.

The Follow-up

After a convention begins, newspapers report its progress. Important speeches and debates are reported, and the outcomes of votes watched. Minor speeches, such as the address of welcome and the response and the humorous after-dinner talks at the banquet, may be ignored by press associations and correspondents, unless someone disregards custom and selects such an occasion for an important statement. Scientific papers and speeches must be written up so as to be understandable to the average reader.

Entertainment provided for delegates and their wives, the convention parade and minor business matters pertaining only to the organization are not given much space. If the organization awards prizes of any sort, the names of the winners are desired by various outside papers whose readers are likely to be interested. Such prizes may be for the best showing in the parade, for the largest delegation, for the delegation coming the longest distance, for drill team, band, or fife and drum corps competition, for the chapter that has increased its membership the most during the year, for the chapter that has contributed most to a certain fund and so on.

The results of the election of officers and selection of the next convention city usually are of general news interest. Papers in cities that bid for the convention or whose chapters have candidates for offices, frequently arrange for prompt coverage of elections, depending upon the importance of the convention.

Estimating Crowds

At athletic contests and other events to which admission is charged, there is no difficulty in obtaining accurate figures on total attendance. If admission is not charged, and especially when the audience or crowd is outdoors, the reporter often must make his own estimate of its size. Police usually estimate the numbers to watch a parade, take part in a demonstration or riot or similar event; but police are no more competent to do so than a trained newsgatherer. Furthermore, their bias is evident, as they underestimate attendance when they are unsympathetic with the purposes of the demonstration and overestimate it when they are sympathetic. So, of course, do newspapers, notoriously so when antiwar demonstrations were popular.

The simple process for audience or crowd estimation is to separate it into sections. That is, count the number of persons occupying a particular area. This is easy when the spectators are seated in a grandstand or auditorium, as all that is needed is to multiply the number of seats in a row by the number of rows, then subtract the apparent number of empty seats. Then cast the eye over the entire assemblage and see how many blocks of similar size there are.

The crowd-counting reporter has it easiest when s/he has an elevated position as a press box or platform. If the reporter is on the ground, s/he will do well to reach an elevated spot if possible. Otherwise, s/he will have to move about. S/he still uses the multiplied bloc system. The beginner can practice by estimating the attendance at athletic contests or the like so as to check his ability when the official attendance announcements are made. A skilled journalist comes very close to the mark. In fact, trained reporters frequently are better counters than police or public officials. For weeks before Pope John Paul II celebrated daytime mass in Chicago's Grant Park, fear was expressed that the million or more expected to attend would cause the underground parking garage to collapse. During the ceremony police gave reporters estimates ranging from 500,000 to 1,750,000. After it was over they said 800,000. The Chicago *Tribune* then hired four different teams of government photo intelligence experts, who examined pictures and came up with estimates of 65,000, 167,000 and 350,000. Major James Lindsay, commissioner of inspection for the Federal Park Police, who had estimated crowds at the Washington Monument for 12 years, said there could not have been more than 100,000 there.

Annually on New Year's Day all 104,000 Rose Bowl seats are occupied and huge crowds line the streets to watch the parade which precedes the football game. The Los Angeles *Times* made the following effort to determine just how many spectators there were.

By Robert Gillette

The 91st Tournament of Roses Parade is history now, Pasadena workers have swept 40 tons of litter from the streets, and most of the 1.4 million spectators who dropped it on New Year's Day have decamped.

Or was it 600,000?

Or maybe 400,000?

"Actually, there were 1,406,038 people," Rocky McAlister, a spokesman for the Pasadena Police Department, said Wednesday. "It's very scientific. William R. Wilson (commander of the city's uniformed police) spends about 10 hours out there counting 'em. Don't know how he does it."

Nettled by skeptics who persistently contend that there is not room for more than about half a million people along the route of one of America's preeminent parades, Pasadena police are turning to scientific techniques this year in the hope of demonstrating that its annual guesstimate of the crowd stems more from shrewd instinct than from civic boosterism.

McAlister said Pasadena will ask professional photo interpreters to estimate the crowd size, which the city has consistently reported to be between 1 million and 1.5 million since at least 1975. This year's official estimate of 1.4 million spectators is approximately 10 times Pasadena's population in 1976.

"We're trying to do something different this year, post-parade," McAlister said. "We're trying to be scientific and prove we're not in error." He explained that the city now uses as a gauge space occupied by the Rose Bowl crowd of 104,000.

"It wouldn't cover one-tenth of that (parade) crowd," McAlister said. He acknowledged that pre-1975 estimates of one million were "probably strictly magic" but insisted that current figures are reasonably accurate.

The size of the parade crowd has been the subject of a modest controversy in the Pasadena newspaper, the Star-News. Its editor, Charles Cherniss, touched it off by relaying an anonymous reader's calculation that no more than 400,000 people could fit in the space along the 5.5-mile route.

Another reader wrote that 500,000 was tops and still another unearthed a 20-year-old news clipping reporting that three holders of Ph.D. degrees at Caltech had calculated a maximum crowd size of 500,000.

McAlister, the police spokesman, bounced back off the ropes on Dec. 31 with the rejoinder that, "We do know that 40 tons of trash is left by parade watchers. And if this mess isn't left by a million people, then those who do attend should be ashamed of themselves."

But arithmetic and at least one law of physics—the notion that no two objects can occupy the same space at the same time without serious complaint from one of them—would seem to favor the skeptics.

The 5.5-mile parade route is flanked on both sides by 23 feet of standing room for spectators, as measured by a Times reporter. The space is marked at the front by a strictly enforced blue line painted on the street and at the back by buildings.

By these measurements, the parade route provides 1,336,000 square feet of standing room. (Not all of it is used, however. People in many places walk freely between buildings and the back rank viewers.)

Assuming that each person is two feet wide and a foot thick—and, therefore, occupies two square feet of standing room—the parade route could accommodate 668,000 people.

Packing each spectator into 1.5 square feet of standing room would allow 891,000 viewers. But, according to one transportation engineering text ("Pedestrian Planning and Design," Maudep Press, 1971), a crowd this dense would be immobile, and many in it would find themselves pressed upward with their feet off the ground.

A more generous three square feet per person would allow 445,000 viewers.

Grandstands, according to spokesman McAlister, allow 80,000 people to sit where 60,000 once stood—a net gain of only 20,000.

Pasadena police insist that great but inestimable numbers of spectators jam into buildings and onto rooftops along the parade route. Reminded that office windows above street level accommodate only a handful of viewers at a time in one or two ranks, McAlister said there are many hidden spectators who do not watch the parade directly.

"Look, there are parties going on in a lot of buildings, with people who don't even look out the windows . . . And motorhomes. We have a lot of people who drive here, just to be here, but never get out. They watch the parade on television."

But even if another 200,000 people wedged themselves into the predominantly one- and two-story buildings that line the parade route, or remained like troglodytes in their darkened Winnebagos, the total leaves another 600,000 spectators to be found.

Some certainly may be on rooftops. But the combined weight of 600,000 people at an average weight of 150 pounds each would total 90 million pounds—raising the troubling possibility of engineering overload, even if people 23 feet back from the roof edge could see the parade below.

One of the parade's few objective measurements is the amount of trash discarded, mostly in the form of paper and cans, by however many people attended. But if, as Pasadena police contend, 1,400,000 people dropped 40 tons of litter, it was a remarkably clean invasion: The average spectator dropped about one ounce of litter.

Editor Cherniss, for one, having opened the discussion in Pasadena, says he's weary of the subject and wishes it would go away.

"The plain truth is that I just don't know and actually don't care . . . Whether 500,000 or 1 million or 2 million are in person doesn't matter at all," Cherniss wrote in an exuberant column on Dec. 31. "I've never counted the hairs on a beautiful woman's head . . . I've never measured the miles in a brilliant sunset nor the stars in a clear summer sky."

SPEECHES

The Preliminary Story

In obtaining information for a story about a speech to be given, the reporter must pay special attention to the following:

1. Adequate identification of the speaker.
2. The occasion for the speech.
3. The exact time and place.
4. The exact title of the speech.

Identification of the speaker in the lead may not be lengthy, but the body of the story should contain those facts which indicate that the person is qualified to discuss the subject. The opinions of other persons may be obtained and quoted to emphasize the speaker's ability, but the reporter should not say that "he is well qualified" or "is an authority on his subject." It is better to give an adequate account of the speaker's experience and let it speak for itself.

The speaker's name usually is more important than the subject and, therefore, should come first in the lead. Sometimes, however, the subject may be more important, but rarely is it advisable to begin with the exact title in quotation marks. Note in the second example below how the writer emphasizes the subject and at the same time the importance of the speaker:

WEAK: "Commercial Aviation" will be the subject of a speech to be given. . . .
BETTER: The causes of several recent commercial airline accidents will be analyzed by. . . .

Sometimes the occasion is more important than either the speaker or the topic, as

> The 55th anniversary of the Milltown Salvation Army will be celebrated at 3 P.M. Sunday at the Municipal Opera house with Commander A. K. Asp delivering the principal address, a resume of the Army's rise to second position among local charities.

In addition to a further identification of the speaker, the body of a preliminary speech story should contain the program of the meeting at which the speech will be given and additional details about the occasion.

In the following example of a well-written preliminary speech story, the lead emphasizes the speaker's name, and the body explains the importance of both speakers and the occasion.

> State Sen. Charles H. Bradfield, Rushville, will speak on the state parole system at the monthly meeting of the Council of Social Agencies at 12:15 P.M. Thursday at Hotel Wolseley.
>
> A member of the joint legislative committee which recently recommended a complete overhauling of the existent parole system, Senator Bradfield has been a severe critic of Gov. Herbert Crowe for his failure to make a public statement on the committee's report.
>
> "It was Senator Bradfield, more than any other member, who was responsible for the recommendation that a board of alienists be substituted for the present board," declared Maurice S. Honig, president of the council, in announcing Thursday's meeting.
>
> The council's committee on legislation, of which Mrs. Arne Oswald is chairman, will report on the results of its study of the legislative committee's recommendations.

The Follow-up

After the speech has been given, the emphasis should be upon what the speaker said, rather than upon the fact that s/he spoke. Never write

> Bruce Paddock, Prescott city manager, gave a lecture Thursday on "Municipal Government" to the Kiwanis club of Greensboro.

Such a lead is vague and indefinite. It is only a preliminary story lead put into the past tense. It misses the feature entirely.

The feature should be found in something that the speaker said. The reporter must follow the orthodox rule of important details first and must disregard the chronological order of a person's remarks. No good speaker ever makes his/her most important point in the introduction. The reporter should play up the speaker's most startling or important remark, which may come at the very end of the speech. Such expressions as "The speaker continued" or "In conclusion the speaker said" do not appear in a well-written story.

Every speaker tries to make a point, and the news writer should play up the speaker's attitude toward the subject as a whole. This is not a hard-and-fast rule, however, as frequently it is better to pick for the lead some casual statement or remark that has strong local interest. In playing up an aside or incidental remark, however, care must be taken not to give a wrong impression. It is easy to misrepresent a speaker's attitude by picking a single sentence which, when printed alone, has a very different meaning from that conveyed when the sentence appears in context.

The timeliness of a speaker's remarks may determine selection of the feature. If the speaker refers to some vital public problem of the moment, his/her opinion regarding it may be more important than anything else said. This, of course, is contingent upon the speaker's prestige as an authority on the subject under discussion.

During political campaigns, it is difficult for a reporter who travels with a candidate to write a different story daily, because the aspirant for office gives nearly the same speech day after day, possibly hour after hour. The same difficulty is met with in reporting public lectures by persons who speak frequently on the same subject. If the writeup of the speech is for local consumption only, the feature may be selected on its face value, provided an account of a similar speech by the same person has not been printed recently. The reporter, however, should not play up, as something new and startling, a remark that actually is "old stuff" to both speaker and auditors.

As preparation for speech reporting, there is no substitute for adequate knowledge of both the speaker and the field of interest. A reporter with little or no background in science, for instance, would be completely unable to evaluate the relative importance of points made by a nuclear physicist, some of which might be of great potential general interest. An uninformed reporter in any field might write that a speaker "revealed" or "made known" something that could be found in elementary textbooks on the subject.

To localize the appeal of a speech means to play up any reference that the speaker makes to the immediate locality. Thus, if in the course of a lecture on geology, the speaker declares that the vicinity is a very fertile field for research, that remark may be the most interesting, from the standpoint of his audience, of any the speaker makes. The same speech, written up for a press association, might have an entirely different lead.

The time and place need not be stated so definitely in the follow-up as in the preliminary story, and the identification of the speaker should be brief.

The Lead

Possible rhetorical leads for a follow-up speech story include

1. The speaker's name.
2. The title.
3. A direct quotation.
4. A summary statement of the main point or keynote.
5. The occasion or circumstances.

If there is reason for emphasizing the authority of the speaker, the story may begin with the name, as

> Chief of Police Arthur O. Shanesy last night told members of the Chamber of Commerce at their monthly meeting that traffic accidents in the downtown business district are largely the fault of merchants.

Ordinarily, it is weak to begin with the speaker's name, because by so doing the importance of his/her remarks is minimized. For the same reason, the lead seldom should begin with the exact title unless it is stated in an unusual way or in a way which makes a title lead effective, as

"America's Weakness" is her failure to realize that the frontier has disappeared, according to Prof. Arnold L. Magnus of Booster college's political science department, who spoke on the subject last evening to the Milltown Lions club.

Opinions differ regarding the direct quotation lead. Jackson S. Elliott of the Associated Press once said, "Show me a news story that begins with a direct quotation, no matter how striking it is, and I will show you how it could be improved by taking the quoted statement out of the lead and placing it in the body of the story."

Other editors condone the direct quotation lead when the intention of the writer is to play up some startling statement rather than to epitomize the speaker's general attitude. Obviously, it is seldom that a speaker summarizes the entire speech in any one sentence contained in the speech itself.

The following is a fairly good use of the direct quotation lead:

"World War III is inevitable within five years," Harold E. Paulson, professor of political science at Booster college, told the World Affairs club last night in Memorial hall.

The partial-quotation lead is a way to avoid lengthy direct quotations which would lack definiteness, as

Schools, by failing to develop to the full the "creativeness" of all their students, are responsible in large measure for "countless not fully developed humans," Dr. John L. Tildsley, retiring assistant superintendent of schools, told 1,800 art teachers and students yesterday. He spoke at the opening session at the Hotel Pennsylvania of the 28th annual convention of the Eastern Arts association.

The best lead for a speech story is one that summarizes the speaker's general attitude toward the subject or gives the keynote of the speech.

Kindergarten reading is out of place in high school and college, even if the students are coping with a foreign language.

So a University of Illinois professor told his fellow teachers of French, Friday, in a national meeting in the Palmer House.

"The books we're reading with our students in the first few years of French are far below their intellectual level, and below the seriousness of things, they are reading in other classrooms," declared Prof. Charles A. Knudson, head of romance language at Urbana.

"In short, in French classes we are reading tripe."

The lead may emphasize the occasion or the ovation given the speaker, the crowd or some unexpected circumstance that occurs during delivery of a speech.

A well organized group of about 50 hecklers last night failed to persuade State Sen. Roger Parnell to discuss loyalty oaths for public employees.

Instead, the Republican candidate for reelection stuck to his announced topic,

"The State's Proposed Highway Program," and police evicted the troublemakers from an audience of about 500 in Masonic hall.

The Vernon County Republican club sponsored the meeting.

If several speech stories are to appear on the same page, as a page in a Monday edition including stories of Sunday's sermons, there should be variety in the use of leads. The average sermon is difficult to report because there seldom is a well-defined feature or keynote. A "title" or "speaker's name" lead may be used for a sermon story.

Beginnings to avoid in writing a speech story include:

The feature of the Chemical society meeting last evening in Swift hall was a speech by . . .

Lieut. Amos Andrews spoke to members of the Chemical Society in Swift hall on the subject . . .

"Shakespeare" was the topic of an address given last evening in Swift hall by . . .

Speaking at a meeting of the Chemical society last evening in Swift hall, Lieut. Amos Andrews declared that . . .

Pennsylvania limestone was discussed last evening at a Geology society meeting in Swift hall by . . .

All these leads are vague and indefinite. They do not satisfy the reader's curiosity as to what the speaker thinks about his subject.

The Body

Prominent persons, as public officials, usually speak from prepared manuscripts, copies of which often are distributed to reporters before actual delivery. This enables a reporter to write part or all of his/her account in advance. The danger of going to press prematurely is obvious, as the speaker may make last-minute changes or digress from the text.

The safe way is never to publish a speech account until word has been received that delivery actually has begun. Even in such cases, and especially if it is impossible to obey the rule of delay, it is wise to use in the first or second paragraph the identification "in a speech prepared for delivery" on such and such an occasion. This offers protection in case there are unexpected developments. If there is none, the reporter, manuscript in hand, can follow the speaker and make note of any modifications necessary in the story already written.

The second paragraph of a speech story ordinarily should explain the occasion on which the speech was given, if the lead does not do so. The rest of the body should consist of paragraphs of alternating direct and indirect quotation. The first paragraph of direction quotation well may be an elaboration of the indirect quotation lead.

If, as often happens, the reporter has an advanced copy of the speech, there is no difficulty in obtaining direct quotations. Otherwise, one must develop facility in taking notes.

The reporter needs to exercise his/her best judgment in selecting the parts of a speech to quote directly. Ordinarily it is best to quote directly

1. Statements representing a strong point of view, especially if related to a newsworthy controversial matter. Often it is more forceful to use the material in indirect quotation first, possibly in the lead, as "Mayor Brinton will not be a candidate for reelection." Readers, however, like to know the exact words which a speaker used and they should be given in the body of the story even though a verbatim account appears elsewhere in the paper.
2. Uniquely worded statements, including ones which might become aphorisms or slogans, as "Lafayette, we are here," "I do not choose to run" and the like.
3. Statements of facts not generally known, perhaps in statistical terms.

Ordinarily, statements that are merely ones of evaluative opinion or that contain old or easily ascertained information can be summarized in a reporter's own words if they are newsworthy at all. It would be foolish, for instance, to quote a labor leader as saying, "Unions are the hope of America." If, however, the president of the National Association of Manufacturers were to say so, it would be a sensational news story lead.

Instead of quoting directly a statement containing an old fact, the reporter can say, "The speaker reminded the audience that white-collar workers are the most difficult to organize" or "He recalled that the governor vetoed the measure two years ago."

How often a "he said" or synonym should be inserted in the body of a speech story depends on the length of the article. In paragraphs of indirect quotation a "he said" should be used as often as needed to make it clear that the ideas expressed are those of the speaker rather than of the writer. Direct quotations should be preceded, broken or followed by a "he said" or its equivalent.

The writer should try to use the most forceful synonym for the verb "to say." Any good dictionary of synonyms or a thesaurus includes many score. Since no two verbs have exactly the same meaning, great care must be exercised in their selection. If a speaker "roared," the interpretative reporter owes it to readers to say so. If, however, the speaker merely raised his/her voice normally, grave injustice can be done by a reportorial magnavox.

Substance can be given to the speech story only by the reporter who knows something about the speaker and the subject. Otherwise it is impossible to comprehend the speech as a whole, to digest it with proper emphasis or to convey the proper impression of the occasion on which it was delivered. A speech is an event and the superior reporter comprehends its significance. The factual material of a series of phrases in a sentence or paragraph may come from a half-dozen widely separated portions of the speech as a whole, yet be properly grouped so as to give a complete and accurate summary of the speaker's point of view. Note the knowledge and understanding displayed by the writer of the following story:

By Pat McGuire

NEWS STAFF WRITER

Land use planning in Birmingham is still in its infancy, a planning expert told members of the League of Women Voters of Greater Birmingham at a Thursday luncheon meeting.

"Most cities this size have been into planning for 35 or 40 years," said Charles Shirley, deputy executive director, Birmingham Regional Planning Commission. "We probably could have saved some of the more prominent structures around Birmingham if we had gotten started earlier."

Land use will be a major item in the U.S. Congress this year, Shirley said, adding that if the Jackson bill is approved, land planning will be required in every state. There are no federal regulations on land planning at the present time, he said.

Shirley explained the organization of the BRPC and Jim Scott, public information officer for the agency, showed slides detailing the structure of the BRPC.

The Birmingham Regional Planning Commission has no power to enforce, but may only make recommendations to municipalities on land planning, Shirley said. "Our biggest single problem is that by law we are advisors. But in most cases, regional comprehensive planning is required to receive grants."

About 80 to 85 municipalities are now participating in the BRPC program, and a citizen's advisory committee is now in the process of being organized, Shirley said.

Shelby County is the only county in the six-county region served by the commission that employs a planner, Shirley said. A primary land use plan has been developed for the Shelby County area, but has not yet been approved by the citizens, he said.

Current projects the commission hopes to get the go-ahead on include a long-range transit study; a strip mining study, to be funded by the Appalachian Regional Council; and a water quality study on the Cahaba and Warrior rivers, under a grant from the Environmental Protection Agency. "The EPA wants the local governments to agree to abide by the results of the study if they are to fund it," Shirley said. "This is where we're having our problem."

Mrs. William Williams is land use study chairman for the league and Mrs. Kenneth Bohannon is league president. [Birmingham *News*]

13
ILLNESS, DEATH, DISASTERS

PUBLIC HEALTH

There is hardly a newspaper, daily or weekly, without a column, mostly syndicated, by an outstanding medical expert who is cautious about diagnosing ailments on the basis of symptoms submitted by readers. Just as they discourage self-medication by patients, so do reputable doctors deplore sensationalism by the press in handling stories of unusual illnesses or treatments, as artificial hearts, organ transplants and the like. Newspapers provide the medium whereby public health officials advise the public on such matters as threats to the purity of the water supply, possible heat prostration and the presence of epidemic diseases.

> Seventeen persons will begin the painful 24-shot series of rabies vaccine today after two baby skunks taken as "pets" died and were found to be rabid, the Payne County Health Department announced.

The exposure has been called the largest in the state since more than 50 persons were exposed last year in another part of the state.

Ray Russell, sanitarian for the county, said the 17 include nine members of a local family, a grandmother of the family, several local friends, four members of a Kay County family and two relatives of that family. Two additional persons have been identified as "possible" contacts, he said.

Cost for shots will average approximately $500 per person, Russell said. Though chance of contracting rabies in this incident is small, he said, if the disease were contracted, certain and horrible death would result.

[Stillwater (Okla.) *News-Press*]

WASHINGTON (AP)—Heavy users of saccharin or cyclamate, whether they smoke or not, significantly increase their chances of contracting bladder cancer, warns a new government report.

The National Cancer Institute report released Thursday characterizes the two controversial sweeteners as weak carcinogens that enhance the likelihood of bladder cancer.

The study was done at the request of the Food and Drug Administration, the agency that tried to ban saccharin as a food additive in 1977.

The study, the largest of its type ever conducted, was based on interviews of more than 9,000 people about their habits over a period of 15 months. It cost $1.5 million and was supposed to help resolve the controversy over the safety of saccharin. . . .

By Charles Seabrook

Georgia health officials say this winter's flu vaccine will provide protection against the three types of flu that are expected to cause most of the misery in the coming months.

The vaccine will contain protection against the A Brazil flu strain, a variant of the so-called Russian flu and the predominant strain last winter.

The A Brazil type caused outbreaks in schools, colleges and military bases in Georgia and the rest of the nation.

This coming flu season's vaccine also will contain protection against A Texas flu and B Hong Kong flu, which were not as widespread as the A Brazil strain.

According to the Georgia Immunization Unit of the Department of Human Resources, an ongoing program has been initiated targeting the 996,000 Georgians over 65 years of age and those with chronic diseases for flu vaccination.

The chronic illness group includes those with ailments such as bronchopulmonary disease (asthma or cystic fibrosis), heart disease, renal disease, diabetes and other metabolic disorders, neuromuscular problems, malignancies and immunodeficient disorders.

The elderly and the chronic disease sufferers are those who are considered to be at risk to the complications of flu.

State health officials say that only about 20 percent of that group has been immunized adequately against flu in the past.

The flu vaccine, according to the health officials, will be available to private doctors for use in their offices, or it may be obtained through local county health departments.

It should be available this month.

Health officials say there is no charge for the vaccine for those in the high risk groups. Doctors may not charge the patients for the vaccine but may charge for administering it.

Officials at the U.S. Center for Disease Control in Atlanta also report that they are keeping an eye on a new strain of flu that surfaced earlier this year and caused some outbreaks in nursing homes during the summer. [Atlanta *Journal*]

Private organizations that support research into various diseases are a source of information for locally written articles.

By Steve Smith

A stroke can be devastating.

It can alter a human mind, render a once-active person helpless and change the lives of those close to the victim.

Every year, one out of every 10 Americans falls victim to a stroke. And one out of every 10 victims dies.

In Anderson County, that translates to 1,500 persons a year suffering from strokes and 150 dying.

The American Heart Association estimated this year:

- 2,000,000 Americans will suffer strokes.
- 200,000 will die.
- 1,000,000 stroke victims will be paralyzed permanently, although 750,000 will regain some use of the paralyzed area.
- 800,000 will suffer only temporary paralysis.

The Heart Association said a stroke occurs when blood enriched with oxygen is blocked from reaching part of the brain. Strokes are caused either by a clot blocking an artery in the brain or a diseased artery bursting and flooding the surrounding brain tissue with blood.

When this happens, brain cells become damaged or die, according to the association. Depending on what part of the brain has been damaged, the result of a stroke can be death, difficulty in speaking or walking, memory loss and, almost always, paralysis of both limbs on one side of the body.

Health experts agree one of the major causes of strokes is hypertension, known as high blood pressure. If hypertension is diagnosed and brought under control, many fatal strokes can be prevented. [Anderson (S.C.) *Independent/Daily Mail*]

By Earl Lane

The unsightly problem of varicose veins traditionally has been a concern primarily for women. By a 4-to-1 ratio, women suffer the problem more than men, and for cosmetic reasons, women tend to seek medical help more often.

But Dr. Howard C. Baron, a New York vascular surgeon, says more and more men also are starting to express concern about the looks of their legs. "With the jogging craze, they are concerned about how they will look in running shorts," Baron said recently. "A lot of men are coming in for help." Baron said he serves as a sort of informal consultant for two or three running clubs.

Roughly 20 per cent of Americans (including about half of the population over age 50) suffer from varicose veins to some degree. While even some physicians consider varicose veins to be primarily a nuisance disease, Baron said, there are good reasons for taking the problem seriously.

Beyond the cosmetic concerns, varicose veins sometimes can lead to troubling complications, including phlebitis—an inflammation of vein walls, most often accompanied by blood clots in the veins as well.

Phlebitis of the legs' superficial veins sometimes can precede an even more serious condition: involvement of the legs' deep veins with inflammation and blood clotting (thrombosis). Portions of the clots may break loose and travel up the bloodstream to lodge in the pulmonary artery, which serves the lung. If these emboli, as they are called, are massive enough to severely restrict blood supply to the lungs, death can result in minutes. [*Newsday*]

ILLNESS

Although the illness story may seem to be routine, it frequently is one of the most difficult to report and write. This is because the medical profession is reluctant to give out information about the condition of patients or about its own discoveries, unusual surgical performances and the like. Physicians hold that they are duty bound to protect the privacy of those under their care, and the ethics of the profession forbids anything suggesting personal publicity. They may feel that knowledge of a patient's condition, gained through a newspaper account, would be detrimental to that patient's recovery, and they do not trust the average reporter to report medical news accurately.

Relatives of a prominent person who is ill usually can be persuaded to authorize the physician in charge to release periodic bulletins regarding the patient's condition, but these may be in scientific language, which must be translated. Until newspapers can employ reporters capable of handling medical news with the same understanding that baseball writers have in handling their specialty, the only safe way is to ask the doctors themselves for popular "translations," or to consult a medical dictionary. Because in many cases physicians and surgeons have gone to extremes in refusing cooperation with the press, they must share the blame for inaccuracies that occur in news concerning them. The press also has learned that attending physicians may not be entirely truthful in their discussion of the nature of an ailment when a prominent person, say a president of the United States, is involved. If the doctor has written a book, it can be consulted to detect differences between what the man writes and what he says.

Chambers of commerce also are a handicap to adequate coverage of medical news because of the pressure they often exert on editors to play down news of epidemics. Fortunately, few newspapers listen to such requests, holding their social responsibility to be too great and the loss of prestige they would suffer if the contagion reached sizable proportions to be an offsetting consideration. The paper with a sense of responsibility, of course, must take care not to frighten readers unnecessarily.

Medical Successes

Certain to arouse reader interest is any account of proof of the efficiency of a new drug or surgical technique.

By Cal Turner

Being part of "a medical first" might not even land Lavere Wolf's name in the footnotes of a future textbook, but he's not peeved.

Wolf, a 54-year-old grandfather and former assistant manager of a fertilizer plant, is alive and well and living in York. To say he has a cardiovascular glow is to put it lightly. Wolf beams.

Wolf's life was saved in June when a cardiothoracic surgeon—during a five-hour-plus heart operation at Penn State's Hershey Medical Center—made innovative use of a heart-assist pump.

Wolf and the surgeon, Dr. Grant Van S. Parr, were "given the works" by the press Thursday at a conference in a Medical Center auditorium. With the aid of a blackboard, the 37-year-old Parr, whose seriousness carries wit and unstudied precision, told how it was done. . . . [Harrisburg (Pa.) *Evening News*]

By Marcia Kramer

Doctors are hopeful that a father of nine whose hands were severed in an industrial accident will regain their use as the result of a 23½-hour operation.

Natalio Alamillo, 47, of 2342 S. Millard, was in the intensive care unit of Billings Hospital at the University of Chicago Tuesday after the surgery.

The injury occurred early Monday at Clearing Die Casting Co., 6220 S. New England, where Alamillo was working on a punch press. He reportedly had just started his shift and was inserting the first piece of metal in the machinery when the accident occurred.

Both hands were trapped in the press for several minutes as the machinery was dismantled.

Dr. James D. Schlenker, who headed two surgical teams of 10 doctors who reattached the hands, predicted that Alamillo will regain 60 per cent use of the hands. . . . [Chicago *Sun-Times*]

Seattle (UPI)—Jon Brower Minnoch weighed 1,400 pounds last year. That made him the heaviest human being in medical history, and he says he never expected to survive.

But today, the 6-foot-1-inch Minnoch weighs only 475 pounds—a loss of 900 pounds—and he says he won't pose for pictures until he loses a lot more.

Minnoch, 38, has spent most of the last 15 months in bed at University Hospital in Seattle fighting a daily, painful struggle with his body to lose weight and learn how to move again.

It was March, 1978, when a crew of fire fighters rushed to Minnoch's Bainbridge Island home, removed a window, lifted the obese, ailing man onto a thick piece of plywood and carried him to an ambulance.

When he arrived at the hospital, he was in severe pain, suffering from heart, circulation and respiratory problems and unable to move or speak.

"Actually, I was being crushed by my own weight; you could put it like that," said the soft-spoken, mustachioed Minnoch from his hospital bed.

A few hours after he got to the hospital, Minnoch said, the horrible pain strangely lifted for a few moments, as though he were dying. When he was tugged back to reality, he said, it was "almost like getting a second chance," and he resolved to stay alive. . . .

By Pat Borden

Charlotte, N.C.—On the blustery Friday after Thanksgiving, Robin Rowland heard a strange new sound. "Mama," she asked as leaves danced around her feet in a hospital parking lot, "does the wind make noise?"

That Friday, Nov. 23, Robin heard the whistling wind for the first time in her 15 years.

She was born without ears. She had only little nubs, with no openings. The canals that carry sound toward the brain were missing. Doctors predicted she would always be stone deaf.

But in a three-hour, seven-minute operation Nov. 19, doctors created an ear canal. And today, Robin not only listens to the wind, she also has new, delicately painted silicone ears she glues on each morning and takes off each night.

"I was just hoping I'd get my hearing," Robin said a few days before going to Duke Medical Center in Durham, N.C., to have new ears fitted. "For so long, I thought I never would. But now I've got my hearing, and now I'm going to get my ears. It's all happening so fast!" . . . [St. Louis *Globe-Democrat*]

Medical Law

During the past century the life expectancy of Americans has increased by more than 50 per cent. Specifically, in 1850 the average life span for white males was 38.3 years; for white females it was 40.5 years; for nonwhite males, 32.54 years and for nonwhite females, 35.04 years. In 1977 the comparable figures were: 70.0, 77.7, 64.6 and 73.1. According to the Metropolitan Life Insurance Company, an American born in 1980 could anticipate living 73.8 years. Life expectancy for a newborn boy was 70.1 in 1980; for a newborn girl it was 77.5 years. The 1980 census revealed that 49.99 per cent of Americans are over 30. So skilled have doctors become in keeping people alive that it is becoming necessary to go to court for permission to pull the plugs on life-supporting equipment that allows heart beats and breathing to continue after a patient otherwise would be considered dead.

According to the Uniform Brain Death Act approved by the National Conference of Commissioners on Uniform State Laws, death occurs "when there is irreversible cessation of all functions of the brain." Some relatives and religious groups refuse to accept this definition and their defiance often is newsworthy.

Madison, Wis. (AP)—Sen. Red Risser, D-Madison, is asking that a bill defining death as the irreversible cessation of all brain activity be sent to the Wisconsin Senate early next year.

The Wisconsin Catholic Conference almost simultaneously asked for a different kind of bill, one absolving doctors and hospitals from liability for disconnecting life-support systems from a patient in good faith.

Both requests were prompted by a weekend order of Judge Daniel Moser for removing biological support equipment from David Campbell, an infant who had been kept breathing in a Madison hospital for almost a week.

He was three weeks old when admitted to the hospital Nov. 10, suffering from skull fractures and a broken leg. Investigators said they were checking the possibility of child abuse.

The Circuit Court judge had been asked by attorneys representing the child and the father to disconnect the life-support equipment. The mother's lawyer had asked that the equipment be kept operating. . . .

The courtroom may become a newsworthy battleground when medical authorities encounter parental, religious or other opposition in cases involving blood transfusions, inoculations or vaccinations, sterilization or some other controversial matter.

Morristown, N.J. (AP)—A judge ruled Thursday that the parents of an 18-year-old mentally retarded woman should be allowed to have her sterilized.

In a 37-page opinion, Superior Court Judge Bertram Polow approved the request of Edward and Luanne Grady of Sparta that Morristown Memorial Hospital be allowed to perform a tubal ligation on their daughter, Lee Ann.

She is a victim of Down's syndrome, also known as mongolism, and in five days of testimony last month medical experts said there is up to a 50 per cent chance that her offspring would inherit the condition.

Both the New Jersey public advocate's office and the attorney general's office argued against the procedure. They pointed out that the woman lives at home and said it was extremely unlikely she would find herself in a situation where she could have sexual relations.

Because advances in medical science make it possible for doctors today to make more exact diagnoses, patients are increasingly bringing malpractice suits when a diagnosis is inaccurate. A five-year survey of 19,417 malpractice suits against doctors insured by the St. Paul Fire and Marine Insurance Company revealed that diagnostic errors accounted for 24.9 per cent of all claims. Errors in treatment, however, accounted for 49.8 per cent. St. Paul experts said that many physicians fail to keep up with new tests, equipment and drugs.

By Lillian Williams

An 11-year-old mentally retarded boy from Lake Geneva, Wis., will receive $3.8 million, the largest malpractice settlement in Illinois history.

The boy, Michael Pesche, son of Fred and Shirley Pesche, is suffering from phenylketonuria (PKU), a chemical imbalance that can be detected at birth and treated. The disease is prompted by lack of an enzyme known as phenylalanine hydroxylise.

The boy's lawyer, John D. Hayes, said that Ravenswood Hospital failed to discover the disease when the boy was tested after his birth. If the disorder had been diagnosed, the child could have been put on a low-protein diet to overcome the chemical imbalance, Hayes said.

The disease was finally discovered at the University of Wisconsin in Madison when the boy was 5½ years old, too late for treatment, the lawyer said.

Cook County Circuit Court Judge James Murray approved the settlement Thursday. The parties decided to settle the case after three weeks of trial in which two experts spoke on preventive measures to combat the disease.

Ravenswood Hospital will pay more than $3 million of the settlement, while insurance companies for two pediatricians, Dr. Patricia Conrad and Dr. Elfriede Horst, will contribute the rest.

The boy's parents operate a floral business in Lake Geneva.

Authorities say one in every 12,000 newborns has the disease. [Chicago *Sun-Times*]

Reportorial Rules

Journalists in reporting medical news must be as careful as doctors who make it. Precautions to take to reduce the likelihood of error include the following:

1. Be cautious about announcing cures for important diseases. The hopes of millions of cancer victims have been raised cruelly through newspaper publicity for discoveries that turned out to be false alarms.
2. Be certain that a newly announced discovery actually is recent. Cases have been reported of some cure or method's being ballyhooed as a startling find when it has been familiar to medical men for years.
3. Go easy on accrediting dogmatic statements to any medical researcher. Few of them ever speak in positive terms. Their efforts may be directed toward a certain goal, but they are extremely cautious about claiming credit for having reached it. Often they report to their scientific brethren on the progress of work they are doing; the newspaper should not credit them with having completed something that they have only begun.
4. Do not use without verification stories of miraculous cures.
5. Do not ascribe a pestilential disease to a person without absolute authority, as such a story, if untrue, is libelous.
6. Do not say a person died "from" instead of "after" an operation, as such a statement may be libelous.
7. Everyone dies of "heart failure." There are diseases of the heart and such a thing as a heart attack.
8. A person does not "entertain" a sickness; and not everyone "suffers" while under a physician's care.
9. Very seldom does a person "have his arm cut off." Rather it is cut off contrary to his plans and wishes.
10. Injuries are not "sustained" but are "received."
11. The nature of a diagnosis ordinarily should be stated unless there is weighty reason for omitting it. "Natural causes" tells little. Some wag once said that according to the press there are only two causes of death: a long or lingering illness or a short illness.
12. Scientific names of diseases may be used provided the popular names also are given.
13. Attach statements of diagnoses and of the seriousness of an epidemic to an authority.
14. Do not mention the name of a physician except in stories of the illness of a prominent individual.

15. Avoid stories of medical freaks unless authorized by a medical association. Expectant mothers can be frightened dangerously by accounts that advance public understanding little or not at all.

MENTAL HEALTH

The fastest growing field of medical knowledge probably is that of mental health. Although the supply of competent psychiatrists still is woefully inadequate, during the past few decades the thinking of many, within and without the medical profession, has been profoundly affected by discoveries and theories regarding the motivations of human behavior.

Among those most influenced by developments in the mental health field have been journalists. They have helped expose bad conditions in many hospitals for the mentally ill and have assisted psychiatrists, social workers, probation and parole officers, educators, judges and others in enlightening the public regarding the many ramifications of the newer knowledge. In its reporting of crime, juvenile delinquency, school problems and similar matters, the press has become much more understanding and consequently more intelligent in its exercise of news judgment.

For "depth" reporting in this field, considerable specialized knowledge is necessary. A typical error of the uninformed is to confuse feeblemindedness with mental illness. The former is lack of intellect, either from birth (amentia) or as a result of brain injury in later life (dementia). The feebleminded today are called "retarded" or "exceptional" and special schools exist for those who are educable—that is, the high-grade morons, not to be confused with lower-grade imbeciles and idiots for whom only custodial care is feasible. Under pressure from mental health authorities, newspapers generally have ceased using "moron" as a synonym for "sex pervert," which it is not.

The trend in mental health work is away from categorizing specific diseases—dementia praecox, schizophrenia, manic depression, catatonia, paranoia and the like—as long study reveals the existence of few pure types. Rather, the psychiatrist recognizes and speaks of symptoms of abnormal behavior. Outstanding book tracing the development of expert thinking is *The Vital Balance* (Viking, 1963) by Dr. Karl Menninger with Martin Mayman and Paul Pruysen, subtitled, "The Life Process in Mental Health and Illness." Long gone, of course, is belief in possession by evil spirits to be exorcised, malicious lunar influence, emotional suffering as a punishment for sin and similar unscientific and superstitious notions.

Although the teachings of Sigmund Freud, stressing the strictly behavioral aspects of mental disease, still influence modern psychiatric thinking more than those of any other scientist in the field, an increasing number of practitioners today are coming to believe that Freudian psychoanalysis is good research to determine the causes of a patient's emotional disturbance but that it falls short as a cure; that, in fact, it may merely provide a patient with a scapegoat, as a parent, for his condition and a rationalization for not making proper effort to correct irresponsible behavior. See *Reality Therapy* (Harper & Row, 1965) by William Glasser.

Experiments continue in the search for ways to cure, or at least alleviate, symptoms through insulin, electric and other types of shock treatments, glandular extracts, tranquilizers and so forth. Newspapermen can do a great disservice by sensationalizing any results of isolated experiments. They also must be careful to distinguish between psychoses (major mental disorders whose victims lose touch with reality) and neuroses, of which most of us may be victims at times. Psychosomatic illnesses are physical disorders that have an emotional base; work toward their understanding and cure progresses but has a long way to go.

Historical examples, notably that of Nazi Germany, give credence to the assumption that large groups, perhaps entire nations even, can act insanely. Certainly there are social psychological causes for the widespread success of fads and fashions, for the popularity, especially if it is sudden, of political and other movements and for crazes of all kinds. Seemingly separate phenomena may be related because of the conditions giving rise to them. For instance, in times of insecurity and fear some people may become strong activists to promote reform or change, whereas others may become escapists. It is not merely coincidental that contemporaneously there are movements of protest and revolt in many fields: on college campuses in almost all parts of the world; among schoolteachers who are unionizing and striking for the first time; within the Roman Catholic church, where nuns and priests are protesting centuries' old conventions. There are the civil rights, peace and women's liberation movements. Mostly all segments of these groups to date have advocated peaceful tactics, but the patience of many has been strained by the failure of the Establishment to respond and because of the violence, including murder, with which the protestors have been answered.

On the other hand, those who seek solace by some form of escape become beatniks or hippies, exalt their egos by esoteric forms of dress and behavior, by the use of narcotics and by other "cop-out" techniques. Still others, who can no longer find security in the traditional religions, are attracted by revival movements, new cults, astrology, ESP, spiritualism and other forms of superstition. Many different responses, all to the same motivation.

The mine-run reporter cannot be expected to be an expert analyst of public opinion and morality; but some understanding of such matters can enable him to avoid gross error in perpetuating ignorance. This author had his say in his *Understanding Public Opinion,* Sigma Delta Chi research prize winner, now published by Wm. C. Brown Co., Dubuque, Iowa. Erich Fromm's *Escape From Freedom* (Rinehart, 1941) and *The Sane Society* (Rinehart, 1955) have stood the test of time as outstanding treatises on the nature of collective irresponsibility.

OBITUARIES

After a three months' strike ended, the Vancouver *Sun* printed a list, in five solid pages of agate type, of all funeral notices it could gather for the period during which publication had been suspended. It did so because that was what readers missed the most, according to Stuart Keate, publisher. Nevertheless, during the past decade or so, death notices have been processed through the classified advertising departments to which they are submitted by funeral directors. The few deaths considered newsworthy are written up by formula. What may develop as a countertrend is the addition of a Monday obituary page in the Los Angeles *Times*. Editor William F. Thomas said the page will feature the obits of the famous but also will report the deaths of "ordinary people who may not have been famous but led interesting lives." He added that the page stems from "a realization that we are not doing a proper job with obits because of time and space limitations."

Basic Elements

The size obituary a person gets depends upon his/her importance as news. Even the shortest, however, must include these basic facts:

1. Name of deceased.
2. Identification.
3. Time of death.
4. Place of death.

Two other facts really are essential for even a one- or two-sentence notice:

5. Cause of death.
6. Age of deceased.

Unless death occurs in some unusual way the name (*who*) always is the feature of an obituary. Identification in the brief notice may be by address or occupation only. No authority need be stated unless the dispatch comes from an obscure place or is third- or fourth-hand. Then "it was learned here today" or some similar statement should be used. The paper must be on guard against false rumors of a person's death started by enemies or jokesters.

In giving the age of a dead person some papers permit the form "Henry Baxter, 61, died today," whereas others object to this form on the ground that placing the age after the name indicates the present tense. Papers with this attitude prefer a phrase "at the age of 61 years" or a second sentence, "He was 61 years old."

> Rutherford Regal, 414 Oates street, a City Yards employee, died at 3 A.M. today at his home following a week's illness from pneumonia. He was 43 years old.

A person's importance or the achievement by which s/he will longest be remembered ordinarily should be used in identifying him/her as

By Paul L. Montgomery

Martyn Green, the British actor who set the standard in Gilbert and Sullivan interpretation for half a century, died early yesterday of a blood infection at Presbyterian Hospital in Hollywood, Calif. He was 75 years old. [New York *Times*]

Sometimes a reporter discovers an interesting circumstance in the life of a relatively unimportant person who has died. Perhaps, for instance, s/he was present at the assassination of a president, was a pioneer of the locality or a former millionaire or in some other way a romantic figure, as

William Dickinson, 81, lifelong Milan resident whose grandfather laid out the village and founded and built the Presbyterian church here, died at 6 P.M. yesterday in his home on Dickson Street.

James Mauris, whose restaurant at 1464 E. 57th street has for many years been a rendezvous for faculty members and students of the University of Chicago, died suddenly of a heart attack last night. He was 70 years old.

See Warren J. Brier's "Delicate Art of Writing Obits," in the 1964 *Montana Journalism Review,* for advice on how to write colorful obituaries with dignity.

Circumstances of Death

When a person is known to a large number of readers, the circumstance of death should be related as that is one of the first things about which a friend inquires when hearing of another's demise. Circumstances of death include

7. Bedside scene.
8. Last words, messages and so forth.
9. Account of last illness.

In a full-length obituary, according to the formula being developed, these facts usually follow the lead.

Allen E. Schoenlaub, 57, cashier of the First National bank, died suddenly about 8 P.M. yesterday at his home, 1146 Elm street, from a heart attack.

He was found in the kitchen by his wife after she heard him fall while in quest of a drink of water. About a half hour before the attack, Mr. Schoenlaub complained of feeling queer. He had spent a normal day at the bank and ate dinner with his wife, son, Robert, 22, and daughter, Flora, 28, apparently in excellent health. He had had no previous heart attacks nor any other recent illness.

A physician whom Mrs. Schoenlaub summoned declared death was due to coronary thrombosis and that Mr. Schoenlaub probably died instantly.

In addition to his wife and two children, he is survived by a brother, Herbert, Kansas City, Mo., and a sister, Mrs. R. S. Bostrum, Chicago.

Mr. Schoenlaub was connected with the First National bank for 26 years, the last 18 of which he was cashier. He was born Jan. 30, 1925 at Ann Arbor, Mich., and was graduated from the University of Michigan in 1947. He moved here in

1956 after nine years as teller and cashier of the State Bank & Trust Co., of Dowagiac, Mich.

Mr. Schoenlaub was an active member of the First Baptist church, having been president of the Men's club from 1971 to 1978. He also was a member of Keystone Lodge No. 14, B.P.O.E., and of Milltown Lodge No. 150 F. & A.M.

Funeral arrangements have not yet been made.

Note in the above the presence of three other important elements:

10. Surviving relatives.
11. Funeral plans.
12. Biographical highlights.

Reviewing a Life

Ordinarily the body of an obituary consists mostly of an objective biographical résumé of the deceased's career. Eulogies and reminiscences may be included or run as sidebars.

If, however, the death is that of a nationally known or world-famous person, one whom history will remember, the trend is toward interpretative pieces which blend the details of death with attempts to evaluate the person's importance. The purpose is to "place" the subject in history with emphasis upon lasting contributions. The interpretative obituary is not an editorial, although it is impossible for a writer qualified to pass judgment upon the subject to avoid evaluations.

Leading advocate of this type of obituary writing is Alden Whitman, recently retired from the New York *Times,* who has written:

> For openers, let's tell what the deceased was really like in life. If he was a saint, let us by all means say so. Or if he choir-lofted with the comely soprano, let's say that, too. If he was modest and unassuming, let's tell it. Or if he was a braggart and a bore, let's also tell that. If he was a handsome donor to charity, we should make that clear, along with the tax advantages his munificence garnered him. If he was a statesman, let the bells ring out. Or if he was a fixer who put up public buildings for the profit of his friends, let the bells clang too.

Whitman expanded on his views in a book, *The Obituary Story* (Stein & Day). A typical Whitman obituary follows:

By Alden Whitman

Alfred C. Fuller, founder and retired chairman of the Fuller Brush Company and one of the foremost promoters of door-to-door salesmanship, died yesterday in Hartford Hospital of myeloma, a bone-marrow disease. He was 88 years old and lived in nearby West Hartford.

A transplanted Nova Scotia farm boy, Mr. Fuller developed a basement brush-making concern into a giant business, with yearly sales of more than $130 million. In the process he created the Fuller Brush Man as a fixture in American Folklore—the subjects of hundreds of quips and jokes—while elaborating a system of salesmanship that spread throughout the Western world. And Mr. Fuller himself became a storybook success, a man who started out with $375 and amassed many, many millions.

The company's basic product was brushes, but over the years its salesmen's sample cases have grown to include cosmetics and household chemicals. Some products have been phased out by changing life-styles—there is no longer a brush for cleaning derbies, for example—but the concept of bringing wares directly to the consumer, chiefly the housewife, has persisted. There are now about 25,000 salesmen in the United States, Canada and Mexico, each operating as an independent dealer in a fixed territory.

Mr. Fuller owed his success to his grasp of a few key business principles. One was that a few cents worth of bristles and other inexpensive materials, plus hard work, could create a much larger market value. Another was that a politely phrased sales pitch—carefully rehearsed—could almost always break down a buyer's resistance. And a third was that salesmen, if they were sufficiently motivated, could perform wonders.

The ubiquitous Fuller Brush Man (later joined by the Fullerette) paid calls on 85 of 100 American homes. He made deliveries in Alaska by dog team; he sold a doctor who set a dealer's fractured leg; he changed a customer's tire, pulled a tooth, dressed a chicken, hung out the wash. Inevitably, he was also a film subject.

Red Skelton, the comedian, played the title role in "The Fuller Brush Man" and Lucille Ball was the heroine of "The Fuller Brush Girl." In addition, Walt Disney's big bad wolf in "Three Little Pigs" disguised himself as a Fuller Brush Man.

11TH OF 12 CHILDREN

Mr. Fuller, according to his own account, was once almost enticed by a red-haired woman. "Don't lead me into temptation," she remarked invitingly after viewing his brushes. His response, he recalled, was to say, "Madam, I'm not leading you into temptation, but delivering you from evil." The woman purchased three brushes.

In his autobiography, "A Foot in the Door," Alfred Carl Fuller recounted that he had been born on a hardscrabble farm in Berwick, Nova Scotia, Jan. 13, 1885. He was the 11th of 12 children, and grew into a tall, handsome youth. With nothing but a grammar-school education and ambition to live in a more bustling world, he left home for Boston when he was 18.

After a succession of jobs, he went to work in 1905 for the Somerville Brush and Mop Company as a salesman. Having saved $375 in a year, he decided to venture on his own and set up a workshop in the basement of his sister's home. At night he turned out twisted-wire brushes for clothes, the hands, the floor, and sold them house to house by day.

His sales approach then was little different basically from that employed today. Recalling his early experience, Mr. Fuller said:

"I started out by trying to be helpful. I would knock on the door and say, 'Good morning, madam, if there is anything wrong in your house that a good brush could fix, perhaps I could help you.' "

The woman bought a long-handle brush and used it immediately to get at the dust between the flanges of a radiator. "After that," Mr. Fuller went on, "I studied a housewife's needs, and we made a brush for every need."

Later Mr. Fuller perfected ways to get inside the front door. On a rainy day he wore overshoes a size too large so he could get them off quickly. He was polite—

"I'll just step in for a moment." And, starting in 1915, he and his dealers gave away a vegetable brush, known as "The Handy." They cost each dealer 3 cents apiece and were presented, of course, inside the door. In a recent year 7.5 million of them were pressed into housewives' hands.

After a selling trip to Hartford early in his career, Mr. Fuller decided to set up a company there in a shed he rented for $11 a month. By 1910 he had 25 salesmen and 6 factory workers. A year later he placed a small advertisement in a national magazine and was swamped with replies from would-be salesmen.

Then and later, those who sold Fuller products were independent dealers buying at wholesale and selling at retail at a profit of about 30 percent. Their incomes varied, depending on their enterprise, but they were (and are) supercharged by company pep talks. At one time, indeed, they were gathered to sing songs, one of which was "Fuller Land; Our Fuller Land," sung to the tune of "Maryland, My Maryland." Even so, dealer turnover was high, running to as much as one-fifth of the total.

PROFITED DURING DEPRESSION

With the proliferation of Fuller Brush Men, the company's sales rose to $5-million yearly by 1920, and to $12-million in 1924. The company did poorly in the Depression year of 1932, but it bounced back to record sales of $10-million in 1937, with a net profit of $108,000. Ten years later the gross was $30-million, and it has been rising since.

Mr. Fuller, who was a kindly and dignified man, even-tempered and agreeable, liked to remind visitors that the word "American terminates in I Can and Dough begins with Do." His own motto, he once said, was:

"With equal opportunity to all and due consideration for each person involved in every transaction, a business must succeed."

In his business life Mr. Fuller joined a score of organizations and clubs. Outside business, his biggest interest was the Christian Science Church, which he joined in 1921. Another concern was education—the University of Hartford, to which he contributed money, and the American School for the Deaf, of which he was a trustee.

Mr. Fuller was president of his company until 1943, when he turned the post over to his older son, Howard, and became chairman of the board, a post he held until 1968. On Howard Fuller's death in 1959, the presidency went to Avard E. Fuller, his younger brother. The company was sold to the Consolidated Foods Corporation in 1968.

Mr. Fuller's first marriage was to Evelyn W. Ellis of Nova Scotia. It lasted from 1908 to 1930, when the couple was divorced. Two years later he married Mary Primrose Pelton, who survives, as does his son Avard by his first marriage. Also surviving are two brothers, Harry of Newburg, Ore., and Chester of Kentville, Nova Scotia; five grandchildren, and four great-grandchildren.

Morgue Stories

It is quite likely that Whitman's piece was written before Fuller's death, possibly months or years earlier. Most newspapers have on file biographical sketches of prominent people. It is because they once contained little else except such sketches that newspaper libraries came to be called morgues.

As the Fuller piece illustrates, the morgue story actually is an interpretative biographical sketch in which the writer attempts to evaluate the person and assign him his proper historical importance. In composing it, the reporter has an opportunity to do some of his/her best writing. The best source of material about the basic facts of a person's life, is, of course, the person. Since the morgue sketch is prepared during its subject's lifetime, it usually is written following an interview. Also, the writer consults previously written material about the person and makes his own impartial estimate of the highlights of the career under review. Most prominent people are willing, even eager, to cooperate in preparing morgue material, and do not consider the experience macabre.

Emphasis in writing should be upon the outstanding characteristics, achievements and activities of the person. The temptation of the young writer is to begin with the fact of a person's birth and to continue with a chronological narrative. In interviewing a person for material about himself or herself it may be convenient to have the subject narrate in such a way but, in writing, the principle to be followed is the same as in all other news writing: most important facts first. The fact of birth seldom is the most important.

When only a short bulletin of an important person's death is received in time for an edition, the morgue part of the printed story may constitute almost the entire printed story.

Side Features

In addition to the obituary proper, a newspaper may print several other related items.

1. It is the habit of newspapers, for instance, to print encomiums of prominent individuals who die. Those acquainted with the career and reputation of the deceased are solicited for statements, which usually are included in a single story with a comprehensive lead. Many of these statements are prepared in writing by the persons quoted: others are written following interviews by reporters who express the interviewee's attitude if not the exact words. Expressions of appreciation of certain persons may be published as separate items. If the president of the United States makes a statement, it usually constitutes a separate item. Dispatches from foreign countries carry separate datelines.
2. Sometimes the death of a prominent person leads to an official proclamation by a public official, ordering flags to be flown at half staff or suggesting the cessation of business on the day or during the hours of the funeral.
3. When messages of condolence are received by members of the dead person's family, a newspaper obtains them for publication, either in place of or in addition to the statements that it gathers itself.
4. Resolutions of sympathy passed by organizations with which the deceased was affiliated usually are given to the press for immediate publication.

5. When a businessman dies, especially in a small community, those who had any dealings with him are interested to know whether the establishment will remain open. Newspapers print notices of how long, if at all, the business will be suspended, and whether other business places will close for any length of time as a gesture of respect.
6. The death of a prominent person is the excuse for a recitation of anecdotes. Persons who were close to the deceased frequently write first-person reminiscences. In smaller communities, newspapers try to find citizens who were acquainted in some way with a prominent person who dies. In after years, on the anniversary of the famous person's death or birth or of some outstanding event more anecdotes are sought.

The Second-Day Story

The second-day story is primarily the preliminary story of the funeral. When more than a day intervenes between death and the funeral, there may be two follow-up stories.

Details to look for in the funeral arrangements include

Time and place.
Who will officiate?
Will services be public or private?
How many will attend?
Arrangements for handling a crowd.
Names of relatives.
Names of notables who will attend.
Will any club, lodge, etc. have a part?
Organizations to attend in a body or to be represented.
Names of musicians and selections.
Who will preach a sermon or deliver a eulogy?
Pallbearers, active and honorary.
Where will burial take place?
What will be the program of the services?

The second-day story also may include additional details of the last illness and death, additional panegyrics, letters of sympathy received by the family, resolutions, memorial services and the floral offerings. If the family requests that friends omit flowers, the newspaper should include the request. If floral offerings are sent, the newspaper should obtain a list and description of the important pieces and the names of the individuals or organizations sending them. Sometimes potential senders of flowers are asked instead to contribute to some worthy cause.

In virtually every case of death, friends of the dead person are given an opportunity to view the body before the time of the funeral or, if the body is not placed on view, to visit with members of the family in a funeral establishment. Newspapers should find out when such visits can be made. Organizations that will not be formally represented at the funeral may pay their respects in a group at an earlier hour.

When a member of Congress dies while in Washington, both houses pass resolutions and appoint committees to accompany the body home. Sometimes they adjourn out of respect. The practice of holding a separate memorial service for every deceased congressman has been dispensed with, and only one memorial service now is held every year at which all members of Congress who have died during the year are eulogized. Many clubs and lodges have a similar custom.

The Funeral Story

When a collection is made of the outstanding newspaper stories of history, it will include more than one account of a funeral. The story of the burial of the unknown soldier by Kirke L. Simpson of the Associated Press has become a classic, as have stories of the funerals of most of the presidents of the United States. The following is a straightforward and dignified account of an important funeral:

By Jack Jones
TIMES STAFF WRITER

A celebrity-hungry crowd of perhaps 2,000 persons surrounded a glass-walled chapel at Hillside Memorial Cemetery in Culver City Sunday to stare at the famous who came to say goodby to comedian Jack Benny, 80.

At the conclusion of the short service in which old friend George Burns broke down and in which Bob Hope called Mr. Benny a genius, many of the curious pressed forward to join the line of mourners passing the closed coffin.

The doors to the chapel finally were closed "in respect to the family" and the spectators were asked to leave. But they clung, making it difficult for entertainment stars to reach their limousines.

Comedian Burns, friend of 50 years to the violin-playing Mr. Benny (Born Benjamin Kubelsky in Waukegan, Ill.), tried to offer the first tribute, saying, "I don't know whether I'll be able to do this."

Then he murmured some words which were inaudible to those outside depending on loudspeakers. He lapsed into sobs and silence and was helped away from the microphone by Rabbi Edgar F. Magnin.

Comedian Hope was more successful in delivering his prepared eulogy, saying the famed Mr. Benny who died Thursday night of cancer of the pancreas was a "national treasure."

He said of Mr. Benny, "He was stingy to the end. He only gave us 80 years, and that wasn't enough."

Hope said that Mr. Benny was a genius who "didn't just stand on a stage—he owned it."

And his tribute contained a gentle almost lighthearted joke, the salute of one comedian to another. "His first love was the violin, which proves—as Jack used to say—you always hurt the one you love."

But he noted, Mr. Benny raised large amounts of money for various causes with his violin playing.

Hope concluded with, "God keep him; enjoy him. We did—for 80 years."

Among those who reached the service as hard-pressed Culver City police cleared walking space were:

Actors Raymond Massey, Cesar Romero, Frank Sinatra, Gregory Peck, James Stewart, Edgar Bergen, Jack Lemmon, Henry Fonda, Andy Griffith, Walter Matthau. . . .

Dinah Shore, Rosalind Russell, Lucy Arnaz, Candice Bergen, and Merle Oberon were there. So were Gov. Reagan, U.S. Sen. John V. Tunney (D-Calif.), and former Sen. (and actor) George Murphy.

His fellow comedians were there: Milton Berle, Hope, Jack Carter, Morey Amsterdam, George Jessel, Groucho Marx, Danny Thomas, Johnny Carson. . . .

And, too, the every-Sunday regulars of his old radio (and TV) show gathered: bandleader Phil Harris, singer Dennis Day, Eddie (Rochester) Anderson, announcer Don Wilson and Mel Blanc.

Benny's wife Mary, who played his girlfriend on the show, arrived with their adopted daughter, Joan, and three grandchildren. But the widow had to sit in the car for a few minutes before the service when the overwhelming scent of lavish floral pieces caused her to feel faint.

At the end of the 20-minute service inside the packed 350-seat seethrough chapel, the crowd pushed in so close that police had to again clear the way so the casket could be moved to the hearse carrying Mr. Benny to private entombment up the hill.

Berle, Peck and Sinatra were among the pallbearers struggling through the onlookers, as were Benny's business manager Irving Fein, Mervyn LeRoy, director Billy Wilder, Leonard Gershe, Fred DeCordova, Hilliard Marks and Armand Deutsch.

"Can you believe this?" one dismayed spectator asked another as some in the crowd ran forward to get close to the casket, pallbearers and the family.

But another woman with a small camera was complaining, "Just as we get up to the chapel, they shut the doors." [Los Angeles *Times*]

Follow-ups

A number of other stories may grow out of that of a death. Virtually everyone who is worthy of an obituary has held some position that will have to be filled. Before a speaker of the house is buried, newspapers print stories speculating as to who will be the successor. Frequently there are changes in business organizations after the death of an executive. A smart editor reads the account of an executive's death and notes the organizations, business, fraternal and otherwise, in which s/he held an office, and assigns reporters to learn how that person's place will be filled in every case.

The courthouse reporter watches for the filing of wills and follows carefully every legal step up to and including the final settlement and discharge.

Memorial services may be held weeks or months after a person's death, schools and clubs may be named for the deceased, monuments and tablets erected to his/her memory.

The Obituary Blank

The obituary may seem an important assignment, yet it is one of the first that a cub reporter receives. Most newspapers have an obituary blank for reporters who gather facts about deaths. These printed forms also are given to undertakers, who cooperate in obtaining information for newspapers. A sample blank follows:

OBITUARY REPORT

Full name ....

Residence ....

Place of death .... Time ....

Cause of death ....

Duration of illness ....

Present at deathbed ....

Circumstances of death ....

....

Date of birth .... Place ....

Surviving relatives: Wife or husband ....

Parents .... Address ....

Brothers .... Address ....

.... Address ....

and

Sisters .... Address ....

.... Address ....

Children .... Address ....

.... Address ....

.... Address ....

Date of marriage .... Place ....

Came to this country .... Naturalized ....

Residence here since ....

Previous residence and duration ....

Last occupation ....

Previous occupations ....

Education, with degrees and dates ....

Fraternal orders, clubs, etc. ....

Distinguished service, fraternal, educational, industrial, political, etc. ...

....

....

....

Church affiliations ....

War record: Division, war ....

When discharged .... Rank ....

Honors ....

Time of funeral .... Place ....

Who will officiate ....

Organizations to attend in a body ....
Body will lie in state: When .... Where ....
Active pallbearers ....
....
Honorary pallbearers ....
....
Music ....
....
Burial place ....
....
Prominent floral pieces ....
....
Attending from away ....
....
Additional information ....
....
....

No blank can include every question that a reporter may want answered, and so it is better not to rely entirely upon an undertaker but to interview the nearest living relative.

To rely upon another to obtain facts means to risk missing the feature of the story, especially if death resulted from violence or an accident. Possible features not suggested by the questions on the blank include failure of a close relative to reach the bedside in time; a letter written by the dead person containing instructions for his own funeral; the last words of the deceased; some request made shortly before death; any coincidence in the date, place or manner of death and some other event in the history of the individual or his family.

Language and Style

The language of the obituary should be simple and dignified. The verb "to die" is the safest to use. No religious group can take offense at it but can interpret it to suit its own tenets. "Passed away," "passed on," "called home," "the great beyond," "gone to his reward," "the angel of death," "the grim reaper," "departed this life," and similar expressions should be avoided. Also, let it be repeated, attempts at "fine" writing may be only maudlin. A man does not leave a widow; he leaves a wife.

SUICIDES

In covering a suicide, the reporter seeks the same information about a person's career, funeral arrangements, when the body will lie in state, etc., as in the case of an ordinary obituary. Elements peculiar to the suicide story, however, include

1. The motive.
2. The method.
3. The probable circumstances leading up to the act.
4. The coroner's inquest or medical examiner's report.

The Motive

A person who commits suicide usually is despondent because of financial difficulties, ill health, marital unhappiness, a mental disorder, or a philosophic attitude of discouragement toward life in general.

If the person does not leave a letter explaining motive, the reporter must investigate whichever motives seem most probable. A person's banker or doctor, business associates and friends and relatives should be interviewed. The reporter should ask if the person made any previous attempts at suicide, ever mentioned suicide, appeared to be in good health recently, especially the day before the suicide. How did s/he take leave of family and friends? Was there anything at all suspicious about the person's actions or remarks recently? If s/he had not consulted a physician recently, others who knew him/her can pass judgment upon his/her state of health. The person's appetite, sleep, recreation or hours of work may have been affected noticeably.

When there is no apparent motive, the news writer should say so and should quote those whom he/she interviewed to that effect. The reporter should not attempt to concoct a motive and must be particularly careful not to ascribe a suicidal motive when none was present. Legally, no suicide is a suicide until so called by a coroner's jury or a medical examiner's report, depending on the system in vogue. If there is a doubt, the account of death should be qualified by a statement as "thought to be suicide."

Even when the suicidal motive is present beyond a doubt, some newspapers hesitate to use the word. The editor of a paper in a small community may attempt to protect the feelings of surviving relatives by covering up the suicidal intent. Seldom is such an attempt successful, as an unprejudiced statement of the facts surrounding death indicates either suicide or murder. Only by deliberate fabrication is it possible really to "protect" the widow and other survivors.

It is doubtful, furthermore, whether the paper does as much good as harm in "hushing up" a suicide story. Anyone who knew the dead person will become acquainted with the facts anyway, and if one encounters an effort to deceive as to what actually happened, there is a tendency to conjecture. The rumors that circulate as to the motive of a suicide usually are much more damaging to a person's reputation than the simple truth would have been. A frank newspaper account puts an end to rumors.

The Method

The method by which suicide was accomplished usually is obvious. A newspaper should not dramatize the means of a suicide or print a story that might encourage another to do the same. A poison used for a suicidal purpose should not be mentioned by name, and if suicide by any other method is prevalent, newspapers should cooperate with authorities by omitting the method.

The coroner or physician summoned to examine the body can estimate the length of time the person has been dead. Members of the family and friends can provide clues as to what actions preceded the accomplishment of the act. The reporter should try to find the person who last saw the deceased alive.

By Fred Ferretti

Robert A. Morse, United States Attorney for the Eastern District of New York, plunged to his death from his fifth-floor Brooklyn Heights apartment yesterday afternoon, hours after he had told the chief judge of the district that he intended to resign.

His death was termed an "apparent suicide" by the police, who said he had told associates and friends that he was "despondent" and "distraught."

Mr. Morse had been United States Attorney since Aug. 3, 1971. He was 45 years old and divorced.

Last night Chief Judge Jacob Mishler and other Eastern District judges met to name an acting United States Attorney for the district, which comprises Brooklyn, Queens, Staten Island and Nassau and Suffolk Counties.

Judge Mishler said last night that Mr. Morse had come to his chambers at 10:30 yesterday morning and told him he intended to resign. "He was agitated, depressed," the judge said. "I asked him why?"

"He mentioned some litigation in Surrogate Court. I didn't want to pry. I tried to comfort him, to tell him things sometimes look worse than they are. But if you've made up your mind, submit your resignation to the President and send me a copy."

The judge said that Mr. Morse had been with him until 11 A.M. "and he only spoke about three or four minutes—the rest of the time he just sat and stared."

His former law partner, Norman Turk, was reported to have told Brooklyn political leaders yesterday that Mr. Morse was "extremely distraught" and had told him he was going to resign.

According to the Brooklyn Republican chairman, George Clark, Mr. Morse was "elated" last Friday when Mr. Clark informed him that his name had been submitted for a Federal judgeship to replace Judge John R. Bartels, whose retirement takes effect Jan. 1.

Mr. Clark said Senator James L. Buckley had told him Mr. Morse would be "very favorably considered" for the judgeship that Mr. Morse, a politically ambitious man, had sought. But a spokesman for Senator Buckley said Mr. Morse's name was but "one of many names dropped into the hopper" of political consideration.

The police said that they did not know the reason for his despondency and that he was not in ill health. Both the police and District Attorney Eugene Gold of Brooklyn said last night that no investigation of Mr. Morse was under way.

According to the police, Mr. Morse leaped to his death at about 2:10 P.M. from a casement window of his fifth-floor, three-and-a-half room apartment at 57 Montague Street.

Two young women saw him fall onto the pavement of Pierrepont Place, on the west side of the apartment house, a 12-story nineteen-fifties vintage white brick building called the Breukelen.

He was shoeless, wearing gray trousers, a blue oxford shirt, dark blue socks, and his glasses, and apparently cracked his skull as he hit the pavement.

He was identified by the superintendent of the building, Luciano Lopez. According to the police, there were no signs of a struggle in Mr. Morse's apartment. A note was found and was turned over to the medical examiner.

One investigator said, "From the looks of the place it had all the marks of a classic suicide."

POLICIES LAID OUT

He said Mr. Morse had apparently taken out his insurance policies and laid them neatly on a table next to the window from which he plunged. Next to them was his United States Attorney's identification card. He had emptied his wallet and laid the contents on the table. He had removed his shoes and taken off his tie. The door was double-locked.

"We've seen the pattern before," the investigator said.

A police source said last night that "some of his fellow workers tell us he was very depressed, he was down at the mouth lately."

Mr. Morse had been on a crash diet, under a doctor's care recently and had lost 35 to 40 pounds, according to the police, and "he was very proud of that." However, others said that Mr. Morse, who was 5 feet 5 inches tall, "had looked terrible" since he dropped from 180 to 140.

Mr. Morse was a Brooklyn-born man who made good on his home ground. President Nixon appointed him United States Attoreny in 1971, but Mr. Morse was not averse to telling friends that he longed for either statewide office or a Federal bench appointment.

The police said that Mr. Turk was in the Morse apartment early in the afternoon. According to them, it was shortly after Mr. Turk left that Mr. Morse plunged to his death. Last night Mr. Turk was questioned by the Federal Bureau of Investigation.

In Washington, Robert H. Bork, Acting Attorney General, issued a statement that said in part: "I was shocked to learn of the tragic death of Robert A. Morse. . . . The Department of Justice extends condolences and regrets to his family, friends and associates." [New York *Times*]

Inquests

The coroner, a county official whose duty it is to investigate cases of unusual death, usually orders an inquest into a case believed to be suicide. Sometimes this is delayed until an autopsy is performed on the body and until circumstances of the death are fully determined. The coroner's jury may determine the motive as well as the manner of death. If in doubt, it returns an open verdict.

The trend is toward replacing the coroner with a professional medical examiner attached to a police department or some other law-enforcement agencies. Nearly half the states have adopted the medical-examiner system, in full or in part. Small counties are more likely than large population centers to retain the coroner system, but it may be required that he be a physician. Either a coroner or an examiner must determine the cause of death in cases in which an attending physician cannot sign a death certificate. Neither a coroner's jury verdict nor a medical examiner's report has any more weight in a criminal case than a grand jury cares to give it.

ACCIDENTS, DISASTERS

There always have been catastrophes: volcanic ash annihilated Pompeii; earthquake and fire destroyed San Francisco; floods killed or made homeless millions of Chinese; an iceberg sank the unsinkable *Titanic;* the Zeppelin *Hindenburg* exploded; and so on. Not until the nuclear age, however, did some disaster occur somewhere almost every day: oil slicks, poison gas released from the wreckage of railroad cars or trucks; leakage of radioactive material from nuclear plants. How some papers covered the Three Mile Island crisis and the DC-10 airplane crash was told in Chapter 9.

Part of the price that moderns pay for the benefits of a highly industrialized society is the danger of sudden, violent injury or death. Automobile accidents result annually in nearly 60,000 deaths and nearly two million injuries. Wrecks of common carriers—railroads, buses, trucks, airplanes, boats—are fewer but are more destructive than in the days of slower speed and less delicate mechanics. Homes, public buildings, industrial plants and mines are better protected against fire and explosions, but an undetected minor flaw may result in a catastrophe without warning. Because of lack of foresight on the part of our grandfathers, we who live in the United States today are facing a national crisis as to how to control floods, dust storms and soil erosion, which cause tremendous losses of life and property and, some say, are turning our country into a desert. "Acts of God," such as hurricanes, tornadoes, earthquakes and cyclones, continue to occur with their same frequency, and society has not yet learned how to protect itself adequately against them. The growing journalistic, as well as general interest in the problem of protecting the environment against pollution will be considered in Chapter 22.

The magnitude of an earthquake is measured by the scale that Prof. Charles F. Richter, California Institute of Technology seismologist, invented in 1927. It compares earthquakes with each other in terms of the size of the sweeping lines seismographs use to measure the amount of ground motion. The height of the lines when correlated with the distance from the quake's epicenter, determines the Richter magnitude. Every increase of one number on the open end scale, as from 6.5 to 7.5, represents a tenfold increase in magnitude.

Elements of Interest

Although they differ from each other by types, and although no two disasters of any kind are alike from the standpoint of news interest, news events pertaining to loss of life and property have in common numerous aspects that a reporter must bear in mind. Among the possible angles that no reporter can overlook are the following:

1. Casualties (dead and injured).
   a. Number killed and injured.
   b. Number who escaped.
   c. Nature of injuries and how received.
   d. Care given injured.
   e. Disposition made of the dead.
   f. Prominence of anyone who was killed or injured or who escaped.
   g. How escape was handicapped or cut off.
2. Property damage.
   a. Estimated loss in value.
   b. Description (kind of building, etc.).
   c. Importance of property (historical significance, etc.).
   d. Other property threatened.
   e. Insurance protection.
   f. Previous disasters in vicinity.
3. Cause of disaster.
   a. Testimony of participants.
   b. Testimony of witnesses.
   c. Testimony of others: fire chief, property owner, relief workers, etc.
   d. How was accident discovered?
   e. Who sounded alarm or summoned aid?
   f. Previous intimation of danger: ship or building condemned, etc.
4. Rescue and relief work.
   a. Number engaged in rescue work, fire fighting, etc.
   b. Are any prominent persons among the relief workers?
   c. Equipment used: number of water lines, chemicals, etc.
   d. Handicaps: wind, inadequate water supply or pressure, etc.
   e. Care of destitute and homeless.
   f. How disaster was prevented from spreading: adjacent buildings soaked, counter forest fire, etc.
   g. How much property was saved? How?
   h. Heroism in rescue work.
5. Description.
   a. Spread of fire, flood, hurricane, etc.
   b. Blasts and explosions.
   c. Attempts at escape and rescue.
   d. Duration.
   e. Collapsing walls, etc.
   f. Extent and color of flames.
6. Accompanying actions.
   a. Spectators: number and attitude, how controlled, etc.
   b. Unusual happenings: room or article untouched, etc.
   c. Anxiety of relatives.
   d. Looting.
7. Legal action as result.
   a. Inquests, post mortems, autopsies.

b. Search for arsonist, hit-and-run driver, etc.
c. Protest of insurance company.
d. Negligence of fire fighters, police, etc.
e. Investigation of cause.

In all stories of disaster there is human interest. In most of them, there also are suspense and a recognition of combat between man and the elements. Disaster stories, furthermore, are action stories and contain considerable details as to exactly what happened. If these details are not presented in chronological order, they at least are so arranged as to leave no doubt in the reader's mind regarding the sequence of the most important of them.

Few other types of stories offer the writer greater opportunity for descriptive writing. Although major disaster stories are illustrated, the writer does not rely upon a photograph to do the work of 1,000 or even 100 or 10 words.

Picking the Feature

No formula for writing a disaster story—or any other type of story for that matter—should be accepted as absolute. In general, however, the lead of the disaster story should follow the orthodox rule of playing up the five *w*'s, giving identification and authority and emphasizing the feature. Any one of the elements listed may be the feature of the story at hand. Regardless of what is played up, the occasion must be identified in the lead by the amount of loss, either in lives or property. The reader judges the importance of the disaster by the size of the casualty list or the number of digits after the dollar sign. When the casualty list or inventory of property is long, it is impossible to be specific in the lead. Names, however, must be high in the story. If their number is not prohibitive, they should come immediately after the lead; otherwise, they should be included in a box either within or next to the story proper. If included in the story itself, they should be followed by explanations as to how every casualty or item of damage occurred.

Precautions

The reporter must be careful not to assign blame in an automobile accident, the type of disaster story that s/he has most frequent occasion to write. Police reports are not adequate protection against libel in such a story as the following:

> Disregarding a traffic signal and a policeman's whistle, Alex Winser, 1421 Talcott street, crashed into an automobile driven by Miss Ruth Hazelhurst, 1191 W. Villas court, at 11 o'clock this morning at Third and Hamilton streets.

The following is a much safer way:

> Two automobiles, one driven by Miss Ruth Hazelhurst, 1191 W. Vilas court, and the other by Alex Winser, 1421 Talcott street, collided at 11 o'clock this morning at Third and Hamilton streets. Neither driver was injured.

Some editors insist on the form "the automobile driven by" or "the automobile in which the couple was riding," instead of "his automobile" or "the couple's machine." This is a precaution against possible libel action when the driver or occupant of a car is not the owner. Other editors consider the precaution unnecessary.

Care must be exercised in using "crashed," "demolished," "destroyed," and other descriptive verbs. The reporter should study the definitions of such words to avoid misapplying them. The makes of automobiles should not be mentioned unless pertinent.

It must be remembered that to collide two bodies must be in motion. Thus, if a moving automobile hits one parked at the curbing, there is no collision; rather, the car in motion strikes the other.

In the attempt to make drivers more careful and thus reduce accidents, some newspapers print daily tables or charts to show the total number of accidents and casualties by comparison with the preceding year. Likewise, since a magazine campaign against automobile accidents a few years ago, newspapers have been more inclined to include frank details of such mishaps to emphasize their horror. Much more gruesome pictures also are being used than formerly.

In the belief that they are performing a public service as well as fostering both reader interest and friendship, some newspapers undisguisedly editorialize in accident stories, as

> The danger of bicycle riding on public streets again was illustrated about 7 p.m. yesterday when Harold, 13-year-old son of Mr. and Mrs. Emil J. Bornstein, 636 Carbany street, was seriously injured in the 1200 block of Chicksaw avenue. He was struck by an automobile driven by O. S. Patrick, 802 Lunt avenue.

What follows is a very skillful handling of a delicate story after a masterly job of fact-gathering.

By Tom Rademacher

James Wilson, a hero, is dead.

The 36-year-old area resident died early Wednesday at Blodgett Memorial Medical Center's Burn Unit, less than 24 hours after he rushed repeatedly into a flaming home to rescue a family friend and her children.

Wilson was staying with Julie Ann Croff, her son and two daughters at the Croff's home at 12013 Lincoln Lake Ave. NE in Oakfield Township when a gas furnace in the single-story dwelling exploded and ignited a fire about 5 A.M. Tuesday.

Wilson led Croff, 33, and her son, Kevin, 6, to safety, then went back into the home to save Croff's 1½-year-old daughter, Christina.

He rushed back in again in an attempt to save Christina's twin sister Regina, but the heat was too intense and he was forced to exit alone, according to Kent County sheriff's deputies.

Wilson suffered second- and third-degree burns over 50 percent of his body, mostly on the head, neck, torso and arms, according to a hospital spokesman. He was admitted Tuesday in critical condition.

About 10 a.m. Wednesday, he had a cardiac arrest and died 45 minutes later, the spokesman reported.

Christina Croff remains in critical condition at the center's burn unit.

The destroyed home had no basement and the furnace was located on the main floor, adjacent to the living room, deputies said. Regina's bedroom was separated from the furnace by a thin retaining wall.

Harvard Fire Chief Dale Cole said a babysitter told Wilson and Croff when they returned home Monday night that the furnace had been making strange noises.

The couple intended to have the furnace checked by a maintenance man Tuesday morning, a deputy said.

The fire remains under investigation.

Wilson's body was taken to Marshall Funeral Home in Greenville, where services are scheduled for 11 A.M. Saturday. Burial will be at Rest Haven Memory Gardens.

He is survived by a wife, Kathleen of Greenville; three children, Gina, Denise and Scott, all at home, and parents, James and Myra Wilson of Florida.

Funeral services for Regina Croff are scheduled for Saturday at 10 A.M. at the Pierce-Pederson Funeral Home in Rockford. Burial will be in Blythfield Memory Gardens. [Grand Rapids (Mich.) *Press*]

Side Features

Any one of the elements that go to make up a complete disaster story conceivably could be played up in a sidebar: acts of heroism, miraculous escapes, rescue and relief work, coincidences, etc. It is customary to use boxes or separate stories for long tabulations of casualties or damages and for lists of previous catastrophes of a similar nature. Eyewitness accounts are provided by victims who had narrow escapes and by bystanders, rescue workers, reporters, and others. When the disaster occurs outside the circulation area of the publication, it is customary to use a sidebar or in some other way play up the names of any local persons who were involved.

Perspective

Many disasters can be prevented by such obvious precautions as straightening highways, repairing defective electrical wiring and posting warning signals. Others cannot be controlled without scientific study and analysis and action on a much broader scale. The media of communication can help the public understand why a certain type of disaster is prevalent in a community, area, state or nation by "digging deeper" than the facts related to a specific news event.

> Behind last summer's great natural catastrophe, the devastating floods in Kansas and Missouri, is a simple story. The sweeping tragedy of 44 persons killed, 500,000 persons displaced, 2,000,000 acres flooded, 45,000 houses damaged or destroyed, the teeming Kansas Citys gutted by water and flame, and a $2.5 billion loss is only an effect. Underlying it all is the tale of three dams that became lost in politics in Kansas and the District of Columbia, and never got built.

Sociological phenomena are interrelated. Why flood control projects are not constructed involves consideration of more than selfish political interests.

The stories of the depletion of natural resources, chiefly forests and grazing lands, and of soil erosion and other bad consequences of unscientific methods of farming are intricate ones.

Slum area fires usually can be blamed on faulty building codes and/or their improper enforcement. Probing deeper, to obtain perspective, however, the interpretative reporter may discover the origin of overcrowded housing in the heavy migration of Negroes, Puerto Ricans or others into areas where segregation is enforced and programs for integrating newcomers into the economic and social life of the community are inadequate. The machinations of some real estate operators to reap personal profit by playing race against race or nationality group against nationality group may be revealed. Tracing the ownership of tenement property, often concealed by "dummy" titleholders, may be enlightening and a first step toward removal of fire hazards.

At a different level, newspapers can lead the way in educating home owners and tenants in how to preserve and renovate property so as to remove hazards. The famous Baltimore Plan of urban renewal could not have succeeded without the vigorous support of the *Sunpapers*.

Those concerned with safety on the streets and highways still stress the *three E*'s: engineering, education and enforcement. Increasingly, however, researchers are paying more attention to so-called human factors. The psychology of the automobile driver is being studied with remarkable results. The causes of "accident proneness" often are deep-seated within the individual and, for proper understanding, may require study of social factors external to the individual. Only a start has been made toward understanding the interrelationships in this field.

The same is true of most other aspects of the problem as a whole. Too many explanations of why teenagers are more reckless drivers than adults are superficial and contradictory. Simple explanations and answers should be avoided until much more study has been completed. In the meantime, the interpretative journalist can help keep the public informed as to the status of that research.

In 1966 the book *Unsafe at Any Speed* became a best seller and its author, Ralph Nader, was a key witness at congressional hearings that resulted in legislation to compel the automobile industry to pay more attention to the safety of its products. After private detectives hired by the automobile industry failed to uncover anything with which to smear or blackmail him, Nader continued to expose many other shortcomings in the operation of the economic system and encouraged many young journalists to ask why their editors failed to give them more constructive investigative assignments.

The newspaper is the greatest medium for medical education of the public. Practically all of our other modes of medical education reach their largest audiences through the press. . . . It is a question whether the newspaper is playing fair with its readers in issuing feature stories (relating to medical news) without determining first whether such stories emanate from writers of known honesty or from publicity agents.

—DR. MORRIS FISHBEIN, editor, American Medical Association *Journal*

14

POLICE, CRIME, CRIMINAL LAW

As the traditional beat system has been superseded or at least supplemented by "subject matter" or "field of interest" beats, and as routine crime has come to be considered comparatively less important by editors whose scope must include the whole world, the stationary police headquarters beat has become comparatively less important. Nevertheless, if for some unimaginable reason a newspaper were compelled to remove all of its beat reporters but one, it would be the person at police headquarters who would remain at the post. This is so, not because crime news is considered so overpoweringly important, but because in addition to learning of homes that have been broken into, checks that have been forged and murders that have been committed, the police reporter usually is the first to turn in tips of accidents, attempted suicides, missing persons, rabid dogs, strikes and many other events about which newspapers carry stories.

Because the police are in close touch with more phases of everyday life than any other news source, the police beat affords excellent training for the beginning reporter and, fortunately, is one which he or she is likely to get. In the small community, covering police means visiting the police station two or three or more times a day, visiting the scenes of the infrequent important crimes that occur, verifying and amplifying the comparatively meager reports contained on the official police blotter or bulletin and writing all police news worth mention. In a large city, covering police has meant to remain all day at headquarters or at a district station, watching the steadily growing day's report and phoning tips of the most important items (perhaps 25 per cent of the total) to the city desk. When anything happens that the paper wants more about than the beat reporter can obtain from the police bulletin or by interviewing members of the force or witnesses brought to the station, an assignment reporter is sent out; the writing is done by a rewrite person.

The life of neither the police reporter nor the average police detective resembles very closely that depicted by the comic strips and mass market paperbacks. After one has seen one sobbing mother, one hardboiled harlot, one repentant gunman and one of all of the other types who frequent police headquarters, one has seen them all. When this fact dawns upon the reporter and as s/he becomes accustomed to the intransigence of all parties concerned in the diurnal police drama; s/he may have to struggle against both cynicism and discouragement. A good turn at police reporting is the best hazing possible for the callow graduate and aspiring author of the world's greatest novel. There are few newspapermen of importance who did not take the test and pass. An attitude of detached studiousness will enable the beginning reporter to make this police reporting experience what it should be: the most valuable of his/her entire journalistic career. One must not let a hardboiled attitude blind him/her to the fact that human beings are not merely statistics and that there is a story about every unfortunate person who runs afoul of the law. It is impossible to obtain any sizable proportion of those stories, but frequent visits of professional novelists and other imaginative writers to police courtrooms show that there is no better place for the writer in search of material.

LEARNING THE ROPES

The Police System

The police reporter has got to know who's who and why at headquarters or at the district station. The setups of police departments differ in details but not fundamentally. At the top is always a chief of police, superintendent of police, police commissioner or some other individual appointed either by the mayor with the approval of the lawmaking body or by a police commission so appointed. Whatever its title, this office is a political one, and its holder may have little or nothing to say about the formation of general policies. If the higher-ups decide that certain "places" are to be allowed to remain open, they remain open until the word comes from above, either as a result of public pressure or for other reasons. The same is true as regards parades, rallies and demonstrations. Under orders from their superiors, police either protect or harass participants. Whenever any change in policy is made it is, of course, the chief who fronts, making the announcements and receiving the credit; likewise, when something goes wrong he is the scapegoat unless it is possible to "pass the buck" down the line to some underling.

This realistic picture of how the law enforcement system operates may be disturbing to young reporters with an idealistic or reformist nature, but until the public insists on an extension of the civil service system to include heads of police departments and upon strict observance of discipline and honesty throughout the entire system, the situation will not change. The trouble is that the element in the population who might favor an improvement either is unaware of the true state of affairs or is too indolent to do anything about it. The irate citizen who fulminates against the patrolman who looks the other way for a slight consideration or because of orders from above is the same who, when he receives a ticket for parking his automobile overtime, starts on a hunt for someone who knows someone who knows someone. The practice of frightening children into proper behavior by threatening to call a policeman also is not conducive to a helpful attitude on the part of the same children when they become adults.

"Law and order" and "support your police" have been recent political slogans. Usually they mean that their users would like to stifle dissent by groups with views different from theirs. A major problem of honest law enforcement today is to maintain neutrality and not contribute to violent disturbances. Several excellent reports have been made by presidential commissions and it would do the beginning reporter good to take them off the shelves, where they unfortunately rest, neglected, and study them. The best include these:

The Challenge of Crime in a Free Society, a report by the President's Commission on Law Enforcement and Administration of Justice, Nicholas deB. Katzenbach, chairman, February 1967.

The Politics of Protest, by Jerome H. Skolnick, director of Task Force on Violent Aspects of Protest and Confrontation of the National Commission on the Causes and Prevention of Violence, 1969.

Report of the National Advisory Commission on Civil Disorders, Otto Kerner, chairman, March 1968.

Rights in Conflict, the Violent Confrontation of Demonstrators and Police in the Parks and Streets of Chicago During the Week of the Democratic National Convention, a report submitted by Daniel Walker to the National Commission on the Causes and Prevention of Violence, December 1968.

To Establish Justice and to Insure Domestic Tranquility, final report of the National Commission on Causes and Prevention of Violence, Dr. Milton S. Eisenhower, chairman, December 1969.

Violence in America, Historical and Comparative Perspectives, an official report to the National Commission on the Causes and Prevention of Violence, by Hugh Davis Graham and Ted Robert Gurr, June 1969.

Despite modern training methods, many if not most policemen adhere to the "catch 'em and lock 'em up" school of criminology. Understandably, they want every arrest they make to lead to a conviction in court. They find it difficult to accept the principle of everyone's being considered innocent until proved guilty. They chafe under court restrictions regarding the gathering of evidence that forbid entering a place or searching a suspect without a proper warrant and applaud "no knock" laws, which increase their authority. They believe some eavesdropping, wire-tapping and even entrapment to be necessary. They also want more time than the United States Supreme Court says they should have to question or "work over" a suspect before filing charges against him. The police reporter cannot allow himself, while making friendships, to adopt the policeman's psychology. His homework to justify himself psychologically should include Karl Menninger's *The Crime of Punishment* (Viking, 1965), Estes Kefauver's *Crime in America* (Doubleday, 1951) and Ramsey Clark's *Crime in America* (Simon and Schuster, 1970).

These books, as well as the reports cited earlier, all date from the '50s and '60s. Unfortunately there are no similarly valuable references from the '70s except perhaps Jessica Mitford's *Kind & Usual Punishments, The Prison Business* (Knopf, 1975).

Paid more poorly than would be necessary to attract a higher type of public servant, "coppers" off their assumed dignity are pretty good fellows. Fraternizing with them, the reporter learns to like them. A policeman friend is a real asset and usually can be obtained through mention of his/her name creditably in connection with some story. Without friends in the department the reporter is worthless, as the formal reports and notations on the police blotter are grossly inadequate in case of an important story. In such instances it is necessary to talk to the policemen assigned to the case or to the principals; to see anyone in custody of the police, of course, requires permission.

A police captain is in executive control of a station that is organized in semimilitary fashion. In small communities, the chief may assume this responsibility or there may be a captain performing the function of chief at night. In large cities, every precinct station is directed by a captain. The lieutenants usually head up the different operating divisions, such as traffic, detective and patrol. The sergeant is a "straw boss," who may have charge of a switchboard over which he directs the activities of patrolmen on beats or may take charge of a small squad of patrolmen on some errand or duty. Inspectors may have roving assignments to check up on the operations of district stations or may perform the functions described as usually assigned to lieutenants; it is largely a matter of terminology. Inspectors in the traffic division are an entirely different type, being responsible for investigating the circumstances of traffic accidents.

If there is more than one station in a community, all keep in touch with headquarters by means of a ticker or printer telegraph system, and a central record is kept of all important cases. Police departments even in small cities have two-way radio systems to enable headquarters to talk with cruising patrolmen in police automobiles. Also increasing are bureaus of identification in which photographs, fingerprints and possibly Bertillon records are taken and kept and ballistic and chemical studies made of clues.

To check up on minor occurrences, the police reporter telephones the district stations at intervals throughout the day. For the most part, however, s/he watches the blotter or bulletin on which appears promptly everything of prime importance; assignment reporters are sent to district stations when necessary. Most large police departments now have elaborate electronic reporting equipment so the reporter has prompt notice of the occurrence of a crime. It still, however, is necessary to use ingenuity to interview the arresting policemen, the detectives assigned to a case, an assistant district attorney and/or others. Mechanical recording devices do not do the fact-finding job essential for good coverage of a case.

Entirely separate from the city police is the sheriff, who is the law enforcement officer for unincorporated areas within a county. Theoretically, the sheriff can intervene in municipal criminal affairs, but actually seldom does so except when invited or when local law enforcement breaks down. When such happens, it is extremely newsworthy and someone inevitably charges "politics."

Sheriff's raids are made mostly to break up dope peddling centers and illegal gambling establishments outside city limits. Sheriff traffic police also patrol the highways along with a limited number of state police. In states where the township unit of government persists, the law enforcement officer is the constable and the local judicial officer is the justice of the peace.

County prosecuting attorneys are called circuit or district attorneys or state's attorneys. They are elected locally but are responsible to the state attorney general in the enforcement of state law. Federal prosecutors are district attorneys; federal law enforcement officers are marshals; and preliminary hearings are conducted by commissioners.

What Constitutes Crime

As important to the reporter as knowing police procedure is a knowledge of what constitutes crime. A breach of the law may be either a felony or a misdemeanor. As the law differs in different states, the same offense may be a felony in one state and a misdemeanor in another; and a felony or misdemeanor in one state may not be considered a crime at all in another. A felony always is a serious offense, such as murder, whereas a misdemeanor is a minor offense such as breaking the speed law. Felonies are punishable by death or imprisonment, whereas a misdemeanor usually results in a fine or confinement in a local jail. A *capital* crime is one punishable by death; an *infamous* crime is one punishable by a prison sentence.

Crimes may be classified as follows:

1. Against the person.
   a. Simple assault: threatening, doubling the fist, etc.
   b. Aggravated assault: threat violent enough to cause flight.
   c. Battery: actually striking a person or a rider's horse, spitting on another, etc.
   d. False imprisonment: liberty unlawfully restrained by anyone.
   e. Kidnaping: stealing away a person. (May use *abduction* for women or children.)
   f. Rape: unlawful carnal knowledge of a woman forcibly detained; statutory rape occurs when girl is a minor even though she consents.
   g. Maiming (mayhem): disabling or dismembering of the victim by an attacker.
   h. Homicide: killing when the victim dies within a year and a day.
      (1) Matricide: killing one's mother.
      (2) Patricide: killing one's father.
      (3) Fratricide: killing one's brother or sister.
      (4) Uxorcide: killing one's wife or husband.
      (5) Justifiable: in self-defense or in line of duty.
      (6) Felonious: either murder or manslaughter.
   i. Manslaughter.
      (1) Voluntary: intentionally in the heat of passion or as the result of extreme provocation.
      (2) Involuntary: unintentional but with criminal negligence.
   j. Murder.
      (1) First degree: with expressed malice and premeditation.
      (2) Second degree: with no premeditation but with intent to kill or inflict injury regardless of outcome.
   k. Abortion: interfering with pregnancy except as permitted by United States Supreme Court decisions.
2. Against habitation.
   a. Burglary: entering another's dwelling with intent to commit a felony therein; often extended to include any building.
   b. Arson: malicious burning of another's real estate.
3. Against property.
   a. Larceny: taking and converting to use with felonious intent the property of another.
   b. Robbery: larceny with intimidation or violence against the person.
   c. Embezzlement: larceny by means of a breach of confidence.
   d. False pretenses: confidence games, impostures, swindles.
   e. Receiving stolen goods: for sale or concealment; recipient called "fence."
   f. Forgery: altering or falsely marking a piece of writing for private profit or deception of another.

g. Malicious mischief: killing animals, mutilating or defacing property.
h. Extortion: blackmail; obtaining illegal compensation to do or not to do any act.

4. Against morality and decency.
    a. Adultery: sexual relations between a married and an unmarried person.
    b. Fornication: sexual relations between unmarried persons.
    c. Bigamy: second marriage without dissolving the first.
    d. Incest: sexual relations between persons so closely related that they are forbidden to marry.
    e. Miscegenation: marriage between races forbidden to intermarry.
    f. Seduction: inducing an unmarried girl to engage in sexual relations by false promises or deception.
    g. Prostitution: promiscuous indulgence in sexual relations by women for profit.
    h. Sodomy: homosexual relations between men.
    i. Obscenity: anything offensive to one's sense of chastity.
    j. Indecency: anything outrageously disgusting.
    k. Contributing to delinquency of a minor: encouraging or permitting any waywardness in youths.
    l. Sabbath laws restricting commercial and other activities on Sundays.
5. Against the public peace.
    a. Breach of the peace. (May cover disorderly conduct and a variety of nuisances.)
    b. Affray: fighting in a public place to the terror of the public.
    c. Unlawful assembly: gathering for purpose of planning or committing illegal act.
    d. Rout: unlawful assembly that begins to move.
    e. Riot: unlawful assembly or rout that becomes tumultuous or violent.
    f. Disturbance of public assembly: interference with legal meeting.
    g. Disorderly conduct. (Statutes stipulate acts forbidden.)
    h. Forcible entry and detainer: illegal seizure or holding of property.
    i. Defamation: libel if written, slander if spoken.
    j. Concealed weapons. (May be listed as disorderly conduct.)
    k. Gaming: playing games for money or games of chance.
    l. Gambling: betting on outcomes of events over which bettors have no control.
6. Against justice and authority.
    a. Treason: breach of allegiance to country; giving enemy aid.
    b. Perjury: false testimony under oath in judicial proceedings.
    c. Bribery: attempt to influence public official in his duties.
    d. Embracery: attempt to influence a juror.
    e. Counterfeiting: making false money that is passed as genuine.

f. Misconduct in office: extortion, breach of trust, neglect, etc.
g. Obstructing justice: resisting arrest; refusing to aid arresting officer.
h. Obstructing punishment: escape; prison breach.
i. Compounding a felony: agreeing not to prosecute felon or assisting him in evading justice.
j. Exciting litigation: stirring up lawsuits for profit; barratry; maintenance; champerty.
k. Election laws: fraud or illegal interference with voting.
l. Conspiracy: planning or plotting to commit crime.
m. Contempt: improper respect for court.

7. Against public safety, health and comfort.
   a. Nuisances: annoyances.
   b. Traffic regulations.
   c. Food and drug acts.
   d. Health regulations.
   e. Safety laws for common carriers; use of explosives, etc.

The police reporter must understand these popular definitions of criminal offenses, the names of which may or may not correspond to the statutory titles, which differ somewhat by states.

Criminal Slanguage

Gangster motion pictures have made some underworld slang familiar: "contract," for instance, is "to hire a murderer" and "hit" means "to commit murder." A dictionary of such terms would be thick and under constant revision. What follows is a glossary of terms referred to in the numbers racket operations that originated with the Indianapolis *News*.

Numbers. A form of paper gambling such as baseball tickets, bank and lottery tickets based on a select group of numbers.

Paper gambling. Any form of gambling where the only device needed is paper.

Bank. A form of paper gambling where numbers are written on specially designed slips and the results are based on stock market tallies. The word *bank* is derived from gamblers years ago who used bank clearing house tabulations to pick winning numbers.

Lieutenant. The second-in-command of a numbers racket who picks up numbers and collects money and takes them to a location called a drop.

Pick-up man. He does essentially the same thing as the lieutenant, but usually does not know who is the head man or bank.

Drop. A place where numbers betting is tabulated and winners are decided.

Counthouse. Same as a drop.

Numbers writer. A person who takes numbers bets.

Hit. A winning number.

Flashback. When stock market results are changed by undisclosed business or business late at the stock market that is not immediately recognized, changing the number and sometimes making the house pay two bets.

Cut. Certain numbers are cut in bank gambling. Cut numbers are those either barred or paid one half of their winning value when they hit because they have shown a consistency in hitting. There are good odds of hitting the number.

Bagman. The alleged payoff middleman between police and racketeers.

Baseball tickets. A form of paper gambling based on either current baseball games or last year's games.

Blue book. A book that records last year's baseball run totals for the professional leagues which determines the winner in baseball tickets.

Pea shakes. A way of selecting a winning number for baseball tickets and other gambling.

Layoff. If a certain number is played heavily, one gambler may have his employees bet the same number with other gamblers to absorb part of the loss if the number should hit.

Lid. A limit on amount of a bet.

ELEMENTS OF CRIME NEWS

The Police Blotter

Despite the quantity of news emanating from police headquarters which gets into print, much more that appears on the blotter or bulletin is disregarded by the police reporter. Whereas it is possible to give feature treatment to almost everything that is reported to police, there is so much sameness in most of the routine of law enforcement that such entries on the bulletin as complaints against peddlers, small boys or dogs, notices from the police of other cities to be on the outlook for a certain person or automobile, reports of suspicious characters and lost and found articles go unheeded. The usual style is that followed by the Appleton (Wis.) *Post Crescent,* in which the following items appeared, almost verbatim, from the police bulletin:

> Gary S. Haugen, 515 N. Meade St., reported that his 1964 Rambler was stolen Wednesday or Thursday from in front of his home.
>
> John E. Livingston, 2400 N. Drew St., told police that his home was broken into on Thursday and $214 in cash and some small items were stolen.
>
> Appleton police are investigating an indecent exposure complaint that occurred about 6:45 p.m. Thursday in the children's section of the Appleton Public Library. A man exposed himself to an 11-year-old girl and then left.
>
> Janice L. McDaniel, 526 N. Rankin St., reported that her wallet with $250 in cash and personal papers was stolen from 106 W. College Ave., on Thursday.

By contrast the Evanston *Review* generally omits names and exact addresses.

Bulletin	**Review**
Kay Peterson, 1217 Hull Terrace reported between 6:30 a.m. and 3:30 p.m. on April 30, someone broke the glass in back door and took $40 cash from her apartment.	Forty dollars was taken April 30 from an apartment in the 1200 block of Hull Tr.

More nearly complete records are turned in on regulation forms in all such cases, and these blanks may be consulted by the police reporter. Usually, however, s/he prefers to talk to the policemen involved if s/he can find them, or with the principals. It is not safe practice to rely upon the police bulletin as authentic because policemen are notoriously bad spellers and make numerous mistakes in names and addresses.

If attempts at verification fail, the reporter should accredit his/her story to the police bulletin. It is presumed, of course, that s/he knows the law of libel which offers no protection if s/he uses the expression, "police say." It is not safe to print news of an arrest until a person has been taken into custody and booked on a certain charge; then the newspaper can relate only what has happened. It is impossible to say without risk that a person is "wanted for having fled the scene of an accident." Rather, the reporter should write that the person is wanted "in connection with the accident . . ." Every item of police news should be verified before being used.

Usually for an adequate account of any item appearing on the police bulletin, more details than given there are needed.

Picking the Feature

All crime stories involve action. They relate to incidents that are potentially exciting when read about, provided the reporter has been resourceful and thorough in newsgathering. Until a case reaches court, knowledge of law is secondary to ability to observe, describe and imagine all of the angles needing investigation and the sources from which information may be obtainable. The crime reporter, in other words, must possess some of the qualities of a good detective although the purpose is entirely different. S/he is not out to solve the crime but to learn all that it is possible to find out about it.

Because anything can and constantly does happen, the following list of potential elements of interest in news of crime cannot possibly be complete. It is only suggestive.

1. Casualties.
   a. Lives lost or threatened.
   b. Injuries and how received.
   c. Description of any gun play or fighting.
   d. Disposition of dead and injured.
   e. Prominent names among dead and injured.

2. Property loss.
   a. Value of loss.
   b. Nature of property stolen or destroyed.
   c. Other property threatened.
3. Method of crime.
   a. How entrance was effected.
   b. Weapons or instruments used.
   c. Treatment of victims.
   d. Description of unusual circumstances.
   e. Similarity to previous crimes.
4. Cause or motive.
   a. Confessions.
   b. Statements of victims.
   c. Statements of police, witnesses and others.
   d. Threats.
5. Arrests.
   a. Names of persons arrested.
   b. Complaint or policeman making arrest.
   c. Charges entered on police blotter.
   d. Police ingenuity.
   e. Danger incurred by police.
   f. Arraignment.
6. Clues as to identity of criminals.
   a. Evidence at scene of crime.
   b. Testimony of witnesses.
   c. Statement of police.
   d. Statements of victim and others.
   e. Connection with other crimes.
7. Search for offender.
   a. Probability of arrest.
   b. Description of missing persons.
   c. Value of clues.
   d. Contact with criminal through ransom notes, etc.

Juveniles

The first juvenile court in the United States was established in Chicago in 1899. Leader of the citizens' group that had agitated for it was Jane Addams of Hull House, where the Juvenile Protection Association was founded to lobby for better laws affecting children. One law that most states adopted forbade publication of the names of juveniles involved in crime. Even newspapers in states without such a law adhered to the policy.

Today, the pendulum is changing as a result of drastic increases in juvenile crime. In a case involving a 17-year-old girl arsonist, the Colorado Supreme court declared that state's law unconstitutional. In doing so it cited a 1976 United States Supreme Court decision that courts cannot suppress facts about even normally secret juvenile proceedings if the facts have been made public. In that case the court overruled the Oklahoma Supreme Court, which had upheld the conviction of Oklahoma City papers for reporting a hearing for an 11-year-old boy who fatally shot a switchman.

The decisive case was that of the Charleston (W.Va.) *Gazette* and *Daily Mail,* in whose behalf 11 journalistic organizations filed *amicus* briefs in the United States Supreme Court. The papers had published the name of a 14-year-old boy arrested for fatally shooting a classmate in the presence of seven witnesses. In June 1979 the Supreme Court declared the state law unconstitutional.

Bills to repeal laws forbidding publication of the names of juvenile offenders have been introduced in the legislatures of many states. The Florida law was amended to allow publication but does not require law-enforcement agencies to release names. City commissioners of Coral Springs, Fla., authorized the release of the names of the parents of children involved in crime.

In November 1980 Judge Willard Hogan dismissed a $75,000 libel suit against the Lebanon (Tenn.) *Daily Democrat* for using the name of a 15-year-old boy suspected of participation in a murder. Said the judge: "A newspaper has not only the right but the duty to print the names of juveniles involved in newsworthy events."

Regardless of what the courts decide it is unlikely that most newspapers will abandon all restraint in publishing juvenile crime news. It is more likely that they will follow the lead of the Peru (Ind.) *Tribune* as follows:

> The *Tribune* will publish the names, ages, and addresses of all youthful offenders thirteen years of age or older provided:
>
> 1. in the opinion of the court there is no valid reason for such information to be withheld from publication
> 2. the offenses are not of an extremely minor nature
> 3. the offenders are actually charged with a specific offense.
>
> These facts will appear, along with all other pertinent facts of the case released by the proper authority.
>
> The *Tribune* will follow up with stories which tell whether or not the youth charged has been found guilty or not guilty.

Human Interest

In every community, no matter how small, there occur minor brushes with the law or situations reported to police which, in the hands of a skilled writer, can be made into extremely bright copy. In writing brevities originating on the police beat, the rewrite person is permitted considerable stylistic leeway as the emotional appeal outweighs the news interest.

> The dire possibilities of equipping residential structures with an inadequate number of baths was demonstrated here today when two indoor bathers were arrested for causing a riot through the too-prolonged use of the only bathtub in the rooming establishment of which they were tenants.

Unfortunately, the two offenders chose Saturday night for a general overhauling. The operation consumed so much time that the regular weekly indulgence of the other ten guests, awaiting their turns outside the bathroom door, seemed in jeopardy. After a long wait, during which epithets of an uncomplimentary nature were hissed through the keyhole, disorder broke out among the would-be bathers, and soon took on such proportions that a riot call was sent into police headquarters.

When a sufficient number of patrolmen who were not at the moment taking their Saturday night baths could be corralled and sent to the scene, the two bath monopolists were taken into custody, charged with inciting riot and fined the goodly sum of $3, plus costs.

Leonard Rawlings, 45, of 1968 Winthrop avenue, stepped into a saloon Friday and, between beers, told a fellow he'd sure like to have a new car. And as a result, Leonard's $1,070 poorer.

The fellow, a character in a snappy sports jacket, said that it so happened he had a car to sell. If Leonard would meet him the next day at Division street and Wilmette avenue, he'd accommodate him.

Yesterday, Leonard showed up with his $1,070. The other showed up too, saying, "Let me have the money and I'll be back in a jiffy with the car."

That was 6 P.M. By 10 P.M. Leonard got tired of waiting and trudged to the Central police station. He reported his loss to Sgt. Michael Thomason, who promptly informed Leonard that he undoubtedly had been swindled by a confidence man.

Other Police News

Not all news originating in police headquarters has to do with lawbreaking. Police engage in a variety of noncriminal activities, many of which may be newsworthy. For instance, the missing persons bureau of any large department receives hundreds of calls weekly. Children who leave home in search of adventure, old people who wander off and spouses and parents who desert their families often are news. The first intimation that a crime has been committed also may come from a report that a certain person is missing.

New traffic rules, warnings concerning dangerous intersections, demands that householders make better disposal of their garbage and innumerable similar announcements come from police headquarters. Then there are additions to the staff, retirements, promotions, demotions, citations and social activities within the department itself. Monthly, annual and other reports contain statistics and other information of public interest.

By Joe Dolman

Dwindling police manpower and a work slowdown earlier this year have taken a $411,000 bite out of Atlanta's parking and traffic fines.

Fines collected during the first eight months of 1979 totaled 21 percent less than fines collected during the comparable period of 1978, according to the city's monthly revenue and finance report.

The number of traffic cases declined 29 percent between Jan. 1 and Sept. 25 when compared with the same period last year, police figures show.

The drop represents a significant loss of revenue, city officials admit, but it likely will have little impact on the total city budget. Revenue from all city fines and penalties accounts for about 2.8 percent of the budget.

"We're not in the revenue business. We're here to keep our citizens safe," said Eldrin Bell, who directs the police bureau's Field Operations Division.

"Every little bit helps," remarked City Finance Commissioner Charles Davis.

Beat officers are spending most of their time answering citizen complaints, but they are not ignoring their traffic duties, Bell said.

So far, this year, however, only 43,757 traffic cases have been made, including 2,865 for driving under the influence and 5,671 for speeding. By Sept. 25 last year, 61,989 cases had been made, including 3,502 DUI charges and 10,101 speeding cases.

The city collected $1,535,000 in traffic and parking fines through Aug. 31 this year, compared with $1,946,000 during the first eight months of last year.

Falling revenue should not be blamed entirely on the police, some officers maintain. Fewer motorists are being convicted in the city's Traffic Court, and when they are convicted, their fines often are smaller than in past years, said one high-ranking officer in the traffic section.

Traffic Court officials could not be reached for comment.

Georgia State Patrol officers have been helping Atlanta's beleaguered force in recent weeks, and the state troopers have been focusing on traffic enforcement. Revenue from the tickets they write within the city limits goes into Atlanta's coffers—not the state's.

The manpower shortage is the most obvious culprit in the declining number of cases and falling revenue. With fewer officers, the bureau has been forced to concentrate on serious crimes and citizen complaints, to the exclusion of traffic problems.

Despite a restricted hiring program that was approved by the federal courts, Atlanta's police force in mid-September was short 218 officers.

And the bureau continues to lose more officers than it gains. In September 1978, Atlanta employed 1,125 sworn officers. The bureau listed 1,099 policemen in mid-September this year.

Low morale is also a major problem contributing to the declining number of traffic cases. [Atlanta *Journal*]

Crime Statistics

Since 1930, the Federal Bureau of Investigation, in cooperation with the International Association of Chiefs of Police, has published *Uniform Crime Reports*. Great caution must be exercised in using the statistics therein contained because they are submitted voluntarily by local police departments. As the FBI itself warns, "In publishing the facts sent in by chiefs of police in different cities, the FBI does not vouch for their accuracy. They are given out as current information which may throw some light on problems of crime and criminal law enforcement."

For several years, the crime figures for New York City were so patently inaccurate that the FBI refused to include them in its reports. After the Chicago police department was reorganized under a new commissioner, its improved reporting system indicated crime had increased 85 per cent in a year. Newspaper investigation, however, previously had supported the Chicago Crime Commission's contention that the old department had been officially reporting only about one-third of the crimes it actually handled. Among the devices used to minimize the situation were listing automobiles and other objects as lost instead of stolen, making burglaries seem to be larcenies, making grand larcenies seem to be petty larcenies by "writing down" the amount of loss and so forth.

"With reference to the volume of crime—number of offenses—pressures are always present to keep the figures low," the Chicago Crime Commission warns. In addition, the same source declares, numerous known crimes never are reported, including (1) various types of sex offenses because the victims wish to avoid the embarrassment of publicity, (2) those that private citizens fail to report because of lack of confidence in the police, (3) those unreported by citizens who do not wish to become involved in extended court actions and (4) matters that are handled by private police or protective agencies.

Negroes and members of other minority groups are especially reluctant to summon policemen to their neighborhoods. This fact counterbalances, in part at least, the greater avidity with which police often arrest members of minority groups.

All these and numerous other factors contribute to making the best crime statistics of questionable validity. They suggest the caution with which newspapers should handle such news and the opportunity that exists for investigative reporting to uncover the truth.

Whenever there seems to be an increase in crime, especially violent crime, there is likely to be a clamor, to which editors often contribute, that the size of the police force should be increased. It is to conjecture, however, how much good huge forces, even large enough to provide a bodyguard for every citizen, would accomplish inasmuch as approximately three-quarters of all homicides are committed indoors by relatives, friends or acquaintances of the victims, and the really big crime, white-collar corporate crime, is stonewalled until a congressional hearing is held.

Situation Stories

One type of interpretative writing open to the police reporter is that in which s/he describes, not one or a number of specific crimes, but a situation related to antisocial conduct or law enforcement of continuous public interest.

By Marjean Phillips

A woman's handbag is the sleek complement to a costume, a necessary sack to carry half the paperwork of a household, and an object of convenience, responsible for money, keys, identification and quick aids to beatuty. True, it's useful, but this cache is a threat to woman's peace of mind. Why? The thing is always disappearing! Half the trouble, women agree, is due to their own forgetfulness. Also, there is the real danger of a purse thief, particularly now when stores and buses are more crowded with holiday shoppers.

What often happens, according to Miss Betty Lou Martin, retail store buyer, is that women put their purses and coats on a counter and turn away to a mirror to try on a blouse.

"They might not even leave the floor," she said, "but someone sees the temptation, picks up the purse, and is away before anyone notices."

AN EASY MISTAKE

Occasionally, a shopper thinks her purse is lost when it's really on her arm, Miss Martin pointed out.

"With a lot of packages you can't get the feeling of where each item is located," she said. "It's natural to think the purse was left behind. Just like looking for glasses on the forehead!"

Lieut. Ora Gregg of the police department cautions that shoulder-type bags are easy prey for the pickpocket.

"If a woman has that style she should be sure to keep her hand on top," he said. "A pickpocket could bump her and easily flip the purse flag and get the billfold. Bumping is to distract the person. If a thief sees he is failing in an attempt, he is likely to go on and say, 'excuse me.' "

Sometimes a woman takes out her money purse, lays it on the counter, and thinks about something else. Then, it is hard to tell whether this is a lost article or a real purse theft, he pointed out.

"The best thing is to always hold on to the purse, as well as packages," he urged.

LOCK PACKAGES IN CAR

Lieutenant Gregg, who commands the general assignment unit of the detective bureau, also advises women to lock their purchases in the trunk of a car, instead of leaving them out in the back seat or floor. That merely tempts a thief to take out a screw driver and go to work.

The street is the scene of other trouble. A purse thief may approach women walking home alone late at night. Miss Margaret F. Richardson, 3304 Wabash avenue, former policewoman, has this advice: "Scream or throw a fit if someone bothers you."

Miss Richardson recalled an incident when she was surprised by a teenage boy, who worked as a team with another youth. He pulled on her purse (a box type hanging over her arm), and failed to take it because she kept jerking and yelling at him. Then the partner came up and asked to help her pick up a package she dropped in the struggle. Suspicious, she warned, "You get away or I'll scream again!" The two-man system is a common tactic, she explained.

TROUBLES IN OFFICES

Office workers, Miss Richardson says, invite disappointment by leaving pocketbooks out on desks. The purses are safer in a locked drawer. If there is no lock, a secretary can place the handbag in a large manila envelope in the desk farthest from the office entrance. The noise of the drawer opening might alert others.

Women have worked out their own safety rules for homes, such as pulling down window shades before counting money. Also garage doors are closed when the homemaker drives out to go downtown.

It's an achievement for young mothers to get out of a grocery store with a child in one arm, parcels in another and the purse, hopefully, someplace in between.

Mrs. J. M. Bills, 7902 Fairway drive, manages by using a shoulder bag; the safest way is to place its closing side against her body. At home, she doesn't leave her purse in the kitchen where it could be spotted by an intruder.

Mrs. Bills recalled that a friend who frequently lost her purse had the unusual habit of going to the movie and placing her purse on the seat next to her.

Another example of carelessness was cited by Mrs. Ed G. Freed, 5820 the Paseo, who observed that women hang large handbags on the backs of their chairs in restaurants. Mrs. Freed keeps her purse on her lap.

LEFT ON BUSES

Handbags are numerous in the thousands of articles left on buses and streetcars. Of course, some never reach their owners again. Proof of honesty, however, are the 10,000 to 12,000 items returned by the lost articles department of the Public Service company each year. The clerks at the main office are Mrs. Mary Knight and Mrs. Georgia Ashenfelter.

"Operators turn in lost articles at the car barns each day," Mrs. Knight explained. "A quadruple record is made there and the objects are brought to the general office at Eighth and Delaware for thirty days.

"If there is identification, letters are written asking persons to come in. If unclaimed, after thirty days, the articles are sent back to the finder or the operator," she said.

Even Mrs. Knight has lost her purse . . . on a street car.

"Yes, I lost my purse and it beat me home. The person who found it on the street car took it to my home. I had gone back to look for it," she recalled.

[Kansas City *Star*]

CRIMINAL PROCEDURE

When a person is arrested and charged with a crime s/he is taken immediately to a jail or police station where s/he is held pending arraignment. If the arrest is made upon the complaint of another person, the magistrate or judge already has provided the arresting officer with a *warrant,* which commands him to bring the defendant to court. Anyone seeking the arrest of another must affirm under oath that s/he has reasonable grounds for belief in the guilt of the accused. A *search warrant* permits search of a premise where there is reason to believe evidence of a crime may be found. Unless police on raids have search warrants, their testimony is worthless in court. By a *motion to suppress* the evidence the defense obtains the right to question the arresting officer as to the means by which s/he gained admittance to the place where the arrest was made. Even though the entrance was legitimate, the case still may be dismissed if *entrapment* (inducing someone to commit a crime) is proved.

Arraignment

A person has a constitutional right to be brought into court promptly to be confronted with the charge against him. When that is done, s/he gives his/her legal answer to the charge. If s/he remains mute, a not guilty plea is entered. Then the court proceeds according to its authority.

Easton—Robert Fehnel, 29, of 1236 Bushkill St., was arraigned Thursday before District Justice David T. Reibman on a bad check charge. He was released on his own recognizance for the next term of court.

The charge was filed by Easton National Bank and Trust Co. He was accused of having insufficient funds in his account for his $400 check which he cashed Sept. 27.

[Easton (Pa.) *Express*]

Andrew Konstans, 19 of 5700 Michigan avenue, stood mute on arraignment on a murder charge before Recorder's Judge W. L. Swanson. A plea of not guilty was entered for him and he was remanded without bond for examination Dec. 1.

The murder charge resulted from the death of Policeman Arthur Kendricks, 44, of 156 South Wells street. Kendricks died of three gunshot wounds suffered when he interrupted the holdup of a grocery store Nov. 15.

Preliminary Hearing

If the offense is one over which the inferior court does not have jurisdiction, it holds a hearing to determine whether there is enough presumption of guilt to *bind over* the case for grand jury action in the higher court. If it decides differently, it dismisses the case and frees the suspect. In such a case, either on a coroner's jury verdict or on the initiative of the prosecuting attorney, the case still can be presented to the grand jury. Persons charged with indictable offenses frequently waive preliminary hearing.

By John McCarroll

Des Moines—Merle Bennett, formerly of Brooklyn, was bound over to a federal grand jury in Des Moines Monday on charges of armed bank robbery and conspiracy stemming from the Nov. 12 robbery of the Grinnell State Bank. . . .

[Cedar Rapids (Iowa) *Gazette*]

If the court in which the prisoner is arraigned has jurisdiction, it holds, not a preliminary hearing, but a trial. Inferior court trials provide abundant human interest material, more than a paper can use.

Frank Peterson, 30, of 2231 Wells street, was called "the lowest of criminals" today by City Judge Raymond C. Owens who sentenced him to a year in Bridewell for obtaining money under false pretenses.

Peterson was found guilty of taking $10 from Mrs. Sarah Thornton, 619 Clybourn avenue, on the promise that he would go to St. Louis to seek her missing husband.

Pending hearing, the prisoner may be released on *bail,* usually requiring a bond of cash or security. Sometimes a person is released on a *recognizance,* which is merely his/her written promise to appear when wanted or forfeit a stipulated sum.

The Grand Jury

The grand jury must be distinguished from the petit jury. It does not try a case but merely investigates crimes that have been committed and decides whether there is enough evidence to warrant the expense of bringing the accused persons to trial in the circuit or district court. The grand jury hears the evidence of the prosecution only, and, on the basis of that *ex parte* (one-sided) evidence, it may indict the accused.

An *indictment* may take the form of a *true bill* in case the evidence has been submitted by the prosecuting attorney. If the jury itself gathers evidence of a crime, the indictment is called a *presentment*. A grand jury is supposed to investigate the conduct of government in the territory served by the court and to consider conditions that it thinks should be remedied by law.

In some states, accused persons may be brought to trial upon *informations* submitted by the prosecuting attorney under oath and without a grand jury investigation.

Whenever a crime has been committed and the guilty person has not been ascertained, a *John Doe hearing* is held by the grand jury in the attempt to discover the identity of the person wanted. The prosecuting attorney has the power to summon witnesses to any grand jury hearing.

Grand jury proceedings are secret, but there frequently are leaks from which the reporter benefits. It is contempt of court, however, to publish the results of a grand jury action before it is reported in court. Often, newspapers withhold information even longer so that indicted persons not in custody of police can be arrested on a *bench warrant* (or *capias*) without tipoff.

The reporter should watch (1) the number of indictments naming the same person, (2) the number of counts or charges in the same indictment, (3) the number of persons included in the same indictment. By standing outside the jury room, s/he can determine who the witnesses were and, on his/her past knowledge of the case, can speculate as to what their testimony must have been. The law under which indictments are returned and the punishment, in case of ultimate conviction, frequently should be obtained. Some states have immunity laws to permit a witness to testify without incriminating herself/himself. The power of the prosecutor in determining what evidence shall be presented to a grand jury makes him an important political figure, and a trained reporter keeps an eye on his office as a public watchdog. In writing the story, the reporter must use great care to accredit every statement to the true bill.

> Five police officers and six private citizens appeared before the special grand jury investigating police department activities in the jury's second consecutive meeting of the week, Tuesday night at East side court.
>
> One of the first police officers to be called was Detective Sgt. Thomas Buzalka who remained closeted with the jury for more than an hour. While awaiting call, Buzalka chatted with Robert Hull, head of the police garage, and Patrolman R. L. Lincoln, who also appeared before the jury.

Emerging from the jury room, Buzalka left the building hurriedly with a brief "good night" thrown over his shoulder to those awaiting their turns.

Six indictments charging five companies and 14 individuals with illegally obtaining 800,000 gallons of cane syrup were returned by the federal jury yesterday before Judge Peter Ennis.

The indictments followed an investigation by the Agriculture and Justice departments to determine how the companies were complying with a supplement to the federal sugar rationing order.

Pleas and Motions

When someone is arraigned on an indictment, or at any time thereafter up to trial, there are numerous pleas and motions that may be made, chiefly by the defense. Those which merely seek delays are called *pleas in abatement.* One such is a *challenge of the panel* (or *to the array*) which contends that the grand jurors were selected or acted improperly. A motion for a *continuance* is merely a request for a *postponement.* A *severance* may be asked so that a defendant will not have to stand trial with others named in the same indictment.

A *plea to the jurisdiction* challenges the authority of the court. A motion for a *change of venue* asks that the case be transferred to another court or locale or that a new judge be assigned to it. Motions that would stop all action are *pleas in bar.* One is a *demurrer,* which contends that even though true the acts alleged in the indictment do not indicate crime. A *plea of former jeopardy* is an assertion that the accused previously has been tried on the same charge.

The two common pleas, of course, are *guilty* and *not guilty.* A modified form of the former is *nolo contendere* by which the accused says he will not contest the charges. It is frequent after a test case when others awaiting trial realize that they have no chance to "beat the rap." It keeps the defendant's record clear of an admission but otherwise is the equivalent of a guilty plea. If any civil action is brought, this plea cannot be used against the defendant.

There is no legal plea of "innocent," but some newspapers use the word instead of "not guilty" as a precautionary measure. They fear that the "not" might get lost in the composing room, thereby committing possible libel.

The one important plea that the prosecution can make is *nolle prosequi* (*nol pros*) which means "do not wish to prosecute." It is made when new evidence convinces the prosecutor of the accused's innocence or when there is insufficient evidence to convict. If it occurs under any other circumstances, an alert newspaper should expose the fact.

Fifteen to 60 years' imprisonment was in prospect for Frankie Waters, 24-year-old fugitive from a Georgia chain gang, who pleaded guilty yesterday to a charge of robbery in the first degree to cover a 15-count indictment alleging robbery and assaults on women passengers in taxicabs he had stolen.

Waters entered his plea before General Sessions Judge T. L. Bohn. After the plea had been made by Waters' court-assigned counsel, Charles Shueman, Judge Bohn asked:

"Do you realize that if you plead guilty I can give you no less than 15 years and up to 60 years?" . . .

Circuit Attorney Franklin Moore today dismissed in Circuit Judge Harry Jamieson's court, indictments against six precinct officials in the Fifteenth precinct of the Fourth ward, charged with fraudulent removal and secretion of ballots in the primary election, Aug. 7.

The indictments were returned Nov. 3, but the cases have been continued from time to time by the defendants who said they were not ready for trial. The cases were originally assigned to Judge Charles R. Watson, but transferred to Judge Jamieson on a change of venue.

The last continuance was sought Monday by the state, which said it was not ready for trial, in view of the fact that the State Supreme court had not yet acted on applications for permanent writs of prohibition to prevent the Madison grand jury from examining ballot boxes and other election records of the Fourth ward. Moore told a Journal reporter that the records were needed to prosecute the cases.

Those indicted were. . . .

Other Preliminaries

When a fugitive from justice in one state is arrested in another, s/he may be returned to the jurisdiction where s/he must answer charges by *extradition*. The procedure is for the governor of the state seeking custody of the fugitive to request the governor of the state in which s/he is apprehended to return him. It is newsworthy when such a request is denied, as it sometimes is by a northern governor reluctant to send a prisoner back south; or in the case of an exconvict who has lived an exemplary life for years since a prison break. In federal courts, the equivalent of extradition is *removal* from one jurisdiction to another following hearing before a commissioner.

A description of torture allegedly inflicted upon him in the Georgia State penitentiary was given yesterday by an escaped prisoner as he opened a fight against extradition proceedings to return him to that prison.

He is Leland Brothers, 35, who was released Tuesday from the Stateville penitentiary after serving a one-to-three-year sentence from Brown county for armed robbery.

Yesterday he filed a petition for a writ of habeas corpus in the Wayne County Circuit court.

Wardell Morrison, 31, 5387 N. Culver, has waived extradition proceedings in Seattle and will be returned to Milltown to face charges in connection with separate assault incidents on two Milltown men, according to Pelican County Sheriff Walter Stanchfield.

In both criminal and civil cases, *depositions* may be taken with court permission when there is a likelihood that a witness will be unavailable during trial. A deposition differs from an *affidavit* because it is conducted by a court appointee, both sides are notified and the rules of evidence are followed. In other words, the witness testifies under the same conditions that he would in court; the transcript of his testimony may be introduced as evidence.

Witnesses who do appear in court usually are there as the result of *subpoenas* (court orders), which either side may obtain as a matter of right. A *subpoena duces tecum* orders a witness to produce certain real evidence, usually documents and records.

CRIMINAL TRIALS

Most criminal trials (same is true of civil trials) last only a few hours or minutes. Some, however, take days, weeks or months. The story the day before or on the day of trial may forecast its probable length, based on statements by attorneys for both sides and what the reporter knows of the probable evidence.

First Stories

The reporter should include (1) careful tie-back to the crime itself—time, place, names, events; (2) the charges as stated in the indictment; (3) the possible outcome, meaning the minimum and maximum penalties fixed by law for all of the possible verdicts in the case; (4) the probable evidence with names of witnesses and attorneys' statements, if obtainable, as to what they will attempt to establish; (5) any unusual angles, as possible difficulty in obtaining a jury—for instance, one side may be expected to favor persons of ages, occupations, religion or politics different from those favored by the other side—or maybe this is the first trial of its kind, or the first in a long time, or a new law may be applied to some part of the proceedings. The possibilities are limitless.

Picking the Jury

After the indictment has been read and the plea entered, and after any last-minute motions have been disposed of, selection of the jury begins. The jury of twelve is picked from a panel of *veniremen* prepared by the jury commission or its equivalent. They are questioned by attorneys of both sides and, if found unsatisfactory for reasons that are obvious, may be *challenged for cause*. In addition, each side has a stated number of *peremptory challenges* for which no reasons need be given; usually the defense has twice as many as the prosecution. The questioning of prospective jurors is called the *voir dire* (to speak the truth). Clues to future tactics may be obtained from the types of questions asked veniremen. If, for instance, the prosecutor does not inquire whether they are prejudiced against the death penalty, it is apparent s/he does not intend to ask for that punishment. If the original panel of veniremen is exhausted without a jury's being completed, additional persons are summoned; they are known as *talesmen* and in inferior courts may be brought in off the street or selected from courtroom spectators.

Opening Statements

The state leads with a statement of what it intends to prove and the nature of the evidence to be introduced. The prosecutor presents no evidence. The defense may make its reply immediately or may wait until after the prosecution's evidence has been presented.

Evidence

First witnesses for the state are called for the purpose of establishing the *corpus delicti,* or proof that a crime was committed. All testimony is given in answer to questions by attorneys. After *direct examination* by attorneys for the side calling him, a witness is subjected to *cross-examination* by attorneys for the other side. They must restrict their questions to matters about which he already has testified and they often attempt to *impeach a witness* by catching him in contradictory statements. Objections to questions frequently are made by counsel; the judge is the arbiter. Occasionally, the jury is taken from the room while arguments on the admissibility of evidence are heard. A *jury view* is the taking of a jury to the scene of a crime or any other place outside the courtroom for the purpose of observing anything pertinent to the case.

By Vanessa Shelton

Identifying persons involved in a May 20, 1978, incident at a southeast-side tavern was difficult, a Cedar Rapids police officer said today in the Linn District Court trial of Edward Williams.

However, he added, there was no mistake about Williams or his actions.

Williams and six other men were charged with rioting in connection with a brawl involving police and patrons of the L and H Lounge (formerly the Brown Derby), located at 601 12th Ave. SE.

Williams is the first of the seven to stand trial on the rioting charge. Trials were delayed while awaiting a state supreme court ruling on the constitutionality of the riot statute in Iowa's new criminal code. In its July ruling, the court held that the statute requires the prosecution to prove a person within a group actually participated in the group's violent acts.

In opening statements today, defense attorney Mike Vestle said the arrest of Williams was a mistake and that he did not participate in any violence occurring the day in question. For his trial, Williams, 26, was transported from the Iowa Men's Reformatory where he is serving a two-year term on an unrelated charge.

Cedar Rapids police officer Michael Klappholtz, testifying as the state's first witness today, said he was able to identify Williams as one of several persons outside the tavern who were "pushing and shoving" him and two other officers.

Prior to opening statements, a twelve person jury was selected. The state was expected to rest its case this afternoon. Attorneys expected the trial would last about two days. [Cedar Rapids (Iowa) *Gazette*]

After it has presented all of its evidence, both through the testimony of witnesses and by exhibits, the state *rests*. Then the defense usually automatically makes a motion for a *directed verdict of acquittal* on the ground that the state has failed to prove its case. Most such motions are denied as automatically as they are made; when they are not, there is a news story. A *mistrial* can result in cases of gross irregularity, as an attempt to bribe a juror.

The overzealous interest of a juror in a robbery case before County Judge Nova in Brooklyn caused a mistrial yesterday, and brought a reprimand from the court. The juror was William E. Rejall, 54 Tompkins place, Brooklyn, who had sat for two days in the trial of Joseph Fernandez, charged with holding up Felix Orrusti, 173 Washington street, Brooklyn.

When the trial opened yesterday, Rejall stood up and asked if he might question the complainant.

"I took the trouble to visit the scene and I want to ask the complaining witness how he could identify anyone in the dark," the juror explained. Judge Nova appeared surprised.

"You are entitled only to the evidence that is submitted in court in the presence of the defendant," the court said. "You should not have gone to the scene. I must declare a mistrial." [New York *Times*]

All motions having been denied, the defense presents its case, beginning with its opening statement if not already made. Direct and cross-examination proceed as before. There follow *rebuttal* witnesses by the state and frequently the recalling of witnesses by either side for further questioning.

By Ron Ebest

City policeman Robert Squires testified Thursday in U.S. District Court that he hit Richard G. Miller in self-defense before arresting him on Nov. 23, 1978.

Squires, on trial on charges that he violated Miller's constitutional rights while making the arrest, said he punched Miller twice in the forehead in the kitchen of Miller's home.

But Squires testified the punches were thrown in self-defense: "I hit him before he could hit me."

The charges against Squires stem from an incident in which Squires and two other officers were called to Miller's home to settle a family dispute between Miller and his daughter Cindy.

Miller earlier testified that he was heavily intoxicated during the incident, having drunk more than 20 bottles of beer during the day.

Miss Miller testified Squires shoved her father into the kitchen of the residence after Miller asked for Squires' badge number. According to Cindy Miller, Squires told her father, "You can push the women around, but you can't push me around."

Squires testified he pushed Miller into the kitchen of the house after Miller made a threatening gesture toward Squires' eyes. . . .

[Springfield (Ill.) *State Journal-Register*]

Closing Statements

The prosecuting attorney usually has the right to go first and then to follow the attorney for the defense with a brief rebuttal; frequently s/he waives his/her right to speak twice and lets the defense go first. These final statements by attorneys are argumentative. Then the judge *charges* the jury, explaining the law in the case, the possible verdicts it can return and the meaning of each. Often the law stipulates the exact wording a judge must use in at least part of his/her charge. Judges have little right to comment on the evidence itself but by facial expressions, gestures and verbal emphasis they often can prejudice a jury without the fact being evident in a written transcript.

Reporting Trials

In reporting trials of long duration, the reporter bases every new lead on the most important new development since the last preceding story. Factors to consider are

1. Does some new testimony or other evidence contradict or supplement some preceding evidence?
2. Do the questions asked by defense counsel on cross-examination portend what the constructive defense case will be?
3. Is any of the evidence surprising; that is, has it been unreported in connection with either the crime itself or the trial?
4. How do the versions of what happened as presented by both sides coincide or differ?
5. Is there consistency of purpose in the types of objections raised by counsel and in the judge's rulings on them? Is the defense laying the ground for possible future appeal?

Seeking answers to these and similar questions involves an interpretative approach to the assignment. Much of the reporting "on deadline," however, is likely to be strictly factual. Often testimony can be presented in Q and A (question and answer) form if there is space; otherwise, it can be summarized briefly or the important parts quoted. The courtroom scene, including the attitudes of principals, witnesses, relatives, friends and spectators, is newsworthy, especially if there are any disturbances. In capital cases, the way the defendant acts when the verdict is announced is of interest.

> While Vincent Cilenti, 32-year-old ex-convict was in County Jail awaiting trial on a first-degree murder charge, he allegedly attempted to "shakedown" Mrs. Mary Carmigiano a second time in connection with the bombing of Angelo Pappalardo's home.
>
> This was the testimony today of Albert P. Lauerhaus, alleged confederate of Cilenti, who is on trial for blackmail and bombing of the Pappalardo home.
>
> The trial was interrupted shortly before noon when John Draggo of 3861 Montevista Rd., Cleveland Heights, a state witness, repudiated a statement he made to police in 1942 accusing Cilenti of "shaking him down" for $100.
>
> Common Pleas Judge Alva R. Corlett excused the jury, summoned attorneys into his chamber and warned them he would not permit perjury in the courtroom.

TELLS OF BULLDOZING

After the noon recess, Draggo reluctantly told a story of being bulldozed by Cilenti into signing papers which Draggo thought made him cosignor for a loan for purchase of an auto. Later, he said, he learned that he had actually been the one to sign the papers and that Cilenti had placed both car and license in Draggo's name, forcing Draggo to make the payments.

Lauerhaus, 32, said it was in November, 1942, while Cilenti was waiting trial in the murder of Peter Laduca (of which he was acquitted) that he sent for Lauerhaus to visit him at County Jail.

"I want you to see Mrs. Carmigiano," Lauerhaus said Cilenti told him. "She owes me some money. Go out and get it for me."

Q. What did you do then?

A. I went out and she said she didn't owe Cilenti any money. I didn't get any money from her.

Lauerhaus said he couldn't remember the exact amount of money Cilenti said she owed. Mrs. Carmigiano said in testimony yesterday that after paying Cilenti $300 she was approached for $600 more.

Lauerhaus confirmed Mrs. Carmigiano's testimony about how he drove her to see Cilenti in September after the Pappalardo home had been bombed.

Then James P. Hart, assistant county prosecutor, asked him: "Did you ever have any conversation with Cilenti about the bombing?" Lauerhaus said he did, talking to him about how Mrs. Carmigiano had complained that Cilenti had bombed the home without telling her about it or getting her approval.

"What does she think I am, a damn fool?" Lauerhaus said Cilenti told him. "Does she think I'd tell her when I'd be there so she could be in the window waiting for the explosion?"

Mrs. Carmigiano, 1392 SOM Center Rd., Mayfield Heights, yesterday told how Cilenti extorted $300 from her for bombing a neighbor's home without her knowledge or approval.

Mrs. Carmigiano, a real estate agent, said Cilenti first came to see her early in 1942, when she lived on Arrowhead Ave., about renting a house. Later, she related, he returned saying he understood she was having trouble with a neighbor.

Mrs. Carmigiano said she told him of arguments she had with the family of Angelo Pappalardo, 19408 Arrowhead Ave.

A. He said I should punish the people next door.

Q. What did you say?

A. Well, I don't know how to punish them. I'm only a widow. There's nothing I can do about it.

Q. What did Cilenti say to this?

A. He said: "I can take care of it for you." I asked him in what way. He replied: "Just leave it to me. We know how to take care of it for you." I told him I didn't want anybody hurt.

Mrs. Carmigiano moved from Arrowhead Ave. in May, 1942. The Pappalardo home was bombed July 8. She told De Marco she read of the bombing in the newspapers. Then Lauerhaus came to see her several times, she said, telling her: "Cilenti wants to see you."

On the second or third visit he came at night and pushed his way into her house, Mrs. Carmigiano said.

Q. What happened then?

A. He took me in his car to 82d St. and Quincy Ave. He left me in the car awhile. I waited about an hour, so I went into a cafe and asked for Cilenti. They said they didn't know where he was. I went back to the car and someone came out and took me to Cilenti. Cilenti said to me, "The job is done. The boys want their money."

Mrs. Carmigiano said she asked: "What money?"

"They want $300."

"For what?"

"For the Pappalardo job," she said Cilenti replied.

ASKED FOR RECEIPT

The interview, she testified, closed with Cilenti driving her home and telling her to get him the money by 2 P.M. that day. She said she borrowed the money from a friend, took it to Cilenti's home, accompanied by one of her sons. She said she gave the money to Cilenti and when she asked for a receipt she testified he told her:

"Oh, no. We don't do business that way."

Mrs. Carmigiano denied she was operating a still in 1941, but added that Cilenti's purpose in wanting to rent a house from her was to establish a hideout for operation of a still. S. M. Lo Presti, defense attorney, sought to show that the money transaction between Mrs. Carmigiano and Cilenti involved a bootlegging deal rather than a bombing. [Cleveland *Press*]

Verdicts

The jury leaves the courtroom and deliberates, with the foreman presiding. After the case is over, the reporter may find out, by questioning jurors, how many ballots were taken and how the vote stood every time. The length of time it takes a jury to reach unanimity is newsworthy. If no decision ever is reached, the jury is said to be *hung,* and there is a *mistrial.* Some indication of how a jury is thinking may be obtained if it returns to the jury room to ask further instructions or to have part of the evidence read to it again. The reporter's best tipster as to what goes on in a jury room is the bailiff standing guard at the door.

The defendant must be in court when the verdict is read. If a verdict is reached late at night, it may be written and *sealed* and left with a court official, so that the jurors may leave. All, however, must be present when the envelope is opened and the verdict announced. The losing side may demand a *poll* of the jury, which requires every juror to declare that s/he concurs. If any juror changes his/her mind during such a poll it is "hot" copy.

By Win Sims

A six-woman, six-man jury took about 2½ hours Thursday to find Keith Pontseele guilty of second-degree murder in the sniping death of 12-year-old Billy Mills in Merrill on Sept. 16, 1978.

The charge carries a maximum sentence of life in prison but the average term served is about eight years.

After the verdict, Circuit Judge Hazen R. Armstrong sent the 30-year-old Merrill-area bartender back to jail to await sentencing, expected to be sometime in the next four to six weeks.

The jury also found Pontseele guilty on two counts of assault with a dangerous weapon, a 4-year felony, in the wounding of Delphine Merritt, 16, and Michael Brown, 4, by shrapnel from the two bullets which killed Mills.

The prosecution had asked for a verdict of first-degree murder and the outcome was in doubt until the jury foreman rose to speak. The proven elements of the crime—that Pontseele crouched on a rooftop and fired at the children below—might have been construed as killing by "lying in wait," a sort of first-degree murder by definition.

Those searching for signs might have noticed that while the jurors listened to Assistant Prosecutor Patrick M. Meter, seven leaned their heads on their left hands. When they listened to the defense attorney, Thomas J. Demetriou, six heads rested on right hands.

"I guess it could've been a lot worse," Pontseele's older brother, Tom, remarked on the way out.

Despite two confessions in which Pontseele admitted being on the roof and doing the shooting, no motive was ever offered why he shot Mills.

There was ample testimony about a romantic entanglement between Pontseele and Miss Merritt, and testimony that he claimed to be the father of her child—a claim she disputed.

And there was testimony from Miss Merritt that in the week before the shooting, Pontseele told her he loved her and that she had rejected his advances.

But the testimony about Pontseele and Miss Merritt didn't add up to a reason for shooting a boy Pontseele didn't even know, the jury apparently decided.

Meter proposed that in the darkness (the shooting took place at 1:20 a.m.), Pontseele mistook the 150-pound boy for a rival, but he admitted it was only a theory.

Meter tried to get a conviction on first-degree murder by citing a part of that law which says murders committed by "lying in wait," like all murders by poisoning, are first-degree murders.

In rejecting this and voting to convict on second-degree murder, the jury in essence said that when Pontseele pulled the trigger, he acted on "a purpose to kill, formed suddenly," but "without that deliberation and premeditation which distinguishes first-degree murder." [Saginaw (Mich.) *News*]

Sentences

Unless it is "not guilty" in a felony case, a jury's verdict is advisory only; the judge accepts or rejects it. He may grant a defense motion to *set aside* the verdict and grant a *new trial* if there have been errors that he knows would cause an appellate court to reverse the verdict and *remand* the case. A motion for *arrest of judgment* accompanies such motions to postpone sentencing.

The leeway permitted a judge in pronouncing sentence is established by statute for every crime. In some cases, s/he may have no choice at all; convictions on a certain charge may mean an automatic sentence of a certain kind. A *suspended sentence* is one which the convicted person does not have to serve pending good behavior. It is rapidly being replaced by *probation,* which gives the convicted person limited freedom of action under the supervision of probation officials; if anyone violates the conditions of his/her probation, s/he serves not only the original sentence but an additional one also because of the violation. Probation is most common for minors and first offenders. It should not be confused with *parole,* which is the supervised conditional release of prisoners who already have served part of their prison terms.

If someone is convicted on more than one count, s/he may serve several sentences *concurrently* or *consecutively*. If the former, s/he serves only the longest of the several sentences; if the latter, s/he serves the accumulated total of them all. An *indeterminate* sentence sends a convicted person to the penitentiary for "not less than" a designated number of years, and "not more than" another number of years. The exact time of release is determined by the state board of paroles. Usually s/he is not eligible to apply for parole until after at least one-third of his/her time has been served, so judges often give maximum penalties to run consecutively to make release on parole unlikely.

> Clarence Whittle, 20, of 187 South Water street, was sentenced by Judge John S. Anthony in Criminal court yesterday to serve a term of not less than 10 years to life in the penitentiary for armed robbery.
>
> Judge Anthony overruled a motion for a new trial before pronouncing the sentence. Whittle was convicted by a jury Jan. 10 of holding up a tavern at 1700 Ashland avenue, on Sept. 1 and taking $190.
>
> Whittle faces charges of murdering Michael Storms, 50, a tavern owner of 5800 Market street, on July 15. Four others have pleaded guilty to participating in the shooting of Storms and a fifth is under sentence of 20 years in prison.

Punishments

Despite the trend toward individualized treatment of lawbreakers and the substitution of theories of reformation and protection of society for theories of retaliation and expiation, the criminal law still requires that a convicted person "pay his debt to society." To carry out any sentence is to *execute* it, although the popular connotation of the word limits it to cases in which capital punishment is inflicted. The death penalty was virtually outlawed by the United States Supreme Court but it was being neglected anyway because judges and juries are reluctant to impose it. Recently the court has upheld some new state laws permitting the death penalty in certain cases. It is within the power of a governor to *commute* any sentence: that is, to reduce it, as from death to life imprisonment. A governor also can issue a *reprieve* which, however, is merely a postponement of execution. A *pardon* is a granting of freedom. If absolute, it restores civil rights. If conditional, it prescribes limits to the ex-convict's behavior. Few states as yet have adequate systems for recompensing persons proved to have been imprisoned wrongly.

Appeals

The appellate court system will be described in Chapter 15. Mostly, the appellate courts do not review evidence introduced in a lower court, only procedural matters. Nevertheless, the results often are newsworthy.

By Gordon Winters

The Nebraska Supreme Court Tuesday rejected arguments that an Omaha man was unfairly convicted of killing his wife because hearsay evidence was used against him.

Dean L. Beam was found guilty of second-degree murder and sentenced to 15 years in prison after he shot his wife in the head in an argument in the kitchen of their home on Jan. 15, 1979.

The record in the case was that the emergency communications center in Omaha received a phone message in which the caller said in part, "I shot my wife . . . 3817 Monroe . . . get here fast . . . my wife is dying."

When police arrived Beam told them, "You guys are too late. I have already shot my wife. You can't help me and you can't help her because she is already dead."

Beam said he remembered one shot being fired as his wife tried to take the .22-caliber pistol from him, but police said they found six empty shells in the revolver and five bullet holes in the floor near the body. A bullet lodged at the base of Mrs. Beam's skull.

Beam's attorneys appealed the case on the ground that testimony from Mrs. Beam's attorney, a deputy sheriff who aided her after her husband beat her and a co-worker was inadmissible hearsay evidence. . . . [Lincoln (Neb.) *Star*]

The state's 3rd District Court of Appeals has refused Outagamie County Dist. Atty. William Drengler's request to admit into evidence a more precise method to determine the father of a baby.

Drengler, who had hopes that the paternity case could establish a national precedent, filed the notice of appeal in August after a local judge refused to admit the results of the test into evidence. Drengler assisted the state attorney general's office in the writing of the briefs.

In a release from his office today, Drengler said the 3rd District Court of Appeals refused to consider the merits of the test case. However, Drengler said he has contacted the attorney general's office and is strongly urging that the case be appealed to the Wisconsin Supreme Court.

Drengler claims that the present law being applied in paternity cases is "outmoded" and says that "hundreds of thousands of tax dollars are at stake."

The new test, called the Human Leukocyte Antigen (HLA) system, can provide probabilities of paternity with an accuracy rate that quite often approaches 99% or better, Drengler said. The standard ABO red blood cell test that is admissible in court under existing state statutes cannot prove fatherhood.

It only proves that the alleged father can or cannot be excluded from possibly being the father. Since a large percentage of the population carries similar blood types, this test can only establish the possibility, not the probability, that the defendant is the child's father. . . . [Appleton (Wis.) *Post-Crescent*]

THE ETHICS OF CRIME NEWS

No ethical problem connected with newspaper publishing has been more thoroughly discussed by both newspaper and lay persons than the treatment of crime news. Upon his/her superiors' attitudes toward the problem depends largely the type of occurrences to which the police reporter pays particular attention and the manner in which s/he writes his/her articles. A few papers, notably the *Christian Science Monitor,* generally ignore antisocial behavior; others have experimented with leaving crime news off the front page or of playing it down in the writing. Familiar, on the other hand, is the type of newspaper that considers a sensational crime story as second to few other types in potential reader interest.

It is not so much a question of the amount of crime news but of how it is presented. Contrary to popular opinion, only a small proportion of the total offering of the average newspaper relates to lawlessness. Several sociological studies have revealed that whereas readers guess from 25 to 50 per cent of the contents of the newspaper is crime news the actual proportion is hardly 5 per cent.

A Fair Trial *v* A Free Press

Some newspapers, magazines, and radio and television stations have been accused of inciting to crime by glorifying and making heroes of criminals; of assisting criminals to escape by relating detailed accounts of the activities of police; of interfering with the administration of justice by emphasizing the horrible aspects of brutal crimes, by quoting the prosecuting attorney as to the severe punishment s/he is going to demand and by editorial comment; of causing unfair suffering on the part of the relatives and friends of principals in a criminal case; and of offending public taste by relating lurid details of crimes and scandals.

The sensational and often inaccurate reporting in the '20s and '30s of several murder trials, especially that of Bruno Richard Hauptmann for the murder of the infant Charles A. Lindbergh, Jr., led to the formation of a joint committee from the American Bar Association and the American Newspaper Publishers Association and American Society of Newspaper Editors. As a result there was agreement regarding a long list of rules to prevent recurrence of objectionable behavior by both press and bar. Nevertheless, by far the most important issue today is how much pretrial publicity there should be so as not to interfere with a defendant's right to a fair trial before an impartial jury in an unprejudicial atmosphere. Several United States Supreme Court decisions and adverse criticism of the press contained in the Warren Commission report on the assassination of President John F. Kennedy renewed the debate. Law enforcement officers, although not liking the restrictions placed on them by the court, have nevertheless become cautious about discussing cases with reporters and scrupulous in obeying the rules imposed upon them as regards questioning of suspects, especially that a suspect must be warned immediately of the right to remain silent and have a lawyer. On the other hand, some newspapers toned down quite a bit after the United States Supreme Court ordered a new trial for Dr. Sam Sheppard of Cleveland on the ground that the Cleveland newspapers had made a fair trial for him impossible. Said the court in this case: "The press does not simply publish information about trials, but guards against the miscarriage of justice by subjecting the police, prosecutors and judicial processes to extensive public scrutiny and criticism.'' At issue, however, is how far the press should go in exercising this function without jeopardizing the rights of the defendant. Neither legal nor journalistic leaders are unanimous in their opinions on the matter or regarding the Warren Commission's statement that ''the news media, as well as the police authorities . . . share responsibility for failure of law enforcement in Dallas.''

In October 1966 the Advisory Committee on Fair Trial and Free Press of the American Bar Association, of which Massachusetts Judge Paul C. Reardon was chairman, issued a preliminary report that most newspapers felt recommended too-narrow restrictions on the press during a pretrial period. Shortly before the report appeared, the Toledo *Blade* adopted a code that other papers have emulated. It includes the following:

> Before a trial begins, the Toledo papers pledge to publish only the following data:
>
> ¶The name, age and address of the accused.
>
> ¶How, when and where the arrest was made.
>
> ¶The charge and the identity of the complainant.
>
> ¶The fact that a grand jury has returned an indictment and that a trial date has been set.
>
> The policy will be to provide detailed coverage so that information perhaps held back at the time of the arrest may be published later in the proceeding if and when it will not interfere with the judicial process.
>
> During the progress of the case, unless very special circumstances dictate otherwise, the following types of information will not be published:
>
> ¶Any prior criminal record of the accused.
>
> ¶Any so-called confession the accused may have made other than the fact—if it is one—that he has made a statement to the authorities, but with no indication of the nature of the statement.
>
> ¶Any statements by officials construed as detrimental to the accused.
>
> ¶Any statements by lawyers either detrimental to the accused or concerning any defense that is to be made during trial.
>
> ¶Any names of jurors selected for a particular trial.
>
> ¶Any arguments made in court in the absence of the jury, or evidence excluded from the jury.

Other papers have publicized policy changes. The St. Louis *Post-Dispatch* no longer prints the house number of a burglary victim; nor will it report whether a burglar overlooked other valuables. The Boston *Globe* will print the name of a street on which a crime victim lives but not the house number. In common with most other papers, the New York *Times* will not print the name of a rape victim unless she wants it used in alerting the community. The Peru *Tribune* withholds publicity concerning telephoned bomb threats to businesses, industries and public institutions, believing that most such calls are by publicity seekers.

In January 1981 The U.S. Supreme Court unanimously ruled that it is permissible for a state to allow cameras and television coverage of trials. It did so by affirming the refusal of the Florida Supreme Court to hear a challenge to Florida's law permitting the electronic coverage of court proceedings brought by two Miami Beach policemen who blamed their convictions for burglary on the disturbing influence of photographers in the courtroom.

This was a landmark decision and made obsolete the canon adopted by the American Bar Association in 1937 after the trial of Bruno Richard Hauptmann for the kidnap-murder of Charles A. Lindbergh, Jr. In 1964 the court had reversed the conviction of Texas financier Billy Sol Estes, ruling that the televising of the trial had denied him due process.

Understanding the Criminal

Perhaps the most important adverse criticism of the press in the past has been that it has not taken sufficient cognizance of modern criminological and penological thought. By advocating harshness of treatment as the only corrective, by labeling every sex offender (even before apprehended) as a moron (a scientific term meaning high-grade feeble-minded), by pointing to every paroled prisoner violating his parole as proof of the unsoundness of the parole principle, by ridiculing leading thinkers as maudlin sentimentalists, and in other ways, the media, it is charged, are a sizable obstacle in the movement to replace a barbaric philosophy and methods of curbing antisociability with a scientific approach.

Following a scientific study of the life history of Giuseppe Zangara, the psychopathic immigrant who attempted to assassinate President-elect Franklin D. Roosevelt in 1933, Sidney Kobre said, in part, regarding the manner in which the American press handled the story:

> Newspapers, in theory, print the news as it occurs, head it according to its significance, and comment on its important aspects. Here, certainly, was an opportunity for them to get at the root of a social evil—to insist, rather than on laws to prevent purchase of guns or enforce deportation of aliens, on the essential nature of the problem. Zangara, had the influences under which he labored been understood (and they might have been discovered when he entered the Italian army, when he passed through the immigration bureau, when he was admitted to citizenship, when he was a patient in a hospital), might have been headed off, his physical and psychological ailments corrected. Suggestions for the isolation and treatment of the class from whom are "recruited the criminal types and cranks" might have been made, along with emphasis on the fact that the class is not composed exclusively of aliens. . . .
>
> The newspapers had opportunity to examine the impulse behind the shooting at its root. . . . For the most part they did not do so. Instead they seized upon the "red" stereotype, or proposed police or legislative methods of dealing with the evil once it had arisen, rather than psychiatric or medical methods of preventing it from arising. . . . Most American editors handling this story chose stereotypes and superficialities rather than the more subtle but certainly more fundamental implications. . . .

Since Kobre wrote this article, later expanded for inclusion in his *Backgrounding the News,* there has been considerable improvement on many newspapers. World War II awakened interest in psychiatry and acquainted millions with the fact that abnormal behavior does not necessarily result from malicious willful choice. Sociological research, furthermore, has proved that what is considered criminal in one environment may be perfectly normal in another, and that, particularly in large cities, there are communities in which the incidence of crime remains virtually constant although the racial or nationality complexion of the population changes many times. Gone is belief in born criminals, feeble-mindedness as a major cause of criminal behavior, and many other unscientific explanations. Today, psychiatry is throwing light on the peculiarities of the individual offender and sociologists are examining slums, economic status, marital relations and other social factors that breed misbehavior.

In tune with the times, few newspapers any longer consult phrenologists, handwriting experts, fortunetellers and other quacks whenever a major crime occurs. Instead, they interview scientists and they are adding steadily to their own staffs specialists able to do more than invent "cute" headline-fitting nicknames for murderers and their victims.

Indicative of the greater journalistic enlightenment are the first few paragraphs of a full-page article that appeared in the *National Observer* for August 8, 1966.

AUSTIN, TEXAS

The record will show that Charles Joseph Whitman was not a simple man. But who is?

Whitman was, as the world knows by now, a good student, a conscientious husband, an Eagle Scout, a Marine Corps sharpshooter, a hard worker, handsome, strong, fun to be with, popular.

Then last Monday, in the scorch of a 100-degree Austin day, from near the peak of a 341-foot building, he took a deer rifle and killed 13 people and wounded 31. This was a few hours after he had stabbed to death his pretty wife and shot to death his mother. Then police shot him to death.

Gov. John Connally of Texas has announced that the state will convene in a few weeks a conference of psychiatrists and psychologists who will attempt to piece together the reason for such an action. They may never be able to explain Whitman fully, but perhaps their research will tell something more about the murderous mind.

For never in the annals of mass murder has there been such a clean-cut example of a man run amok. If anything, the lesson of Charley Whitman is to remind us how delicate is the human mind, and how little we know of it.

Reflecting last week on the rampage, a medical authority on mental health said he was not surprised that everyone who knew Whitman described him as such a pleasant person.

"The common way of destroying someone [with this hostility] is over a period of 25 or 30 years. This boy just did it suddenly."

A FIERCE WILL POWER

It is only now apparent that Whitman's strains and vices were present all the time—suppressed, no doubt, by a fierce will power finally incapable of holding them in check, creating a pressure-pot that erupted beyond civilized understanding.

Unfortunately, says one doctor, the whole story will never be known. The data are forever incomplete. There will be theories, but no one will be certain how valid any of them are.

Before the experts have a crack at it, here are a few of the pieces to the puzzle, some not widely known, which contributed to this deadly state of mind. . . .

It is commonly said that the reporter meets a great many interesting persons. This is true; but the persons he meets show to him their least interesting side. He meets them as an interviewer, or as one of a battery of interviewers. To such questions as, What is your favorite flower? or Do you advocate the cancellation of the international debts? or Is equal suffrage the answer to social unrest in the Balkans? the interviewee (unless a publicity agent has prepared a handout in advance) presents a hostile or perplexed front. In my own talks with many celebrities in many walks of life, I have never enjoyed but one interesting experience, and that was when I was a cub, utterly ignorant of national politics, and was assigned to interview William Jennings Bryan. I sat on the edge of a hotel bathtub while Bryan shaved and suggested questions as well as answered them. This was an honest interview, because one man did it all. It was not a hybrid, representing truthfully neither party to the transaction.

—SILAS BENT in *Ballyhoo*

Perversion does not consist merely in distorting facts but also in omitting facts which should have been mentioned, or sometimes even in stating facts as they happened but with exclamatory or interrogatory marks, or putting certain words in italics. The journalist should be careful to see, in short, that his news columns serve the purpose for which they are intended, that they give the news in a clear, pithy and truthful manner and do not mislead the public in any manner whatsoever.

—RUSTOM N. VATCHAGHANDY, editor, *Evening News*, Bombay, India

15
COURTS, CIVIL LAW, APPEALS

Just as it is essential for a sports reporter who covers baseball to understand the rules of the game, so is it necessary for the reporter assigned to the courts to know the basic structure of American law.

KINDS OF LAW

Roughly, all laws can be divided into *public* and *private* (usually called *civil*), the distinction being whether the state (organized society) is a party to the litigation. The dichotomy is not exact because government can be a party to certain types of civil actions. In general, however, the distinction holds. Branches of public law include constitutional, administrative, international and criminal, with the ordinary reporter, of course, being most interested in the last.

The two major divisions of private, or civil, law are *common law* and *equity*. The former is that law which was developed through the centuries in judicial decisions in English courts, and—roughly again—it can be divided into *real* and *personal* law. Real law relates to the possession of and title to property whereas personal law relates to attempts to recover damages for injuries received, to enforce a contract, to bring about the return of property and to settle similar matters. The two major divisions of personal law relate to *contracts* and *torts* (all injuries received other than by violation of contract). Equity law, as developed in the equity (or *chancery*) courts of England, begins where common law leaves off. One does not go to equity to recover damages for injuries to self or property, but to compel someone to do or to refrain from doing something. Modern equity courts handle such matters as injunctions, foreclosures, receiverships, partitions etc.

The law administered in the courts originates either (1) in the acts of Congress, of a state legislature or of some other lawmaking body, such law being known as *statutory,* or (2) in the accumulated decisions of courts both here and in England, such law being known as *common law.* Courts adhere to the principle of *stare decisis* (let the decision stand), which means that lawyers quote at length from decisions in earlier cases in the attempt to show that the case in hand should be decided similarly. When there has been a pertinent decision by the Supreme Court of the United States or some state appellate court, the issue may seem clearcut. Usually, however, such is not the case. Either the matter at hand differs in some essential from the previously decided case, or the appellate court decision is limited in scope. Also, there may be conflicting decisions in apparently identical cases.

Young reporters should know that, despite the apparent inconsistencies in both the written (*basic*) law itself and common law decisions, and despite their ability to find citations to substantiate both or all sides of almost any argument, lawyers as a whole profess belief in the existence of absolute justice, and hold that the purpose of any court case is to find the abstract principle that applies. Such lawyers are not conscious rogues, whose main interest is to "play a game" and win a judgment for their clients at all costs. They have been trained to think in a precise specialized manner that makes it easy for them to rationalize their actions, even though to the layman the results may not seem tantamount to anything resembling common sense or justice.

THE COURT SYSTEM

A knowledge of the court system of the state in which s/he works is essential to the reporter assigned to cover the courts. If s/he moves from one state to another the reporter will discover that even the names of generally similar courts may differ. For instance, what is known as a circuit court in Indiana is called a district court in Nebraska, a superior court in Massachusetts and a supreme court in New York.

The jurisdictions of courts also differ, even between counties of different sizes within the same state. For instance, there may be a separate probate court in one county or state whereas probate matters may be handled by the circuit court or its equivalent in another place. One court may handle both civil and criminal matters or there may be different courts (*common pleas* courts are civil courts; courts of *oyer and terminer* are criminal courts). Similarly, law and equity courts may be separate or combined. The practice is growing of establishing special branches of courts to handle particular kinds of cases, and these branches may be referred to in news stories by their specialized names, such as Renters' Court, Juvenile Court, Traffic Court, Divorce Court. To the reader, it makes little or no difference that such courts really are only branches of a circuit, municipal or county court, but the reporter should know their nature.

It is particularly important that the reporter know which are *courts of record,* that is, ones that keep a permanent record of their proceedings. What happens in *courts not of record* is not privileged and the newspaper that covers them must be careful to avoid committing libel.

Differences in both *substantive law* (defines what is and is not proper behavior) and *adjective law* (defines legal rules and procedures) also provide potential snares for unwary journalists. For instance, in one state grand larceny may be defined as stealing anything worth more than $15 whereas in another state stealing anything worth less than $100 or $1,000 may be petty larceny. Since inferior courts generally can handle petty larceny cases but not grand larceny cases, the same offense committed in one jurisdiction will be tried in one type of court whereas if it happens in another jurisdiction it will be tried in a different type court. In one jurisdiction, a civil action may be considered to have begun with the filing of a complaint, whereupon the reporter is safe in reporting it; in another, however, the action is not considered to exist until the other party has been notified. Similar rules may affect all motions by attorneys and court rulings.

Fortunately, the similarities between the 50 court systems are greater than their differences. Roughly, the typical system is as follows:

Inferior Courts

Inferior courts have the least amount of jurisdiction. Generally they can handle criminal cases involving misdemeanors for which the punishment is a fine only. Their jurisdiction in civil matters generally is limited to cases in which the amount of money does not exceed a few hundred dollars. Among the most common of such courts are the following: *justice of the peace* (townships); *police magistrates* (limited to a city or a section of a city); and *city* and *municipal* courts, which, however, in some larger places may have much greater jurisdiction.

County and Probate Courts

The jurisdiction of a county court depends upon what other state courts exist. Thus, it may be an inferior court or a court of first instance, with unlimited jurisdiction in civil and criminal matters. In other cases, it may operate mostly as a probate or juvenile court or as overseer of the election machinery and county institutions and agencies concerned with poor relief, adoptions and similar matters. Probate courts supervise the disposition of the estates of deceased persons and may also handle adoptions, lunacy hearings, commitments of feeble-minded and insane persons and guardianships for minor and incompetents.

Courts of First Instance

The "backbone" courts are the circuit, superior, district, supreme or whatever they are called. In them, all kinds of civil actions may be brought and, unless there are separate criminal courts, criminal matters as well. In some states, there are separate equity, divorce and other courts, but in a large majority of states the court of original jurisdiction either has separate calendars or branches for different kinds of civil actions. The criminal court may be set up separately or may be a branch of the circuit court. It may handle all kinds of criminal matters, or there may be separate courts for felonies (as the Court of General Sessions in New York). The number of circuit or district courts in a state is dependent upon the state's size and population. A large city or county may be a circuit in itself and may be permitted a large number of judges, the exact number being established by constitution or statute. Outside of thickly populated areas, a circuit may include two, three, ten or more counties and the judges may hold court at different times in different county seats. The number of terms annually, and often their length, are established by constitution or statute.

Appellate Courts

Appellate courts do not try cases originally, but only review decisions reached by courts of jurisdiction in the first instance when defeated parties, dissatisfied with lower-court decisions, appeal to the higher courts. In smaller states, there is likely to be only one appellate court, usually called supreme, ranging in size from three to twenty-three judges, either appointed by the governor with the consent of the state legislature or elected (at large or by divisions). In larger states, there are intermediate courts of review, often called circuit courts of appeal, which, however, seldom if ever receive appeals involving constitutional or other important matters. Some of the decisions of the intermediate court may be appealed a second time to the highest appellate court, either as a matter of right or with that court's permission. The three, five, seven or more members of an intermediate appellate court may be appointed or elected, or they may be regularly elected circuit or district court judges assigned to appellate court duty by the supreme court. Appellate courts do not try cases as lower courts do; they merely pass on the arguments of attorneys in the case as presented to them in written form (*briefs*) and orally (at *hearings*). The practice is growing to permit new evidence not introduced in an original trial of a case to be presented to an appellate court, but this is not yet common practice. All appellate court decisions are by majority vote of the judges; there never is anything resembling a jury trial in an appellate court.

Federal Courts

Although the federal judicial system is growing in importance with the passage by Congress of an increasing number of laws defining as federal crimes certain offenses of which formerly only the states took cognizance, and with the establishment of additional federal court districts, the federal judicial system is outside the worries of the average small-city reporter. Anyone arrested for a federal offense is taken for arraignment to the nearest city in which a federal court is situated.

Despite the activities of the Federal Bureau of Investigation in recent years, kidnaping is not a federal offense because Congress does not believe the Supreme Court would hold constitutional a law declaring it such. The so-called Lindbergh law makes the transportation of a kidnaped person across state lines a federal offense, which, together with the federal law against sending ransom notes through the mails, allows the FBI to enter kidnaping cases.

Similar technicalities permit federal agents to participate in other criminal cases. For instance, automobile theft is not a federal crime but transporting stolen automobiles across state lines is prohibited by the Dyer act; seduction is not a federal offense but transporting a female across state lines for immoral purposes is prohibited by the Mann act. The notorious Al Capone was convicted in a federal court not for gangsterism but for failure to make a faithful federal income tax return. Law enforcement officials and others are prosecuted in federal court not for murder but for depriving a dead person of his civil liberties.

In addition to those suggested, cases commonly handled by the federal courts include (1) frauds against the federal government, including embezzlements from national banks; (2) citizenship and denaturalization cases; (3) violations of federal income tax and other revenue laws; (4) violations of post office regulations, including sending threats and other improper material through the mail, rifling mailboxes and other interferences with the mails; (5) violations of federal statutes such as the food and drug acts, antitrust act, Securities and Exchange act, Interstate Commerce act, narcotics act and Railway Labor act; (6) bankruptcy proceedings.

Officers of the Court

Officers of a circuit court or a court with similar jurisdiction are as follows: (1) The *judge* presides during trials, decides points of law, rules on the admissibility of evidence, instructs juries as to the law, pronounces final judgments and sentences, admits criminal defendants to probation. In fact, the judge *is* the court and even his/her oral orders are authoritative and violations of them constitute contempt of court. (2) The *clerk of court* receives applications and motions made formally for the record, preserves pleadings until used in a formal trial, prepares a court docket and trial calendar with the cooperation of the judge, during a trial records all motions and prepares records and orders of the judge, receives moneys paid to the court as fines, damages and judgments. (3) The *prosecuting attorney* prosecutes all civil and criminal actions in which the state is a party, defends actions brought against the county, examines all persons brought before any judge on habeas corpus, gives legal opinions to any county officer or justice of the peace and, in general, represents the constituency electing him in all legal matters. The prosecuting attorney usually is called *district attorney* or *state's attorney*. (4) The *public defender* is paid by the state to defend persons unable to afford private counsel; where no such officer exists the court often appoints a member of the local bar to serve in that capacity. (5) The *bailiff* acts as sergeant-at-arms, announces the opening of court (''Hear ye, hear ye,'' and so forth), keeps order in the courtroom, calls witnesses, ushers jurors from the jury room and acts as messenger. Many bailiffs really are *sheriff's deputies,* assigned to the courts. In justice of the peace courts the comparable officer is the *constable,* in federal courts it is the *marshal.* (6) The *masters, referees* and *commissioners* act as ''assistant judges'' in civil matters. They hear protracted testimony and make recommendations to the judge who has final authority. Masters act in *chancery* (equity) matters and referees in *common law* matters. Commissioners in state courts are appointed for particular tasks, mostly investigative; federal commissioners are examining magistrates in criminal matters. (7) The *court reporter* is not an elected official but a licensed stenographer authorized to take verbatim testimony and prepare notes in a transcript of evidence called a record. The court reporter may sell copies of his transcript to parties engaged in a trial; in cases of appeal, several copies of a transcript are necessary. (8) A *friend of the court* is a temporarily appointed adviser to the judge who serves during the particular case for which s/he is selected. The Latin translation of friend of the court, *amicus curiae* is used to designate someone, not a party to the litigation, who volunteers to advise regarding it, usually by filing a brief with the court's permission. (9) The *jury commissioners* make up a jury list or panel consisting of the names of a certain number of voters in the territory served by the court for each term of court. In smaller counties, the board of supervisors appoints the commissioners; in larger counties, the county judge does so.

CIVIL LAW

Through codification and/or passage of civil practices acts, many states have simplified both substantive and adjective law. Whereas formerly it was necessary to bring parts of the same action in different courts, in the federal courts and many state courts, it now is possible to ask for both legal and equitable relief in the same action. For instance, you can ask for *damages* (legal relief) and for an *injunction* (equitable relief) to prevent continuation of the cause of injury in the same complaint.

The reporter must be warned, however, that such is not universally true. Several Atlantic seaboard states in particular still adhere to old common law and equity definitions and procedures. In those states one would not bring a simple action to set aside a contract or to force compliance with it or to recover damages because of its breach. Rather, one would bring an action in *covenant* (to recover money damages) or *debt* (to recover specific sums) or *assumpsit* (for damages if the contract was not under seal) or *detinue* (to recover specific chattels). Similarly, a damage suit (tort action) would be one in *trespass* (for money damages) or *trespass on the case* (if injuries were not the direct result of the action complained of) or *detinue* (to recover specific chattels) or *replevin* (a statutory right to recover both property and damages), or *trover* (damages in case the property is lost, destroyed or otherwise incapable of return), or *deceit* (damages for a wrong committed deceitfully).

Starting an Action

In noncode states a common law action is an *action at law* whereas a case in equity is a *suit in equity*. In federal courts and states with civil practices acts, there is just one *civil action*. To start it the *plaintiff* (who brings the action) files a *petition* (also called *declaration* or *complaint* or *statement of claim*) stating clearly the alleged cause for action and the relief the court is asked to grant. Every paragraph of the complaint is numbered and is called a *count*. When one files an *answer*, as must be done within a specified period to avoid the plaintiff's winning a *judgment by default*, the *defendant* (often called *respondent*, with any third parties mentioned as equally guilty being *co-respondents*) must admit or deny each count. In the old days, litigants could continue arguing a case on paper almost indefinitely. Under simplified procedures, the *pleadings*—as all such written arguments are called—are limited to two or three by each party.

By Mary O. Bradley

A Lower Paxton Twp. mall is suing one of its tenants to compel it to be open on Sundays.

The case apparently is the first of its kind in Pennsylvania since the state Supreme Court struck down the ban against Sunday sales 1½-years ago.

The suit was brought by Union Deposit Center Equities Limited, owner of the Union Deposit Mall, against Warren R. and Helen Heidelbaugh, owners of Stretch and Sew Fabrics, a retail fabric store operating in the mall since September 1973.

Heidelbaugh's attorney plans to argue that forcing someone to work Sundays is unconstitutional because it is an illegal restriction on the free expression of religion.

According to documents filed at the Dauphin County Courthouse, the mall's owners want to enforce uniform hours for tenants, including opening on Sundays during the Christmas season.

The suit contends that the Heidelbaughs are violating their lease by not opening on Friday and Saturday evenings and "by not operating their store on the designated Sundays during the Christmas season as required."

[Harrisburg (Pa.) *Evening News*]

A judgment for $50,000 against Lang's Bar, 179 E. 3rd St., and Roger Brown, also for $50,000, was filed last week in the Winona County District Court clerk's office by Steven Meyer.

Meyer claims that on Sept. 11, 1978, he and the defendant, Brown, were at Lang's Bar and at approximately 10 P.M. Brown assaulted Meyer as a direct result of Lang's selling intoxicating liquor while Brown was in an intoxicated condition.

[Winona (Minn.) *Daily News*]

Defending an Action

A defendant who has been properly served by *summons* (law) or *subpoena* (equity) must answer within a prescribed time or at least file an *appearance,* which is an acknowledgment and indication that s/he will answer later. When the answer is filed the reporter scans it for its contents.

To avoid answering, the defendant may enter a *motion to dismiss* the action, contending that the plaintiff has no legal right to bring it. In such a motion, the defendant may challenge the jurisdiction of the court or the sufficiency of the process by which s/he was notified of the beginning of the suit; or, most importantly, s/he may contend that the plaintiff has failed to state a ground for action. Under old procedures, the defendant may enter a *demurrer,* which is a plea that, even if true, the facts alleged do not constitute a cause for action. S/he also may plead that the *statute of limitations,* which sets the time limit within which such action can be brought, has been violated.

To delay or postpone the case, the defendant may resort to dilatory tactics by a *plea in abatement,* which may (1) *challenge the array*—that is, question the procedure by which the panel of veniremen (potential jurors) was selected as the case nears trial; (2) ask a *change of venue,* which is a transfer to another court or branch of the same court on the grounds that judge or jurors are prejudiced; (3) ask a *continuance,* or postponement, for any of a variety of reasons, the merits of which the judge must decide; (4) be a *motion to quash* because the summons was defective.

A special kind of answer is one in *confession and avoidance* wherein the defendant admits the facts but declares s/he acted within his/her legal rights. A *counterclaim* is an answer in which the defendant not only denies liability but contends that the plaintiff is obligated to him/her. Counterclaims are frequent in damage cases involving automobile accidents; each driver blames the other.

When several actions related to the same incident are begun, the court may order that there be a *joinder of parties* or *joinder of causes*. On the other hand, on its own motion or that of one of the parties, the court may grant a *severance* when co-defendants make separate answers. A third party who believes his/her interests are affected by the action may petition the court for permission to file an *intervening* petition to become either a plaintiff or defendant.

To understand what is going on, the reporter should be familiar with a few other types of motions: (1) a *bill of particulars* may be demanded by the defendant if the complaint is unclear or not sufficiently specific; (2) a *bill of discovery* may be asked if the defendant wishes to examine documents or other material in the plaintiff's possession; (3) either party may ask permission to submit an *interrogatory,* or set of questions, to the other to obtain necessary information; (4) scandalous, redundant, irrelevant or otherwise objectionable portions of any pleading may be eliminated if the court grants a *motion to strike*.

Civil Trials

Unless there is a *default judgment* (or *decree*) because of failure of the defendant to answer or a *summary judgment* because the answer is inadequate or a *judgment by confession* because the defendant admits the plaintiff's charges, the issue becomes joined and, upon motion of either party or the court itself, the case is placed on the trial calendar.

Most civil trials today are heard by a judge alone. In fact, it generally is necessary to make a formal request and pay a court fee at the time of filing a complaint or answer to obtain a civil trial by jury. Except for the preliminary step of selecting the jurors, theoretically the procedure is the same. The steps are as follows:

1. Opening statement by plaintiff, through his attorney, of what he expects to prove.
2. Opening statement by defendant. (Often waived.)
3. Direct examination of plaintiff's witnesses.
4. Cross-examination by defendant of plaintiff's witnesses.
5. Direct and cross-examination of defendant's witnesses.
6. Redirect or rebuttal witnesses for plaintiff.
7. Closing statements by both sides, plaintiff speaking first, then the defendant, and, finally, rebuttal by plaintiff.

In actual practice, a hearing before a judge usually is informal. With all of the principals and their attorneys and witnesses clustered about the bench, the judge may interrupt, change the usual order of procedure and take a hand at questioning. Then s/he either takes the case under *advisement* (meaning s/he wants to think it over before deciding) or s/he enters a *judgment* for either plaintiff or defendant, in a law action, or a *decree* if the case is one at equity.

Even if there is a jury, it can only recommend what *damages* are to be assessed against the loser in a law action; the final decision is up to the judge and, upon motion of the losing party or on his/her own initiative, s/he can disregard the jury's findings and enter a *judgment notwithstanding the verdict*.

Damages may be (1) *general,* meaning they are the same as might be expected to compensate anyone for the type of loss proved to have been incurred; (2) *special,* those peculiar to the particular case; (3) *nominal,* which are trifling and for the purpose of moral vindication only; or (4) *exemplary,* assessed in addition to the general or *compensatory* damages, to punish the other party.

> A judgment for $119,358 against the Global Securities & Holding company as stockholders in the Acorn National bank, was ordered by Federal Judge Frick today in favor of Gerald Swayne, receiver of the bank. The amount of the judgment represented a double assessment against the company as holders of 1001 shares of the bank's stock and $9,358 accrued interest.

A civil action may end in a *nonsuit* if at any time the plaintiff fails to continue; such a judgment naturally is for the defendant. So is a *dismissal,* the difference being, however, that in case of a nonsuit the plaintiff may begin another action whereas a dismissal is a final disposition of a case, unless it is a *dismissal without prejudice,* which usually comes upon request of the plaintiff himself. A *consent* judgment is entered when the court approves an out-of-court agreement between the parties. A *declaratory* judgment, obtainable in federal courts and some state courts, is an informatory opinion in advance of any legal action; by means of it the court declares what its decision would be in the event action were brought. Its use prevents much expensive and useless litigation.

An ordinary judgment or decree is either (1) *final,* or (2) *conditional,* which means certain acts (as exchange of property) must be performed before it becomes final, or (3) *nisi* (unless), which means it becomes final after a certain lapse of time if certain forbidden acts do not occur, or (4) *interlocutory,* in which case restrictions on behavior—as against remarriage—are designated.

Enforcing Civil Law

There is no imprisonment for debt in the United States, so a plaintiff may not be much better off after s/he receives a judgment against a defendant than before. By applying for a *writ of execution,* the judgment creditor can force sale of the judgment debtor's property to satisfy the claim, but if the debtor does not possess enough assets to meet the obligation it is often better to allow the judgment to stand as a lien against what s/he does have until the day when it is wise to enforce it. To discover a debtor's assets, a creditor may obtain a court *citation* ordering the debtor to appear in court for questioning by a referee. Failure to comply means that one may be cited for *contempt of court* which, in some cases, may be punished by imprisonment. In such cases, however, the judgment creditor usually has to pay for the debtor's keep. The inmates of "alimony row" in the county jail are contemptuous divorcees.

Either at the beginning of a suit or after a judgment has been obtained, the plaintiff may obtain a *property attachment,* placing the defendant's assets under control of the court to prevent their conversion. A *body attachment* or *execution* is a court order to arrest a principal to prevent his/her untimely departure from its jurisdiction. A *ne exeat* decree is an order forbidding such departure. *Garnishment* proceedings are for the purpose of attaching a debtor's income, usually his/her salary, for the benefit of the creditor.

If a court becomes convinced that a supposedly closed case should be reopened, it can entertain a motion to *reinstate* a case that has been dismissed, to *set aside* a verdict, to *vacate* a judgment or to *review* a decree. A *writ of audita querela* stops execution of a judgment when new evidence is presented. A *writ of supersedeas* orders a court officer to stop execution which has not gone too far.

Many damage suits contain a *malice* count, which means that the alleged injury was committed intentionally or because of gross negligence. If the court upholds the contention, the guilty defendant may be jailed if s/he fails to satisfy the judgment.

The following feature story illustrates how an interpretative court reporter can help inform the public regarding legal and judicial matters.

By Leigh Morris

Winning in the courtroom may be the simplest part of a personal injury suit against the city.

Difficulty arises when the victim attempts to collect.

According to City Controller Otto Loser, the city is now 2½ years behind in payment of judgments over $1,000. Those who are to receive less than $1,000 are paid within a few weeks in accordance with state law.

As a result, the individual with a major claim has two options. He may decide to wait out the 2½ years for his money—money that may be needed to pay medical expenses and support a family.

The other option allows the victim to collect his award shortly after the trial, but this may prove expensive. About 60 percent of those with claims choose this method.

Several law firms in the city will purchase judgments, retaining anywhere up to 15 percent for themselves. Thus, a person who has been awarded $10,000, may only get $8,500. Of course, legal expenses must still be paid out of the remaining amount.

"We are actually rendering people a service by buying their claims," said Jonas Wolfberg, a partner in the law firm of Wolfberg & Kroll, 10 N. Clark St.

"We are providing them with money they need and we are entitled to a profit of 15 percent for the time we must wait for the money. I fear we may have to raise the percentage we retain if the tight money market continues."

The source of the problem is the city's tax collection machinery.

For example, in December of 1969 the city appropriated $4.5 million, the maximum allowed under state law, for the city's judgment fund. That money was to cover judgments awarded before December.

However, the city will not receive any of that tax money until May of 1971, and not until September of that year will all tax monies be collected.

The city has moved to ease part of the problem by selling tax anticipation warrants to raise funds to pay judgments.

The city may sell warrants during the same year the taxes are to be collected, but the warrants may only total 75 percent of the tax yield. [Chicago *Today*]

CIVIL ACTIONS

There are a seemingly interminable number of kinds of actions. Judges and lawyers with years of experience pore over ponderous legal tomes for hours to refresh their memories regarding many of them. The lay reporter cannot be expected to master the intricacies of even an appreciable number of them. If s/he understands the basic differences between the major types of actions and can translate the most frequently used legal language, s/he can get along. There are several good law dictionaries which s/he can consult when s/he "encounters a new one." What follows are a few suggestions concerning some of the kinds of actions that are most newsworthy.

Damage Suits

The news interest usually is in the incident giving rise to the action: an automobile accident, a surgeon's error and so forth. If so, perhaps the paper carried a story at the time, which means the account of the filing of the complaint should contain a careful tie-back. The reporter should get names and addresses of principals; the plaintiff's version of exactly what happened, all charges being carefully accredited to the complaint; the comments of the defendant on the charges; the amount of money demanded. And he/she should find out if there is a malice count.

Howard Bates filed a $30,000 damage suit in Lanchester District Court Wednesday in connection with a fall he incurred while loading furniture belonging to the defendant, Harold Bride.

Bates who operates a long-distance moving firm, alleges that on Aug. 3, 1980 while in the process of loading the van to move Bride from Littleton, Colo., to Lincoln, he requested Bride to get him a ladder so he could inspect the load on top of the van.

He contends that the defendant was negligent in setting up the ladder and, as a result, it collapsed and he suffered a fractured wrist.

He alleges 20% permanent partial disability.

Strong warning against this type of reporting was included in a letter from Thomas F. Driscoll, assistant managing editor of the Peoria *Journal Star:*

I have been trying for several years to try to make a dent in the journalistic practice of making a great to-do over damage suits in which the plaintiff seeks sizeable damages. Editors are suckers for a story like this, and lawyers have found that they are virtually certain of getting a story published if they ask for absurdly high dollar damages. You can hardly avoid picking up any paper, any day, in any city without finding a story that so-and-so filed a $9 million damage suit, or a $90 million suit, or $900 million, or $9 billion. Of course, the plaintiff can ask for whatever amount he wants, in punitive damages at least, so the amount sought really is meaningless. But if the lawyer adds enough zeros, even if the suit makes the most outrageously absurd or trivial allegations, he can be sure that an editor will give it big play. The amount of damages sought has come to be an adjective modifying "damage suit"—as in, "a $5.5 million damage suit"—as though that were the price tag—as in, "a $5,000 Buick." . . . Ridiculous.

When Driscoll complained to the Associated Press for playing up a so-called $3 billion suit, the answer read in part: "All I would have to do is throw the story in the kill drawer and within minutes we'd get 'Need matcher to NY Times special on $3 billion suit filed over bank credit cards'."

Libel

Newspapers are reluctant to give much publicity to libel suits against other publications so as not to encourage similar actions against themselves. Such a policy naturally cannot apply at all times. Here is the way the Denver *Post* handled both the beginning and the end of a libel suit against itself:

Stanley Furs, Inc., 1600 E. Colfax Ave., and Stanley Calkins, president of the firm, filed libel suits Wednesday morning against the Denver Post and The Rocky Mountain News.

In the complaints filed in Denver District Court, damages are being sought in behalf of Calkins and the firm as a result of articles published April 13 in the two newspapers.

The complaints charge the articles about the firm in a U.S. District Court action were "an unfair, false and malicious account" of the court proceedings.

The stories exposed Calkins and his firm to "public wrath, hatred and ridicule and deprived the business of the benefits of public confidence," the complaints charged. In the suit against The Post, damages of $550,000 are sought in behalf of the firm and an additional $500,000 is sought in behalf of Calkins.

The suit against the News asks for $1.3 million in damages in behalf of Calkins.

A $1 million libel suit brought against The Denver Post by Stanley Furs, Inc., was dismissed Thursday in Denver District Court.

Judge Zita Weinshienk granted the motion to dismiss at the conclusion of presentation of evidence at a three-day trial. The dismissal motion was made by the newspaper's attorneys, Richard Hall and Thomas Kelley.

The judge held that the evidence had failed to meet the tests needed for proof of libel under Colorado law.

The required standards of evidence, the judge explained, must show the statements were known to be false or printed with reckless disregard as to whether they were true or not.

"There was not sufficient evidence to take the case to the jury on these points," the judge said.

The libel suit was filed by Stanley Calkins, president of the firm, as the result of an April 1973 article. The story discussed a U.S. District Court consent judgment against Calkins and his firm.

A similar lawsuit seeking $2.3 million was filed by Stanley Furs against the Rocky Mountain News as a result of that newspaper's story on the same judgment. A June trial is scheduled in that case.

J. Richard Nathan, the Stanley attorney, said Friday no decision had been made yet on whether the case would be appealed.

Driscoll warns against carelessness in reporting the filing of damage suits, pointing out that the contents of a complaint may not be privileged at the time it is filed and that newspapers thereby publish stories at their own risk. "Some day," he comments, "somebody is going to be sorry for it. Even if not libelous, I think the press ought to be careful about letting people make scurrilous charges against others just because they make them in the form of a lawsuit."

Divorce

Distinguish between *divorce* and *annulment*, and between *separate maintenance* and *alimony*. What are the grounds (desertion, cruelty and so forth)? Watch out for libel when reporting specific incidents cited as grievances (beatings, criminal behavior). The reporter should obtain names and addresses of both principals; dates of marriage and of separation; names and ages of children and what the bill requests regarding them; suggested disposition of property; whether alimony is requested; whether wife asks court to authorize use of her maiden name. When a case comes to hearing, testimony, of course, can be reported; state whether defendant contests case or allows decree to be obtained by default. States are slowly but steadily passing no-fault divorce laws, making the decree obtainable by mutual agreement without one party's having to state a case against the other.

Two suits for divorce were filed in circuit court Thursday. Cruelty is charged in both cases.

Sandra Neisen alleged James Neisen struck her several times. They were married Sept. 30, 1961, and separated Tuesday. She asked the court to order a division of the property in the residence at 26 South Granview, farm machinery and a checking account. She asked for the custody of three children and that a car be given to her.

Rochelle Williams alleged James N. Williams struck her and ordered her to leave the house and not return. They were married Sept. 13, 1958, and separated in March, 1965. She asked that she be given her equity in real estate in New Jersey. [Quincy (Ill.) *Herald-Whig*]

Foreclosures

A person who defaults in payments on a mortgage stands to lose the property through foreclosure proceedings. In most states, however, s/he has an *equity of redemption*—a period of time in which to pay up, even though a court has awarded the property to the mortgage holder.

Evictions

The Renters' Court always is a fertile source for human interest stories. The legal name for actions to evict is *forcible entry and detainer*. During housing shortages, renters' courts are crowded. The reporter does well to examine the statutes of the state for sections pertaining to the rights of landlords to evict or refuse to rent to families with children or pets. S/he also should read up on statutes and court decisions mostly outlawing restrictive covenants whereby property owners agreed not to sell or lease to Negroes, Jews or members of other minority groups or otherwise restrict the use of property.

Inadequate inspection and inability, under the statutes, of judges to assess heavy penalties mean that large city slumlords consider this court as only a minor nuisance. Reporters are handicapped by protective secrecy laws covering trusts to determine who the real culprits are when outrageous housing conditions are exposed. Urban renewal projects have caused urban center slum areas to increase and worsen as real estate interests use residential land areas for more lucrative purposes and friendly public officials offer little or no interference. Tearjerking, albeit accurate, stories can be written about unfeeling landlords and others who exploit poor and ignorant tenants. One device is to purchase tax delinquent bills so as to make evictions legal. Seldom, however, is the greedy action considered morally commendable.

Especially in Florida and Illinois where secret land trusts are allowed to conceal ownership, arson is suspected when abandoned or dilapidated buildings are destroyed by fire.

Despite supposedly protective legislation, blockbusting and redlining persist. The former is the practice of enabling a single Negro family to move into a white neighborhood by making the purchase price extremely low. Then the remaining white property owners are panicked into selling their property at low prices after which it is resold to Negroes at a considerable profit.

Redlining is making geographical boundaries within which banks and other lending institutions do not make loans for building construction or repairs, in the belief that the neighborhood is deteriorating. Residents who continue to deposit money in such institutions complain because their deposits are used for loans outside the area and are a major factor in bringing about deterioration.

Condemnation Suits

When a new street or highway or public building is planned, the proper government agency uses its right of *eminent domain* to purchase—at a fair price—any privately owned land needed for the improvement. Property owners often resist such taking of their property or hold out for higher compensation.

Public clamor may cause a change in official plans, as happened when property owners in Connecticut objected to the headquarters of the United Nations being established there. Scandals occur when some public officals use prior knowledge of governmental plans to purchase certain property. They purchase it themselves and consequently reap a profit when its value increases. The insider may not technically be a part of the spending agency but such behavior obviously is not in the public interest.

Receiverships

Creditors or stockholders of a corporation or individuals in financial difficulties may apply to an equity court for appointment of a receiver to conserve assets and rescue the business. A chancery receivership, intended to put a going concern back on its feet, must be distinguished from a receiver in bankruptcy, who is in charge of liquidating a defunct institution. Many banks, hotels, transportation companies and others continue operating under receiverships for years. Often newspapers uncover scandals regarding political favoritism in appointment of receivers or companies with which they do business. Reporters should watch the periodic reports that receivers must make to the courts appointing them.

Bankruptcy

A financial failure may file a *voluntary petition* in bankruptcy, or his creditors may file an *involuntary petition* in his case. The reporter should examine the inventory filed with the petition, to obtain total assets; total liabilities; nature of the assets (stocks, real estate, controlling interest in other companies, etc.); nature of liabilities; clues as to reasons for failure. Bankruptcy matters are handled by the federal courts. Every petition is referred to a *referee in bankruptcy,* a permanent court officer; the *trustee* is elected by the creditors and, if approved by the court, takes over the task of liquidating the assets and distributing them on a pro rata basis. Instead of dissolving a business, a company may undergo *reorganization* under a court-approved plan. Usually, some creditors are "frozen out" when such happens, and the legal jockeying between them to avoid that happening is newsworthy when the company is important. Since every action of a trustee must be approved by the court, the reporter can keep close to the situation.

Since 1960 there has been a phenomenally steady increase in personal bankruptcy petitions, about 20 times as many as in the '40s. The Consumer Bankruptcy Committee of the American Bar Association blames abuses of credit by both recipients and grantors and would tighten the laws to make such petitions more difficult to file. In this area, as in so many others, the interpretative reporter can find valuable in-depth situation and trend stories. What follows is about one-third of an excellent explanatory article in this area.

By Robert Enstad

The payoff plan was simple enough. For $84.21 a week he could pay off his creditors, maintain his standard of living, and still hold his head high as a man who pays his bills.

His financial crunch had come about easily enough. An overwhelming craving for material goods and merchants who extended him credit had pinched his wallet.

Now the man was before Richard L. Merrick, a federal bankruptcy judge in Chicago. Merrick looked at the repayment plan and then looked down from the bench at the debtor.

''I'm familiar with your plan and I think you will be able to complete it all right,'' the judge said.

With those few words from the judge, the man was on his way, not as an adjudicated deadbeat, but as a man given another chance to make ends meet. In bankruptcy parlance, the man had undertaken a ''Chapter 13'' reorganization of his debts.

Going into debt is becoming more common, less of a social stigma.

''Indebtedness has grown like a cancer,'' says Leonard Gesas, a veteran Chicago bankruptcy lawyer. ''It is hard to find a family that has not been exposed to it.''

The ominous signs of a consuming public that is charging more and saving less are all over. For example:

- Consumer debt soared a record $4.45 billion in September. This year's growth in consumer debt is expected to be about 16 per cent.
- Bankruptcy filings in U.S. District Court in Chicago are expected to be up 20 per cent this year. The total of about 12,000 cases will be the highest number in recent years. Bankruptcy courts in other metropolitan areas report the same upward trend.
- For the third quarter of this year, consumers put only 4.1 per cent of their disposal income into savings, the lowest level in years. In September, withdrawals from savings accounts exceeded deposits by $200 million.

Why the changes in the way people manage their money? . . .

The rising consumer debt, which is rapidly approaching $400 billion [not counting home mortgages] has triggered concern about whether Americans are assuming more bills than they can handle. . .

However, for a small minority the urge to ''pay with plastic'' and to say ''charge it'' leads to bankruptcy court. In the Chicago area, the chances of being in that court this year are one in 666.

A year ago, the odds were one in 800.

Part of the increase in bankruptcy filings this year has been attributed to the new Chapter 13 federal bankruptcy law. The law, which is debtor-oriented, enables the debtor and his lawyer to devise, with court approval, a plan for paying back the debts.

If all goes well, the debtor avoids liquidation of his assets and an adjudication of bankruptcy.

Chapter 13 filings are up 10 per cent in Chicago, according to court records.

''The debtors run the gamut from the very poor to very rich,'' says Craig Phelps, the Chapter 13 trustee in the bankruptcy court. . . [Chicago *Tribune*]

Injunctions

Distinguish between a *preliminary restraining order,* which is issued by a judge on ex parte evidence only and without notice, and *temporary* and *permanent injunctions.* The orthodox procedure is for the court to issue a temporary order to the defendant to appear in court and "show cause" why it should not become permanent. In the meantime, the alleged offensive conduct must cease. Injunctions are used to prohibit government agencies and officials from exceeding their authority; to test the constitutionality of a law; to restrain picketing and other activities by labor unions; to restrain corporations from acts injurious to stock- or bond-holders; to compel persons to keep the peace and not interfere with the civil liberties and other rights of others; to stop and prevent nuisances; and for other purposes.

By Frank Clifford

U.S. Circuit Court of Appeals Judge Irving L. Goldberg temporarily stopped FBI agents Tuesday from seizing records of Maxwell Construction Co., a local firm under federal investigation for its multimillion dollar business dealings with the Dallas Independent School District.

Tuesday afternoon, during a seesaw struggle between government lawyers and attorneys for Maxwell to gain control of the records, U.S. District Judge Sarah T. Hughes ruled that the records must be turned over to the government and authorized FBI agents to proceed immediately to the Maxwell offices at 3722 Bowser. . . .

[Dallas *Times-Herald*]

By Sharon Hanks

The battle between local minority contractors and the city over construction of the $25 million Convention-Entertainment Center resumed Wednesday in federal court.

Once an affidavit from a Maryland congressman arrives, U.S. District Court Judge Douglas Hillman is expected to act on a request for a temporary restraining order to halt the downtown construction.

Local attorney William Jackson told Hillman Wednesday the affidavit will be the final evidence for the minority contractors. The affidavit is from U.S. Rep. Parrin Mitchell, who drafted the bill governing minority requirements for federal grants.

The $50-million class action suit was filed Sept. 28 against the City of Grand Rapids, the City-Kent County Joint Building Authority and Owen-Ames-Kimball Co., the project's general contractor. . . .

[Grand Rapids (Mich.) *Press*]

Contracts

There follows a typical complaint:

STATE OF ILLINOIS }
COUNTY OF COOK } SS

IN THE SUPERIOR COURT OF COOK COUNTY

IRIS GARDNER,
Plaintiff
—VS.—
CHARLES W. WRIGLEY,
Defendant

NO. 42 s 10542

COMPLAINT AT LAW FOR
BREACH OF CONTRACT

Now comes IRIS GARDNER, plaintiff in the above entitled cause, and complains of the defendant, CHARLES W. WRIGLEY, as follows:

1. That the plaintiff was, on the 15th day of October A.D. 1937 temporarily sojourning in the City of Chicago, County of Cook and State of Illinois; and, on the date aforesaid, she was about to depart from the said city, county and state, and return to her domiciliary city and state, to-wit: St. Louis, Missouri.

2. The plaintiff had a long social acquaintance and friendship with the defendant, CHARLES W. WRIGLEY, prior to October 15, A.D. 1937, when, on the date, aforesaid, she, the plaintiff, at the special instance and request of the defendant, CHARLES W. WRIGLEY, met the defendant, CHARLES W. WRIGLEY, in his offices, located at 400 North Michigan Avenue, in the City of Chicago, County of Cook and State of Illinois, and that at the place and on the date aforesaid, plaintiff entered into a verbal agreement with the defendant, CHARLES W. WRIGLEY, the substance of which agreement is hereinafter verbatim alleged.

3. That the defendant, CHARLES W. WRIGLEY, was then, and is now, engaged in the advertising business, and was then, and is now, reputed to have considerable material wealth.

4. That the plaintiff was then, and is now a woman possessed of pulchritude, charm, and numerous other attributes and qualities to enchant, charm, and grace any person; or, in fact, any social circle.

5. That the defendant, CHARLES W. WRIGLEY, met the plaintiff, at the place and on the date aforesaid, at his special instance and request, and then and there the defendant, CHARLES W. WRIGLEY, was expressly charmed and enchanted by the plaintiff, because of plaintiff's charm, graciousness, and other womanly qualities and attributes and thereupon the defendant, CHARLES W. WRIGLEY, informed plaintiff that she was the person for whom he had been searching to assist him, socially and in his business. Whereupon, the parties entered into a verbal agreement, which, in words, figures and substance, is as follows:

a. The defendant, CHARLES W. WRIGLEY, verbally agreed with the plaintiff to pay plaintiff the sum of One Thousand Dollars ($1,000) per month, either in cash, or by letters of credit, or in any other mode or manner the plaintiff might see fit provided the said sum was paid in full to the plaintiff before the expiration of each and every month, commencing on the 1st day of November, A.D. 1937, during the rest of her natural life; and the defendant, CHARLES W. WRIGLEY, further agreed, in order to protect plaintiff, in the event of predeceased plaintiff, to create a trust in the sum of Two Hundred and Fifty Thousand Dollars ($250,000.00), said trust to be evidenced by a trust agreement, the provisions of which trust agreement were to provide that the plaintiff would be entitled to receive the proceeds, rents, profits, and emoluments accruing therefrom, during the plaintiff's natural life.

b. That in consideration of the said verbal agreement, the plaintiff was to cancel her then imminent departure, as aforesaid from the City of Chicago, County of

Cook and State of Illinois; and it was further agreed that the plaintiff should reside and domicile continuously in the City of Chicago, County of Cook and State of Illinois, during the natural life of the defendant, CHARLES W. WRIGLEY, in order to assist the defendant, CHARLES W. WRIGLEY, in his social activities, as the defendant might, from time to time, direct, which social activities, according to the defendant, CHARLES W. WRIGLEY, could be efficaciously performed only by the plaintiff, or by some other member of the fair sex with abilities co-equal to those possessed by the plaintiff.

c. That in pursuance of said verbal agreement, the plaintiff remained, resided and domiciled, and continues to remain, reside and domicile, in the City of Chicago, County of Cook and State of Illinois; that the defendant, CHARLES W. WRIGLEY, in pursuance of the terms of said verbal agreement, obtained or rented an apartment on behalf of the plaintiff, at the St. Clair Hotel, and paid plaintiff (in cash or by check, or paid the expenditures of the plaintiff directly to plaintiff's creditors) the stipulated consideration thereof to wit: One Thousand Dollars ($1,000.00) per month, including the rental for said apartment; and that the defendant, CHARLES W. WRIGLEY, continued to comply with the terms of said agreement until on or about the 30th day of May, A.D. 1943, on which date the defendant, CHARLES W. WRIGLEY, expressly repudiated the same, verbally informing and advising plaintiff that he would no longer continue payment thereof, in view of his reduced financial status.

6. That in pursuance of the terms of said verbal agreement, the plaintiff heretofore has exerted much effort, and expended her youth, grace and charm, to the end of ameliorating defendant's social as well as esthetic, well-being.

7. That at the time the aforesaid agreement was entered into defendant was approximately twenty (20) years plaintiff's senior.

8. That the plaintiff has performed each and every condition of her contract with the defendant, CHARLES W. WRIGLEY, whether precedent or subsequent, and she is not in default thereof.

9. That the defendant, CHARLES W. WRIGLEY, has wilfully and maliciously, and without any just cause, but merely whimsically, breached the provisions of said verbal agreement.

10. That the plaintiff has sustained damages, by reason of the breach of said agreement by the defendant, CHARLES W. WRIGLEY, in the sum of Five Hundred Thousand Dollars ($500,000.00) and costs.

This is how the Chicago *Sun* handled this news:

Suit for $500,000 charging breach of contract, was filed in Superior Court yesterday against Charles W. Wrigley, 71, brother of the late William Wrigley Jr., chewing-gum magnate, by a woman who described herself as possessing "pulchritude, charm, and manner."

She is identified in the bill as Mrs. Iris Gardner, 41, of the St. Clair Hotel.

Her complaint, according to the bill, alleges that Wrigley is not paying her $1,000 a month. He agreed to do this back in 1937, she said, and kept up the payments for six years before quitting.

WRIGLEY INDIGNANT

Wrigley, head of an outdoor advertising firm, with offices at 400 N. Michigan av., indignantly denied the entire alleged transaction. Reached at his home, Canterbury ct., Wilmette, he said:

''It's an outrage to file a suit like that. The lady's husband worked for me 15 years ago.

''She never worked for me. As to the payments of $1,000 a month, why, that's crazy! Where would I get the money? She started after me just after Charlie Chaplin's trouble.''

ASSERTS TRUST FUND PLEDGED

According to the bill, Wrigley, uncle of Philip K. Wrigley, owner of the Chicago Cubs, agreed to pay Mrs. Gardner $1,000 a month for life and, if he died first, leave a $250,000 trust fund to provide the income.

In return, the bill continued, Mrs. Gardner was to ''assist him socially and in his business.'' The agreement, Mrs. Gardner said, was verbal.

Note that (1) the reporter obtained information other than that contained in the complaint, and (2) he exercised great care in ascribing every fact based on the complaint to the complaint itself, by means of such phrases as ''according to the bill'' and ''the bill continued.'' It is absolutely necessary never to allow any statement in a story based on a legal document to stand by itself, even at the risk of boring repetition of references.

EXTRAORDINARY REMEDIES

The equitable relief provided by an injunction originated as an extraordinary remedy, but has become so common it no longer is extraordinary. Almost the same is true of *habeas corpus,* whereby a jailer is required to produce a prisoner in court to answer charges against him. Dating from Magna Charta, it is one of the great Anglo-Saxon democratic protections.

Other so-called extraordinary remedies follow.

Prohibition

Prohibition is a writ issued by a superior court to one of inferior jurisdiction commanding it to desist in handling any matter beyond its authority to consider.

Certiorari

Certiorari also is an inquiry into the behavior of a lower court after it has taken some action. Thus, it usually operates as an appeal, to bring about a review of the lower court's action in the higher court. In granting a writ of certiorari or *writ of review,* as it also is called, however, the higher court merely agrees to look into the matter. It may return the case later.

Mandamus

A *writ of mandamus* is directed by a higher court to administrative officers, corporations or an inferior court ordering some action required by law. It does not specify what the action must be—as in a case where a required appointment is overdue—but it does demand that some action be taken.

Quo Warranto

By a *quo warranto writ,* a higher court inquires into the right of a public official to hold office or of a corporation to exercise a franchise.

PROBATE PROCEEDINGS

When a person dies, the state supervises payment of his/her debts and distribution of his/her property. If s/he dies *testate* (that is, if s/he leaves a will), unless someone can prove that the contrary should be done, the court sees that its provisions are carried out. It usually appoints the *executor* named in the will to supervise settling the estate; that official, often a relative of the deceased, posts bond for about one-and-a-half times the estimated value of the estate and receives a commission when the work is done. If there is no will (deceased died *intestate*) the court appoints an *administrator*. In many states there now are public administrators. Either executor or administrator receives *letters testamentary* to authorize the work, which includes notification of beneficiaries named in a will or legal heirs if there is no will, advertising for bills against the estate, collecting money due the estate, preparing an inventory of the estate and so forth.

Filing a Will

The first step in probate proceedings is the filing of the will by whoever has it in custody or finds it. Reporters watch for such filings of wills of prominent persons recently deceased. In their case, it is news whether the estate is large or small. As a matter of fact, it usually is difficult or impossible to determine an estate's size from the will itself; it is not known with certainty until an appraisal is made months later. The first public information may come with the filing of an inheritance tax return.

> The estate of Henry B. Ritter, Milltown construction contractor, totaled $3,062,182, according to an inheritance tax return filed Thursday with the Vernon County clerk.
>
> Ritter, uncle of former county treasurer Herbert C. Ritter, died Dec. 19, at the age of 77. He lived at 345 W. Fullerton.
>
> The estate was left in trust to the widow, Lillian, with a provision that upon her death one-half of it to go to their children, Mrs. Marjorie O'Neil of 706 S. Sheridan, Barton, and Henry Jr., of 12 E. Scott.
>
> The federal tax on the estate was $358,659 and the state levy, $117,328.

An ingenious reporter in some cases can estimate value by determining the market value of securities or the assessor's valuations of real estate and by similar investigation. Frequently, the nature of an estate is newsworthy as a person may be revealed to be the owner of property that he was not known to possess. From the will, the beneficiaries can be determined, and often a will contains surprises. The first news story should mention when and where the will was drawn and possibly the witnesses. In small places, virtually every will is newsworthy; in larger places, only those of important persons or involving large estates receive mention.

Admitting to Probate

The reporter must not confuse filing a will and admitting a will to probate, which is done by court order upon petition of the executor or someone else. Before such a petition is granted it must be proved to be genuine and there also must be proof of heirship; usually referees supervise such routine matters. If anything happens to disturb the routine, it probably is newsworthy.

> The will of Richard W. Young, founder and chairman of the board of the Young corporation, who died March 1, at the age of 70, was admitted to probate today by County Judge Thomas Sullivan.
>
> The executors are Thomas B. Young and R. L. Waters. Waters declined to place an estimate on the size of the estate, but it is generally understood to be in the millions.
>
> SETS UP TRUST FUND
>
> The will sets up a trust fund on behalf of 11 relatives of the industrialist. The division is as follows:
>
> One-sixth of the estate to Thomas B. Young, now president of the Young corporation, a nephew. One-eighth to Frank Young, a nephew, One-eighth to Ruth Young Stoddard, a niece.
>
> One-twelfth to Louise R. White, a niece. One-twelfth to Margaret Rolnick, a niece. One-twelfth to Nancy Young, a niece. One-twelfth to Mary Sheridan, a niece. One-twelfth to Robert Carpenter, a nephew. One-twelfth to Richard Sheridan, a nephew.
>
> One-twenty-fourth to Patricia Young, a grand-niece and one-twenty-fourth to Kent Young, a grand-nephew.
>
> MAY BE LIQUIDATED
>
> The will provides that the Young Investment company, established by Young, may be liquidated within 12 months of his death and the assets distributed to the stockholders, this with the approval of the executors. It also provides that the entire estate shall be liquidated within 20 years and may be liquidated, if the executors approve, in ten years.

Contesting a Will

By law an interval that varies from three months to two years must elapse between the time a will is admitted to probate and a *final accounting*. During that period, suit may be brought to break the will, perhaps by a disgruntled relative who was disinherited. Common charges are that the deceased was unduly influenced when he made the will, or was not in full possession of his mental faculties. Sometimes it is charged that the will filed was not the most recent. Such suits usually are filed in courts other than that handling routine probate matters.

> Suit to contest the will of Mrs. Margaret W. Winchester, widow of Charles B. Winchester, an official of Scott & Co., whereby she left most of $100,000 to friends, was filed in Circuit Court yesterday by six relatives, including three sisters and a brother. Mrs. Winchester plunged to her death from a room in the Bacon House last July 27 at the age of 68.
>
> The suit charges she was "eccentric and peculiar" and "susceptible to influence and blandishments," and that undue influence was put upon her in making the will. Attorney G. A. Yates, co-executor under the will, who was left a $20,000 bequest, was her close financial adviser, and Attorney Allan E. Mack, also left $20,000, was his associate, the bill points out.

RULES OF EVIDENCE

To "feel at home," as s/he should whenever s/he steps into any courtroom, a reporter must understand the fundamental rules of evidence.

Nature of Evidence

Most evidence is in the form of testimony by witnesses. Other forms of evidence include objects and written material introduced as exhibits. Together they constitute the *proof* whereby it is intended to influence the court's decision. All evidence must be (1) *material*—have a direct relation to the case; (2) *relevant*—pertinent; and (3) *competent*—authoritative. Otherwise, the court will uphold an *objection* to its introduction.

Burden of Proof

In a civil action it is *preponderance of evidence* that counts; in criminal cases, the state must prove guilt *beyond any reasonable doubt.* At all times, the burden of proof rests with the side that must refute evidence that if allowed to stand, would be injurious to it.

Presumptions

The law presumes that any situation known to exist at one time continues to exist unless proof to the contrary is provided. Thus good character and impeccable behavior on the part of all citizens are presumed until disproved.

Judicial Notice

Common knowledge—such as the organization of government, size and location of cities and countries, business practices and the like—need not be proved in court. Instead, the court "takes notice" of them unless challenged for doing so.

Qualifications of Witnesses

Children, wives, husbands, insane persons, felons, dependents, interested lawyers and other parties once were barred from testifying. Today, the restrictions are much lighter. Almost anyone competent at the time of trial or hearing can be a witness; the credibility to be attached to the testimony is a different matter.

Privilege

The Fifth Amendment to the Constitution of the United States protects anyone from being compelled to testify against oneself. In actual practice, refusal to testify because to do so might incriminate oneself often is a "dodge." No lawyer can be compelled to reveal what a client has told him/her in confidence. Similar protection is afforded physicians and clergymen in many cases and, in several states, newspapermen.

Leading Questions

Witnesses tell their stories in response to questions by attorneys. Those questions cannot be so worded as to suggest the answers desired.

Hearsay Evidence

A witness can testify only to that of which s/he has firsthand knowledge. S/he cannot draw inferences from the facts. Exceptions to the rule include dying declarations, spontaneous declarations, confessions and admissions against one's interest.

Opinion Evidence

Anyone is an authority on matters that s/he has witnessed or that are within the knowledge of an ordinary person. Experts must be qualified before their testimony is considered credible. An expert's opinion often is obtained by means of a *hypothetical question* in which a situation comparable to that at issue is described.

Real Evidence

Clothing, weapons and objects of all sorts are introduced as exhibits. So are models and photographs.

Circumstantial Evidence

Correct inferences often can be drawn from evidence pertaining to a person's behavior both before and after a crime is committed and from his/her known capacities and predilections. A great deal of the evidence in both civil and criminal cases is circumstantial rather than eyewitness accounts.

Best Evidence

Copies of documents are admissible only when there is proof that originals are unavailable. In every case, the court demands the best possible evidence regarding any point.

APPEALS

Since the trial judge passes on motions for new trials, not many are granted. Only in rare cases, however, does a judge refuse to grant a dissatisfied party the right to take his case to the appellate court. In criminal matters, no appeal is possible by the state in the event of acquittal, but a convicted defendant can appeal; and in civil matters either side can do so.

The distinction between *appeal* (of civil law origin) and *writ of error* (of common law origin) is virtually nonexistent today. Where it exists, it means that in the former instance a case is removed entirely from the lower to the higher court, which then can review both the law and the evidence; a writ of error, by contrast, is an original proceeding, not a continuation of that in the lower court.

Appeals are either *as of right* or *by permission* of the upper court as the statutes designate. Common grounds on which an appeal can be made are (1) irregularity of the submission of evidence, (2) new evidence discovered since the trial ended, (3) misconduct of the jury, (4) lack of jurisdiction of the court, (5) an error by the judge in instructing the jury, (6) incompetent witnesses, (7) excessive damages allowed (in civil cases) and (8) influencing or packing of the jury by the adverse party.

A bill of exceptions (also called *statement of the case* or *certificate of reasonable doubt*) must set forth clearly and completely the grounds on which appeal is taken. It may be accompanied by a *brief* in which the details are made more elaborate and the case as a whole summarized although the trend is toward simplification of procedure so that only one document is necessary. Certified copies of *transcripts* and *abstracts* of lower court records also are submitted.

The party taking the appeal is known as the *appellant* or *plaintiff in error* and the other party (usually the winner in the lower court) as the *appellee or defendant in error*. It is good practice for a reporter always to ask a defeated party in an important case whether s/he intends to appeal. Otherwise, s/he first learns of such action by a *notice of appeal* filed in the appellate court. Today, such notice acts as an automatic *stay of proceedings* or *supersedeas* to hold up execution of any lower court judgment or sentence. In some jurisdictions, however, it is necessary to petition for such writs.

If the higher court's permission is necessary, whatever the court decides regarding a petition is news. If it agrees to review a case, it sets a date for *oral arguments* by attorneys. Then it takes the case *under advisement*. Every justice studies the case independently before the court meets to discuss it. After a vote is taken, the chief justice assigns one justice to prepare the *majority opinion* supporting the court's *decision*. Other members may prepare *concurring opinions* or *dissenting opinions*. Any part of a decision that deals with background not directly pertinent to the case at hand is called *obiter dictum;* it explains the mental processes by which the justices formed their opinions.

By its decision, the appellate court *upholds* or *reverses* or *modifies* the lower court's decision. A *mandate* is an order to a lower court to take any kind of action, and the upper court *remands* the case to the lower so that it can act.

Only an experienced reporter is likely to be assigned to cover appellate court proceedings. By the time s/he has mastered the art of handling lower court news, s/he will be thoroughly qualified to do so.

A panel of three judges is pondering a case which will affect 1,600 mass tax appeals in Shelby County and could affect the financial solvency of the county government and all its agencies and schools.

The Fifth Appellate Court at Mount Vernon Wednesday heard oral arguments in the tax appeals case filed by the state Attorney General's office in a move to defend the decision by the state Tax Appeals Board that county tax assessments and tax bills were illegal because of a late publication date.

Representatives of the county Taxpayers Assn. apparently are unhappy because they were not notified of the hearing in the case which directly affects their individual tax appeals.

Wednesday's oral arguments represent the last step in the court, before a written decision is to be handed down by the three judges. [Shelbyville (Ill.) *Daily News*]

The U.S. Supreme court Tuesday, Oct. 30 heard arguments on an appeal by the village of Schaumburg of a lower court ruling concerning the constitutionality of its solicitation ordinance.

Outcome of the appeal is expected to set a precedent for local solicitation ordinances across the country and the way charitable organizations solicit their funds.

A lower district court had ruled that the village violated the first amendment free-speech rights of groups by denying them a solicitation permit unless they can prove that 75% of their receipts were used for charitable purposes.

The case, Village of Schaumburg vs. the Citizens for A Better Environment (CBE) was brought by a group in 1976 which claimed their first amendment rights of free speech were violated when they were denied a solicitation permit after refusing to submit to a certified audit to prove that 75% of the collected contributions went for charitable purposes. [Lerner-Voice Newspapers]

A state Court of Appeal has overturned a lower court ruling dismissing charges against a Jewish activist accused of soliciting the murder or maiming of American Nazis. The decision has the effect of reinstating the charges.

A Superior Court judge had earlier dismissed the charges against Irv Rubin, West Coast director of the Jewish Defense League, saying the comments were protected by the First Amendment.

Rubin had waved five $100 bills in the air at a Los Angeles news conference last year and offered them to anyone who "kills, maims or seriously injures a member of the American Nazi Party."

Last January, Superior Court Judge Carlos Velarde dismissed the charges, saying Rubin's statement was permissible under constitutional guarantees of free speech.

The California Court of Appeal ruled Monday, however, that Rubin's offer was not constitutionally protected. [San Francisco *Chronicle*]

To consent to the right of judges to punish criticism of their past ineptitudes would be to concur in the establishment of a judicial oligarchy such as has not afflicted us heretofore.

—Editorial, Baltimore *Sun*.

There are times when judges need some plain speaking to, and upon such occasions an alert, fearless, and vigorous press is a public godsend.

—Editorial, Wheeling (W. Va.) *News*

16

POLITICS, ELECTIONS

A. Political Philosophy
B. Political Public Opinion
C. Political Organization
   1. Local
   2. Precinct, Ward
   3. County
   4. State, National
D. Precampaign Activities
   1. Petitions
   2. Registration
   3. Primaries
   4. Conventions
E. Campaigns
   1. Candidates
   2. Issues
   3. Tactics
   4. Speeches
   5. Records
   6. Roorbacks
   7. Polls
   8. Predictions
F. Elections
   1. Election Day
   2. Results
   3. Post-Mortems

One beneficial consequence of the disappearance of local competition has been an increasing trend toward political independence on the part of surviving newspapers. It is both good business and in the public interest that the news be presented accurately, objectively, impartially and completely. Conscious of past criticisms for bias during campaigns, most newspapers now attempt to give rival candidates equal treatment.

The American politician is a practical businessman or woman. What the politician sells is his/her public service, which the public purchases with its ballots. The politician's remuneration is employment by the electorate with all the emoluments that the position entails. As a merchant, the politician is responsive to consumer demand and, in turn, attempts to influence that demand. Independents in other lines of business have plenty of difficulty in withstanding the competition of Big Business with its holding companies, chain stores and conglomerates. The lone wolf in politics is virtually hopeless. Any success s/he attains is temporary; to get far s/he must align with one of the two large rival organizations that, since the Civil War, have divided the nation's political profits with very little loss to third parties.

Almost any reporter can cover routine political news: announcements of candidacies, issues and platforms, rallies, speeches, registration, electioneering, voting and results. Competence in handling such assignments is necessary preparation for expert specializing later.

Truly interpretative political writing consists in explaining the immediate phenomenon in terms of long-range trends, national or international. Accepting the fact that practical politicians still do not operate with any appreciable awareness of such trends, pragmatic interpretative political writing consists in identifying leaders with movements and groups—political, economic, religious, ethnic and others—and in "seeing through" motives and actions to discover their probable meaning and effect upon political fortunes.

In preparing to derive the most benefit from his/her experiences, the newspaper political reporter should (1) know something about political philosophy; (2) be a student of public opinion, its nature and manipulation; (3) understand practical political organization and election machinery; (4) be sufficiently on the "inside" to distinguish the bunkum from the realities of political phenomena.

POLITICAL PHILOSOPHY

Plato, in describing a highly disciplined perfect state in which philosophers would be kings, Aristotle, in advocating a balanced democratic government, and political theorists ever since, have expressed points of view that the enlightened political reporter will detect in substance in the arguments of contemporary seekers for public office. Heaven forbid that the college-trained reporter should be a pedantic idealist passing judgment upon twentieth-century practical men of affairs in terms of a favorite thinker of the past. Nevertheless, historical perspective is indispensable in enabling one to make sense of modern affairs. Being conversant with the history of political thought, especially with how it has been affected by practical considerations, at least provides the political reporter with the tools for making his/her work personally instructive.

In the writings of many contemporaries, the aspiring political reporter will find plentiful interpretative analyses of the modern scene. A superabundant amount of material concerning capitalism, communism and fascism, of course, exists. The average person may not be able to tell the difference between these and other political theories, but no political writer can be so ignorant. S/he should at least know when a demagogue is incorrect in branding an opponent as socialistic or fascistic or the like.

Political writers are a potent force in educating the public regarding the pros and cons of such matters as the two-party versus multiple-party systems, permanent registration, proportionate representation and the direct primary. Nobody, however, can write on such subjects without deep understanding of them.

POLITICAL PUBLIC OPINION

Before formulating an opinion about the nature of public opinion, one must understand what is meant by each word. What is a public? And what is an opinion? Unless one knows the results of scholarly attempts to answer these questions, his/her own conclusions are invalid. Consequently, a minimum of training in sociology and psychology, or in the dual science social psychology, is essential to the political writer. From a good course or textbook s/he will learn that few modern thinkers in the field share the faith formerly held in instincts or a group mind as the explanation of why men behave similarly. Instead, inspired by the revelations of the behaviorists, psychoanalysts, anthropologists and other specialists, they are impressed by the importance of cultural conditioning, which involves traditions, customs, myths, legends, taboos, superstitions and the like of which most people are dimly conscious if at all. The present author evaluated these factors in *Understanding Public Opinion*.

The politician as a psychological phenomenon was first effectively treated by Harold D. Lasswell in *Psychopathology and Politics* and by A. B. Wolfe in *Conservatism, Radicalism, and the Scientific Method.* Walter Lippmann's *Public Opinion* and *The Phantom Public* resulted from his observations as a newspaperman. Lincoln Steffens' momentous *Autobiography* was inspired similarly. There is a sizable library on modern propaganda, including political propaganda, and abundant reading material on all other phases of the subject.

Failure of the professional pollsters to predict correctly the outcome of the 1948 presidential election gave impetus to research into the motivations of voting behavior. Paul Lazarsfeld and associates at Columbia University stress the effects of group interrelationships (*The People's Choice, Voting*). Louis Bean emphasizes longtime economic trends (*How to Predict Elections*). Samuel Lubell thinks the effect of nationality and cultural background has been underestimated (*The Future of American Politics, The Revolt of the Moderates*). Angus Campbell and associates demonstrate in *The American Voter* that voting preferences are consistent with a person's total personal and cultural conditioning.

Theodore H. White's quadrennial *The Making of the President* books, beginning with the campaign of 1960, "did more to explain the political process of manipulating the news and the reporter than anything else I've read," according to Patrick Graham, political writer for the Milwaukee *Journal.* White's fans, however, received a shock when 20 years later he confessed in *In Search of History* that in his 1960 book he had "cast Nixon as the villain as in a novel" and not only hero-worshiped Kennedy but also advised him on campaign tactics.

No other "behind-the-scenes" book ever got a better response than Joe McGinniss' *The Selling of the President* after 1968. Bob Greene's *Running* and Timothy Crouse's *The Boys on the Bus* revealed facts about the 1972 campaign that were recalled during the Watergate hearings. Definitive books about the breakup of the Nixon-Agnew administration include *A Heartbeat Away, the Investigation and Resignation of Vice-President Agnew* by Richard M. Cohen and Jules Witcover, *All the President's Men* by Carl Bernstein and Bob Woodward and *The Great Cover-Up* by Barry Sussman.

POLITICAL ORGANIZATION

Local

Municipal political affairs in recent years generally have become dissociated from major party organizations. Candidates for mayor and other city officers run as independents but may be identified in state and national politics as members of established parties that tacitly lend them support. In smaller communities, the rival groups in a municipal campaign are more likely to cross established party lines and to be dissociated from all but strictly local issues.

Because of the nonpartisan character of municipal elections, it should be the newspaper's function properly to identify candidates by the interests of the persons or groups backing them. Local political groups may take names as the People's Party, but these have little or no meaning until party members have held office and given indication of what they represent. A local candidate's backing may be racial, religious, economic, geographic or in some other way classifiable. In preparing slates of candidates, political parties try to have as many of the important elements as possible represented. Furthermore, it is customary to run a Catholic against a Catholic, a Jew against a Jew, someone of Swedish extraction against another with similar ancestry and so on. In this way, awareness of nationality, racial and other backgrounds is kept alive as well as taken advantage of politically.

Precinct, Ward

To assist the party to power in elections involving established political parties, cities are organized by wards and their subdivisions, precincts. The lowest rung on the political organization ladder is that of precinct worker, who carries the responsibility of ringing doorbells, talking to voters, handing out campaign literature, watching at the polls and assisting voters to and from polling places. Ambitious workers are conscious of their positions between elections and "talk up" the party or some of its prominent members on all occasions; intensive work, however, is only during the few weeks or months before an election.

Precinct workers are most effective in getting votes for local candidates about whom voters know little and often care less. They are influential in determining party policies and selecting candidates for city and court clerks, assessors, recorders of deeds and other offices that dispense patronage. In general elections it is not unusual for precinct workers to ask voters who support the rival party's candidates for president, congressmen, governor and other national and state offices to split their tickets sometimes "as a favor" to help elect local candidates of the precinct worker's party. Sometimes there are deals whereby workers of different parties seek split votes for local candidates.

Procedure for selecting precinct and ward captains differs, but ordinarily both are elected by registered members of the party in the sections. It may be, however, that only the ward or township captain or chairman is elected and given the responsibility of appointing precinct captains. A precinct, created by the election board, usually contains from 500 to 2,000 voters, and it is the precinct captain's job to carry the precinct in both primary and general elections. Most precinct captains have patronage jobs that depend upon their continued satisfactory performance on election days.

Precinct workers are paid for their work during campaigns by the precinct captain, who gets the money from the ward leader, who gets it from the city or county committee, which raises part of it and gets more from the state or national committee. Original sources of the millions spent annually to assist candidates to get elected are the candidates themselves, public officeholders and others who have obtained employment with the assistance of the party, businessmen who have profited by providing goods and/or services to the party's officeholders, and interested outsiders who believe they have more to gain if a certain candidate is elected than if the opponent were to win. Some large donors, mostly potential recipients of official largess, bid for the friendship of whoever occupies an important political office and may contribute to the campaign funds of both major parties.

The precinct captain generally is credited with controlling at least 50 voters among friends and relatives, the families of those whom he has been helpful in obtaining positions on election day as judges and clerks at the polls and other recipient of political favors. Unlike the ordinary worker, the precinct captain is active between elections, obtaining minor favors for voters in his precinct, such as assistance when they run afoul of the law, financial help in case of illness or death, advice on how to obtain employment, and any other services that the strength and wealth of the organization permit.

Although the nonpolitically minded person doesn't realize it, if the power of a political party machine is to be broken it must be done in the primary. In the general election, the voter merely has a choice between two or more machine-picked slates. Under any circumstances, bucking the efficiently organized party is virtually impossible; so-called reform slates result from fusions of political cliques or parties out of office at the time and with no hope of victory without each other's cooperation. The history of such fusion movements is one of temporary successes only. The primary laws in many states, furthermore, make starting a third party virtually impossible.

Most candidates for public office at the local level who receive regular party endorsement have earned the reward by hard work in the precincts. Not always, however, is this the case. Sometimes, a ward committeeman becomes jealous of the growing popularity of a subordinate and maneuvers to get him/her into a public office where s/he will be less of a personal power threat. Usually, this means a judgeship or some appointive job whose incumbent is required by the Hatch act or other laws, or by tradition, to minimize politicking.

County

County chairmen usually are elected by ward and township leaders, some or all of whom constitute the county executive committee. No political leader whose concern is a unit smaller than the county merits the unofficial title of boss. All bosses, furthermore, are not officeholders or even party officials; they may be influential dictators who prefer to operate in the background. By whatever type of person occupied, the political boss' office is the clearing house for finances and information. Reporters may obtain tips from underlings but seldom get anything official except directly from headquarters.

''Getting next to'' a political boss is not impossible, as Lincoln Steffens discovered. How to do it, however, is an individual matter dependent upon the reporter's particular personality. Just as the boss must be cautious about making promises but scrupulous about keeping them once made, so must the political reporter become resigned to learning more ''off the record'' than on and to not learning anything about a great deal of important party business. It is because newspapers are unable to obtain the information that they do not give more ''inside dope.'' Furthermore, to get what s/he does, the reporter cannot incur the displeasure of a source. Instead, it often is necessary to report seriously what is known to be the insincere remarks of some demagogue, overlook personal foibles, correct bad grammar and in general ''cover up.'' The alternative is openly to defy and fight the party machine; a newspaper finds it difficult to take that attitude against all political groups without discrimination.

The newspaper reporter's task is magnified whenever television cameras are present. In such instances the interviewee, from the president down, usually dominates the occasion. It is his prerogative to designate who his questioners shall be and he can cut off a probing reporter before s/he has a chance to put all of the questions necessary for a complete story. Political candidates are particularly astute about making the arrangements conducive to their presentation of prepared statements and controlling the entire experience.

State, National

State and national committees nominally exist continuously but are quiescent most of the time, arousing from their lethargy about a year before an election. Most active are potential candidates who are ''pulling strings'' to obtain machine backing when nominating time comes around. With feigned modesty, the aspirant gets some friend or group of backers to ''front'' for him/her so that the suggestion that s/he run for office may seem to emanate from someone other than him/herself. To reporters, the aspirant is evasive and unambitious and is so quoted by a press, which, of course, knows better. Until an official announcement is made, however, it is dangerous to go too far in surmising anyone's intentions.

PRECAMPAIGN ACTIVITIES

Petitions

To have one's name placed on the printed ballot as a candidate for office, a person must obtain the signatures of a certain proportion of the voters on nominating petitions that must be filed before a certain date with the proper public official—city clerk, county clerk, secretary of state and so on. Because top positions usually are given to candidates filing their papers first, candidates stand in line waiting for the hour at which it is legal to file them.

It is news both when petitions are taken out and when they are filed. The candidate's name, address, occupation, political experience and general background are included in the first story about his/her intentions. Sometimes the candidate already has prepared a statement or platform regarding his/her candidacy although generally that comes later. In city elections, the first petition stories should contain information as to the deadlines for filing, the number of signatures needed and possibly something about the position at stake. The names of prominent signers of a petition are newsworthy.

The next clerk of the Milltown Municipal court will be either the incumbent, Andrew L. Ziegler, or Constable Eustace L. Cohen for whom nominating petitions containing the required number of signatures, were filed yesterday, the deadline, in the office of City Clerk Jerome Z. Day.

Mr. Ziegler, who has been court clerk since establishment of the municipal court three years ago, filed petitions containing 1,416 names, 11 fewer than the maximum permitted. Cohen's petitions contained 1,043 names. Minimum number of names required was 892, or 5 percent of the vote cast at the last general election.

Graham R. Olson, 146 Arnold avenue, insurance man who took out petition forms last week, failed to file. His name appeared on one of Cohen's petitions. Feature of Ziegler's petitions was one sheet containing only the names of Milltown's 16 aldermen.

Until late yesterday, it was believed petitions would be filed for a candidate backed by the Milltown Democratic organization which took out blanks several days ago.

The election for Municipal court clerk will take place Nov. 3 at the same time as the state and national elections. There will be a separate ballot, however, for the office.

By Peggy Reisser

State Rep. Ralph Duncan, R-Decaturville, the first minister to sit in the Tennessee legislature, filed an invalid petition for re-election and will not be on the Aug. 7 primary ballot, state Election Coordinator David Collins said today.

Collins, a Democrat, said Duncan, the only Republican in the race in District 65, filed his qualifying petition on time, with the proper number of signatures from registered voters, but without the addresses of the signers.

State law requires persons signing nominating petitions to list their addresses, Collins said.

Collins said there are about 40 signatures on the petition, but only three have the addresses of the signers. A qualifying petition must have at least 25 signatures of registered voters indicating their wish for a candidate to run . . .

[Nashville *Banner*]

Registration

Eligibility to vote differs by states but some sort of registration usually is required. On certain specified days, all otherwise eligible voters (those who have resided in the state, county and precinct a sufficient length of time, have paid certain taxes, given evidence of literacy, and so forth, as the case may be) appear at their polling places to have their names recorded. Such registration may be quadrennial, annual or permanent; for municipal elections no registration at all may be necessary. Voting by affidavit also may be permitted in case a voter is unable to register on the designated days. If there is permanent registration, the voter merely notifies election officials of a change of address.

The total number of voters registering is news. Knowing that only about 60 per cent of the nation's eligible voters take the trouble to register, crusading editors often investigate abnormally large registrations. Pulitzer prizes have been won by newspapers that checked registration lists to discover "ghost" votes from empty lots, abandoned buildings and transient hotels.

Despite the all-day rain, Saturday's registration of voters for the Nov. 3 election was slightly higher than normal for a first registration day when 21,678 Milltown voters registered, according to City Clerk J. M. Blackburn.

John A. Burgess, Republican township committeeman for Milltown, declared that this total should be 340 greater, to include additional registrants from the Seventh ward: the clerk's office, however, reports that its figure is accurate.

The 21,678 total represents about 70 per cent of the total vote cast in Milltown in 1976. A registration of 65 per cent of voters normally is expected on the first registration day. Final registration day this year will be Tuesday, Oct. 6, when the polling places again will be open from 6 a.m. to 9 p.m. Registration is essential in order to be eligible to vote in November; no affidavits will be accepted. According to the city clerk's office, Milltown's registration by wards was as follows. . . .

Ghosts also walk in the Eighth ward, at least on municipal election day.

To be specific, Tuesday, April 2, at least three nice spooks materialized in the southernmost ward of Milltown and helped the voters there select their aldermen and other city officials.

One of them called himself Hugh Hillis and gave 130 Elmwood avenue as the apartment building he haunts.

The second and third identified themselves as Thomas Long and Nicholas Reding and claimed to be neighbors in the closets of 333 Howard street, also an apartment building.

Thus it is seen that the ethereal denizens of the Eighth ward differ from those of the Fifth ward, where you will recall from my article of last Friday, the dusky unrealities preferred empty lots as their mundane habitats for the day.

This is not surprising, of course, when it is realized that the Eighth ward is predominantly an apartment house section, whereas the Fifth ward is punctuated with wide open spaces.

Here is the dope on Spooks Hillis, Long, and Reding. . . .

Primaries

With the notable exception of the national tickets every four years, most candidates for important office are chosen by party primaries instead of by convention as formerly. Any citizen may enter a primary election as a candidate for the nomination of any party. A voter, however, can participate in the primary of one party only. The names of only those candidates who have filed nominating petitions appear on the ballot, but the voter can add the name of anyone else. It is seldom, however, that a "write-in" candidate is elected.

In some states, if no candidate receives a majority, runoff primaries are held of the two or three leaders. In most states that have primary laws, a plurality in a single primary is sufficient to nominate.

If there is little contest in his/her own party, in most states a voter may vote in the primary of another although s/he intends to vote for his/her own party candidate in the general election. If too many voters desert it in a general election, however, the party may not receive a large enough proportion of the total vote to receive a place on the ballot at the next election. Likewise, the party voter may forfeit the right to vote in any special primary within the time limit, usually two years, during which it is possible to change party affiliation.

Presidential primaries in about half the states are for the purpose of electing delegates to the national conventions at which the candidates are nominated. Procedures differ considerably. In most cases the delegates' preferences are known and they are pledged to vote for them on at least one ballot. Some delegates, however, may be uncommitted and even if they have choices they may not be indicated on the ballots. In addition there may be "beauty" contests as they are facetiously called, allowing voters to indicate their preferences for nominees. The way the political winds are blowing often, but by no means always, can be judged by the outcomes of the early primaries or those with the largest number of delegates.

Until 1936 when Gov. Alf M. Landon of Kansas carried only Maine and Vermont against President Franklin D. Roosevelt, it was believed that "As Maine goes, so goes the nation." That meant the outcome of a local Maine election early in the year indicated voters' predilections throughout the rest of the country. Since then it is the New Hampshire primary that is analyzed. Runners-up have demonstrated unexpected strength as Eugene McCarthy did in 1968 persuading President Lyndon B. Johnson to withdraw as a candidate; it was in New Hampshire that George McGovern's candidacy got its first boost. In 1980 John Anderson was seen to be a sizable threat to the Republican front runners.

By Mark Ragan

South Carolina has become, in political significance, the New Hampshire of the South.

Voters in the Palmetto State will choose March 8 between six candidates bidding for the Republican presidential nomination.

No one is sure who those voters will be or how many ballots will be cast.

But one thing is certain: The first presidential primary in South Carolina history has emerged among the more important contests in the 1980 Republican quest for a presidential nominee.

Why?

The South Carolina primary is the first to be held in the South.

Three days later, primaries will be held in Georgia, Alabama and Florida, focusing the eyes on the nation on South Carolina first.

Campaign directors for each Republican candidate believe a strong showing in South Carolina will improve chances in the other southern primaries.

And like the residents of New Hampshire, Iowa and other states with early presidential contests, the people of South Carolina are feeling the effects of living in a bellwether state.

That qualifies every South Carolinian as a political pundit.

[Anderson (S.C.) *Independent*]

Conventions

Adoption of a direct primary law does not mean the end of state party conventions, but such conventions (or conferences) are held outside the law and for the purpose only of recommending and endorsing candidates to receive the party's nomination at a primary election. Often rival factions within a party hold separate conventions and endorse different slates.

The news writer can estimate the strength of candidates at a state or national convention by comparing the instructions given to delegates. Delegations sometimes support "favorite sons" from their localities and may deadlock a convention by refusing, after the early ballots, to change their votes to one of the leading candidates.

Knowledgeable political editors suspect deals whenever stubborn delegations suddenly change their positions. Possibly appointment to a cabinet position or judgeship or some other office has been promised someone; or support has been pledged in some future campaign. Maybe the compromise involves stands on issues to be involved in anticipated legislation.

A party convention is called to order by a temporary chairperson who gives a prepared keynote speech. Then a permanent chairperson is elected and also gives a speech. Usually the committee's recommendation for permanent chairperson is taken, but sometimes rival factions may nominate different candidates. The vote for permanent chairman then may be an indication of how delegates will vote later on other important matters.

The group in control of a state or national committee has the advantage of obtaining a personnel to its liking. Through its committee on credentials it determines which delegates are eligible for seats, if rival delegations from the same locality claim recognition.

Vote on the platform submitted by the committee on resolutions is conducted by a roll call of delegations. After the platform is adopted, with or without amendments, the next procedure is the election of candidates. Often, several ballots are necessary for a choice. When a deadlock continues after several ballots, a "dark horse," someone not among the leaders, may be elected as a compromise candidate.

A party convention frequently is interrupted by the demonstrations of different delegations. When the time to nominate candidates arrives, the roll call begins. Every delegation either nominates someone or passes its turn or permits some other delegation, whose turn normally would come later, to use its opportunity. In addition to the principal nominating speech there may be several other speeches to second a nomination. Every speech is the signal for an outburst of enthusiasm by supporters of the candidate. Unfavorable viewers' reactions to the carnival aspects of the televised proceedings have caused the two major political parties to attempt to streamline their quadrennial conventions somewhat. The stage managers, however, may become overly conscious of what is considered prime viewing time and either slow down or hurry up activities with the nationwide television audience in mind. Thus the conventions tend to become entertainment rather than serious exercises in statesmanship.

In 1972 the networks spent about $8 million to cover the Democratic convention in Miami; the Democratic party and candidates spent less than $3 million. In *The Boys on the Bus,* Timothy Crouse relates the consternation which the Republicans experienced when a British Broadcasting Company reporter obtained a minute-by-minute script of the convention which, Crouse wrote, "simply confirmed what everyone already knew, that the convention was a totally stage-managed coronation of Richard Nixon. . . . The script instructed speakers when to pause, nod and accept 'spontaneous' cheers. It stipulated that at a certain time, a demonstration would interrupt the convention secretary in midsentence." In obedience to the traditional rules of objective reporting, both electronic and print reporters report such incidents straight.

A party *conference* is for the purpose of discussing an important matter. A party *caucus* differs from a conference because all who attend it, by their attendance, pledge themselves to support the decisions of the majority. Insurgent members may stay away from party caucuses because they do not wish to commit themselves to the support of what the majority will favor.

By Betsy Cook

The Republican 3rd Congressional District convention on Saturday may have lacked the fireworks of the Democratic convention, but there was a lot of horn-tooting and banner-waving as delegates from 14 counties unanimously elected Mick Staton as the Republican candidate for the late Rep. John Slack's unexpired term.

"Let's act like Republicans and whoop it up," convention chairman Dale Casto told the crowd of more than 600 at the Municipal Auditorium. "Have a little fun."

And after all 552 eligible votes were cast for Staton, the aisles filled with parading Republicans, waving hats and banners and tooting party horns. Alongside the Staton campaign paraphernalia were Ronald Reagan banners and stickers.

Staton thanked the crowd for the "support, loyalty and kindness. My wife, Lynn, and I will thank you for the rest of our lives," he said. . . .

[Charleston (W. Va.) *Gazette*]

CAMPAIGNS

Socially responsible coverage of a political campaign involves providing readers with as much pertinent information about candidates and issues as possible. This means more than merely reporting speeches and platforms. Significant facts that may not appear in a candidate's own biographical sketch or news releases must be published and the importance and ramifications of issues analyzed. What is ignored or soft-pedaled may be a better clue to what a candidate believes than what he stresses, possibly to an exaggerated extent, in public statements.

Candidates

Who the candidates are and how they differ from each other must be reported.

By Ed Jahn

The six-term Democratic incumbent in the Texas House District 78 race may seem assured of another win, but his youthful, headhunting Republican opponent is planning an upset for election day.

Contender Ed Emmett, 29, is the first Republican opposition Rep. Joe Allen, 38, has faced in 12 years. And the newcomer already has state and national Republicans interested in the race.

District 78, which covers most of northeast Harris County and includes Baytown, Crosby and Kingwood, has seen rapid residential expansion in the last few years and Emmett claims the new arrivals have a conservative outlook.

He points out that the district has been willing to split the vote and cross over to the Republican side with some county and state level candidates in the past.

Emmett has received money from the Republican National Committee and state and local party coffers. He said his party's growing interest proves the race will be a forecast of a Republican resurgence in the area.

So Emmett is trying to bring up issues and question Allen about what he says are his "problems of ethics."

Allen, however, says, "My opponent has nothing to talk about. The dominant issue here is experience."

Allen, who lives at 1306 Ward Road in Baytown, is sixth in House seniority and is a member of the Appropriations Committee. He is a Lee College graduate, a public relations executive for a Baytown bank and is active in business development and real estate.

Emmett lives at 3307 Riverlawn in Kingwood and was a special assistant to the Department of Health, Education and Welfare secretary during the Ford administration. He completed undergraduate work at Rice University and graduate work at the University of Texas. Presently Emmett is on leave from his job as a public affairs specialist for a locally based national oil company.

What Allen calls his experience, Emmett terms ''my opponent's tenure.'' Emmett says voters should look at effectiveness first. The contender says Allen's ''ineffective past'' and the rapidly changing district will be the one-two punch needed to knock him out of the race.

But Allen says he can get things done and points to many bills he has supported. He said he pushed for the Public Utilities Commission, fought for homestead exemptions for people over 65, and authored legislation allowing better means of absentee voting in the state.

Allen said he authored sales tax reform legislation and fought a refinery tax that would have affected one of the largest refineries in the state that is located in the district.

Emmett questions Allen's influence in the Legislature despite his seniority and says he already has more education and experience in political work and private industry than his older opponent.

As for Allen's position on the important Appropriations Committee, Emmett claims ''there is at least a problem of ethics when a man has that position, works for a bank and gets private loans from banks for personal use.''

Emmett also brings out Allen's admitted debt of $108,000 on loans to buy a home, antiques, automobiles, art and jewelry.

But Allen says Emmett is misinformed about finance and explains the debts are more than offset by assets that have a market value twice what they are listed at.

About the only things both men seem to agree on are what they feel are the concerns of the constituents. Both would like to see a Baytown-La Porte bridge and feel the freeways in the district are neglected. And they say the environment must be protected.

Allen wants the state to take over total minimum funding of school districts to lessen the burden on taxpayers. He wants the individual school districts to use their surpluses for capital improvements and state surpluses refunded to taxpayers.

Emmett says the schools are producing ''too many kids who can't read or write.'' He wants public schools to have competency testing.

Emmett is all for trimming the fat in the bureaucracy and contends Allen has only contributed to the problem. But Allen says he has a role not only as a legislator but as a servant to the voters. ''I believe government ought to leave the people alone as much as possible,'' Allen says.

Both men are married and have two children. [Houston *Post*]

Traveling with a candidate enables a political reporter to describe him/her better than one can do by objective reports of speeches and meetings.

By Basil Talbott Jr.

Madison—Bouncing across Wisconsin on the makeshift rear platform of a comic contraption, Lee S. Dreyfus looks more like Captain Kangaroo than a modern politican. Dreyfus' chubby build, frizzy gray hair, mischievous smile and the bright red vest he wears everywhere bring the children's television hero to mind.

The contraption is an old school bus that was rebuilt and painted to look like a railroad locomotive. Another platform was added on the top to carry a changing collection of teen-agers and sub-teens dubbed by Dreyfus ''the rag-tag band.''

As the bus rattles into each town, Dreyfus' public-relations man starts yanking at a rope to clang the large bell hanging out front. Dreyfus goes to the rear platform ready to wave. The children, all dressed in red sweatshirts, climb up to the top with their instruments and begin to play. After each rendition of the theme for the Budweiser beer commercial, the kids chant, "When you say Lee Dreyfus, you've said it all."

Wisconsin political observers found it difficult to take this corny entourage seriously during the summer. Dreyfus, a chancellor at the University of Wisconsin-Stevens Point, was breaking into politics late in life at age 52. He chose as his entry point the Republican Party, which has been withering away here for the last two decades. Before deciding to run, he called himself a Republocrat.

To make the odds appear worse, Dreyfus had very little money and declined to use the little he did raise on conventional political tools. He refused to air 30- or 60-second television commercials and thumbed his nose at polling techniques.

The week before the Sept. 12 primary, polls seemed to confirm reporters' assessments. Dreyfus' Republican opponent, Rep. Robert Kasten, a wealthy, 36-year-old Milwaukee congressman, had lined up the party's backing at its state convention and was concluding a well-funded campaign. A professional pollster hired by Kasten predicted he would win with 58 per cent of the vote.

Bang! On primary election day, Dreyfus pulled an upset by getting nearly 58 per cent of the GOP vote. As the pollsters and pundits scrambled, Dreyfus refueled his bus and started his campaign against a new opponent, Democratic Acting Gov. Martin J. Schreiber.

Dreyfus used an anti-politics appeal to beat Kasten and has continued using it against the acting governor. Schreiber, however, is a more formidable opponent. A boyish 39, Schreiber has the enthusiastic backing of the majority party and its plentiful labor allies. Democrats have held the governor's job for 14 of the last 20 years and have two-thirds of the state legislative seats.

Schreiber, however, has been a career politician, making him a vulnerable target for Dreyfus' anti-politics. Schreiber, the son of a politician, entered politics at age 23 when he was elected a Milwaukee alderman. [Chicago *Sun-Times*]

Issues

Issues cannot be described separately from candidates or their supporters, but the reporter can put the emphasis on what is at stake.

Austin, Texas (AP)—The Texas Railroad Commission—an agency that regulates so many things besides railroads that it may be the most powerful such department in the nation—has two seats up for grabs.

Commissioners John Poerner and James Nugent, both former legislators who were appointed to their posts in non-election years, are now running with all the big industry money and political backing traditionally awarded incumbents.

The challengers are a timber baron's son and a muckraking journalist who used his tabloid to criticize the cozy relationship between the commissioners and the very industries they regulate.

What attracts so much attention to the 1980 statewide races for two $45,200-a-year jobs is the commission's duties.

The three-person agency was created in 1891 to control outrageous rail freight rates. Over the years, the commission kept its name but added duties.

Now it regulates the strip mining of coal, lignite and uranium; the rates and routes for intercity buses and trucks; and the production of liquified petroleum gas such as propane and butane.

But most vitally, it sets prices and regulates production for Texas' oil and gas industry, which supplies 25 percent of all fuel consumed in the United States.

"We know a senator can debate energy policy and we've seen a governor can spill oil on our beaches, but a railroad commissioner actually sets energy prices," says Jim Hightower, 36.

Hightower, given to cowboy hats and boots, touts himself as a candidate who owns no oil wells and gets no dividend checks from "Exxon or Lone Star Gas or one of the railroads."

He quit as editor of the bimonthly Texas Observer to run against Nugent, who was nicknamed "Supersnake" for his maneuvers in the Texas House.

By Kathleen Vitale

The November referendum concerning pari-mutuel betting on horse races in Virginia promises to pit segments of big business against church and family advocates opposed to any form of gambling on moral grounds.

The stakes are high, according to campaign workers on both sides of the issue.

Advocates of pari-mutuel betting point to an anticipated $25 million tax revenue for state and county budgets, thousands of new jobs and a "shot in the arm" for Virginia's agri-business.

Opponents cite studies connecting political corruption and criminal activities with pari-mutuel betting in other states and call the anticipated boost in state revenue insignificant compared to the problems of policing and controlling the scene.

In pari-mutuel betting, the player buys a ticket on the horse he wishes to back. The payoff to winners is made from the pool of all bets on the various entries in the race, after deduction of an operator's commission.

Though approved in various forms in 32 states, gambling has never been legal in the Commonwealth.

For many years, Virginia has ranked among the top five breeders of race horses in the nation.

If voters approve the pari-mutuel referendum in November, a racing commission would be appointed by the governor. The measure would allow development of two major tracks, but would require approval through local referendum for development of a track in any Virginia locality. The local referendum would be held next year if supporters are successful in gaining voter approval in November . . . [Reston (Va.) *Times*]

Tactics

The tactics candidates employ may not be clear until pointed out to readers by perceptive political reporters. The primary elections to determine the Democratic candidate for United States senator from Georgia in 1980 provided the political experts of the Atlanta *Constitution* and *Journal* an excellent opportunity for objective reporting, analysis and commentary.

A runoff election became necessary when none of the six candidates received a majority vote.

By Frederick Allen

CONSTITUTION CHIEF POLITICAL WRITER

U.S. Sen. Herman Talmadge and Lt. Gov. Zell Miller are modeling their runoff campaign strategies on popular notions that don't necessarily hold much water.

Heading toward their Aug. 26 showdown for the Democratic Senate nomination, Talmadge is trying to change Miller's middle name from Bryan to Liberal, while Miller is riding the old saw that incumbents lose runoffs.

The strategies have caused the two men to reverse roles from the primary campaign: Talmadge, who was "senatorial" and above the fray on the first go-round, is now the attacker. Miller, once the hot-breathing critic, is now hoping to broaden his appeal and run on "the issues."

The switch produced a curious situation Thursday. In a marvelous display of pot-kettle politics, Talmadge accused Miller of "shrill demagoguery" in one breath and called him "a proxy for big-time labor bosses and self-anointed Atlanta power brokers" in the next, while Miller was talking about his own "very good record" in office.

One irony in all this is that if Zell Miller is a "liberal," the word has lost its definition.

Anywhere save Georgia and the deep South, true liberals would view Zell Miller as a throwback to the Pleistocene Epoch.

Miller the "liberal" opposes gun-control legislation and federally funded abortions, once called for the wholesale jailing of some 60,000 Iranians in the United States, and freely stole a plank from the Republican national platform in calling for tax-indexing.

On foreign affairs, the old Marine in Miller comes out, and he sounds like the key-noter at a John Birch Society banquet. He would not, he likes to say, have voted to "give away" the Panama Canal as Talmadge did.

Talmadge is trying to tie organized labor and big-city blacks around Miller's neck, but the truth is that the gambit might backfire. Miller would not be the first statewide candidate to run successfully with labor and black backing.

Talmadge runs a profound risk of alienating midstream voters by coming on too strong.

Meanwhile, Miller has taken the 1974 governor's race as his model for the runoff: He equates Talmadge with former Gov. Lester Maddox, who ran first in the primary but lost decisively to George Busbee in the runoff.

The problem is that Georgia history really yields no good case-study for the current election.

Gubernatorial races do not provide a good comparison, because Georgia governors could not succeed themselves until the state constitution was changed in 1976 to benefit Busbee. . . .

That Talmadge, a four-term senator, was forced into a runoff on Tuesday is unprecedented in modern Georgia history. No popularly elected Georgia senator has been forced into a runoff in at least half a century.

Talmadge had held his seat without difficulty since the retirement of Walter George in 1956, and George had kept the seat easily since winning a special election in 1922 to replace the late "firebrand" Tom Watson. . . .

Asked what plans he might have to broaden his support for the runoff, Miller said he expects to publicize his record as lieutenant governor on "frugality, compassion and openness."

He said he will begin a series of press conferences around the state in which he will outline a series of specific issues on which he and the senator differ.

In addition, Miller plans to begin airing a five-minute television "spot."

Miller and Talmadge agreed to meet in a series of televised debates, and their staffs were working out details Thursday afternoon. The senator said he wants the debates to be conducted without any panelists.

Miller said he believes "it would serve the public interest better to have them patterned after presidential debates, with opening and closing statements, questions from impartial panelists and each candidate having an opportunity to respond to the other candidate's answer."

By Charles Hayslett
JOURNAL STAFF WRITER

The change was sudden and complete.

Here was Herman Talmadge, who complained during the primary battle that his opponents were smearing him with "mud and muck and slime," railing against Zell Miller as a "proxy of a big-labor union boss and self-anointed Atlanta power brokers."

And here was Miller, for nearly a year the major fire-breather in the Senate race, responding 24 hours later in such a conservative and somber tone that it might have come from Norman Underwood.

The runoff was on.

Talmadge, who had made it through the primary on the robot-type statements for which he is famous, was coming after Miller with an oratorical meat cleaver.

The sometimes skittish Miller was strangely calm in the face of Talmadge's attack, answering a day later with a call for a tax-indexing plan spawned by congressional Republicans and wondering out loud why Talmadge, the would-be fiscal conservative, had fought it for three years.

The next three weeks should produce more of the same as Georgians decide the most clear-cut political showdown ever.

Talmadge, 67, never really challenged since he took over the governor's office three decades ago, was forced Tuesday into the first runoff of his life when Miller, Underwood and U.S. Rep. Dawson Mathis rolled up nearly 60 percent of the statewide vote.

Miller, 48, serving his second-term as lieutenant governor, led the pack of challengers and earned the right to meet Talmadge head-on. . . .

Speeches

A campaign really gets under way with the first speech of the candidate. In the case of a presidential candidate this is the speech of acceptance of the nomination formerly made at a formal notification ceremony, but in recent years usually at the nominating convention. Although presidential candidates have fresh speeches for every important occasion thereafter, in the case of candidates for less important offices the opening or keynote speech may be the pattern for all others delivered during the campaign. The political reporter traveling with the candidate may be hard put to obtain a fresh angle in reporting the day's forensics, but the local news writers who hear the candidate only once are not so handicapped.

When candidates start calling each other names, hurling challenges, answering each other's arguments and raising new issues, the political reporter's problem is easy. Otherwise, s/he may be forced to rely upon the press releases of political headquarters. If s/he travels with a candidate s/he tells of the crowds, the opinions of local leaders, the reception given the candidate and the like.

In reporting and writing up a political speech the reporter should observe the orthodox rules for such occasions as described in Chapter 12.

Most newspapers try to equalize the space given rival candidates. Often this is difficult to do. William Pride, executive news editor of the Denver *Post,* summarized the difficulty in part as follows:

> Last time around we had a congressional race (suburban) featuring staid, stodgy 3-term incumbent vs. young, sharp, interesting challenger. Problem: how to treat 'em equally. We allotted equal space and traded off reporters following them the last two weeks. The incumbent was a shoo-in from the start, so all he did was stand at factory gates and shopping centers shaking hands. The young guy, full of ideas, uncorked a new major speech about every other day. If we give each half a column, what can we say about the first guy after we say he stood at the entrance to the supermarket all morning? If we give the second guy more space, we get squawks, pickets, etc., so there you are. (I hardly need add that the incumbent was easily re-elected.)

A related problem is how to include all of the candidates for all of the offices that will appear on the ballot. Naturally, the most important—president, governor, senator, mayor, etc.—will receive most attention if for no other reason than the fact that the candidates will campaign more vigorously. But despite the trend to making formerly elective offices appointive the voter still is asked to make a multitude of choices. S/he may stare at a long ballot with scores of unfamiliar names of candidates for public offices about whose duties s/he knows little or nothing.

A traditional method is to print thumbnail sketches of all candidates shortly before election day. These include the essential facts of family background, education, occupational, civic and political experience. They seldom include statements on issues. In local elections when there is a short ballot, depth interviews can be obtained with all candidates and the written questionnaire method, soliciting answers regarding key issues, can be used effectively. Space is given the candidates' own words in reply.

Records

Gov. Alfred E. Smith of New York, Democratic presidential candidate in 1928, frequently advised, "Let's look at the record." It's a good idea for politicians, voters and journalists.

By Doug Harbrecht

Washington—A congressman votes against a controversial bill, knowing he will please a bloc of constituents and the hometown newspaper will record his vote.

The next week, in a less publicized and intense atmosphere, he turns around and votes with his party or his conscience.

Thus, he has it both ways. To one group he can say he voted for cuts in public spending, or restrictions on abortion, or foreign aid. To another, he can say he opposed such measures, and his record speaks for itself.

In Washington, it is called the "yahoo vote," the vote that plays to the right audience. Congressional leaders recognize and allow for it, as long as the chickens eventually come home to roost. Sometimes, it works the other way.

The U.S. House has had 530 record votes since January, ranging from routine measures approving the previous day's record to hotly contested amendments.

But if you were to check the Congressional Record for this year, you would find that Rep. Austin Murphy, D-Mononghela, has somehow managed to vote for and against a pay increase for congressmen, for and against the Panama Canal treaties, for and against the 1980 budget resolution, for and against the Department of Education bill, and for and against raising the national debt ceiling.

Murphy, a thoughtful former state senator whose district includes Upper St. Clair, Moon, Findlay and Robinson, as well as Washington and Fayette counties, has an articulate reason for all his votes, as does every congressman who takes seriously his role as U.S. representative.

But his voting record is probably the most checkered of any area congressman and shows a broad range. . . . [Pittsburgh *Press*]

By Jim Riter

Since January, presidential candidate U.S. Rep. Philip Crane has:

- Compiled the fourth worst voting record in Congress.
- Missed about as many roll-call votes as the seven other suburban congressmen combined.
- Skipped at least 80% of the meetings of the influential Ways and Means Committee, the only House unit of which he's a member.
- Spent more time campaigning in New Hampshire than visiting his home district.

As of June 21, the Mount Prospect Republican was present for 48% of the 252 House roll-call votes. The average House voting rate this year is 90%. In 1977, before he officially began his campaign, Crane answered more than 90% of roll-call votes.

Only three of the 434 other House members have worse voting records than Crane. They are U.S. Rep. Daniel Flood (D-Pa.), who participated in 30% of the votes; U.S. Rep. John Conyers (D-Mich.), 35%; and U.S. Rep. John Anderson (R-Rockford), 40%.

Flood, 75, has been hospitalized and occupied with his bribery trial. Conyers has spent several weeks in Michigan for personal and political reasons, spokesmen said. Anderson is running for president.

This year, Crane has been absent from the Ways and Means Committee even more than from the House floor. By his own count, Crane was present for no more than 20% of committee votes. Other Republicans have voted for him in his absence, he added. . . . [Chicago *Suburban Sun-Times*]

Roorbacks

The word *roorback* entered the dictionary as a common noun following the presidential election of 1844 during which a last-minute attempt was made to defeat James K. Polk by newspaper publicity for a fictitious book by a nonexistent author named Roorback supposedly telling of Polk's having bought and branded a number of Negro slaves.

There is a difference between raising false issues and plain lying. The former is for the purpose of misdirecting attention from important to insignificant matters; the latter is sheer falsehood. Roorbacks generally appear as late as possible to be effective and yet permit the opposition insufficient time for an answer. The political reporter always should be wary of a new important issue raised late in a campaign unless it is one that couldn't have been brought up earlier.

May it be said to the credit of newspapermen that they generally have the intelligence to "see through" political humbug, but they are stymied as to what they say, for the reasons that have been enumerated in this chapter. The political reporter who is "taken in" by political bunk is inadequate for the job, which is one for seasoned and not callow persons.

Polls

Because of the apparently uncanny ability of television networks to predict the outcome of elections after only a small proportion of the total vote has been tabulated, newspaper editors, readers and politicians have come to place considerable confidence in polling. Political parties and candidates conduct private polls and some newspapers have their own.

It took the Gallup organization a quarter-century to recover from the 1948 fiasco when it and its rivals predicted an easy victory for Republican Thomas E. Dewey over incumbent Democrat Harry S Truman. There has been no comparable failure of any professional organization in a presidential election since that time. There have, however, been many failures in predicting the outcomes of presidential primaries and local elections. In 1980, for example, the New York *Daily News* final primary poll had Carter beating Kennedy, 55 to 37 per cent. The actual vote was 50 to 43 for Kennedy. The University of Connecticut's Social Science Research Center poll said Carter would receive 34 per cent and Kennedy 18 per cent with 45 per cent undecided. The result was 47 to 41 for Kennedy. Two years earlier the Minneapolis *Tribune* poll showed the Democratic Farmer-Labor party candidates for two U.S. senators and governor to be safely in the lead. After all three Republican candidates won by comfortable margins the Research Information Center of Phoenix broke its contract with the newspaper, which, it said, altered what the polls actually showed.

The success of the networks and some other polls has been due in large part to their adoption of techniques developed by a journalist, Samuel Lubell whose periodic series of articles on the political thinking of "the man in the street'' are supplemented by his uncannily correct forecasts of election results. Lubell's methods confound the professional pollsters and academic political analysts who go to elaborate extremes to be certain those whom they interview represent a correct cross-sectional sample of the electorate as a whole.

Lubell studies election results. When he notes similar significant changes in voting behavior, even in precincts thousands of miles apart, he follows his nose for news to the areas to determine the cause. He has ''pet'' precincts and blocks and even residences in all parts of the country based on past experience of their value as political weather vanes, enabling him to make generalizations. Lubell's main interest is in discovering the reasons for voting behavior rather than merely straw voting. The national pollsters have key or weather-vane districts that are yardsticks by which to predict shifts in voting preferences.

Predictions

As election day approaches, reporters who have followed the campaign more objectively than candidates or party leaders usually are better able to predict the outcome than they. It is customary for large newspapers that assign reporters to travel with candidates to ''switch assignments'' at least once as the campaign progresses. That means that one writer will accompany Candidate A for a few weeks and then trade places with the reporter who has been covering Candidate B. Political reporters note the sizes of crowds and especially their composition; they mingle with and talk to voters as well as to professional politicians and local journalists. Straw votes among political writers have shown them better able to forecast election results than publishers, editors or editorial writers.

The networks almost seem to regard an election as a contest between computers. After every national election there are angry growls from some congressmen who at least would forbid broadcasting the results in Eastern states until after the polls have closed in the West. Critics also contend that the principal function of all journalistic media should be clarification of issues and of candidates' positions rather than bookmaking. In 1956 a team of more than 30 New York *Times* reporters proved it is possible, using traditional reportorial techniques, to forecast accurately. The costly experiment was not repeated and the talents of many who participated in it have since been used more constructively. As for the public, much of it takes as much pleasure from a pollster's error as it does from second-guessing the weatherman. In 1980 everyone had a big laugh when the pollsters were unanimous in predicting a cliffhanger and Ronald Reagan won in a landslide.

In *Precision Journalism* (Indiana University Press, 1973), Philip Meyer of the Knight-Ridder Newspapers explains the necessity of selecting a polling sample scientifically and the value that computers can have in tabulating results and making projections. Despite the new interest in election predictions, the press' obligation remains that of informing voters rather than to concentrate on outguessing the competition.

Throughout the 1980 Georgia Democratic primary, the editorial writers and columnists for the Atlanta newspaper voiced vigorous opposition to Talmadge. The news columns, however, were devoted generally to impartial and objective coverage. About the closest to a propaganda roorback was the following piece, which contains no adequate attribution. It appeared on page one two days before the election.

By Charles Hayslett
JOURNAL STAFF WRITER

An independent survey of more than 400 Georgia Democrats found last week that Lt. Gov. Zell Miller and Sen. Herman Talmadge are running virtually even and that Miller has actually picked up at least a handful of votes that went to Talmadge in the Aug. 5 primary, sources said Saturday.

The survey's respondents, asked how they voted in the Democratic primary, broke out along lines similar to the results of the primary, the source said, and the overall sample approximated the split between Democratic and Republican voters who cast ballots in the two party primaries.

The Talmadge-Miller question was asked as a masking question incidental to a marketing survey conducted by a Midwest consulting firm for a client searching for a new business location in Georgia, the sources said. The question was asked of 436 Georgia Democrats who planned to vote in Tuesday's runoff.

Conducted Thursday and Friday, the survey of registered voters in Atlanta, Savannah, Valdosta and Macon and two rural counties, Sumter and Carroll, found Miller getting 199 (48.06 percent) of 414 likely votes to 186 (44.92 percent) for Talmadge. Seven percent—29—remained undecided, the pollster said.

"I have felt, and I've had some of my folks who have found it, say that they are running into folks who voted for Talmadge who say they are going to vote for Miller," the lieutenant governor said. ". . . I don't understand it either," he added, "but I can feel it."

Among the principal findings of the survey were the following:

- Miller is picking up at least some support that went to Talmadge on Aug. 5, a phenomenon sensed by some political observers but previously unconfirmed by any polling data. The out-of-state pollster said he found 14 of the 168 Democrats who voted for Talmadge Aug. 5 switching to Miller in the runoff. Asked why, nearly every one of the 14 said "Talmadge was the only one they knew" before the runoff, the pollster said. At the same time, only two of the 102 who initially voted for Miller now plan to vote for Talmadge, the survey found.
- The vast majority of Miller's supporters—77 percent—were voting against Talmadge and not "for" the lieutenant governor, the source said, and for "a range of reasons" involving questions about Talmadge's honesty and effectiveness.
- Miller falls heir to most of the support that went to U.S. Rep. Dawson Mathis and former state Court of Appeals Judge Norman Underwood, but not the 80 percent his own pre-primary polls showed. Of the Mathis and Underwood voters who have made up their minds, the out-of-state survey showed: 56 percent plan to side with Miller while 17.5 percent will line up with Talmadge. Nearly 12 percent said they would not vote and the same number said they were undecided.
- Overall, between 4 percent and 5 percent of the Democrats who voted Aug.

5 plan to stay home Tuesday, and another seven percent—29—have yet to decide how they will cast their ballots in the runoff.

On the eve of the voting, the rival candidates, according to custom, issued optimistic statements;

By Frederick Allen and Carole Ashkinaze
CONSTITUTION STAFF WRITERS

In a runoff contest with his career at stake, U.S. Sen. Herman Talmadge faces his most dogged challenger, Lt. Gov. Zell Miller, on Tuesday for the 1980 Democratic Senate nomination.

The winner earns the right to face Republican nominee Mack Mattingly, a St. Simons businessman, in the Nov. 4 general election.

Polls will be open statewide from 7 a.m. to 7 p.m.

Georgia Secretary of State David Poythress is predicting a turnout of about 40 percent—or nearly 900,000—of Georgia's 2.2 million registered voters. However, other observers have forecast a lower showing, despite the record-setting turnout of slightly more than 1 million in the Aug. 5 Democratic primary.

The two candidates spent Monday on last-minute campaigning and bickering about who would benefit most from a high turnout at the polls.

Miller predicted that he would win if there is a "large turnout," which he defined as "900,000-plus."

He added, "I'm not a soothsayer, but I think that less than 2 percent will separate the winner and the loser. I think it's going to be real close."

"I think the lieutenant governor has it reversed," Talmadge said during a press conference in Rome. "I hope every registered voter in Georgia will vote tomorrow."

Most observers call Talmadge the favorite, but agree with Miller that a large turnout would be helpful to the lieutenant governor.

Talmadge finished first with 42 percent of the vote and Miller finished second with 24 percent on Aug. 5, trailing the senator by 185,000 votes. The runoff was required because neither candidate took an outright majority in the field of six candidates.

The runoff is open to any registered voter who participated in the Democratic primary or who did not vote at all on Aug. 5. Voters who cast a ballot in the Republican primary may not vote in the Democratic runoff . . .

ELECTIONS

Election Day

The size of the vote, violence at polling places, amusing anecdotes, the circumstances under which the candidates cast their ballots, last-minute statements and predictions and methods used to get out the vote or persuade voters on their way to the polls provide news on election day before the ballots are counted.

Ordinary newsroom routine is upset on election day as regulars work overtime and extra helpers gather and compile returns. A newspaper may use its news carriers or other employees to wait at polling places until the votes are counted or may receive its returns through campaign headquarters. Often, the police gather returns and release them to reporters. Radio and television have eliminated the newspaper election extra although editions may be set ahead to provide details, background and interpretative material that the electronics media cannot give.

In national elections the three television networks and the two press associations sometimes pool their efforts to gather the returns rapidly. As the results come in by isolated districts they are tabulated, and the political writer prepares a trend story for the first edition. Some outcomes can be predicted comparatively early; often, in a close race, the result is in doubt until the last vote is counted. When the result is apparent, campaign committees and candidates issue statements claiming victory or conceding defeat. Losers send messages of congratulations to winners, and everybody poses for pictures.

If an outcome is close, a loser may demand a recount. Some elections are protested by defeated candidates who charge fraud, stuffing or tampering with ballot boxes and other irregularities. All candidates are required to file statements of campaign expenditures. Investigations of alleged violations of the corrupt practices act during an election are not infrequent.

The mid-election-day story should include the number voting and a comparison with previous elections.

> Candidates were being nominated in today's statewide primary elections for United States Senator and Representatives in Congress, and for some state and local offices in St. Louis and St. Louis county. In the city and county, balloting was generally light, indicating one of the smallest off-year primary votes in years.
>
> By 4 p.m., it was estimated 61,889 ballots had been cast in the city, following 10 hours of balloting in the 784 precincts. This was 18 percent of the total registration of 343,830.
>
> In the county, an estimated 9,936 ballots were cast by 4 p.m., nine hours after the 7 a.m. opening of the polls. The estimated vote was 7.9 percent of the 125,782 registration.
>
> St. Louis polling places will close at 7 p.m. Those in the county will close at 8:07 p.m. with the exception of those in University City, where the closing time is 8 p.m. The hours given are daylight saving time.
>
> SPECIAL WATCH ON TWO WARDS
>
> Special deputy election commissioners are on duty in all precincts of the Fifth and Sixth Wards, in which a recent recanvass of the registration indicated efforts to pad the lists. Chairman Frank L. Rammacciotti of the Election Board said the deputies were stationed in the two downtown wards to guard against any election irregularities.
>
> Ballots and registration lists for the two wards were not delivered to the polling places until early today. Rammacciotti said this was done because many of the election officials resided outside of the wards and they did not have adequate means to care for them. These were the only two wards where this was done, the

ballots and voters' lists having been delivered to election officials in all other wards last night.

The special deputies in the Fifth and Sixth Wards were instructed specifically to guard against ballots being marked openly instead of in the regular voting booth, and to see that all ballots were counted by Republican and Democratic poll officials working together instead of dividing ballots for a separate tabulation by each party's officials.

TWO BALLOTS IN CITY

City voters received two ballots at the polls, a party primary ballot and one for the two amendments to the City Charter and the proposed $4,000,000 bond issue for rubbish collection facilities, each calling for a Yes or No vote.

Proposed amendment No. 1 would permit. . . . [St. Louis *Post-Dispatch*]

Results

When all or nearly all returns are in, so that the outcome is known, the news feature naturally is who won. The story also should emphasize (1) by how much—in total votes and proportions; (2) areas in which different candidates were strongest and weakest; (3) upsets—incumbents with long services who were defeated, candidates on a party slate who lost whereas most of the others won; (4) whether results coincide with predictions; (5) what significance the outcome is likely to have both locally and/or nationally, as the case may be; (6) statements by winners, losers and party leaders, and similar matters.

By Charles Hayslett
JOURNAL STAFF WRITER

In a staggering display of political prowess, Sen. Herman Talmadge rolled up more than 553,000 votes to swamp Lt. Gov. Zell Miller and finally put down the most serious challenge to his three-decade dominance of Georgia politics.

Rebounding from a public bout with alcoholism, a sensational divorce and a damaging Senate probe of his personal and official finances, Talmadge swept at least 140 of Georgia's 159 counties as he polled 58 percent of the runoff votes Tuesday and nailed down the Democratic nomination to a fifth straight six-year term in the Senate.

He now faces Republican Mack Mattingly, a former GOP state chairman making his first bid for public office, in the Nov. 4 general election. . . .

Sidebars in the same edition included the scenes in the headquarters of both winner (Roar of Crowd: Talmadge, Talmadge, Talmadge) and loser (Zell Miller: "I Feel Good About the Race I Ran"), plans of the Republican nominee and first indications of how the fall campaign would be conducted.

Post-Mortems

A great deal of postelection interpretative writing is of the "I told you so" or "We should have known it" type. By analyzing the vote in different sections where the electorate is predominantly of one type—workers, members of a particular racial, national or religious group—it is possible to imagine which campaign issues or attitudes antedating the campaign were most effective. The skilled political writer analyzes results in the search for trends. Often, s/he has to compare local with state and national results to interpret correctly.

When a new officeholder or party takes over a city hall, county building, state or national capitol, the citizenry expects that "there will be some changes made." Party platforms and campaign speeches provide clues as to what they will be, but voters have become suspicious of politicians' promises. Personality sketches and reviews of the past records of successful candidates are valuable.

The leads of three of the next-day stories after the Georgia runoff primary follow. One can only wonder why the analysts refrained from displaying their erudition before election day.

By Frederick Allen

Constitution Chief Political Writer

Lt. Gov. Zell Miller symbolically lost his chance at capturing Herman Talmadge's Senate seat on the afternoon of March 20, 1980, when he accepted the poisoned kiss of endorsement from Atlanta Mayor Maynard Jackson.

However, the story of Miller's punishing loss in Tuesday's runoff is considerably more complicated than the easy explanation of white backlash and antipathy for liberal ideas.

A leading factor, of course, was the tremendous political strength demonstrated by Talmadge, while Miller's own flawed strategy played a leading but misunderstood role.

With all 2,251 precincts counted Wednesday, Talmadge had 553,244 votes, or 58.5 percent, to 393,931 votes, or 41.5 percent, for Miller. Turnout in the Democratic runoff was nearly 950,000 voters, or 42.5 percent of Georgia's 2.23 million registered voters.

The main component of Talmadge's strategy was a record amount of money. He spent about $1.5 million, swamping all of his pursuers combined.

However, Talmadge also demonstrated considerable finesse, deciding early on a risky but effective advertising campaign that dealt directly with his personal problems.

Knowing he was the front-runner, he avoided direct reference to his challengers until the runoff, when he went for Miller's jugular in a series of television debates.

The senator ran a masterful "retreat" campaign—limiting potential losses of support among his traditional followers. No farmer failed to hear about Talmadge's chairmanship of the Senate Agriculture Committee, no constituent went uninformed about Talmadge's years of answering requests for help, and no Georgian was allowed to forget Talmadge's seniority.

In the runoff, Talmadge saw quickly that Miller could be shredded as a "big spender," and the debates were a showcase for the senator's abilities at making Miller sound like U.S. Sen. Edward Kennedy on a buying spree.

Talmadge also realized the potential damage from anti-Talmadge voters, so he limited his advertising in the last three weeks and relied instead on a telephone canvassing operation aimed at pinpointing his followers and spurring them back to vote again.

About the only mistake Talmadge made was misreading his own polls and thinking he would win without a runoff. It took Talmadge about three days to recover from his initial panic and realize that the numbers made him a prohibitive favorite against Miller. While his decision to debate Miller was a mild error, he recouped by winning the debates . . .

By Charles Hayslett

JOURNAL STAFF WRITER

It was in Augusta that Zell Miller first began to crawl onto the limb that would put him to the left of his foes and ultimately collapse under him.

Answering questions at a convention of Georgia's Young Democrats, Miller said he, like the others, favored balancing the federal budget, but finally admitted that he would vote against any budget that had to be balanced on the backs of the nation's poor.

In the weeks and months ahead, Miller edged farther and farther out onto that limb, pledging to support an extension of the federal Voting Rights Act, openly accepting the support of controversial black leaders despite predictions of a white backlash and refusing to abandon his less-than-conservative positions on spending issues that would most benefit the state's black and poor.

Tuesday, Zell Miller got his reward. One out of five registered black voters cast a ballot for him.

There were many stories in Tuesday night's numbers, but none more stark than that one. While the statewide turnout was again bubbling over the 40 percent mark, Georgia's black voters were turning out at a much slower pace.

A survey of 14 black precincts in Fulton County showed the black turnout averaging only 25.9 percent. Miller got 79.1 percent of that, but the raw math of those numbers—if that trend held throughout the county—would put no more than 25,000 votes in Miller's column.

In the low income areas the story was even more dismal. Worst of all for Miller was Atlanta's precinct 4C, which has 1,929 black registered voters and 10 white registered voters. Herman Talmadge got 10 votes. Zell Miller got 109.

Late Tuesday night, while those numbers and others were rolling out of the state's computers and spelling an end to Miller's Senate hopes, Miller was on a podium at the Atlanta Stadium hotel, flanked by Maynard Jackson and a dozen other supporters, several of them black. He would not have done anything differently, he told the roomful of supporters.

"You are the future of Georgia," he said, "and history will prove us right.

"Some have the job of planting seeds, while others reap the harvest. We have planted the seeds, and in future years others will reap the harvest."

And in the cool morning hours after Tuesday's runoff, it indeed appeared that Zell Miller might never reap that harvest. The seeds he planted with his highly touted coalition of blacks, teachers and union members, raised, if nothing else, grave questions about his future in Georgia politics.

While Miller has established himself as the pre-eminent maverick-populist in Georgia politics, and won two statewide races along the way, the truth is that he has never seen competition like he faced in the Senate campaign or would face in a 1982 bid for the governor's office.

17 GOVERNMENT

A. City Government
   1. Mayor
   2. City Council
   3. City Clerk
   4. Corporation Counsel
   5. Public Works
   6. Finances
   7. Other Offices and Boards
   8. Urban Renewal
B. Schools and Education
   1. Integration
   2. Religion
   3. Delinquency
   4. Student Unrest
   5. Exceptional Children
   6. Automation
   7. Academic Freedom
   8. Teachers
C. County Government
   1. County Board
   2. County Clerk
D. State Government
E. Federal Government

As population increases and all phases of life become more complex, ''closing the gap'' between governed and governors becomes a major problem in a democracy. The journalistic media have a great opportunity and responsibility to stimulate interest and participation on the part of the citizenry in governmental affairs.

Journalism's first obligation is to report fully the activities of public agencies and officials. As all public issues ultimately are decided by public opinion, the duty includes presentation of the pros and cons of all important matters and expert analysis of them. In other words, interpretative reporting and writing are essential in the field of governmental affairs.

To prepare for the role of expert in this field, the aspiring interpretative reporter must be thoroughly grounded in political history and theory. S/he must understand the nature and purpose of all governmental agencies and the political connections and motivations of public officials and their backers. No matter how public spirited or socially conscious officeholders may be, they are candidates for re-election or reappointment; they do not cease to be politicians and become statesmen suddenly the day they take office.

The interpretative reporter who specializes in governmental news makes use of all of the devices of the interpretative reporter anywhere. To place an immediate occurrence in proper perspective, s/he may give its historical background. Even before legislators or administrators take action, s/he may describe the existence of a problem. When a proposal is pending, s/he explains its nature, the arguments pro and con and the political alignment as regards it. S/he describes the functions of various offices and officers and reviews the records of the representatives of the people.

CITY GOVERNMENT

Closest to the average newspaper and its readers is city government. The oldest and still most prevalent type of city government is the *mayor-council plan.* Members of the city council (or board of aldermen) are elected from wards, one or two from a ward, their terms usually staggered so that half of the members always are carryovers. The mayor is elected at large. The trend is toward nonpartisan elections rather than contests between nominees of political parties. When political parties do exist at the city level they usually are not affiliated with the national parties and have names with local significance. Once elected, in some places the mayor has almost unlimited power of appointment of subordinates; in other places the legislative board exercises tight veto power.

If the city has the *commission plan,* instead of the aldermen there are two, four or six commissioners, usually elected at large, and fewer appointive officers, the duties usually performed by them being assigned to the full-time commissioners. If the city has the *city manager plan,* the important officer is not the mayor but the city manager who performs the duties, in a small city, of many appointive officers under the mayor-council plan. Under the city manager plan, the office of the mayor, if it is retained at all, may be little more than that of presiding officer at council meetings. A city manager runs a city as a general superintendent operates a business or as a superintendent of schools directs a school system. He is chosen for his expert knowledge of municipal business affairs and is not necessarily a resident of the city at the time of appointment.

Although city hall still is a beat, large city newspapers, especially, have learned that it is impossible to rely on beat men alone to cover local government. Rather, the trend is toward so-called urban affairs reporters who cover events that overlap governmental levels, as urban renewal, public housing, model cities, etc. Otherwise, the city hall reporter is frustrated when the urban renewal director complains about federal "red tape" and bureaucracy. The "issues" reporter must have a sound background in Housing and Urban Development rules and regulations and other federal and state governmental operational procedures.

Mayor

Under the mayor-council plan, which still exists in a majority of American cities, the mayor is chosen, as is a governor of a state or a president of the

United States, by popular election every two or four years. A significant change has taken place in recent years, however, in that city politics has been divorced from state and national. Except in the larger cities, candidates for mayor generally do not run as Republicans, Democrats or Socialists but as independents, their backing crossing party lines.

Wealthy businessmen and industrialists who live in the suburbs provide financial support for mayors and other city officials who promote measures, as urban renewal and zoning laws, of benefit to their financial interests. Although these pillars of the Establishment cannot vote in the city, they must take an interest in what happens within the city limits because that is where they do business. In recent years staunch diehard suburbanite Republican conservatives have been the financial supporters of strong big-city Democratic political machines, the most notorious example being Chicago under the late Mayor Daley.

As the executive head of the city, the mayor is the chief news source in the city hall. S/he should be aware of every important occurrence in all city departments, most of them headed by persons whom s/he has appointed with the approval of the city council. For details, the reporter should see the department heads themselves, or subordinates in closer touch with the news at hand.

As municipal affairs become more complex and the bureaucracy grows in size, the reporter's access to primary news sources becomes more limited. S/he has to learn to circumvent press agents alias publicity directors alias public relations counsel alias public affairs vice presidents or directors of information. So s/he finds it smart to cultivate the good will of telephone operators, receptionists and other potential tipsters, vulgarly known as "leaks."

Because the mayor is called upon to take part in most important nongovernmental activities in the city, s/he is a potent source of miscellaneous tips. The mayor is visited by delegations of all sorts and receives letters of complaint and inquiry; s/he buys the first Red Cross button, proclaims special days and weeks, welcomes convention delegates, attends meetings and gives speeches.

If s/he is a strong mayor, s/he has a program for the city which s/he reveals in his/her reports, messages and remarks to the city council. Usually s/he is close to certain aldermen who introduce motions, resolutions and ordinances embodying his/her ideas. Unable to speak on legislative matters without leaving the presiding officer's chair, the mayor who is a leader has spokesmen in the council who present his/her point of view.

City Council

Councilmen or *aldermen* usually devote only part time to their official duties, possibly doing little more than attend weekly or semimonthly meetings. Committee meetings are held council night before the general session and may be closed to reporters. Chairmen of important committees, such as finance, streets and welfare are compelled to give some attention to the aldermanic duties throughout the week, at times at least, and may be interviewed in case of important news. A typical order of business for a city council meeting follows:

Roll call by the city clerk.
Minutes of the last meeting.
Communications read by the city clerk.
Standing committees (reports called for in alphabetical order.)
Special committee reports.
Call of wards (each alderman brings up any matter pertaining to his ward that needs council or executive attention.)
Miscellaneous business, including mayoral reports.
Adjournment.

The rules for covering a city council meeting do not differ from those that apply to any other type of meeting. Because of the importance of council meetings, however, it frequently is necessary to write two or more stories adequately to play up different matters affecting the public. It is seldom that a reporter can write a story entirely from the notes s/he is able to take as motions are made and argued and matters are referred to different committees. Usually the reporter must verify names, the wording of motions and resolutions, the outcome of votes and other matters by consulting the city clerk or his stenographer at the end of a meeting.

In an advance story of a council meeting, the nature of business likely to come up should be emphasized. The experienced reporter usually can anticipate the nature of debate and the lineup of votes. S/he also should attempt to interpret the significance and possible aftermath of any controversial matter.

By Raul Reyes
CHRONICLE STAFF

When the new expanded Houston City Council assumed office early this year, few city observers expected a proposed sign ordinance to become the focal point that it now is.

The proposed ordinance has caused tempers to flare and produced shouting matches among members of council, and split council down the middle.

The ordinance, if passed, would prohibit the construction of any new so-call off-premise signs (billboards not at the locations of the businesses they are advertising) and effectively outlaw portable, mobile signs, and high-voltage, ''spectacular'' signs. Also, within six years, existing signs would have to conform to strict height and size requirements.

The ordinance's third and final reading is scheduled for this Wednesday and proponents on both sides of the issue will be maneuvering for any advantage.

On Wednesday a number of possibilities can occur. It is possible that sign industry representatives will persuade council members to defeat the ordinance. Several amendments are expected to be introduced which could dilute the ordinance. Or, a completely new version of the ordinance—some say a weaker version—could be introduced for consideration. Still another possibility is that the entire matter could be delayed for at least a week. [Houston *Chronicle*]

It is the responsibility of the press to explain the nature of council actions, as well as to report them.

By Brad Frevert

Contracts totaling more than $100,000 were awarded at Monday night's Winona City Council meeting, but the council rejected all bids on two items and ordered specifications rewritten to allow local firms another shot at the contract.

Five contracts totaling $101,967 for equipment and supplies were awarded with little discussion by the council. But when the bids for two 72-inch mowers for the park-recreation department were reviewed the matter was no longer cut and dried.

Six bids were received on the contract for the two mowers. One mower was to include a snowblower attachment, the other a broom. Both are to have cabs. The two lowest bids were received from local firms, Feiten Implement and Winona Fire and Power Equipment Co., but the bids did not meet specifications.

Outgoing 3rd Ward Councilwoman Jan Allen said, "If we write specifications that exclude Winona bidders, it's wrong."

Park-Recreation Director Robert Welch disagreed. "If we don't write specs for equipment to do the job, we're missing the boat," he said.

The mowers from local dealers did not have a "true zero turning radius," meaning the wheels on each side operate independently. The machine could turn in its own wheel base, Welch explained, but only by using the brake on one side, which leaves a divot on grass and makes for difficult operation on ice.

The only bid that met specifications came from Edwin Johnson Co., Minnetonka, Minn.

The council voted 6–1, with At-Large Councilman James Stoltman opposing, to reject all the bids on the mowers. The only legal way the council can keep from accepting the lowest responsible bidder is to reject all bids and readvertise.

The council then voted a number of times on a motion and related amendments—splitting 4–3—with Mayor Earl Laufenburger, 1st Ward Councilwoman Susan Edel, and 4th Ward Councilman Jerry Borzyskowski voting no—to have the bids rewritten to allow for a water-cooled engine and not restrict the specifications to one brand. One of the local firms has a machine with a water-cooled engine.

Phil Feiten, owner of Feiten Implement, was in the audience but did not address the council.

Apparently the council's action will result in the specifications for the mowers being redrawn, making them broader so as to allow more than one brand of mower to fit. [Winona (Minn.) *Daily News*]

Readers should be told how governmental actions affect them.

By Bernie Peterson

Appleton homeowners will be hit with a 20% sewer user fee increase in 1980, according to a budget of more than $3 million approved Thursday by the Common Council's Finance Committee.

Similar hikes will be felt by industrial customers, as Appleton feels the impact of full-fledged operations at the sewage treatment plant, which is close to completing a $31 million renovation started in 1976.

According to Public Works Director Robert Miller, the quarterly bill for a "typical" family of four persons using 2,800 cubic feet of water will increase from $17.64 to $21.28.

He also cited three specific industries, which he did not identify by name. [Appleton (Wis.) *Post-Crescent*]

The collective effect of governmental activity is important.

By Dean Mayer

The city of Green Bay's refusal to part with a sewer interceptor could raise the dollar figure and alter the timetable for extending sanitary sewers into a portion of the town of Scott.

It could also lead to a court battle between Green Bay and the Metropolitan Sewerage District Commission following action approved at the MSD's meeting Monday.

Green Bay owns the Scott-Bayshore sewer interceptor on the city's Northeast Side along lower Green bay and, in some portions, in the bay.

An interceptor is a sewer line that has no direct user hook-ups but serves to connect a number of sewers.

The Scott-Bayshore interceptor currently serves only Green Bay residents. But the Metropolitan Sewerage District needs to acquire it from the city to extend sanitary sewers to a portion of Scott recently annexed by the MSD.

The annexed portion affects about 240 persons, many of whom face severe sewage problems. The segment runs south from the Wequiock School area to the town limits and includes parts of the Scott-Bayshore and Wequiock drainage basins.

[Green Bay (Wis.) *Press-Gazette*]

Disgusted reporters of legislative bodies and governmental agencies at all levels—municipal, county, state and federal—sometimes write in the spirit of the following first half of a Minneapolis *Tribune* news story:

By M. Howard Gelfand
STAFF WRITER

By 8 p.m., when the show begins, there isn't an empty seat in the house. And no wonder. The most popular repertory company in the suburb of Dayton never does the same show twice.

Not that the cast—the five members of the Dayton City Council—doesn't repeat its favorite lines from time to time: lines like, "Shut up," and "You're out of order," and "What was the motion?"

This week's Monday-night meeting was such a hit that after a five-hour, three-act performance, the Dayton City Council decided to continue the drama next Monday.

When the decision was made it was 1 A.M., and the council hadn't even plowed halfway through its agenda. Still, only a few in the standing-room only audience of 50 had left.

The central issue at the meeting was whether to grant a zoning variance to Dayton developer Erland Maki. Maki wants to build an addition to a development on which he already has constructed 30 houses. The problem is that since he began the development, the council passed a law prohibiting houses on lots of less than 2½ acres. He wants to build 42 more houses on lots of half-an-acre each.

The council never did decide what to do. It seems likely, though, that some sort of compromise will be reached next week.

On one side of the issue is the mayor, Mrs. Gene Nelson. (Mrs. Nelson, 50, is also the police chief, and . . . but that's another story. More of that later.) Mrs. Nelson wanted to grant the variance, and it was partly her refusal to accept a compromise that resulted in the stalemate.

On the other side of the issue—and just about every other issue—is maverick Councilman Gerald Barfuss, a junior-high school art teacher. He contends that granting the variance would be illegal and environmentally unsound. He further says that Maki is guilty of a conflict-of-interest because Maki sits on the city's planning commission.

The scene for the bi-weekly sessions in the northwestern Hennepin County Community is the Dayton City Hall, a blue metal structure that houses two caterpillar trucks but no telephone.

Mrs. Nelson conducts the meetings like a stern schoolmarm, scolding audience members and Barfuss for laughing or talking out of turn.

Barfuss, 33, is her sassy pupil, the incorrigible class wit who accepts the titters of his friends as payment for the admonishments he constantly endures.

Barfuss walked out of a special hearing on the matter held by the council last month, but before he did so he outlined his case against the variance. Mrs. Nelson told him last night:

"You have prematurely presented your opinion at the hearing and unless you've had a change of heart that can stand."

"I'm a council member," he responded, "and I intend to speak."

"I'd like to hear what the other council members have to say," she said.

City Clerk

The *city clerk,* an elective officer, might be termed the city's secretary. S/he attends council meetings and takes minutes, receives communications addressed to the city, issues licenses (dog, beach and the like), receives nominating petitions, supervises elections and preserves all city records.

Corporation Counsel

A lawyer, the *corporation counsel* is legal adviser to the city and its representative in court in major matters. In smaller communities these duties are performed by the *city attorney,* who, in larger places, is the prosecuting attorney in criminal cases: much of the work relates to minor court cases. The title may be *city solicitor*.

Public Works

The tendency is toward consolidation, under a *commissioner of public works,* of the departments of streets, water, public buildings, local improvements and the like. If the offices are not consolidated, the commissioner of public works has charge of new construction of streets, sewers and so on, whereas the *street commissioner* has the responsibility of seeing that the streets are kept clean and in repair and usually has charge of garbage collection. The *city engineer* works under the commissioner of public works.

Finances

The elected officials are usually the mayor, city clerk and city treasurer; other city officers also may be chosen by the voters but usually are appointed by the chief executive with the approval of the council. It is the duty of the *city treasurer,* of course, to collect taxes and other moneys due the city and to pay bills upon executive order. There also may be a *city auditor,* who keeps detailed records of the city's financial setup and acts as financial adviser. Also there may be a *city collector,* who is chiefly a desk clerk to take in money, and a *purchasing agent,* in charge of buying material authorized by the city council.

The financial setup of a city requires study to be understood. The reporter struggling to comprehend it has the consolation of knowing that many city officials don't know what it's all about. State law limits the taxing power of a municipality, usually by restricting the rate at which each $100 of assessed valuation of real and personal property can be taxed for each of several different purposes. The city's budget cannot call for expenditures beyond the total tax collection possible for a given purpose, such as streets, parks and libraries. The financial operations of a city furthermore are limited by state laws, restricting the city's bonding power. A city, for instance, may be allowed to issue tax anticipation warrants to only 50 or 75 per cent of the total amount which would be realized from the collection of taxes if all were paid. Financial houses that purchase these warrants, however, may not be willing to approve the issuance of as many as the law would permit. In Illinois, a city's bonding power is limited to 2½ per cent of assessed valuation.

The reporter with a good grounding in economics and commerce courses has an advantage in comprehending municipal finance. Any reasonably intelligent reporter, however, can grasp it if it is explained clearly.

The reporter should not feel embarrassed to ask some city official qualified to do so—the city treasurer, auditor or chairman of the council finance committee perhaps—to give an hour's time to outline the basic principles of the system. Once the reporter has mastered the essentials s/he will be in a position to perform a valuable public service by making every story related to city finance a lesson in an important phase of government for tax-paying readers. With training, one may even be an authority on the finances of one's own city at least.

Three financial stories annually are of "sure fire" interest. They are (1) announcement by the assessor of the assessed valuations of real property, (2) announcement of tax rates and (3) passage of the city budget.

The assessment story may not be an annual one, as many places have new assessments biennially or quadrennially. There invariably follow interminable appeals to the board of tax appeals by property owners seeking reductions, and there always is at least one additional news story regarding the quantity of such suits. It is in the public interest that those who pay taxes understand the procedure by which they are levied.

When one knows the valuation placed on a piece of property and the legally adopted tax rate (the amount one will have to pay for each $100 worth of assessed valuation), the tax payer can figure out his/her own tax bill. Taxpayers' suits to set aside a tax rate in whole or part on the basis that some item in the city budget is improper are frequent. Usual practice in such cases, and when appeals are pending from the assessor's valuations, is to pay the tax under protest. If the protest is allowed, often after an appellate court decision, refunds are made. To postpone tax collections until after all appeals are decided would be to deprive the city of revenue.

The following is an example of a journalistic attempt to explain the tax-assessment process:

By Dolores McCahill and Lillian Williams

There was bad news for some Cook County property owners Monday when the Illinois Department of Revenue authorized an almost 7 percent increase in the multiplier used to compute real estate tax bills in the county.

The multiplier, a mathematical device designed to make property taxes equal for homeowners throughout the state, was set Monday at 1.6016, compared with last year's 1.4966.

Assuming the tax rate this year was identical to the rate a year ago, the tax on a $60,000 home in Chicago would rise to $1,386 under the new multiplier, as compared with $1,295 under the old multiplier, according to the Civic Federation, a taxpayer watchdog group.

However, the federation noted, most homeowners wouldn't have to pay the increase because the first $3,000 in increased taxes would be exempted under a new state law.

The Civic Federation said the owners of industrial plants, commercial buildings and large apartment buildings wouldn't escape the tax increase.

Cook County Assessor Thomas C. Hynes immediately criticized the boost in the multiplier as too high.

"I am concerned because this decision of the Department of Revenue could result in an unwarranted and objectionable property tax increase even without any increase in assessment or tax rates," Hynes said.

However, Hynes said most homeowners would be cushioned against the higher multiplier by the so-called homeowners' exemption, which exempts up to $3,000 in increased assessed valuation from real extate taxes. Hynes sponsored the exemption when he was president of the state Senate.

Frank Coakley, executive director of the Civic Federation, criticized the multiplier increase as "excessive and unjustified."

The tax multiplier, also known as the county equalization factor, is a mathematical formula that is supposed to make property assessments equal in each of the state's 102 counties.

The 1.6016 multiplier announced Monday was higher than the tentative multiplier of 1.5917 announced earlier. The previous figure also had drawn criticism from Hynes as too high.

Barbara Moore, of the state Revenue Department, said the higher multiplier was made necessary by "a considerable number of cutbacks" in property assessments by the Cook County Board of Tax Appeals.

She said the board granted a total of $355 million in reductions from assessments made by Hynes' office.

On April 30, Hynes' office announced that total assessments in the county stood at about $15.9 billion, up 6.4 percent from the previous year.

Tax experts said it was difficult to estimate the impact of the higher multiplier on individual tax bills because of the varying rates set by taxing agencies in the many county taxing districts.

The multiplier will be applied to 1979 tax bills payable this year. Property owners already have paid the estimated first installment on the 1979 tax bills. Bills for the second installment, which will reflect final tax rates and the impact of the multiplier, will be mailed later this summer. . . . [Chicago *Sun-Times*]

The newspaper that takes seriously the watchdog function should keep a constant eye on the assessor's office. It should insist on learning, so as to inform the public, what rules the assessor follows in so-called special cases. Too often it seems that political friends of the administration are the chief beneficiaries. In large places the Establishment is more concerned over who controls the assessor's office than it is over most other offices. This is especially true now that the old central business districts are fighting to maintain their financial supremacy over the suburban and outlying shopping centers. Provided that property is not assessed too high, urban renewal projects may make it possible for older people, potentially good spenders, to live near the old central shopping areas. Expensive high-rise apartments often replace slums where the purchasing power of the residents was negligible. Public buildings and recreational centers also attract upper- and middle-class people.

Other Offices and Boards

The police and fire departments and the courts already have been discussed and schools will be the subject of the next section. There remain the offices of the building commissioner, commissioner of health, superintendent of playgrounds and recreation, other minor officers (sealer, purchasing agent and so forth) and the numerous official and semiofficial boards and commissions.

The first requisite of the city hall reporter is to be aware of the existence of these offices and boards and of their functions. In no two communities is the setup exactly alike, although the following are generally to be found: civil service commission, zoning board, park board, board of tax appeals, liquor control, library board and planning commission. The number of land clearance commissions, urban renewal and housing authorities is increasing. So also are various types of pollution-control agencies. There may be any of the following boards or commissions: traffic safety, local improvements, recreation, health and quite a few more.

In some cities, these groups are active and newsworthy; in others they are dormant, their existence seeming to serve little purpose other than to provide the mayor with the opportunity to appoint minor political followers to prestige positions. A live chairperson, however, can make any one of the groups a vital factor in municipal affairs. The civil service commission, for instance, can cease being the rubber stamp for political appointments that it is in many places and can become a real watchdog of the merit system by insisting that all jobs that should be filled by civil service examinations be so filled, that the spirit of civil service not be defeated through repeated temporary appointments in lieu of holding examinations to fill vacancies, that too much weight not be given in the final ratings of candidates to the ''intangible'' qualifications as contained in the recommendations of political friends, that dismissals from city employment be for valid reasons rather than as a result of trumped-up charges and that the conduct of examinations be absolutely honest.

Most large city newspapers now have welfare beats that take reporters to a multitude of local, state and national offices engaged in operating a variety of programs. According to Lois Wille of the Chicago *Sun-Times,* in the past several years the welfare field has become an important offshoot of political reporting. The fact that government agencies, rather than privately supported agencies, are the biggest supplier of welfare services puts welfare in the political arena and makes it a key function of governments. Says Mrs. Wille: ''Groups struggling to compete with an established machine have learned to use welfare services as a means of gaining political power. For example, the movement to give free medical care to the poor through 'people's health clinics' has a dual purpose: to mobilize physicians and nurses and other volunteers to give genuine service to the poor, and to organize viable political action groups in poor communities that often have no 'clout' in city hall. And, as a result, City Hall may react by trying to sabotage the clinics. Thus, we have a good political story going as well as a welfare story.''

Advises Mrs. Wille: ''Treat welfare reporting as the big story it is. An occasional feature story about a child whose brain has been damaged because he nibbled lead-poisoned paint crumbling from tenement walls is not enough. You have to find out who owns the building, whether city officials have enforced housing codes to repair the broken walls, who, if anyone, will treat and cure the child, and who, if anyone, will fix the house so he won't get sick again.''

Increasingly since New Deal days federal funds have become available for local projects. With the largess have come standards that states and municipalities must observe. Perhaps the most newsworthy situations resulting from conflicts over whether federal rules are being obeyed relate to charges of discrimination against minority groups regarding employment compensated for in part by money from Washington.

Urban Renewal

No aspect of local governmental operations in the large cities has grown more in importance in recent years than slum clearance and urban renewal. Federal, state and local funds are involved and many metropolitan centers are undergoing wholesale renovations costing into the millions or billions of dollars. Whereas a generation ago the strength of a political machine was its ability to act as a welfare and relief organization—the Tammany Hall method—today municipal political leaders feel that their strength comes mostly from their ability to remake the appearance of their bailiwicks by tearing down and rebuilding. Mayors and their planning, housing and land clearance boards trot to Washington to seek approval of "workable plans," the first step in obtaining federal funds for any program. There follow an interminable number of steps, including legislative and administrative action at three levels of government, condemnation proceedings, letting of contracts, demolition, housing of dispossessed tenants, haggling over plans for buildings, streets, the location of parks, schools and the like. Civil libertarians and human relations groups often are apprehensive over the futures of Negroes and members of other minority groups who are most frequently affected by slum clearance projects dubbed "people removal."

The movement of whites to the suburbs means that the proportion of nonwhites within the big city limits is becoming greater. Political as well as social and economic upheavals result. Inevitably, despite the fear of racists, little revolutionary fervor has developed among the underdog groups. Negroes and other minorities don't want to overthrow the system; they just want to become a part of it and benefit fairly therefrom. Most so-called liberated blacks unfortunately act just like white people. They haven't reformed much of anything any more than did the women a half century ago when they obtained the suffrage or than did the 18-year-old new voters more recently.

So intricate and important has urban renewal become that large newspapers increasingly are hiring or training reportorial specialists to keep up with developments.

Some critics, notably Jane Jacobs in *The Death and Life of Great American Cities,* contend that federally supported urban renewal programs are destructive of small independent businesses and are a weapon used by large commercial interests in central business districts to combat the growth of suburbs and outlying shopping centers and to preserve their economic power. A new gimmick to attempt to bolster the traditional central business district is the mall, a closed-off street where vehicular traffic is forbidden and there is plenty of shrubbery.

Journalistic watchdogs should probe to determine the extent to which uprooting people from old neighborhoods has created new social and economic problems. Martin Anderson wrote in *The Federal Bulldozer* that during the 1950–60 period 126,000 dwelling units in good condition were destroyed to make way for urban renewal projects that resulted in public or private commercial construction. Only 28,000 new housing units were built in the same areas.

What is the quality of the new housing to which displaced persons go? Consider health, educational and other facilities. Do dislodged families merely form new slums in other localities? Is there any hope for the small businessman? What leadership is being provided and with what success by church, political, community and other groups, including aggressive self-help councils?

SCHOOLS AND EDUCATION

Routine coverage of school news is not too difficult. It consists of watching such items as enrollment figures, bond issues, faculty and curriculum changes, new buildings and equipment, commencement and other programs, student activities and the like. What follows is a routine story of a board of education meeting.

Stephen Construction company of Glenwood was named last week to construct a new addition to Brookwood junior high school, school district No. 167. The board of education awarded the contract to the company in the amount of $520,918. Base bids had been received from 13 firms on the addition.

Stephen Construction company built the original school building at Longwood, board president Weldon Nygren noted.

At the board's continued meeting on Wednesday, Superintendent Louis M. Prevost announced that 1,662 pupils presently are enrolled in the district, an increase to date of 122 students. He also reported Brookwood elementary school enrollment at 630 and pointed out that grade three had class sizes of 34 and 35 students.

Anticipated additional enrollments during the course of the present school year, due to construction of 62 more homes in the district, will require an additional mobile unit to house the students, Prevost said. He was authorized by the board to obtain bids for the additional unit to alleviate crowded conditions in the third grades.

The board discussed participation in the building program for trainable mentally handicapped of the South Cook County Special Education cooperative (SPEED), and endorsed the joint-agreement program. A resolution was adopted specifying that District 167 shall bear a share of the program's cost not to exceed the yield of tax levy of two percent for five years.

Board president Nygren selected the board professional negotiations committee and named Gene Kappel as chairman. Robert Brady and Kathleen Huck were appointed to serve for the 1970–71 school year.

In other actions, the board directed Prevost to obtain a bid from Horace Mann before deciding an award of insurance coverage for all school district employes, awarded a contract for $425 to Lustig Construction company to install a window in the Longwood school kitchen and authorized purchase of 18 desks from Lowrey-McDonnell company for Brookwood junior high school.

Raymond Brejcha reported that life safety construction work at Brookwood elementary school was "essentially complete."

The board also approved the hiring of personnel. Approval was granted for the employment of Mrs. Karolyn Margerum as an elementary librarian at $7,800 per year, for the hiring of a full time library clerk at Brookwood elementary school to assist the librarian and for the payment of $400 to Mrs. Janet Dart to supervise girls' extra-curricular physical education activities.

The board approved a motion to support a memorial fund drive by the PTA to be conducted in tribute to Mrs. Lucile Barron. Mrs. Barron, who taught in District 167 for more than 17 years, died September 5.

In final action, the board appointed Kappel, Barton Herr and John Dougherty to represent the school district at a meeting of the Chicago Heights planning commission.

[Park Forest (Ill.) *Star*]

Helping citizens—over 50 per cent of whose local tax dollars go to maintain the public schools—understand what's going on educationally is a different matter. When the children of World War II veterans began reaching school age in the '50s, there was hardly a school district in the United States which did not find it necessary to expand its educational facilities. Nevertheless, in many places there persisted grave shortages in buildings, classrooms, equipment and teachers. By the mid '70s the war babies were graduated and many communities faced with financial problems considered closing some schools and firing some teachers. Protests by parents and others made many school board meetings much livelier than ever before.

As the total tax burden—federal, state and local—grew during the cold war period and the Vietnam War, taxpayers became reluctant to approve school bond issues and little progress was made toward obtaining financial aid from the federal government. Whereas formerly school elections aroused only meager interest, by the mid '60s exactly the opposite was coming to be the case in many places. Many voters, furthermore, voted against proposed bond issues or proposals to raise the tax rate as a protest against heavy taxation, most of it federal income tax, about which ordinary people lack the opportunity to express themselves directly at the polls. So they vote against any and all taxes presented to them, regardless of their own immediate best interests.

In addition to the basic problem of finances, other educational issues have become controversial and, consequently, newsworthy.

Integration

In the '50's the entire world knew, from news reports and pictures, of the violence connected with attempts to implement the United States Supreme Court decision that racial segregation must end in schools. In the '70s the nation's image as the citadel of democracy suffered again when violence flared in the aftermath of court orders that school children be bussed to foster integration.

In the interim there were incessant court battles and incidents to make the international headlines, as the goals of equality still eluded millions. School segregation exists in many places as a result of housing segregation. Some bond issues for the construction of new schools were defeated in the suburbs to discourage the migration of Negroes and other minorities.

Most newspapers are moderate or liberal in their attitude toward the school integration issue and generally strive for strict objectivity in reporting news of the controversy. Most agree that the quality of education in ghetto schools must be vastly improved. Aroused black parents have brought pressure resulting in benefits to all students as a result of abolition of so-called tracking systems whereby children are assigned to classes on the basis of intelligence and other tests now generally discredited.

Religion

Public taxpayers' assistance to parochial schools became a political issue in the '70s as the schools, mostly Roman Catholic, pleaded inability to continue to exist without it and exerted pressure on Congress, state legislatures and delegates to constitutional conventions to find ways to circumvent the constitutional separation of church and state.

The parochial school crisis followed a considerable increase in their number and enrollment in the '50s and early '60s, the period of war babies. As the need for public assistance grew, traditional Catholic opposition to bond issues to support public schools diminished, and promotion of shared-time plans—whereby parochial school students take some studies in public schools—grew. Catholics also became candidates for public school boards, causing bitter campaigns in some places.

The Catholics' argument is that their children should benefit from free bus transportation and similar services and that such assistance is "child aid" and not "church aid." Catholics have traditionally fought federal aid to education programs in Congress because their schools were not included on an equal basis. The Catholic church is very secretive about its finances and wealth.

In opposition, the crying need of public schools for more funds, especially in the ghettoes and rural areas, is argued; the contention is advanced that two school systems, both financed by public funds, obviously cost more than a single system and are likely to be inferior. Furthermore, it is argued that the religious education presumably provided parochial school students is outdated and the existence of the dual system is divisive and undemocratic.

Leading the opposition to parochiaid is Americans United for Separation of Church and State, which publishes the magazine *Church and State,* and lobbies. It applauded the United States Supreme Court decisions that forbade use of school property for released-time religious instruction and outlawed prescribed prayers and bible readings in the public schools. Bound to become an increasingly crucial issue are the tax exemptions for church-owned real estate not used for religious purposes. Not only the parochial schools but municipalities are in a financial bind, and more than 50 per cent of the potentially taxable land in many of them is tax exempt.

Delinquency

From one standpoint, the history of public school education in America could be written to show how, step by step, the schools have assumed responsibilities formerly considered the prerogative of the home, factory or other institutions. Most broadening of the curriculum has resulted from outside pressure, including statutes requiring that this or that—American history, the dangers of dope addiction, automobile driving and the like—be taught. As a consequence, the student's free choice is limited, especially if s/he is among the increasing number who seek to meet college entrance requirements. Were it not for compulsory attendance laws, the already serious dropout problem would be greater. Problem children are generally ones in revolt against regimentation, real or imagined. In the huge high schools of today, potentially disturbed adolescents develop intense feelings of frustration. Despite physical education and intramural athletic programs, participation in varsity sports is limited to an increasingly smaller proportion of the student body. The same is true of other school activities, with opportunities to become officers or star performers restricted to the minority. In several large cities, post-athletic ccntest riots between fans representing rival schools have become serious. The emphasis that rooting alumni insist colleges and universities place on sports, especially football, sets a nationwide pattern. Exposures of widespread professional gambling activities, which include attempts, successful and otherwise, to bribe players, occur frequently.

Maintaining discipline has become a major problem at all levels. Teachers and pupils alike are the frequent victims of violence and police and security guards are necessary to preserve order and protect property. Teachers often blame indifferent parents, who in turn say the schools are too permissive and should straighten out any disturbed youngsters.

Even if the schools solved all the problems suggested in this section, of course, the problem of juvenile delinquency would continue to exist because its social and economic causes are mostly outside, not inside, the school walls.

Student Unrest

It would be a grave error also to conclude that widespread unrest among college and high school students is instigated or led by delinquents or those academically deficient. Exactly the contrary is the case. The picket lines, sitdowns and other manifestations of discontent have attracted the best, not the poorest, students throughout the United States and the rest of the world, in many parts of which there have been disturbances much more serious than any in this country, as, for example, Tokyo, Mexico, Paris and Rome. After all, foreign students and teachers traditionally have been much more alert to social injustices and much more active in attempting to correct them than have their American counterparts.

The revolt of the students is matched by that of public school teachers, who have finally overcome their prejudice against labor unions and are organizing and joining them to bargain collectively and to strike in all parts of the country. It is foolhardy to limit coverage of such incidents to the immediate overt incidents as unrelated to other forms of protest: the civil rights movement, the peace movement, the women's liberation movement, uprisings of American Indians, Mexican-Americans (Chicanos) and other minority ethnic groups, unionization of priests and nuns, unionization of policemen, nurses and many others. Economic and social unrest is worldwide. The newspaper reporter does not have the perspective of a historian or a cultural anthropologist of a century from now, but s/he can avoid overemphasis of minor incidents and help readers to be aware of the fact that many apparently isolated events actually are related.

Many high school dropouts charge that the curricula are not relevant to contemporary life. Now that 18-year-olds are eligible to vote, the question arises as to how well the public schools have acquainted them with even the existence of the issues about which they will be expected to have opinions in a democracy. Pressure groups, mostly conservative, in the past have influenced school authorities to soft-pedal the so-called controversial and, as a result, curricula have continued to stress rote learning, nonfunctional English theme writing, foreign languages, mathematics and pre-World War II history. This corrupts the original concept of the free public school system, which was to prepare citizens for participation in a democracy. Teachers' colleges have gone in for so much theory and methodological experimentation that students in many places are little more than human guinea pigs for pedagogical game playing. Character education, personality development, vocational training, sensitivity experiences and similar programs may possess some value but they contribute little to producing perceptive voters.

Exceptional Children

Counselors, psychologists, psychiatrists and other advisers deal with individual problems of disturbed and other children. Special classes or instructions exist for physically handicapped children—the deaf, dumb, blind, crippled and mentally retarded—and the gifted child is attracting more and more attention. Opinions differ as to whether children should be grouped according to potential ability, usually determined by intelligence or other tests, or achievement. On the one hand, the consciousness of being labeled superior, medium or inferior is considered disturbing to some children who will have to compete in a world of unequals. On the other hand, it is contended that fast learners are held back if instruction has to be kept at the level of the slowest. The pros and cons of this matter have been debated by educators and parents for a number of years in many parts of the country.

Automation

Related to this issue is the controversy over the extent to which instruction should be standardized in the interest of reducing teaching burdens. Under the influence of teachers colleges during the past generation, testing of many kinds—intelligence, aptitude, achievement and so forth—has developed considerably. The results are used for placement of students in classes in the grades and high schools and by colleges and universities to determine admissions. Criticism is growing that if improperly used these tests result in "giving a student a number" at an early age and prejudice teachers' attitudes toward actual classroom work. Also, and more seriously, it is contended that the tests do not measure a student's ability to organize his thoughts, his total understanding of a topic, imagination, ingenuity or originality. Devised for fast grading by machines, the tests require the student merely to put an *x* after which of three of four answers to a question is correct. University professors, especially in the professional schools such as law and medicine, complain that students are coming to lack the ability to express themselves and that automatized teaching makes for conformist robots. Teaching machines, airborne television programs and the like ease the teacher problem, it is admitted, but stultify initiative and creativeness.

Impetus to the "back to fundamentals" movement has come about because of growing evidence, noted by employers and others, that Johnny really can't read, or spell or compose a grammatical sentence; and that furthermore, he has little or no knowledge of history, geography or contemporary social, economic and political problems. The protests have led to the abandonment of many fads that originated in the teachers colleges: Dick and Jane, gestalt reading, no alphabet, no syllables, New Math, Marshall McLuhan, and programmed learning by lesson plans mechanized by commercial companies.

The tests on which teachers have focused attention are discredited by revelations that they measure exposure to the upper-middle-class. A few years ago children who scored from 700 to 800 on college board tests had a mean family income of $24,124; those with 700 to 740 scores had income levels of $21,980; those with 550 to 590 had levels of $19,481, and at the bottom those who scored 200 to 249 had income levels of $8,639.

Academic Freedom

There is hardly an American community that has not had a "case" involving a teacher with allegedly heretical ideas, a reading list that someone does not like or a textbook or magazine under attack by a patriotic or other pressure group. The best way to keep abreast of developments is by reading the *Newsletter on Intellectual Freedom* of the American Library Association. The situation unquestionably has made teaching less attractive to many young men and women and has contributed to the development of the strong administrator type of school superintendent. As in all other aspects of contemporary complex society, rules and regulations and forms and reports have multiplied in the school system. Teachers often complain that they are left too little time to teach and that they have increasingly less to say about the determination of educational policy. In huge school systems, not only pupils but teachers as well run the risk of becoming merely numbers.

Teachers

For firsthand observation of the classroom, reporters sometimes obtain assignments as substitute teachers. The following is the first third of one article that resulted from such a stunt.

By Helen Kimmel

Working as a substitute teacher in several neighboring school districts in California, my work has taken me to scores of classrooms each year. I've had a chance to see firsthand what students today are learning—and what they are being denied.

In the first few grades of school, students are labeled as good students (gifted or college-bound) or bad students (learning-impaired, behavior problem, unmotivated), or are lost in the mass of students who are mostly ignored because they don't stand out in either direction. Very early on, students come to understand that they are viewed in a certain way, and come to expect to be treated and separated into groups accordingly. A brief glance at any MGM ("Mentally Gifted Minors") class or remedial class, anywhere in the country will reveal that racial and economic lines are major factors in the students' placement.

Many teachers view their assignment to remedial or "review" classes as a form of punishment, and certainly many principals assign teachers to these classes as punishment or as a form of harassment. Working with these classes is often exceptionally difficult, not because the students placed in them are slow learners, but because they are dumping grounds for bright students with behaviour problems, the handicapped, or recent immigrants who may have potential to be excellent students but don't speak English well yet. Teachers are assigned not according to their strengths and weaknesses, but according to the needs and convenience of the administration.

Teachers new to a district can expect to be assigned to schools in the poorer parts of the district, generally in minority areas. Special grants to pay for college expenses are given to teacher trainees who sign contracts to teach in "inner-city or special problem" schools. Now some districts use "combat pay" to lure teachers to what are considered difficult or physically dangerous schools. These are working-class, mainly minority schools.

The students know what's going on. Can you imagine how it must feel to know that your teacher gets extra pay because you are considered a threat?

One day during a social studies class on "the contributions of Black Americans to society," a 15-year-old Black student, silent until then, got up at her desk at the back of the room and said, "How dare you talk about Black people in this school?"

For the next 10 minutes, with tears running down her cheeks, she described some of the racist treatment she had been subjected to at the school. When she got to the part about how the school secretary had refused that very morning to touch her to put change in her hand, but had pushed it across the counter with distaste on her face, the young woman just sat down and sobbed.

[New York *Daily World*]

COUNTY GOVERNMENT

The county building is what ordinarily is known as the courthouse because the county court is the most important room in it. The same building probably also contains the circuit court and possibly the municipal court, if there is one, and the court of a police magistrate or justice of the peace. There also are other offices of county officials.

County Board

Corresponding to the city council (or *board of aldermen*) of a city is the *county board,* sometimes called *board of commissioners* or *board of supervisors,* which is the governing body of a county. Its president (or chairman) may either be elected by the voters or be selected by the board members who are elected by townships or at large. In smaller places, the board may meet infrequently, as bimonthly or semiannually; in large places it meets almost as frequently as the city council. Its powers are limited because the county is primarily an agent of the state in collecting taxes, enforcing laws, recording documents, constructing and maintaining highways, providing poor relief, administering rural schools, supervising nominations and elections, guarding public health and performing other similar functions. These duties are the responsibility of the elective county officers.

By Roland Krekeler

The Linn County Board of Supervisors decided today to negotiate for a contract with Associated Engineers of Cedar Rapids for remodeling of the courthouse.

Supervisors Ken Schriner and Joe Rinas voted for the attempt to work out a contract with the company, which was one of several that were interviewed by the board recently. Supervisor Jean Oxley did not vote on the matter.

There was no discussion on the motion, and Mrs. Oxley did not explain her failure to vote, saying simply that she would "pass."

The supervisors plan to remodel the courthouse to provide more court space after most of the county administrative offices move to the Courthouse South, the former Penick and Ford administration building, later this year.

Federal revenue sharing funds totaling about $1.2 million are to be spent on the remodeling over a period of several years. Purchase and remodeling of the former Penick and Ford building also is being financed with $1.1 million in revenue sharing funds.

In other action, the board:

- Received a notice from Teamsters Local 238 that a majority of persons doing administrative assistant work for the county had voted to designate the union as their bargaining representative with the county. A total of eight persons were listed in the category.

Teamsters business repesentative Bob Schorg said a petition has been filed with the Iowa Public Employees Relations Board to set up the bargaining unit and asked the supervisors to sign a stipulation about the makeup of the unit.

However, Assistant County Attorney Glenn Johnson advised the board that the employees appear to be confidential employees and would thus not be allowed to organize for bargaining under state law.

Schorg said that matter would be taken up by the state board.

- Gave permission for Bob Jeter of 1635 Park Towne Lane NE to set up a two-chair shoeshine stand under the shelter for bus riders at the west edge of the Witwer Building at Second Avenue and Third Street SE.

The supervisors set a 90-day limit on the endeavor, saying they wanted to review the matter since only handicapped persons and the city previously had been allowed to use space in that area.

- Officially declared that the $1 million Squaw Creek Lake bond issue last Tuesday had failed to get the 60 percent approval required. A canvass of the election showed the official vote to be 4,574 in favor and 3,485 against. The unofficial figures on election night were 4,571 in favor and 3,485 against.
- Accepted with regret the resignation of Beth Reed of Cedar Rapids from the Health Center Board. She submitted her resignation for health reasons.

[Cedar Rapids (Iowa) *Gazette*]

County Clerk

Secretary of the county board, the *county clerk* also issues licenses (wedding, hunting and the like), accepts nominating papers, supervises the printing of ballots, receives election returns and keeps county records. If there is not a separate elective officer, *a register of deeds,* s/he also records articles of incorporation, receives applications for corporation charters and keeps all other records and documents of private transactions. It is to him one writes for a copy of one's birth certificate or to prove ownership of a piece of property.

Duties of the *sheriff, prosecuting attorney* and *coroner* and the operation of the county court already have been explained. The sheriff usually has his/her office in the county jail and the coroner may be a practicing physician or undertaker with a private office.

The *county treasurer* is an agent of the state, collecting taxes that s/he forwards to the state capital. S/he pays county employees out of funds reallocated to the county from the state and meets other obligations in similar fashion. The *county assessor* assesses the value of property in the county, prepares maps to show real estate ownership and reports his/her findings to the state.

The *county highway commissioner, county engineer, county surveyor, county superintendent of schools, county health officer, county agricultural agent* and other county officials perform duties suggested by their titles.

With the population explosion into the suburbs, county government has had to pay more attention to unincorporated areas because they inevitably are involved in problems related to water supply, transportation, recreation, policing and the like. Counties also operate poor farms, homes for the aged, jails, general hospitals, special hospitals for the tubercular, mentally ill and others, nursing homes and other institutions that cities and states also maintain. The awarding of contracts must be watched carefully as well as the quality of service performed. Illegal operations, as gambling, banned from the cities, may flourish in nearby areas.

An authoritative interpretative reporter may goad public officials to take action at the same time s/he enlightens readers regarding a governmental function.

By Len Kholos

Erie County commissioners' refusal to enter into regional planning with the city is not only hampering efforts to attract new industry, it is actually costing Erie taxpayers extra thousands of dollars.

In an interview with The Erie Dispatch last week, J. Cal Callahan, of Morris Knowles Inc., disclosed that the federal government is willing to pay half the cost of developing a workable program when more than one community is involved.

"The federal government feels that regional planning is the only sensible vehicle for progress, not only to promote orderly growth of an area but to prevent mistakes that will be costly in future years," Callahan said.

How is refusal of the county leaders to cooperate costing Erie taxpayers money?

Before the government will forward funds for redevelopment, whether it be for industrial or residential purposes, the communities involved must prepare a workable program.

Erie has already spent $5,000 and has contracted to spend $25,000 more to prepare this program in order to become eligible for federal planning money.

Assuming that the cost of work within the city would cost the same amount in a regional planning setup, the federal government would then have paid $15,000 plus half the costs incurred outside the city limits.

Can the individual communities in the county do anything to protect their own futures?

County Solicitor Jacob Held has told county commissioners that they cannot spend any money for planning. This came as a surprise to local government observers.

Held may also claim that the boroughs and townships are not allowed to spend money to plan for themselves.

On the other hand, the government will pay half the costs of preparing a workable program for communities of less than 25,000 population or, if they join in the city's planning efforts, half of the cost of the joint project.

We have explained why the federal government wants communities to have a workable program before it will forward funds for redevelopment. Now, here is what a workable program includes:

1. Sound local housing and health codes, enforced; an end to tolerating illegal, degrading, unhealthy substandard structures and areas.

2. A general master plan for community development, an end to haphazard planning and growth, a road map for the future.

3. Basic analysis of neighborhoods and the kind of treatment needed, an inventory of blighted and threatened areas upon which a plan of treatment to stop blight in its tracks can be developed.

4. An effective administrative organization to run the program, coordinated activity toward a common purpose by all offices and arms of the local government.

5. Financial capacity to carry out the program, utilizing local revenues and resources to build a better community for the future instead of continuing to pay heavily for past mistakes.

6. Rehousing of displaced families; expanding the supply of good housing for all income groups, through new construction and rehabilitation, so that families paying premium prices for slums can be rehoused.

7. Full-fledged, community-wide citizen participation and support, public demand for a better community and public backing for the steps needed to get it.

[Erie *Dispatch*]

STATE GOVERNMENT

Unless the beginning reporter works in one of the 50 state capitals, s/he has little contact with state governmental offices. If s/he is ambitious to become the state capital correspondent for a metropolitan newspaper as a possible step toward a similar position in Washington D.C., covering the city hall and local politics provides excellent training.

Although the reporter does not attend legislative sessions or visit the offices of state officers, some member of the editorial staff of the small city newspaper follows what is happening at the state capital as the local community is certain to be affected. City officials, civic organizations and other individuals and groups discuss state governmental matters and make known their opinions to their representatives in the legislature. Often it is necessary to obtain passage of a state law before it is possible for the city council to take some desired action; the corporation counsel may write such laws, which members of the legislature from the district introduce and push to adoption.

The following are examples of how to localize what is happening at the state capital so as to emphasize its importance and the role played by local persons:

> Mayor Walter E. Lewis today urged State Rep. Oscar R. Fall and State Sen. James L. Born to support the bill pending in the state legislature which would permit Milltown and other cities in the state between 25,000 and 100,000 population to establish a municipal court.

> All doubt as to the legality of Milltown's compulsory automobile testing station was removed today when Gov. Dale O. Hart signed the enabling act prepared by Corporation Counsel V. K. Kenwood and passed unanimously last week by both houses of the legislature.

> Representatives of The Crib, Milltown's foundling home, will go to the state capital tomorrow to join the lobby fighting passage of a bill which would establish a state department of public welfare. The bill is considered a threat to the local institution because it is believed a state department with power to direct all such establishments would insist upon regulations which The Crib could not meet and continue to exist.

> Killing of the remaining state library appropriation in Springfield last night in the term-end jam by a legislature anxious to adjourn late tonight, will deprive Milltown of the purchase of books and periodicals to the amount of $6,000 during the next two years, Miss Edith Delancey, city librarian, revealed today.

Local newspapers use, often by rewriting to play up the local angle, press releases from state offices. State representatives may write weekly newsletters to summarize legislative activities. Press associations in state capitals handle special queries from newspaper clients regarding matters of special interest. Only the largest papers, however, can afford to maintain bureaus in the capitals, either while the legislatures are in session or at any other time. Such assignments almost invariably go to reporters with experience covering local politics and government. They can educate their paper's readership regarding the realities of lawmaking, as in the following example:

> **By Pete Plastrik**
> NEWS LANSING BUREAU
>
> Lansing—The art of pork barreling, as practiced by lawmakers with the approach of Christmas, is to get the most fat with the least blood and fuss.
>
> In a flurry of last-minute deals, lawmakers carved plenty—grants costing from $5,000 to $10 million each—out of the state budget.
>
> Little political blood was shed. Rather than battling over who got what, law-

makers simply shoved something for just about everyone into the $770-million grants-and-transfers bill.

"We're going to give the governor a busy time with his pen (vetoing items)," quipped Rep. Dominic J. Jacobetti, D-Negaunee. Jacobetti is chairman of the House Appropriations Committee and the legislator in charge of "stuffing the stocking."

The bill had to be passed because 80 percent of the spending was for the state's revenue-sharing program for local governments. That made it an easy target for pork barreling, adding on special projects for the ride through the Legislature and to the governor's desk. Biggest add-on was an estimated $40-million package for the City of Detroit.

Then came other projects, a way to deliver "goodies" to non-Detroit lawmakers and to get their votes, which were needed to approve the package.

This year, the Muskegon area almost was knocked out of the bill because Jacobetti was miffed with Sen. Phil Arthurhultz, R-Whitehall.

Jacobetti tried to squelch an $800,000 grant to build a dock at Whitehall, even though it also would go to a Democratic representative's district.

He said he had been offended by remarks belittling his power that were attributed to Arthurhultz.

"I don't like the senator from that area," Jacobetti barked before relenting.

He also was bristling over being forced to strip projects for his Upper Peninsular district from the bill because of adverse publicity.

"I'm a dammed fool for what I did. Look at what you guys put into the bill," he snapped at other lawmakers.

Then Jacobetti slipped $75,000 into the bill for study of an Olympic training site at Northern Michigan University in Marquette.

He planted $250,000 for what was called the "Sturgeon River Sloughs Wetlands Development" project.

Lawmakers and staff aides weren't sure what that project is. It would help create a sanctuary for geese on state-owned land, suggested an aide.

But Jacobetti had the answer. It went back to a $250,000 grant to build a cultural-recreation center in Pelkie which he had been forced to remove from the bill earlier: "They didn't like the name Pelkie so I changed it," he said.

The buck-grabbing didn't stop with Jacobetti.

Sen. Bill S. Huffman, D-Madison Heights, squeezed a $4-million item into the bill to buy computer terminals for the state lottery.

Outside lawmakers plugged in $25,000 for a rape-crisis center in Saginaw; $10,000 for a halfway house for female convicts in Grand Rapids; $1 million for the Gerald R. Ford Museum; $150,000 to build a waterline across the Muskegon River; and more.

When the bill was before the legislature, little opposition surfaced.

[Saginaw (Mich.) *News*]

Mike Royko gave some Illinois ladies an even more realistic civics lesson.

I was talking to an ERA lady recently. She was fretting that the amendment might again fail in Illinois, after all of her hard work.

She showed me a list of about a dozen legislators and asked if I had any idea what kind of approach would work in bringing them around to her side.

I said: "Make the drop."

She looked puzzled and asked: "Make the what?"

"The drop. Give them some money."

She still didn't understand. "Money? For what?"

"Bribes."

She looked horrified and gasped: "Bribes?"

"Well, you can call it a campaign contribution, if it will make you feel better."

Then she laughed and said: "Oh, you're just kidding."

That's the trouble with the ERA crowd and most do-gooders. They are earnest, diligent and energetic. But they don't have much sense.

Throughout the history of this state, sly people have been getting what they want out of Springfield. They haven't done it by being honest, earnest, diligent and energetic. All those qualities get you is laughed at by the legislators and called a goo-goo.

They have done it by throwing a shoebox full of money through the transom of a Springfield hotel room.

Bet the ERA ladies don't understand that. As I told the lady mentioned above:

"It would be much cheaper, too. You could probably buy the votes of the dozen guys on that list for $5,000."

"I can't believe that," she said.

See? They don't even read about the bribery trials of legislators. They have no idea what a real bargain Springfield can be.

When the ready-mix concrete companies wanted their trucks to carry heavier loads, they bought some legislators' votes for as little as $200. Most of the individual bribes weren't higher than $500. Their total bankroll for co-operation was only $30,000. One legislator leader told the concrete people that he could deliver both sides of the aisle for only $20,000. The fact is, you shouldn't ever offer a legislator too much money. It might scare him. He'll think you want him to commit treason or kill somebody.

In contrast to the concrete people, the ERA forces in Illinois have a war chest of about $200,000. . . [Chicago *Sun-Times*]

FEDERAL GOVERNMENT

Of the major divisions of the federal government only one has a peacetime representative in the small city or town. That is the Postal Service, which in 1970 replaced the Post Office Department, which had existed since colonial days. In moderate-sized cities, at least for a few days before April 15, representatives of the Internal Revenue Service of the Department of the Treasury may be there to assist taxpayers in making the filing deadline.

A record high in the number of federal income tax returns filed and payments received was reported yesterday at the office of the collector of internal revenue here.

The approach of the midnight deadline brought thousands of persons to the office and there was sufficient extra help to take care of taxpayers who needed assistance in filling out the forms. Extra cashiers were on hand to accept payments. Because taxpayers had familiarized themselves with their problems, comparatively few had to wait long in line.

The peak in the day's business came in the early afternoon, but there were long lines in the early evening. Early closing of offices and manufacturing establishments, as well as the complete shut-down for some for the entire day, also helped make easier the trips of the last-minute visitors to the tax offices.

Payments in cash, money orders and checks totaling $150,000,000 were received yesterday. One check was for $1,000,000. In the two previous weeks $50,000,000 had been paid in person and through the mail.

In the internal revenue offices there were hundreds of bags of mail waiting to be opened. The opening of this mail, containing millions of dollars in checks and money orders, will begin tomorrow and will be finished by the end of the week.

With the exceptions noted, the federal government as a local news source in a small city hardly exists. As its power increases and that of the states declines, however, the lives of American citizens are more and more affected by it. Whereas the press associations and special column writers from Washington must be relied on for interpretations of major current events in the national capital, intelligent handling of much local news requires an understanding of national political issues and events.

Work for the unemployed, for instance, in depression years was provided through funds supplied by the federal government. In wartime there was the Office of Price Administration. Financial assistance also has been obtained through such federal agencies as the Home Owners Loan corporation and the Federal Housing administration, and the bank deposits of almost everyone today are insured through the Federal Deposit Insurance corporation. Most far-reaching, perhaps, is the federal Social Security act, which provides for old age pensions, Medicare, unemployment insurance, aid for dependent children, widows, the blind and other needy persons, and the Fair Labor Standards (wage and hour) act.

To write about how the local community is affected by these and other federal governmental activities without understanding them is not conducive to effectiveness.

It was the suburbs' turn today to absorb some criticism from the United States Public Health Service.

Milk sanitation conditions in several of them were found to be below a high standard set by Milltown, the federal agency said in a report released by the Advisory Committee of the Milltown-Wayne County Health survey.

Richmond had a rating of only 75.01 per cent for raw milk from 40 dairy farms under control of its health department and 73.15 per cent for three pasteurization plants, the report showed.

This compared with Milltown's rating of 91 per cent compliance with conditions set up in the recommended USPHS ordinance and code.

"The weighted rating for all milk sold in Richmond was 86.74 per cent," the surveyors declared, "the increase being due to the fact that 80 per cent of the milk sold in the city was being produced under the control of other agencies maintaining a more efficient control.

"It is advisable that Richmond adopt the standard ordinance and limit sale of milk to Grade A pasteurized in order to be in line with the state, Milltown, and other communities in the county."

Sanitation control of milk also was found to be "less than satisfactory" in Bluffs, Blytheville and Lakeside.

Milltown's milk control was praised by the surveyors, and the report commented, "there has been no communicable disease epidemic traced to the Milltown milk supply since 1936."

Nevertheless, the USPHS declared improvement in inspection services is needed immediately "if these high standards are to be protected."

The report also criticized an ordinance recently adopted by the county commissioners requiring all milk and milk products to be pasteurized, but not specifying grading.

We do not confer an odor of sanctity and guarantee infallibility when we elect men to office, and we properly reserve the right to consider them subject to such criticism as we may choose to make concerning their actions while in public service.

—Editorial, Cincinnati *Enquirer*

The system has made of the American politician a privileged character, a man whose private life becomes sacrosanct and inviolate, unless he is so clumsy as to be drawn into a lawsuit or arrested. . . . The American politician could become intoxicated nightly, beat his wife, use snuff, write free verse, or indulge in any other vice, I maintain, with slight danger of exposure.

—HENRY PRINGLE, New York *World*

PART FIVE

SPECIALIZED REPORTING

(requiring particular knowledge and expertise)

THE CITY EDITOR AT HOME

by B. F. Sylvester

"You had a good paper tonight, Dad."

"Thanks, Junior. It was just fair. Not enough local."

"Isn't national and world news good news?"

"You have to have a certain amount. But what people want to read is what is happening to their neighbors."

"If anything happened to Mr. Wilkins, would that be news?"

"Wilkins, the janitor? It would have to be important; the mayor's car run over him, or something."

"Why don't you put in the paper that Mr. Thomas is painting his house?"

"The necktie manufacturer? That wouldn't be news."

"Was that chorus girl suing the former millionaire important news?"

"Not important, exactly. It was the story of a woman—"

"We'll let that one go, Dad. Tell me about this interview with Senator Loke. He says the country needs real patriots. What does he mean?"

"I suppose he means real leaders."

"Why didn't your reporter ask him what he meant?"

"It might have sounded impertinent."

"The reporter didn't know what he meant, did he?"

"Oh, he must have had an idea."

"Let's get back to Mr. Thomas' house, Dad. Why isn't painting his house important?"

"It doesn't mean anything except to Thomas. Things must be looking up for him."

"Then, Dad, maybe it means something to others. If business is better, perhaps the 1,000 men he laid off in January are going back to work. That would mean business stimulation in our city, grocery bills paid, home installments paid up, new cars sold. And look, Dad, if people have begun to buy neckties, it might mean a new spirit throughout the country. It might be the turning of the tide."

"Now, Junior, run along. You talk like an editorial writer."

"Junior, I want to thank you for that tip on Thomas painting his house."

"Then it was important? Did he put the men back to work? Is there an upturn in business?"

"Sorry, Junior, we didn't get around to that. Our story is that Mr. and Mrs. Thomas couldn't agree on the color so she's painting her side blue and he's painting his orange. It's a pip."

Editor & Publisher

18
BUSINESS, FINANCE

A. Business
   1. Routine News
   2. Localization
   3. Trends
B. Finance
   1. Stock Exchanges
   2. Seeking Explanations
   3. Definitions
C. Problems and Policies
   1. Secrecy
   2. Puffery
   3. Codes
   4. Economic Experts

Since the end of World War II the number of shareholders of publicly owned corporations in the United States has more than doubled, peaking at 30 million in the '70s and numbering about 29.8 million today. This does not mean that control of the management policies of American businesses and industries has passed into the hands of housewives, widows, factory workers and middle-class shopkeepers. In fact, in monetary terms, the total ownership of stocks and bonds by small investors still is but a minute fraction of the invested wealth of the nation. It does mean, however, that millions of newspaper readers who formerly ignored the financial and business pages now have a vested interest in them. As a result, such pages are being expanded and their contents geared to appeal to the average reader and not just to the broker or banker.

The New York Stock Exchange reports that the typical shareholder in 1980:

> Is likely to be a male, although men outnumber women by only a narrow margin (14.0 million vs. 13.5 million). Men recaptured the edge held in 1970, but women have outnumbered men in each of the other six shareownership surveys the Exchange has conducted since 1952.
>
> Is 45½ years old. This was the median age of all shareowners in 1980 and the lowest median age in any of the surveys.
>
> Probably lives in a populous state and in a metropolitan area with a population of

one million or more. California, New York and Illinois by a wide margin are the states with the largest numbers of shareowners. New York, Chicago and Los Angeles are the only metropolitan areas with more than one million shareowners.

Had a median household income of $27,700 last year, about 67 per cent higher than the estimated national median household income of $16,600. In 1975, the annual median income of shareowners was $19,000, 70 per cent above the national median income of $11,200.

Is a professional or technical worker. This was the largest occupational group, as it was in 1975.

Probably attended college or a business or technical school.

Has a portfolio of equity holdings with a median value of $4,000 in mid-1980. The median value of shareowners' portfolios in the 1975 survey was $10,100.

The New York Stock Exchange also reports:

Twenty-two per cent of shareowners today, 6.5 million individuals, are new investors, compared with 9 per cent in 1975.

The median stock portfolio has declined to $4,000 from $10,100 in 1975, largely as a result of the growth in the number of younger, less affluent owners.

More than 12 million of today's shareowners have obtained stock through employee stock purchase plans at some time, far more than ever before.

Male shareowners now slightly outnumber females, reversing the finding in 1975.

The proportion of housewives, retired and non-employed people dropped from 40 per cent of the total number of shareowners to 30 per cent today.

Every geographic region of the country except New England gained shareowners over the past five years.

The popularity of some syndicated columns in this field and the phenomenal increase in the circulation of the *Wall Street Journal* to replace the New York *Daily News* as the American daily with the largest circulation have helped to inspire many newspapers to give greater attention to business and financial news, and specializing in this kind of journalism has become much more attractive to active newspapermen, especially beginners.

In 1980 *Editor & Publisher* noted, "In recent months many newspapers have moved their economic and financial news out of the shadows behind sports and into the spotlight with separate sections offering expanded coverage. The sections have strengthened the papers' appeal to affluent readers and provided new sources of retail and national advertising revenues."

Alan Nagelberg, Chicago *Tribune* financial editor, explained, "Business news is on the main page. The need to explain the economy has increased and that gave a push to our expansion." The types of news the paper's staff of 26 handles includes profiles of business personalities, industry trends, foreign news, money management, taxes, coping with recession, Chicago's options markets and features about companies or trends with a Midwest aspect.

Whereas a generation ago ability to read a financial ticker tape, bank statement and annual report of a corporation was about all that was required, today's business or financial page reporter must be able to explain as well as report what goes on in this field. Several developments have made almost nonexistent the strictly local business news story. Among these have been the growth of retail chain stores that are parts of nationwide operations or conglomerates, the mushrooming of shopping centers serving more than one community, the specialization of factory production so that few products any more are manufactured all in one plant, the growth of dependency of small industries upon large ones for subcontracts and of large industries upon the federal government for orders, the increase in foreign trade and investments, multinational corporations, government aid to underdeveloped countries and other similar trends, which add up to this: what happens almost anywhere else in the world today can affect the prosperity of the small town, which is no longer self-sufficient economically as it may have been in grandfather's day.

Reader interest is heightened when economic conditions affect a person's standard of living. The journalist should be expected to provide accurate information regarding the extent of a recession or inflation and analysis of important factors affecting employment, wages, prices and the like, together with the opinions of experts.

BUSINESS

Despite the trend toward localization of as much as possible of what appears on the business-financial pages, there is no business beat as such. That is, the reporter's day is not spent making regular stops comparable to those that other newsgatherers make at police headquarters, city hall and so on. Rather, covering a story for the business page means mostly investigating a tip or following up an idea, and every assignment may require making contacts with an entirely different set of news sources. Thus, the business page reporter must be fully conversant with the public and private agencies from which information of all kinds can be obtained.

Typical examples of how the business reporter obtains information would be the following: a railroad shipping clerk knew that a company that was close-mouthed was on the decline because its shippings had fallen off; a city assessor provided information on plans for a major shopping center with which the reporter confronted the developer who persuaded him to postpone publication in exchange for a promise of an exclusive story eventually; a department store official had an informed guess on the sales volume of a statewide chain that did not disclose sales or earnings; a paragraph in a routine quarterly report of a company indicated a major change in marketing plans; a union official confirmed rumors of a reduction in a plant's production as indicated by the laying off of a large number of employees. Frequently, a business reporter can persuade a company to talk even though it at first declares, "We don't want to say anything for competitive reasons," by pointing out that s/he can dig out the information s/he wants from Dun & Bradstreet reports or from other sources available to competitors as well as everyone else.

Even in the case of a routine story, the explanation may be the feature.

For example, businesses have been known to move to avoid the disturbance caused by jet airplanes. A concern once changed location because the vibrations from trucks on nearby highways interrupted the manufacture of delicate parts. More significantly, a major appliance store pulled out of a shopping center, saying that shopping habits had changed and customers did not care to hunt for major durable goods in the midst of other commodities.

A routine story could be written:

> XYZ Cola reported lower earnings, etc.

More significant would be

> The coldest weather in 79 years cut XYZ Cola sales to the lowest in 20 years, etc.

If stories are written in this way, one leading business and financial editor commented, "Aunt Jane with her 1½ shares of XYZ Cola stock won't be so prone to seek to oust the dumb bunny management."

The reporter must not be so naïve as to accept uncritically whatever s/he is told. An electric plant once moved out of the state saying that the "labor climate" was unfavorable. Several months later it advertised its plant for sale, citing as an advantage, "skilled, stable labor." One Wisconsin business editor has this warning note:

> Business executives pressed for "why?" usually tell reporters that it's all due to high taxes, unreasonable wage demands by labor, too much government interference, not enough tariff protection and spiraling costs of goods and services. Never mentioned in public (it's been called the "conspiracy of silence") is the fact that other factors may have had a more important part in lower profits, salary cuts, layoffs, production cutbacks, plant moves and shutdowns, etc. The other factors include bad guesses by management on product acceptance, excessive production costs, poor scheduling, bad design, insufficient market research, lack of quality control and/or generally poor management.

Routine News

Publicity departments of businesses, industries, trade organizations and governmental agencies voluntarily supply the bulk of the routine news in this field: new advertising campaigns; new products; stock sales; production figures; expansion programs; comments on pending legislation, court decisions or other events affecting business; big orders received; reports on dollar sales; new models; personnel changes in partnerships, corporation officials, managerial appointments, promotions and the like; new building or other expansion plans; moves to new locations; public shows and exhibits.

Trade associations and institutes make reports covering entire industries monthly, quarterly, semiannually and annually. The weekly reports on department store sales have been taken over by the Commerce Department from the Federal Reserve banks and are regarded as a "holy index" even though they do not include suburban stores or discount houses. Federal Reserve bank monthly reports are an index to the state of the overall economy and usually include profiles of particular industries. Some university business schools issue composite weekly reports on department store sales using percentages instead of dollars. For instance, the University of Pittsburgh School of Business issues a composite weekly report on sales of three major department stores. Sales are listed for the preceding week, for the preceding four weeks, for Jan. 1 to date and for how they compare with similar periods of the previous years. There is a breakdown of downtown and suburban sales along with the total metropolitan percentages.

The monthly Federal Reserve index of industrial production gives information regarding the outputs of mines, mills and so on. Also up-to-date are the reports put out by some state agencies—for example, the *Illinois Business Review,* a monthly summary published by the Bureau of Economic and Business Research of the College of Commerce of the University of Illinois. Its summaries are made public from two to six weeks after the data are gathered whereas government figures may be two or three months old. Similar first-rate reports are put out in Indiana and Texas, among other states.

Other good overall business and economic indicators are monthly and weekly reports on carloadings; reports of shipments of folding paper cartons; reports on shipments of collapsible metal tubes; weekly Edison Electric Institute reports on electrical production and percentage changes. Gross national product reports (dollar values of all goods and services produced) are widely used.

Monthly employment reports from state bureaus are economic indicators. The Pittsburgh bureau covers the four-county metropolitan area. Although the figures are a month to six weeks late, they suggest how the local economy is doing. Included is the unemployment rate, the number of people looking for work, new filings for benefits, size of the local work force and a breakdown of employment in industries with a comparison to the same month in earlier years.

Since so much of this news originates or at least is announced in New York or Washington, it first reaches local newspaper offices throughout the country via press association financial wires. The business page editor must be highly selective and naturally considers the particular interests of the readers in the paper's circulation area. It is easy to clutter a page with indiscriminate use of commodity market reports—livestock market prices, dairy, poultry, produce, grains, prices of various futures, dividends and earning tables and the like.

The journalistic expert who wrote the following story combined interpretation with reporting.

Washington (UPI)—Fueled by the government's tight money policy, the long-anticipated slump in the home-building industry is now under way.

Before the plunge ends, hundreds of thousands of construction jobs could be lost, homebuilding industry officials said Tuesday after reviewing new Commerce Department housing figures.

Housing construction last month fell by nearly 14 percent from the October level and were off by about 28 percent from a year earlier.

Construction of new homes and apartments was at an annual rate of 1.52 million units in November, the lowest rate since bad weather brought building activity in some sections of the nation to a virtual standstill last February.

"There is no question the recession in the housing industry is under way," said Michael Sumichrast, chief economist for the National Association of Homebuilders, the industry's major trade group.

Association President Vondal Gravlee said, "Hundreds of thousands of construction workers could be laid off their jobs in the months ahead" because of the abrupt housing slowdown.

Housing starts had held up pretty well throughout the first nine months of this year, mainly because of federal housing aid and new high-interest money market certificates offered by mortgage lending institutions.

Earlier this month, the government reported the median sales price of a new, single-family home in October was $61,900. That represented a 7 percent drop from September.

The Commerce Department reported Americans' personal income last month rose at the fastest pace since mid-summer, but their savings rate fell sharply. At the same time, consumers spent far more of their income on goods and services in November than in October.

On top of that, the National Association of Realtors reports sales of previously occupied single-family homes fell 12 percent in November to an annual rate of 3.55 million units.

In the face of all that, the Department of Housing and Urban Development announced Tuesday that it would ask Congress today to update its standby authority for dealing with recessionary slumps in housing.

But the Federal Reserve's Oct. 6 decision to drastically tighten credit sent interest rates skyrocketing to record levels and sharply reduced availability of mortgage funds. . . .

A similar story concerning the local situation appeared in the Fort Lauderdale *News/Sun-Sentinel:*

By Bruce Ellison

The home-building industry, long a mainstay of the South Florida economy, has fallen on hard times.

While Washington policy makers argue over whether the recession has arrived, those who build or sell homes for a living in Broward or Palm Beach counties know that it already is here.

"There is no question that the recession is here," said Harris Friedman, an officer of Miami Beach-based American Savings. "(Mortgage) loan demand has fallen to near zero."

State-wide mortgage lending activity bears him out. Florida savings and loan associations closed $647 million in mortgages in October, $580 million in November and $422 million in December.

Closings plunged to $436 million in January and dropped again to $431 million in February. Since the lending volume reflects mortgage interest rates committed several months prior to closing, S&L officials expect April to show the first disastrous impact of record 16 percent mortgage rates.

The rates resulted from the second effort by the Carter administration to fight inflation and inflationary expectations with higher interest rates and tighter credit. The first effort, in October, also took its toll in construction.

"The housing recession across the country began months ago," said Friedman. "Only Florida and Texas escaped it then." No state is escaping it now.

New home sales "have come to a screeching halt," said Carl Palmisciano, president of the housing division of Development Corp. of America, a major builder of moderate-price shelter in Broward County.

Only a few kinds of shelter are selling these days on the Gold Coast:

- Luxury homes and condos, in the $150,000 and up price range.
- Condo units in retirement areas, being delivered now to people who had contracted for them some time ago.
- Homes on which financing commitments at low interest rates were obtained by the builders months ago.

The market is being held up in large measure by cash buyers—retirees who use the proceeds of homes sold up north to buy in Florida, and foreigners who see the market here as a bargain.

Virtually the only building going on in South Florida today is for dwelling units that were ordered some time ago. Buyers contracted for the units then and put money down on them. . . .

Localization

Famine in India, an earthquake in Japan, revolution in Venezuela or the peaceful overthrow of a government anywhere can affect local business conditions. This it may do directly if an industry sells or buys abroad, or indirectly if anyone with whom it does business is directly affected.

Local opinion should be sought whenever important new legislation is proposed, introduced, passed or tested in the courts. Always the desideratum should be "How will this affect us locally?" The same is true of work stoppages from strikes or for other reasons. If the commodity is coal, oil, steel or some other basic that is used locally by manufacturers or the public, estimates of stockpiles should be obtained.

The direct relationship between the politics of a foreign nation and an American business was stressed by Donald K. White in the following column in the San Francisco *Chronicle:*

Gillette Co. looks sharp, feels sharp and is sharp as a result of the Tory victory in the British elections last month.

The company's stock was down to $66.37½ a share the day before the election and the prognosis was for a rough go if the voting went against the Tories.

But it didn't and investors took heart and brought the stock back up to $72.50 a share last week.

On the surface there doesn't seem to be much connection between elections in Britain and razor blades, the Friday night fights, VIV lipstick, Pamper shampoo and Toni home permanents. The last three items are also Gillette products.

The connection becomes clear when you realize Gillette got 43 per cent of its net profit from overseas sources last year. And the bulk of that profit came from the clean-shaven British, who voted back into office the party Gillette investors felt was better for their interests.

Tom Wolf explained to readers of the Anderson (S.C.) *Independent* what effect changes in the prime interest rate would have on them.

People will pay still more for mortgages and consumer loans, after major U.S. banks Tuesday hiked the prime interest rate to 15 percent.

Area financial officials agreed the impact on consumers would not be immediate but the trend is for higher rates in the future.

The boost in the prime rate will mean that:

- Consumer loans for new autos and home improvements are likely to rise from their current 11¾ to 12½ percent available at area banks.
- Home loans could go up further from the 13 to 15 percent rate available at South Carolina savings and loans.
- Higher costs for business borrowers could bring higher costs for consumers—from the clothing they wear to food they buy.

The prime rate, which banks charge their best customers, rose from 14½ percent to 15 percent Tuesday as banks were faced with higher costs for the funds they lend.

South Carolina National, the state's largest bank, said it will increase its prime rate to 15 percent effective Wednesday.

"The move by the banks was thoroughly anticipated," Thomas Schaap, a Clemson economist, said.

Schaap said the move was precipitated by the Federal Reserve Board's action Oct. 6 to slow the price rises by discouraging consumer purchases through higher interest rates.

"The purpose of the Fed's move is to make prices and interests rates lower in the future," Schaap said. . . .

Trends

Any old-timer knows that methods of doing business have changed considerably during his/her lifetime. It requires journalistic perception, however, to become aware of a new development when it is still new. In the early '60s it was apparent that speedier transportation, including "piggy backing" by trucks and railroads, had made it expedient for local businessmen to maintain smaller inventories than formerly. Both the Chicago stockyards and railroad passenger service were in decline, much more foodstuffs of all kinds were being rushed in refrigerator cars from place of origin to place of consumption, one-industry towns were disappearing, chambers of commerce were more intent on attracting diversification and other changes were occurring that affected the entire social as well as the economic life of communities.

Two of the most significant new businesses were retail discount houses and leasing companies. The former originated shortly after the end of World War II in New England in abandoned factory towns, most of them depleted as industries moved south, often as a result of strong state governmental inducement to obtain cheaper, usually nonunion, labor. Some smart operators bought the distress merchandise of retailers who faced bankruptcy and made fortunes. Through their operations it was learned that customers take to self-service in department stores as well as in groceries and this type of merchandising spread, mostly in the suburbs where automobile parking was made available.

Another situation was the subject of an investigative interpretative piece by Kim Upton for the Chicago *Sun-Times,* about the first one-third of which follows:

> It's called coupon fever and it is a way in which the little man (make that person) can speculate without jeopardizing home, savings or jewelry collection.
>
> The stakes may not be big, but they could be free. And the possibilities are making people crazy.
>
> "The average refunder can save $500 to $2,500 by using coupons and refunding," Jan Leasure, a Chicago refunder, said. "I saved close to $3,000 in 1979 by refunding."
>
> It's done by utilizing money-off coupons published in newspaper food sections, in magazines and on pads dangling from supermarket shelves. As an additional way of bringing in money, labels from those products can be mailed in for cash or for a free-product coupon.
>
> There is evidence that refunding and couponing may be found in a wide variety of income and social situations. Coupon queen Mary Anne Hayes, a New Jersey homemaker, says she knows a woman who sends her housekeeper to market with a fist full of coupons.
>
> "I do not want people to think refunding is just for domestic engineers," said Gail Vierneisel, a refunder. "I have two children, am a full-time college student, write a newsletter and lecture. I worked for a supermarket and I used to think, 'What's the matter with those people, they're coming with a seven-cents-off coupon?' I realize now how smart they were."
>
> The availability of all this something-for-nothing stuff has given birth to a whole world of techniques for getting our hands on it.
>
> There are groups that collect coupons for charity. There are exchange clubs for couponers. There are books on couponing.
>
> And there are newsletters. Usually six to eight pages in length, usually slightly homespun in literary tone, one estimate places the number in circulation at 200. No self-respecting couponer would be caught dead without one.
>
> The reason for this is that it contains listings of coupons manufacturers have just released into the market. An experienced couponer and refunder will take this list to his or her files, extract the necessary coupons and mail them in for a cash refund or for a free-product coupon.
>
> Then there are label banks. Like a giant bank-by-mail operation, the saver sends in labels and his account is credited for a cash value against future withdrawals.
>
> Then, too, there is a whole new language that has built up around the coupon craze. It is possible, for example, to *exchange* a *cash-off* for a *hang tag* or a *pop* or a *refund form* with correct *qualifiers* through a *classified* for a *complete deal.* This, in case you're interested, means $$.
>
> Need we not say more?
>
> If you think this is kid's stuff or tea-time entertainment for not-too-bright domestic engineers, you know not of what you speak. There is complexity enough for a certified public accountant.

A *triple play,* just one item in the bag of couponing and refunding tricks, might involve a 71-cent product, discounted with a 25-cent coupon on a coupon-and-a-half day, giving it a 37-cents-off value. To achieve the third move of the triple play, the universal product code is removed from the box and turned in for a refund, possibly a free-product coupon that will mean that 34-cent product (originally 71 cents) actually costs 17 cents, or two for the price of one with 37 cents off.

Thus we come to a sort of elitism in the world of coupon and refunding. A refunder is not to be mistaken for a couponer and will most likely correct you if you fail to make the distinction. Big-time operators like Mary Anne Hayes don't waste their time on couponing.

FINANCE

Until they broadened their scope to include business news, most newspaper financial pages contained little more than listings of transactions on the New York and/or other stock exchanges. Such charts still are used and every editor must exercise judgment as to what items to include in the limited amount of space available. The editor does so by editing the listings transmitted by the press associations or obtained from local brokerage houses to include those securities in which local readers have the greatest interest, because they are those of outstanding nationally known companies or of companies that have plants or do business in the community.

Stock Exchanges

Elementary is ability to read stock quotations. A typical line as follows:

High	*Low*	*Stocks Div.*	*Sales in 100's*	*High*	*Low*	*Close*	*Net Change*
26⅞	18⅝	Jeff. 1	278	20¾	19⅛	20	−1¼

This means that the highest price for which one share of Jefferson company stock sold during the current year was $26⅞ and the lowest price was $18⅝ per share. The "1" means that the stock paid $1 per share in dividends last year. This day, 27,800 shares were sold on the exchange, at prices which ranged from $20¾ to $19⅛ per share. The last day's sale was for $20, which was $1¼ less than the closing sale the preceding day.

This is the raw material on the basis of which the financial reporter describes the "ups" and "downs" of the market. Since perhaps 90 per cent of all stock trading takes place in New York, what happens on the New York Stock Exchange is, of course, of primary importance. There are also, however, the American Stock Exchange, with about one-third the amount of trading as the New York Stock Exchange, the Midwest Stock Exchange in Chicago and numerous small exchanges in different cities throughout the country. Before a corporation's securities can be listed on an exchange, it must register under the Securities and Exchange act of 1934, which means it must meet minimum standards of financial soundness. Then its application must be approved by the exchange's board of governors. This act does not guarantee the value of the stock but, because of the double scrutiny by federal government and exchange, listed stocks generally are considered more secure. Over-the-counter sales, however, more than double the accumulated total of sales on all the exchanges combined. Such stocks, although registered with the SEC, are not listed on any exchange, so the transactions in them are conducted between brokers on behalf of their clients, away from the formal setting of a trading floor. For each OTC company there are a number of brokerage firms that act as market-makers to execute trades in its stock. The salesmen are supervised by their own self-regulatory agency, the National Association of Securities Dealers, which provides information to the press, as does the National Quotation bureau. The NASDAQ has a computerized network of traders dealing in about 1,800 OTC companies, to provide an "instant market" for any issue on a list. There are more than 50,000 OTC stocks and they remain a risky investment, but NASDAQ has added credibility, at least to companies on the list, which include Hoover, Tampax, Pabst Brewing and some other giants.

The advantages of a stock exchange are said to be (1) to provide financial facilities for the convenient transaction of business, (2) to maintain high standards of commercial honor and integrity and (3) to promote just and equitable principles of trade and business. This is decidedly not to say, however, that most other trading is unethical, dangerous or otherwise undesirable. As a matter of fact, the extent to which what happens on the large exchanges actually reflects the state of the nation's financial health is a matter of considerable dispute. Certain it is that the exchanges respond emotionally to political and other news and the prices of particular securities may fluctuate widely within a matter of hours or minutes. Some skeptics say that a great deal of what goes on is just dignified or aristocratic gambling.

Seeking Explanations

Whatever the truth may be, the financial reporter has the responsibility to seek reasons for important fluctuations. S/he is aided in the first instance by the Dow Jones & Co. ticker-tape news service, which continuously transmits selected stock quotations, late news on the grain, meat and foreign markets, sometimes baseball scores and top national and international news. Its most important function is reporting business news of all kinds and its averages of what stocks are doing in accumulated major categories—industrials, railroads, utilities—are widely accepted as indices of the financial market as a whole. The purpose of the Dow Jones averages—industrial, railroad and utility—is "to give a general rather than precise idea of the fluctuation in the securities markets and to provide a basis of historical continuity of security price movements."

Of the stock averages compiled by Dow Jones, the industrial average is the one investors most carefully scrutinize. It is made up of the stock prices of 30 industrial corporations, generally regarded as "blue chips."

These are: Allied Chemical, Aluminum Co., American Can, American Telephone, American Tobacco, Anaconda, Bethlehem Steel, International Business Machine, Merck, Du Pont, Eastman Kodak, General Electric, General Foods, General Motors, Goodyear, International Harvester and International Nickel.

Also included are International Paper, Johns-Manville, Owens-Illinois Glass, Procter & Gamble, Sears Roebuck, Standard Oil of California, Standard Oil of New Jersey, Swift, Texaco, Union Carbide, United Aircraft, U.S. Steel, Westinghouse Electric and Woolworth.

The average goes back to Jan. 2, 1897, when Dow Jones began publication of the daily average closing prices of 12 active stocks. This continued until 1916 when the list was increased to 20. This list was increased to 30 on Oct. 1, 1928.

The stocks in the average now and then are changed to stay modern. Otherwise, the average today might have a buggy whip manufacturer among its components. Substitutions also are made when a stock becomes too inactive or its price is too low.

When, in 1979, IBM and Merck replaced Chrysler and Esmark, the *Wall Street Journal* said of the first major membership change in 20 years,

> As is the case with stock splits, these substitutions would distort the average if they were made without a change in the divisor. The divisor is the number used instead of 30 to divide the total price of stocks in the list to arrive at an average. Over the 50-year history of the 30-stock average, the divisor has been reduced by stock splits and substitutions to its current level of 1.443.
>
> Here is how the change will be calculated at the close of trading today: The stock prices of all the issues in the current list will be totaled and then divided by 1.443 to arrive at an "old" average. Then the prices of pre-split Du Pont, Esmark and Chrysler will be subtracted from the total and the prices of post-split Du Pont, IBM and Merck will be added in, for a new total.
>
> This new total is then divided by the "old" average and the quotient becomes the new divisor. The new divisor is then used regularly until another change is required.

The comparative values of the indices were described by William Gruber in the Chicago *Tribune* as follows:

> **By William Gruber**
>
> To judge only by the Dow Jones industrial average, investors made little money from stocks in 1979.
>
> The most widely watched market barometer is winding up a roller-coaster year with a gain of less than 5 per cent after rising and falling between the 800 and 900 levels during all but two trading days in November.
>
> Its most striking action was a plunge of more than 58 points in the week ended Oct. 12—after a sharp tightening of credit by the Federal Reserve Board—which briefly revived memories of the great market crash 50 years earlier.
>
> But the performance of the Dow average of 30 blue-chip industrials tells only part of the 1979 market story.

The broader New Stock Exchange composite index has climbed 15 per cent, and the Standard & Poor's 500-stock index shows a gain of 12 per cent with one session to go in the year.

Far more spectacular records are being posted by the American Stock Exchange index, which soared this week to an all-time high that is up more than 62 per cent from the end of 1978, and by the NASDAQ index of over-the-counter stocks, up about 27 per cent.

"The Dow Jones does not reflect what really happened in the market," said Newton Zinder, analyst of E. F. Hutton & Co. "It was a year for the stocks of small- and medium-sized companies rather than the big names and blue chips."

The year's best performers have been energy-related firms, such as those that produce oil-drilling equipment; natural gas exploration companies; makers of machine tools, aerospace products, and fertilizer; and mining firms reaping the benefits of soaring prices for gold, silver, platinum, and copper.

Turning in the worst records were electric utilities, especially those with nuclear facilities, in the wake of the Three-Mile-Island accident last spring; and some gambling, real estate, retail, brewing, distilling, and steel stocks.

Larry Wachtel, analyst at Bache Halsey Stuart Shields, Inc., said the "real story of 1979 was not what happened to the Dow—it did very little—but to the secondary issues on the New York, American, and over-the-counter markets.

"The market did very well, provided you were in the right place at the right time," he added.

"It was a year in which stock selection was more important than ever," said Alan Shaw, of Smith Barney Harris Upham & Co. "A lot of fertilizer stocks jumped 50 per cent and some oil stocks soared 300 per cent. The real buzz word was 'energy' and anything to do with it."

Many investors who chose the stocks of companies with the idea they would be acquisition candidates also came up with sizable profits. More than 2,000 mergers or acquisitions were announced during the year, second only to 2,400 in 1978, Wachtel noted.

Interest rates and economic activity, both within the United States and abroad, affected much of the market's activity during 1979. . . .

The American Stock Exchange and the New York Stock Exchange use rapid computers to transmit indexes based on all stock transactions, not just those of selected stocks. The American Index reflects the average price changes of more than 1,000 common stocks and the New York Exchange Index does the same for approximately 1,250 common stocks and it also has special common stock for transportation, utility, finance and industrial.

Another valuable source of business and financial news is Dun & Bradstreet, which, among other things, issues a monthly report on business failures based on data from 25 large cities. The emphasis is on explanation as is also true of the Dun & Bradstreet annual and other reports.

Since January 1968 Dow Jones has had competition from the Reuter Financial Report, which is oriented to the information needs of the financial community—banks, insurance companies, mutual funds and other "institutional investors" as well as brokerage houses—with a few newspaper clients. The Reuter General News wire, however, carries a considerable amount of economic news under the Business Beat tagline so Reuter press clients can pick up the major business news and exclusive feature stories written for the financial wire. The result has been to "sharpen" the Dow Jones service. The new financial service is only one aspect of the British news agency's increased coverage of American news since dissolution of its exchange agreement with the Associated Press, so the competition may be expected to become keener.

One reason why the number of shareholders has declined from 30 million to 25 million during the past decade before recovering is the great increase in trading by institutional investors, such as pension funds, profit-sharing plans, unions, religious groups, insurance companies, banks, governments, universities, mutual funds etc. Institutions overshadow the individual investor on Wall Street. The value of securities owned by the institutions equals one-third the value of all stocks listed on the Big Board.

Institutions are by far the most active traders. It's difficult to pinpoint how much trading they do, but a NYSE spokesman estimates 50 per cent by institutions, 25 per cent by individuals and 25 per cent by members of the NYSE. That breakdown would apply to the Big Board. Also, a lot of trading is done in the so-called "third market" with buyers and sellers negotiating directly outside the exchange. This avenue is taken frequently by institutions when a large position in a stock is sought.

Because institutions buy and sell large blocks of stocks, they have a tremendous impact on prices. At the same time, because of the size of their trades, they lack the flexibility of an individual. This inhibits their ability to move quickly. Sometimes their holdings of a given stock are so large that they get locked in. This was apparent in the recession of '75 when bank trust departments suffered huge losses in the value of their portfolios as stock prices tumbled.

Willard F. (Al) Rockwell, who put Rockwell International together, believes corporations must cater to institutional buying preferences to keep their stocks popular. One of those preferences, according to Rockwell, is "buying industries" such as chemicals, drugs, oils, textiles etc. Rockwell believes a conglomerate is at a disadvantage unless its businesses are clearly defined. If not, it may be overlooked by the institutions.

Another reason why individuals cooled off on the market was the disastrous experience so many had in the mid-70s—a slide that was comparable to and in some cases worse than the '29 fiasco.

Also, there is disillusionment with stocks as a hedge against inflation. This was one of the grand ideas of the '60s, and it appeared that common stocks did stay ahead of inflation then when it was in the 1½–3 per cent range. But as inflation worsened in the '70s, stock values sank and a lot of people were left holding the bag.

As a consequence afternoon papers are cutting back on stocks. Some print only a selected list of the Big Board. Some omit stocks completely. Of course, morning papers have the advantage of listing the previous day's closing prices. Complete listings are much more prevalent in morning editions.

To keep abreast of the inflation, in the late '70s and early '80s investors withdrew bank savings and abandoned the stock and bond market to invest in treasury notes, money market certificates of deposit and money market mutual funds.

A T-note is a short-term loan to the United States government, the minimum being $10,000.

Money market certificates of deposit are offered by commercial banks, mutual savings banks and savings and loan associations. Again the minimum investment is $10,000 but the interest rate, which is tied to T-bill rates, is high. Also, these special CDs are insured by the Federal Deposit Insurance Corp., the same as any savings account. These are six-month certificates.

The money market mutual funds have become very popular with banks, corporations, unions, pension funds, individuals and others as a refuge for cash. A money market fund really is a checking account that pays high rates of interest. If U.S. Steel had $4 million in cash, it might invest it in one of the money market funds for a few days at 15 per cent, or whatever, and earn a few thousand dollars. The minimum usually is $1,000 to get in and there are no fees. The funds invest in large bank CDs, the ones that sell for $100,000 each and once were restricted to the very wealthy.

Definitions

Because of the financial injury that might otherwise result, the business-financial page reporter must be deadly accurate. Among other precautions s/he must observe is not to use business or financial terms unless s/he thoroughly understands their meaning. S/he should not hesitate to ask a news source to define and explain unfamiliar words and expressions. Among the fundamentals in his/her lexicon are the following:

Arbitration. Submitting a dispute to a third party to decide and agreeing to abide by his/her decision.

Articles of incorporation. The charter granted by the state permitting the organization of a corporation. It usually contains details relating to such matters as the purpose or purposes for which the corporation is formed, its principal place of business, the number of its directors and the amount of its capitalization.

Audit. Verification of records and accounts.

Balance sheet. The report of a company's assets and liabilities, profits and losses.

Bankruptcy. Abandonment of one's business and assignment of its assets to creditors, which discharges the debtor from future liability, enables the creditors to secure title to all the debtor's assets and provides a pro rata distribution of the assets among all creditors. A petition in bankruptcy may be voluntary if initiated by the debtor, or involuntary if initiated by the creditors.

Bear. (Stock or produce exchange.) One who believes the market will decline and contracts to sell securities or commodities at some future date at a certain price in the belief one will be able to buy them for resale at a lower one. In a bear market, the average price of all stocks drops because of widespread selling.

Big board. New York Stock Exchange.

Blue chip stock. Well-established stock, leading and essential industries stock.

Bond. A formal promise, always under seal, by the maker, usually a corporation, to pay a principal sum of money at a specified time and interest at a fixed rate at regular intervals. *Registered bonds* are paid only to the party named in the instrument and recorded on the corporation's books. A *coupon bond* is payable to bearer and may be transferred by mere delivery.

Broker. A financial agent who buys and sells securities for others, usually on a commission basis.

Bucket shop. A phony securities exchange that really engages in speculation or gambling on the ups and downs of the market.

Bull. (Stock or produce exchange.) One who expects, or tries to effect, a rise in prices. Sometimes a great number of people decide more or less at the same time to buy stocks. Such general buying action raises the average price of all stocks. If the price rise is big enough and lasts long enough, it is a bull market.

Call loans. Loans subject to payment upon demand.

Cash flow. "Net income after taxes, plus depreciation, depletion, amortization, extraordinary charges to reserves. An important figure, because it measures the company's real ability to pay dividends. A company which is reporting modest earnings can still pay a large dividend if income pouring into the corporate treasury is great because large amounts are being written off within tax impact." . . . from glossary in Donald Kirsch, *Financial and Economic Journalism.* New York University Press, 1978.

Cats and dogs. Highly speculative and usually low-priced stocks that do not pay dividends.

Check off. Reduction from employee's pay checks of union dues, which the employer then transmits to union officials.

Clearing house. A device to simplify and facilitate the daily exchange of checks and drafts and the settlement of balances among associated banks.

Closed shop. One in which labor force is either all union or all nonunion.

Collateral. Stocks, bonds and other evidences of property deposited by a borrower to secure a loan, as a pledge or guarantee that the loan will be repaid at maturity.

Collective bargaining. Bargaining between an organized group of workers and an employer instead of between each individual worker and an employer.

Conciliation. The attempt to settle a dispute by consultation with rival parties who do not pledge themselves to abide by any third person's decisions.

Controlling ownership. A controlling owner is one who owns sufficient shares to give the stockholder voting control, which may sometimes be less than 50 per cent of the total stock.

Corporation. Any body consisting of one or more individuals treated by the law as a unit. The rights and liabilities of a business corporation are distinct from those of the individuals that comprise it.

Craft union. A labor organization of skilled workers doing similar work. Called a horizontal union because no one craft union would include all workers in any one large industry.

Credit. Postponed money payment; a promise to pay money or its equivalent at some future time.

Curb. A market for securities not listed on any regular exchange.

Debenture. Similar to a bond except that the security is the company's earnings only.

Deficit financing, debt management. Financial arrangements by United States treasury, companies operating at a loss to borrow new cash, consolidate debts, shift from short- to long-term loans, refinance and so forth. The objective generally is to reduce interest charges, put loan repayments on regular basis, assure enough funds to meet payroll costs and bills for raw materials.

Depletion. Exhaustion or using up of assets, such as raw materials used for production.

Depreciation. Loss of value through use or disuse.

Discount. Receiving payment on an acceptance or note from bank for a consideration. The indorser still is responsible in case the maker of the note or acceptance defaults.

Discount rate. The interest charged for discounting a note.

Dividend. The share of the surplus distributed to a stockholder.

Dumping. The sale of products abroad at prices lower than those charged at home.

Escalator clause. A provision in a union contract whereby wages fluctuate with the cost of living.

Feather bedding. Union rules to slow up or reduce work and to prevent speed-up so as to protect jobs and avoid unemployment.

Federal Reserve banks. Banker's banks dealing only with member banks and the government, the purpose of which as set forth in the preamble of the act creating them is "to furnish an elastic currency, to afford means of rediscounting commercial paper, to establish a more effective supervision of banking in the United States, and for other purposes."

Foreign exchange. A clearing house to adjust balances between countries.

Futures. A contract for future delivery.

Hedging. Selling or purchasing a security or commodity to offset the purchase or sale of another security or commodity.

Holding company. A corporation that produces nothing for the market but merely invests in the securities of other corporations.

Hot issue. A security that meets a heavy demand on being sold publicly for the first time. Price rises sharply and original buyers, if they sell, make a quick profit.

Hung up. The plight of an investor who has capital tied up in a stock that has slumped below his purchase price. S/he can't sell without taking a loss.

Income, earnings or profit. Must be used with modifiers: net, gross, operating, nonoperating, etc. Net profit is figure most people are interested in. Gross profit is sales less cost of selling the goods. Operating profit is gross profit less operating expenses (overhead). Net profit is operating profit less income taxes, any other charges or extraordinary expenses.

Index numbers. An index number represents the price of a group of commodities, or the average price during a given period, which is used as a basis or standard with which to compare the prices of these commodities at other dates.

Industrial union. A labor organization in which membership is open to all workers, skilled or unskilled, within any industry. Called vertical instead of horizontal because of its inclusiveness.

Insolvent. Unable to pay one's debts.

Insurance. A contract whereby one party, for a consideration, promises to indemnify another party in the event a specified loss occurs.

Interest. The price paid for the use of capital.

Interlocking directors. Individuals who are on the boards of two or more corporations that do business with each other.

Investment club or house. One in which small investors pool their resources, usually by monthly payments, for the purpose of purchasing securities. They profit in proportion to their investment.

Jurisdictional strike. Strike in which members of one union refuse to work if those of another union are employed.

Lamb. A beginner at speculation. S/he follows the flock, blindly.

Liquidation. Conversion of available assets into cash.

Lockout. The wholesale exclusion of workers from a plant by an employer.

Long or short. A customer is "long" in securities that he owns, or "short" in securities s/he has sold but does not own.

Maintenance of membership. Requirement that workers must remain union members during life of contract with employer.

Majority owner. One who owns 50.1 per cent or more of the stock of a company.

Margin. To buy securities on margin means to do so without putting up the full purchase price in cash, with a broker lending the rest.

Mediation. Third party attempts to end a dispute by persuasion.

Monopoly. That substantial unit of action on the part of one or more persons engaged in some kind of business which gives exclusive control, more particularly, though not solely, with respect to price.

Mutual fund. A corporation that invests members' capital in securities and pays dividends on the earnings.

Net income. See *Income*.

Nonprofit. Yielding no dividends or financial advantage to owners.

Odd-lot investor. A broker who combines small requests for sales or purchases by several customers to be able to make an adequately sized bid on the exchange.

Open and closed shop. An open shop is one in which both union and nonunion workers are employed. A closed shop is one in which either nounion or union workers only are employed.

Option. The right to have first chance, as in the purchase of property, usually obtained by a money payment that is not returnable if the deal falls through.

Overhead. Expense of equipment, stock and maintenance, which is relatively constant regardless of production.

Premium income. In insurance, the income of an insurance company from premiums paid by policy holders. Interest and dividends from investments are the other major source of revenue.

Prime rate. The interest rate charged by banks to customers—business firms and individuals—who have the best credit ratings and solid collateral. Prime rate generally is one percentage point higher than the discount rate—the interest rate that federal reserve banks charge on loans made by commercial banks from the reserve bank.

Profit and loss statement. It summarizes income and expenses of an organization or business, to show net profit or loss for the fiscal period covered.

Profit sharing. Sharing with workers the profits of good years; in effect, a bonus based on profits.

Proxy statement. A signed document to give another authority to act for the signer. Proxy fights develop at stockholders' meetings when rival groups solicit proxies from absent stockholders.

Receiver. A temporary court-appointed officer to conduct a bankrupt business in the interest of the creditors.

Receivership. Operation of a business by the creditors when the debtor otherwise would be bankrupt or in danger of bankruptcy.

Rediscounting. The purchasing by one bank of a note or bill of exchange held by another.

Rent. The price paid for the use of land or anything else.

Reserve. Lawful money or other liquid assets that a bank must keep on hand to insure prompt payment of its deposits and liabilities.

Revenue. Generally, the cash received in any fiscal period. It may include cash from sales of goods or services (operating revenue) and cash from investments, sale of property or from other sources such as patent rights, royalties and license agreements (nonoperating revenue).

Right-to-work laws. Open-shop laws.

Sabotage. A conscious or willful act on the part of workers intended to reduce the output of production or to restrict trade and reduce profits by the withdrawal of efficiency from work and by putting machinery out of order and producing as little as possible without getting dismissed from the job.

Scab. A strikebreaker.

Sell short. To contract to sell securities one does not own in the expectation of being able to buy them later more cheaply.

Speculation. Taking a risk when making a purchase in the hope that future developments will make the deal profitable.

Stock certificate. A stock certificate represents one or more shares of the corporation's capital. Its price is determined by the market, usually a stock exchange, where securities are bought and sold. *Preferred stock* holders have a prior claim on the company's assets before the *common stock* holders in the event of bankruptcy. *Cumulative stock* arrears are paid before the common stock receives a dividend in case dividends are omitted at certain periods. *Participating preferred stock* entitles the holder to a share in the profits, in addition to the stated dividend.

Stock split. Increasing the total number of shares of stock, usually by doubling the number and dividing the par value of each share. This has the same effect as a stock dividend but is treated differently for taxation purposes. It enables small investors to buy more easily.

Stockholders' equity. Merrill Lynch Pierce Fenner & Smith's *How to Read a Financial Report* defines stockholders' equity as "the corporation's net worth after subtracting all liabilities. This is separated for legal and accounting reasons into three categories: capital stock, capital surplus, and accumulated retained earnings."

Surplus. The equity of stockholders in a corporation above the par value of the capital stock.

Sweetheart contract. One between management and a labor leader that benefits them at the expense of the rank and file.

Trademark. The name or symbol by which a merchandised product is distinguished from all others. It always must be spelled with at least the first letter capitalized. See *Publishers' Auxiliary* for Dec. 1, 1980.

Trust. A company that deals in capital and handles funds that are principally inactive, thus conserving existing wealth.

Trustee in bankruptcy. Court-appointed officer who converts a bankrupt's assets into cash and pays the creditors.

Underwriting. Insuring against loss, to guarantee to meet an obligation if the original party fails to do so.

Wildcat strike. One not authorized by union officials.

Yellow dog contract. A contract for labor in which the worker is required to promise not to join any labor union during the term of employment.

PROBLEMS AND POLICIES

As the scope and consequently the readership of the business-financial page increase, so do the problems of the editor and the need for a strong sense of social responsibility. Tips are received from many sources—brokers, lawyers, union leaders, competitors, shipping agents, trade associations and the like—and some of the tipsters may be motivated by other than pure public-spiritedness. Misinformation or injudicious handling of news may be injurious to innocent persons. Premature disclosure regarding a pending real estate transaction, for example, may ruin a potential deal. And then there is the little old lady who reads a story about the profits being made by raisers of soybeans and wants to cash in her small savings to speculate on the grain market. She calls the editor for further information and advice.

Secrecy

Increasingly, the business reporter is likely to be stymied because of federal government security regulations that make it impossible for even the most cooperative official or public relations counsel to provide information. Often the editor suspects that there is too much "hush-hush" about what happens to be common knowledge in his community, so he may contact the Freedom of Information Committee of the American Society of Newspaper Editors or some such group to see what can be done about "knocking some sense" into the heads of some Washington bureaucrats. Seldom, however, does he dare defy requests from officials with proper credentials.

Puffery

Biggest perpetual problem is how to distinguish between legitimate news and free publicity. "Business Office Musts" from the advertising department are distasteful to any editor who wants to use only the yardstick of legitimate public interest. This means that s/he wishes to keep no blacklist of nonadvertisers whose news is to be ignored or played down and s/he resents any successful attempt to persuade him/her to use a spurious story whose only effect is to increase someone's sales.

Especially in the sections devoted to real estate and main business district news, the business-financial page may seem to be a booster page and its editor to be interested in promoting the best interests of the community—much as the sports editor usually promotes the success of the home-town team. Despite the opposition of the National Association of Real Estate Editors, there is a trend toward removing the newspaper real estate sections from editorial control to advertising department management. The association declares ". . . real estate news is a hot commodity today with the citizen activists fighting over concerns such as displacement, condominium conversion, redlining, rent control, land use policies and no-growth policies. . . . These are the kinds of articles which are better handled in a real estate section than spread throughout the paper on a catch-as-catch-can basis."

In special real estate and similar sections the copy may be unashamedly free publicity. Advertisers generally believe that such "good will" material enhances the value of their advertisements. Many skeptical newspapermen believe that a good obituary or other legitimate story would serve their purposes better; but they are still to be convinced. One doesn't need to attend a school of journalism or even go to college to learn to produce that kind of tripe. In fact, he would be well advised not to do so.

Some businessmen who employ expensive public relations men want to be relieved of responsibility. They expect the highly paid help to maintain relations with the press and both boss and public relations men resent it when a journalist attempts to circumvent this line of authority. Often, however, it is imperative to do so. One of the best places is the cocktail party. This is a genteel type of payola to which many business enterprises are addicted. The business reporter may be as bored as the society reporter who attends a tea party a day, but he might otherwise not get the opportunity to rub elbows with top executives. More naïve than their public relations men, these officials often provide tips and information of importance, and possibly exclusive as far as the imbibing newsman is concerned. It is a constant source of amazement to newspapermen how ignorant those who make the news usually are as regards its reporting and editing. They do, however, understand that any business enterprise must operate in accordance with rules and, although not understanding, are often prone to accept the explanation "That is not done," when a reporter diplomatically rejects a suggestion.

Codes

What follows are extracts from a memorandum on "Business News Policy," issued to the staff by Creed C. Black, then executive editor of the Wilmington (Del.) *News-Journal*.

> One of the traditional and thorny problems of newspapers is distinguishing between legitimate news of the business world and free advertising. Wilmington has its share of both legitimate business news stories and space-grabbers. The aim of our newspapers is to get the legitimate news in and keep the puffs out.
>
> Our policy is based on the premise that the decision on whether an item will be published will rest with the news departments.
>
> Advertising salesmen have been instructed to explain that they have no connection with the news departments, and advertisers are being requested to deal directly with our city desks when they have stories they consider newsworthy.
>
> Our decisions will be based solely on news value. If it's news, no amount of advertising will keep it out of the paper; if it isn't news, no amount of advertising will get it in.
>
> To follow such a policy successfully, consistency is absolutely essential. If we slip up in one instance, we're putting ourselves in a position that's hard to explain the next time somebody wants similar treatment and wants to know why we won't do thus-and-so for him when we did it for so-and-so. . . .
>
> There will be no attempt here to set down a comprehensive list of hard-and-fast rules, for that's obviously impractical. But here are some general guidelines on various types of items we encounter:
>
> *Personnel Changes*. Appointments, promotions, resignations, etc., are news up—or down—to a point, depending on how important the job is. Obviously we can't

cover all personnel changes in the business and industrial community, so we must be selective.

New Business. A new business or a change in ownership is news. So is a major expansion of an established firm, or a major remodeling project. Let's not get sucked in, however, by somebody who's just added another showcase or finally put a badly needed coat of paint on the walls.

And when pictures are justified, let's strive for something besides ground-breakings and ribbon-cuttings.

Giveaways. Everybody who's giving something away seems to think we should provide full coverage, including photos of the jubilant winners. We shouldn't and we won't.

Our first consideration here is the lottery laws. If anything must be bought to make one eligible for the prize, the drawing is legally a lottery and we can't touch the story.

Beyond that, our general policy is that we aren't interested in giveaways unless there's something unusual enough to give the story an angle that will enable it to stand on its own as a readable human interest feature. And even when a story is justified, the name of the firm giving away the prize should be only an incidental part of the story.

Business Anniversaries. The fact that a firm has been in business for *x* number of years hardly excites our readers, even though some businessmen have the idea this qualifies as big news every 12 months. We will not report such anniversaries except on special occasions—such as a 50th, 75th, or 100th anniversary.

Dealerships. It is not news when a men's clothing store adds a new line of shirts; it is news when an auto dealer takes on a new car. The distinction (and it can be applied generally) depends on both the nature of the product and the type of business. A clothing store, for example, handles scores of products; an auto dealer handles only one or two lines, and usually he is the exclusive dealer for these.

Company Awards. If a company could get newspaper coverage of awards it makes or prizes it gives its own employees, there would be no limit on the number of plaques, scrolls, certificates and gold keys gathering dust in Wilmington households. So let's help fight the dust menace by covering only very special awards within a company—a recognition of 50 years of service, for example—or genuine honors bestowed by professional organizations embracing more than a single company.

Special Sections. Special sections are somewhat of a case apart, since their aim is frankly promotional. Even so, no editorial content will be devoted to a special section event unless participation in it is broad enough to give it general interest. And in *all* special sections, remember, the editorial content is as good—or as bad—as *we* make it. If it sounds like advertising, that's our fault.

Trade News. Strictly apart from the question of what is and what is not a legitimate business news story, there's the problem of whether to use commercial names of businesses or products in other news stories.

No pat rule is possible here. A good general guide is to use commercial names only when the story would be incomplete without them. You don't have to say, for instance, that thieves looted a Buick parked in front of the Wilmington Dry Goods; a car parked on Market Street would do. But if an elevator falls in a store, name the store; if a man jumped out of a hotel window, name the hotel.

There has been a tendency in our papers to go out of the way not only to describe a car as a compact car but to name the make as well. Only if the size of the car is an important element of the story is it necessary to designate it as a compact, and the make is almost never relevant. . . .

We will not use stories on the sale of individual homes unless historic interest or something similar makes them especially newsworthy. The sale of such a home or of commercial property should be reported immediately and not saved for the real estate pages. Prices are permissible if known.

Stories and photos on the real estate pages should be confined to developments or general trends instead of to individual homes for sale. That is, a picture of one home in a new development would be permissible, but we would want to avoid using a single home that's come on the market in an established neighborhood. Price ranges of homes in a development are permissible.

Let's be sure we don't use repeated pictures or stories on the same development and let's also avoid follow-up stories on crowd turnouts at individual developments and stick to general roundups on the state of the real estate market.

Several years ago, the Atlanta newspapers got together to draw up a statement as to how to reduce the puff evil to a minimum. In part, the agreement read as follows:

The following items are specific types of publicity which we will NOT carry in the future:

a. Fashion shows, cooking schools, garden schools or any similar promotion of any kind originated by or which has any commercial connection with any business.
b. Beauty specialists.
c. Pictures of salesmen or managers who change jobs or pictures of new members of organizations.
d. Pictures of buyers.
e. Pictures of either the exterior or interior of stores except in those cases which might be considered in the light of real estate news.
f. Interiors of buildings.
g. Special promotions such as the "Bell Ringers," "Hour Glass" teasers, etc.
h. Luncheons or store promotions.
i. Entertainment of prominent people by stores.
j. Receptions for authors in book departments.
k. Pictures of merchandise. It is understood that this not only includes retail but distributors' publicity; as, for example, pictures of distributors holding a can of beer, etc.
l. Pictures of grocery chain new members.
m. Santa Claus promotions.
n. Robots and trick automobiles disguised as locomotives, etc.
o. All promotions on the part of stores which feature the Junior League, the debutantes or other social celebrities.
p. All commercial promotions such as state fairs, carnivals, auto races, flower shows, etc. This does not apply to civic enterprises or those enterprises which are operated strictly for charity, as for example, Scottish Rite hospital, but it is understood that where publicity is given these promotions the names of no retail or commercial organizations are to be used.

q. Photograph contests, dancing schools, insurance stories, stories and pictures of used car lots.
r. Elimination of travel, resort publicity.
s. Any paid local ads simulating news matter must take the word "Advertisement" spelled out in 8-point black.
t. No automobile publicity will be carried in daily paper. All must go Sundays.
u. All special sections for advertisers cannot carry over 30 per cent publicity.

Special: Photographs of meetings of business organizations, which hold conventions in Atlanta; pictures will be used of men of prominence who attend. These will be run in one column cuts only.

Publicity on wrestling matches will be limited to 3 inches on week days and 3 inches on Sunday before the match, but story after the match will be based on news value as determined by sports department.

Advertisers should not be given preference over any other teams in soft ball leagues. No requests will come from business office on soft ball stories.

Economic Experts

Governments, businesses and individuals have economic advisers to whom they turn for practical advice, especially in critical times. Unfortunately, the experts are better at theorizing concerning historical trends than they are at explaining current phenomena and predicting the immediate future.

This is distressing to journalists, who, increasingly since the Great Depression, have sought help. The tragic fact is that the supposed best economists, from the left to the right, have been consistently wrong about everything during the past half-century. With the exception of Roger Babson, a newspaper columnist who forecast a stock-market crash in 1929, though not a depression, the professional economists did not understand what had happened. Even with 14 million people out of work, they convinced President Herbert Hoover that the classical law of supply and demand as expounded by the 18th-century economist Adam Smith would operate, so Hoover declared that "prosperity is just around the corner." Then came Franklin D. Roosevelt's New Deal and his adoption of the philosophy of the 20th-century British economist John Maynard Keynes, who taught that when business is depressed, government must provide jobs, by deficit spending if necessary.

The Keynesian New Deal did not end the depression; it was our participation in World War II that did. And when the war ended the virtually unanimous prediction of the economists was that the return of 14 million servicemen would glut the employment market and cause depression. Actually, the goal of Henry A. Wallace and F.D.R. of 60 million postwar jobs was realized to confound the experts.

After the war the National Association of Manufacturers argued that unless the classical laws of supply and demand were allowed to operate there would be inflation, and they persuaded Congress to repeal price controls. The National Association of Real Estate Boards did the same in order to end rent controls and to discourage low-cost veterans' housing. When Marriner Eccles refused to go along with demands that restraints on credit be lifted, President Truman removed him as chairman of the Federal Reserve Board. In his State of the Union message in January 1948, the president had to admit that between July 1946, when the controls were lifted, and October 1947 wholesale prices had gone up 60 per cent and retail prices 33 per cent, and by the time he reported they had both gone up another 10 per cent, all contrary to what the economic advisers had predicted.

So after inflation came, despite the experts, the next wave of predictions concerned imminent deflation, possibly depression. So forecast Standard & Poor; so also did the Public Affairs Institute, founded by the Brotherhood of Railroad Trainmen. In its issue of Jan. 20, 1956, *Newsweek* asked, "What's Wrong With the Top U.S. Economists?" and ran a chart to indicate with a red line, "What really happened in industrial production" from 1946 and 1956, with arrows pointing in the right direction.

A similar graph at any time from then to now would show the same discrepancies between economic theorizing and economic fact. On Aug. 15, 1967, the Associated Press reported: "This has been a rugged year for the forecasters, most of whom have been kept busy updating, correcting, painfully readjusting and, in the U.S. Treasury's case, revising downward." May 20, 1962, the AP reported: "As stocks have sunk lower in recent weeks some technicians said that all the clues and guidelines they rely on to forecast probable market movements had gone by the board."

When the magazine *U.S. News & World Report* asked four American winners of the Nobel Prize in economics to offer suggestions on how the Reagan administration could achieve prosperity without inflation, it got four different answers. The Chicago *Tribune* editorialized: "Not even the Nobel Prize pretends to reflect a judgment on what is right or wrong. It is awarded rather on the basis of what is novel, what is appealing and what contributes to the never-ending debate on the subject."

In summary, economics is not an exact science. The classical laws—iron law of wages, supply and demand, ordinary prudent man, marginal utility and so forth—exist in the minds of believers and only coincidentally in real life. The journalist wishing to become an expert in this field must study actual occurrences. S/he should cover the business-financial beat with as much as, or more, skepticism than s/he covers any other. S/he must realize that demands that the power of regulatory agencies, as the Federal Trade Commission, be curtailed are motivated by those whose practices led to the creation of the commission in the first place, beginning with the Interstate Commerce Commission in 1890. The only safe theory to expound is this: people support what they think will serve their own best interest. That is what is called free enterprise.

No economist or system of prediction is infallible. The caution a reporter should exercise in making judgment is illustrated by the following article from the Pittsburgh *Press:*

By William H. Wylie

PRESS BUSINESS EDITOR

Was the inflation rate 13.3 percent or 9.9 percent last year?

Joseph C. Lang Jr., associate economist for Pittsburgh National Bank, raises this question in the bank's publication, Business News And Trends.

He points out that there are two barometers for measuring inflation. One is the well known and widely used Consumer Price Index. The other is the GNP (Gross National Product), deflator for personal consumption expenditures.

The CPI showed a 13.3 percent inflation rate for the 12 months ending Dec. 31, while the PCE put the price spiral at 9.9 percent.

If you go by the PCE, inflation isn't as bad. For example, during the first three months of this year, the Consumer Price Index soared to an annual rate of about 18 percent but the deflator showed a reading of only 12 percent for the same period.

The difference is important because big dollars are involved.

"Social Security payments, food stamps, welfare payments and most negotiated cost-of-living adjustments in labor contracts which affect over 60 million persons are indexed to the CPI," the economist says.

How can differences in the two indexes be explained? Lang does it this way:

"There are a number of differences involved in the calculation of the two indexes of consumer price changes. Many of these differences are traceable to the fact that the population groups covered and the weights used are different between the measures.

"In addition there are further variations between the two that stem from differences in the definition of expenditures and in some cases the choice of prices. Each index also uses its own method of seasonal adjustment."

Lang notes that the PCE deflator is tied to quantities of goods and services actually purchased. On the other hand, the CPI is a "fixed-weight" price index. "It does not and cannot account for changes in individual buying habits that are caused by changes in relative prices."

In other words, the deflator acknowledges that when prices of clothing or food increase, consumers have a tendency to "buy down." The person who prefers tailor-made shirts may switch to a ready-to-wear brand, or eat hamburger instead of steak, or buy a Chevy, Ford or Plymouth instead of a Buick, Mercury or Chrysler. By the same token, cloth coats may be "in" while furs are "out."

"The most substantial difference between the CPI and the PCE can be seen in the category for shelter. By including new home prices and mortgage costs, the CPI gave almost twice the weight to shelter in the base period," Lang points out.

The economist suggests that the CPI gives too much weight to the effect of housing on the cost of living. He notes that "relatively few American consumers" actually buy, finance or refinance a home during any given month.

"The personal consumption deflator also attempts to measure prices paid by consumers for housing," he says, "however, its basic measure of change in housing costs for both rental and owner-occupied dwellings is an index of rents." The deflator doesn't reflect mortgage rates, which often rise or fall quickly.

In addition to housing prices and mortgage rates, the CPI was jolted by energy prices. "These three components accounted for well over 50 percent of the increase in consumer prices in January and February," Lang said.

Despite heavy criticism of the Consumer Price Index, it's not likely to be replaced, Lang feels. But he believes the CPI should be amended to reflect housing costs more accurately.

Tax selling occurs near the end of the year when investors get rid of securities to establish a loss for income-tax purposes, which suggests the importance to the financial reporter of understanding the effect tax laws have on market operations. For instance, the layman often is mystified by sales of what from all indications are profitable businesses. Often they occur so that the seller can pay a capital gains tax on the difference between the value of the property when he purchased it and its value at the time of his own sale. This, his financial advisers have figured out, means a greater long-run return on his investment than staying in business and paying the graduated corporation income tax. Put in laymen's language this means it sometimes is bad business to be too successful provided one wants to stay in the same line of work.

The possible assignments for the business-financial page are interminable. The alert interpretative reporter constantly asks "why?" especially when any form of behavior seems to become widespread, as investing capital abroad, establishing branch banks, splitting stock, purchasing government bonds or shares of an investment club or mutual fund rather than investing directly in common stocks, and so forth.

The consumer price index and the wholesale price index disclosed every month by the United States Bureau of Labor Statistics are called major yardsticks for determining the success or failure of government policies. The CPI, often erroneously called a cost of living index, is a report on the prices of 400 goods and services, from butter and beef to bowling balls. It is compiled after checking 15,000 retail stores and outlets throughout the country every month. Vital to understanding the index is its use of weights for every commodity or service. Food, for example, is calculated to be 24.8 per cent of a consumer's budget, housing 33.3 per cent and transportation 12.6 per cent.

Chicago *Tribune* expert Alvin Nagelberg describes the indices.

> The CPI is a handy way to assess the erosion of the dollar's purchasing power. And for some people it also is a defensive tool to protect their income against advancing prices.
>
> Today, more than 5.1 million workers are covered by labor contracts providing for wage increases when the CPI affects the income of:
>
> Some 29 million Social Security beneficiaries.
>
> Two million retired military and federal civil service employes and survivors.
>
> About 13 million food stamp recipients.
>
> It guides the national school lunch program, sets the poverty threshold level for health and welfare programs, has been used as an escalator for rental payments, and has played a role in divorce settlements.
>
> It is estimated that the income and benefits of one-half of the population is affected by the CPI.
>
> A one per cent change in the index triggers at least a $1 billion increase in income under escalation provisions. An error of only 0.1 per cent can lead to a misallocation of more than $100 million.

The CPI and WPI reports have often sent the stock market off in one direction or another. . . .

The Bureau of Labor Statistics first developed a CPI after World War I as a way of arriving at a fair pay scale. Quarterly indexes were started in 1935 and monthly indices in 1940. The CPI was revised in 1940, 1946, 1953, and 1964 and is due for another change in 1977 when two indices are scheduled to be published.

The problem today is that the population has grown so fast and the buying tastes and patterns have changed so much that some features of the CPI are obsolete. Also, there is a drive to get a more comprehensive and thus more accurate CPI. . . .

On the other hand, the WPI is basically a collection of prices solicited by mailed questionnaires to firms and trade associations. It's a compilation of 2,000 individual prices at the primary market level. That means the price of an item—whether a raw material product or finished product—the first time it is sold into the marketplace.

The CPI is not a true cost of living index because it does not take substitutions into account. If the price of beef goes sky high, the consumer may switch to buying more chicken. If the cost of repair services soars, the consumer may postpone repairs. Yet the CPI continues to reflect the same purchases, in the same proportions, each month. . . .

Here is another article that interprets as well as describes:

Washington (AP)—The third-steepest monthly decline in history in the nation's Index of Leading Economic Indicators was recorded in March, the Commerce Department said Wednesday, providing more evidence that the nation may face a deep recession.

The index fell 2.6 percent last month. It was the eighth decline in the past 12 months and the steepest for any month since September, 1974, when it fell 3 percent as the economy sank into the 1974–1975 recession.

"It means forces are very much tilted toward recession," said Feliks Tamm, a Commerce Department analyst.

The index declined 0.4 percent in February. It was unchanged in January, on the basis of a revision, but declined during the previous three months.

Tamm said there are similarities between the behavior of the index in recent months and its behavior in the last recession, although it does not yet give much indication of the severity of the new downturn.

The index is designed to indicate future trends in the economy. Tamm said it has been pointing to sluggish or negative growth for the past 17 months.

The only other time the index fell by more than 2.6 percent was in September, 1953, when it dropped 2.8 percent.

Tamm said that since October, the average monthly decline has been 0.8 percent, which he said is "particularly important" in reflecting weakness of the economy.

Seven of the 10 individual statistics used in the index declined in March, led by stock prices and building permits. Also negative were the average work week, the job layoff rate, raw materials prices, the money supply, and new factory orders.

On the positive side were sales deliveries, cash and other liquid assets and plant and equipment orders.

The index stood in March at 131.3 with a 1967 base of 100.

Meanwhile, government officials hope an improvement in the nation's trade balance will help keep the U.S. dollar attractive overseas, despite the drop in interest rates that is now well under way.

The Commerce Department reported Tuesday the trade deficit narrowed to $3.16 billion in March, down sharply from the February deficit of $5.6 billion and the lowest monthly deficit in four months.

At the same time, several major U.S. banks on Tuesday became the latest to lower their prime lending rates to 18½ percent, and there were predictions the rate will soon drop below 18 percent.

Interest rates have been falling steadily in recent weeks, mostly because the recession trend in the economy is reducing demand for loans.

The Commerce Department's Index of Leading Economic Indicators is designed to show which way the economy is headed. This index is a composite of 12 leading indicators. These are:

Average Work Week of Production Workers, Manufacturing
Contracts and Orders for Plant and Equipment
Index of Net Business Formation
Index of Stock Prices, 500 Common Stocks
Index of New Housing Permits, Private Housing Units
Layoff Rate, Manufacturing
New Orders, Consumer Goods and Materials
Net Change in Inventories On Hand and On Order
Per Cent Change in Sensitive Prices
Vendor Performance, Per Cent of Companies Reporting Slower Deliveries
Money Balance (M-1)
Per Cent Change in Total Liquid Assets

It is clear that in dealing with such complicated relationships and interactions of cause and effect as exist in our complex financial and industrial structure, it is necessary to make a careful analysis and explanation of the entire situation. To do this necessitates looking behind the scenes. The economist believes that in this material and industrial age it is necessary to understand the economic factors. In this way the newspaper man can give his readers a correct interpretation of otherwise misunderstood events.

—Ernest L. Bogart, professor of economics

19
LABOR

The history of the American labor movement is as much that of a struggle of different ideologies for supremacy within the ranks of labor itself as it is that of a fight between capital and labor for a share of the national wealth and income. In its early stages, organized labor was handicapped because of its control by leaders of foreign birth or influence and by native-born intellectuals who lacked experience as workers and were discredited further because of their known unorthodoxy in other fields.

In the middle half of the nineteenth century, labor was too prone to espouse every new economic or political theory that offered a possible step upward on the economic scale. Agrarianism, idealistic cooperative plans, greenbackism, the single tax, free silver and syndicalism were among the ideologies with sizable followings within the ranks of labor. Until the American Federation of Labor emerged as powerful under the leadership of Samuel Gompers late in the nineteenth century, organized labor hardly was an important permanent factor in American economic and political life.

The AFL's triumph over the Knights of Labor represented a victory for the craft union as opposed to industrial unionism, of the "aristocracy of labor" idea over the "one big union" idea. Gompers and his followers believed in working within the existent capitalistic system, seeking through unions of craftsmen organized horizontally throughout industry as a whole to obtain the maximum benefits for the workers. The Knights of Labor had admitted unskilled as well as skilled workers.

Craft unionism remained dominant until 1936, when, under the leadership of John L. Lewis, the Committee (later called Congress) for Industrial Organization began to organize many large basic industries, such as mining, automobile and steel, in which large masses of unskilled workers were not eligible for membership in craft unions. CIO unions were industrial or vertical unions because membership in them was all-inclusive within a given plant in which there might conceivably be numerous craft unions.

In December 1955, the two big organizations reunited as the AFL-CIO, but today many old units of each, at all levels from international to local, still operate with virtually unchanged autonomy. Also, still independent are the railway brotherhoods and a number of other large groups, as the miners, automobile workers and teamsters and several mavericks that were expelled as left-wing by the CIO in 1949.

Despite the comparative contemporary strength of the labor movement as a whole, only about 20 per cent of the entire labor force belong to unions. Little progress ever has been made among white-collar (professional) workers whose proportion of the total labor force continues to grow with the expanding service industries and as mechanical automation reduces the ranks of the blue-collar workers.

In the United States, with its rugged individualistic frontier tradition and its democratic open-class social system, there never has developed strong class consciousness at any social or economic level. Despite considerable demagoguery to the contrary, socialistic and communistic ideas never have attracted any appreciable number of rank-and-file working people. There is no political labor party as in many other parts of the world, and organized political activity by labor always has been condemned by the rest of the populace. Because of the absence of class consciousness as a welding force, there has developed a strong type of labor leader in the United States. Whoever happens to be the leading labor figure at any time is bound to be considered a "public enemy" by anti-laborites. Regardless of the justice involved, this has been true of such widely different labor leaders as Samuel Gompers, Eugene V. Debs, John L. Lewis, Sidney Hillman, Walter Reuther, James Petrillo, Harry Bridges and James Hoffa.

Because organized labor never has enjoyed the confidence of an appreciable proportion of the American people, it has been faced with the problem of avoiding mistakes that are more costly to it than similar ones are to any other segment of the population.

LABOR LAWS

The National Labor Relations (Wagner) act of 1935 was called labor's Magna Charta because it gave federal protection to the right to organize and bargain collectively and to maintain closed shops. It was mostly under its protection that the CIO became established in the mass production industries, using the Gandhi-inspired sit-down strike strategy. The Taft–Hartley act of 1947 and the

Landrum–Griffin act of 1959 considerably weakened the basic law from the standpoint of labor. Among other things, the former outlawed jurisdictional strikes (one union against another), secondary boycotts, strikes for union recognition and the closed shop except by majority vote of eligible employees. It also stipulated penalties for breaches of contract and boycotts by unions, forbade union contributions and expenditures for political purposes, forbade the services of the National Labor Relations board to unions that had not registered financial information and filed anticommunist affidavits for all its officers, allowed employers greater freedom to campaign against unionization of workers and gave the federal government the power to use injunctions to compel an eighty-day "cooling-off" period before a strike could be called.

The Labor-Management Reporting and Disclosures act (Landrum–Griffin) of 1959 was aimed at racketeering labor officials. Among other things it required annual reports from all unions, gave the FBI power to enter cases of suspected violations, forbade "hot cargo" pacts in which a trucker, for example, refused to handle cargo from another trucker if the union labeled it forbidden, outlawed extortion or blackmail publicity, outlawed "sweetheart" contracts between unscrupulous employers and labor leaders and provided for secret ballots in union elections, machinery for ousting crooked union officials and a ban against arbitrary raising of union dues or assessments without a secret ballot vote of the members.

In the 1950s, several states adopted "right-to-work" laws. These were a misnomer for open shop as they guaranteed nobody a job and were intended to forbid closed union shops under any circumstance. In its behalf, organized labor increased agitation for the guaranteed annual wage, shorter work week and strengthening or recovery of old protections as maintenance of membership clauses, seniority rights, check-off systems for the collection of dues, pensions, longer vacations, profit-sharing plans and the like.

COVERING LABOR

Important as all these other factors indisputably are, the basic issue involved in most contract disputes is wages. As in the case of business, there is no regular labor beat. The smart labor reporter notes in a futures book the dates of expirations of contracts between important unions and industries and, weeks or months in advance, starts interviewing both management and labor officials to determine what exactly will be at stake when the new contracts are up for negotiation.

Newspaper headlines naturally emphasize conflict, especially when it leads to strikes and lockouts. It is easy to overlook the fact that the overwhelming majority of labor-management affairs are conducted harmoniously and that there are numerous companies and even entire industries in which there has been little or no trouble for decades or longer. Labor leaders have traditionally charged that when matters do come to a point of conflict, the press underplays its side of the story. During the day-by-day account of a strike, the issues causing it often become lost because of the emphasis given incidents of violence, hotheaded statements by leaders and human interest accounts.

LABOR PROBLEMS

Any major or protracted shutdown in any part of the American economy today would be catastrophic throughout the entire economy, so interrelated have all parts of it become. How to preserve the dignity and freedom to work or not to work guaranteed all Americans in the Thirteenth Amendment to the Constitution and at the same time protect the innocent masses from the repercussions of a strike or lockout is a major social and political issue. Through its Mediation and Conciliation Service, the federal government investigates and provides leadership in bringing about peaceful settlements of most disputes. During periods of comparatively full production of high prosperity, as during a cold war with huge government expenditures to keep industry going, its successes far outnumber its failures. Organized labor has been a leading supporter of American foreign policy and local unions prod employers to be diligent in seeking good government contracts to maintain full employment. If such a condition continues, organized labor may be expected to devote more of its energy to worker education programs and to plans to assist workers to participate in community affairs.

Greatest obstacle to such activities continues to be the matter of racial integration. AFL unions were discriminatory against Negroes and the unskilled foreign born. The CIO forbade such discrimination, but unions must share with management the blame for the slowness with which Negroes and members of other minority groups obtain equal job opportunities, are upgraded and are given seniority rights, not to mention managerial positions.

STRESSING THE PUBLIC INTEREST

In covering many aspects of labor news, the reporter should consider the public interest as parmount.

Union Affairs

Aside from the same reader interest that exists regarding the activities of any large organization, in the cases of unions there is the additional public interest as regards their control and policies.

> **By Andrew Ross**
>
> Concord—After working for months without a salary contract, some of the 1,500 central county employees of Chevron USA are shaking their fists in anger—not at management, but at the union.

It's the union of Oil, Chemical and Atomic Workers, which has been representing workers in Concord, Walnut Creek and other West Coast cities since May of this year.

Six months and 28 negotiating sessions later, the effectiveness of OCAW is being questioned by workers in Contra Costa County.

The employees complain that they haven't had a pay increase for 18 months and inflation is quickly catching up with them.

The company has offered an 8 percent wage increase retroactive to February of this year, but the union repeatedly has turned down the offer because of dissatisfaction over contract language pertaining to items such as grievance procedures and merit raises.

"From what we've seen, we're happy with the company offer," said Mike Hicks, a head computer operator at the Chevron accounting center in Concord. The Pittsburg resident said his feelings are representative of a majority of workers locally.

But Bob Boudreau, the international representative for the OCAW, dismisses their complaints.

"The company has been playing games in Concord," he said. "Since becoming the bargaining agent, I haven't had a chance to talk to the these people."

"They (the company) sit them down and tell them what they want to tell them," he added. "They have a captive audience."

Ironically, though, local employees say they are being held captive by the union. Employees like Mike Hicks don't belong to the OCAW, but the union does represent them at the bargaining table.

Boudreau won't say how many of the 2,700 hundred Chevron employees he represents belong to OCAW. He says it's a significant number, but concedes "the degree of organization here is not as high as everywhere else." . . .

[Contra Costa *Times*]

Public Statements

Organized labor is a strong political force. Candidates for public offices seek its endorsement. When a labor leader makes a public statement on a matter affecting the general public it is newsworthy.

By Michael Flannery

The Chicago Federation of Labor called for a massive campaign to defeat a proposed ordinance written by Mayor Byrne's advisory committee on collective bargaining for city employees.

Federation President William A. Lee, who resigned from Byrne's committee last summer to protest its alleged anti-union bias, said the proposal "is so bad it can't be amended" into acceptable form.

Byrne last month sent the proposal to the City Council, where it is pending before the Finance Committee, along with a counterproposal drafted by attorneys for the federation, a local central body of the AFL-CIO. No hearings have been scheduled for either measure. . . .

[Chicago *Sun-Times*]

Grievances

Even wildcat strikes are not spontaneous but the culmination of incidents to which workers object. A sharp labor reporter has inklings of increasing discontent long before there is overt action. It usually is in the public interest to acquaint readers of impending trouble.

> One of the Black Hawk County Health Department employees active in a movement to oust Rita Burbridge, county health director, from her job has been fired by Mrs. Burbridge.
>
> The discharge of Karen Blonigan, a public health nurse, occurred the same day the County Board of Supervisors received notice that the employees have taken steps to form a union.
>
> Mrs. Burbridge's attorney, David Nagle, Tuesday denied Ms. Blonigan's claim she was fired because she was helping to line up support for a union. Instead, he said it had to do with the health director's "obligation to maintain an ongoing department."
>
> Nagle refused to be more specific and Mrs. Burbridge declined comment.
>
> [Waterloo (Iowa) *Courier*]

Conflict

Too often strikes or lockouts occur to the inconvenience of the public. Too often the issues in the dispute are not clear and frequently if the strike continues for a protracted period, the issues are forgotten.

> **By Ted Schafers**
>
> As at least five construction sites in St. Louis were padlocked Friday, contractors accused union officials of the striking equipment operators of demanding "pure and simple featherbedding" to make work for themselves "at the expense of other AFL-CIO building trade unions."
>
> And "the real long-term issue," said Edward L. Calcaterra, president of the Associated General Contractors of St. Louis, "is the survival of the AFL-CIO unions and contractors."
>
> Negotiations entered the 51st day Friday.
>
> It was the strongest management statement issued since the beginning of the strike, which has idled nearly 10,000 union building tradesmen in St. Louis and the eastern half of Missouri. It came as federal mediator Beryl Carlew announced that a tentative agreement had been reached early Friday between the Associated Contractors of Missouri, an outstate organization, and Local 513 of the International Union of Operating Engineers. The agreement involves mainly road construction.
>
> Among the five St. Louis projects on which construction work was halted were the $20 million, 22-story addition to the Marriott's Pavilion Hotel downtown, a visitor's center for Missouri Botanical Gardens, and hospital additions to St. Luke's West, Incarnate Word and St. Mary's Medical Center.
>
> "It simply is no longer feasible to work the other trades," said Tom Dollar, senior vice president of construction for McCarthy Brothers Constructions, whose contracts are involved.

The latest agreement is similar to that reached last weekend with Fred Weber, Inc., also a road builder. If accepted by both parties, it could open road jobs to as many as 1,000 members of Local 513 outstate. Carlew emphasized the agreement will not become operative until both the union and management groups ratify it, and said he expected that to begin next week.

Union officials could not be reached for comment Friday.

The Globe-Democrat learned the latest agreement provides for a wage increase of $4.15 an hour spread over three years on work in St. Charles, Jefferson, Franklin, Lincoln and Warren counties, with $4.30 more for equipment operators employed in surrounding outstate counties. . . . [St. Louis *Globe-Democrat*]

Negotiations

When management balks at union demands, a strike is always a potential threat. State and federal conciliators may step in to attempt mediation; one side may offer to arbitrate. In all such cases, the reporter should seek the versions of both union and management as to the issues: what the union asks and what management offers. This involves comparing the new conditions sought with existing ones. A résumé of the past history of relations between the particular company and the union may suggest the possibility of peaceful settlement in the current situation.

By Edward Peeks
BUSINESS/LABOR EDITOR

Chances are that members of the United Mine Workers will ratify the latest contract offer by a sound majority vote, although the contract will be weighed and found wanting by many miners.

For one thing, pension and health care benefits fall short of demands, despite improvement over benefits in the previous offer turned down by the UMW membership.

For another, a demand for the right to strike fell early by the wayside in the course of bargaining between negotiators for the UMW and the Bituminous Coal Operators Association.

The UMW Constitutional Convention at Cincinnati in 1976 voted overwhelmingly for a right to strike clause in the new contract now up for ratification. Miners spoke of the clause as a means of tightening up the grievance machinery that had become an object of anger and a trigger of wildcat strikes.

Arnold Miller and other top UMW officials favored such a clause. They saw it as a way of controlling unauthorized work stoppages and confining them to the mine where a labor dispute arose. A strike would be authorized at the source of the dispute upon majority vote of the UMW local after other measures had failed. The strike, in the framework of the grievance machinery, was regarded as a last resort by Miller and other proponents.

Moreover, it was looked upon, from the standpoint of the union, as a way to curb roving pickets and to stop miners from genuflecting at the sight of every picket or picket line. It was meant to strengthen UMW local leadership and make members themselves more responsible for stability in the workplace.

But coal operators wouldn't or couldn't buy the limited right to strike. Some held that there was nothing in the history of the UMW that argued for the right to strike as a measure against wildcats in the coalfields.

The 1974 contract, operators say, offered UMW members one of the best grievance procedures in the country, but miners wouldn't abide by it. All too often if they didn't like an arbitrator's decision, members of a local would go on a wildcat strike and spread it across the coalfields.

In addition, from the view of operators, miners take umbrage when they are hauled in court for violation of the union contract. They defy court orders and some miners even have the gall to try to deny an operator his constitutional right to go to court in a labor contract dispute.

Against this backdrop of labor-management relations, the new UMW contract has nothing that promises to forestall wildcat strikes in the coalfields.

Nevertheless, the new BCOA offer makes improvements in pension and health care benefits over the two previous offers found unacceptable by the union.

[Charleston (W. Va) *Gazette*]

Settlements

The account of a settlement must contain the provisions and some analysis of their probable effect.

By John Junkerman

The city of Madison and its public employee unions are batting .500 at the bargaining table, having settled contracts in the past week for the firefighters and public works employee unions while requesting state mediation for the police and general city workers.

Members of Firefighters Local 311 and Laborers Local 236 (public works employees) both ratified 1980–81 contracts that will increase earnings by 17.5 per cent over the duration of the pact and increase base pay by 22 per cent by the end of 1981. The city also agreed to pick up the increase in health insurance premiums and will continue to pay about 88 per cent of the cost.

The firefighters contract also establishes a new physical fitness program that will require a 45-minute exercise period per 24-hour duty period, to be administered by Madison General Hospital. The firefighters will be tested for agility and fitness, but will not be disciplined for failure to meet the standards during the term of the new contract.

A somewhat different city proposal has been the major barrier to a negotiated settlement with the Madison Professional Police Officers Association. MPPOA president Gordon Hons has said the union is willing to accept the same plan that the firefighters have agreed to, but city negotiator Tim Jeffery contends the two jobs require different levels and qualities of fitness.

Firefighters president Joe Conway said the union proposed a fitness program four or five years ago, but the city rejected the idea. According to Jeffery, the city's new interest in the programs is a result of the lifting of mandatory retirement at age 55. Public safety employees are now allowed to work beyond 55 if they meet the fitness standards.

There are also fitness requirements to be met at the time of recruitment onto the force. ''Since there are standards at the front end and the back end, we are legally required to have them throughout,'' Jeffery said. The parties will meet Wednesday with Wisconsin Employment Relations Commissioner Herman Torosian to begin the mediation process. [Madison (Wis.) *Press Connection*]

Strikes

Unless it is a "wildcat," a strike is preceded by a strike vote of the membership. This vote may be taken long in advance of the actual walkout and may consist in authorizing the officers to use their own discretion. In states with "cooling off" periods it may be necessary to file notices of intention to strike weeks or months in advance. One result of such laws may be that a union keeps an industry under almost perpetual notice, as was the case frequently under the wartime Smith-Connally act.

After a strike begins, the reporter describes factually what happens: (1) how many members of what unions walk out, when and where; (2) what is the status of picketing—number engaged, location and activities; (3) police handling of the situation and comment by both union and management on the handling; (4) violence or threats of violence; (5) the effect upon the public because of curtailed production or services; (6) efforts to settle the strike. A fair treatment of labor disputes requires constant contact with both sides and equal space to comments. Also, good reporting consists in frequent reminders as to the issues involved; that is, the union's demands and the company's counterproposals. Too often tempers become so inflamed that by the time a strike ends nobody remembers what it was all about in the first place. The newspaper which never forgets that no one, including the participants, really wants a strike contributes toward peaceful settlement by not contributing to the incipient ill will.

> A strike at Beach Products, a Kalamazoo producer of paper tableware, headed into its sixth day today as Teamsters and management have reached an impasse on the wage issue.
>
> The 157 production workers, members of Teamsters Union Local 7, walked off the job Thursday morning following the overwhelming rejection of the company's contract offer.
>
> Management proposed an increase of 25 cents an hour per year for three years, according to Teamsters Local president Jack Brand. In a ratification vote at 7 A.M. Thursday, the Teamsters rejected the offer by a 132–12 count.
>
> "The only issue on the table is money," Brand said. "We can't live with 25 cents a year. We'll need at least 45 cents."
>
> Brand said the average production worker at Beach now earns about $5 an hour.
>
> The striking workers have been picketing at the plant at 2001 Fulford since last Thursday's walkoff.
>
> Production at the plant has been totally shut down, with only the 15–20 clerical workers and administrators reporting for work.
>
> Frederick Hanse, president of Beach Products, declined to comment on the strike.
>
> Brand said no date has yet been set for further negotiations.
>
> [Kalamazoo (Mich.) *Gazette*]

Public Effect

There are many ways in which the general public is affected by developments in labor circles.

By Herb Gould

Politicians, from President Carter on down, pay lip service to it. But it took a strike to get it rolling in Chicago.

It is car pooling. And it was an idea whose time came with the CTA walkout.

The Chicago Area Transportation Study, a government planning and research group for the six counties, has been counting noses inside autos entering the downtown area and has collected some impressive statistics.

To make sense out of them, you have to know that under ordinary circumstances, 15 per cent of the cars coming into town during the morning rush hour contain at least one passenger in addition to the driver.

On Monday, the first day of the Chicago Transit Authority strike, 45 per cent of those cars carried at least one passenger. On Tuesday, the figure was 57 per cent.

And it's even more impressive than that because there have been more swimmers in the pools, the study found. While observing some 4,100 inbound autos at nine downtown locations, study sleuths determined that four times as many cars as usual carried two or more passengers.

Even when the driver is not alone, a spokesman said, there is seldom more than one rider.

And all this has been happening without much help from employers, most of whom generally encourage car pooling but only do a bit more about it than they do about the weather. . . . [Chicago *Sun-Times*]

By Michael Curtin

OF THE DISPATCH STAFF

The city of Columbus will not suffer substantially from Sunday's cutoff of federal Comprehensive Employment and Training Act (CETA) funds to pay employee salaries.

Federal regulations require that cities must cease using CETA funds for most employee salaries as of Sunday.

However, the city plans to retain 275 of its 319 workers who until Monday will have received paychecks from CETA payrolls.

Congressional reauthorization of CETA in late 1978 resulted in new regulations limiting CETA participants to no more than 78 weeks in the program. Salary limitations also were put on CETA salaries. And those salaries generally fall below those paid by the city. . . . [Columbus (Ohio) *Dispatch*]

YOUNGSTOWN, Ohio (UPI)—When Mike Mignogna heard that U.S. Steel Corp. was closing its huge McDonald Works, his first thought was, "I wish I hadn't bought that house."

Mignogna is one of 3,500 Youngstown-area steelworkers who are facing a less-than-happy holiday season this year because they will lose their jobs at the McDonald Works and the Ohio Works when U.S. Steel shuts down the two mills in 1980.

The closings are part of a nationwide series of cutbacks announced Nov. 27 by the nation's largest steel manufacturer.

The McDonald Works has been more than a place to work for the 30-year-old Mignogna; it has given him everything he has, and now he sees it all being taken away.

"The night I told my wife I was going to lose my job I sat down and cried. My wife cried. I owe everything we have to U.S. Steel and now I'm terrified, more than afraid, of what's going to happen.

"On June 18, (U.S. Steel Chairman David) Roderick said U.S. Steel had no intention at all of shutting down the Youngstown Works. I told my wife, what the hell, let's buy a new house. So we did. We used my whole life savings. That $4,000 might not seem like much to some people, but it would have kept us going for a while and now it's all gone," Mignogna said.

From mortgage payments to doctor bills to gasoline, the economic squeeze facing the average American family has turned into a suffocating financial crush for Mignogna and his fellow steelworkers.

"What are you going to do? We'll just have to start over. I can probably make a go of it for a little while, but we will probably end up losing our home," Mignogna said.

Suppose they have a strike and nobody cared?

The attitude around Detroit was not quite that blase Thursday as a strike by 9,000 garbage workers, bus mechanics and other city workers went through its third day. But while uncollected trash continued to pile up, so did evidence that the walkout has not yet made a significant impact on the lives of most Detroiters.

"I guess I've noticed it, but it hasn't really affected me," said a clerical worker for City National Bank who would identify herself only as Diane.

"I called the city on Tuesday to get some dead trees picked up, and they said it would be two or three weeks," she said. "But they probably would have said the same thing if they weren't on strike."

She said she usually rides a city bus to work from her east side home, but has had no problems getting rides from friends or co-workers.

While Detroiters were hitching rides and ignoring garbage pileups, bargainers for the city and union members were continuing to talk. Negotiation sessions were expected to continue over the holiday weekend. . . . [Detroit *Free Press*]

William Eaton, who handled labor news for the United Press International in Washington for many years, gives the following advice:

The reporter starting on the labor beat needs a certain persistence to overcome (1) the mild paranoia of most labor leaders toward the commercial press, and (2) the timidity of most management spokesmen in dealing with the nosey newspaperman. A new labor reporter also should:

Walk a picket line—and listen.

Find a friend on each side of the bargaining table and not neglect the mediators, either.

Be cautious about predictions on the length of strikes and the imminence of settlements.

Learn to wait for hours outside a bargaining room and eat cold hamburgers at 3 o'clock in the morning.

Keep the faith with the rank-and-file.

Never violate a trust.

20
AGRICULTURE

An area of potential news that is generally neglected by city daily newspapers is the rural, farm or agricultural sector. Generally such papers rely on the press associations to cover Washington and state capital developments regarding farm legislation. Some press releases from agricultural organizations are rewritten to stress local angles and, especially in smaller places, columns written by local county agents are sometimes run. By comparison with the treatment given business and/or labor, this coverage is meager. As a result the press is accused of neglecting its responsibility by ignoring changes that have occurred in farming. "Too many daily papers run farm news as if it were a running battle between farmers and the secretary of agriculture or between farmers and town people—or between farmers themselves," according to former Secretary of Agriculture Orville Freeman.

Most newspapers that formerly gave greater coverage to farm news have long since ceased the attempt to instruct farmers in how to farm, leaving that area to the farm magazines. Commenting on Freeman's criticism, B. B. Watson, farm editor of the Hannibal (Mo.) *Courier-Post,* emphasized a "conflict of objectives" as follows: "Farm news as such is primarily local or at least regional in character, is pedantic, repetitious, highly compartmentalized and is seldom productive of advertising revenues in proportion to other elements in the news."

Other editors explain that agricultural news is slanted to interest the public as a whole. As Stanley Lantz, farm editor of the Bloomington (Ill.) *Pantagraph,* put it, it is "not written in 'farmer talk' to the mythical man in the overalls and straw hat."

THE RURAL POPULATION

That such a man is mythical is seen in the statistics regarding changes in rural America since the country's origin. Whereas in colonial days 90 per cent of the population was rural, today about 2.8 per cent is, down from 18 per cent at the end of World War II. American farm units reached their all-time peak of 6,500,000 in 1935. A quarter century later there were only 2,300,000 units, approximately half of them marginal and not needed to supply the nation's food needs. The small independent farmer is almost nonexistent today. Since 1945 an average of 330,000 farmers have gone out of business annually. Agriculture has become Big Business, very big. The top 35 so-called farmers have larger incomes than the bottom 350,000.

"Every day 12 square miles of American farmlands vanish forever," according to Peter J. Ognibene. "Where crops, barns and silos once stood, roads, subdivisions and shopping centers have sprouted. In the past decade we have lost farmlands equivalent to the combined areas of Vermont, New Hampshire, Massachusetts, Rhode Island, Connecticut, New Jersey and Delaware. Today we still have 24 million acres in reserve—currently unfarmed land that could be brought under cultivation within a short time. If the present rate of loss continues, however, that reserve will evaporate by 1990."

According to the Council on Environmental Quality, since 1935 "100 million acres have been degraded to the point where they cannot be cultivated, and on another 100 million acres more than 50 per cent of the topsoil has been lost."

THE SOCIAL EFFECT

R. C. Longworth summarized and analyzed the nationwide ramifications of these changes in the Perspective section of the Chicago *Tribune* for March 2, 1980.

> There have been warnings for years that the family farm is dying. If the situation in northwestern Iowa is a reflection of the rest of the Midwest, the family farm may be all but dead—with a permanent impact on our economy, our diet, and on the values and philosophy of the entire region.
>
> Even many urban Midwesterners have in the past identified with the independent spirit and self-sufficient individualism of the family farmer: if the typical farmer turns out to be a sharecropper, what does that say about us?
>
> James Rhodes, a University of Missouri economist, has noted that this process may be creating a class and a problem that the United States, almost alone among nations, has never had—a "landed aristocracy."
>
> There has been much printed about the rape of the land in other parts of America. We know that the eight largest energy companies own 64.6 million acres of American land, that railroads hold questionable title to 23 million acres, that 80 per cent of Maine is owned by absentee landlords, that the 25 biggest landowners in California (mostly corporations) hold 58 per cent of that state's land.

We also know that this concentration has severe consequences for those areas—the deaths of small towns as huge corporate farms replace smaller spreads, the creation of large numbers of unemployed in cities of the North as corporations force Southern blacks off their lands, the transformation of whole counties into the fiefdoms of powerful coal companies, and the cultivation of the square tomato and other tasteless food by corporations more interested in profit than nutrition.

Farm land has become another investment commodity and a particularly valuable one. In the Midwest, crop land costs $2,000, $3,000, or more per acre. The size of the average American farm, once about 160 acres, is now 400 acres and growing fast: the number of farms under 500 acres is shrinking while the number over 500 is growing.

This means it costs $1 million or more to buy a farm. No young farmer has that kind of money, nor can he afford to borrow it at current rates of interest. Farming is still a profitable business, but speculators have bid up the price of land to three times its value in crops produced.

So the young man rents. Sometimes he is the farmer's son. Once upon a time, he would have taken over the farm from his father.

But farmers, like everybody else, are living longer; the average age of Midwestern landowners these days is an incredible 57 years. More and more, farmers are holding on to their land, even after they retire.

Farm groups report an increasing number of farmers' sons who remain in tenancy to their fathers until they are 50 or older. Often the sons, weary of such servitude, simply leave the farm and the old man rents to somebody else.

Then one day, the old farmer dies and leaves the land to his children. But inheritance taxes on $1 million worth of farm land are murderous. Even if the family has forestalled the tax problem through family corporations or other devices, most of the heirs have already left the land and want only to sell their inheritance and take the money.

At this point, a neighboring farmer, wealthy and able to borrow $1 million, steps in and buys the land. Many Iowa and Illinois farmers have spreads of 2,000 acres or more and are looking for more.

And so the neighboring farmer buys. Two family farms are incorporated into one. A farm family leaves the land.

Time passes and the wealthy farmer ages. He has farmed part of his holding, rented out the rest. When he dies, the tax burden is crushing. If he has one heir who already owns land, the farm may stay in the family. But if there are several heirs or if all the heirs have left the land, the pressure to sell is strong.

But a farm of this size costs millions. A wealthy buyer is sought—and often found among businessmen, doctors, or lawyers in town. Sometimes a syndicate of such investors buys the land, and rents it out.

Now the process is complete. Land that once was owned a century ago by some 50 families, and was consolidated over the years until it was owned by just one family, now is owned by no family at all.

"So a farmer, by wanting more and more land, is actually cutting his grandson's throat," says Curt Sorterberg, assistant to the president of the National Farmers Organization.

Studies on Midwestern towns also show that as family farms die out, so do the local businesses that support them. For every six family farms that are swallowed up, one local business expires—and Iowa alone is losing some 4,000 farms each year.

When a farm gets big enough, it finds it easier to bypass local businesses altogether. Instead of dealing with the local feed dealer, implement salesman, bank, or grain elevator, it goes directly to the head office, buying in bulk from a big supplier hundreds of miles away.

Absentee landlords skew local economies and local tax rolls. In 1968, the Department of Agriculture reported that two-thirds of the 66,000 richest persons reporting farm income claimed a net farm loss.

Among experts in the field, there is no dispute at all about what is wrong. The culprit is decades of federal and state laws that have had the result—intended or not—of encouraging big farms, penalizing small or medium-sized farms, and driving family farmers off the land.

On this, even Secretary of Agriculture Bob Bergland agrees.

"The truth is, we really don't have a workable policy on the structure of agriculture," Bergland admitted before the National Farmers Union convention last year.

Past policies created an American food-producing system "that is the envy of the world," Bergland said. But he said this system, for all its fecundity, seems to "have worked to the disadvantage of small and medium-sized farmers."

The pressure is on for "larger and larger and fewer and fewer farms that will increasingly dominate and control production." Bergland said.

He told of 21 farmers who came to Washington recently to lobby for higher price supports "to save the family farm." Yet 20 of these farmers had annual sales of more than $200,000 and several claimed that a farm should have sales of at least $100,000—a minimum level that would eliminate 90 per cent of all U.S. farms.

Bergland quite clearly shares the view of almost all land reformers—that well-intentioned federal policies, designed to increase farm output, have inadvertently driven small farmers out of business and created a cult of bigness.

These policies include the inheritance tax laws. They include other tax policies that encourage land ownership by non-farmers as a tax shelter. They include tax laws that encourage big farmers to buy yet more land.

The policies include farm research carried out by land grant colleges that focuses on produce and machinery intended to increase profits on big farms.

They include government credit policies that favor big farmers, with a reluctance to lend to smaller, less profitable, farmers.

They include, especially, farm price supports. In 1976, 36.5 per cent of these payments went to the richest 5.5 per cent of American farmers.

ROUTINE NEWS

Typical of the kind of news that is important in farm areas are the following from news stories in the Lincoln (Neb.) *Journal* and *Star*.

Lancaster County referees heard Thursday from a number of disgruntled farmers, who said the 1980 values placed on their land only add to the burden of the farmer, already plagued by inflation and declining grain prices.

"The taxes are too darn high for my income," said Theodore Meyer, who owns 282 acres northwest of Emerald. "I have as good equipment and farm as good as anyone else, but the income just isn't coming in."

A whopper crop of hoppers could be hatching out on Nebraska's rangeland if unseasonably warm and dry weather continues. The first pale-green grasshopper nymphs are emerging from their eggs this week.

According to a U.S. Department of Agriculture survey, Nebraska has the potential for a severe grasshopper infestation on more than 6 million acres of rangeland. The best hope of nipping the hopper problem in the nymph stage lies in the weather.

A siege of cold, rainy weather just as the nymphs emerge from the eggs could make the young hoppers sick. A large number of them could fall prey to fungus diseases, according to Tim Miller, entomology technician at the University of Nebraska-Lincoln.

The hope for rainy weather is shared by Nebraska farmers, who are growing concerned that dry field conditions could jeopardize their young crops. . . .

Nebraska farmers have been nibbling away at the $44.7 million available from the Farmers Home Administration for 14 percent economic emergency loans like rats at prime cheddar.

The FmHA has loaned out about $30 million in economic emergency funds since the funds became available last month. The sum represents two-thirds of the amount received by Nebraska FmHA as its share of a $1 million federal appropriation to help farmers caught in the credit crunch obtain operating capital.

About 500 Nebraska farmers have received loans from FmHA, according to Doug Horrocks, assistant to the state FmHA director. The agency still has 800 economic emergency applications pending—more than enough to use up the remaining funds.

Nebraska remains the undisputed corn-reserve king of the nation.

The state's farmers have placed more than 262 million bushels of corn in the federal grain reserve, according to Harold Rademacher of the state Agricultural Stabilization and Conservation Service office.

The price-support and loan specialist said Nebraskans also have 17 million bushels of wheat and 32 million bushels of grain sorghum in reserve.

Storage bins around Nebraska are groaning with more grain under federal loan than any other state. Not even Nebraska's corn-growing rivals, Iowa and Minnesota, can match the total, although they rank second and third with 220 million bushels and 180 million bushels, respectively.

POLITICAL POWER

Several United States Supreme Court decisions in the '60s led to considerable changes in the rural-urban balance of political power. States have had to reapportion congressional and legislative districts in accordance with the equal representation rule: one voter, one vote. Previously, through gerrymandering and refusal of the rural-dominated legislatures to reapportion, the farm areas were represented way out of proportion to their population strength. For instance, a Georgia farmer's vote was 62 times more effective than that of a Georgia city voter. A typical situation existed in Michigan where an upper peninsula congressman represented 177,431 persons whereas a Detroit congressman spoke for 802,994.

Logrolling by members of the Farm Bloc, representative of noncompetitive agricultural interests as cotton and cattle, wheat and vegetables, no longer is so effective with total rural representation reduced. No drastic changes have occurred yet; but as the power structure is altered by deaths and elections, cities should find it easier to obtain needed laws from state legislatures and possibly will be able to rely less heavily on Washington. The lobbies should become less active. The Big Three of such lobbies are the American Farm Bureau of over three million members, generally sympathetic to the larger and wealthier farm owners; the National Farmers Union with about 330,000 members, a gadfly New Deal-born organization of small and independent farmers; and the National Grange, whose 700,000 members regard it mostly as a social group instead of as a militant political force as it was when it began shortly after the Civil War. There is also the National Farmers Organization with almost 200,000 members, which has aspects of both a cooperative and a labor union. Formed in 1955 in Iowa, it has engaged in several holding actions (keeping a commodity off the market) and in 1979 from $650 to $750 million worth of farm products were marketed through the organization, which acted as agent for blocks of production.

Today's federal agricultural policy is still substantially the same as that established in early New Deal days by Henry A. Wallace and associates. The essential feature is to keep farm income high by payments to farmers for participation in the Soil Conservation program whereby part of their acreage is kept idle and by loans through the Commodity Credit Corporation secured by products that can be forfeited in case the market price stays low.

These and similar efforts are geared to what is called parity, the relationship between the well-being of the farmer and nonfarm population using the period 1910–14 as the base. Devised years ago by the American Farm Bureau, it has been called a statistical monstrosity, and the Bureau in recent years has favored reduction or elimination of federal farm supports. The small independent farmers, however, insist that the present policy is necessary for their continued existence, even though the large corporate farms admittedly benefit more from it and do not need it to survive. Ceilings on federal governmental subsidies to big producers are favored increasingly by urban-suburban members of Congress, who now outnumber their rural area colleagues.

Critics of the present policy correctly point out that it is handicapped in achieving its aims because it still is based on acreage rather than productivity. Today an hour of farm labor produces five times as much as it did a generation ago and crop production by acres is up about 75 per cent. All of this has been accomplished by the technological revolution that began in the late nineteenth century with the threshing machine, reaper and similar machines and by the experimental work of the land-grant agricultural colleges, which have made higher education an essential for farming today. Contemporary farming is Big Business and expensive. The family farm is becoming obsolete.

THE URBANITE'S STAKE

Today more workers are engaged in transporting, processing and selling food than are engaged in producing it, and the farmer receives only about 35 cents of every dollar that the housewife spends in the supermarket. Her interest is many-sided. She wants the best for the least cost. William Longgood of the New York *Times* with his *The Poisons in Your Food* (Simon and Schuster, 1960), Rachel Carson in *Silent Spring* (Houghton Mifflin, 1962) and many others since then have made the housewife aware of the health hazards resulting from many current agricultural practices. Nutritionists have made her conscious of vitamins, calories and balanced diets. Recipes are an indispensable part of most publications today. The developing field of consumer reporting was described in Chapter 11. What follows is an attempt to interpret a matter of concern to "city slickers" so they can understand it.

By Roger Croft

If beleaguered housewives are hoping for an early relief in the soaring price of sugar they are in for a bitter disappointment. And if any would-be economic sleuth is searching for sinister, speculating gnomes in Zurich his mission is likely to be unsuccessful.

Sugar prices, to be sure, are running rampant. Today, housewives are paying about 70 cents a pound compared with 13 cents a pound at the beginning of this year.

The refining companies are similarly having to fork out about six times the money they pay for raw sugar—now about $1,300 a ton against $328 a ton last January. Such a 600 per cent take-off in the price of sugar for the housewife makes current inflationary trends of 10 per cent to 12 per cent a year in food costs look puny indeed.

What is really behind this phenomenal rise in the price of one of our basic foodstuffs?

First and foremost it's a question of supply and demand. Crop failures, rapidly rising demand from developing countries and the inability or reluctance of producers to react quickly to changes in demand are the major causes of today's sugar shortages.

GLIMMER OF HOPE

Prospects for an early fall in sugar prices are therefore slim. But there is one glimmer of hope on the horizon.

Sugar brokers report that sugar "futures" (contracts to buy sugar several months from now) are beginning to drop a little. For example, in London spot sugar (today's price) is 570 pounds sterling a ton. Next month's price is a discouraging 581 pounds sterling. But by August, 1975 the price drops to 519 pounds a ton and for October of next year the slide continues to 490 pounds a ton.

The slight weakening in the futures prices reflects the prospect of a better sugar crop next year—the beet crop is harvested in the early fall. The European and the Soviet Union's beet crop this year was hit by early frost and a wet spring. The sugar cane producers, which account for roughly 60 per cent of world supplies and are mainly the tropical countries like Cuba, Mauritius and the Philippines were physically unable to boost their production to make up for the short-fall in beet supplies.

One reason producers find it difficult to boost the supplies of sugar in one part of the world to make up for a shortage elsewhere is that a sugar-making plant costs around $50 million—and that's a lot of money to invest to produce a commodity whose price, given a good crop, could spiral downwards as fast as it has rocketed skywards this year.

Apart from such hefty capital costs, production costs have climbed sharply for the sugar growers this year. Fertilizer prices have increased sharply, partly because of the quadrupling in the price of crude oil—and labor costs, even in the developing, tropical nations, are on a steep upward trajectory.

On the heels of the OPEC nations' collective price-fixing for crude oil, the question in many people's minds is still whether there has not been some conspiratorial cartelization moves by the producer countries.

"No way," says Leslie Palmer, president of Czarnikow Montreal Ltd., worldwide sugar brokers.

"Why would anyone want to hoard sugar now that the price is up five or sixfold? They would be unloading, taking their profits. But there is no sign of this whatsoever.

"As to cartels, they fix prices. The price of sugar has been rising inexorably all year."

There has been heavy buying from the Middle East and this has given rise to guesses about Arab sugar speculations. . . . [Montreal *Star*]

Profile of the Average Farmer

The Iowa Farm Bureau Women constantly monitor the changing role of the farmer and the following statistics have been prepared by the association.

The average farmer in Iowa is 49.7 years of age. He farms 266 acres, earns $56,000 in gross income and $7,600 in net income annually.

The average farmer also has $458,969 invested in land, machinery, buildings, crops and livestock.

Iowa farmers spend $6.5 billion on production expenses, $1,083 million on feed, and $579 million on repairs, maintenance, etc.

In addition, $548 million is spent on fertilizers.

The Farm Bureau Women also found that Iowa has 25 percent of the Grade A land in the United States. Iowa cropland represents 7 percent of the total U.S. cropland and is equal to the combined cropland of 20 other states.

Hogs are raised on about 60,000 Iowa farms—about one-half of the farms in the state.

Also according to the Farm Bureau Women, the diets of Iowans are more varied than in the past. We are eating 31 percent more poultry and 16 percent more beef per persons than we did 10 years ago.

We are also eating 6 percent more vegetables and 16 percent more fruits.

Finally, the expenditures for food amount to approximately 16.8 percent of the disposable income of the average family in Iowa.

[Ft. Madison (Iowa) *Democrat*]

21 RELIGION

A. Modern Liberalism
B. The Conservative Reaction
C. Cults
D. Church and Politics
E. Religious Group Pressure
F. Church News
G. Reportorial Qualifications
H. Correct Nomenclature

Less than a generation ago a standard Friday or Saturday feature in almost any daily newspaper was a column or page of church notices, listing the times of Sunday services and possibly sermon subjects and announcements of meetings of church organizations throughout the week to come. Today, this Saturday ghetto, as it came to be called by church editors, has disappeared from all except some small dailies and community and suburban weeklies. Newsworthy events involving churches and churchmen, such as appointment or installation of a new pastor, dedication of a new building, a public concert or lecture or the like, are reported throughout the regular news sections on any day of the week.

This desegregation of church news is a consequence of one of the most important changes in journalistic news practices in recent or perhaps all times. It involves a shift of interest from church news to news of religion, including religious ideologies and controversies. Abandoned is the traditional hush-hush policy as regards religious conflict and supercaution to avoid giving the slightest offense to anyone, the longtime policy that had as its commendable purpose the avoidance of ill will and conflict. As Gustavus W. Myers detailed in *A History of Bigotry in the United States* (Random House, 1943), religious intolerance has been severe throughout American history, with virtually every one of the 300 or so denominations that exist in this country having suffered from some sort of discrimination at one time or another. On the whole, however, freedom of religion and separation of church and state, as guaranteed by the Constitution, have worked well for two centuries and nobody, least of all the press, has wanted to stir up trouble.

MODERN LIBERALISM

The abandoning of taboos against anything but gingerly handling of matters involving religious differences does not mean journalistic incitement to bitter divisiveness. Quite the contrary, for the first time normal reporting techniques are being applied to religious news with the intent of transmitting information "across the closed borders of denominational differences and thus making for better mutual understanding," in the words of George Cornell, Associated Press religion editor. To quote him further,

> Since religious education is denominationally segregated for the average person, and since prevailing practice in this country has kept the subject out of the public school classroom, most people have been left largely uninformed or misinformed about each other's religion, and dependent mostly on hearsay or backfence supposition. This has caused one of the deep social sores in America's religiously heterogeneous makeup, and informative reporting across the compartmentalized lines has helped and is helping to make for fuller all-around understanding. And this is one of the values in the information business. Now that the ecumenical movement has exploded all over the map, it is extending the process.

The single event which, more than any other, caused the revolution in the journalistic treatment of religious news was the Second Vatican Council, from 1962 to 1965. The 2,300 Roman Catholic bishops were revealed to have sharp differences on a multitude of matters, both theological and social, thus dispelling the myth of unanimity among the leaders of a supposedly monolithic medieval institution. Although Pope John XXIII died in 1963, the liberal reformist spirit that he espoused grew, and among the revered ancient practices that were modified was secrecy of deliberations. Perspicacious newsmen explained that most of the supposed new positions, as collegiality, had been debated for decades in scholarly journals, largely in Latin, and the council merely affirmed a consensus that had developed and in some cases, as the role of bishops, represented the unfinished agenda of Vatican Council I in 1870. Commenting on the continued debates, Edward B. "Ted" Fiske of the New York *Times* declared:

> Some future council will have to ratify a new consensus. The difference is that while the last debate was carried on in private, the current one is going on under the glare of publicity and the media in fact become factors in the consensus that will emerge. Many Catholic bishops, among others, will not accept this and still cling to the idea that responsible deliberations can be carried on in secret. This, however, will have to change and already is. Witness the new policies of financial disclosures, semiopen bishops' meetings, conferences, etc.

It is estimated that because of disagreement with the Vatican II reforms, 45,000 American nuns left the convents and 10,000 American priests resigned. Other nuns and priests have been active in civic affairs, visible in the streets with civil rights and antiwar demonstrators. Until John Paul II forbade it in

1980, some ran for public office, several successfully. They also now participate in ecumenical movements with Protestants and Jews and openly debate each other regarding such issues as divorce, abortion and birth control, despite the Vatican's oft-repeated conservatism. For years the Vatican tolerated the heretical teachings of the Swiss Prof. Hans Kung, who challenged the infallibility of the church on matters of faith. Finally, in May 1980, Kung was barred as a Catholic theologian.

It is not only Roman Catholics who are questioning long-established creeds, dogmas and taboos. Disputes between traditionalists and reformers are considered newsworthy, as the following illustrates.

> It's OK for Lutherans to have sex.
>
> It's also OK to mention it.
>
> That's the word from the Church Council of the American Lutheran Church (ALC), which recently recommended positive attitudes toward human sexuality.
>
> "We reject the view that sexual behavior in and of itself is evil, lustful, unmentionable, a duty to be done, a burden to be born," said a statement adopted by the council and recommended to the ALC convention next October.
>
> "We repent for the fact that Christians so often have taught such false views. We do not, however, accept the view that sexual intercourse or sexual satisfaction is the highest or noblest goal in human life."
>
> Nor does it mean wild nights on the town.
>
> "Scriptures set the standard of a lifelong monogamous marriage of one man and one woman, and that sexual intercourse reaches its greatest potential only within the committed trust relationship of marriage," said the document, prepared by ALC's Office of Research and Analysis.
>
> The report also rejects homosexuality as proper Christian behavior.
>
> The Lutherans said sexuality includes "all that we are as human beings—biologically, psychologically, culturally, socially and spiritually." They said birth control could "enhance" sexual enjoyment but criticized "willful abortion."
>
> [Detroit *News*]

Similarly, some Jews are questioning practices centuries older than Christianity. Modern religion editors tend to humanize events, as in the following example:

> At 11 a.m. last Wednesday, Susan Snyder, a 29-year-old Evanstonian, and three rabbis made local Jewish history.
>
> The rabbis, after hearing Snyder's story of why her first marriage ended in a civil divorce in 1976, took her Jewish divorce certificate, read it to her in Hebrew, folded it in the prescribed way, and cut it two times.
>
> In this ritualistic act, the rabbis, all trained at the Reconstructionist Rabbinical College in Philadelphia, granted a Jewish divorce (known traditionally as a "get") to the young Jewish woman who was married by a Conservative rabbi in 1975.
>
> As a result, when Snyder fulfills her plans to marry Michael Gonzales, a convert to Judaism, sometime in the near future, she no longer will be considered a "chained woman" (agunah) and can be married by a rabbi.
>
> The Wednesday action was historic because it was initiated by Snyder, not by her former husband, Gary Klein.

In the past, all such initiatives had to be taken by the male partner to a marriage.

The Reconstructionist Rabbinical Assembly voted to change that tradition last January.

Not long ago, an East Coast woman became the first to take advantage of the change in the centuries-old tradition. When Snyder heard about that case, she decided to follow suit.

Her search led her to Rabbi Arnold I. Rachlis, spiritual leader of the Jewish Reconstructionist Congregation that has been meeting at First Baptist Church in Evanston and soon will move its offices and worship center to Covenant United Methodist Church in north Evanston. Snyder is delighted by the recent turn of events in her personal life.

"When Michael and I decided to be married," she said the other day, "I first thought we would be married by a judge.

"But that didn't seem sacred to me. When I looked into the process of getting a Jewish divorce, it all seemed very long and complicated until I heard about the action the Reconstructionist had taken."

Snyder and the Evanston rabbi got together to discuss her first marriage, the reasons that led to her divorce, and her hopes for the future.

At the end of the conversation, Rachlis agreed to ask Rabbi Gary Gerson and Rabbi David Brusin to join him in constituting a marriage court that could take the necessary action.

Sometimes called the fourth branch of Judaism, Reconstructionism was founded in 1934 by Rabbi Mordecai M. Kaplan, who stressed the necessity of translating the Jewish tradition into humanistic and naturalistic terms.

"The past has a vote, but not a veto," he declared.

For many years, the Reconstructionists have attempted to update the Jewish tradition in ways that acknowledge the importance of equal rights and equal rites for women.

It was Reconstructionism, for example, that pioneered in the development of bat mitzvah ceremonies for Jewish girls.

Rachlis reflects this evolving heritage.

"Life requires ceremonies," he said this week. "In terms of both marriage and divorce, the civil procedures are so crude.

"What we did Wednesday was something that enabled a person to feel released from the past. In a way, it's a purging experience.

"The legalistic aspects of the ceremony concern me less than the need to resolve the difficulties of the past in an atmosphere that is unpolluted by layers of tradition, courtroom procedures and money.

"By our action, we were saying that the community has recognized her as a person free to marry in a religious ceremony."

Rachlis believes the revised tradition has cast an affirmative vote for Susan Snyder. And Susan Snyder is grateful for a tradition that can change and for chains that can be broken. [Chicago *Tribune*]

In the December 1979 *Quill,* William C. Simbro of the Des Moines *Register* and *Tribune* enumerated some other "Unheralded Religious News" as including the continuing doctrinal struggle in the Lutheran Church–Missouri Synod, the growing political muscle of "pro life" groups and of those combining fundamentalist religion with right-wing politics, efforts to introduce "scientific creationism'' in the public schools, and the explosion of the ''electronic church'' of television form are but a few of the legitimate areas of coverage-areas ''too often poorly reported or not reported at all.''

THE CONSERVATIVE REACTION

Simbro also chastised the press for not having been aware of the resurgence of conservative Christianity long before ''born-again'' Jimmy Carter became president. Gallup pollsters in fact say 47 per cent of all Americans have been ''born again'' and evangelical Christians in the United States now total about 45 million.

Whereas some revivalists still fill large tents and auditoriums, these audiences are meager by comparison with the 150 million who are served by 1,300 radio stations, one of every seven in the country, which are owned by fundamentalist religious groups. About 150 million Americans are in areas served by two fundamentalist television networks; Praise the Lord, headed by Ted Bakke, and Pat Robertson's Christian Broadcasting Network. Some of the sermons warn of hell's fire and eternal damnation, others stress the healing effect of faith. Almost without exception the programming is overwhelmingly conservative as regards political, social and economic issues. The financial return is tremendous, several of the most successful preachers grossing $50 million or more annually. Their critics charge that only a small portion, if any, of the profit goes for constructive or charitable purposes. The United States Better Business Bureau has a list of approximately 50 evangelical movements of which it disapproves.

Bruce Buursma, religion editor, traced the development of the Video Church in the Chicago *Tribune* for Dec. 7, 1980. Thirty years ago the only important religious leader to use television was the Roman Catholic Bishop Fulton J. Sheen. Then came the evangelist William Franklin ''Billy'' Graham. Since then, according to Buursma, television ''has changed the face of American church life forever.'' One of the most successful broadcasters today, Dr. Ben Armstrong, a Presbyterian pastor and executive director of National Religious Broadcasters, says, ''All this is the most exciting development in the world today. . . . Don't fight the electric church—join it.''

CULTS

Commenting on the more than 600 members of the People's Church who committed suicide at the command of the Rev. Jim Jones in Guyana, Aryeh Neier wrote:

> We find them interesting not because we think they were freaks but because we think they may be representative of a great many other Americans who would welcome the opportunity to dedicate themselves to a cause. The power that Jim Jones achieved over them did not emanate from him. It came, we think, from their

desire to endow him with qualities deserving of the sacrifices they were prepared to make.

Similarly Simbro wrote:

> In recent years we have been moving through a time of stress on personal, experiential religion and a de-emphasis on denominational distinctiveness. It was and is a time of spiritual hunger. It hasn't been reported all that well.
>
> That hunger has expressed itself in myriad forms: the movement of the "Jesus freaks" from drugs to religion, the charismatic movement in the Roman Catholic Church and "mainline Protestantism," the attendant growth of the Pentecostal churches, and the fascination with Eastern religions, cults, mysticism, meditation, spiritualism, astrology, soul travel, revival of the old religion of witches.

Events in the Middle East, mainly Iran and Saudi Arabia, indicate that Islam as well as Christianity is undergoing a reactionary religious reformation. In the United States there has been a proliferation of new movements or cults, which appeal mostly to youth. These phenomena are not strange. Similar ones have occurred throughout history during times of insecurity and fear of the future. During these times many people turn to the supernatural for comfort. Prior to the current trend to adopt new religious movements, American young people tried activism, participating in political activities and liberal movements such as those promulgating civil rights and peace. Often discouraging failure resulted from their efforts. Therefore, many who had been unsuccessful in attempting to reform the world, rejected it. They became indolent beatniks and hippies, hedonists. They scorned orthodox dress, hairdos and morals, music and language. Under the influence of LSD and other narcotics they "took trips" and came as close to complete rejection of their environment as possible. And when the rotten world was still there after their revolt they found solace in fanatical movements that promised peace of mind on earth and salvation in the beyond. Bewildered parents have gone to court and have hired kidnappers to deprogram their sons and daughters. Belatedly, interpretative journalists have attempted to make the strange new cults understandable in terms of their recruits.

By Elaine Markoutsas

Sri Lekha devi dasi and Sri Govinda das, who used to be Stephanie O'Henly and Robert Lindberg, respectively, have been married happily for about three years. They're the parents of a 2½-year-old son, whom they'll send away to a special out-of-state boarding school when he's 5. They don't gamble, drink, smoke, or eat meat, fish, eggs, and chocolate. They don't own a house or a car, and they don't go to movies or nightclubs. In fact, they shun all material things. And they sleep in separate quarters.

Lekha and Govinda are members of the International Society of Krishna Consciousness [I.S.C.O.N.], a religious sect based on 5,000-year-old Vedic scriptures and founded 10 years ago by spiritual master A. C. Bhaktivedanta Prabhupada of India. Approximately 100,000 Hare Krishnas [named for the chant the followers intone] live in temples scattered across the nation.

The Hare Krishnas' unusual appearance and austere lifestyle have made them conspicuous. The men shave their heads and wear saffron-colored robes; the women wear multicolored saris, and some pierce their noses. They all smear clay on their foreheads and greet you with a "Hare Krishna" instead of a "Hi."

Anything that might dull the senses to Krishna [or Krsna, another name for God] is taboo. Inferior pleasure must be given up for "a superior bliss." That includes sex.

Even in a Krishna marriage, sexual relations are allowed only for the purpose of procreation. Husbands and wives generally live apart. There is no spiritual divorce, and if one partner leaves the sect, remarriage is not possible for the other.

When they are 5, children are sent to a Krishna boarding school in Dallas, where they become wards of the community and are immersed in the religion until they're about 15. Parents are permitted to visit only twice a year. . . .

[Chicago *Tribune*]

If you've ever been approached for a donation by the pamphlet-peddling Children of God, you may have noticed canvas bags dangling from their shoulders. Those are their survival kits.

Whenever they leave their Gold Coast commune, the young zealots take with them toothbrush, first-aid kit, packets of vegetable seeds, waterproof boxes of matches and a Bible.

If there is a group of them, usually one will be toting a small tent, and perhaps a fishing rod and reel.

They have to be ready, they say, in case their enemies should give chase—or in case the world should suddenly end.

"That's the battlefield out there, the battle for souls," says 24-year-old Raquel Thunder (the name she picked for herself when she quit her graduate studies in psychology at the University of Puerto Rico to join the Children of God.).

"The devil wants to stop us," adds Raquel. "We must be alert."

This us-against-the world philosophy, plus the firm belief that they are an elite group that will survive the coming holocaust, binds them to their cult, according to a theologian who has studied the group since its birth in 1968. . . .

[Chicago *Daily News*]

By James H. Bowman

Three years ago, Jack Burback, a 39-year-old tool and die maker from Homewood, sat at home reading and thinking about Jesus Christ, and it dawned on him that Jesus really loved him. Robert J. Butcher, 42, of Lansing, a trial lawyer, felt he was created "for God's amusement" until he came to the same realization as Burback and began to love his "brothers and sisters."

Kathy Follett, 32, of Country Club Hills, a homemaker, had the same big realization four years ago and since then has begun to appreciate herself as "not so bad."

The three are Roman Catholics, born and raised in a church that prides itself on its grip on divine reality achieved through a "reasonable" faith.

Instead, they are moving in the spirit of a wholly different Christian tradition, that of the Pentecostals—once known to Catholics and other mainline Christians as "holy rollers."

They have embraced the faith of enthusiasm over that of the cold, clear intellect—the difference, says Butcher, between being saved and being damned.

And as Christian lay people who have found something to cheer about in their religion, they represent a potential within their church for new life and vigor.

Today, they are known as Charismatics, or participants in the Charismatic Movement, who believe in that special contact with God known sometimes as Baptism in the Holy Spirit, or second baptism.

This is basically an inspirational moment in which the believer has the sensation of being loved by God, of being bathed in a holy glow.

Its Biblical foundation lies mainly in the experience of the apostles and others on the first Pentecost, when the Holy Spirit—the third entity of the Trinity—descended in the form of tongues of fire and people understood each other's foreign languages. . . . [Chicago *Daily News*]

CHURCH AND POLITICS

The timid role of the Roman Catholic church in Mussolini's Italy and Hitler's Germany has been criticized by several recent historians who correctly point out that the wartime and post-wartime power of the Vatican was a matter of widespread alarm, assuaged only by the Vatican's strong anticommunist policies, and regardless of the ironic fact that outside the Soviet Union—in such nations as Italy, Hungary, Poland and others—the majority of Communists are also Catholics. Postwar fears grew as the American Catholic church became the principal financial support of the worldwide Catholic missionary efforts and contributed heavily to other causes operated from headquarters in Rome. So great was the Protestant protest that President Truman had to abandon plans to name an ambassador to the Vatican. The first Catholic president, John F. Kennedy, helped diminish anti-Catholic fears, especially because of his disagreement with church leaders regarding federal aid to parochial schools and other measures that might infringe upon the traditional principle of separation of church and state.

Nevertheless, it is a historical fact that religious peace up to the immediate past was more apparent than real. For more than a century, religious controversy was at a minimum because the United States was predominantly a Protestant nation. Split into almost 300 sects, Protestants could proselyte each other but, except for the Know Nothings just before the Civil War and the Ku Klux Klan immediately afterward, few felt great alarm over Roman Catholicism. In the late 20th century, however, there is visible evidence of the extent to which the two major divisions of Christianity are pulling even. The best available figures indicate that between the two campaigns, 1928 and 1960, in which Catholics were nominees for the presidency, the American Roman Catholic population increased from 19,000,000 to 40,000,000. By 1980 it had reached 49,812,108 or 22.48 per cent of the entire population, 60.8 per cent of which belonged to some religious body. Protestants numbered 72,382,737. Total membership for all denominations was 132,812,470 or about 61 per cent of the total population. Gallup polls show that church attendance has declined slowly but steadily from a high of 49 per cent in 1958 to 41 per cent today; in contrast the percentages for church attendance in some foreign countries were as follows: Canada, 44; Netherlands, 36; Greece, 26; Australia, 25; Great Britain, 20; Uruguay, 18. Still, total church attendance in the United States during 1973 was 4.4 billion whereas only 290 million attended sports events. Contributions to churches and synagogues totaled $11 billion compared to $221 million in gate receipts at sports events.

All statistics regarding church membership are unreliable because of widely different methods of counting members—some from birth, others from adolescence, etc.—and of dropping nonparticipants from the roles (once a member, always a member is the rule for some but not all). Nevertheless, the best evidence seems to indicate that organized religion is not the factor in the everyday lives of people that it was up to a generation ago. In January 1975 Gallup pollsters reported 62 per cent of all Americans believed religion could answer most of the problems of the day. In 1957 the proportion was 81 per cent. Lip service still is paid to oath taking, prayers and other acts involving faith; but there is not the constant fear of hellfire or of offending unseen deities, nor the desire to placate them by ritual, sacrifice, penance or ordeal. There is less attention to dogma, creed and ceremony, less susperstition and mythology and consequently less fanaticism, possibly less or at least a different type of intolerance and/or bigotry. And few if any inquisitions or pogroms. As pot (drugs) lost popularity with youth, esoteric gurus, faith healers, prophets, Satan cultists and lots of hallelujah increased to rival the established churches.

Because the Republicans were entrenched among the upper economic classes, during the second half of the nineteenth century the Democrats made strong appeals to the immigrants who came in waves and settled in the large urban centers to do the most menial work. The social welfare services, developed by Tammany Hall in New York and by other urban Democratic organizations, resulted in the recruitment of most of these new citizens into the Democratic party. They were predominantly from southern Europe and were Roman Catholics. Today, their grandchildren run the city governments of virtually every large city in the United States, although the exodus of the older white elements to the suburbs is increasing the importance of the urban Negro voter and has resulted in the election of several black mayors. The relationship that exists between parishioners and their church is suggested by the appellation usually given the local Catholic archdiocese office. It is Powerhouse, and its opposition to any important public issue jeopardizes its success. Public health commissioners do well to clear promotional matter related to venereal diseases, birth control and some other matters so as not to risk public chastisement. The hierarchy is concerned over assignment of judges to such courts as Juvenile, Divorce, Domestic Relations and Family, and with the attitudes of social welfare workers, hospital administrators and the like.

During the 1980 campaign several fundamentalist religious groups were active in support of Ronald Reagan for president and helped defeat several liberal senators, including George McGovern of South Dakota, 1972 Democratic candidate for president, and Birch Bayh of Indiana. Most vigorous group was Moral Majority organized by the Rev. Jerry Falwell, described as a rightist vigilante group. There also were the National Conservative Political Action committee and the Life Amendment Political Action Committee. The last named was especially adamant in its opposition to members of Congress who opposed an anti-abortion amendment or legislation. Although these groups may not have been as influential as they claimed to be, they frightened the American Civil Liberties Union, the Union of American Hebrew Congregations and other liberal groups into launching campaigns to counter the growth of fundamental religious and other right wing organizations.

RELIGIOUS GROUP PRESSURE

At all levels of government, the activities of religious groups interested in censoring motion pictures, plays, magazines, books and the like are opposed by civil libertarians, most strongly represented by the American Civil Liberties Union. A generation ago it was Protestant groups that were most active, censoring books in Boston and fostering laws forbidding the teaching of Darwinism in the South. More recently Catholic groups, as the Legion of Decency and the National Organization for Decent Literature, brought pressure on motion-picture theaters, libraries and bookstores and advocated the establishment of official censorship boards. Today, in a period of comparative freedom in the arts, religious groups concentrate on encouraging good works rather than condemning poor productions. The Broadcasting and Film Commission of the National Council of Churches (Protestant) and the National Catholic Office of Motion Pictures still comment on films but motion-picture critics are not intimidated by them as they were once. Instead, they pay attention to the Motion Picture Association of American reviews and ratings. Pressure from numerous groups, as Parent-Teacher association is growing to restrict the showing of pornographic films, especially when juveniles are involved. The revival of Sunday blue laws, forbidding certain commercial operations, as the sale of used automobiles, is more economic than religious in origin. Such groups as the Jews and Seventh Day Adventists, however, are in opposition for religious reasons. Differences in religious viewpoints certainly are paramount in legislative and public discussion of many matters, as dissemination of birth control information, abolition of anti-abortion laws, easier divorce laws, elimination of restrictions on adoptions by parents with religious backgrounds different from those of the children involved and many more. Growing journalistic practice is to cover such news on its merits, identifying adversaries but emphasizing issues.

The schools probably are the battleground for more religious controversies than any other institution. In the late '40s the United States Supreme Court ruled that school properties cannot be used for religious instruction but that so-called released-time programs, whereby children are excused from school to go elsewhere for religious instruction, are legal. Originally supported by Protestants who feared the effect of the decline in Sunday School attendance, released-time programs now are also approved by Catholics especially in areas where there are no parochial schools. Jews are unalterably opposed. Still to be tested in the United States Supreme Court are shared-time programs whereby parochial school students take some of their work in public schools.

Although the state and federal governments already contribute considerable sums to local boards of education, through such programs as those which provide hot lunches and through the National Defense act and similar legislation, "federal aid to education" is a controversial phrase whenever a bill is before Congress to provide large-scale federal expenditures for school building construction, teachers' salaries or other services. Many Catholics oppose such federal aid unless it is provided parochial as well as public schools and have succeeded in blocking several proposals, even when they were endorsed by the nation's first Roman Catholic president. Catholics argue that free transportation for parochial school students and similar benefits are proper governmental expenditures as they are made to benefit children rather than churches. Under President Johnson's War on Poverty programs such grants multiplied, but not without protest from such organizations as Americans United for Separation of Church and State. That group also is attacking sales or gifts of public property to religious institutions and much tax exemption of church-owned property, especially that not used for strictly religious purposes.

United States Supreme Court decisions declaring that neither the federal nor a state government must pay for abortions by welfare recipients were hailed as a victory by the Right-to-Live proponents. The fundamentalists, both Catholic and Protestant, also are pleased with the progress they are making in persuading public schools and colleges to teach "scientific creationism" as well as the conventional Darwinian evolutionary theory. The Scientific Creationists believe that God created the world in seven days as related in *Genesis*. Presumably this viewpoint was discredited during the 1925 Scopes trial in Dayton, Tenn., when Clarence Darrow cross-examined William Jennings Bryan.

United States Supreme Court decisions outlawing a New York Regents Prayer and compulsory Bible reading in public schools have been followed by attempts, so far unsuccessful, to amend the United States Constitution to permit such practices. Leader of movements to extend prohibitions of religious influences is Dr. Madalyn Murray O'Hair, founder and head of the Society of Separationists and the American Atheists whose headquarters are in Austin, Tex. Atheists oppose chaplains in Congress and the military establishments, would remove "under God" from the pledge of allegiance to the flag and strike "in God we trust" from coins. They also, of course, oppose laws restricting their right to hold public office or testify in court.

Other controversial matters that may have local angles include compulsory flag salutes or other patriotic exercises to which Jehovah's Witnesses and others may object; compulsory blood transfusions for Jehovah's Witnesses and some others; vaccination and other health requirements repulsive to Christian Scientists; what religious emphasis can be given to Christmas programs without offending Jews; the propriety of Catholics' serving on public school boards; inspection of the quality of education in parochial schools and, most importantly perhaps, legalization of abortion. The lobbying activities of some religious groups may make important journalistic copy.

Offensive to some churchmen, as it is to many others, is the newspaper practice of running daily horoscopes despite the protest of those who say astrology, in addition to being made obsolete by astronomy, involves fatalistic concepts inimical to religious ideas of free will and individual responsibility. Some papers also like to play up claims of visions, revelations and apparently miraculous escapes. Journalistic critics assert that when someone says that the "Man Upstairs" heard his/her prayers and was responsible for his/her escape from death, the implication is that others who prayed in vain deserved the fate that befell them and is a blasphemous assumption. Neverthless, some newspapers feature such claims and may be prone to inquire of anyone who confronts disaster or experiences sorrow whether he or others involved had premonitions. Superstition may be perpetuated by the attention paid ESP (extrasensory perception), spiritualistic seances, flying saucers, astrology, Loch Ness and other nonexistent monsters, haunted houses and on the treatment given Friday the 13th, Ground Hog day and similar occasions. A frequent problem is how to handle the remarks of a public speaker who insists that God is on his side and condemns others as irreligious, sacrilegious or atheistic. So many prominent men of affairs take this line that it is difficult to edit their remarks to delete all such unfounded, unfair and unprovable expressions. In all probability they speak carelessly rather than from belief in predestination, which is contrary to the teachings of most churches.

CHURCH NEWS

Although church pages have disappeared from most large and many small daily newspapers, they still are to be found in small dailies and weeklies. They usually specialize in announcements of Sunday observances to come but also publicize special events and meetings of church organizations.

Handling all of this routine church news is time-consuming and easy to the extent that church authorities cooperate in preparing material adequately and on time. Personal acquaintanceships between reporter and news sources are important so that ill will does not result from mistaken ideas regarding deadlines and space limitations.

Covering all of the sermons delivered any Sunday in any place of any size is impossible. Some papers ignore them all. Others "take turns," reporting a minimum but different sample every week. Still others run "A Reporter Goes to Church" piece written by a staff member who attends a different church every week. Sometimes these pieces are more than accounts of particular services and include historical background regarding the church and possibly an explanation of the major tenets of the denomination. Always, however, great care is taken not to offend, to explain dogma and ritual sympathetically from the standpoint of the believer.

Most people know little about religions other than their own. Helping them understand the faith of others, however, never has been considered to be a function of periodical journalism. About the only occasion on which this rule is broken is on a widely observed religious holiday.

The Fall season symbolizes the dwindling of the old year for most people, but for those of the Jewish faith, October is the beginning of the new year 5737.

The solemn new year rites for Jews are known as the High Holy Days and begin this year the first day of the new year, Oct. 1, ending Oct. 10.

The High Holy Days are especially rich in tradition and symbolism, not only for those who are Jewish, but for all religions. Described as a period of confession by Rabbi Bernard Gold of the Parkway Jewish Center, the High Holy Days are a "time of individual personal stock-taking." They are 10 days of repentance, he said.

The High Holy Days differ from other Jewish holidays because of their personal relevancy. Holidays such as Passover, which marks the exodus of the Jews from Egypt, and the Tabernacles, a special day for the people of Israel, are historical and agricultural. But the High Holy Days may really be observed by all those of all faiths who desire forgiveness from sins against God and man.

"The Jewish religion concentrates on the sins against man," explained Rabbi Gold, "because we feel these are the hardest to forgive and be forgiven."

The High Holy Days begin with the Jewish New Year, Rosh Hashanah. Rosh Hashanah, according to the Bible, is the first day of the seventh month of the year. Because the Jewish calendar is partially lunar and partially solar, it differs from the standard Gregorian calendar. And so the seventh month falls sometime during September or October.

"Tradition," explained Rabbi Gold, "says that the world was created on the first day of the seventh month, which would be Rosh Hashanah."

Beginning with Rosh Hashanah, the Jewish petition to be inscribed in the Book of Life, a legendary book in Jewish religious life. Ten days later, on the Day of Atonement, Yom Kippur, worshippers petition to be sealed in the Book of Life. The Jewish religion has three ways of securing this petition—prayer, repentance, and charity.

Yom Kippur is observed by a complete day of services in the synagogue. When it falls on the Sabbath day it is often called the Sabbath of Sabbaths to signify the importance of the Sabbath.

The service on the eve of Yom Kippur is often called the Kol Nidre service, named after the prayer that begins the service.

A fast is observed beginning at Sundown on the eve of Yom Kippur and continuing until sundown of the next day. The purpose is "to put the mind completely on prayer," explained Rabbi Gold.

Yom Kippur also marks the handing down of the second set of Ten Commandments to the Jews. Moses broke the first set given at Pentecost when he discovered the people worshipping a golden calf at the foot of Mt. Sinai. Moses received the second set at Yom Kippur.

The symbol of the zodiac sign of Libra (Sept.–Oct.) the scales, also plays an important role in the Jewish rites. The scales symbolize justice and mercy, which are the emphasis of the High Holy Days.

"The High Holy Days are universal," says Rabbi Gold, "Because anyone may take this time to evaluate his life, whether Jewish or not."

[Penn Hills (Pa.) *Progress*]

An important consequence of the broadened journalistic interest in this field is consideration of theological issues even when there is no specific news peg. Outstanding recent example was the space given in the feature as well as news sections and on the editorial page to the God Is Dead movement. Similarly, it is no longer uncommon to read pros and cons regarding the virginity of Mary, the divinity of Jesus, the probability of miracles and immortality. Even seminarians today debate the necessity of a belief in God. Such issues are quite different from those that engaged the theologians in the past: the proper form of baptism, the reality of transubstantiation, of angels and the like.

Church news is put to the same test as all other news: the extent of its appeal. Thus, an item of interest to only one congregation seldom is used unless it involves something innovative. Comings and goings of pastors and rabbis are news in the same way that changes in business and industry leadership are news. Churches long have been involved in social and welfare work, operating charities, hospitals and other institutions, which often are newsworthy. Even such news is more valuable if related to outside issues and interests. The leadership provided civil rights, antiwar and other groups by church leaders such as Martin Luther King in Alabama, Father James Groppi in Milwaukee, the Berrigan brothers and others made plenty of front-page news.

REPORTORIAL QUALIFICATIONS

According to the late Richard Cardinal Cushing of Boston, "It is not too much to suppose that the time is coming when we will expect the religious news reporter to have attended, for some time at least, a school of theology or divinity or religion; that he is in simple terms an expert in his own work."

Quite obviously Cardinal Cushing believed that a journalist with training in any religion would be able to report fairly news of other denominations. Editors are coming to be of the same opinion. Edward B. "Ted" Fiske, until recently religion editor of the New York *Times,* was a Presbyterian minister, Roy Larson of the Chicago *Sun-Times* was a Methodist minister, William B. MacKaye of the Washington *Post* had a year at General Theological Seminary and other religion news writers similarly have had specialized training. All leading publications are represented among the 100 plus members of the Religious Newswriters' Association, formed in 1945. The object of its Newsletters is to advance professional standards in the secular press.

The Religious News Service was established in 1933 as an independently managed agency of the National Conference of Christians and Jews. It provides daily news reports and various features and a photo service for an estimated 800 news outlets. Subscribers include the religious press of all denominations, various church agencies and major secular media. It is served by a network of stringer correspondents in the United States and abroad.

There are also the Catholic Press Association, which operates the National Catholic News Service, and the Associated Church Press for Protestants. Since 1953 there has existed the James Supple award given annually by the Religion Newswriters Association for excellence in reporting religious news in the secular press. The award was named in honor of James Supple of the Chicago *Sun,* who was killed in an air crash in 1950 while en route to Korea. Since

1970 there also has been an award memorializing the late Harold Schachern, religion editor of the Detroit *News*. It is given for editing a church page or religion section in the secular press. In 1974 the Louis Cassels award was created in honor of the late UPI religion writer. It is for papers with circulations under 50,000.

George Cornell, religion editor of the Associated Press, believes that modern readers are much better educated and informed so that they recognize words related to science and technology—as radiation, astronaut, genealogy and electrocardiograph—but are stumped when it comes to such elementary religious terms as atonement, apostolic succession, mystical body, presbyter and justification of faith. It is the responsibility of the specialist religion writer to promote public enlightenment.

A *Christianity Today* survey resulted in replies from 180 religion news reporters for the secular media out of 460 who were queried. Of them 146 said they hold church or synagogue membership; 107 said they are active in local congregations and 25 are active in a larger unit of their denomination.

Dr. Don Ranly, associate professor of journalism at the University of Missouri, concluded a report on his analysis of what 57 religion editors declared in a questionnaire as follows:

> The editors perceive their role of reporting religion news as relevant and significant. Their attitudes toward religion news and toward their jobs as religion editor indicate that they can perform their duties fairly and objectively. Because, for the most part, the editors are happy with their jobs and consider them important, they are motivated to do their jobs well.

CORRECT NOMENCLATURE

When he was religious news editor of the Nashville *Tennessean,* the Rev. James W. Carty Jr., professor of journalism at Bethany (W.Va.) College, prepared the following warning:

> Incorrect use of titles in the reporting of church news discourages reader interest, but correct use helps build confidence in the reliability of the news, feature and interpretative articles.
>
> In fact, the wrong designations can draw some hot protests. The appropriate bring grateful letters or phone calls.
>
> A reporter has to be cautious lest he uses the wrong synonym for the sake of variety.
>
> An example concerns the different designations for the spiritual heads of the church. Many terms are available. They include the Reverend, Rabbi, priest, minister, pastor, evangelist clergyman, father, brother. Actually, these concepts have different meanings. Some are interchangeable with different denominations; others are not.
>
> A Catholic priest would be called the Reverend or Father and lives in the rectory. A Monsignor is the Rt. Rev.; a bishop, the Most Reverend; a nun, Sister.

Christian Science has practitioners, lecturers, readers. A title would be Reader John Jones.

The words reverend, pastor, doctor, or clergyman would not be used for the Church of Christ minister or evangelist. Two other correct terms for addressing them are preacher or brother.

An Episcopal clergyman, a deacon or priest, would be called the Reverend, and lives in the rectory. A dean is the Very Reverend. A bishop is the Right Reverend; an archbishop, of which there are none in the United States, would be called the Most Reverend.

A Jewish clergyman would be called Rabbi or Doctor if he holds that degree.

The Lutheran designation would be Pastor John Jones or the Reverend.

A Methodist pastor, minister or preacher also would be called the Reverend. The Episcopal head is Bishop John Jones, never the Right or Most Reverend.

Seventh-day Adventist pastors are addressed as Elder.

Presbyterian ministers also are called the Reverend Mister. Their residence is the manse.

Groups also are concerned about their title. Most resent being called a sect.

America's two largest indigenous groups, the Christian Church (Disciples of Christ) and Church of Christ, do not want to be called denominations. They prefer brotherhood or religious movement.

Other groups are careful about stating the power of conventions. For example, Southern Baptists and Christian churches (Disciples of Christ) are careful to point out that the convention resolutions are not binding on congregations, which are autonomous. Both groups use the title the Reverend for pastors, preachers, ministers.

And editors, remember also not to displease women. Don't call their presbyterial a presbytery.

I have never been able to see why the utterances of an outstanding preacher should be not only reported, but reviewed as carefully and regularly as the concerts of a great musician or the writings of a great author.

—The Reverend John Haynes Holmes

Clergymen are rarely misquoted in the more reputable and careful newspapers. These papers go to great pains and expense to see that preachers are not placed in a false position. There have been instances (I wonder if the clergy would ever be as considerate of the press) of a city editor, reading on Saturday night an advanced copy of a sermon to be delivered the next day and encountering in the manuscript a gross misstatement of fact which might have got the preacher into trouble, telephoning the preacher and giving him opportunity to correct his text before the damage was done.

—Stanley Walker, city editor, New York *Herald Tribune*

22
SCIENCE

A. The Contemporary Challenge
B. Newsgathering Problems
C. The Newspaper's Responsibility
D. Energy and The Environment
E. Definitions
F. Nuclear Age Hazards
G. Space Exploration
H. Reportorial Qualifications

Mankind's progress at any stage throughout history can be calculated by the extent to which scientific discoveries made known what previously was unknown and old, ignorant and superstitious explanations of the origin and nature of life on this planet and in the universe were abandoned.

Long-lived beliefs, myths and legends do not disappear quickly. Many heretics, both before and since Copernicus and Galileo, have been vilified, persecuted, punished and killed by those whose faith they have shaken. Even today, more than 300 years later, there is a Flat Earth Society with a growing membership that believes news accounts and photographs of astronauts on the moon were fabricated. And, despite the victory Clarence Darrow supposedly won over William Jennings Bryan in 1925 at Dayton, Tennessee, there is considerable organized pressure to forbid the teaching of Darwinian evolution in the schools or at least to offset it with the creationist theory in Genesis. In March, 1981 Arkansas became the first state to pass a bill to require public schools to teach two theories of man's beginnings: evolution and creation by a supreme being.

Considering the extent of their knowledge, primitives were rational when they invented a multitude of gods, devils, angels, ghosts, leprechauns, trolls, witches, fairies and other supernatural forces to explain the sun's diurnal movement across the sky, life and death, day and night, the powerful invisible wind, the seasons and other phenomena.

THE CONTEMPORARY CHALLENGE

Contemporary journalists are not so easily excused for their contributions to the perpetuation of ignorance and superstition through daily horoscopes and sympathetic treatment of astrology, clairvoyance, fortune telling, faith healing, extrasensory perception (ESP), witchcraft, spirtualism, haunted houses, miraculous escapes, premonitions, reincarnation, prophecies by professional psychics and soothsayers, UFOs, Loch Ness and other sea monsters, Big Foot, the Abominable Snowman and other animal freaks, good- and bad-luck charms and spells and similar sensational or hysterical news features.

The tangible evidences of applied science, however, are not so easily disregarded as the philosophical and ethical implications of scientific knowledge. Since World War II, no matter what the effect on their preconceptions, few have been able to ignore (1) the threats to the environment from polluted air and water, hazardous waste and depletion of natural resources in an overpopulated world, (2) atomic and nuclear energy problems and (3) space exploration.

Ours is called an Age of Science. In view of the stubborn refusal of many to accept the deeper implications of reality, the present world more properly should be called an Age of Technology. Today the average person tinkers with a television set, automobile and household electrical appliances, takes motion pictures, dreams of owning his or her own airplane and uses scientific or technical language unknown just a few years ago. The Jules Verne science fiction novels of great-grandfather's day and the Tom Swift and Boy Aviators yarns that commanded grandfather's attention are old stuff to modern youth. So, in fact, are the science fiction magazines of one's own boyhood, so rapidly has fact caught up with imaginative fiction.

Actually there is no such thing as Science. Rather, there are sciences, scores of them, man-made categorizations for convenience in studying and utilizing knowledge. A generation ago high schools offered courses in physics, chemistry and biology and that was presumed to about cover the field. Today it takes three solid pages just for the table of contents of *A Guide to Science Reading* (Signet Science Library), compiled and edited by Hilary T. Deason of the American Association for the Advancement of Science. Take one of the shortest main sections, ''Earth Sciences.'' Listed are History of Geology, Geophysics, Oceanography-Physical, Meteorology and Paleontology. So specialized is knowledge becoming that the experts, who know more and more about less and less, find it difficult to converse with each other, even in closely related fields.

NEWSGATHERING PROBLEMS

As the awful power of science to make the planet uninhabitable became apparent, the absolute necessity for everyone's understanding something of the implications of scientific progress (?) became recognized.

Even before the atom bomb and sputniks, newspapers had awakened to their social responsibility as regards science. The remarkable improvement, in completeness of coverage, in accuracy and clarity of writing and, in general, in social purpose, followed years of misunderstanding and consequent inadequate cooperation between scientific writers and scientists. Out of the name-calling came a mutual decision to get together in a common program to protect the public against false science and to assist it in obtaining the maximum benefit from what the experimental laboratories and the scholars' studies are revealing daily, almost hourly.

By assigning to scientific news, reporters with sufficient training to talk the language of those whom they must interview, newspapers have broken down much of the reluctance of inventors, medical personnel and theoretical scientists to give information to the press. Whatever hesitancy to cooperate remains results from several factors: fear of being considered a publicity seeker, fear of revealing the nature of an experiment before absolute proof has been obtained, a feeling that one's fellow scientists deserve to hear of a new scientific fact or theory for the first time at a learned gathering, fear of being misquoted, doubt of the reporter's ability to translate a technical matter into popular terms, fear that improper emphasis will be given to sensational, unimportant aspects of a news item.

On the other hand, partly through the pressure of well-intentioned journalists, many leading scientists have come to realize the value to them of sharing their findings with the public, of their social obligation to do so and of the sincerity of a vast majority of present-day journalists attempting to do a completely honest and creditable job. Scientists and writers cooperate to combat quacks.

Dr. Irvine H. Page described the lingering doubts of many medical men. After expressing shock because of a television offer of $50,000 to a patient for exclusive rights to broadcast his heart transplant operation, Dr. Page wrote,

> There are two aspects of reporting. The one concerns publicity after a discovery is reasonably established and reported in a scientific publication; the other concerns the precipitate announcement to the press of the discovery of a new procedure, especially one of magnitude, before it has been adequately tested. An example of the first was the discovery of insulin and its use in diabetes. The most recent example of the other is the artificial heart.

Only by adherence to the highest ethical principles can editors and reporters retain the confidence of public-spirited scientists in all fields. It is unrealistic to condemn the press for sensationalizing science when so much science news cannot be described by any word other than sensational. To be guarded against is the faker or publicity seeker. A century and a half ago the New York *Sun* could get away with its hoax concerning life on the moon because of public ignorance. Today such a hoax would succeed for exactly the opposite reason: because the "impossible" has happened so many times there is nobody willing to doubt anything. If the astronauts had declared the dark side of the moon, never visible to earthlings, is inhabited, they would have been believed. The same is true of virtually any item of science fiction posing as fact. In some regards science has made people more, not less, gullible and credulous.

On the other hand, there must be caution so as not to uphold orthodox scientists who are as adamant as religious fundamentalists in resisting new ideas destructive of some of their own pet theories and systems of thought. Scientists can be as fanatical and narrow-minded as defenders of the faith, no matter what. A classic example was provided by the threat of several of America's leading astronomers to boycott all Macmillan textbooks unless the company discontinued publication of *Worlds in Collision* by Immanuel Velikovsky. Similar violent opposition also was shown the same author's other books, all published by Doubleday, which has no textbook department. They are *Ages in Chaos, Earth in Upheaval* and *Oedipus and Akhnaton*. More than a decade later many of Velikovsky's theories were validated by Mariner and other space flights.

Journalists also must be mindful of the depth and breadth of the revolt within the organized ranks of scientists by peace-minded and socially conscious, mostly younger, persons who object to the extent to which their older colleagues have cooperated with the military-industrial establishment in promoting the war effort, mainly by the development of weapons inimical to the continuation of life on this planet. Newsgatherers must realize that in great part they are dealing with businessmen, that few pure scientists have kept their purity. Rather, they seek to make discoveries of value to their commercial or military employers. Student recognition of this situation is a strong contributing factor to widespread campus unrest.

In view of the attention now given atomic energy, other energy sources, space exploration, pollution control and other recent scientific topics, it is difficult to recall that newspapers of the past virtually ignored Robert Fulton, Charles Darwin, Samuel F. B. Morse and the Wright brothers.

THE NEWSPAPER'S RESPONSIBILITY

In the stories of sufferers from virulent diseases who have been given pathetic false hope because of premature announcements of new cures, of lives and fortunes that have been lost because of misplaced confidence in inventions, and of persecution and injustice resulting from unscientific superstition is implied the social responsibility of the newspaper as regards scientific news. Likewise, for that matter, is implied the duty that the reputable scientist has not only to maintain proper caution himself but to discipline his fellows as well.

What scientists deplore is reporting that they consider "shallow, inept and totally lacking in scope and understanding," to use the phraseology which Dr. Jonathan Karas of the Lowell Technological Institute applied to the radio and television handling of the first manned Soviet orbital space flight.

Scientists are appalled when some journalist refers indiscriminately to a new scientific announcement as a "major breakthrough" or "major advance" or "a key to life." They deplore journalistic playing up and exaggerating the significance of a medical or scientific contribution.

A point the scientists have conceded, in the face of evidence, is that dramatizing an item of scientific news does not destroy its educational value. Austin H. Clark, eminent biologist, for instance, once confessed that he would not object to a newspaper article beginning

> Those unfeeling mothers who leave their babies on the doorsteps of prosperous people's houses have their counterparts among the birds. . . .

as a popular translation of a scientific paper in which he might declare

> Most cuckoos, the honey-guides of Africa, the weaver finches, some hangnests, our cow birds, the rice-grackle, a south American duck, and, according to recent information, one of the paradise birds, lay their eggs in nests of the other birds which hatch these eggs and raise the young.

Most people, including readers and editors, live in the here-and-now. Much science news, however, is important because of what it portends for the future. Casey Bukro explained the plight of the environment reporter, which is what he is for the Chicago *Tribune:*

> In the old days, stories were more obvious. A murder, a fire, or financial ruin. These obviously are stories. But is the snail darter a story? Especially in Chicago? A radioactive leak at a nuclear power plant? The ozone content of the air on any given day? Polychlorinated biphenyls (PCB) in Lake Michigan?
>
> These are matters of degree and long-range impact. A newspaper editor wants to know what is happening NOW! They don't want to hear about something that MIGHT happen 10 or 20 years from now, which is the incubation period for some cancers. It all sounds pretty iffy, and that turns off an editor.
>
> But one thing both environment and energy have in common is the danger of long-range consequences. Some of the problems are fairly immediate, like gasoline lines or the polluted Cuyahoga river in Cleveland. Those are obvious stories. But a major part of both beats deals with things off in the future. And in both beats, there are no obvious answers. . . .
>
> Journalism has thrived on single-dimension stories, writing about a single event, in a single time, in a single place.
>
> Now we're into multi-dimensional journalism. Our environmental impact statements require alternative choices. What is the best spot for a nuclear power plant? Is there a better spot? Would it be better to build a coal-burning plant? What are the advantages in fuel? The advantages in pollution control? The advantages in waste disposal? Relative costs? Impact on neighboring communities? Public sentiment? Is the utility economically able to support the project? How much power is expected? Do future power demand projections justify building another power plant? What does it mean to electric bills?
>
> And so on. We are getting into a lot of detail in these stories. We once called it in-depth reporting. That's becoming more routine.

The following thoughtful observations on the reportorial hazards in this field were made by Jerry Ackerman, environment/energy editor of the Boston *Globe:*

> As with most everything, the environment is a subject area which is often better developed by feel. Geography, politics, events, economics and personalities pretty well decide what is important for the moment and what is not. Water-diversion in the sense of the perennial war among the Colorado River states is certainly of only peripheral interest in the East. Similarly, offshore oil drilling and the issues that surround it will find little interest, among either lay readers or opinion shapers, until it is a clear and present danger close to home. The Boston Globe wouldn't have agreed to send me to Mexico for the Bay of Campeche blowout in 1979 had it not been a harbinger for future petroleum development being planned on Georges Bank. Timing is a crucial determinant of what should be done, too—except in the Rockies, coverage of the environmental questions surrounding oil-shale would have been premature and probably lost before the nation's energy awareness was heightened in 1973.
>
> On the other hand, there is an array of environmental issues with universal appeal and implications—national parks, national land policies, endangered species, air pollution, the threat of a carbon-dioxide "greenhouse" effect, melting polar ice caps are among the obvious ones. A caveat is in order, though: I am reluctant to write in much depth on any of these without being able to do some first-hand, on-the-spot reporting. While the ivory-tower view is tempting, all too often it is likely to be erroneous, with oversimplification the greatest pitfall. The issues are seldom as clean-cut as they seem from afar. Thus I don't think I could have written well on the snail-darter controversy without having visited the Tellico Dam and talking with the principals—managers at the TVA, environmentalists at the University of Tennessee—in more relaxed circumstances than the best alternative, telephone interviews, would have allowed.
>
> The biggest problem facing a conscientious environmental reporter is the far-flung field that demands coverage. To keep one's sanity, the reporter must pick and choose what he'll be doing, and shove all the rest to the back of the desk. . . .
>
> Yet the environmental reporter must also be in a position to swing into new areas on a moment's notice. The first alert, all too often, is an emergency one. Contamination in the wells. A chemical accident. A harbor suddenly polluted. An oil well run amok. A nuclear power plant shut down for other than obviously routine reasons. In a sense, it was sinful that so few journalists in America were prepared to ask the right questions about nuclear safety when the Three Mile Island balloon went up. . . .
>
> And there's simple observation. Not every new real estate development is going to be worth a full-scale environmental story, of course. But each bulldozer, smokestack or oil tanker you see around you is likely up to little good from an environmental point of view. It's up to you to decide if a little good reporting might not be in the public interest.

Journalism professors Michael Ryan of Temple University and James W. Tankard Jr. of the University of Texas studied "Problem Areas in Science News Reporting, Writing and Editing" and made these recommendations:

1. Science reporters, like reporters in other areas (such as government), should dig for information beyond the publicity handout.

2. Science reporters should use journal articles and published reports to verify and improve the accuracy of their stories. They should not rely solely on interviews with scientists.

3. Science reporters should resist the temptation to exaggerate or oversimplify in a lead sentence for the purpose of attracting reader interest; many scientists report that "catchy" leads distort their findings.

4. Science reporters should pay particular attention to quoting sources accurately and in context. This may be more important in science than in other areas of news because of the care with which scientists use language.

5. Science reporters should be cautious in introducing lay terminology that the scientist himself did not actually use. Scientists often object to such terminology and find it inaccurate.

6. Science reporters should be wary of interpreting a scientist's technical conclusions, as scientists often think such interpretations are misleading.

7. Science reporters should avoid the temptation to sensationalize information about science. As one responding scientist pointed out, progress in science is slow and often does not make "good copy."

8. Science reporters should avoid using the words "cure" and "breakthrough" unless the scientist himself approves the use of the words in describing his work.

9. Science reporters should consider giving information sources an opportunity to review articles or parts of articles for accuracy before publication. Such a review can be done with the reporter still making the final editorial decision, and it might help prevent serious inaccuracies.

10. Headline writers should resist the temptation to put simplistic, cute, or "scare" headlines on science stories.

11. Make-up editors should be aware that the practice of cutting news stories from the bottom to fit available space may not apply very well to science stories, as science articles often need to be reported completely to make sense.

12. Finally, scientists themselves should accept their share of the responsibility for accurate communication of science information to the public. In the words of one of the responding scientists, they should learn to "think about their work [in] a simple and adequate manner that the layman can understand."

Dr. Dael Wolfle, executive officer of the American Association for the Advancement of Science, has lamented: "The chief thing wrong with science news writing is the audience. The average reader does not know enough about science to let the reporter do his best job."

That is the challenge. That is the opportunity.

ENERGY AND THE ENVIRONMENT

For many Americans the first warning of a national energy shortage came Nov. 9, 1965, when the lights flickered out in New York City and 30 million people in eight Northeastern states were plunged into darkness. The next day they heard the term "energy crisis" for the first time.

Many heard about an "environmental crisis" for the first time a few years later, Jan. 28, 1969, when an offshore oil well blew out off the Pacific coast. The million-gallon oil spill that followed fouled the harbor and beaches at Santa Barbara, Calif., killed thousands of shore birds and marine creatures, and alerted the nation to the dangers of a polluted environment.

It was some time after these two headline events—the New York blackout and the California blowout—that the American press began to realize how the energy and environmental crises are interwoven: It is impossible to produce energy without some degradation of the environment—the land, the water, or the air—and so there is a constant conflict between our demand for energy and our desire for a clean environment.

After the landmark National Environmental Policy Act was signed into law by President Nixon on New Year's Day, 1970, and millions of Americans demonstrated against air and water pollution in the first national observance of Earth Day, April 22, 1970, many newspapers established energy/environmental beats and assigned reporters to cover the conflict on a full-time basis.

Reporters on that beat are covering what might be called the Survival Story—man's effort to provide enough energy for the ever-growing human race without degrading the planet to the point where it is uninhabitable. The beat has produced a plethora of big, long-running stories—the passage by Congress of laws setting national clean air and water quality standards, regulating strip-mining and the disposal of toxic wastes, protecting wild and scenic rivers and endangered species of wildlife; the eight-year fight over the Alaska Pipeline, which threatened the delicate ecological balance of the 49th state; the Supreme Court decision halting construction of the Tellico Dam to save the tiny snail darter fish, a decision subsequently overridden by Congress.

It has also produced many local stories that quickly worked their way on to the "A" wires; the discovery in 1978 of birth defects in families living along the infamous Love Canal in upstate New York and the near-disaster at a nuclear power plant on Three Mile Island, near Harrisburg, Pa., in 1979, are examples.

To keep the Survival Story in perspective, the environmental movement did not begin with the publication of Rachel Carson's *Silent Spring* in 1962 or with Earth Day in 1970. Rather, a part of the modern conservation movement began early in this century under such leaders as Theodore Roosevelt and Gifford Pinchot, the first head of the U.S. Forest Service. Most early conservationists were hunters and outdoorsmen who perceived that in nature "everything is connected" and thus became interested in the wise use and management of all natural resources.

Many of the old-line conservation organizations, such as the National Wildlife Federation, the National Audubon Society, and the Izaak Walton League, still have a special interest in wildlife. NWF, the nation's biggest nongovernment, nonprofit conservation group, was founded at a 1936 conference called by Franklin D. Roosevelt "to bring together all interested organizations, agencies and individuals in behalf of restoration of land, water, forests, and wildlife resources." Now it can call upon 4.6 million members and supporters in 50 states to bring pressure to bear on the White House or Congress, not just on wildlife issues, but for a stricter strip-mine law, tougher requirements for nuclear waste disposal, or more solar energy research.

When such groups as the NWF, the Audubons, and the "Ikes" join forces with the Sierra Club, the Wilderness Society, Friends of the Earth, the Natural Resources Defense Council, and other smaller specialized groups in a lawsuit or lobbying effort, they comprise a potent force—though they are not so formidable, financially, as the National Association of Manufacturers, the U.S. Chamber of Commerce, and others who are often aligned against them.

The Conservation Directory, listing more than 11,000 officials of approximately 1,700 conservation groups and government agencies, is an indispensable reference tool. It is published by the National Wildlife Federation, 1412 16th St. NW, Washington, DC 20036. Charles Roberts, who provided most of the foregoing, is its director of information.

A leading figure in the campaign to preserve wildlife and protect endangered species is the writer Cleveland Amory. Among the concerns of his Fund for Animals are the burros in the Grand Canyon, baby seals traditionally slaughtered on the shore and whales that will soon be extinct unless commercial killing of them is halted. There also are Greenpeace, the Whale Protection Fund, the Seal Rescue Fund and the Animal Protection Institute of America. The Cousteau Society fights pollution of the oceans and waterways. Ralph Nader's Public Interest Research Group has ongoing projects in water pollution and nuclear power. It is engaged mostly in litigation, whereas some of the other groups lobby or engage in public educational activities.

DEFINITIONS

Among the important terms with which the energy/environment reporter must become familiar are the following:

Accelerator. A device that increases the speed (and thus the energy) of charged particles such as electrons and protons.

Alpha ray. The nucleus of the helium atom, consisting of two protons and two neutrons. Emitted from certain heavier nuclei as radiation.

Atom. The smallest unit of a chemical element, approximately 1/100,000,000 inch in size, consisting of a nucleus surrounded by electrons.

Background radiation. Radiation from natural sources (cosmic rays, rocks and from minerals inside the body). Normal background radiation for Americans is about 100 to 200 millirems per year, with the higher figure occurring at higher altitudes.

Baryon. A type of strongly interacting particle. The baryon family includes the proton, neutron and those other particles whose eventual decay products include the proton. Baryons are composed of 3-quark combinations.

Base gas. Gas that cannot be extracted from gas storage reservoirs.

Beta ray. An electron or positron emitted when weak interaction causes a nucleus to decay. The neutron, for example, decays into a proton, an electron (beta ray), and an antineutrino.

Boiling water reactor (BWR). A reactor in which water, used as both coolant and moderator, is allowed to boil in the core. The resulting steam is used directly to drive a turbine.

British thermal unit (BTU). The quantity of heat necessary to raise the temperature of one pound of water one degree Fahrenheit.

Bubble chamber. A particle detector in which the paths of charged particles are revealed by a trail of bubbles produced by the particles as they traverse a superheated liquid. Hydrogen, deuterium, helium, neon, propane and freon liquids have been used for this purpose.

Catalyst. A substance that increases the rate of a chemical reaction without being consumed in the process.

Charm. The distinguishing characteristic of the fourth type of quark, also called the *C-quark*. Each *quark* is characterized by a number of properties including familiar ones like mass and electric charge and less familiar ones, which were arbitrarily given names like *charm* and *strangeness*.

Cladding. The outer jacket of nuclear fuel rods. It prevents corrosion of the fuel by the coolant and the release of fission products into the coolant. The most common cladding material is a zirconium alloy.

Condenser. Apparatus in which steam that turns the turbines is cooled and condensed to liquid state for return to steam generator.

Control rod. A rod, plate or tube containing a material such as cadmium, boron etc. used to control the power of a nuclear reactor. By absorbing neutrons, a control rod prevents the neutrons from causing further fission.

Cooling ponds. An artificial lake into which the heated cooling water from a power plant is pumped and from which cooler water is extracted to resupply the cooling loop.

Cooling tower. A tower designed to aid in the cooling of the water used to condense the steam after it leaves the turbine of a power plant.

Core. The central portion of a nuclear reactor containing the fuel elements.

Crude oil. Oil as it is recovered from oil wells.

Cyclotron. In this type of accelerator, magnets cause particles to travel in circular orbits and to pass repeatedly through a constant-frequency alternating electric field, which adds a small amount of energy each time the particles travel through it. In these low-energy machines, the time for a particle to make one orbit is constant.

Deuterium. Heavy hydrogen, the nucleus of which contains one proton and one neutron.

Electromagnetism. A long-range force associated with the electric and magnetic properties of particles. This force appears to be intermediate in strength between the weak and strong force. The carrier of the electromagnetic force is the *photon*.

Electron. An elementary particle with a unit negative electrical charge and a mass 1/1840 that of the proton. Electrons surround an atom's positively charged nucleus and determine the atom's chemical properties. Electrons are members of the *lepton* family.

Electron volt. The amount of energy of motion acquired by an electron accelerated by an electric potential of one volt: MeV = million electron volts; BeV = billion electron volts; TeV = trillion electron volts.

Fast-breeder reactor. A reactor that operates with fast neutrons and produces more fissionable material than it consumes.

Fission. A process in which the nucleus of a heavy atom such as uranium splits into two small nuclei, with the release of energy.

Fuel rods. Long hollow rods, usually of a zirconium alloy, into which are packed thimble-sized pellets of uranium.

Fusion. A process in which two light nuclei are joined or fused together to make a heavier nucleus, with the release of energy.

Gamma rays. Penetrating electromagnetic radiation emitted in radioactive decay, similar to radiation produced by X-rays.

Gravity. The weakest of the four basic forces and the one responsible for the weight of matter and the motion of the stars and planets.

Half-life. Term used to describe the time rate at which radioactive materials decay into stable elements.

Helium. A light colorless nonflammable gaseous element found primarily in natural gases.

Hydrocarbon. An organic compound containing only hydrogen and carbon commonly found in petroleum, natural gas, and coal.

Ion. An atom or molecule that has lost or gained one or more electrons and therefore becomes electrically charged.

Isotope. One of two or more atoms with the same atomic number (the same chemical element) but with different atomic weights because of a difference in the number of neutrons.

J. A particle made of a *c-quark* (see *Charm*) and an *anti-c-quark*. It is also called the *psi particle* and is three times as massive as the proton.

Kilowatt hour (*KWH*). The amount of electrical energy involved with a one-thousand watt demand over a period of one hour. One kilowatt hour is equivalent to 3,412 BTU of heat energy.

Melt-down. The overheating of a reactor core, usually as a result of loss of coolant, to the extent that uranium melts through the metal cladding on the fuel rods. It is believed in extreme cases that heat in the core could become so intense that the core would melt through the reactor vessel and down through the concrete floor of the containment vessel.

Methane. A gaseous compound (CH_4) that is the primary constituent of natural gas.

Millirem. A measure of radiation. A millirem is one-thousandth of a *rem*

(Roentgen), the basic measure of radiation. A chest X-ray exposes a person to between 20 and 30 millirems.

Molecule. A unit of matter made up of two or more atoms.

Nuclear reactor. The device in which a fission chain reaction can be initiated, maintained and controlled. Heat from the fission process is used to turn generators for production of electricity.

Neutron. An uncharged baryon with mass slightly greater than that of the proton. The neutron is a strongly interacting particle and a constituent of all atomic nuclei, except hydrogen. An isolated neutron decays through the weak interaction to a proton, electron and antineutrino with a lifetime of about 1,000 seconds.

Nucleus. The central core of an atom, made up of neutrons and protons held together by the strong force.

Particle. A small piece of matter. An elementary particle is a particle so small that it cannot be further divided—it is a fundamental constituent of matter. *Quarks* and *leptons* now appear to be the only elementary particles, but the term is often used in referring to any of the subnuclear particles.

Particle detector. A device used to detect particles that pass through it.

Photon. A quantum or pulse of electromagnetic energy. A unique massless particle that carries the electromagnetic force.

Positron. The antiparticle of the electron.

Pressurizer. Vessel designed to control pressure level in the reactor vessel and main coolant system.

Pressurized water reactor. The most common type of commercial nuclear reactor in the United States. Coolant in the primary loop is kept under pressure to prevent its boiling. TMI Units 1 and 2 are pressurized water reactors.

Primary loop. The loop through which the reactor coolant circulates. Coolant is heated in the reactor and then pumped under pressure to the steam generator, where it heats water in the secondary loop (see below) into steam that turns the turbines.

Propane. A hydrocarbon that exists under normal pressures and temperatures as a liquid; however, it gasifies easily and for many purposes it is an excellent substitute for natural gas. The main source of propane is from the refining of crude oil.

Proton. A baryon with a single positive unit of electric charge and a mass approximately 1,840 times that of the electron. It is the nucleus of the hydrogen atom and a constituent of all atomic nuclei.

Psi. A particle made of a *c-quark* (see *Charm*) and an *antiquark* and three times as heavy as the proton. It is also called the *J particle*.

Radioactivity. The spontaneous decay or disintegration of an unstable atomic nucleus, usually accompanied by the emission of ionizing radiation.

Reactor vessel. Steel-walled (8–10 inches thick) container housing the nuclear reactor fuel core and control rods.

Refinery. An industrial plant that processes crude oil and manufactures refined petroleum products (i.e., gasoline, wax, fuel oil).

Relief valve. Device designed to reduce excess pressure in the primary loop.

Solar cell. A device, usually made of silicon, that converts sunlight into electrical energy.

Secondary loop. The loop through which water circulates from steam generators to turbines, then through condenser and back through the steam generator.

Solar energy. The energy produced by the fusion reaction occurring on the sun, which reaches the earth as radiant energy.

Thermonuclear reaction. A reaction in which very high temperatures allow the fusion of two light nuclei to form the nucleus of a heavier atom, releasing a large amount of energy.

Thermodynamics. The physics (science) of the relationship between heat and other forms of energy.

Turbine. The device that converts heat energy into electrical.

Upsilon. A particle believed to be made up of a *b-quark* and an *anti-b-quark*. It is approximately ten times as massive as the proton.

Volatile. Vaporizing readily at a very low temperature.

Waste (radioactive). Equipment and materials from nuclear operations that are radioactive and for which there is no further use.

Watt. An electrical unit of power or work equal to one ampere flowing under a pressure of one volt. Approximately 746 watts are equivalent to one horsepower.

X-rays. Photons produced when atoms in states of high energy decay to states of lower energy.

NUCLEAR AGE HAZARDS

William Laurence, New York *Times* science editor, was in the air over Nagasaki when the second atomic bomb was dropped on Japan in August 1945. He had been privy to the secret experimentations at Oak Ridge, Tenn., Los Alamos, N.M., and other places and had the confidence of both the military and scientific authorities. By now it is known to every schoolboy that there is no secret regarding how nuclear energy is released. The atomic armaments race was over the technological details of the destructive weapon, and the speed with which the Soviet Union produced its own bomb proved that the scientists who opposed secrecy were correct.

From the start the tremendous scientific breakthrough, for which basic credit goes to Albert Einstein, has served the purposes of politicians and militarists more than it has private industry or the common man. It was a shocker when the Nobel prize-winning Englishman P. M. R. Blackett published his *Fear, War and the Bomb* in 1948 and revealed that the strategic purpose of bombing Hiroshima was to try to keep the Russians from honoring their Yalta

Conference pledge to enter the war; the bomb's use was unnecessary in order to defeat the Japanese. Since then many others, including former Secretary of State James F. Byrnes, have confirmed the Blackett revelation. A foreign journalist, Robert Jungk, wrote two books to depict the awfulness that the atomic age already had produced. They are *Brighter Than 10,000 Stars* and *The Future Is Already Here*.

During the past quarter century there have been many incidents to worry people not about what an enemy might do but about what we have done to ourselves. Japanese fishermen were contaminated by fallout from American tests of nuclear bombs in the South Pacific. As radioactive materials from American, Russian, British and other atmospheric tests began raining onto farmlands and waterways, President Kennedy negotiated a treaty with the Soviets to restrict further testing to underground. Since the injurious effects of contamination may not show up for generations, widepread frustration has replaced mere alarm. Revelations of improper disposal of waste materials, frequent leakages of poison gases and chemicals in transit by rail, sea, air or road have caused large areas to be cleared of civilians for hours, days or weeks.

The difficulties reporters encountered in covering the Three Mile Island nuclear plant disaster were described in Chapter 9. Similar obstacles are met with when flocks of sheep die mysteriously in Utah near testing grounds. When Lake Erie and other waterways become contaminated by industrial waste, the water is unfit for drinking, bathing or fishing. A widely publicized case that caused Americans to lose further confidence in the federal government was the pollution of the Love Canal at Niagara Falls. The following is part of a story relating an aspect of the situation.

By William Hines

Washington—The possibility that a dangerous poison gas used in World War I may be included in the devil's brew of chemicals dumped into the Love Canal was raised last week in a report made public by the New York Legislature.

The report, which casts doubt on the truth of Army denials of earlier charges of illicit dumping, could seriously weaken the federal government's efforts to stick the Hooker Chemical Co. with financial responsibility for the nation's worst toxic-waste crisis to date.

The poisonous gas is phosgene (also known as carbonyl chloride), which Webster's dictionary defines as "a severe respiratory irritant [whose] deadliness is increased by the fact that serious symptoms appear only after some hours following the exposure."

The report, released Thursday at the New York state capital of Albany, challenged statements made by the Army two years ago when it absolved itself of earlier charges of illegally dumping toxic chemicals in the abandoned canal in Niagara Falls, N.Y.

Faced with the challenge from Albany, the Army late last week said it would analyze the report "for new evidence and then make a decision as to whether to reopen the [1978] investigation."

In 1978, the Army stated that it did not produce phosgene in the Niagara area during or after World War II. The new report says that declassified documents from the War Production Board dated 1943 show "that phosgene was being manufactured under the direction of the Army with a coordinating officer by the name of Maj. Willard."

The Army's 1978 disclaimer may have been a quibble. "Phosgene was being produced at the Niagara Chlorine Plancor in Lockport and Hooker Electrochemical Co.," the report says. "The [Army] Chemical Warfare Service was receiving phosgene from both locations to meet their requirements."

One of these "requirements," the World War II documents indicate, was to supply this chemical to the Soviet government, apparently under the lend-lease arrangements in force at the time.

Phosgene was not used in combat in World War II, but it was stockpiled, and troops undergoing combat training learned about it and other chemical-warfare agents and how to defend against them.

The declassified documents "indicate extremely dangerous chemical substances were being produced in the area of the Love Canal, substances dangerous to personnel," the Albany legislative task force report added.

Also, according to the documents, phosgene was being shipped in unorthodox ways in Army vehicles to get around safety regulations of the Interstate Commerce Commission. . . . [Chicago *Sun-Times*]

The following article from across the continent relates other ways in which shortsighted citizens and governments injure themselves.

By Charles Gay

Salmon spawning grounds are being ruined, creeks are spilling over their banks during heavy rains, and streams are turning into open storm sewers.

The question is, "How can King and Snohomish County governments reverse the trend and how much are people willing to pay to save their creeks?"

The public will get a chance to speak on the subject Thursday night at a hearing of the Snohomish Subregional Council to the Puget Sound Council of Governments.

The subregional council will be considering recommendations on how to solve stormwater problems and manage streams and lakes at the hearing, which begins at 7:30 in the first floor hearings room of the SnoCo Administration Building in Everett.

"We've got a lot of small streams that are dying, and no one seems to care," said Tom Murdoch of the Snohomish County Surface Water Management Program. "People just don't know what's there."

Murdoch is interested in the creeks and streams that flow down from Snohomish County through King County to empty into rivers like the Sammamish and eventually into Lake Washington.

He insists that citizens have to act now to save the creeks and the salmon that live in them.

The planner said development activities in the two neighboring counties are killing the creeks. The more land that is cleared, the more streamside vegetation is stripped. Banks erode, and in the winter, creeks turn into flood channels.

Silt flows into creekbeds where it settles and eventually kills salmon eggs. "There's salmon going to McAleer Creek (in Lake Forest Park), but that's sad, because it's so silted up," Murdoch said. "They'll dig a hole and lay their eggs, but the eggs won't survive."

"And once you rid the streamside of vegetation, you lose the insects that live there, so there's no food when the fish do hatch, anyway." . . .

[Bothell (Wash) *Northshore Citizen*]

In all parts of the country there are newspapers that are expending considerable effort to expose conditions about which citizens should be demanding that public officials act. Among the leaders is the Chicago *Tribune,* whose environment editor, Casey Bukro, wrote the following stories of which only the first few paragraphs can be reproduced here:

A torrent of potentially dangerous wastes pours out of Illinois industries each year—3.8 million metric tons by official estimates—enough to fill a tankcar train 123 miles long.

That puts Illinois in a second-place tie with Ohio among the nation's top hazardous waste producers, at a time when careless toxic waste disposal is considered the country's biggest environmental problem.

To make matters worse, at least a dozen states send more than 500,000 tons of industrial wastes to Illinois each year for disposal. About the same amount is sent by Illinois to other states.

This bewildering pattern of hazardous waste shipments around the country explains, in part, why state and federal officials don't know where those millions of tons of wastes produced by Illinois oil refineries, steel mills, and chemical plants are going.

"We're not really all that sure, to be honest," says Michael Mauzy, chief of the Illinois Environmental Protection Agency, when asked to explain where Illinois hazardous wastes are going for final disposal.

The crisis of chemical waste management has grown so rapidly, Chicago's environment code does not even mention hazardous waste—though city officials are deeply involved in the national drive to stop illegal or indiscriminate dumping.

Uncertainty over where all of that waste ends up raises fears that there could be another Love Canal disaster. . . .

The rolling fields around south suburban Crete seem an unlikely place for an environmental mystery that has Illinois officials searching for answers to:

- What killed 16 horses at Rita Battenhauser's stable?
- What is causing Mike Brown and his wife, Mary, to have blurred vision, headaches, and feelings of disorientation?
- Is any of this related to Crete Metals Co., a scavenger operation that sent billowing clouds of black smoke over the countryside while burning electrical cable and film to recover copper, silver, and other metals? The burning was stopped by a court injunction April 1.

No one knows if there is any connection between Crete Metals and the unexplained sickness and animal deaths that have stricken this area about 35 miles south of downtown Chicago. Crete Metals contends that any problems caused by the plant must have occurred before it took the plant over last fall.

The series of unexplained events started in 1976 at the Springwater Hills School of Horse Management, operated by Rita Battenhauser.

There were 60 horses in her stable that she owned or boarded. Then the legs of some horses swelled. Some seemed to be suffering from sunburn. Then they began to die.

"Their skin broke open and peeled off like sunburn, in big sheets," she said. "It was not anything we've ever seen. I've lived around horses all my life." Eleven horses died.

The crisis seemed to pass until the following spring, when some more horses began losing their hair.

Then, one by one, some were paralyzed in the rear end," she said. "That was the end of them within a couple of hours." Five more horses died. All the stricken horses had been in a pasture together . . .

SPACE EXPLORATION

The debate over how much and what next in the space exploration program also has been more political and financial than scientific, much to the disgust of many journalists as well as scientists. Too often it has seemed that the launchings at Cape Canaveral were conducted in a circus atmosphere. Hundreds of journalists seated in bleachers had less opportunity to observe details than television watchers. The reporter has had to be alert to distinguish between a publicity or political propaganda stunt and a genuinely important event; and the science writer's task has been made difficult by extravagant announcements of innovations in several governmental programs, space and missiles prominently. The idea altogether too often has been to beat the Russians regardless of need or value of the venture. Government-imposed secrecy has, of course, been the biggest handicap of all to adequate coverage.

No further proof of the extent to which journalistic science writing has developed exists than the book *We Are Not Alone* (McGraw-Hill, 1964) by Walter Sullivan, science editor of the New York *Times*. It is a masterful job of collating the evidence for conscious life somewhere else in outer space. It made predictions that Mariner flights verified. No amateur scientist Sullivan, and he is not alone. Another masterly job by Sullivan is *Continents in Motion, the New Earth Debate* (McGraw-Hill, 1974).

News of early space explorations caused considerable excitement. Consternation is a better word to describe the reaction of hawkish Americans when the Russians launched the first sputnik well ahead of our first rocket. Since the moon flights, the reception has been calmer as many nations are responsible for millions of tons of hardware circling the earth or flying on to explore Mars and other planets. The use of satellites in space has greatly increased the speed of transmission of news reports and pictures of events occurring anywhere on earth. The following is a typical subdued account of a partial failure.

By Stuart Ozer

Sometime between July 10 and 14, the 76-ton Skylab space station will skid along the upper layers of the earth's atmosphere.

Within minutes, the craft will disintegrate from intense heat and about 500 pieces will fall to the earth at speeds up to 260 miles-per-hour. At least 10 pieces will weigh over 1,000 pounds, and two large chunks will be capable of digging craters 100 feet deep if they hit land.

Although a great deal of anxiety has been generated worldwide by the imminent fall of Skylab, at least one government agency has not been caught by surprise.

When Skylab was launched in May 1973, NASA had already decided to let it fall to earth. Even though the odds of debris hitting a city of 100,000 or more people are one in seven, a plan to add steering rockets to the craft was rejected because it would have delayed the launch and would have been "too expensive." Actually the precaution would have added only 1% to the $2.6 billion Skylab budget, according to NASA figures, while eliminating any risk of debris striking populated areas.

PINNACLE OF TECHNOLOGY?

Skylab, the first habitable space station, was originally lauded as a pinnacle of technological achievement. Nevertheless, the project has been plagued by miscalculations and disregard of safety measures.

At first, NASA expected the craft to stay in orbit until 1983, despite calculations by the National Oceanographic and Atmospheric Administration and by Soviet scientists that Skylab would come down sooner. When officials finally realized they had three fewer years than originally planned to solve the problem, they designed a last-ditch rescue mission. An astronaut was to be sent up in a space-shuttle carrying booster rockets which could be attached to Skylab.

But Skylab continued to drop faster than expected and the space shuttle program slipped behind schedule. In January, the plans to avoid an uncontrollable crash were scrapped and the spacecraft was rotated into a position designed to quicken the fall.

Skylab's debris is expected to land within a 20-minute period. Remnants will be scattered over an area 100 miles wide and 4000 miles long. . . . [*Guardian*]

The United States Atomic Energy Commission has an 80-page book. *Nuclear Terms, a Brief Glossary,* whose original compiler was James D. Lyman of the AEC Division of Public Information.

The basic authority for writers in the space exploration field is the *Dictionary of Technical Terms for Aerospace Use,* National Aeronautics and Space Administration SP-7, 1965. What follows is a condensed version of the glossary attached to the press kit for Apollo X.

Ablating materials. Special heat-dissipating materials on the surface of a spacecraft that vaporize during reentry.

Accelerometer. An instrument to sense accelerative forces and convert them into corresponding electrical quantities usually for controlling, measuring, indicating or recording purposes.

Adapter skirt. A flange or extension of a stage or section that provides a ready means of fitting another stage or section to it.

Antipode. Point on surface of planet exactly 180 degrees opposite from reciprocal point on a line projected through center of body. In Apollo usage, antipode refers to a line from the center of the Moon through the center of the Earth and projected to the Earth surface on the opposite side. The antipode crosses the mid-Pacific recovery line along the 165th meridian of longitude once every 24 hours.

Apocynthion. Point at which object in lunar orbit is farthest from the lunar surface—object having been launched from body other than Moon. (*Cynthia,* Roman goddess of Moon.)

Apogee. The point at which a moon or artificial satellite in its orbit is farthest from Earth.

Apolune. Point at which object launched from the Moon into lunar orbit is farthest from lunar surface, e.g.: ascent stage of lunar module after staging into lunar orbit following lunar landing.

Attitude. The position of an aerospace vehicle as determined by the inclination of its axes to some frame of reference; for Apollo, an inertial, space-fixed reference is used.

Burnout. The point when combustion ceases in a rocket engine.

Canard. A short, stubby winglike element affixed to the launch escape tower to provide CM blunt end forward aerodynamic capture during an abort.

Celestial guidance. The guidance of a vehicle by reference to celestial bodies.

Cislunar. Adjective referring to space between Earth and the Moon, or between Earth and Moon's orbit.

Closed loop. Automatic control units linked together with a process to form an endless chain.

Deboost. A retrograde maneuver which lowers either perigree or apogee of an orbiting spacecraft. Not to be confused with deorbit.

Declination. Angular measurement of a body above or below celestial equator, measured north or south along the body's hour circle. Corresponds to Earth surface latitude.

Delta V. Velocity change.

Down-link. The part of a communication system that receives, processes and displays data from a spacecraft.

Entry corridor. The final flight path of the spacecraft before and during Earth reentry.

Ephemeris. Orbital measurements (apogee, perigee, inclination, period, etc.) of one celestial body in relation to another at given times. In spaceflight, the orbital measurements of a spacecraft relative to the celestial body about which it orbited.

Escape velocity. The speed a body must attain to overcome a gravitational field, such as that of Earth; the velocity of escape at the Earth's surface is 36,700 feet-per-second.

Fairing. A piece, part of structure having a smooth, streamlined outline, used to cover a nonstreamlined object or to smooth a junction.

Fuel cell. An electrochemical generator in which the chemical energy from the reaction of oxygen and a fuel is converted directly into electricity.

g or *g force*. Force exerted upon an object by gravity or by reaction to acceleration or deceleration, as in a change of direction: one g is the measure of force required to accelerate a body at the rate of 32.16 feet-per-second.

Inertial guidance. Guidance by means of the measurement and integration of acceleration from on board the spacecraft. A sophisticated automatic navigation system using gyroscopic devices, accelerometers, etc., for high-speed vehicles. It absorbs and interprets such data as speed, position, etc., and automatically adjusts the vehicle to a predetermined flight path. Essentially, it knows where it's going and where it is by knowing where it came from and how it got there. It does not give out any radio frequency signal so it cannot be detected by radar or jammed.

Injection. The process of boosting a spacecraft into a calculated trajectory.

Insertion. The process of boosting a spacecraft into an orbit around the Earth or other celestial body.

Multiplexing. The simultaneous transmission of two or more signals within a single channel. The three basic methods of multiplexing involve the separation of signals by time division, frequency division and phase division.

Optical navigation. Navigation by sight, as opposed to inertial methods, using stars or other visible objects as reference.

Oxidizer. In a rocket propellant, a substance such as liquid oxygen or nitrogen tetroxide which supports combustion of the fuel.

Penumbra. Semi-dark portion of a shadow in which light is partly cut off, e.g.: surface of Moon or Earth away from Sun where the disc of the Sun is only partly obscured.

Pericynthion. Point nearest Moon of object in lunar orbit—object having been launched from body other than Moon.

Perigee. Point at which a Moon or an artificial satellite in its orbit is closest to the Earth.

Perilune. The point at which a satellite (e.g.: a spacecraft) in its orbit is closest to the Moon. Differs from pericynthion in that the orbit is Moon-originated.

Reentry. The return of a spacecraft that reenters the atmosphere after flight above it.

Retrorocket. A rocket that gives thrust in a direction opposite to the direction of the object's motion.

S-band. A radiofrequency band of 1,550 to 5,200 megahertz.

Selenographic. Adjective relating to physical geography of Moon. Specifically, positions on lunar surface as measured in latitude from lunar equator and in longitude from a reference lunar meridian.

Sidereal. Adjective relating to measurement of time, position or angle in relation to the celestial sphere and the vernal equinox.

State vector. Ground-generated spacecraft position, velocity and timing information uplinked to the spacecraft computer for crew use as a navigational reference.

Terminator. Separation line between lighted and dark portions of celestial body which is not self luminous.

Umbra. Darkest part of a shadow in which light is completely absent, e.g.: surface of Moon or Earth away from Sun where the disc of the Sun is completely obscured.

Up-link data. Information fed by radio signal from the ground to a spacecraft.

Yaw. Angular displacement of a space vehicle about its vertical (Z) axis.

REPORTORIAL QUALIFICATIONS

It would be utterly impossible for anyone, including both journalists and scientists themselves, to be expert in more than one or a few of the multitudinous branches into which scientific knowledge is separated. What scientists of all kinds have in common is a belief in the importance of science and the scientific spirit of open-minded inquiry, which survives despite any prostitution to business or military interests by many scientists.

The science reporter must know enough about the fundamental sciences, physical and organic, to be able to converse with professional scientists. If s/he is well grounded in any scientific field, s/he will find it easier to grasp meanings in other fields. S/he must win the respect and confidence of the scholars s/he interviews by his/her knowledge and attitude. S/he must overcome the risk of acting as apologist for scientists.

The public interest is the prime consideration of the science reporter as it should be of any responsible journalist. This means critical analysis of scientific proposals and it may mean warning and shocking readers.

In 1934 the National Association of Science Writers was founded under the leadership of David Dietz, who in 1921 was employed by Scripps-Howard to become the nation's first science writer. At present the association, with a membership of about 950, publishes a bimonthly *Newsletter,* which provides a forum for the discussion of problems of scientific newsgathering. There also exists the Council for the Advancement of Science Writing in Journalism Schools. Leading journalism educator to promote the training of science writers is Emeritus Prof. Hillier Kreighbaum of New York University.

Already there is accelerating realization of the high moral sense that both scientists and science writers must develop. Today it is not what next but to what end shall we use what we already know or are on the verge of finding out. In *Harper's* for March 1975 Horace Freeland Judson, writing mostly on molecular biology, asks, "What are we afraid of?" The opportunity and/or obligation of the science writer is made clear as Judson becomes specific:

> We are now into the third or fourth cycle of alarms about all this; the subject is intrinsically sensational, as can be seen from the examples that recur. What do you think, then, of choosing the sex of your children-to-be? Of growing human embryos outside the body and experimenting with them? Of genetic screening, to

skim the trash out of the gene pool by determining who shall be permitted to breed? Of cloning, or the multiplication of large numbers of genetically identical individuals—what one entirely serious writer has described as the "asexual reproduction of 10,000 Mao Tse-tungs?" Of genetic engineering, or the creation of posthuman creatures with new or magnified bodily or mental strengths—what another serious writer has called "parahumans, or 'modified men' . . . chimeras (part animal) or cyborg-androids (part prosthetes)"?

The late Arthur Snider, science editor of the Chicago *Sun-Times,* noted that "the content of newspaper science writing has shifted to ethical and social science stories. Questions such as these arise: When is a patient dead? Shall genetics be used to make a super race? Shall a substitute mother carry the fertilized egg of another woman to term? Who shall get the kidney?"

The following are extracts from a statement directed to potential science writers by Casey Bukro, environment editor of the Chicago *Tribune:*

Look at what they did to Lake Erie.

Look at what they did to the air in Los Angeles.

Look at what they did to the American bison.

If you're not moved by these classic examples of America's indifference to the destruction of the earth and life upon it, then you're not cut out to be an environmental writer. . . .

Resist. Ask why these things happen. Don't settle for fuzzy answers. Don't shrug and say you can't fight city hall. Don't let them snow you. There are answers somewhere. Find them.

The cornerstone of the environmental beat is questioning and testing so-called conventional wisdom: That growth is good, that more is better, that biggest is best, for example.

The environmental beat had a part in exploring national policies that put economic values above human values. The need for this kind of exploration will go on. But you've got to be ready for it. . . .

Environmental reporting needs a modern generation of Renaissance men and women without tunnel vision who can understand complexities, who can see how many subtle forces move gargantuan issues like strings on a puppet. . . .

Accuracy is not served by publishing raw lists of facts and figures and two opposing viewpoints. Environmental reporters will be asked to explain "what it means." In doing this, environmental reporters—whatever their label—have a chance to forge a link between our ancient natural world and our modern technological society.

Some experts believe we'll avoid environmental blunders in the future by getting doctors, lawyers, sociologists, engineers, city planners, and others to rule on the consequences and benefits of urban development projects.

Prepare for that day so you'll know what they're all talking about and pull it all together.

And Bukro, the veteran expert, has this advice for the beginner who wants to follow in his footsteps.

As for how to prepare. I'd still be a journalism student. You still have to be able to report and write. I'd take some courses in natural resources, urban affairs, economic reporting. I'd spend some time at a wire service to pick up some practice in writing fast and clearly.

I'd get some basic reporting skills, like police reporting. Then move on to specialize. I can't help but feel that extra attention must be given these days to writing skills. Technical writing is almost self-defeating if it is not conveyed in an understandable way. The more complex the issues, the more readable the writing must be. People have to be drawn in by stories that catch their eye and hold their attention. It has to be interesting. You can't expect the reader to stay with it if the reading is painfully dull.

Now, when do I get to be the expert? I'm an expert first and foremost when I know the right questions to ask, and when I know where to go to ask them. When I come to the interview with sufficient knowledge and training to be able to pass all the elementary stuff, and get on with an interview that will keep the interviewee as interested as the reader. You get the best out of a source when he's interested, not just plodding through some basics. If I were to interview Einstein today, I'd know a heck of a lot about his theories even before going into the interview.

This is where journalists earn the contempt of scientists. They know when we have not done our homework. Conversely, they know when we have done our homework and are not trying to write another trite piece.

Being an expert does not mean I get a chance to shoot my mouth off everytime I write a piece. The old rules of objective writing still apply when doing a piece for the news section.

One of my old editors at City News Bureau would say: "Don't tell me what you think; tell me what you know." A reporter or a specialist still must report facts for the news section.

My status as an expert becomes more obvious when I write a series, or when I do an op-ed piece allowing me to give some opinion, or when doing a signed column. In those, I can comment on issues reported in the news, or even give some behind-the-scenes insight. But the news itself still must come unadulterated with opinion, and reflect all sides of the issue.

I must explain patiently that the news stories do not reflect my own views, but that signed columns are a bit different. Even so, I am mainly a reporter of events. I am not a columnist. I am not an editorial writer. Being a specialist does not mean I am free to write my opinions. It places a very special obligation on me to somehow bridge a gap between the old-time reporter, who only gave facts, to a new kind of reporter that gives the facts and tries to explain what they mean. But explaining what they mean often means another round of reporting or two, talking to experts, who in turn explain what they mean. I have to put that all together by way of detecting significant developments, asking the right questions, and writing it clearly.

To which should be added the comments of Jerry Ackerman, who became environment/energy editor (technically ecology specialist) of the Boston *Globe* in 1975 after ten years as a general reporter and small town editor.

It took me two years just to get a feel for what the principal issue is. Not surprisingly it's money.

But wrapped into this is all sorts of consciousness-raising trickery and chicanery not only on the side of developers (nuclear, oilfield, housing, highway, whatever) but those who grind axes against them (environmentalists of all colorations). More than anything, a writer on these subjects has to understand the sciences and economics behind things which have impact on the environment.

This doesn't mean the writer must also be a working chemist, physicist, economist or financier. But a firm grasp of the principles is essential as a guide to asking the right questions.

Politics naturally follows but the arguments therein are all built on the various ways available to massage hard data to suit one's own purposes. A good reporter in this field, as any other, needs to stoke up with a wealth of information whose principal purpose is only to sort out the crap as the stories come along. It often is necessary to report the discrepancies on one's own authority—something that can be done only if the writer is confident he understands the issue to at least the same depth as the bullshit artists who deal out the position papers.

An illustration of what such understanding can tell me:

Texaco currently advertises (in *Newsweek, Time,* and elsewhere) that it's one company that is Doing Something about developing oil shale, and we all should be patriotically proud.

Bullshit.

Texaco has purchased rights to use a microwave oil-extraction process developed by Raytheon which has yet to be tested outside a laboratory. It worked there, but that doesn't mean it will function efficiently in a large-scale deployment.

What's more, it hasn't yet locked up the leases on land that it proposes to mine out in northeastern Utah. There is absolutely nothing going on there, according to my Western sources.

Beyond this Texaco isn't going to do too much until it can be sure it pays. Texaco folks will be right in the pack when and if Washington makes tax credits available for oil-shale development. And they'll also be at the door with the others when and if the Energy Mobilization Board gets around to choosing "priority" projects to avoid sapping national capital resources. In that contest Texaco will be competing with about eight other big oil operators—each with its own pet technology and self-styled claim to fame.

Needless to say, it helps to be a curmudgeon in looking at all these shenanigans.

We see in the public interest in science a most interesting change. . . . Heretofore the public interest in science has been very largely centered on those forms that promised a more or less immediate return in dollars or in materialistic comforts. But the purely materialistic view of science is now giving way to a wholly different view. We are now beginning to assume the philosophical attitude toward science.

—DR. AUSTIN H. CLARK, Smithsonian Institution

23
WEATHER

With maps, charts, illustrations and other devices, serious and "happy talk" television announcers often calling themselves expert meteorologists have made the weather into a major journalistic interest. Newspapers continue soberly to correct the record but all journalistic soothsayers get their information from the same source, the National Weather Service of the National Oceanic and Atmosphere Administration, a part of the Department of Commerce. That agency was long known simply as the Weather Bureau. If, as is often the case in small places, there is no local representative of the Service to provide official information, the newspaper obtains the most reliable data available from other sources. Possibly a college or high school can provide it; if compelled to rely upon its own resources, the newspaper at least can make certain that its thermometer is properly set up. As any conversationalist knows, the weather is interesting even when there are no hurricanes, floods or droughts. Since people lived in caves their life has been dependent to a large extent upon the behavior of the elements: the machine or power age has not reduced their dependency in this respect. In fact, in many aspects of life, it has increased the dependency, as delicate machines may require certain atmospheric conditions for proper operation.

ELEMENTS OF INTEREST

It is not necessary to read a newspaper to know that it is abnormally hot or cold or that there has been a thunderstorm, but the reader does expect a newspaper to supply authentic statistics about the weather, the widespread consequences of any unusual climatic condition and predictions as to a change in the situation.

To meet this reader demand, newspapers print weather reports and forecasts daily. The maximum and minimum temperatures for the preceding twenty-four hours and the next day's forecast frequently are printed on the first page with detailed hourly readings, reports from other cities, wind velocity, rainfall and other details on an inside page. If the weather becomes unusual in any way, a full-length news story is written.

When the weather becomes extreme, the reporter should seek information including the following:

1. Statistics and explanation.
   a. Maximum and minimum for day.
   b. Hourly readings.
   c. Comparison with other days during the season.
   d. Comparison with all-time records for the same date, month and season.
   e. Comparison with situations in other localities.
   f. Humidity, wind velocity, etc.
   g. Predictions: when relief expected.
   h. Official description of nature of phenomenon.
2. Casualties.
   a. Illness and death directly caused by the weather.
      (1) Heat prostrations.
      (2) Freezing.
      (3) Lightning.
      (4) Tornadoes, cyclones and hurricanes.
      (5) Floods.
      (6) Sleet and hail.
   b. Injuries and deaths of which the weather was a contributing cause.
      (1) Drownings.
      (2) Spoiled food.
      (3) Accidents from slippery pavements, snow, wind etc.
      (4) Fires.
      (5) Heart disease from heat exhaustion or exertion.
3. Property damage.
   a. Telephone and telegraph wires.
   b. Water craft sunk.
   c. Bridges and highways, pavements buckling.
   d. Farm buildings and animals.
   e. Automobiles, buses and other public conveyances.
4. Interference with ordinary life.
   a. Transportation.
      (1) Railroads.
      (2) Buslines and streetcars.
      (3) Airlines.

(4) Highways and bridges.
(5) Private automobiles.

b. Communication.
(1) Mail service.
(2) Telephone.
(3) Telegraph.
(4) Cable.
(5) Radio.
(6) Stoppage of food and other supplies.

c. Public utilities.
(1) Electric lights.
(2) Gas pressure.
(3) Water supply.
(4) Fuel shortage.

5. Methods of seeking relief.
   a. Increased demands on water supply.
   b. Bathing beaches and parks.
   c. Trips.
   d. Sale of fans.
   e. Children cooled by hydrants, hoses etc.
6. Methods of handling situation.
   a. Police activity.
   b. Volunteer groups: Boy Scouts, Legionnaires etc.
   c. Red Cross, Civil Defense and other relief agencies.
   d. Use of ashes and other materials.
   e. Public warnings on driving, diet, etc.
7. Freaks.
   a. Narrow escapes.
   b. Undamaged property surrounded by desolation.
   c. Unusual accidents.

THE LOCAL SUMMARY

Because the weather affects every reader, no matter what unusual features are included or how the story is written, the reporter must include as many of the preceding elements as are pertinent. Emphasis should be on the effects of an unusual weather condition—casualties, damage, disrupted service—and on the basic statistics such as temperature, inches of rain or snowfall and wind velocity.

By Ancella Bickley Jr. and Steve Mullins

The earliest snowfall in 18 years hit the Mountain State today, downing power lines, destroying timber, and closing schools and airports.

Hardest hit by the snow were Braxton, Nicholas, Greenbrier, Webster, Randolph and Tucker counties where snow in some of the mountainous regions reached depths of 12 inches.

The heavy wet snow, falling on trees still burdened with foliage, caused limbs to fall, many onto power lines, and causing sporadic outages throughout the night.

Monongahela Power Co. reported that between 10,000 and 20,000 of its customers were without power. Appalachian Power Co. reported that about 20,000 customers in the Beckley area were without power.

Both the Beckley and Elkins airports had to shut down because of the power outages. The National Weather Service said heavy snow fell in the higher elevations from Beckley to the Pennsylvania border.

The weather service reported at mid-morning that 12 inches of snow fell in Canaan Valley in Tucker County. Eight inches was reported in Pickens in Randolph County, six inches at Summersville in Nicholas County and four inches at Green Bank in Pocahontas County.

Three inches was reported in Elkins, and one inch was reported in White Sulphur Springs, Greenbrier County, and Oak Hill, Fayette County.

Phil Zinn, with the National Weather Service in Charleston, said the last comparable snowfall was in October 1961.

"Limbs are out in the road and power lines seem to be snapping just as fast as they can," said Jim Beaver, a dispatcher at the Nicholas County Sheriff's department. "Every once in a while the sky lights up blue and we know that's another power line that just went. Whenever we see one we chase it down, but they're all over the place. There's no school in Nicholas County. The roads are slick and all of Summersville, Richwood and Craigsville are without power."

School in Randolph, Webster, Greenbrier, Tucker and Barbour counties also was canceled because of the weather and power situation.

Trooper B. A. Vaughan said the roads in Raleigh County were bad. "It's freezing up here. There's about an inch of snow. The roads are all slick and we have a lot of power out. Power poles have been falling all over and some have been on fire."

A spokesman for the Greenbrier Sheriff's department said power was out throughout the county. He also said that the snow is about four inches deep in Rainelle and six inches deep on Sewell Mountain.

Deputy E. E. Skidmore of the Webster County Sheriff's Department said as much as seven inches of snow may have fallen on Point Mountain between Webster Springs and Elkins.

Sen. Richard Benson, D-Randolph, said power was down, highways were impassable and timber was badly broken in his area. "I don't think I have a shade tree left on my lawn."

Minor flooding was reported on the Tygart Valley River between Daley in Randolph County and Philippi in Barbour County. Minor flooding also was expected along the Cheat, West Fork, Little Kanawha and Elk rivers.

The speed limit on the West Virginia Turnpike was reduced to 45 mph and snow was reported on the road in the Beckley and Princeton areas.

In the Charleston area snow is not expected but the National Weather Service said the cold weather will remain for the next few days.

The weather service predicted rain to end this morning with skies becoming partly cloudy late this afternoon. The temperature will reach a cool high in the low 50s. It will remain partly cloudly tonight and tomorrow with chance of showers tomorrow. It will be cold tonight with lows mid to upper 30s. Highs tomorrow mid to upper 50s.

The chances of rain is 20 percent tonight. [Charleston (W. Va.) *Daily Mail*]

A brighter and/or informal style often is appropriate in weather stories.

It was inevitable that the thermometer should dip below zero sometimes this month. Those cold temperatures just took longer than usual to arrive on the Green Bay scene.

This morning's 7-below marked the first time this season the mercury dropped under the zero mark. Usually that happens sometime around the first week in December. Occasionally, it takes place in November, according to the National Weather Service.

But even though it was frigid this morning, the subzero conditions aren't here to stay. The area is expected to benefit from southerly air tonight. The overnight low should be between 5 and 10 degrees above zero, the Weather Service predicts.

Temperatures are expected to continue rising. By Thursday, a high around 40 degrees is expected. Therefore, chances for a white Christmas probably rely on getting another snowstorm because what's on the ground now is likely to melt.

This winter's relatively mild conditions are a welcome break from the last three years, when the cold and snow came early and stayed. This year, the jet stream is unusually far north, keeping the cold air away from the Great Lakes region, according to the weatherman. [Green Bay (Wis.) *Press-Gazette*]

By Lisa Stein

For children, it is the beginning of a journey through the Looking Glass, a wonderland of snow queens and ice maidens—a time when all imagination comes to life.

For their parents, it is the beginning of headaches and worries about heating bills and treacherous driving.

It is today, the first day of what Noah Webster describes as "the colder half of the year, the season between Autumn and Summer."

At 6:10 Saturday morning, the wild west winds of autumn officially became the quiet north winds of winter.

And quiet is what the National Weather Service is forecasting for this winter, at least in this part of the country.

According to meteorologist Dan Hurley of the service's Harrisburg Bureau, this winter is expected to have normal or above normal temperatures. The forecast means that all those dreaming of a white Christmas may be in for a disappointment.

Hurley predicts there will bc cloudy skies and possibly rain, rather than snow, this Christmas day, with temperatures expected to reach the 50s.

Perhaps those in for the greatest disappointment this winter are the children, for whom winter and snow seem to be one and the same.

"I love the winter," said 8-year-old Raquel Beverly, of 1440 South 13th St., "because winter means snow, and when there's snow you can make snowballs and snowmen and chairs out of it."

Nicole Eubanks, also 8, concurred with her friend.

"I like the winter, because we can do lots of things with the snow. I wish we'd have five feet of snow."

To the children, winter is a sort of fairy tale, a time when they can ice skate through the fantasies of Hans Christian Andersen and the Brothers Grimm.

"I like to sleigh ride, and then lie down in the snow and spread my arms and make believe I'm an angel. And I lie in the snow, and look up at the snow falling and at all the icicles hanging from the houses,'' said 9-year-old Melissa Santos.

The children from the city stop for a fleeting moment in the county with Robert Frost to ''watch his woods fill up with snow,'' openly defying Ralph Waldo Emerson's command ''not to be overbold when you deal with arctic cold.''

For the children, snow is no deterrent; rather, it makes them even more bold. It gives them the courage to travel into the world of make-believe to see what new creations they can form from the white delight.

However, even the children realize nothing, including snow, is perfect.

''I'm worried about my mother driving in the snow, it is slippery and she does not have snow tires on her car,'' said a concerned Raquel.

Poet Percy Bysshe Shelley comforts the child.

''The trumpet of a prophecy! O, Wind,
If Winter comes, can Spring be far behind?'' [Harrisburg (Pa.) *Patriot*]

INTERPRETATIONS

Public curiosity concerning unusual weather conditions is a form of scientific interest. To satisfy it, the communication media cannot be expected to define every meteorological term as it appears in a news account, as many of the most common must be used almost daily. When occasion seems to demand, however, parenthetical inserts, sidebars and longer feature articles can be used, mostly for the benefit of middle-aged readers who went to junior high school before its curriculum was enriched by elementary instruction in this field.

After many decades of stubborn refusal to popularize its vocabulary, the National Weather Service has relented in recent years. It takes cognizance of popular usage now by permitting such phrases as ''unusually fine weather'' and ''clear and bright'' in its forecasts.

Explanations of natural phenomena can be given in scientifically accurate but easily understood language.

By Cathie Huddle

It sounds like the roar of a freight train and the sky turns green.

That's a fair description of a tornado striking, according to Orval Jurgena of the National Weather Service office in Lincoln.

Each year tornadoes add an ugly twist to spring in Nebraska and it's that time of year again. Time to get ready, time for some facts.

The sky turns green as sunlight reflects from the hail that often falls to the Northeast of a tornado, Jurgena said.

He dispelled a myth—that there is always a deathlike silence before the twister hits. That isn't always the case, he said. When a cold front passes through, the strong south winds drop before the north winds set in, sometimes causing the ''quiet before the storm.''

One dictionary's ''tornado'' definition is ''a violently whirling column of air extending downward from a cumulonimbus cloud . . . almost always seen as a rapidly rotating, slender, funnel-shaped cloud that usually destroys everything along its narrow path.''

Between 1974 and 1978, 246 tornadoes touched down in Nebraska, killing four persons and injuring 195, according to a recent report.

Nebraska had more tornadoes than any of the other eight states in the central southwestern region during that time, according to a report from the U.S. Commerce Department's National Oceanic and Atmospheric Administration.

Tornadoes form where air masses of contrasting temperature and moisture clash, often creating severe thunderstorms that produce high winds, hail and torrential rainfall. About 5 percent of all thunderstorms produce tornadoes and scientists are not sure what triggers them, according to NOAA.

Tornadoes are usually easy to identify by the familiar funnel, which drops from its apparent cloud overhead like a dark rope or elephant trunk. Larger storms, however, may appear as a general black mass from the sky to the ground.

There is almost complete devastation wherever a tornado touches ground. The winds, which can exceed 200 mph, can roll cars end over end, flatten mobile homes and lift the roof from a house before smashing its walls to splinters. They also bring a lethal barrage of flying mud, sticks, rocks and other debris, including glass from shattered windows. . . . [Lincoln (Neb.) *Sunday Journal and Star*]

FORECASTS

Important decisions such as whether to take an umbrella to work, postpone a trip, or cancel an outdoor picnic depend on weather conditions and make expert forecasting important. Not even the best forecasters, however, can guarantee the accuracy of any prediction, which makes life more uncertain but perhaps more interesting.

The cold, snowy weather that has plagued northern Wisconsin this week has made its move into the Madison area. And only more of the same frigid temperatures have been forecast for the weekend.

According to the National Weather Service, a low pressure system moving east over Lake Superior is causing most of the mischief. That weather system, followed by a cold front bringing extreme Arctic-like temperatures and gusty winds from Canada, will keep weekend temperatures from going much above the low 20s.

Rush-hour motorists got their first taste of what was to come when the temperature dropped 15 degrees in one hour—from 43 degrees at 7 a.m. to 28 degrees at 8 a.m. By 9 a.m., the temperature was 20 degrees, producing a wind chill of 17 below zero.

Winds between 20 and 40 mph battered Madison throughout the day once the cold front moved into the area, and gusts as high as 51 mph were reported in some areas.

Blizzard warnings were issued for west-central Wisconsin, and travelers' advisories covered the rest of the state in the morning. But by mid-day, the National Weather Service had moderated its forecast, lifting the travelers' advisories. Although temperatures will remain cold, much of the bluster of early morning will have moderated considerably, making the roads less slippery.

The Wisconsin State Patrol said I-94 from the Minnesota border to Osseo in Eau Claire County was closed to travel earlier today. A patrol spokesman said the road became impassable due to snow over glare ice. That condition, combined with blowing and drifting snow, cut visibility in the area to zero.

Difficult driving conditions plagued an area north of a line from La Crosse to

Wisconsin Dells to Green Bay. Scattered slippery spots were reported south of that line.

Although highways in the southern third of the state were reported in wet but good winter driving condition, the patrol warned that the rapid drop in temperatures could produce icy road surfaces in a short period of time. The National Weather Service reported that the weather system was moving east at about 50 mph.

A weather service spokesman said Madison should miss the brunt of the snow expected in the central and northern part of the state. Although snow flurries will continue through tomorrow, there should be no accumulation.

The forecast called for temperatures to continue to drop, with a predicted low tonight of zero to 5 below. On Saturday, Madison's temperatures are expected to be in the low 20s, under sunny skies. . . . [Madison (Wis.) *Capital-Times*]

By Chris Satullo

They weren't denying they'd blown one, but the free spirits at the National Weather Service station didn't sound very penitent today.

"What can I tell you? We goofed," said weather specialist Ed Karpinski about the 4 to 6 inches of snow that fell Wednesday morning with no warning. "Actually, I don't feel bad at all. I just got back from vacation today. If you want to talk to the guy who really messed up, I'll get him."

The mistake, Karpinski said, was that the weather service thought a low pressure system would pass farther north than it did. When the pocket dipped south, the snow came, causing dozens of minor traffic accidents, catching most road departments unawares and cutting into school attendance.

Karpinski ventured a forecast calling for partly sunny skies and warmer temperatures Friday followed by highs in the 40s over the weekend.

Fender-benders were the order of the day throughout the Express area, but luckily they caused no major injuries.

Accidents continued today. A multiple-vehicle crash occurred at about 9:10 A.M. today on the Lehigh Valley Thruway near the Route 191 interchange. There were several injuries, but no further details were available. . . .

Ordinarily, a snowstorm like this means no school for most students. However at 6 A.M. Wednesday, the time most superintendents make the decision whether to call a snow day, only a dusting of snow was on the ground and the forecast was for flurries. [Easton (Pa.) *Express*]

Some forecasts are in the form of warnings, thus performing a valuable public service.

By Casey Bukro
ENVIRONMENT EDITOR

Smog-sufferers need a scorecard these days to tell whether Chicago's ozone levels are dangerously high.

Because city and state environment officials cannot agree on how to quantify ozone levels, the information they report often is confusing.

Chicago's Department of Environmental Control reports ozone in micrograms per cubic meter, while the Illinois Environmental Protection Agency reports it in parts per billion [PPB].

Chicago's highest ozone reading of the 1978 season was reached at 4 P.M. last

Monday at Taft High School, 5625 N. Natoma Av. It was reported without comment by the city as 350 micrograms, and by the state as 179 parts per billion.

"Is that high or low?" asked Mrs. H. B. Bergman of Winnetka, one of many Tribune readers who say they don't understand the city's or state's ozone reports. An Illinois official recently admitted it was "stupid" that the two agencies cannot agree on a standard ozone reporting method that makes sense to the public.

Until last year, the city and the state reported ozone in parts per million. But then both changed their reporting methods this year, and neither is willing to change again.

To add to the confusion, the federal Environmental Protection Agency reports ozone limits in parts per million, and much of its data on the health effects of air pollution is expressed in parts per million.

The Illinois clean air code created a four-stage air pollution emergency plan, calling for progressively stricter controls as air filth rises dangerously. In the final stage—an emergency—traffic could be halted and businesses could be closed.

Weather conditions and changes of continuing air filth also are taken into account when sounding the various stages of the emergency plan.

A health advisory or warning—the first stage—is issued to alert persons in weak health of rising smog levels, since ozone can cause breathing problems among the old and young and among persons suffering from lung and heart disease.

Health studies show that ozone begins burning eyes and noses at the yellow-alert stage, and the effects become worse as ozone rises. Coughing and sore throats are likely at the red-alert levels, while some people would expect to be hospitalized with breathing problems in an ozone emergency. [Chicago *Tribune*]

DEFINITIONS

To write understandable weather accounts, the reporter must know the meaning of the most important meteorological terms. The following list was prepared especially for this chapter by J. R. Fulks, who retired recently after many years in the Chicago office of the United States National Weather Service: It has been updated by William M. L. Briggs, meteorologist in the forecast office of the National Weather Service in Chicago where Raymond R. Waldman is meteorologist in charge.

Barometer. An instrument for measuring atmospheric pressure. There are two types. In one, the mercurial barometer, pressure is measured as the height (commonly expressed in the United States in inches) to which the atmosphere will lift mercury in a vacuum. An average height of the barometer at sea level is about 29.9 inches, and in the lowest several thousand feet one inch less for each thousand feet above sea level. The other type of barometer is the aneroid which measures air pressure by the expansion or contraction of one or more metal vacuum cells. Pressure is also measured in millimeters of mercury, but the international unit used by meteorological services is the millibar (1 millibar equals 1000 dynes; 30 inches of mercury equals 1015.92 millibars). An airplane altimeter is a high-precision aneroid barometer.

Blizzard. Strong wind accompanied by blowing snow. The National Weather Service uses this term for winds greater than 35 mph, and visibilities less than ¼ mile. The snow may be either falling or may be picked up from the ground by the wind.

Ceiling. An aviation term used in the United States to designate the height above ground of the lowest opaque cloud layer which covers more than half the sky.

Contrail. The name of a cloud which forms behind high-flying aircraft.

Cyclone. Same as a *low*. The term *cyclone* refers to its system of rotating winds. It is a moving storm, usually accompanied by rain or snow.

Degree days. The number of degrees that the day's mean temperature is above or below 65° F. Heating degree days are the number of degrees the day's mean temperature is below 65° F. These are totaled monthly and seasonally to obtain a measure of heating needs. Cooling degree days are the number of degrees the day's mean temperature is above 65°; they indicate air conditioning needs.

Dew point. The temperature to which air must be cooled for fog to form. It is an index of the amount of moisture in the air.

Fog. A condition of lowered visibility caused by minute water droplets suspended in the air. It is a cloud resting on the ground.

Forecasts, weather. Statements of expected weather, prepared by specially trained professional meteorologists. They are based on weather data collected rapidly over a large portion of the world. To obtain the most probable expected weather, the forecaster uses prognostic computations made by the electronic computer, considers other physical and statistical factors and applies judgment based on long experience. Specific forecasts are generally for periods of one to three days at the most, but the National Weather Service issues both five-day and monthly forecasts of *average* conditions. Weather forecasts are of many types, such as public, aviation, marine, agricultural and forest-fire weather. The National Weather Service also prepares and issues flood forecasts, watches and warnings.

Front. A boundary between two different air masses, one colder than the other. A *cold front* moves toward the warmer air, a *warm front* toward the colder air. When a cold front overtakes a warm front, they form an *occluded* front.

Frost. A deposit of ice crystals on outside objects caused by condensation of moisture from the atmosphere on clear cold nights. Killing frost is defined as the first frost of autumn sufficient to kill essentially all vegetation in the area.

High. An area of high barometric pressure, usually several hundred to a thousand miles or more in diameter. In the Northern Hemisphere, winds blow clockwise about a high center. The approach of a high generally means improving weather—the ending of rain or snow, then clearing, colder and finally somewhat warmer as a result of sunshine. The weather in highs, like lows, varies from one high to another and will differ depending on where the center passes. A slow-moving high may cause fog, and often accumulation of air pollution, in and near its center.

Humidity. A general term applying to any of various measures of the amount of moisture in the atmosphere. See *Relative humidity.*

Hurricane. The name applied in the Caribbean Region, Gulf of Mexico, North Atlantic and eastern North Pacific (off Mexico) to a tropical cyclone in which the strongest winds are 75 miles per hour or greater. The same type of storm in the western Pacific is called a typhoon.

Inversion. An increase of temperature with height, in contrast to a normal decrease with height. Inversions at or near the ground trap pollutants by preventing their upward dispersion.

Jet stream. A line or band of maximum wind speeds high in the atmosphere, generally somewhere between 30,000 and 40,000 feet. The speeds are often in excess of 100 mph.

Lake breeze. A relatively cool breeze which frequently blows, on warm afternoons, from a cool lake onto adjacent warmer land. It may extend less than a mile or as much as several miles inland.

Lake effect. A general term which applies to any effect to a lake on weather. Near the shores of the Great Lakes a sometimes spectacular effect is that of heavy snowfall over a small area (perhaps a county). It is caused by moisture-laden air in winter moving from the lake onto the land, the air having been originally very cold, probably much below 0° F, before it moved onto the lake.

Local storm. Any storm of small scale, such as a thunderstorm. *Severe local storms* are those likely to cause damage, including severe thunderstorms, damaging hail and tornadoes.

Low. An area of low barometric pressure usually a few hundred miles in diameter. In the Northern Hemisphere, winds blow counterclockwise around a low center. Typically, the approach of a low means worsening weather—increasing cloudiness and finally rain or snow, but the pattern of weather varies for different lows and will be different depending on how far away the center actually passes. The low may affect weather up to several hundred miles from its center. Usually, as a low approaches, the weather becomes warmer, then colder as the low passes; this is typical of a low that passes to the north, but there may be little or no warmer weather if the low passes to the south.

Mean temperature. The average temperature over any specified period of time, such as a day, month or year. The United States National Weather Service uses the average of the lowest and highest temperature of each day as the mean temperature—an approximation that is very close to the true mean.

Mist. A condition intermediate between fog and haze—a thin fog. Also, in the United States, often applied to drizzle (fine rain).

Precipitation. Water droplets or frozen water particles falling to the ground. It includes rain, drizzle, freezing rain, freezing drizzle, snow, snow pellets, snow grains, hail, ice pellets (in the United States, sleet) and ice needles. The term *precipitation* is applied also to total measured depth of precipitation for which purpose any frozen form is first melted.

Precipitation probability. In the United States National Weather Service forecasts, the probability that .01 inch or more of precipitation will fall at any one point in the forecast area during the specified time period, usually 12 hours.

Relative humidity. A commonly used measure of atmospheric humidity. It is the percentage of moisture actually in the air compared to the amount it would hold if completely saturated at the given temperature. High humidity contributes to human discomfort at high temperatures but only slightly so if at all at low temperatures. Indoor relative humidity is sometimes applied to the relative humidity which outside air will have when heated to indoor temperature (usually taken as 72°F).

Shower. A rain of short duration, such as with a thunderstorm. Typically, showers begin abruptly and the intensity of precipitation varies considerably. There may be many separate showers on a day of showery weather. The term is also used with other than rain, for example, *snow shower* or *sleet shower*.

Sleet. In the United States frozen rain drops, but in Great Britain a mixture of rain and snow.

Smog. A contraction of the words "smoke" and "fog." It is, however, applied commonly in large cities or industrial areas when the pollutants may include other types in addition to smoke and fog.

Squall. A strong wind which begins suddenly and lasts a matter of minutes—somewhat longer than a gust. Also, especially in nautical usage, a sudden strong wind and an accompanying cloud mass that may produce precipitation, thunder and lightning. A *squall line* is a line or band of active thunderstorms.

Storm. A general term that may mean a cyclone, thunderstorm, wind storm, dust storm, snow storm, hail storm, tornado, hurricane or the like.

Storm warning. Can be a warning of any type of storm, but is applied more specifically to warnings for mariners. Marine storm warnings are of four types. *Small Craft* (less than 39 mph), *Gale* (39–54 mph), *Storm* (55–73 mph) and *Hurricane* (74 mph and greater). On the Great Lakes, the term *Small Craft Advisory* is used instead of *Small Craft Warning*, and *Storm* is used for any speed above 54 mph (*Hurricane* is not used). The figures refer to wind speeds.

Temperature-humidity index. A measure of human discomfort in warm weather. It takes into account the effect of both temperature and humidity. The THI is found by adding the dry bulb temperature and the wet bulb temperature, multiplying this sum by 0.4 and adding 15. With a THI of 70, nearly everyone feels comfortable; at 75, at least half the people become uncomfortable; at 79 or higher, nearly everyone is uncomfortable. Fewer people, however, are uncomfortable if there is a good breeze.

Thundershower. A thunderstorm accompanied by rain.

Tornado. A small, violently rotating storm, commonly a few hundred yards in diameter. It accompanies a thunderstorm, but only a very few thunderstorms have tornadoes. Direction of rotation is usually the same as that of a Low, and the strongest winds range generally 100 to 300 mph. In addition to wind effect, some damage to structures is caused by low atmospheric pressure in the tornado center which causes buildings to collapse outward.

Water vapor. Water in gaseous form. The atmosphere always contains some water vapor, but the amount varies greatly. In hot humid conditions, it sometimes constitutes as much as 2 per cent (by weight) of the air. At low temperatures, the amount is much less. Water vapor is invisible, but when it condenses it forms water droplets that become visible as clouds or fog.

Watch. A bulletin issued by the United States National Weather Service to alert the public to conditions which may require issuance of later warnings. The warnings, when issued, are generally for smaller areas and give more specific locations and times.

Wind direction. The direction *from* which wind blows.

Not all of them (readers) have thermometers. Comparatively few of them do business on top of a skyscraper. When it's hot they prefer to be told it's hot—and how hot. The health commissioner tells them what to wear, what to eat, and how to take it easy when a heat wave comes. There is one thing to be said for printing the number of deaths from prostration in a day. It is negligible compared with the totals of 40 years ago, when, as in 1886, the death rate was disquietingly high. No one worries now. A year ago there was a record summer for heat, and the whole country learned where the very hottest places were.

—Editorial, New York *Times*

Replying to protests from some readers that weather forecasts are not always exact, the Brooklyn Eagle *declared editorially, ''Newspapers are to blame for enough without being made responsible for that. . . . Convenience aside, it is perhaps just as well that in this age of mechanization there remains a slight margin of error in weather forecasting. Nature retains few secrets to herself; her moods cannot be discounted in advance. Life would be monotonous if it never rained. The two most monotonous places on earth are the Arctic and Antarctic, where it is forever cold. Life on the Equator, where it is forever hot, is described as engaging. Let us comfort ourselves with that thought, imagine a few palm trees, and relax.''*

24
ENTERTAINMENT

When they are not working to earn a living, Americans engage in a variety of activities for self-improvement, relaxation or pleasure. In their enjoyment of hobbies and games and other diversions they are either active participants or spectators. In either capacity they have easy access to a quantity of printed material written by journalistic experts to enhance their enjoyment. Newspaper columns and special-interest magazines appeal to the home gardener, interior decorator, pet owner, collector of stamps, coins, antiques or objects of art, players of games such as chess and bridge, book collectors and readers and so forth: hunters, fishermen, campers, hikers, yachtsmen, canoeists, swimmers, joggers, golfers, tennis enthusiasts, bowlers, bird-watchers, tourists, nature-lovers and others.

SPORTS

Greatest journalistic attention is paid to professional sports. This means that sports pages contain mostly free publicity for commercial enterprises. Several newspapers have attempted to reduce the attention paid professional sports but reader complaints invariably have resulted in a reversal of policy. Some technically amateur sports activities, as college football and other athletic contests, are actually huge financial ventures that cannot be ignored. Small city papers can pay more attention than the metoropolitan press to high school and other really amateur events. The increase in sports activities for girls and women has created new readers for the sports page. Even in smaller communities, however, it is impossible to give equal treatment to intramural or sandlot athletics.

The Sports Reporter

High value is put upon the experience gained in writing sports, generally for two reasons: (1) only the critics and reviewers have anywhere near comparable freedom as to both what they say and the manner of saying it, and (2) there is no audience more critical than that consisting of sports fans who demand of a writer absolute accuracy and soundness of critical judgment.

Knowledge of the fine points of a game, which comes from having played it oneself, increases a person's interest in the skill of experts at the sport. Baseball became established as the national sport at a time when it was the most common sandlot pastime; in later years, the boys who played it relived vicariously the thrills of their adolescence through the achievement of Christy Mathewson, Babe Ruth, Ted Williams and others. Today, with young and old enjoying golf, tennis, bowling, swimming and other sports, interest in professional experts in these fields is growing. This means that there are more readers who like to second-guess the umpire and the reporter also.

Remaining Cool

Everyone who attends an athletic event does so in quest of pleasure—that is, everyone except the sports reporters. This does not mean that sports reporters do not enjoy their work; it does mean that they cannot permit their enthusiasm to approach that which the fan displays. The press box is not a cheering section because its inhabitants have all they can do to follow closely what is happening so as to explain the difficult plays and decisions for fans who were too busy spurring on alma mater to notice exactly what happened. It is pleasant for the reporter to view sports events from the best seats and without paying admission, but s/he never is able to assume the carefree attitude of the casual fan.

Following Plays

From his or her superior vantage point, the sports reporter should be expected to observe accurately. In many sports, the action is so fast that spectators cannot always follow it. The news story should let the bleacherite know what kind of pitch went for a home run or should tell the fans who sat in the cheap seats how the knockout blow was struck. At major sports events, the work of sportswriters is facilitated by the assistance of an official scorer who decides whether a hit or an error is to be scored. There also will be statisticians to prepare details in addition to those going into the official score book. At minor events, however, the reporter usually has to compile most of his/her own statistics. If, in addition to a general story of an event, a play-by-play account is desired, customary practice is to assign two reporters. An indispensable part of any featured sports story is a summary or box score, as the particular sport requires, which is run separately or at the end of the story proper. To the fan, the summary or box score is a complete account in itself.

Knowing the Rules

The sports fan not only attends contests but also receives considerable pleasure from discussing the past performances and future chances of players and teams. A favorite pastime is to second-guess the coach or manager and to pass judgment upon the abilities of referees and umpires. Just as popular among fans is criticism of the write-ups of sports reporters. In other words, the sports writer has to "know his stuff" just as much as do players and officials. It is inconceivable that a reporter not understand the rules of the game to be covered. Writers of business news can make mistakes that only economists recognize; sports writers produce copy for readers who think they know as much as they.

Knowing the Records

To keep up with what is expected, the sports reporter not only must understand the rule book but also must know the record book cotaining the statistics of what players and teams have done in the past. Otherwise, the reporter will not know whether a particular achievement is unusual. The sports expert whose mind is a storehouse of information regarding the history of sports is in a position to enrich copy considerably. The old-timer can compare players of today with those of yesterday and frequently may remember "way back when" something, recalled by an immediate event, occurred. At the oldster's disposal, in case memory weakens, are numerous sports record books in the newspaper's morgue.

Talking the Language

A New York sports writer of a generation ago, Charles Dryden, is given credit for having been first to introduce on the sports page an informality and originality of language that would scandalize readers if found in the regular news sections. The credit for genius due Dryden has been dimmed because of the banal depths to which thousands of imitators, consciously or unconsciously, have sunk since then. Stanley Walker, longtime New York *Herald Tribune* city editor, wrote: "If it is true, and it appears to be, that Dryden was the father of whimsical baseball reporting, then the man has a great deal to answer for. He may have freed some reporters and afforded them the chance to do their gorgeous word-painting with a bold and lavish hand, but for every one he liberated he set demons to work in the brains of a dozen others—demons which made American sports writing the most horrendous mess of gibberish ever set before the eyes of a reader."

Today critical analysis of sports writing relates to the widespread practice of delaying the lead. The assumption is that the reader already knows the outcome of the contest, perhaps has heard or seen it on radio or television. If, however, the reader has retired early or for any other reason missed the news, s/he is required to peruse the account in the morning newspaper for several paragraphs to learn who won.

By Phil Hersh

Notre Dame, Ind.—The mood was sedate, and Larry Brown blended into it. His burgundy tweed sport coat was draped across a couple of bench chairs. The rookie UCLA coach talked of what was about to happen.

It was 45 minutes before the 24th meeting in what has become America's major intersectional basketball rivalry. The Notre Dame band was silent, the raucous student rooters yet to arrive in their seats high behind one basket. Players from the fourth-ranked Irish and seventh-ranked Bruins were warming up and it was still quiet enough that the thumps of basketballs on hardwood resounded through the Alumni and Convocation center.

Larry Brown could hardly wait for the calm that would follow the storm. And when the tumult and shouting finally died, Notre Dame (5–0) emerged a 77–74 winner as freshman guard John Paxson hit four free throws in the final five seconds. . . . [Chicago *Sun-Times*]

By Bob Smizik

The day started for this Pitt football team with several crucial questions that didn't have nice answers: For starters, could the defense, the strong point of the team last season, overcome the loss of five starters, three of whom made the pros? And, could the offense overcome the presence of a group of injured, inexperienced and untalented receivers who had caught the combined total of 20 passes on the collegiate level?

The answers came in a hurry yesterday in the opener against Kansas. The defense allowed not a point and the passing game, led by Ralph Still's three touchdown catches, clicked for 277 yards.

Any more questions?

It was a classic season opener for the Panthers. Their whole game came together as they rolled to a 24–0 win over outclassed Kansas, a team with an excellent chance of doing worse than last year's 1–10. [Pittsburgh *Press*]

On the same page appeared the following orthodox lead.

Leetsdale—John Morrison scored every Quaker Valley point during a come-from-behind, 17–7 Quaker win that snapped Leechburg's 12-game regular-season win streak and gave QV (1–8 a year ago) its second win of the season.

Morrison, a 6-2, 215-pound linebacker, scored Quaker Valley's first touchdown by returning an interception four yards. Also the fullback, Morrison then gave his team the lead by running for a two-point conversion.

A 32-yard field goal by Morrison, also the kicker, widened the margin and a 12-yard fourth-quarter touchdown run by Morrison, again the fullback, cemented Leechburg's fate.

Morrison proved fallible, however, when he was stopped short of the goal line while attempting to follow that final score with another conversion run.

Sam LoFaso, the Quaker coach who this season welcomed eight offensive and six defensive starters from last year's squad, said a month ago that his team should show much improvement. With a win against defending AIC East champion Leechburg, his Quakers have made their coach a prophet. . . .

[Pittsburgh *Press*]

Writing Sports News

One advantage the sports writer has over the reporter who specializes in political, governmental, business, scientific or any other type of news: the rules are definite and, despite occasional minor changes, remain the same year after year in all parts of the country. This situation, which contributes to the ease of sports reporting, also may lead to monotony. It is the belief of many successful writers that the opportunity to develop an individual writing style, which sports reporting affords more than any other kind of newspaper work, exists up to a certain point only, after which the sports reporter should do the more serious writing for which earlier work has provided training.

On the other hand, however, there are scores of first-rate sports writers whose copy seems just as fresh as ever after years of writing. Outstanding is Walter (Red) Smith, whose syndicated column originated with the New York *Herald Tribune* and survived the paper. In late 1971 he became a regular New York *Times* columnist.

In reporting amateur or local sports, the sports reporter almost invariably supports the home team. Any criticism of local heroes is constructive and usually is consistent with what a large number of fans believe. The tendency to "build up" local players may be overdone to the detriment of both the players and writer when performances do not square with predictions. The sports writer has a friendly attitude and makes it clear that s/he, as well as the readers, wants the home team to win. On the other hand, the journalist must not act as a virtual public relations counsel for a coach or manager who may wish to use a reporter to send up deceptive trial balloons to confuse opponents, or to promote his own interests.

Although all contests of a particular sport are played according to the same rules, the major news interest of an individual game might be any one of a number of potential elements. In determining the feature of a game, the sports reporter considers the following:

1. Significance.
   a. Is a championship at stake?
   b. Effect of the result on the all-time records of the contestants.
   c. Effect of the result on the season's records of the contestants.
   d. Are the contestants old rivals?
   e. Are they resuming relations after a long period?
   f. Will the outcome suggest either contestant's probable strength against future opponents?
2. Probable outcome.
   a. Relative weight and experience of contestants.

b. Ability as demonstrated against other opponents, especially common ones.
c. Improvement during the season.
d. New plays, tactics, etc.
e. New players, return of injured players, strength of substitutes, etc.
f. Former contests between the two contestants.
g. Weather conditions favorable to either contestant.
h. Lack of practice, injuries and other handicaps.
i. Tradition of not being able to win away from home.
j. Recent record, slumps, etc.

3. How victory was won.
   a. The winning play, if score was close.
   b. The style of play of both winner and loser.
   c. Costly errors and mistakes of judgment.
   d. Spurts that overcame opponent's lead.
4. Important plays.
   a. How each score was made.
   b. Spectacular catches, strokes, etc.
   c. The result of "hunches."
   d. Penalties, fouls, etc.
   e. Disputed decisions of umpire or referee.
5. Individual records, stars, etc.
   a. Records broken.
   b. High scores.
   c. Players who "delivered" in pinches.
   d. Teamwork.
   e. Players not up to usual form.
6. Injuries.
7. The occasion or crowd.
   a. Size of crowd; a record?
   b. An annual event?
   c. Enthusiasm, riots, demonstrations, etc.
8. The weather.
   a. Condition of track or playing field.
   b. Effect of heat or cold.
   c. Effect of sun on fielders, etc.
   d. Which side was more handicapped? Why?
   e. Delays because of rain, etc.
9. Box score, summary and statistics.

REVIEWING AND CRITICISM

If the college-trained cub reporter is not ambitious to become a foreign correspondent or a sports columnist, s/he is likely to want to be a critic—motion picture, dramatic, musical, literary or art. Unfortunately for the youngster with talent that might lead to success in such writing, the average small newspaper offers inadequate opportunities for either experience or editorial guidance. As a result, many—including some of the best that the schools of journalism turn out—redirect their energies into other channels.

This section is intended both for the few who create opportunities for themselves, perhaps by developing a column of motion picture or book criticism in addition to their other work, and for the regular staff members who draw the assignments to cover the annual high school play, the local art club's exhibits, the occasional Broadway cast that makes a one-night stop and the home talent Gilbert and Sullivan light opera.

The Reporter-Critic

Essayists

The lure of critical reviewing, in addition to free tickets, probably is the opportunity it seems to offer for self-expression. The great critics, including Matthew Arnold, Stuart Sherman and George Bernard Shaw, also were creative artists and social philosophers. In addition to explaining to their readers how some muralist, playwright or composer regarded life, they chronicled their own reactions.

To prevent "spouting off" too much on the basis of only textbook knowledge and classroom discussions, it is perhaps fortunate that the beginning reporter is hampered in his critical writing. Before one can be a competent critic s/he must first serve an apprenticeship as a reviewer. When one covers a dramatic, musical or any other kind of aesthetic event, one does well to accept the assignment as one in straight news reporting. That is, while s/he is learning.

The purpose of the average member of a small-town audience at a motion picture, play or concert is pleasure seeking. A safe guide for the tyro in reviewing, therefore, is the reaction of audiences; no matter how high s/he rises in critical writing, it supplies an element of news interest of which s/he always must take cognizance. What got applause? What evoked laughs? Regardless of what the reporter thinks of the audience's taste, to make a fair report of the occasion s/he must mention what indisputably were its high points from the standpoint of those for whom it was presented.

This advice is not tantamount to condoning the practice of building a review upon fatuous sentences or short paragraphs lauding every performer, but it is intended as a brake for those who might be tempted to use a night at the opera merely as an inspiration for an essay upon the fallacies of hedonism as demonstrated by *Faust* or a dissertation on the evidence regarding Hamlet's insanity.

The following is an example of a straightforward, objective report:

By Elaine Markoutsas

Christmas trees and lights. Candy canes. Sleigh bells. Angels, Reindeer. Santa Claus.

It wouldn't be Christmas without them. And it wouldn't be Christmas without

"The Nutcracker," which opened Thursday night for 24 performances [thru Jan. 4] at the Arie Crown Theater.

The classic late 19th-century ballet, set to the superb Tchaikovsky score and updated by Ruth Page, has become a tradition in Chicago, juxtaposed with other important works of art. Some make it an annual addition to their holiday fare. Others, present company included, are dazzled by the event as first-time-first-nighters. It's for everybody, and you don't have to know a thing about ballet or music to enjoy it. [Chicago *Tribune*]

FORMULAS

The critic with a bias is as dangerous as the political or labor reporter whose prejudices forbid interpreting fairly the activities or viewpoints of more than one side in a controversy. In criticism, application of a formula as to what an artistic form should be often results in conclusions as grotesque as condemning a cow for not being a horse.

An example of a critic with a formula is one who believes art should exist for art's sake only and that no artistic form ever should be utilized for propagandistic purposes. As a result, if the hero of a modern picture or play happens to be identified with a particular racial, nationality, economic or other type or group, the critic is likely stupidly to condemn the entire production as propaganda, even though it be an honest and perhaps brilliant attempt to describe sympathetically a certain segment of life.

Even worse than the opponent of propaganda is the exponent of it who is sympathetic only when a certain theory is promulgated by the particular art form under review. Such critics dismiss books, plays or other artistic creations with (to them) derisive adjectives, as "romantic" or "too realistic," with a condescension that, in the small community at least, cannot but brand them as supercilious or, as the critics' critics may put it, "half-baked highbrows."

The critic with a formula is bound to be mostly a negative, carping, constantly dissatisfied one. Because a Hollywood production does not square with his/her conception of what the Old Globe players would have done, s/he sees no good in the result. Regretting that some artistic hero did not execute the idea, s/he is likely to make absurd comparisons between what is and what might have been.

The essence of competent reviewing of any kind is understanding an artist's purpose so as to interpret it to others. Any art form—painting, drama, the novel, music—is a medium of communication. No artistic creation should be condemned merely because of inability to understand its language, although those who hold that the artist should use a vocabulary that it is possible for others to learn have a valid point.

The duty of the reviewer or critic, in addition to that of describing a piece of art or an artistic event, should be to assist readers in an understanding of the artist's motives, to enhance their enjoyment of it. This obligation is prerequisite to that of passing expert judgment upon the artist's success in an undertaking; the role of evaluator is one that the critic-reporter should postpone until s/he has reached maturity in objective understanding, and not even then if the public consists largely of laymen. The greatest service the newspaper that gives space to artistic news can perform for both artists and spectators or auditors is to interpret the former to the latter. The educational background that such service requires easily may be imagined.

The writer of the following example attempted to explain motives without passing judgment:

By Bob Rohrer

The political side of America's struggle for independence receives engrossing and frequently amusing treatment in the Broadway musical play "1776," now being performed with patriotic gusto by the road show company at the Atlanta Civic Center.

The plot covers the last months of the second Continental Congress in Philadelphia, which—after considerable political maneuvering—approved the Declaration of Independence as war raged between Colonial and British troops.

Authors Peter Stone and Sherman Edwards have skillfully blended a wealth of historical detail—much of it humorous—with imaginative dialogue and warm-blooded, affectionate parodies of the men who supported and opposed independence.

The production itself moves vigorously; the staccato pacing of the deftly-handled ensemble scenes alternates effectively with strategically placed slower interludes, and the surging action never backs over itself.

There are quite a few fine individual performances. Particularly outstanding are the efforts of Don Perkins, who is convincingly choleric as the irascible John Adams; Paul Tripp, who turns in a wry performance of an earthy Benjamin Franklin; Reid Shelton, who livens the production with an explosively uninhibited portrayal of the unabashedly egotistical Richard Henry Lee of the Virginia Lees, and Larry Small, who is effective in a small part as a courier who sings a moving anti-war ballad—just about the only memorable musical number in the show.

[Atlanta *Constitution*]

Reviewing

The difference between reviewing and criticism has been implied in the discussions under both previous headings. No matter how critical s/he may become with experience and expert judgment, no writer of the arts can overlook his/her duty to supply the answer to the question "What is it like?" to the reader who has not read the book, attended the play or viewed the exhibit in question.

Is it a book about Russia or about how to raise puppies? A farce or a tragedy? A painting in imitation of Cézanne or one suggestive of Norman Rockwell? The reader who must select the books s/he reads, the motion pictures, plays and musical events s/he attends, expects the newspaper to tell him/her the answers. The reader wants, furthermore, an honest, fair statement, not an advertiser's blurb; and s/he doesn't want his/her pleasure spoiled by being told too much. That is, if the success of the playwright or novelist depends upon an unusual plot incident, it is unfair to both artist and audience for the writer to reveal its nature. How to convey an adequate impression of the nature of an artistic creation without spoiling one's fun demands only that quality known as common sense.

WOMAN OF VIOLENCE. By Geula Cohen. Translated by Hillel Halkin. 275 pp. New York: Holt, Rinehart and Winston, $5.95

Reviewed by Emily C. McDonald

"Woman of Violence" is the story of Geula Cohen and the life she led as a member of the notorious Stern Gang—which fought for the liberation of Palestine from the British. The gang—also known as the Lechi—was composed not only of terrorists, but also of idealists.

Geula Cohen was no exception.

She left her comfortable family life while still a student to join the freedom fight. First she tried the sanctioned organization—Betar. Then she turned to the more revolutionary Estel. Still not satisfied, she finally let herself be "recruited" into the Lechi.

From that day on her life changed completely. She went underground and rarely emerged from hiding except under cover of night. Geula learned to fight, to hide, to recruit, and—perhaps most important of all—to put dreams and ideals into action.

Finally, Geula became one of the "voices" on the Hebrew underground radio. Her voice brought news and inspiration to thousands of Jews eagerly awaiting news of the freedom fighters.

Although her work was dangerous, she never feared the danger. Her family was under surveillance, her friends were captured and put to death—still she went on with her broadcasts.

Then she too was captured. Through the Lechi underground, however, her escape was planned and finally brought about. She immediately returned to work.

Geula's memoirs end on the eve of Independence Day, 1948. Her active work in the Lechi ended then, too. She watched the celebrating but couldn't take part in it. The independence gained was not the Lechi ideal. As she put it:

"But I would remain outside. An ancient, heady melody that had started long ago would continue to resound far beyond these voices and frontiers."

[Nashville *Banner*]

CRITICISM

To pass judgment on the merits of a book, play, painting, musical number, motion picture or any other attempt at art demands expert judgment. To be an expert, one must have a specialist's education and training. This does not mean necessarily that the newspaper critic must be able to produce masterpieces to be qualified to pass judgment on the efforts of another, but it does mean that s/he must have a thoroughgoing understanding of the field s/he writes about.

It is not peculiar that supposedly expert critics often do not agree. Neither do political theorists, economists or scientists. A difference of opinion among specialists, however, is based upon sound principles whereas philistines have as their premises only stereotypes.

The critic who wins the respect of readers usually is one who has proved his/her ability to report an artistic event correctly and to review fairly the nature of a piece of art. If s/he can observe correctly and interpret with understanding, s/he also may be trusted as an artistic "tipster." If s/he lacks either of the other qualities, however, his/her starred selections will be ignored.

These, then, are the three responsibilities of the finished critic, which the ambitious beginner would do well to master one at a time in order (1) to describe objectively an artistic object or event, (2) to explain what the artist intends it to convey and (3) to pass expert judgment on the artist's success in achieving his purpose.

Note in the following example how the writer, although passing critical judgments, remained aware of his role as reporter:

By Albert Goldberg
TIMES STAFF WRITER

The differences in technique among dancers qualified to be principals in such an organization as the Bolshoi Ballet are generally so minute as to defy anything except pedantic expert analysis.

But the differences in personalities can be enormous and readily apparent, and it was this factor, with six changes of cast in the leading roles, that made the Bolshoi's second performance of "Don Quixote" in Shrine Auditorium Thursday night a much livelier and more convincing affair than the one of the previous evening.

Type casting is not ordinarily one of the basic principles of ballet, but it was utilized to maximum advantage by placing Ekaterina Maximova and Vladimir Vasiliev in the roles of Kitri and Basil the Barber. Seldom has a couple—they are Mr. and Mrs. in private life—been better matched in every respect than this irresistible pair of handsome youngsters.

THEIR YOUTH

Naturally they capitalize on their youth and beauty, but their skills go far beyond the physical aspects. Though quite different in other respects, Miss Maximova has something of the radiance of Margot Fonteyn. She lights up the stage with her petite, mischievous sparkle, and she dances with a buoyancy that completely reflects her personality. . . .

It is characteristic of the ensemble principle on which the Bolshoi operates that Natalia Bessmertnova, the troupe's third-ranking ballerina, should turn up unannounced in the comparatively minor part of the Queen of the Driads. Though brief, she made its opportunities count with a serene elegance of style and technique that aroused anticipation of more extended roles.

Alexander Lavreniuk took over the Toreador with a welcome addition of refinement and aloofness, and Rimma Kerelskaya, the Queen of the Driads on opening night, injected more variety and less routine into the street dancer. Maya Samokhalova, the previous street dancer, did the first variation in the last act, but we'll have to take that on faith.

[Los Angeles *Times*]

HANDLING THE ASSIGNMENT

Two factors that the reviewer-critic must bear in mind are these: (1) Are those upon whose work s/he is to pass judgment professionals or amateurs? (2) Is the performance (dramatic or musical), production, presentation or object of art an original creation or a copy or imitation?

It is unfair to judge an amateur by professional standards. The home talent cast usually gets as much fun out of rehearsing and acting as do the relatives and friends who witness the result. Generally, amateur events should be reported objectively with the audience's reactions as the guide.

Whereas Broadway first-nighters are as interested in the work of a playwright as in the excellence of actors, when the local dramatic club puts on something by Oscar Wilde or Somerset Maugham, it is stupid to place the emphasis in the review upon the familiar plot or problem with which the dramatist was concerned. Rather, it is the acting and staging that should command attention.

The broader the critic's background, the better able s/he is to make comparisons between immediate and past events. If s/he has seen several actresses play the same part, s/he can explain the differences in interpretations. When a motion picture is adapted from a novel, short story or stage play, s/he can point out the changes made in plot and artistic emphasis. The same orchestra under different conductors behaves differently in rendering the same musical masterpiece; two authors handling the same subject may have little in common as to either method or conclusions.

The following was a clever handling of the home-town performance of a familiar play.

By Elaine Cloud Goller

P-C ARTS WRITER

The *Pajama Game* has some tops—and some bottoms.

Dress rehearsal Tuesday night of Jonesborough Repertory Theater's current production had some wrinkles, but for the most part, provided a delightful musical evening that stirs mid-1950's memories of Doris Day.

The story line of *Pajama Game,* based on Richard Bissell's novel *Seven-and-a-Half Cents,* is a familiar boy-meets-girl, girl-rejects-boy, boy-gets-girl plot. Although it may hail from 25 years ago, the situation is one that we in 1980 can all identify with.

Management versus labor—the employees want a 7½-cent raise, but the boss isn't about to negotiate. (Sound familiar?)

Sid, the handsome new superintendent in the Sleeptight Pajama factory finds himself to be the third fellow in a year in his position. But it is easily understood. The boss, Mr. Hasler, hassles everybody over every little thing. (What makes this man so mean?)

Sid's fancy has been caught by Babe, the leader of the factory grievance committee. She is concerned about the conflict of interests—her love life, or the issue of the raise—and denies the taunts of the other girls by declaring that "I'm Not at All in Love." Which of course isn't at all true.

The pairing of efficiency expert Vernon Hines, with Hasler's prim bookkeeper Gladys creates a very funny couple. Secretary Mable, who sees and understands all in a matronly cupid's role, tries to illustrate to Hines that he is far too quick to jump to green-eyed conclusions in a comic softshoe duet, "I'll Never be Jealous Again."

Considering himself the greatest lover of all time is the sex-crazed, daffy factory workers' union "Pres"—who appropriately works in ladies pants. He flirts with every skirt. One unwilling victim of his attentions is Gladys in his hilarious come-on, "Her Is."

By far the singing star of the heavily scored play is the crooning Sid, in such songs as "A New Town is a Blue Town," "There Once Was a Man," and the heart-rendering "Hey There." Perhaps due to the first night before an audience, Babe had some difficulty with some of her songs, although there were moments when her almost operatic voice was evident.

Chorus singers of note include Anita Irvin, Barbra Dawson and Frank Stith.

But the chorus in general seemed unsure of itself, especially in the opening number "Hurry Up," a difficult vocal counterpoint, granted, but practicing the words and timing would go a long way to improve the song.

There were some wonderful bits of comic activity, although some of the members of the large cast appeared nervous about little mistakes. They need reminding *anything* is likely to go wrong on stage, and learn to improvise and go on as if nothing had happened. There seemed a bit too much standing around awkwardly, exchanging glances that said "I don't know what to do," slowing the flow of action drastically. (For heaven's sakes, don't look at your feet!) Stage business is not the sole property of leading characters, it is an art to be practiced by everyone. Discovering a character's personality and then projecting it to the audience without disrupting the action is just as important (if not more so) for those who have few lines.

On the other hand chorus singing and dancing in "Hernando's Hideaway" was a spiffy production, as was the sizzling "Steam Heat." Choreography by Sheila B. Cox added much to the show.

The use of a small jazz combo has promise, but again, a little more rehearsal with the entire cast seemed necessary.

Among the minor problems Tuesday were an unfinished set and a short-handed stage crew. Perhaps the most obvious technical problem was with lighting—which was later explained to have been due to last minute rewiring that caused a blackout when lights should have come up. Panic-city in the control booth, but all was quickly returned to normal.

Then of course, the garage adjacent to the theater was once again inhabited by an inconsiderate neighbor playing a radio and racing an engine during the performance.

But despite the difficulties (many of which will undoubtably be corrected—after all, it *was* a rehearsal), the play is rousing, happy-ending family entertainment, with lots of comedy and familiar songs to brighten an audience.

[Johnson City (Tenn.) *Press-Chronicle*]

Motion Pictures

There are few places large enough to support a newspaper that do not also have a motion-picture theater. For the assistance of small-town editors, motion-picture producers issue publicity material descriptive of their films and performers. Obviously, however, much to be preferred is the locally written review or criticism composed from the standpoint of the audience rather than that of the advertiser; fearlessness is a quality without which motion-picture reviewing is likely to be jejune.

By Janet I. Martineau
News Entertainment Editor

"Kramer vs. Kramer" is, quite simply, one of the best movies in a year which started out with a whimper and is closing with a bang.

A nicely crafted script, which never allows pathos to overshadow humanity and laughs; sensitive direction and virtuoso acting on the part of three of our brightest actors give the movie its strength. Who could ask for more?

Well, there's the cinematography—capturing the ins and outs of life in New York City. And then there's Justin Henry, the child who in the end pits Kramer vs. Kramer. Picked out of a New York school, with absolutely no acting experience, he is a charmer—and a charmer without resorting to constant tears like his counterpart did in the sudser "The Champ."

In the storyline we view the lives of Ted and Joanna Kramer (Dustin Hoffman and Meryl Streep). On the surface they seem happily married, and he is a highly successful advertising agency artist (too successful, perhaps).

On the eve of winning a big promotion, his wife of eight years states simply she is leaving him—and her child—to find herself.

What follows is a lovely story of a father finally learning to know and appreciate his son—the hard way. His career begins to take second place to PTA meetings and doctor appointments, making his boss nervous. His whole life is changed around, but he copes.

And, then, she comes back, announcing she wants the child now.

To writer-director Robert Benton's credit, and to the credit of Hoffman and Miss Streep, there are no clear-cut good guys and bad guys in this film. There are only grays. [Saginaw (Mich.) *News*]

The Stage

What has been said about the motion picture applies also to the legitimate stage. If the play is a much-acted one, the reviewer should not devote any appreciable amount of space to relating the story of the plot or to describing the general motive. Rather, s/he should perform the difficult task of distinguishing between the acting and the actor's role and should consider stage management and direction. Obviously, to criticize effectively s/he must have some acquaintance with the technique of play production.

If the play is a production, the critic rightfully evaluates the playwright's success in achieving his purpose. Is there proper congruity in settings, costumes, language and plot? Is the action logical or is the happy ending arrived at by a series of unnatural coincidences? Are exits and entrances merely artificial devices to get characters on and off the stage?

If the production deals with a problem, is it met squarely or is it falsely simplified? Are the characters truly representative of the types they portray or are they superficial or caricatures? Is the play propaganda? If it points a moral, is the playwright sincere or naïve or bigoted? Is anything risqué just smut for smut's sake or is it essential for dramatic completeness?

These are just a few of the questions the critic must ask him/herself. For whatever conclusions s/he reaches s/he must give sound reasons.

Truly great dramatic critics have been students of life as well as of the drama. "Ideally," according to Norman Nadel, critic for the old New York

World-Telegram, "the theater critic should be a Renaissance man," meaning one "with a knowledge of architecture, sculpture, painting, music, government, history, philosophy and other liberal arts subjects." Nadel suggested that college students finish their four-year course with a good classical and historical background so as "to have perspective and to understand the art form in relation to the world as it exists." He urged a knowledge of philosophy because "people turn to a play to express a philosophical question," and a knowledge of history of the theater and playwriting "to recognize a play's originality and importance and to acquire an intellectual appreciation of the play form."

Walter Kerr, long with the New York *Herald Tribune* and now drama critic for the New York *Times,* believes a drama critic must have an extensive background in dramatic literature on a broad humanistic base. John Mason Brown felt that critics should be able to "feel, touch and have sight of the world." He advised students aspiring to be drama critics to get a thorough knowledge of history. Richard Watts of the New York *Post* emphasized the value of studying the English language as well.

By John Neville

Witches wrought havoc in Salem, Mass., in 1792 and some of their devilment carried over to Wednesday night's Community Theaters of Greater Dallas production of "The Crucible."

However, the happenings at the Rotunda Theater in the First Methodist Church are more deserving of a short session on the ducking stool than the ultimate noose or burning stake.

In fine, CTGD's first cooperative effort which united talents gleaned from the seven "little theater" groups that comprise the organization is better than amateur, yet far from professional. This is to be understood, yet there were too many things that smacked of the "let's get some of the gang together and put on a play" about the production.

Again to elucidate, lines were blown, scene changes were slow and considering the sparcity of properties, too much scenery was chewed.

Dr. Burnet M. Hobgood, chairman of the SMU drama department, who directed "The Crucible," was confronted with the problem of welding a large number of part-time players from seven companies into a cohesive whole. This he did admirably. But he is no miracle worker, so there were many loose ends. For one thing, none of the players and seemingly few of the technical people were conversant with the intricacies of theater-in-the-round. Also, the Miller drama, which deals with the hysteria generated by the claims that witches (and warlocks) were destroying the children of Salem, can reach such heights of excitement that the actors can be caught up in the maelstrom and lose their stage discipline. Both of these factors were present in the CTGD production.

This is not to say that Dallas' most recent attempt at community theater was not successful. It was . . . [Dallas *Morning News*]

Entertainment Places

Today the form of entertainment closest to the old-time vaudeville program is found in night clubs, cabarets, hotels, summer resorts and similar places. Performers appear solo, delivering monologues, making music, dancing, engaging in pantomime or even acrobatic and other circus-type acts. The skill of the performer is what's at stake and that occupies the attention of the critic-reviewer more than perhaps anywhere else in the entertainment or artistic world today.

Marty Allen has the body of a Japanese wrestler gone to seed, the face of a troll and a hairdo inspired by a Brillo pad.

But he comes across beautifully in his act at the Holiday House, where he is substituting for Joan Rivers, whose week-long engagement was canceled at the Monroeville supper club.

Allen mixes up his fast-paced act well. One moment he bombards the audience with one-liners (his delivery is so good that you laugh even at jokes you've heard before); at another moment he might be doing a character sketch, like "Johnny Money," a hilarious spoof on Johnny Cash. He also does an interesting pantomime routine about an aging clown and hoofs it up in a finale about the sights and sounds of New York City.

Assisting Allen is Colleen Kincaid, who sings while he takes costume breaks, and she comes across well.

A fine singer, she also is an excellent dancer (she's a former member of the Golddiggers) and has not only an engaging stage presence but also an engaging physical presence.

Allen does one number with Kincaid called "Hey Big Spender" from "Sweet Charity." In this bit Allen is in drag, wearing platinum blonde wig, red silk shift and rhinestone earrings. He camps it up heavily looking like an aging hooker who would have trouble turning on a lightbulb.

Allen, a Pittsburgher, localizes some of his jokes and each area reference is met with guffaws. Also drawing a big response is a segment in which a bewigged and bejeweled Allen does a bewitching satire of Elvis Presley.

[Mike Kalina in Pittsburgh *Post-Gazette*]

Radio and Television

Newspaper criticism of television still is experimental. No orthodox formula has become widespread. Much of the columnar material is anecdotal or program announcements. The job of critically commenting on any appreciable amount of what is presented viewers is staggering. Celebrity interviews regularly make news for the news pages. The critic generally concentrates on dramatic performances, as in the following first-rate example:

By Robert C. Marsh

Are you sure you saw the new Lyric Opera version of Gounod's "Faust"?

Don't answer until you have had a second look at the telecast, which WTTW (Channel 11) will air (with stereo sound on WFMT) at 7:30 p.m. Wednesday. This "Faust" was a controversial stage production but it makes an extremely effective TV show.

Why? The camera gives you a different perspective on the work than was possible in the theater. In the Opera House, Pier Luigi Samaritani's settings dominated the stage. On the tube, for most of the evening the stage does not exist. You are

> tightly focused on the singers. Their facial expressions have a vitality and impact impossible in the Opera House (unless you carry a telescope), and the costumes become more important. (Faust's is silly but most of the others are good.)
>
> Some of the moments that seemed odd in the theater are powerful here; for example, the spinning rose window in the church scene becomes, by a superimposed image, a symbol of Marguerite's anguish. The final scene is softened just enough that the angelic chorus can be taken impressionistically rather than as an illustration from a Sunday school tract. On the other hand, the descent of Faust and Mephistophiles into hell on stage elevators is rather pale. We expect better special effects on the tube. . . . [Chicago *Sun-Times*]

Books

The first task of the editor of a book review page is one of selection of those few of the 25,000 or more new titles published annually that are to receive mention. Harry Hanson, veteran newspaper and magazine book reviewer said:

> The daily book review lifts a book from an overtowering mass of printed material and makes it an integral part of life. It often becomes news of the first order. Between the covers of all these volumes there may be an authoritative voice touching on our vital problems, and if this is true, that voice certainly deserves a hearing. The book reviewer's job, it seems to me, is to sort this flood of titles, find the one that fits in the day's news, and then write about it as news.

That the first duty of the writer about books is to assist readers to select those they wish to read also was the viewpoint of another leading reviewer, Joseph Wood Krutch, who said,

> The best review is not the one which is trying to be something else. It is not an independent essay on the subject of the book in hand and not an aesthetic discourse upon one of the literary genres. The best book review is the best review of the book in question, and the better it is the closer it sticks to its ostensible subject. . . . However penetrating a piece of writing may be, it is not a good review if it leaves the reader wondering what the book itself is like as a whole or it is concerned with only some aspects of the book's quality.

As to the style of book reviewing or criticizing, there is no formula. The writer is free to use virtually any method he chooses, the only test being the effectiveness of the style used. Somewhere in the review or criticism the writer should be expected to classify the book as to type—fiction, philosophy, biography—to describe its contents, communicate something of its quality and pass judgment upon it.

A temptation that even seasoned reviewers sometimes do not resist is to use the writing as opportunity for personal therapy, with the result that seems sophomorically sophisticated or pseudo-intellectual. Take, for instance, the first paragraphs of Godfrey Hodgson's review of *The Glory and the Dream* by William Manchester in the Washington *Post:*

> When this Brobdingnagian work first thumped on my desk for review, I took note of its bulk and of the inflated rhetoric of the title, and my first impulse was to dismiss it as the ultimate *Guiness Book of Records* champion nonbook.
>
> I would count its pages, I said to myself, and I did. There are 1302 of them. That is not counting end pages, forematter, acknowledgments, bibliography, copyright acknowledgments, and index.
>
> All of which it is provided with so lavishly that one might suppose that it is as scholarly as the *Monumenta Germaniae Historica,* which it is not. At something over 500 words to the page, that is more than two-thirds of a million words.
>
> Next I thought I would weigh it on the kitchen scales. And that, too, I did, though it proved harder than I imagined since the chic little brass weights that I gave my wife for Christmas a few years ago only go up to two pounds avoirdupois, and Manchester is out of that division. As far as I was able to determine with the help of a pound of beans and a can of grapefruit segments, however, *The Glory and the Dream* tips the scales at around three pounds, eight ounces.
>
> And then, I supposed, I would write a savage little review, commenting on the economics of book publishing, and ending, perhaps, "A book, however, this is not."
>
> And yet I was wrong. It is even rather a good book of its kind, so long as one does not expect too much from it.

Another standard method is to relate the current volume to earlier works by the same author, as John Brooks did when he reviewed the Manchester book in the Chicago *Tribune:*

> William Manchester is famous for *The Death of a President,* the "Kennedy book" of the 1966 headlines remembered less for its hair-raising account of the assassination of John F. Kennedy than for the prepublication objections to it by the fallen President's relatives and friends. Among his other books are *The Arms of Krupp* and a novel of much merit, *The City of Anger*.
>
> Now he has written an enormous (1,300 page) popular history of the United States over four recent decades. Thru the sheer nerve of his undertaking and the dogged persistence of his execution of it, he almost batters the reader's critical faculties into submission and brings him to a helpless nod of assent. Almost, but not quite.
>
> Prominent among the pitfalls of popular history-writing are the following:
>
> (1) Drawing instant mood-pictures of past years with the help of phrases like "It was a time of . . ." and "It was that kind of year."
>
> (2) Evoking instant nostalgia by writing down old song titles.
>
> (3) Sounding like *Time* magazine.
>
> (4) Sounding like Dos Passos in *"U.S.A."*
>
> (5) Contriving corny melodrama by withholding a famous name until the end of an anecdote ("And that man's name was. . . .")
>
> (6) Trying to convey a sense of destiny by faking detailed knowledge of the playpen days of people later to be famous ("Fifteen-year-old John F. Kennedy heard the long, plaintive wail of the steam whistle at the Choate School in Wallingford, Conn.").

A more scholarly approach is to compare a new book to others dealing with the same subject, as illustrated by the following from what John P. Roche wrote for *Saturday Review:*

> Historical chronicles come in different styles, perspectives, and sizes. Frederick Lewis Allen, for example, utilized the principle of parsimony in his *Only Yesterday*. He made no effort to cover everything, but he did write a book. Cabell Phillips, in his *1929–1939: From the Crash to the Blitz,* drew extensively on *The New York Times* (the volume is one in a series called *The New York Times* Chronicle of American Life), but the result is far more than a scissors-and-paste job; reading it, one gets the distinct impression of a mind at work, of priorities established and maintained. Then, of course, there are specialized works, such as Irving Bernstein's *The Lean Years,* which view American life through the prism of the working class.
>
> Now comes William Manchester with an immense narrative history of the United States 1932 to 1972. I began reading it with great interest, because the time frame is precisely the span of my political consciousness. This could be the story of my generation. Unfortunately it is not. By the time I emerged from the seemingly interminable 1,300 pages, I was convinced that Manchester had simply taken a vacuum cleaner to his task and swept up every bit for information, meaningful and trivial, and had never sat down to sort out the wheat from the chaff.

How different experts can react differently is illustrated by the following examples. The first is by Alfred Kazin, author of *Bright Book of Life: American Novelists and Storytellers from Hemingway to Mailer:*

> This fluent, likeable, can't-put-it-down narrative history of America from the Bonus Army to Watergate is popular history in our special tradition of literary merchandising. It is all about the audience that will read it. Mr. Manchester is a steadier and more reliable source on American vicissitudes than photograph books, Theodore H. White, Time and Life, Frederick Lewis Allen, The New York Times Op-Ed page, Norman Mailer, Betty Friedan, Peanuts, et al. But his real virtue is not just that he is a dependable fact man with an eye for the unexpected fact and that he tells his story with all the ease of a practiced rewrite man who has been inspired by Dos Passos. He is really obsessed by the American audience, the great American consensus, the mass, the popular mind itself. He is confident that there is an all-present character called the American people and that he can describe 40 years of simultaneous experience. He identifies with this character and makes you believe that your whole life has been lived inside it. Reading Manchester, you run with the Bonus Army, lift up your chin like Roosevelt, put up the flag at Iwo Jima, and nervously dismiss MacArthur. You are against Communism *and* the Cold War. You participate!
>
> Manchester is always thinking about *you,* you who are reading him, you who read history and can afford 20 dollars for a book. This book is your life.

By contrast, the author of this book—who also wrote *Hoaxes* and *Gideon's Army, the Story of the Progressive Party of 1948*—wrote the following for syndication by Field Enterprises:

Just about everything that happened for 30 years—in politics, diplomacy, education, science, labor-management relations, public health, the arts, entertainment, fads and fashions, civil rights, civil liberties, law, sports and all else—receives at least brief mention in this 1,397 page narrative.

There are some editorial jibes, such as that Elvis Presley was lewd and vulgar, Lyndon Johnson "characteristically said one thing while believing the exact opposite," the Prince Rainier-Grace Kelly wedding was an M-G-M press agent's dream. Typical of longer evaluative comments are:

"He (Eisenhower) was a backslapper; Nixon was a brooder. In economics and political ethics the general was a fundamentalist. The senator was a relativist, an opportunist, and a fatalist," and "by 1961 the space race no longer had any bearing on national security . . . or on the pursuit of knowledge."

Mostly, the tome is objective reporting of what appeared on the front pages. William Manchester has no inside dope, no behind-the-scenes facts, no skeletons dragged out of closets. He makes no sociological interpretation of the era as a whole, notes no trends nor relationships between the multitudinous events he summarizes. Without historical perspective, he merely records the "what" and leaves the "why" to abler scholars.

Music

The reporter who is timid about covering a musical event because s/he lacks technical training in music at least has the consolation that by far a majority of his/her readers, both those who attended the event under review and those who didn't, know no more than s/he. The superior musical review, of course, is written for both the professor of music and the music-lover. The qualities demanded of the music critic were summarized as follows by the late Lawrence Gilman, long music critic for the New York *Herald Tribune:*

> The best music critic is a good newspaperman. Of course, he must know music, deeply and thoroughly and exactly; he must know what he is talking about. But the first and indispensable requirement of any article written for a newspaper, no matter on what subject is that it must be readable—it must be interesting as well as clearly intelligible to the lay reader of average education. A professional musician might be able to write a competent, technical account of a composition or a musical performance. But his review would probably be interesting only to other musicians.
>
> The chief aim of a newspaper critic must be to interest the general reader. And if he can interest those readers who have not heard the performance, as well as those who have, he is entitled to call it a day. Quite apart from its value as a report and estimate of a musical performance, his criticism must be able to stand alone as an interesting, readable story.

It is the musician in whom the musical critic primarily is interested, because only occasionally, even in the large cities, is s/he required to pass judgment upon a new symphony, opera or other musical creation. Thus, if the audience includes musically trained auditors, s/he may well take a cue from their reactions as to the merits of the performance. If s/he is woefully lacking in musical training, s/he can make his/her entire story descriptive of the audience or the personalities of the musicians.

By Donal Henahan

When Alexander ran out of worlds to conquer, he could think of nothing better to do than to sit down and cry. But Leontyne Price, who has enough musical conquests to her credit to satisfy most sopranos and then some, took a more constructive approach Tuesday night at Carnegie Hall: she sang the "Liebestod" with the Chicago Symphony Orchestra.

Miss Price, as you must know, is one of this era's premier singers, but until now she has not ventured into the weightiest Wagnerian repertory. She built her opera career mostly in moderately heavy roles such as Leonora and Aïda, and has gone so far as Turandot in the area that the Italians designate as lirico spinto, the hinge between the purely lyric and the truly dramatic voices.

But, under the baton of Sir Georg Solti, that tested and proven Wagnerian, Miss Price did what all the greatest artists do: she took a chance. Whether at age 53 there is an Isolde in her future would be risky to say right now, but it can be safely stated that her performance of the famous aria "Mild und leise" from "Tristan und Isolde" carried the day. The audience, its appetite whetted by a suffocatingly evocative reading of the Prelude by the Chicago, gave Miss Price the kind of ovation that most sopranos only get in their reveries. If the Metropolitan Opera chose to announce her as Isolde tomorrow you may be sure seats would go at black-market prices. Miss Price, incidentally, has just completed a recording on which she sings the "Liebestod," and it is entirely possible that she intends to let the matter drop.

Certainly, the voice on this night was splendidly used and wisely husbanded, in the manner most Isoldes learn early if they are to survive. It never did quite become the flood of tone that a Wagnerian soprano of the Nilsson or Farrell type can produce with such seeming lack of strain. Miss Price's more slender soprano could, however, ride the crest of orchestral sound quite thrillingly, and almost invariably did. And there was an ecstatic excitement to it all that probably even benefited from one's consciousness of the effort involved. What would the Love-Death be, after all, without struggle? [New York *Times*]

The Dance

Whereas music is written with complete directions by the composer to guide the virtuoso, and whereas rules for the playwright, novelist, painter and sculptor may be found in textbooks, no way as yet has been devised to score the movements that characterize what, historical evidence proves, was one of the first if not the original form of art. Motion-picture recording may prove the way out for future teachers of the dance who wish to convey the qualities of the work of a Rudolph Nureyev or a Martha Graham.

The medium of the dance is motion, but motion may be either abstract or pantomimic, rhythmic or natural. Folk dancing, being pantomimic, reflects the customs of the people participating in it. Natural dancing consists in such normal movements as running, walking, skipping and leaping without studied posing. What is called the German school of dancing emphasizes strength, endurance and precision of movement. The ballet is rhythmic and repetitious. Greek or classical dancing, revived after World War I by the late Isadora Duncan, is symbolic and involves the entire body, not just the head, arms and legs. Miss

Duncan considered her art interpretative of poetry, music, the movements of nature and of moods and emotions; as such, it defied analysis.

To review a dancing entertainment with any intelligence, the reporter must understand the principles superficially sketched in the preceding two paragraphs. A sympathetic attitude perhaps is more essential than in reviewing any other form of art, if for no other reason than that it is the form with which the average person has the least everyday contact.

By Anna Kisselgoff

A major premiere by Martha Graham is a major theatrical event by any standard, and the premiere of the new "Judith" by the Martha Graham Dance Company Tuesday night at the Metropolitan Opera House was no exception.

There were two stunning moments. The first was spellbinding in its immediacy. Applause broke out and a cry of "fabulous" rang out from the public as the curtains parted. They revealed two works of art—the two sculptures by Isamu Noguchi that make up the set. Beautiful in form but also the counterpart of Miss Graham's genius in functioning on several levels, they suggest many things at once. Smooth and curved, the first piece implies an abstraction of a lyre. The second piece, constructed in the image of a spit and a sawhorse, is clearly reminiscent of an animal.

Of course, these are phallic symbols—true to the tradition of Noguchi-Graham collaborations in the past. This "Judith" is about sex, and Miss Graham is no stranger to eroticism. Yet she takes her story—the seduction and murder of the Assyrian tyrant Holofernes by the biblical heroine Judith—into a larger, abstract plane. The male and female principles embodied in Noguchi's sculpture find their reflection in the two protagonists: Judith, as danced by Peggy Lyman and Holofernes, portrayed by Tim Wengerd.

Miss Lyman, under Miss Graham's direction, is responsible for the second stunning moment. This is the minute in which she takes off the black widow's robe and begins to attire herself alluringly to seduce Holofernes. Halston's costumes, based on Miss Graham's original ideas, offer a flash of brilliant expressive colors here. Miss Lyman removes the black and gold veil in which she has been wrapped. Covered from head to toe, dressed according to our ideas of Jewish heroines of antiquity, she sheds her stance of modesty and determination suddenly in favor of a contemporary frankness.

As she emerges by her lyre, shoulders and arms bare in a red leotard top with a purple skirt, her entire demeanor changes. She sits, legs apart, back up, hand to thigh. If she is not brazen, she embodies a state of sexual forwardness. And, when like a queen going to her execution, she covers her torso with gold snake-coiled jewelry, the change is total.

This transformation was so complete and so extraordinary that one was compelled to go back to the original tale of Judith—who is not a strictly biblical heroine in that her story is contained in the books of the Apocrypha. The corresponding passage, referring to the Jews' reaction, reads as follows: "And when they saw her, that her countenance was altered and her apparel was changed, they wondered at her beauty greatly."

Miss Graham, as choreographer, and Miss Lyman as the dancer, have arrived at the truth of this image—of exterior and moral transformation—so powerfully that their accomplishment goes beyond translation of a literary idea. It is difficult to believe that Miss Lyman, as the woman resolved to free her besieged people, was the same dancer who opened the work. It was a transformation explained by the way Miss Lyman modified the way she held her body—a magnificent example of Miss Graham's use of the body as an expressive instrument. . . .

[New York *Times*]

The Fine Arts

The camera was, to a large extent, the cause of the contemporary ''war'' in the field of painting that has had repercussions among the sculptors and architects as well. Dadaism, futurism, surrealism and other 20th-century ''schools'' of art are revolts against the formal, and a popular explanation given laymen is that the day of a portrait painter is gone and with it a theory as to the purpose of art. It is argued that the role of the 20th-century artist is to communicate an idea or an emotion; the extremes to which some go in upsetting tradition is dumfounding to laymen. In the works of such painters as Grant Wood and Thomas Benton, so-called regional artists, is found an abandonment of the photographic purpose, but the models still are recognizable. Some abstract art has as many interpretations as there are interpreters.

Peter Schjeldahl epitomized recent trends as follows:

The 1960's in American abstract painting was a period of conscientious esthetic and technical pure research, remarkable for its tireless experimentation with hard-edged stripes, disks and polygons of solid color. The avant-garde of a decade ago, having thrived during the abstract Expressionist 50's on seemingly slapdash procedures followed in an intellectual climate of romantic assertiveness and big ideas, took with a sort of cool, evangelical passion to the new use of T-squares and masking tape, and began to couch its self-advertisement in impeccably dry, quasi-scientific language.

How to combine reporting and expert critical analysis is demonstrated in the following:

By Hilton Kramer

The rose is a venerable subject in the history of painting but there are no roses to be found in this history quite like those that appear in the paintings of Bert Carpenter, whose one-man show is now installed at the Zabriskie Gallery, 699 Madison Avenue at 63rd Street.

For Mr. Carpenter, while lavishing a familiar lyricism on the realization of this conventional subject, manages to transform it into something quite different—the materials of ''heroic'' painting.

Mr. Carpenter projects his imagery of roses on a monumental scale, making of each petal, leaf and stem a weighty architectural member. The roses in his paintings are giant roses, monument roses—roses that carry the humble dimensions of nature into the realm of pictorial fantasy. And yet, he effects this magical change in scale without sacrificing anything of the ''realism'' of his depictions. These roses, as large as the head of man, retain all their tender luminosity.

As a sheer technical feat, the exhibition is remarkable. But it is also extremely interesting as virtuoso painting. Mr. Carpenter has adopted something of Alex Katz's pictorial strategy in enlarging his subjects to more than life-size, and the particular "cropping" he employs seems to owe something to Philip Pearlstein's painting—Mr. Carpenter often cuts off the tops and bottoms of his roses the way Mr. Pearlstein crops his views of naked models. But whatever he may have borrowed in the realm of formal ideas, Mr. Carpenter's pictures establish a presence all his own. He is an interesting and powerful painter. [New York *Times*]

Current tendencies in painting, sculpture and architecture are not new. The history of art reveals that throughout the centuries every conceivable theory has been tried out. Likewise, the search for a definition of art is as old as artistic criticism; upon the answer to the question depends largely the nature of what an artist produces.

Through reading and fraternizing with artistic people the reporter can become educated in the meaning of art to the different "schools," the work of whose representatives s/he is called upon to review. In no other field is the responsibility for interpreting the artist to his/her public greater than in that of the manual arts. In fact, such interpretation is about all there is to this kind of criticism.

The opportunity and responsibility of the newspaper today were explained by Herbert Kupferberg, then editor for the arts of the late New York *Herald Tribune*,

> For better or for worse, the world of the arts today is wider than it has ever been. It encompasses not only the patron of the art galleries on New York's Fifty-seventh Street, but the housewife who finds Van Gogh and Renoir reproductions amid the breakfast foods and beauty aids at her local supermarket. It includes the teen-ager buying his first Beethoven symphony at the discount record counter no less than the dowager with a subscription to the Metropolitan Opera. It even touches the millions of visitors who rode the moving platform past Michelangelo's Pieta at the New York World's Fair without being fully aware of whether they were undergoing an artistic or touristic or religious experience, but recognizing that for a brief moment they had entered a realm of beauty. Today a newspaper that makes any pretense at reflecting the life around it, or at appealing to the broad interests of an alert readership, no longer has any real option as to whether it will cover the arts. Its only choice is whether it will cover them badly or well.

There is more action and movement in sports writing than there is in writing news. . . . In a nutshell, the sports fan of today is a different person from the fan of a decade ago. . . . This changed attitude makes the sports writer more responsible. In a good many cases he is just putting into words what nearly every sports fan knows, and there is no stringing that estimable gentleman along. . . . It doesn't take the public long to get wise to a sloppy writer, and such a writer cannot last long. When he loses his following he loses all.

—GRANTLAND RICE, editor, *American Golfer*

INDEX

C

D

E

F

G

H

I

J

K

M

O

P

Q

R

S

Y

Z